THE COMPETITION ACT 1998
LAW AND PRACTICE

THE COMPETITION ACT 1998

LAW AND PRACTICE

by
MARTIN COLEMAN
*Partner and Head of the Competition
and EC Department, Norton Rose, Solicitors*

and
MICHAEL GRENFELL
Partner, Norton Rose, Solicitors

OXFORD
UNIVERSITY PRESS

OXFORD

UNIVERSITY PRESS

Great Clarendon Street, Oxford OX2 6DP

Oxford University Press is a department of the University of Oxford.
It furthers the University's objective of excellence in research, scholarship,
and education by publishing worldwide in

Oxford New York

Athens Auckland Bangkok Bogotá Buenos Aires Calcutta
Cape Town Chennai Dar es Salaam Delhi Florence Hong Kong Istanbul
Karachi Kuala Lumpur Madrid Melbourne Mexico City Mumbai
Nairobi Paris São Paulo Singapore Taipei Tokyo Toronto Warsaw
and associated companies in Berlin Ibadan

Oxford is a registered trade mark of Oxford University Press
in the UK and in certain other countries

Published in the United States
by Oxford University Press Inc., New York

British Library Cataloguing in Publication Data

Data available

Library of Congress Cataloging in Publication Data
Coleman, Martin (Martin A.)
The Competition Act 1998: law and practice / by
Martin Coleman and Michael Grenfell.
p. cm.
Includes bibliographical references and index.
1. Restraint of trade—Great Britain. 2. Antitrust law—Great Britain.
I. Grenfell, Michael. II. Title.
KD2212.C65 1999
343.41'0723—dc21 99–32962
Main work ISBN 0–19–829847–1
Main work with first supplement ISBN 0–19–826874–2 ✓

1 3 5 7 9 10 8 6 4 2

Typeset by Hope Services (Abingdon) Ltd.
Printed in Great Britain
on acid-free paper by
Biddles Ltd., Guildford and King's Lynn

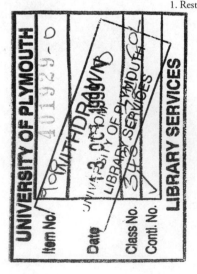

PREFACE

The significance of the new Competition Act 1998 cannot be exaggerated. Widely heralded as the most important change in UK competition law for a generation, it creates new rules and new risks—but also new rights and new remedies—for businesses based or operating in the UK.

This book, as its title indicates, is concerned with both law *and* practice under the new Act. In writing it, we have tried to keep constantly in mind the requirements which our business clients have of the competition law advice which we give on a daily basis in our legal practice. Businesses take it for granted that their lawyers will have a thorough and accurate knowledge of the law, know their way around the procedures, and be familiar with developing policy. They expect, in addition, that the advice provided to them is commercially relevant, practical, and clearly expressed.

We have endeavoured to adopt a similar approach in writing this book. So, for example, as well as setting out the relevant legislative provisions, cases and procedural rules, we have devoted two entire chapters to practical examples of types of commercial agreement and conduct which are likely to be reviewable under the two new prohibitions in the Act (Chapters 7 and 9).

Companies in the regulated utility sectors will face particular new challenges under the Act. In addition to having to comply with the regulatory conditions in their licences, the utility companies will be subject to a new competition regime under the Act, which will be administered jointly by their sector regulators and the OFT; we have included a chapter (Chapter 19) on the special position which relates to the utilities.

Commercial agreements, arrangements and conduct will be governed by the new provisions in the Competition Act 1998, but also by surviving provisions of earlier UK legislation—specifically, the monopoly provisions of the Fair Trading Act 1973 (which are themselves amended under the new Act). From the point of view of a business, the issue of practical concern is whether the agreement, arrangement or conduct complies with *all* the relevant provisions of UK competition law. Businesses cannot look at the Competition Act 1998 in isolation from the other provisions. For this reason, we have included two Chapters (17 and 18) on the rules and procedures under the Fair Trading Act monopoly provisions.

But our intention has been that the whole book, rather than just specific chapters, should be accurate, comprehensive, up-to-date, commercially relevant, practical and clearly expressed. It is for readers to judge the extent to which we have succeeded; and we would welcome any comments and suggestions for future editions.

Although there are just two names on the cover of this book, we could never have written it without considerable help from colleagues in the competition department here at

Norton Rose. A number of trainee solicitors have spent part of their training period in the department while we were writing the book, and they have assisted us in much of the groundwork. This has been of enormous help to us, and we hope that their understanding of competition law has benefited from the research which they have undertaken. Our thanks, in particular, go to Helen Copestick, Andy Edwards, Raj Godfrey-Mahapatra, Jane Keatley, Maria Montaraz-Taus, Nuria Rafique, Claire Rennilson, Christine Tadros, Adam Vause and Patrick Wegerdt.

Among permanent colleagues in our department, we are very grateful for the help we have received from Adam Brown, Helen Kelly and Martin Bailey. Special mention must be made of Mark Jones, who has given us the benefit of his already formidable knowledge of the new legislation, providing us with important and insightful comments on early drafts of the text, and indeed substantially redrafting several passages. His contribution has been invaluable.

Typing a book of this length is obviously no mean feat. In this case, the task has been made more onerous by the many revisions which had to be made in the course of preparing the book—taking account of the various amendments to the legislation as it passed through Parliament, and then the appearance of successive draft versions of secondary legislation and guidelines from the competition authorities. This enormous task has been undertaken by our secretaries Sue Francis, Lisa De Vulder and Penny Revill, who have had to fit it in around their already ample workload in servicing our legal practice. They have produced drafts and redrafts of the text with remarkable speed, accuracy and good humour. We are enormously grateful to them.

The process of issuing secondary legislation and official guidelines on the Act is continuing even as we go to press. There are a number of such documents which are now only in draft form, including the OFT's Procedural Rules. We have included these in the first Supplement that accompanies this book on publication. In due course a second Supplement will be published, including the final versions of these important pieces of secondary legislation. Further updating information will be posted on the Website for this book (see the box at the foot of the page).

In the meantime, businesses already have much to familiarise themselves with in order to be ready for the new environment established by the Competition Act 1998. We hope that this book will be of considerable assistance in the challenges which lie ahead.

MARTIN COLEMAN
MICHAEL GRENFELL
Norton Rose
10 March 1999

This book has an associated web-site on which updating information will be posted on a regular basis.
Visit http://www.oup.co.uk/law/practitioner/competitionact1998

CONTENTS—SUMMARY

PART VIII NEW REGIME FOR UTILITY REGULATION

CONTENTS

PART I CONTEXT

1. Introduction and Background

2. The Institutions

3. Relation with EC Law

PART II RESTRICTIVE AGREEMENTS:
THE CHAPTER I PROHIBITION

PART IV CONSEQUENCES OF INFRINGING THE PROHIBITIONS

10. Consequences of Infringement

PART V TRANSITIONAL PROVISIONS

11. Transitional Provisions

PART VI PROCEDURES UNDER THE PROHIBITIONS

12. Notification

PART VII   MONOPOLY INVESTIGATIONS

17.   Monopoly Investigations—Framework of the Legislation

18.   Monopoly Investigations—Procedure

PART VIII   NEW REGIME FOR UTILITY REGULATION

19.   Changes in Utility Regulation

Appendices

TABLE OF UK LEGISLATION

UK STATUTES

UK STATUTORY INSTRUMENTS AND RULES

TABLE OF EC TREATIES AND LEGISLATION

EC TREATY PROVISIONS

EC SECONDARY LEGISLATION

TABLE OF CASES

EUROPEAN COURT OF JUSTICE AND THE COURT OF FIRST INSTANCE

EUROPEAN COMMISSION DECISIONS AND COMMUNICATIONS

EUROPEAN COMMISSION MERGER DECISIONS

EUROPEAN COURT OF HUMAN RIGHTS

OTHER JURISDICTIONS
Finland

Austria

TABLE OF UK MONOPOLIES AND MERGERS COMMISSION (COMPETITION COMMISSION) REPORTS

PART I

CONTEXT

1

INTRODUCTION AND BACKGROUND

A. Overview

The Competition Act 1998[1] marks a revolution in the United Kingdom's national **1.01**
competition laws. Paradoxically, however, many of its chief features are well-
established in the context of EC competition law; the new UK system, like the
national competition laws of many other EU Member States, is closely modelled
on the competition rules in Articles 81 and 82 (formerly Articles 85 and 86) of the
EC Treaty,[2] although there are also significant differences between the EC and UK
versions, in terms of both law and procedure.

In summary, the main changes introduced by the Competition Act 1998 are as **1.02**
follows:

- Restrictive agreements and arrangements will be subject to a new national pro-
  hibition, similar to Article 81 (formerly Article 85) of the EC Treaty—the
  Chapter I prohibition. The Restrictive Trade Practices Act 1976 and the Resale
  Prices Act 1976 will both be repealed.

- Abuse of a dominant position (also called abuse of market power) will be subject to a new national prohibition—the **Chapter II prohibition**. In addition,
  the monopoly provisions of the Fair Trading Act 1973 will remain in place,
  allowing for the investigation and remedying of 'monopolistic' practices (on the

---

[1] In this book, all references to section numbers and Scheds relate to the Competition Act 1998,
unless otherwise indicated.
[2] The amendments to the EC Treaty made by the 1997 Treaty of Amsterdam have the effect that
Arts 85 and 86 of the EC Treaty are now renumbered Arts 81 and 82 respectively.

part of individual companies or market sectors). The provisions on anti-competitive practices in the Competition Act 1980 will, however, be repealed.

- The main powers of investigation, decision-making and enforcement will rest with the **OFT** (Office of Fair Trading). It will be possible to appeal against OFT decisions to a new body, the **Competition Commission**.

1.03 National merger control in the UK remains unaffected by the new Act, and continues to be governed by the merger provisions of the Fair Trading Act 1973, except that the functions of the Monopolies and Mergers Commission are wholly transferred to the new Competition Commission which replaces it. Merger control is not covered in this book.

> The purpose of this chapter is to describe the background to, and thinking behind, the reforms to the UK's competition law which are embodied in the Competition Act 1998. Discussion of the thinking behind competition law generally—and the arguments for promoting competition—may be found in Chapter 4, paragraphs 4.29–4.37 and (with regard to vertical agreements) in Chapter 5, paragraphs 5.82–5.85.

B. The Need for Reform—the Arguments

1.04 The debate about reform to the UK's national competition laws has continued for years. As early as March 1988, the Conservative Government published a Green Paper[3] proposing reform of the law on restrictive agreements, on the grounds of 'major weaknesses' in the existing legislation.[4] The case for reform has come to be widely accepted, although with more consensus about what needs to be done about restrictive agreements than about abuse of a dominant position. Nevertheless, since that original Green Paper it has taken ten years, one White Paper, a further Green Paper, a Trade and Industry Select Committee report, and two draft Bills, before legislation has finally been enacted.

1.05 There are two main reasons for the reforms embodied in the new Competition Act. First, it was felt that the existing UK legislation was not effective in doing the job of promoting competition in the UK economy, and that EC competition law, as laid out in Articles 81 and 82 (formerly Articles 85 and 86) of the EC Treaty, would do the job better.[5] Secondly, it was felt to be a virtue in itself that national competition law should conform with EC competition law: since many businesses in the UK

---

[3] Green Paper, *Review of Restrictive Trade Practices Policy*, a consultative document, Department of Trade and Industry, Cm 331, Mar 1988.

[4] Ibid, para 1.4.

[5] A brief description of what competition is, and why it is thought worth protecting, is given in Ch 4 paras 4.29–4.37 below.

have to comply with both sets of laws,[6] it would be less burdensome for business if both regimes were to have broadly the same requirements and procedures.

Restrictive Agreements and Arrangements

The deficiencies in the existing UK legislation were particularly pronounced in the case of the law on restrictive agreements and arrangements and cartels. The legislation was contained in the **Restrictive Trade Practices Act 1976 (RTPA)**; in addition, there were specific provisions for resale price maintenance agreements in the Resale Prices Act 1976. **1.06**

Under the RTPA, there was no outright prohibition on entering into cartels or restrictive agreements or arrangements. Instead, there was a system of compulsory notification to the OFT of so-called 'registrable' agreements—that is, agreements which satisfied certain legal criteria set out in the RTPA. The criteria related to the legal form, rather than the actual economic effect, of the agreement: principally, an agreement was registrable only if two or more parties to that agreement accepted restrictions, whether or not those restrictions were actually anti-competitive. The much-criticised consequence of this formalistic definition was that many agreements were registrable, and therefore had to be notified, simply because they satisfied the statutory criteria, even if they had no particular anti-competitive effect—thereby creating an unnecessary regulatory burden on businesses (and on the competition authorities). At the same time, some genuinely anti-competitive agreements and arrangements were able to escape the reach of the RTPA altogether, simply because they were drafted in terms which did not meet the statutory criteria. **1.07**

A further criticism of the RTPA was that, even if a genuinely anti-competitive agreement was 'registrable', the sanctions were weak, so that there was little deterrence: once a registrable agreement was notified to the OFT, the restrictions in it were provisionally valid, and remained so unless and until the OFT brought proceedings in the Restrictive Practices Court to challenge the restrictions in the agreement on the ground that they were 'significant' restrictions—a fairly rare occurrence. It was only if the Restrictive Practices Court then struck down a restriction (or if the parties had failed to notify the agreement in the first place) that the restrictions were rendered void and unenforceable. Moreover, although voidness exposed the parties to civil liability, no fines could be imposed on the parties, until and unless they committed a 'second offence' of purporting to enforce a registrable agreement in breach of an order already made against that agreement by the Restrictive Practices Court; in those cases, there could be contempt of court **1.08**

---

[6] The jurisdictional criterion for the application of Arts 81 and 82 (formerly Arts 85 and 86) EC is that the agreements or conduct 'may affect trade between Member States' of the EU, whether directly or indirectly, actually or potentially. Such an effect on inter-State trade has been held to arise even in cases where all the parties are in the same single Member State.

proceedings resulting in fines on the company concerned and on its directors, as well as possible imprisonment of the directors.

1.09　The case for a national prohibition on restrictive agreements, modelled on Article 81 (formerly Article 85) of the EC Treaty, was that Article 81 solves many of these deficiencies. An agreement only falls within the ambit of Article 81 if it is actually anti-competitive in its economic effect (or its object), rather than merely because it satisfies formalistic criteria. Once an agreement is within Article 81, however, the sanctions are much stronger than under the RTPA: restrictive provisions in the agreement are automatically void and unenforceable, with civil liability to third parties, until and unless they have been specifically exempted. Deterrence is strengthened by the possibility of fines being imposed (by the European Commission) on parties to agreements found to be in breach of Article 81. Notification of an agreement under Article 81 does not confer provisional validity on the restrictive provisions (although it does protect the parties from fines in respect of the period from notification until a decision has been taken on whether there is an infringement).

1.10　Finally, under Article 81 (formerly Article 85) the competition authorities (the European Commission) have stronger powers than existed under the RTPA—(i) to investigate undisclosed cartels and restrictive arrangements than exist under the RTPA, and also (ii) to take preventive action through interlocutory 'interim measures' during the course of an investigation into a suspected infringement which is causing damage.

1.11　In the original 1988 Green Paper, the RTPA was described in the following terms:

> Our present system is inflexible and slow, too often concerned with cases which are obviously harmless and not directed sufficiently at anti-competitive agreements. The scope for avoidance and evasion considerably weakens any deterrent effect the system has and enforcement powers are inadequate. The requirement to furnish insignificant agreements is not only wasteful of official resources but imposes an excessive burden on the firms.[7]

The Chapter I prohibition, based on Article 81 (formerly Article 85), is designed to remedy these deficiencies.

Abuses of Dominant Position

Single-firm Abuses

1.12　The arguments about reform of the law on abuses of a dominant position (or market power) were more finely-balanced. The existing UK legislation on single-firm abuses was set out in the provisions of the **Fair Trading Act 1973 (FTA)** dealing with 'scale monopolies', and in the provisions on anti-competitive practices in the **Competition Act 1980**. The two legislative regimes largely overlapped, although

---

[7]　Green Paper, n 3 above, para 2.8.

the Competition Act 1980 was designed as a somewhat faster procedure, generally used in cases where the abuses by the company concerned were more specific or localised.

The 'scale monopoly' provisions of the FTA apply to companies which account **1.13** for 25 per cent of the supply (or consumption) of goods or services of a particular description, either in the UK as a whole or in a part of the UK; any such company is deemed to be a 'scale monopolist'. The Competition Act provisions on anti-competitive practices—the scope of which was narrowed by exemptions in the years following their introduction in 1980—applied to any company enjoying at least 25 per cent of a relevant market and having an annual turnover of at least £10 million,[8] where that company was engaging in anti-competitive practices. Under both pieces of legislation, abusive conduct could only be prohibited after a lengthy procedure, involving all the following steps: (i) a preliminary investigation by the OFT; (ii) a full-length inquiry by the MMC (Monopolies and Mergers Commission—forerunner of the new Competition Commission); (iii) the MMC concluding in its report that there is a scale monopoly, in the case of the FTA, or an anti-competitive practice, in the case of the Competition Act 1980; (iv) the MMC further concluding that the conduct in question operates against the public interest; and (v) the Secretary of State, on receiving the MMC report, deciding to require or order the company concerned to cease the conduct in question. Until and unless all these hoops have been passed through, the conduct can continue unchecked. The whole process usually takes many months, and often one or two years. There is no possibility of interim measures in the meantime—so that it is quite possible that, by the time abusive conduct is finally prohibited, it is too late to remedy the anti-competitive effects (for example, predatory pricing by a dominant company successfully forcing smaller competitors to exit the market).

The slowness of the process under the old system was compounded by the weak- **1.14** ness of the sanctions. There are no fines under the FTA or the Competition Act 1980, and civil liability to third parties who might be damaged by the abusive conduct arises only if the abusive conduct continues after the Secretary of State has required its cessation. In short, the only sanction for abusive conduct under the old UK legislation, after months or years of investigation, has been a somewhat feeble requirement not to repeat the abuse in the future!

The contrast with the EC rules on abusing a dominant position, in Article 82 **1.15** (formerly Article 86) of the EC Treaty, could not be greater. Under Article 82, abuses of a dominant position are prohibited as soon as they occur—so that, once a company has been investigated and found to have abused a dominant position, in breach of Article 82, it has civil liability to third parties for losses suffered *from the moment the abusive conduct began* (rather than, as under the FTA or the

---

[8] The relevant turnover is that of the corporate group of which the company forms part.

Competition Act 1980, from the moment the authorities, having completed their investigation, ruled against it). As a result, third parties who have suffered such losses may sue in national courts for damages or injunctive relief. Contractual provisions prohibited under Article 82, as well as giving rise to civil liability, are automatically void and unenforceable in national courts. In addition, substantial fines may be imposed by the European Commission on parties which infringe the Article 82 prohibition. The European Commission also has powers under Article 82 to impose 'interim measures' to prohibit conduct while it is being investigated, as well as strong investigatory powers.

1.16 From these clear differences between, on the one hand, the FTA scale monopoly provisions and the Competition Act 1980 and, on the other, Article 82 (formerly Article 86) flowed the arguments about whether to replace the existing UK legislation with a national prohibition modelled on Article 82. The proponents of such change have argued that the existing UK legislation—because of the delays before any conduct can be prohibited, the weakness of the sanctions even where conduct is prohibited, the lack of effective investigatory powers and the absence of interim measures—could not effectively deter anti-competitive behaviour, and thus stifled effective competition in the UK market. Accordingly:

> The chief gain from a prohibition system with penalties is the deterrence of anti-competitive activity. This in itself would make competition policy far more effective.[9]

1.17 However, opponents of an Article 82 (formerly Article 86)-type prohibition have argued that the strong penalties could be counter-productive, and in fact could have an anti-competitive effect. The danger was said to arise because there are no clear-cut definitions under Article 82 of the concepts of 'abuse' and 'dominant position', so that a company will often be uncertain whether its commercial behaviour is legitimate or illegitimate, and therefore uncertain whether its commercial behaviour will expose it to the risk of fines and civil proceedings. The risks created by the combination of uncertainty and the serious sanctions for illegitimate conduct would, it was claimed, make the company excessively cautious about commercial conduct, so deterring it from competing in perfectly legitimate ways. Opponents expressed the danger as being that a national prohibition:

> will, in the worst case, have a chilling effect on competition and commercial response in the market place. If companies are not clear what types of behaviour are outlawed by the prohibition, the law will not act as an effective deterrent and may have the result of preventing beneficial behaviour.[10]

---

[9] *Trade and Industry Committee Fifth Report: UK policy on monopolies* (HC Paper 249–I), 17 May 1995, para 105.

[10] Confederation of British Industry (CBI) response to Aug 1997 draft Competition Bill, Sept 1997, para 34.

'Complex Monopolies'

A further complication in the debate relates to the existence of the 'complex' **1.18** monopoly provisions of the FTA. These provisions allow for investigations by the MMC (now the Competition Commission) into entire *sectors* where there is market failure but where no single firm has a dominant position—and they enable such market failure to be remedied where the MMC concludes that it operates against the public interest. The complex monopoly provisions may be invoked in respect of conduct by a number of unconnected companies which, when taken together, account for at least 25 per cent of the supply (or consumption) of goods or services of a particular description, where their conduct is restrictive of competition in respect of those goods or services—even without there being any agreement or collusion between those companies.

The procedure is the same as under the scale monopoly provisions; but, in the case **1.19** of the complex monopoly provisions, it is thought to be an advantage that there are no fines or retrospective liability, and that the most severe sanction is a requirement that the practice should cease (after all, a company which does not itself have a dominant position, and cannot therefore be deemed to be on notice that it may be liable for abuses of a dominant position, ought not to be 'punished' as a result of the fact that the same conduct is practised by a number of other companies as well as by itself). Without any question of unfair punishment, market dysfunctions can be investigated, identified and stopped for the future. The complex monopoly provisions have been used to investigate and remedy market failures in a wide variety of industries, including brewing, newspaper distribution, private medical services and domestic electrical goods.[11]

There is no equivalent in EC competition law—and both proponents and oppo- **1.20** nents of a national prohibition modelled on Article 82 (formerly Article 86) generally supported the retention of the existing legislation on complex monopolies.

Abuse of Dominant Position—the Outcome of the Debate

The Competition Act 1998 introduces an Article 82-type prohibition: the **1.21** Chapter II prohibition. It abolishes the anti-competitive practices provisions of the Competition Act 1980. However, in accordance with the views expressed by all parties, the complex monopoly provisions of the FTA are retained. The scale monopoly provisions are also retained, but with the express intention that they should be used only in limited cases where: an infringement of the prohibition on abuse of a dominant position has already been held to have occurred; the OFT

---

[11] *The Supply of Beer* (complex monopoly), Cm 651, Mar 1989; *The Supply of National Newspapers* (scale and complex monopolies), Cm 2422, Dec 1993; *Private Medical Services* (complex monopoly), Cm 2452, Feb 1994; *Domestic Electrical Goods: I* (complex monopoly), Cm 3675, July 1997; *Domestic Electrical Goods: II* (complex monopoly), Cm 3676, July 1997.

believes that there is a real prospect of future abuses by the same firm; and a scale monopoly investigation is necessary for structural remedies to prevent such possible future abuses.[12] (The government has also proposed that the scale monopoly provisions may be used in the regulated utility sectors even if there has been no prior infringement of the prohibition on abuse of a dominant position.[13])

The operation of the FTA monopoly provisions under the new system is more fully discussed in Chapters 17 and 18 below.

Conformity with EC Law

1.22 In addition to the specific merits of the EC system as against the existing UK legislation, there was felt to be a benefit in the very fact of having UK legislation which broadly replicated EC legislation. Since the jurisdictional ambit of Articles 81 and 82 (formerly Articles 85 and 86) overlaps with the jurisdiction of national competition law, many businesses would be subject to both regimes—and it would reduce the regulatory burden on businesses if the two regimes could be made as similar as possible. It would be simpler (and cheaper in lawyers' fees) for a company to have to familiarise itself with one body of legal rules rather than two very different sets of rules. Conformity between the EC and national rules would also make the process of submitting notifications to the competition authorities simpler and cheaper: it would be more likely that the same factual and legal points could be made whether the notification was to the EC or the UK authority. Finally, similar sets of rules would reduce the risks of 'double jeopardy'—that is, a risk that conduct, once cleared by one authority, could nevertheless be prohibited by the other.

1.23 These benefits of following EC law were recognised even by the government of Margaret Thatcher, which was not known for seeking to make national laws conform with EC rules just for the sake of it. In 1988 (the same year as the Bruges speech), the government's Green Paper on restrictive trade practices policy said that a national prohibition based on Article 81 (formerly Article 85):

> has the added benefit of alignment with existing EC law for the sake of consistency and simplicity. Increasingly UK companies must have close regard to EC competition rules. Much greater compatibility between EC and UK law than the present system affords will make the latter more easily comprehensible and workable for the business community.[14]

---

[12] Lord Simon of Highbury, Minister of State at the Department of Trade and Industry, *Hansard*, HL, vol 586 no 107, 19 Feb 1998, col 351.

[13] Department of Trade and Industry, 'A Fair Deal for Consumers: Modernising the Framework for Utility Regulation—the Response to Consultation', July 1998, 20. See also: Office of Fair Trading, 'Competiton Act 1988: Concurrent Application to Regulated Industries' (OFT 405), para 4.8.

[14] Green Paper, n 3 above, para 3.15.

The UK Competition Authorities

The debate on reform also extended to the question whether the UK competition   **1.24**
authorities themselves should be reformed. A contrast was drawn between the
tripartite institutional structure in the United Kingdom—where there were separate roles for the Secretary of State, the OFT and the Monopolies and Mergers
Commission (MMC)[15]—and the unitary institutional structure in EC competition law, where all investigatory and decision-making powers under Articles 81
and 82 (formerly Articles 85 and 86) rest with the European Commission's
Competition Directorate (DG IV). For much of the decade after the 1988 Green
Paper, it was argued that the OFT and the MMC should be replaced by a single
competition authority so as to avoid duplication in the current system, enhance
consistency and speed up investigations.[16]

Others, however, saw the 'duplication' between the OFT and the MMC as an   **1.25**
advantage which the British system had over the EC system, and thought that it
ought to be preserved.[17] Their argument was that the 'separation of powers' provided 'checks and balances in the regulatory process', offering protection to companies from possible abuses of regulatory power. The EC system, by contrast,
suffered from the fact that powers were concentrated in one body which was 'simultaneously the detective, the prosecutor, the negotiator and the decision-maker'.[18]

C. The Road to the Legislation—What in Fact Happened

It has taken more than a decade from the original 1988 Green Paper for the reform   **1.26**
proposals to be fully debated and finally enacted in legislation.

On restrictive agreements and arrangements, the intention to replace the
RTPA with a national prohibition modelled on Article 81 (formerly Article 85)
was never in doubt. It was declared to be necessary in the 1988 Green Paper, reaf-
firmed by the government in a 1989 White Paper,[19] supported in 1995 by the all-
party House of Commons Trade and Industry Select Committee,[20] incorporated
in a draft Competition Bill published by the Conservative government in August
1996—and advocated by both the Labour and Conservative parties in their man-
ifestos at the 1997 General Election.

---

[15] Or, in the case of the RTPA, the Restrictive Practices Court.

[16] See, eg, *Trade and Industry Committee Fifth Report*, n 9 above, paras 133 and 135.

[17] *Government Observations on the Trade and Industry Committee Fifth Report* (HC Paper 748),
19 July 1995, p. viii.

[18] House of Lords Select Committee on the European Communities, *Report on Enforcement of
Community Competition Rules*, Dec 1993 (HL Paper 7–I).

[19] White Paper, *Opening Markets: New Policy on Restrictive Trade Practices*, Cm 727, July 1989,
para 1.2.

[20] *Trade and Industry Committee Fifth Report*, n 9 above, para 95.

1.27 The only area of controversy regarding restrictive agreements was the fact that it has taken so long to introduce the widely-supported reforms. The 1989 White Paper promised that new legislation would be introduced 'as soon as Parliamentary time permits'.[21] Six years later, legislation still had not been brought before Parliament, and the House of Commons Select Committee observed that the then government's repeated pledge to introduce the reform when Parliamentary time allows was 'wearing thin'.[22] Although in the summer of 1996 the Conservative government published a draft of a Competition Bill to give effect to the proposed reforms, indicating a degree of commitment to introduce legislation, in the event it did not prove possible to do so in what was to be the final session of the Parliament before the 1997 Election. By 1997, Labour was saying that reform was a matter of 'quite striking urgency'[23]—and within a fortnight of Labour coming to office, the new government announced (through the Queen's speech) that legislation would be introduced in the first session of the new Parliament. That legislation has been enacted as the Competition Act 1998.

1.28 In reality, the delays in introducing legislation on restrictive agreements are largely explicable by the fact that, while there was consensus in that area, there was doubt about how to reform the law in the other major area under discussion—the rules on abuse of a dominant position.

1.29 Reform of the law on abuse of a dominant position had not been addressed by the 1988 Green Paper or the 1989 White Paper. In 1992, however, the government published a Green Paper on the issue. This Green Paper—by contrast with the 1988 Green Paper on restrictive agreements—did not propose a single solution, but instead canvassed three possible options for reforming the law on the abuses of a dominant position:

(i) retention of the existing system, but with stronger investigative powers for the OFT;

(ii) adoption of a prohibition system based on Article 82 (formerly Article 86); or

(iii) adoption of a prohibition system based on Article 82, together with the retention of certain investigative powers under the FTA monopoly provisions.[24]

1.30 In April 1993, following consultation on the Green Paper proposals, the Government indicated that it would not be introducing a prohibition system based on Article 82 (formerly Article 86), but that it favoured option (i)—that is,

---

[21] White Paper, *Opening Markets*, n 19 above, para 1.2.
[22] *Government Observations*, n 17 above, p. v.
[23] Margaret Beckett, Labour spokesman on trade and industry, *Financial Times*, 14 Feb 1997.
[24] Green Paper, *Abuse of Market Power: A Consultative Document on Possible Legislative Options*, Cm 2100, Nov 1992.

retaining the existing system, but strengthening it.[25] The Conservatives broadly maintained this approach during the remainder of their period in office. The draft Competition Bill which they published in 1996 elaborated on how the existing legislation would be strengthened, but contained no proposals for an Article 82-type prohibition. There was, however, a slight softening of the Conservatives' position in a speech made by the Secretary of State for Trade and Industry, Ian Lang, in January 1997: Mr Lang reiterated the Conservatives' preference for reforms of the existing system rather than a new EC-type prohibition, but announced that he did 'not have a closed mind on this issue' and that the Conservatives would 'look further' at the feasibility of a full prohibition.[26]

The Labour Party, meanwhile, was taking the opposite position, and advocated a **1.31** prohibition based on Article 82 (formerly Article 86). In the years preceding the 1997 General Election, Labour was supported in this view by the Trade and Industry Select Committee report of 1995, by the OFT and by the National Consumer Council[27] (the Confederation of British Industry, however, was considerably less enthusiastic). An Article 82-type prohibition was promised in Labour's Business Manifesto at the 1997 General Election, and has been included in the new Competition Act 1998.

In terms of institutional reform, the Conservative government was adamant that **1.32** separation between the OFT and MMC should be maintained, and that they should not be replaced by a single competition authority. This point was made in its official response to the 1995 Select Committee report, and was reiterated in the Conservative manifesto.[28] The Select Committee itself had recommended the amalgamation of the OFT and MMC into a single competition authority[29]—and at that time, in 1995, this had also been the position of the Labour Party. However, in January 1997, Tony Blair acknowledged 'the potential unfairness of a single authority acting as "prosecutor, judge and jury" '.[30] The Competition Act 1998 shows that the idea of amalgamation has been rejected: although there is a new Competition Commission, it has taken on the functions of the old MMC in respect of the continuing FTA monopoly provisions, and will act as an appeals body in cases under the new prohibitions, while the OFT remains as a separate body of preliminary investigation.

---

[25] Department of Trade and Industry press notice; 'Abuse of Market Power', P/93/204, 14 Apr 1993.

[26] Speech by Ian Lang, President of the Board of Trade, to Competition Policy Conference at Skinner's Hall in the City of London, 21 Jan 1997. Summarised in Department of Trade and Industry press notice P/97/52, 21 Jan 1997.

[27] *Trade and Industry Committee Fifth Report*, n 9 above, para 118.

[28] *Government Observations*, , n 17 above, p. ix.

[29] *Trade and Industry Committee Fifth Report*, n 9 above, para 143.

[30] Speech by Tony Blair, Leader of the Labour Party, to the IPPR conference, at the New Connaught Rooms, London, WC2, 21 Jan 1997.

2

THE INSTITUTIONS

A. Overview

2.01 The relevant UK competition authorities for the purposes of the Competition Act are the Office of Fair Trading, the Competition Commission and the Secretary of State.

- *The Office of Fair Trading* (OFT), headed by the Director General of Fair Trading (the Director), has responsibility for the day-to-day operation of the regime under the Competition Act—including conducting investigations; giving guidance on the application of the Act and deciding whether the prohibitions have been infringed; granting exemptions from the prohibitions; and taking enforcement measures including the imposition of fines. Where agreements or conduct being considered under the Act concern the regulated utilities, the OFT shares jurisdiction concurrently with the relevant sectoral utilities regulator(s).[1]

- *The Competition Commission* is created by the Competition Act and given two main functions: first, to hear appeals against decisions made by the OFT or sectoral regulators under the Act; secondly, to take on the duties previously carried out by the Monopolies and Mergers Commission under the Fair Trading Act 1973, regarding the conduct of monopoly and merger investigations following a reference to it by the Secretary of State or the OFT.

---

[1] OFFER, OFGAS, OFREG, OFTEL, ORR, and OFWAT—see Ch 19 as regards concurrent jurisdiction under the Competition Act.

- *The Secretary of State* has an overall rule-making or approving function under the Competition Act—including extending, restricting or removing exclusions from the Chapter I and Chapter II prohibitions; making 'block exemption' orders following a recommendation by the OFT; and approving guidance given by the OFT in relation to appropriate levels of penalties.

This chapter considers the role of each authority in this tripartite institutional structure.

B. The Office of Fair Trading

Structure and Organisation of the OFT

The OFT was established under the Fair Trading Act in 1973. The Director **2.02** General of Fair Trading is appointed by the Secretary of State[2] and supported by the OFT, a non-ministerial department of government.[3] OFT staff are appointed by the Director General, subject to the approval of the Minister of Civil Service as to number and terms and conditions of service.[4] During the 1996–7 financial year, the permanent staff of the OFT averaged 409, including 15 lawyers and 18 economists.[5]

The duties of the OFT extend beyond competition policy to include consumer **2.03** protection matters, and consequently it is structured into two broad operational Divisions: Competition Policy and Consumer Affairs. Within the field of competition policy, in addition to its activities relating to restrictive agreements and abuse of a dominant market position under the Competition Act, the OFT also has duties relating to monopolies and merger control under the Fair Trading Act, and responsibility for liaison with other competition authorities (primarily the European Commission over cases falling under the EC Merger Regulation[6] or Articles 81 and 82 (formerly Articles 85 and 86) of the EC Treaty).

The increased powers and responsibilities of the OFT that the Competition Act **2.04** entails have, on the competition policy side of its role, necessitated significant internal reorganisation, recruitment of extra staff[7] and a programme of economic and legal training for existing and new staff. As regards re-organisation, the OFT is likely to be restructured along the lines of the Directorate-General of the

---

[2] Fair Trading Act 1973, s 1(1).
[3] As with other UK competition legislation, functions under the Competition Act are formally allocated to the Director. However, in practice they are carried out by the staff of the OFT under supervision of the Director and so, in accordance with common usage, references in this book are to the OFT rather than the Director.
[4] Fair Trading Act 1973, s 1(5).
[5] Annual report of the Director General of Fair Trading, 1997.
[6] Council Reg (EEC) 4064/89, as amended: [1990] OJ L257/13 and [1998] OJ L180/1.
[7] The Explanatory and Financial Memorandum for the Competition Bill estimated that approximately 50 new posts would be required.

European Commission concerned with competition (DG IV). The OFT's Director of Competition Policy will now head a Division containing a number of different branches:[8]

(i) *a Policy Branch* similar to Branch A of DG IV, containing substantial economic and legal expertise and charged with overall monitoring of cases and ensuring policy consistency across the other branches. This Branch will also handle non-casework-related EU and international liaison;

(ii) *a Mergers Branch* continuing the OFT's existing duties as regards merger control under the Fair Trading Act and liaising with DG IV over EC Merger Regulation cases;

(iii) *a Cartels Branch* specialising in the exposure and investigation of cartels. This Branch will include specialist investigators to gather evidence, which will then be assessed separately by case officers also within the Branch; and

(iv) *Sectoral Branches* dealing with casework, including the handling of notifications and non cartel-related complaints, across a number of specific industry sectors—eg financial services, media and transport. There are likely to be four sectoral branches. These will also liaise directly with DG IV over casework where appropriate.

There will, in addition, continue to be a separate Legal Division, one half of which will advise on competition policy issues.

General Functions of the OFT

2.05 From its establishment, the OFT has been charged with a number of general duties:[9]

(i) to keep under review the carrying out of commercial activities in the UK in relation to goods or services, and to collect information with respect to such activities and the persons by whom they are carried on, with a view to becoming aware of practices which may adversely affect the economic interests of UK consumers;

(ii) to receive and collate evidence with respect to such UK commercial activities which appear to it to be evidence of practices that may adversely affect the economic or other interests (including health and safety) of UK consumers;

(iii) to keep under review commercial activities in the UK and collect necessary information on such activities, and the persons by whom they are carried on, with a view to becoming aware of monopoly situations or uncompetitive practices;

---

[8] Margaret Bloom, Director of Competition Policy, Office of Fair Trading: paper to 'The Europeanisation of UK Competition Law' conference, 10 Sept 1998, paras 26 and 27.
[9] Fair Trading Act 1973, s 2.

(iv) to give information and assistance to the Secretary of State in respect of the duties described above, where the OFT considers it expedient or is so requested by the Secretary of State;

(v) to make recommendations to the Secretary of State as to action which in the OFT's opinion it would be expedient for the Secretary of State to take in relation to any of the matters in respect of which the OFT has duties.

The Competition Act sets out procedures under which parties to a particular **2.06** agreement or conduct may notify the OFT with a view to obtaining guidance or a decision from it as regards the application of the Chapter I and Chapter II prohibitions.[10] The OFT also has powers to conduct investigations where there is reasonable suspicion that either of the prohibitions has been infringed.[11] Investigations may be instigated by third party complainants or by the OFT acting on its own initiative. The general duties of the OFT outlined above consequently provide an important framework for its role in performing these functions under the Competition Act. The OFT is able to carry out regular monitoring of UK business activity—its staff review newspapers, trade and other journals, on-line information services etc—allowing it to gather information and market knowledge to be used as a basis in deciding whether and how to proceed with investigations, and to assist in assessing the market significance of particular agreements and conduct that have been notified to it.

Specific Functions of the OFT under the Competition Act

The OFT is the key agency in relation to the implementation and enforcement of **2.07** the Chapter I and Chapter II prohibitions under the Competition Act. It has a number of specific responsibilities under the Act, of which the most important are set out below.

In relation to *the Chapter I prohibition*: **2.08**

(i) to give guidance on whether agreements notified to it are likely to infringe the Chapter I prohibition;[12]

(ii) to make decisions whether or not agreements notified to it infringe the Chapter I prohibition;[13]

(iii) to grant individual exemptions to agreements that infringe the Chapter I prohibition, for such duration and subject to such conditions and obligations as it considers appropriate;[14]

---

[10] Ss 12–16 in respect of the Chapter I prohibition and ss 20–24 in respect of the Chapter II prohibition—see Ch 12 as regards notifications.
[11] S 25(1)—see Ch 14 as regards investigations.
[12] S 13.
[13] S 14.
[14] S 4.

(iv)   to recommend 'block exemptions' to the Secretary of State in respect of particular categories of agreement;[15]

(v)   to apply the 'opposition procedure' to agreements that satisfy specified criteria set out in a block exemption;[16]

(vi)   to recommend variation or revocation of block exemptions to the Secretary of State;[17]

(vii)   in the case of agreements benefiting from 'parallel exemption' (broadly, automatic exemption from the Chapter I prohibition as a result of meeting criteria for exemption from the prohibition on restrictive agreements in Article 81 (formerly Article 85) of the EC Treaty): to impose, vary or remove conditions or obligations subject to which such exemptions are to have effect; and to impose additional conditions or obligations, or cancel the exemption;[18]

(viii)   in specified circumstances, to take further action and to remove the immunity from penalties that otherwise benefits agreements in respect of which it has given positive guidance (ie that an agreement is unlikely to infringe the Chapter I prohibition or is likely to be exempted) or made a favourable decision (ie that an agreement does not infringe the Chapter I prohibition or is exempted).[19]

2.09   In relation to *the Chapter II prohibition*:

(ix)   to give guidance as to whether or not conduct notified to it is likely to infringe the Chapter II prohibition;[20]

(x)   to make decisions as to whether or not conduct notified to it infringes the Chapter II prohibition;[21]

(xi)   in specified circumstances, to take further action following positive guidance or a favourable decision under the Chapter II prohibition.[22]

2.10   As regards *investigations and enforcement* of the prohibitions:

(xii)   to conduct an investigation if it has reasonable suspicion that the Chapter I or Chapter II prohibition has been infringed;[23]

(xiii)   during an investigation, to require the production of specified documents[24] and to enter and search premises;[25]

---

[15] S 6.
[16] S 7
[17] S 8(3).
[18] S 10(5).
[19] Ss 15–16.
[20] S 21.
[21] S 22.
[22] Ss 23–24.
[23] S 25.
[24] S 26.
[25] Ss 27–28.

(xiv)   to make infringement decisions and to give directions to the relevant persons to bring the infringement to an end;[26]

(xv)   where such a direction has been given and a person fails without reasonable excuse to comply, to apply to the court for an appropriate order;[27]

(xvi)   in specified circumstances, to take 'interim measures' prior to completion of an investigation in order to prevent serious and irreparable damage;[28]

(xvii) on making an infringement decision, to require the payment of a penalty[29] and take action for the recovery of the penalty;[30]

(xviii) to prepare and publish guidance on the appropriate amount of penalties, with the approval of the Secretary of State;[31]

(xix)   to withdraw the immunity from penalties that otherwise applies to 'small agreements' and conduct of 'minor significance'.[32]

As regards *other functions*:   **2.11**

(xx)   to consider third party appeals against its decisions;[33]

(xxi)   to make Procedural Rules, subject to approval by the Secretary of State;[34]

(xxii) to publish general advice and information (OFT Guidelines) on the application of the Act;[35]

(xxiii) to charge fees in connection with its exercise of its functions under the Act, eg notification fees;[36]

(xxiv) to assist the European Commission in conducting investigations under Article 81 or 82 (formerly Article 85 or 86) of the EC Treaty or carry out such investigations on its behalf.[37]

Under the Fair Trading Act, the OFT's main functions as regards monopoly inves-   **2.12**
tigations are:[38]

(i)   to make a monopoly reference to the Competition Commission;[39]

---

[26] Ss 32–33.
[27] S 34.
[28] S 35.
[29] S 36.
[30] S 37.
[31] S 38.
[32] Ss 39–40.
[33] S 47.
[34] S 51.
[35] S 52.
[36] S 53.
[37] Ss 61–64.
[38] See Chs 17 and 18.
[39] FTA s 50.

(ii) to propose that the Secretary of State accept undertakings as an alternative to the OFT making a monopoly reference in certain circumstances[40] and keep such undertakings under review;[41]

(iii) to investigate by requiring the production of specified documents or information and entering premises, for the purpose of assisting it in deciding whether to exercise its functions under (ii) or (iii).[42]

C. The Competition Commission

2.13 The Competition Commission, established under the Competition Act,[43] replaces the Monopolies and Mergers Commission (MMC). It exercises appeal functions in respect of the Chapter I and II prohibitions under the Competition Act, and carries out the functions previously exercised by the MMC—those in relation to monopoly and merger inquiries under the Fair Trading Act following a referral to it by the OFT or the Secretary of State[44] and for inquiries in respect of the regulated utility industries regarding disputed licence conditions.[45]

Structure of the Competition Commission

2.14 Members of the Competition Commission are appointed by the Secretary of State to one or more of three panels: the appeal panel dealing with appeals from decisions of the OFT regarding the Chapter I and Chapter II prohibitions; the reporting panel performing the other reporting functions of the Commission; and the specialist panel exercising the Commission's sectoral powers in relation to water, electricity and telecommunications.[46] MMC members, of which there were some 40 at the end of 1998, chosen from a wide variety of backgrounds (business, the professions, the trade unions and academia), become members of the reporting panel.

2.15 The Competition Commission has a Chairman and one or more Deputy Chairmen appointed by the Secretary of State from the reporting panel members.[47] There is also a President of the Competition Commission Appeal Tribunals appointed from the appeal panel members by the Secretary of State after consul-

---

[40] FTA s 56A.

[41] FTA s 56E.

[42] FTA s 44 as amended by Competition Act s 66.

[43] S 45. The Competition Commission came into being on 1 Apr 1999.

[44] FTA s 5 and ss 47–56.

[45] Under the Telecommunications Act 1984; the Airports Act 1986 and the Airports (N Ireland) Order 1994; the Gas Acts 1986 and 1995 and the Gas (N Ireland) Order 1996; the Electricity Act 1989 and the Electricity (N Ireland) Order 1992, the Broadcasting Act 1990; the Water Industry Act 1991; and the Railways Act 1993.

[46] Sch 7, para 2.

[47] Sch 7, para 3.

tation with the Lord Chancellor and the Lord Advocate.[48] The President of the Appeal Tribunals is required to have at least 10 years' general legal qualification[49] or equivalent experience in Northern Ireland and must have appropriate experience and knowledge of competition law and practice. Members of the Competition Commission are appointed for periods of five years at a time but may be re-appointed for a further term.[50]

The Competition Commission has a management board, known as the Competition Commission Council and made up of the Chairman of the Commission, the President of the Appeal Tribunals, the Secretary to the Commission and such other members as the Secretary of State may appoint.[51] The Chairman has a casting vote. **2.16**

Like MMC members before them, Competition Commission members are supported by a permanent staff. In 1998 the MMC had a permanent staff of approximately 90; the Competition Commission may have more in view of its increased functions under the Competition Act. **2.17**

As regards its general functions (ie with the exception of its appeals functions), any function of the Competition Commission must be undertaken by a group of three or more members selected by the Chairman from the reporting or specialist panels, and chaired by a person appointed by the Chairman.[52] The Chairman is able to appoint a replacement for any member of a group or appoint an additional member from the reporting panel even if the proceedings of the group are under way.[53] Non-members of a group may also attend meetings if invited by the chairman of the group, although a non-member may not vote or have a statement of dissent recorded.[54] Each group is free to determine its own procedure, including its quorum, subject to guidance given by the Chairman or any special or general directions given by the Secretary of State.[55] The person chairing a group has a casting vote.[56] **2.18**

So far as appeals are concerned, these are to be heard before appeal tribunals consisting of three members and appointed by the President of the Appeal Tribunals on receipt of a notice of appeal.[57] There will be a further panel of appeal panel members appointed by the Secretary of State for the purposes of providing **2.19**

---

[48] Sch 7, para 4.
[49] Within the meaning of the Courts and Legal Services Act 1990, s 71—eg barrister or solicitor.
[50] Sch 7, para 6.
[51] Sch 7, para 5.
[52] Sch 7, paras 15–16.
[53] Sch 7, para 17.
[54] Sch 7, para 18.
[55] Sch 7, para 19.
[56] Sch 7, para 21.
[57] Sch 7, para 27.

chairmen of appeal tribunals.[58] Such persons must have a seven-year general legal qualification[59] and also appropriate experience and knowledge of competition law and practice. Each appeal tribunal will be chaired by a member of this further panel or the President himself.[60]

2.20 The Secretary of State is to make procedural rules with respect to appeals and appeal tribunals, after consultation with the President of the Appeal Tribunals (see Chapter 16 for more details).[61]

Functions of the Competition Commission under the Competition Act

2.21 The Competition Commission's function under the Competition Act (apart from conducting monopoly and merger investigations) is to hear appeals:

    (i)   from parties to an agreement in respect of which the OFT or a sectoral regulator has made a decision or persons in respect of whose conduct the OFT or a regulator has made a decision;[62] and

    (ii) from third parties against a decision of the OFT or a regulator (third parties are required to show a sufficient interest).[63]

2.22 The decisions in respect of which an appeal may be heard are those of the OFT or a regulator relating to:

    (i)   whether the Chapter I or Chapter II prohibition has been infringed;

    (ii)   whether a block exemption or a parallel exemption applies;

    (iii) whether to grant an individual exemption, and as to any condition or obligation in relation to it;

    (iv) whether to extend the duration of an individual exemption and, if so, for how long;

    (v)   whether to cancel an exemption;

    (vi) on the imposition of any penalty or its amount.[64]

2.23 Where relevant, the appeal can also be against any OFT or regulator directions to terminate or modify agreements or conduct which accompany the infringement decision, and against interim measures directions.

---

[58] Sch 7, para 26.
[59] See n 46 above.
[60] Sch 7, para 27.
[61] S 48(2).
[62] S 46.
[63] S 47(6).
[64] S 46(3).

D. The Secretary of State

Statutory convention is to allocate functions to be carried out by Government **2.24** Ministers to the Secretary of State, without specifying which particular Secretary of State should exercise such functions. In practice, all relevant functions under the Competition Act are exercised by the Secretary of State for Trade and Industry as advised by another Minister of State or Under Secretary of State specifically responsible for Competition and Consumer Affairs.

Functions of the Secretary of State

The Secretary of State's functions under the Act are mainly confined to making or **2.25** approving rules and agreeing the scope of exclusions and exemptions. Unlike the OFT and the Competition Commission, the Secretary of State has no obligations under section 60 of the Act to exercise his functions in a manner consistent with EC competition law. The main functions of the Secretary of State are as follows:

(i) to amend Schedules 1 and 3 to the Act so as to add to, amend or remove any of the exclusions from the Chapter I or II prohibitions (and, in specified circumstances, to grant exclusion to individual agreements);[65]

(ii) to make, vary or revoke orders introducing block exemptions from the Chapter I prohibition following a recommendation by the OFT or consultation with the OFT;[66]

(iii) to determine by order the provisions for calculating percentage of turnover of an undertaking for the purposes of imposing penalties,[67] and to approve the general guidance to be given by the OFT in relation to the appropriate amount of penalties;[68]

(iv) to make by order further provisions to those in the Act concerning the dissolution of the MMC and the transfer of its functions to the Competition Commission;[69]

(v) to make procedural rules concerning appeals and Appeal Tribunals following consultation with the President of the Appeal Tribunals and such other persons as he considers appropriate.[70]

(vi) to specify further functions and persons in relation to which the confidentiality obligations in the Act do not apply.[71]

---

[65] S 3(2)–(3).
[66] Ss 6 and 8.
[67] S 36(8).
[68] S 38(4).
[69] S 45(5).
[70] S 48(2).
[71] S 55(6).

3

RELATION WITH EC LAW

A. Overview

3.01 The wording of the new UK Chapter I and Chapter II prohibitions mirrors to a large extent the EC competition law prohibitions in Articles 81 and 82 (formerly Articles 85 and 86) of the EC Treaty. Obligations to ensure that the new UK prohibitions operate consistently with EC law arise, as a matter of EC law, under the EC Treaty and, as a matter of UK law, by virtue of the Competition Act. This chapter considers the policy and legal reasons for achieving consistency between UK and EC competition law, and how far as a matter of practice alignment has been achieved.

B. Policy Considerations

The policies of successive UK governments for reforming UK competition law are **3.02** reviewed in Chapter 1. The following paragraphs examine the broad policy considerations and constraints regarding the specific issue of modelling the Competition Act on EC law.

No Legal Requirement to Conform the Act with EC Law

The European Court of Justice (ECJ) has confirmed on many occasions that **3.03** national competition authorities are fully entitled to examine, under national law, the same case which is being examined by the European Commission under EC law, subject to the important qualification that the national authorities must not prejudice the full and uniform application of EC law or the effects of measures taken to implement EC law.[1] Thus, there was no legal obligation under EC law to model the reform of UK competition law on existing EC competition law—the objective of alignment was based on a business or political case rather than a legal obligation. This case is considered in more detail below.

Reducing the Regulatory Burden for Business

Businesses in the UK can be affected simultaneously by UK and EC law. Clearly, **3.04** where there are concurrent competition law systems applying and these differ, an increased regulatory burden is placed on business. Indeed, this was one of the main criticisms of the regime in the UK prior to the Competition Act. Businesses faced a double regulatory burden—'double jeopardy'—as a result of the existence of two unaligned sets of competition rules. The two systems arose from differing philosophies and policy objectives and so resulted in two quite different sets of requirements and procedures. Since the rules governing the legality of agreements and abuses of market power differed considerably as between the UK and EC, compliance with one regime had little direct impact on compliance with the other. The extra costs arising from having to comply with such divergent regimes, whilst difficult to assess precisely, can reasonably be estimated to have been significant.

There was thus a clear potential benefit in aligning the two systems of law to **3.05** reduce inconsistency, irrespective of the merits in themselves of the EC regime

---

[1] Joined Cases 253/78 and 1–3/79 *Procureur de la République & Ors v Giry and Guérlain* [1980] ECR 2327; Case C–14/68 *Wilhelm v Bundeskartellamt* [1969] ECR 1.

(the case for alignment does not, of itself, confirm any such merits). This was a major reason for drafting the two prohibitions contained in the Competition Act to mirror to a large degree Articles 81 and 82 (formerly Articles 85 and 86) of the EC Treaty.

3.06 Resource Constraints on the Competition Authorities

Competition authorities have only finite resources. In order to maximise the effective use of their resources, both the European Commission and the OFT are keen to avoid having to deal with notifications or complaints that do not give rise to appreciable competition or other policy concerns. A system which gives rise to a significant amount of dual notifications (ie requires companies to notify both EC and UK authorities) or dual complaints is wasteful of administrative resources as well as burdensome on business, and diverts the authorities from focusing on their priorities. Thus, in reducing administrative overlap, alignment of national and EC competition regimes offers significant advantages to the respective competition authorities as well as to business.

3.07 The arguments for reducing administrative overlap between competition authorities have been recognised by the European Commission in its Notice on co-operation between national authorities and the Commission in handling cases falling within the scope of Article 81 or 82 (formerly Article 85 or 86) of the EC Treaty (the Co-operation Notice), in which it states:

> Parallel proceedings before the Commission, on the one hand, and a national competition authority, on the other, are costly for businesses whose activities fall within the scope of the Community law and of Member States' competition laws. They can lead to the repetition of checks on the same activity, by the Commission, on the one hand, and by the competition authorities of the Member States concerned, on the other.[2]

The European Commission goes on to point out in the Co-operation Notice that co-operation between authorities reduces the risk of divergent decisions and gives rise to benefits 'to competition authorities in terms of mobilisation of their resources'.[3] The OFT also recognises in its guidelines on the Chapter I prohibition that notifications to both the Commission and the OFT are 'undesirable in terms of the compliance costs for undertakings and the duplication of effort by competition authorities'.[4] As a result of these considerations, a key objective in drafting the Competition Act was to try and ensure that, as far as possible, only one regime would need to be applied to any particular agreement or conduct.

---

[2] 'Notice on co-operation between national competition authorities and the Commission in handling cases falling within the scope of Art 85 or 86 [new Art 81 or 82] of the EC Treaty' [1997] OJ C313/3, para 10.

[3] Ibid, para 11.

[4] The Office of Fair Trading, 'Competition Act 1998: The Chapter I Prohibition' (OFT 401), para 7.1.

Overlap between EC Law and the Act

One straightforward way to ensure consistency and to avoid duplication would **3.08** have been to set out a clear jurisdictional demarcation—or 'bright line'— between, on the one hand, agreements or conduct which affect trade between EU Member States, which fall under EC law, and, on the other, agreements or conduct which only affect trade within the UK, to which UK law would have been applicable.

The benefits of such a jurisdictional demarcation have already become apparent **3.09** in the 'one stop shop' procedure that exists in the context of EC merger control law: the general rule under the merger control regime is that where specified turnover thresholds are exceeded, only EC law will apply and the European Commission has exclusive jurisdiction in the EU, whereas the Member States' national competition laws do not apply.[5] Conversely, where the thresholds are not exceeded, EU Member States' merger control laws apply and EC law on mergers does not apply. Thus, other than in exceptional circumstances, the parties involved need not concern themselves with any possible simultaneous application of *both* national *and* EC merger rules. However, this mutually exclusive jurisdiction of the European Commission and the Member States is imposed as a requirement of EC law,[6] rather than any bright line drawn by the national authorities themselves. No such exclusive jurisdiction is reserved in the application of Article 81 or 82 (formerly Article 85 or 86), and so the discretion to draw a bright line in the control of anti-competitive conduct and abusive behaviour by dominant companies rests with the national competition authorities themselves.[7]

From the UK's perspective, if the need to ensure consistency and avoid duplica- **3.10** tion were the only policy drivers in shaping the new UK competition regime, the objectives of reform could probably have been achieved by such a bright line. However, they were not the only relevant issues: a further level of resource issues *within* the European Commission's jurisdiction needed to be addressed. It is apparent that, at Community level, resource constraints mean that the European Commission is unable to investigate effectively all potential infringements of Articles 81 and 82 (formerly Articles 85 and 86) that come to its attention, ie even where there is an effect on trade between EU Member States. The European Commission is therefore selective in the cases that it investigates. It will generally investigate only those cases in which there is a 'significant Community interest'.[8]

---

[5] Council Reg (EEC) 4064/89 of 21 Dec 1989 on the control of concentrations between undertakings [1989] OJ L257/13 as amended by Council Reg (EC) 1310/97 of 30 June 1997 [1997] OJ L180/1.
[6] Ibid, Art 21(2).
[7] A division of this type is adopted under Italian law.
[8] See Ch 13 and Case T–24/90 *Automec Srl v EC Commission ('Automec II')* [1992] ECR II–2223.

3.11   Thus, while the 'effect on trade between EU Member States' test provides the jurisdictional basis for allocating responsibility between the European Commission and national authorities, it does not, at least in relation to complaints and own-initiative investigations, provide a practical basis for the allocation of jurisdiction. If the UK were to prevent its competition authorities from considering all cases which affected trade between EU Member States, there would be only a limited number of cases that remained under its jurisdiction because of the wide interpretation given to the effect on trade criterion. Whilst this would significantly reduce the OFT's caseload in terms of notifications, there would be a significant body of agreements and conduct which it would have been concerned should have competition scrutiny—cases that would have a material adverse effect on conditions of competition in the UK—but which would, in practice, be unreviewable. The OFT would not be able to investigate them and, even though these cases affected trade between EU Member States, they would not give rise to a significant Community interest such that the European Commission would investigate either.[9]

3.12   Consequently, the Competition Act provides alignment with EC competition law, but stops short of providing a bright line test for the division of responsibility between the UK and EC authorities. There is therefore a jurisdictional overlap as a result of the category of agreements and conduct which both affect trade *within* the UK and also affect trade *between* the UK and other EU Member States. Such agreements and conduct will fall within the scope of the Chapter I and II prohibitions as well as Articles 81 and 82 (formerly Articles 85 and 86).

3.13   It can be seen, however, that in spite of substantive alignment of competition law regimes this area of overlap gives rise to a tension between the aims of the EC and UK authorities. On the one hand, both the European Commission and the OFT are concerned to have the ability to *investigate* agreements and conduct, and hence the UK authority has retained a capacity to scrutinise cases within the UK which may also satisfy the 'effect on trade between EU Member States' criterion where the Commission has chosen not itself to investigate the case because there is insufficient Community interest. Yet, on the other hand, so far as dealing with *notifications* and the resources burden entailed are concerned, both authorities to some extent encourage notification to the other. Thus the European Commission in the Co-operation Notice indicates that one of its purposes is 'to induce firms to

---

[9] This problem could, at least to some extent, be overcome by giving the UK authorities power to apply Arts 81 and 82 (formerly Arts 85 and 86) directly (under Art 84 (formerly Art 88) of the EC Treaty) but the UK Government has generally been reluctant to endorse this approach, perhaps fearing that if the administration of EC law is delegated to national authorities, many national authorities will be less rigorous in applying it than the UK would be—thus unfairly 'tilting the playing field' to the detriment of UK companies.

[10] See n 2 above, para 8; although this is specifically with regard to national authorities applying Arts 81 and 82 (formerly Arts 85 and 86), this desire can be taken to extend to national authorities applying substantively similar national competition law such as the Chapter I and II prohibitions.

approach national competition authorities more often',[10] but the OFT has advised that the starting point in assessing an agreement will be to consider whether it may affect trade between EU Member States and emphasised the advantages of notifying the European Commission rather than the OFT (advantages which have been intentionally built into the Act).[11]

Other Policy Divergence

A further consideration in framing the Act has been that there are some aspects of   **3.14** EC law which it has been considered undesirable to incorporate at a national level; this has led to divergence from the EC model. Significantly, the Act contains provisions to allow for exclusion or exemption from the UK Chapter I prohibition of vertical agreements (those between parties at different levels of the supply chain, eg a manufacturer and a distributor) and land agreements,[12] even though such agreements fall within the scope of the equivalent EC prohibition in Article 81 (formerly Article 85).

In part, this divergence is because the policy objectives of EC law are not identical   **3.15** with those of UK law. In particular, the completion of a European single market is a fundamental feature of EC law, whereas it is of little relevance under the UK regime. Thus, one of the main reasons for including vertical agreements within the scope of EC competition law—that restrictions in such arrangements can significantly undermine market integration—does not arise under UK law. In fact, the Act, in its more permissive treatment of vertical agreements, is to some extent ahead of developments at EC level, where there are now significant doubts whether it is desirable to apply competition law prohibitions to such agreements.[13]

A further reason for differences between EC law and the UK measure is that the   **3.16** absence from the UK Act of the jurisdictional test requiring an effect on trade between EU Member States, coupled with the fact that the Act will apply to agreements or conduct in the UK regardless of the size of the geographic market,[14] means that certain types of agreement are now potentially captured by competition law in the UK, whereas before they were generally outside the scope of EC competition law. This is chiefly so in the case of land agreements, which would not normally affect trade between EU Member States such that they fall within Article 81(1) (formerly Article 85(1)), but typically contain provisions such as restrictive covenants which would, in the absence of provision otherwise, fall within the scope of the Chapter I prohibition. Without an exclusion for land

---

[11] See Ch 12 para 12.11, and OFT, n 4 above, para 7.4.

[12] S 50.

[13] See European Commission Green Paper on Vertical Restraints in EU Competition Policy, COM(96)721, 22 Jan 1997, and Follow-up to Green Paper [1998] OJ C365/3.

[14] Ss 2(8) and 18(3) make clear that the references to the UK in the prohibitions means any part of the UK, ie however small.

agreements, the Chapter I prohibition would apply to business relationships in respect of land in circumstances that would undermine normal commercial practices.

Consistency in Practice

3.17 It can be seen from an examination of the Act that, in some ways, strong efforts have been made to align the EC and UK regimes—in particular, through the following provisions in the Act:

- the system of *parallel exemptions* (see paragraphs 3.44–3.46 below);[15]

- section 60 of the Act—the '*governing principles*' section (see paragraphs 3.47–3.57 [below);[16]

- the provision that notification of an agreement to the European Commission (for individual exemption under Article 81 (formerly Article 85) confers *provisional immunity* from financial penalties under the Chapter I prohibition as well as from fines under Article 81, until the Commission determines the case (see Chapter 12 paragraphs 12.10 and 12.19 as regards this and other aspects of the EC and UK notification systems where co-ordination arises as matter of policy and subordinate procedure);[17]

- the requirement for the OFT, in determining the level of any penalties for breach of the Act, to *take into account any fines* or penalties which have been imposed by the European Commission or another EU Member States, in order to prevent double jeopardy (see Chapter 10 paragraph 10.44).[18]

3.18 Nevertheless, in spite of the general principle that there should be no duplication between the two jurisdictions and that 'double jeopardy' for business should be avoided, there remain significant areas in which the ambit of the two regimes overlap and significant areas of divergence. The Government's view during the passage of what was then the Competition Bill through Parliament was summarised in the House of Lords as follows:

> As for the question of divergences [from the EC system], we are not importing it 'lock, stock and barrel'. Divergences are possible in three respects. First, I have just explained that the Director [ie the head of the OFT] will be setting out his own rules for the detailed procedural administration of the new prohibition systems. Secondly, it is apparent from the face of the Bill where we have departed. A wider exclusion for mergers than exists under EC law is but one example . . . Thirdly, I explained at

---

[15] S 10.

[16] S 60.

[17] S 41. Consequently, there is no requirement, in the first instance, to notify an agreement to the UK authorities, where the agreement has been notified to the European Commission—although the OFT can still investigate on its own initiative.

[18] S 38(9). See also Office of Fair Trading 'Competition Act 1998: Enforcement' (OFT 407), para 4.40.

Committee that single market objectives would not be relevant to the domestic prohibition system.[19]

The impact of procedural differences, the effects of exclusions (such as those for vertical agreements and land agreements) and the relevance of Single Market objectives to the operation of the Competition Act are all considered below.

C. The EC and UK Prohibitions Compared

The starting point in considering the effects of such overlap and divergence is to examine the prohibitions in the EC Treaty and compare them with those in Competition Act.   **3.19**

Article 81 (formerly Article 85) EC and the Chapter I Prohibition

Article 81 (formerly Article 85) of the EC Treaty contains three separate provisions. First, Article 81(1) (formerly Article 85(1)) prohibits anti-competitive agreements between undertakings in so far as they may affect trade between EU Member States. An agreement of any kind whose object or effect is the prevention, restriction or distortion of competition and which meets the other criteria in Article 81(1) will be caught. Article 81(1) contains a non-exhaustive list of examples of the types of agreements which may be prohibited: price-fixing, limiting markets or production, market sharing, discrimination, and tying. Secondly, Article 81(2) (formerly Article 85(2)) provides that agreements which fall within Article 81(1) are void.   **3.20**

However, this is subject to the *possibility of exemption* under Article 81(3) (formerly Article 85(3)). This third provision under Article 81 (formerly Article 85) states that Article 81(1) (formerly Article 85(1)) shall not apply where an agreement (i) contributes to improving the production or distribution of goods or to promoting technical or economic progress; (ii) allows consumers a fair share of the resulting benefit; (iii) does not impose restrictions on the undertakings which are not indispensable to the attainment of the objectives of the agreement; and (iv) does not create the possibility that competition will be eliminated in respect of a substantial part of the market for the products affected by the agreement.   **3.21**

The **Chapter I prohibition** is set out in section 2 of the Act and the exemption criteria in section 9. These provisions are largely a carbon copy of Article 85. There are, however, two significant differences. First, Article 85 applies to agreements which affect trade between EU Member States whereas the Chapter I prohibition   **3.22**

---

[19] Lord Simon of Highbury; *Hansard,* HL, vol 586, no 116, col 1365 (5 Mar 1998).

bites on agreements which affect trade within the UK; this issue of territorial jurisdiction is considered in more detail in paragraphs 3.28–3.33 below. Secondly, there are a number of exclusions from the Chapter I prohibition, whereas there is no concept of exclusion under Article 81; these exclusions are discussed in paragraphs 3.34–3.35 below.

3.23 Another, minor difference is that the wording of the exemption criteria in section 9 is not limited by a specific reference to 'goods', whereas the wording of the equivalent criteria in Article 81(3) (formerly Article 85(3)) is so limited. However, this is not a material difference as it is clear that, in any event, Article 81(3) applies to agreements relating to services as well as goods.

Article 82 (formerly Article 86) EC and the Chapter II Prohibition

3.24 **Article 82 (formerly Article 86)** of the EC Treaty prohibits the abuse of a dominant position in a substantial part of the common market (EU), where the abuse may affect trade between EU Member States. Although any type of abuse is capable of being caught, Article 82 contains a non-exhaustive list of examples: imposing unfair purchase or selling conditions (including prices); limiting production, markets or technical development; discrimination; and tying.

3.25 There is no equivalent of Article 81(3) (formerly Article 85(3)) in the text of Article 82 (formerly Article 86). Therefore, where all of the conditions for the application of the Treaty provision are met, the prohibition is automatic and there is *no possibility of exemption.*

3.26 The **Chapter II prohibition** is set out in section 18 of the Act. As with Article 81 (formerly Article 85) and Chapter I, the Chapter II prohibition is virtually identical to Article 82 (formerly Article 86) save for the fact that it refers to an effect on trade within the United Kingdom or any part of it, rather than an effect on trade between EU Member States. As with Article 82, there is no possibility of exemption from the Chapter II prohibition. Again, however, there are a number of exclusions from Chapter II, whereas no such concept exists under Article 82.

3.27 One other significant difference is that Article 82 (formerly Article 86), in giving examples of behaviour that may constitute an abuse states 'such abuse may . . . consist in . . . ', whereas section 18 of the Act states 'conduct may . . . constitute such an abuse, if it consists in . . . '. It has been suggested that the specific reference to 'conduct' in section 18 may mean that it only prohibits acts, and does not prohibit omissions—for example, refusals to supply.[20] However, this is unlikely, both on grounds of principle, and as a matter of statutory interpretation. The objection in principle is that a restricted interpretation would involve a significant diver-

---

[20] See, eg, Aidan Robertson, 'UK and EC Competition Laws, Paper to Conference on Europeanisation of UK Competition Law,' 10 Sept 1998.

gence between the UK and EC provisions, contrary to the general purpose of the Act (as expressed in the 'governing principles' section) which is to align the substantive rules of UK law with the substantive EC rules. In any case, as a matter of interpretation, it is arguable that 'conduct' is not restricted to a positive act but also covers a failure to act, at least in circumstances where a request to act is made and a dominant undertaking decides not to accede to such a request. This difference between the wording of Article 82 and the Chapter II prohibition presumably results from the fact that 'conduct' (unlike 'abuse') is a neutral term for a phenomenon which may or may not be considered to infringe the Chapter II prohibition (equivalent to 'agreement' under the Chapter I prohibition) and which may, for example, be notified to see *whether or not* it constitutes an abuse (as in sections 20 to 22 of the Act). Article 82, lacking such a term, creates drafting awkwardness.

Territorial Jurisdiction

Article 81 (formerly Article 85) prohibits agreements which restrict competition within the common market (ie the EU), whereas the Chapter I prohibition applies to agreements which restrict competition within the UK (the Act also makes clear that the Chapter I prohibition applies only if the agreement is, or is intended to be, implemented in the United Kingdom[21]). Similarly, Article 82 (formerly Article 86) applies to abusive conduct by undertakings which have a dominant position within the common market (ie the EU) or a substantial part of it, whereas the Chapter II prohibition applies to such conduct by undertakings with a dominant position within the UK or any part of it. These differences reflect the geographical focus of the respective sets of the prohibitions. In addition, however, both sets of prohibitions also require the agreement or conduct concerned to have an effect on trade before it falls within their scope. The territorial scope of this latter criterion has a more significant effect in demarcating jurisdiction between the EC and UK systems and bears closer consideration. **3.28**

Both Articles 81 and 82 (formerly Articles 85 and 86) are triggered by an effect on trade *between* EU Member States. By contrast, the Chapter I and II prohibitions apply where there is an effect on trade *within* the United Kingdom. As explained in paragraphs 3.08–3.13 above, there is no bright line between the application of the EC and UK systems: where an agreement or conduct meets both territorial criteria, it will fall within both EC and UK jurisdiction. **3.29**

A sensible starting point when looking at a particular agreement or conduct is to consider whether EC law is applicable, ie whether there may be an effect on trade between EU Member States.[22] **3.30**

---

[21] S 2(3).
[22] And the OFT encourages this approach; see OFT, n 4 above, paras 7.4.

3.31 An agreement which expressly prohibits imports or exports between EU Member States can clearly be seen to affect trade between them. However, the concept of an effect on trade between EU Member States has been accorded a much wider meaning than that. The test, as currently applied, was first formulated in *STM v Maschinenbau Ulm*.[23] It was established in this case that, to satisfy the test, the effect on trade may be actual or potential, and may be direct or indirect. For instance, it does not matter that the products or services to which a particular agreement relates are not *currently* traded across EU Member States. Furthermore, the ECJ has given the European Commission considerable latitude in speculating whether trade will develop on a particular market.[24] Where an agreement extends across the whole of a Member State, it will be very difficult to argue successfully that trade between Member States will not be affected.[25] An effect on trade between EU Member States has also been found by the European Commission where a product was only traded in a particular region within a Member State.[26]

3.32 Thus, although in principle the distinction between cases falling under only UK jurisdiction and those falling under dual jurisdiction is clear, the elasticity of the concept of 'affecting trade between Member States' entails that in practice it is not always apparent whether or not the EC test is satisfied. Agreements or conduct possibly falling within both EC and UK jurisdiction create complexities for the parties concerned in terms of notification tactics and the priority with which the respective competition authorities will deal with their case (see Chapter 12 paragraphs 12.72–12.89 for further consideration of these issues).

3.33 In fact, whereas under Article 81 (formerly Article 85) it is quite possible that an agreement may restrict competition within the EU without necessarily affecting trade between EU Member States (ie because the effect on trade is confined to one Member State), it is very unlikely that under the Chapter I prohibition an agreement might restrict competition within the UK without also affecting trade within the UK—particularly given that the United Kingdom is defined to include any part of the UK.[27] In this sense the requirement in the prohibitions under the Act for the agreement or conduct in question to have an effect on UK trade is redundant. Arguably, however, its purpose is to ensure that the UK prohibitions are sufficiently similar to their EC counterparts to facilitate references to the ECJ under Article 234 (formerly Article 177) of the EC Treaty (as to which, see paragraphs 3.79–3.86 below).

---

[23] Case 56/65 [1966] ECR 235.
[24] Case 107/82 *AEG—Telefunken v Commission* [1983] ECR 3151.
[25] Case 8/72 *Vereeniging van Cementhandelaren v Commission* [1972] ECR 977.
[26] Case 123/83 *Bureau National Interprofessionnel du Cognac (BNIC) v Clair* [1985] ECR 391 and Case 136/86 *Bureau National Interprofessionnel du Cognac (BNIC) v Aubert* [1989] 1 CEC 363.
[27] See n 14 above and OFT, n 4 above, para 2.16. This point is discussed further in Ch 4, paras 4.60–4.61.

Exclusions

Articles 81 and 82 (formerly Articles 85 and 86) do not allow for any types of **3.34** agreements or conduct to be specifically excluded from their scope. By contrast, in the Competition Act there are a number of exclusions from the Chapter I and II prohibitions. These exclusions are provided in section 3 in the case of the Chapter I prohibition, and section 19 in the case of the Chapter II prohibition, read with Schedules to the Act; and exclusions may also be created under section 50. They can be summarised as follows:

(a) Under Schedule 1, agreements which constitute mergers and concentrations falling within the jurisdiction of EC or UK merger control laws (the EC Merger Regulation and the merger provisions of the Fair Trading Act 1973) are excluded from the Chapter I and the Chapter II prohibition, together with ancillary restrictions.

(b) Under Schedule 2, agreements subject to competition scrutiny under other legislation, (such as the Financial Services Act 1986 and the Environment Act 1995) are excluded from the Chapter I prohibition.

(c) Under Schedule 3 there are a number of general exclusions:

- planning obligations, agreements in receipt of a direction under section 21(2) of the Restrictive Trade Practices Act, EEA regulated markets and agricultural products are excluded from the Chapter I prohibition;

- services of general economic interest, agreements or conduct in order to comply with legal requirements, and agreements or conduct relating to coal and steel covered by the ECSC Treaty are excluded from both the Chapter I and the Chapter II prohibition;

- the Secretary of State is able to exclude particular agreements or conduct from the Chapter I or II prohibition to avoid conflict with international obligations, and to exclude agreements or conduct from the Chapter I or II prohibition for reasons of public policy.

(d) Under Schedule 4, designated professional rules are excluded from the Chapter I prohibition.

(e) Under section 50, the Secretary of State has the power in respect of vertical agreements and land agreements to make orders for exclusion from the Chapter I or II prohibition (or for exemption from the Chapter I prohibition, or otherwise for provisions in the Act not to apply to them).

Of the general exclusions in Schedule 3, it is noteworthy that the exclusion for ser- **3.35** vices of general economic interest is substantially a duplication of Article 86(2) (formerly Article 90(2)) of the EC Treaty, with the difference that Article 86(2) contains a further sentence: '[t]he development of trade must not be affected to such an extent as would be contrary to the interests of the Community'. This omission is presumably a reflection of the fact that the principle of proportionality does not play as significant a role in UK law as it does in EC law; it also reflects the broader objectives of the EC Treaty extending to trade as well as competition issues—otherwise the exclusion in the Act would have contained a similar qualification with the word 'Community' simply replaced by 'United Kingdom'.

The exclusions summarised above are considered in more detail in Chapter 5.

D. The Framework of EC Law—Obligations on National Law to Follow It

3.36 This section considers the obligations arising as a matter of EC law which constrain the operation of national competition legislation such as the Competition Act.

Supremacy and Direct Effect

3.37 The significant impact in practice of Articles 81 and 82 (formerly Articles 85 and 86) hinges critically upon two concepts of EC law. At one time it was thought that the EEC Treaty (as the EC Treaty was formerly known) applied only as between signatories (ie Member States) in the traditional manner of public international law. As such, EC law would not create rights and obligations to which businesses would be subject directly, but rather create rights and obligations only as between Member States themselves. However, this view was dispelled as a result of the development by the European Court of Justice of two path breaking, parallel concepts: the supremacy of EC law and the direct effect of EC law.

3.38 The **supremacy** of Community law was established in *Van Gend en Loos*,[28] where the ECJ ruled that, by creating the Treaty, Member States had limited their sovereign rights within certain fields. Since then, the ECJ has confirmed that EC law takes precedence over national statutes,[29] and even national constitutions which conflict with it.[30] Consequently, where there is a conflict between national competition law (or indeed any other national law) and EC law, EC law should prevail. This principle has been accepted by all national courts in EU Member States. It was established in the *Wilhelm* case that a conflict arises where national law prejudices the uniform application of EC law and the full effect of measures adopted in implementation of those rules.[31] A conflict does not arise just because there is a

---

[28] Case 26/62 *Algemene Transport- en Expeditie Onderneming Van Gend en Loos v Nederlandse Administratie der Belastingen* [1963] ECR 1.

[29] Case 6/64 *Costa v Ente Nazionale per l'Energia Elettrica* (ENEL) [1964] ECR 585.

[30] Case 11/70 *Internationale Handelsgesellschaft mbH v Einfuhr- und Vorrastsstelle für Getreide und Futtermittel* [1970] ECR 1125.

[31] Case 14/68 *Walt Wilhelm v Bundeskartellamt*, n 1 above.

difference between EC and national law. Nevertheless, the precise circumstances in which a conflict or prejudice arises is a matter of some debate.

Direct effect is the legal mechanism created by the ECJ through which EC law **3.39** can be enforced by businesses (or individuals) in their national courts.[32] Articles 81 and 82 (formerly Articles 85 and 86) EC have long been held directly effective,[33] which means that undertakings can bring actions in UK courts to obtain remedies against other businesses which breach these provisions.

The practical implication of the concepts of supremacy and direct effect should be **3.40** that any *conflicts* between the national and EC competition rules are resolved in accordance with the position under EC law. Furthermore, since the remedies and sanctions granted in respect of EC law must be no less effective than those granted in the case of national law,[34] it is to be expected that there will emerge a good deal of overlap in the rights and remedies available under both regimes. This is of some importance since damages for breach of EC competition law have yet to be given in the UK courts.[35]

The Impact of EC Competition Law on the Operation of National Competition Law

The relation between EC competition law and national competition law is thus **3.41** governed by the twin concepts of supremacy and direct effect, which must be applied in the UK irrespective of the provisions of the Act itself.

It is in fact possible to identify a number of different situations where the obliga- **3.42** tion to follow EC law may or may not arise:

(i) *Infringement: an agreement or conduct infringes Articles 81 or 82 (formerly Articles 85 or 86) and, in the case of Article 81, is not exempted.* Where an agreement or conduct is prohibited under EC law, the agreement or conduct cannot be rendered valid under national law.[36] Thus, if the UK authorities approve under the Competition Act an agreement or practice which also affects trade between EU Member States (either because they found that it did not infringe the Chapter I or Chapter II prohibitions or, in the case of the Chapter I prohibition, because they have formed the view that it was able to benefit from an exemption), the European Commission may subsequently find that it infringes EC competition law and thus is prohibited. The

---

[32] Council Reg (EEC) 17 [1959–62] OJ Spec Ed 87 gives the European Commission the power to enforce Arts 81 and 82 (formerly Arts 85 and 86).

[33] Case 127/73 *BRT v SABAM* [1974] ECR 51.

[34] Case 158/80 *Rewe-Handelsgesellschaft Nord mbH v Hauptzollamt Kiel* [1981] ECR 1005.

[35] Although it has been clearly recognised that damages are possible: *Garden Cottage Foods v Milk Marketing Board* [1983] 3 WLR 143; and, more recently, *Gibbs Mew plc v Gemmel* (NLC 2980712203). See Ch 10 paras 10.23 for further details.

[36] Case 14/68 *Walt Wilhelm v Bundeskartellamt*; n 1 above.

European Commission is not bound to follow the decision of the UK authorities even if, as is the case with the Chapter I and Chapter II prohibitions, the national rules are virtually identical to the EC rules, and even if the evidence available to the European Commission is no different from that which was available to the national authorities.[37] In such circumstances, notwithstanding the decision of the UK authorities, the agreement or conduct is prohibited.

(ii) *No jurisdiction: an agreement or conduct does not infringe Article 81 or 82 (formerly Article 85 or 86) because it has no appreciable effect on trade between EU Member States, or has no appreciable effect on competition.* In this situation there is no EC jurisdiction and the national competition authority is free to apply its own national competition law to the agreement or conduct. The ECJ has held in *Giry & Guérlain* that:

> the fact that a practice has been held by the European Commission not to fall within the ambit of the prohibition contained in Articles 85(1) and (2) [now Articles 81(1) and (2)], the scope of which is limited to agreements capable of affecting trade between Member States, in no way prevents that practice from being considered by the national authorities from the point of view of the restrictive effects which it may produce nationally'.[38]

Thus, the UK authorities will be free to clear or prohibit or (in the case of an agreement) exempt an agreement or conduct under the Competition Act.

(iii) *Other clearance: an agreement or conduct does not infringe Article 81 or 82 (formerly Article 85 or 86) for a reason other than because it has no appreciable effect on trade between EU Member States trade or has no appreciable effect on competition.* The position here is less clear than that in (ii). It is arguable that, as in (ii), in the absence of an EC prohibition the national authority is free to make its own determination. On the other hand, it is arguable that there is a difference because, whereas in (ii) the European Commission has no jurisdiction, here the Commission clearly has jurisdiction but has decided, in exercise of that jurisdiction, that there is no infringement of EC law. It might therefore follow that the *Wilhelm* principle which requires the uniform application of competition law throughout the EU (see (i) above) would be undermined if individual EU Member States took a different view on an agreement that had been considered at EC level.

Thus, for example, if the European Commission had decided that particular conduct of a dominant undertaking did not constitute an abuse and therefore did not infringe Article 82, it could be contrary to this principle for

---

[37] Case T–149/89 *Sotralentz SA v EC Commission*, Case C–360/92P *Publishers Association v Commission* [1995] ECR I–23.

[38] Joined Cases 253/78 and 1 to 3/79 *Procureur de la République & Ors v Giry & Guérlain SA & Ors* [1980] ECR 2327, para 18.

a national competition authority to take an opposite view and seek to prohibit such behaviour.

However, the wording of the ECJ's view as stated in *Giry & Guérlain* (see (ii) above) leaves the matter in some doubt and could be construed as allowing the national competition authority free rein in such circumstances. Indeed, the European Commission appeared to acknowledge this in 1997 when it was consulted by the UK's Monopolies and Mergers Commission (MMC). The MMC—forerunner to the Competition Commission—was investigating selective distribution systems in domestic electrical goods (televisions, hi-fi systems, and so on) under the UK's monopoly legislation,[39] and the European Commission had already issued decisions finding that certain such selective distribution systems did not infringe Article 81. Nevertheless the European Commission told the MMC that it

> will consider whether Article 85(1) [now Article 81(1)] does or does not apply in any case notified to it only in the light of an assessment of the specific features of the relevant market and of the effectiveness of competition in that market . . . If a given selective distribution system does not fall under Article 85(1) [now Article 81(1)] it may be prohibited under national law.[40]

The European Commission, however, takes a very different view about the effect of its decisions granting exemption under Article 81(3) (formerly Article 85(3)), as explained in the following paragraph.

(iv) *Exemption: an agreement or practice infringes Article 81(1) (formerly Article 85(1)) but is exempt under Article 81(3) (formerly Article 85(3)).* The issue in such a case is whether the national authority is free to prohibit the agreement or impose conditions for exemption that are stricter than those imposed by the European Commission. EC law is not clear on this point. The European Commission's view is that a Community exemption must be respected by national authorities. This is supported by the Advocate General in the *BMW* case, where he opined that 'the exemption granted to [the parties] cannot but prevent the national authorities from ignoring the positive assessment put on them by the Community authorities'.[41] A distinction is often drawn between: negative clearance under Article 81(1), as in (ii) and (iii) above, which is a statement that the EC prohibition does not apply at all; and exemption, which is a statement that EC law regards the agreement as having positive economic benefits, and therefore endorses (rather than just

---

[39] See Chs 17 and 18 below.

[40] Monopolies and Mergers Commission report, *Domestic electrical goods: I*, Cm 3675–I, July 1997, paras 2.425 and 2.426.

[41] Opinion of Tesauro AG in Case C–270/93 *BMW v ALD* [1995] ECR I–3439; see also Case C–266/93 *Bundeskartellamt v Volkswagen and VAG Leasing* [1995] ECR I–3477 (observations of the European Commission and Opinion of Tesauro AG). See also *IVth Report on Competition Policy* (1974), para 55; and the Co-operation Notice (n 2 above, para 19).

permits) the agreement. In the latter case, it is said, the national authority in prohibiting the agreement would actually be conflicting with positive EC policy, and this would infringe the doctrine of the supremacy of Community law.

The alternative view is that an exemption is merely a derogation from the application of Article 81(1) and that an EU Member State is therefore free not to apply the derogation if it sees fit; that view is known as the 'double barrier' view, in that an agreement has to be exempted both by national and by EC law in order to be authorised. Whilst the matter has yet to be resolved at ECJ level, the most likely outcome would be that the European Commission's view prevails and that a Member State may not prohibit or restrict an agreement benefiting from an exemption.

The UK authorities and the European Commission have so far sought to avoid putting the issue to the test.

• When the MMC investigated the UK's distribution agreements for perfumes ('fine fragrances'), it 'kept in mind' two European Commission decisions granting exemptions to similar agreements, but asserted that it was 'nevertheless open to us [the MMC] to examine the effects of the distribution system on the UK public interest, to make findings and, if we see fit to make recommendations'—although, significantly for the purposes of the new Competition Act, the OFT had apparently taken a more cautious view and wanted to limit the MMC's inquiry to only those aspects of the agreements which were not covered by the European Commission decisions.[42]

• The MMC's investigation into selective distribution systems for domestic electrical goods (see (iii) above) made its recommendations after consulting the European Commission on the scope of its powers, given that the European Commission had granted some exemptions to such agreements.[43]

• In the case of *P&O/Stena Line*[44] a joint venture between the parties was subject to UK merger control and consideration by the European Commission under Article 81 (formerly Article 85). The joint venture was unconditionally exempted by the European Commission but cleared by the UK authorities subject to conditions—so that, in spite of the EC exemption, the UK imposed more stringent requirements before allowing

---

[42] European Commission decision, *Yves Saint Laurent Parfums* [1992] OJ L12/24; Monopolies and Mergers Commission report, *Fine fragrances*, Cm 2380, Nov 1993, paras 8.6 to 8.7, and 8.35 to 8.38.

[43] Monopolies and Mergers Commission report, *Domestic electrical goods: I*, n 40 above, paras 2.436 and 2.439.

[44] EC Merger Reg Case IV/MAR/36.253 [1997] OJ C80/3; Monopolies and Mergers Commission report, *The Peninsular and Oriental Steam Navigation Company and Stena Line AB*, Cm 3664, Nov 1997.

the joint venture agreement. However, these conditions were expressly stated not to apply during an initial period of Article 81(3) exemption by the European Commission.

It is also noteworthy that the UK Restrictive Practices Court has stated that

> There is clearly a serious argument that it is not open to the national court to condemn under the national law an agreement which has received an exemption under Community law.[45]

In the case of block, as opposed to individual, exemptions, the UK has, following Fair Trading Act monopoly investigations in relation to the supply of beer and of motor cars, applied more stringent requirements before authorising distribution agreements than were required for the agreements to be exempted from Article 81 (formerly Article 85) under the relevant EC block exemption regulations. Indeed, as regards cars, an earlier block exemption expressly indicated that stricter national laws could be applied;[46] however, this can be interpreted as no more than a concession from the Commission's basic view that EC block exemptions take precedence over national law, and the Commission added that it did not affect the primacy of EC law (moreover, there is no such concession in the current motor vehicle block exemption[47]). In the case of beer supply agreements, the European Commission has said that:

> In general, the Commission has always considered that national regulations which are more stringent than block exemption regulations drawn up by the European Commission are compatible with them, provided they do not affect the essential conditions of such exemptions.[48]

However, the difference between 'the essential conditions' and other conditions of the exemption may be difficult to apply in practice. This is even more the case in relation to an individual exemption, where the relative significance of different conditions may not be entirely clear.

The fact that the 'parallel exemption' provisions in the Act can be made subject to additional obligations or cancelled (see paragraph 3.45 below) is itself evidence of the UK authorities' attitude. It is understood that the European Commission has accepted this provision, provided that it is deployed within reasonable limits.

---

[45] *Re Net Book Agreement 1957: The Director General of Fair Trading v The Publishers' Association*, 9 Aug 1995, unreported judgment.

[46] Commission Reg EEC 1123/85 on the application of Art 85(3) [now Art 81(3)] of the Treaty to certain categories of motor vehicle distribution and servicing agreements [1985] OJ L15/16, rec 19.

[47] Commission Reg EEC 1475/95 [1995] OJ L145/25.

[48] EP debates no 3–41/6/192. Question no 8–11070/91.

Conclusion on Conflicts between EC Law and National Law

3.43 Conflicts between EC law and national law may arise in certain scenarios and the position regarding the relationship between the two systems is not entirely settled. As explained in paragraph 3.17 above, in order to avoid such conflicts arising, there are a number of provisions contained in the Act itself which attempt to resolve any tensions where jurisdictions overlap by requiring a large degree of alignment with EC law. The most significant are those dealing with parallel exemptions (section 10) and the 'governing principles' section (section 60). These are considered in turn in the following paragraphs.

E. Obligations to Follow EC Law Arising Under the Competition Act—Parallel Exemptions

3.44 Section 10 of the Act is a key provision in governing the relationship between EC law and the Competition Act. It provides that, where an agreement is exempt under Article 81(3) (formerly Article 85(3)), or would be but for the issue of jurisdiction, the agreement will benefit from *automatic* exemption under the Act. Thus an exemption under UK law is automatically granted where:

(i)   an EC Regulation, ie an EC block exemption, exempts the agreement;[49]

(ii) an individual exemption has already been granted by the European Commission;[50]

(iii) the agreement has been notified under an opposition procedure, and the European Commission has either not opposed the agreement within the time limit, or has withdrawn its opposition;[51] or

(iv) an agreement would have benefited from a EC block exemption but for the fact that it did not have an effect upon trade between EU Member States and so fell outside the jurisdiction of Article 81(1) (formerly Article 85(1)).[52]

However, the Act in addition provides that the OFT may impose conditions or obligations subject to which a parallel exemption may have an effect.[53] It may also vary or remove such additional conditions or obligations,[54] or cancel the exemption.[55]

---

[49] S 10(1)(a).
[50] S 10(1)(b).
[51] S 10(1)(c).
[52] S 10(2).
[53] S 10(5)(a) and (c).
[54] S 10(5)(b).
[55] S 10(5)(d).

The power to impose additional conditions on a parallel exemption or cancel the **3.45** exemption as regards the Chapter I prohibition raises the issue considered in paragraph 3.42 above—namely the extent to which the UK authorities are free, as a matter of EC law, to diverge in national law from an exemption granted by the European Commission:

(a) In the case of *agreements that do not affect trade between EU Member States but otherwise satisfy the conditions of an EC block exemption* (those falling under (iv) above), there is nothing under EC law prohibiting the UK authorities from taking a stricter view of the agreement, since the agreement does not fall within EC jurisdiction at all (see paragraph 3.42(ii) above). In other cases, a distinction must be drawn, on the one hand, between the situation where an exemption is granted by Regulation (in the form of a block exemption) or an individual exemption decision, and, on the other hand, the more common situation where the parties receive a 'comfort letter' from the European Commission.

(b) In a case of an *exemption by way of a decision or block exemption Regulation*, the position under EC law is not certain. As explained in paragraph 3.42(iv) above, the European Commission's basic view is that, where an exemption has been granted, a Member State is not permitted to prohibit the agreement or further restrict the operation of the agreement. If this is correct, it is open to question whether, as a matter of EC law, the OFT could apply stricter conditions or cancel the exemption. However, in practice the Commission has not rigidly insisted on enforcing its view (possibly because of uncertainty that the ECJ would uphold it in the event of a dispute)—for example, as regards beer distribution—and it may be that, provided the 'essential conditions' of the EU exemption are not undermined, some variation is possible.

(c) The position is different where the European Commission has issued a '*comfort letter*'.[56] In such a case, there is no Regulation or decision granting an exemption and therefore parallel exemption under section 10 does not arise. The treatment of EC comfort letters is considered in more detail in paragraphs 3.72–3.78 below.

Lastly, the circumstances in which *parallel exemptions cease to have effect* are **3.46** slightly different from the position with regard to Article 81(3) (formerly Article 85(3)) exemption under EC law. The starting point is that parallel exemptions cease to have effect when the exemption granted under EC law ceases to have effect.[57] However, a parallel exemption will also cease to have effect where any

---

[56] A 'comfort letter' is an administrative letter from the Commission stating the Commission's intention is to close the file. The letter may give a reason: for instance, the agreement may be considered not to fall within Art 81 (formerly Art 85) or it may be eligible for an exemption. Most cases are settled by way of a comfort letter.

[57] S 10(4)(b)(ii).

particular conditions imposed by the OFT are breached[58] or where the OFT revokes the exemption (for which the Procedural Rules provide an express procedure—see Chapter 12 paragraph 12.54–12.55).[59]

F. Obligations to Follow EC Law Arising Under the Competition Act—'Governing Principles'

3.47 Section 60 is one of the most important provisions in the Competition Act. It aims to ensure that the UK authorities and UK courts deal with questions arising under the Act in a manner so far as possible consistent with the approach taken at EC level in relation to Articles 81 and 82 (formerly Articles 85 and 86). However, there are a number of uncertainties about the scope and application of this provision. These are considered below.

Section 60(1)—the Statement of Purpose

3.48 Unusually for an English statute, section 60 starts with a general statement of the purpose of the section along the lines more commonly found in the recital to an EC legislative measure. Section 60(1) states:

> The purpose of this section is to ensure that so far as is possible (having regard to any relevant differences between the provisions concerned), questions arising under this Part in relation to competition within the United Kingdom are dealt with in a manner which is consistent with the treatment of corresponding questions arising in Community law in relation to competition within the Community.

3.49 The object of this subsection is to guide the interpretation of other parts of section 60. To the extent that a literal interpretation of the other subsections of section 60 would, in any event, achieve the purpose set out in section 60(1), it adds little other than a broad declaration of legislative policy. However, to the extent that there is scope for differing interpretations of the other subsections, or that a literal interpretation of them is contrary to the purpose stated in section 60(1), the function of section 60(1) is to require the adoption of the interpretation that best accords with the purpose stated there, even if that requires a 'strained' interpretation of the later subsections.[60] During the passage of what was then the Competition Bill through the House of Lords, the Government stated that: '[s]ubsections (2) and (3) must . . . be read as a package together with the purpose

---

[58] S 10(7).

[59] S 10(5)(d); The Office of Fair Trading, Formal Consultation Draft, 'Competition Act 1998 The Draft Procedural Rules proposed by the Director General of Fair Trading' (OFT 411), R 21.

[60] See F. A. R. Bennion, *Statutory Interpretation* (3rd edn, London: Butterworths, 1997), Part VII.

in subsection (1)'.[61] It is therefore necessary to consider what objective section 60(1) is seeking to achieve.

The general objective is to ensure that questions arising in relation to competition **3.50** in the UK are dealt with consistently with the treatment of corresponding questions arising in EC law in relation to competition in the EU. This is subject to the qualification that regard must be had to any relevant differences between the provisions concerned. The wording of section 60(1) deserves specific scrutiny:

(i) *'Questions'*

The subsection requires consistency in dealing with 'questions arising under this Part' and 'corresponding questions arising in Community law'. The reference to 'questions' is significant. Section 60 applies to situations where the UK authorities 'determine a question' under Part I of the Act. The determination of a question can arise, most obviously, in the context of a conclusion whether the Chapter I or Chapter II prohibition applies to a particular agreement or conduct. A more difficult issue is whether the making of a procedural rule gives rise to a 'question'.[62]

(ii) *'Competition'*

The provision is restricted to questions in relation to 'competition within the UK'. This may be thought to be obvious from the fact that the section applies only in relation to Part I of the Act which deals with competition in the UK. However, it must be read in the context of the obligation to treat such matters consistently with corresponding questions relating to 'competition within the Community'. It is therefore arguable that, to the extent that non-competition issues are relevant under UK law, particularly in deciding whether the criteria for exemption from the Chapter I prohibition are met, there is no obligation to ensure consistency with Community law. Similarly, it would follow that when determining penalties for infringement of the Chapter I or II prohibition, the OFT need not have regard to the fining policy of the European Commission.[63]

In interpreting Articles 81 and 82 (formerly Articles 85 and 86), EC law requires that issues other than competition issues are taken into account—most notably Single Market issues—but, in so far as such decisions or statements of the European Commission or the European Court do take into

---

[61] Lord Simon of Highbury; *Hansard*, HL, vol 583, no 69, col 961 (25 Nov 1997). Ministerial statements before Parliament may be referred to by the court if the legislation is ambiguous, obscure or leading to absurdity: *Pepper v Hart* [1993] AC 593. As discussed below, a number of Government statements may be helpful to the extent that the meaning of s 60 is obscure.

[62] See para 3.58(ii) below.

[63] Although under s 38(9), where there have been EC fines (or fines in other Member States) for a particular agreement or conduct, the OFT has a duty to take to these into account in order to mitigate the level of any penalties it is imposing in respect of that agreement or conduct—see Ch 10 para 10.44.

account these matters, this limitation in section 60(1) means that there is no obligation to ensure consistency as regards the application of the Act. However, this distinction is by no means clear-cut: for example, Single Market questions may give rise to competition issues (see paragraphs 3.61–3.69 below). Uncertainties also arise as regards the import of EC procedure: it is likely that certain underlying principles of EC law which are inseparable from the operation of the competition Articles of the EC Treaty cannot be disregarded (see paragraphs 3.58–3.60 below).

In the sense of this narrow interpretation of section 60(1), the subsection is particularly unusual because no such limitation to questions of competition (only) is made in the following subsections of section 60—section 60(2) refers to '*any* corresponding question of law' (emphasis added). Whereas a purpose clause would normally be expected to give rise to a more expansive interpretation of other provisions, section 60(1) has, on this analysis, a more limited scope than sections 60(2) and (3). As explained above, however, the subsequent provisions should be interpreted in a way which best accords with the prior stated purpose.

A separate argument, which runs counter to this narrow interpretation of section 60(1), is that the requirement for consistency of treatment with questions of competition arising in EC law is actually a broader obligation than a requirement to ensure consistency with (all) EC law, in that it may extend to findings of *fact* on competition issues by EC authorities in proceedings arising under Community law. This is because the subsection refers to 'questions arising under this Part in relation to competition' rather than 'questions of competition law'. Thus a determination by the European Commission as to, for example, the absence of collusion under Article 81 (formerly Article 85) or of predation under Article 82 (formerly Article 86) would prevent the OFT from reaching a different conclusion in respect of the agreement or conduct concerned. This interpretation is not undermined by the later reference in the subsection to 'corresponding questions arising in Community law in relation to competition within the Community'. The reference to 'Community law' is a reference to the context in which the competition question arises rather than the nature of the question. Similarly, the reference to 'arising under this Part' in the earlier part of the subsection is not necessarily a limiting provision in relation to the type of competition issue to which the subsection applies, but simply serves to distinguish questions on competition arising under Part I of the Act from similar questions arising under other parts of the Act.

(iii) *'Manner which is consistent'*
The reference to the requirement to ensure that questions arising are 'dealt with in a *manner* which is consistent' (emphasis added) as opposed to just 'dealt with consistently' suggests that the obligation is not limited to ensur-

ing consistency of outcome but also consistency of approach; ie that the broad principles such as proportionality and fairness which are applied by the Community institutions in dealing with issues of competition law must, so far as is possible, be applied in determining questions under Part I of the Act. This accords with the Government's views on the import of 'high level principles'—see paragraph 3.58(iv) below.

(iv) *'Corresponding questions'*

The obligation of consistent treatment with corresponding questions arising in Community law assumes that a corresponding EC law question can be identified and that there is a Community standard against which consistency of treatment can be measured. This will undoubtedly be the position for many cases that the OFT and the other UK institutions have to deal with. However, there are likely to be a significant number of cases where either there is no obvious corresponding EC law issue or where there is no clear or consistent EC law answer. It is foreseeable that there will be much debate before the OFT, the appeal tribunal and the UK courts as to how the EC authorities apply particular principles, quite apart from the question of how those principles should be applied in the context of UK law.

Such uncertainties at EC level can arise in the jurisprudence of the European Court. Thus, for example, on a matter of interpretation of what constitutes an abuse for the purposes of Article 82 (formerly Article 86), the ECJ held in two cases that a refusal by a dominant proprietor to grant a licence of an intellectual property right did not in itself amount to an abuse,[64] whereas in a third case it held that a refusal to license may constitute an abuse.[65] While it may be possible to reconcile these cases,[66] it is not easy to do so and the result is that this series of cases provides no clear guidance for the UK authorities on how to apply the Chapter II prohibition in similar circumstances. Similarly, there have been a number of situations where the European Commission has interpreted decisions of the European Court in a narrow way not necessarily justified by a reading of the relevant Court decision; indeed, almost every decision of the European Commission under Article 82 (formerly Article 86) has been challenged before the European Court.

This is not to say that there are no consistent principles at EC level. In the majority of circumstances, EC law provides adequate guidance on what is and is not an acceptable practice. However, there will undoubtedly be a number of cases at the margin where there is real uncertainty about the

---

[64] Case 238/87 *AB Volvo v Erik Veng (UK) Limited* [1988] ECR 6211 and Case 53/87 *CICRA v Régie Nationale des Usines Renault* [1988] ECR 6039.

[65] Joined Cases C–241/91 P and C–242/91 P *Radio Telefis Eireann (RTE) and Independent Television Publications Ltd (ITP) v EC Commission* [1995] ECR I–743.

[66] See Ch 9 paras 9.55–9.60.

appropriate position under EC law, and the UK authorities will have to make a choice as to what, in their view, is the proper interpretation. In appropriate circumstances, however, there will be scope to refer such difficult cases to the ECJ for clarification (see paragraphs 3.79–3.89 below).

Another pertinent issue is the extent to which there is a difference between the obligation to avoid conflict with EC law imposed under EC law itself as compared to the obligations under section 60 of the Act, ie whether there is a higher obligation on the UK authorities to follow EC law as a result of the obligation to be consistent imposed under the Act, as compared with obligations already existing under EC law (ie rather than the Act) to avoid conflict with EC law (see paragraphs 3.41–3.43 above). As described above, the obligation to avoid conflict nevertheless leaves scope to prohibit an agreement or conduct under the Act even though it does not infringe Article 81 or 82 (formerly Article 85 or 86). It might be argued, however, that an obligation to ensure consistency offers no scope for divergence at all. So, for example, a finding that a selective distribution system of a type which had been held not to infringe Article 81 infringed the Chapter I prohibition might be contrary to section 60.

(v)   *'Relevant differences'*

The proviso to section 60(1) requires that regard must be had to relevant differences between the UK and EC provisions. There are a number of differences between the Act and the EC provisions. Some of these are institutional, for example, the existence of an appeal tribunal under the Act. Others relate to investigation and enforcement, for example, the power to enter and search under a warrant for which no equivalent exists under EC law.[67] These differences may of themselves give rise to other differences. Thus, for example, it was suggested in Parliament that the existence of the appeal tribunal meant that there is less need for the OFT to give respondents to complaints a right to an oral hearing even though such a right exists under EC law.[68]

There are also a number of substantive differences between the Act and EC law and the question arises which of these are 'relevant' differences. For instance, it might be asked whether the reference to conduct in the Chapter II prohibition (see paragraph 3.27 above) is a relevant difference, such that a divergence between the Chapter II prohibition and Article 82 (formerly Article 86) is permitted, or whether it is just a drafting difference and therefore the Chapter II prohibition should be interpreted consistently with Article 82 (the latter is more likely). The issue of relevant differences also

---

[67]   S 28.
[68]   In fact, the Procedural Rules do give respondents such a right to oral representation, although the UK procedure will differ significantly from that followed by the European Commission; see Ch 12, para 12.17.

speaks to the import of procedural issues (see paragraphs 3.58–3.60 below) and to the treatment of Single Market and other non-competition questions (see paragraphs 3.61–3.71 below).

Section 60(2) and (3)—the Operative Provisions

The operative provisions of section 60 are set out in subsections (2) and (3) as follows: **3.51**

(2) At any time when the court determines a question arising under this Part, it must act (as far as is compatible with the provisions of this Part and whether or not it would otherwise be required to do so) with a view to securing that there is no inconsistency between:

(a) the principles applied, and decision reached, by the court in determining that question; and

(b) the principles laid down by the Treaty and the European Court, and any relevant decision of that Court, as applicable at that time in determining any corresponding question arising in Community law.

(3) The court must, in addition, have regard to any relevant decision or statement of the [European] Commission.

The term 'court' here means the OFT,[69] sector regulators[70] and any court or tribunal.[71] This clearly includes the Court of Appeal and the appeal tribunal of the Competition Commission.[72] **3.52**

Some of the issues that arise under section 60(2) are identical to those arising under section 60(1), namely: the meaning of 'question'[73] and what is meant by a 'corresponding question'.[74] Other provisions of section 60(2) give rise to similar issues of interpretation as related provisions in section 60(1). Thus, section 60(2) requires that a court must secure that there is 'no inconsistency' between the principles and decisions of the UK institutions and those of the Treaty and the ECJ. While an obligation to ensure no inconsistency may import a slightly lesser burden than the section 60(1) obligation to ensure that matters are treated in a manner which is 'consistent' with corresponding questions arising under EC law, as a matter of practice these provisions will be applied identically. **3.53**

---

[69] S 60(4).

[70] By virtue of Sch 10, references in Part I of the Act to the Director are to be read as including a reference to the relevant sector regulator unless the context requires otherwise. There is no reason to believe that the context requires otherwise in s 60(4).

[71] S 60(5).

[72] It should be noted that the Competition Commission when exercising functions other than that of an appeal tribunal is not covered by s 60, as such other functions are not within the scope of Part I of the Act.

[73] See para 3.50(i) above.

[74] See para 3.50(iv) above.

3.54 Similarly, the reference in section 60(2) to 'so far as is compatible with the provisions of this Part' is unlikely in practice to give rise to a different result from that arising from the obligation in section 60(1) to have 'regard to any relevant differences'. Although the section 60(2) obligation is, on a literal interpretation, stronger—that is, it gives rise to more limited scope for divergence between the UK and EC provisions—in practice it is likely to be interpreted in the same way as its section 60(1) equivalent.[75] The following paragraphs review the most significant aspects of section 60(2):

(i) *Securing no inconsistency with principles of the EC Treaty and the European Court*

Section 60(2) requires consistency in outcome ('decisions reached') and consistency in the application of principles ('the principles applied') in determining the outcome. The reference to 'principles' is important. It means that section 60 is not merely laying down a doctrine of precedent by which the UK institutions are required to follow the precedents of the EU institutions in much the same way as lower courts in the English system are obliged to follow relevant judgments of higher courts. It is also requiring the UK institutions to observe general principles of EC law such as the privilege against self-incrimination, proportionality and non-discrimination.[76]

More significantly in the context of a consideration of the relationship of the Act with EC law, section 60(2)(b) imposes an absolute obligation on these UK authorities to ensure that there is no inconsistency with the principles of the EC Treaty and the principles and decisions of the European Court (in so far as is compatible with the provisions of Part I of the Act) when determining a question under Part I.

(ii) *Internal consistency between UK institutions*

Section 60(2) requires consistency between, on the one hand, the UK institutions (that is the OFT, the appeal tribunal within the Competition Commission and the courts) and, on the other hand, the EC Treaty and the ECJ. A more difficult question is the extent to which internal consistency is required between the UK institutions themselves.

It is clear that where a later decision of the ECJ (or arguably the European Commission) is inconsistent with an earlier decision of the UK courts, the UK institutions shall apply the law as laid down by the ECJ (and possibly the European Commission) rather than the judgment of the UK court. This is apparent from the reference in section 60(2)(b) to 'as applicable at that time'.

The more difficult situation is where the UK institution is of the view that a decision of, say, the English court is inconsistent with relevant provisions of EC law for reasons other than the fact that there is a later inconsistent EC

---

[75] See para 3.50(v) above.
[76] See, eg, Lord Simon of Highbury, *Hansard*, 25 Nov 1998, vol 583, No 84, HL cols. 960–962.

decision, for example, where the UK institution is of the view that the English court misinterpreted EC law or failed to take into account relevant provisions.

In such circumstances the UK institution has two possible options. It may take the view that the interpretation of EC law for the purposes of the application of the Act is a matter to be determined by the hierarchy of institutions and courts within the UK system and, to the extent that the precedent of a court in the hierarchy is wrong in EC law, that is a matter for ultimate resolution by the ECJ if necessary following a reference under Article 234 (formerly Article 177) of the EC Treaty.[77] Alternatively, the UK institution may take the view that its obligation is to ensure consistency with EC law, even if this means not following a precedent within the English court hierarchy. The latter approach is probably the one that is more consistent with the spirit of section 60, even though it may, in the exceptional cases where this problem arises, undermine the normal hierarchy of decision-making within the English system. Section 60(2) imposes an obligation on each court or tribunal (ie UK institution) determining a matter to act with a view to securing that there is no inconsistency between its decision making and the principles and relevant decisions arising under EC law. While the fact that a superior English court had taken a particular view on a matter would clearly influence the UK institution in deciding this, the ultimate responsibility for avoiding inconsistency lies with the court or tribunal (ie the UK institution) actually making the particular decision. In this regard the position may be different in relation to decisions or statements of the European Commission where the UK institution is only required to 'have regard' to any such decision or statement, and in this context it may take the view that an apparently inconsistent decision of a superior UK court outweighed its obligation to have regard to the European Commission' decision on the same matter.[78]

(iii) *'Relevant decisions and statements' of the European Commission*
As regards European Commission 'decisions and statements', the obligations are less onerous—the UK authorities are required under section 60(3) to 'have regard' to them. The difference in language between, on the one hand, the obligation in section 60(2) to 'act with a view to securing there is no inconsistency' and, on the other, the obligation under section 60(3) to 'have regard' indicates that a lesser weight is to be attached by the UK authorities to European Commission decisions and statements than to the principles of the EC Treaty and the principles and decisions of the European Court. This suggests that, to the extent that there is inconsistency between the decisions and statements of the European Commission, and the principles and

---

[77] See paras 3.79–3.89 below.
[78] See also para 3.54(iii) below.

decisions of the Treaty and the Court, the UK authorities must follow the Treaty and the Court.

A more difficult question is whether it also means that, whereas the UK authorities must act consistently with the EC Treaty and the European Court, the obligation, in relation to the Commission's decisions and statements, is merely to take them into account—ie to what extent are the UK authorities free not to follow Commission decisions or statements even if there is no contradictory provision of the Treaty or decision of the Court? A literal interpretation of section 60(3) would suggest that the UK authorities have a significant margin of discretion to diverge from Commission decisions or statements: a duty to 'have regard to' does not imply an obligation to follow such decisions or statements—just to give them due consideration. (The fact that only 'relevant' Commission views need be had regard to allows further scope for the UK authorities to depart from the European Commission position.)

If this is correct, it also appears to follow that the UK authorities should accord greater weight to previous UK court and OFT cases than to European Commission ones (even if the latter are more recent). First, the requirement for reference is higher for UK cases under section 60(2) ('securing there is no inconsistency'), than for Commission decisions and statements under section 60(3) ('have regard to'). Secondly, the fact that, unlike in the treatment of the EC Treaty and European Court under section 60(2)(b), there is no reference to Commission decisions and statements 'as applicable at that time' also leads to the inference that the UK authorities have the discretion to diverge from relevant Commission views in favour of earlier UK determinations.

However, if section 60(3) is read in the context of section 60(1), it can be seen that the discretion of the UK authorities to depart from relevant Commission decisions and statements is more limited. As explained above, section 60(1) requires the UK authorities, so far as possible, to ensure consistency of treatment between questions arising under Part I of the Act and corresponding ones under EC law. It is clear that Commission decisions are part of EC law and thus the consistency obligation is likely to apply in relation to such decisions.

(iv) *Principles laid down by the EC Treaty—a superior UK statute?*
It has been suggested, intriguingly, that the wording of section 60(2)(b) may give rise to even more far-reaching implications—that it may have the effect of raising the Chapter I and II prohibitions into superior obligations taking precedence over inconsistent procedural, judicial or administrative rules in other areas of UK national law.[79]

---

[79] Nicholas Green QC, 'Some Observations on the Civil Consequences of the Chapter I and Chapter II Prohibitions', paper delivered at conference on 'The Europeanisation of United Kingdom Competition Law', 10 Sept 1998.

The reasoning seems to be that 'the principles laid down by the Treaty' which are used in 'determining any corresponding question arising in Community law' are not confined to Articles 81 and 82 (formerly Articles 85 and 86) themselves, but extend also to other EC Treaty principles, including direct effect and the supremacy of EC law over conflicting national law (as to which, see paragraphs 3.37–3.40 above). Accordingly, the argument runs, since Articles 81 and 82 have direct effect and supremacy over conflicting national laws, the Chapter I and Chapter II prohibitions will have these attributes too, by virtue of section 60. It follows that, if there were to be subsequent UK legislation which conflicted with the Chapter I or Chapter II prohibition—for example, an Act of Parliament authorising price-fixing in a particular sector of the UK economy—that legislation would be unlawful and could be struck out, because of its inconsistency with the prohibition in the Competition Act.

Although this line of reasoning is ingenious, it seems unlikely that a court would interpret section 60 in this way. It is not obvious that the wording of section 60 is capable of such a broad construction. The obligation, in section 60(2)(b), on the UK courts and authorities to act with a view to securing that there is no inconsistency with 'the principles laid down by the Treaty' applies only in the specific circumstance when the court or authority 'determines a question arising under this Part [of the Competition Act]'; this will be when that UK authority or court determines whether or not there is an infringement of the Chapter I or Chapter II prohibition. The authority or court is obliged to address that question consistently with the way in which a 'corresponding question' would be dealt with under EC law—ie applying the Chapter I or Chapter II prohibition to the case consistently with the way Article 81 or 82 (formerly Article 85 or 86) (respectively) would be applied. However, an obligation to apply the UK prohibitions consistently with the way that Articles 81 and 82 are applied is, it is submitted, altogether different from an obligation to treat the UK prohibitions as *equivalent to* Articles 81 and 82 themselves, such that they are deemed to have all the same attributes as Articles 81 and 82 (including direct effect and supremacy over inconsistent national law).

Moreover, this narrower construction of section 60 is almost certainly in line with what Parliament intended; there is nothing to suggest that Parliament, in passing the Competition Act, intended it to have the kind of fundamental constitutional significance, in terms of its implications for the legality of future statutes, that (say) was clearly intended and understood when Parliament passed the European Communities Act 1972; and it is almost inconceivable that any court would apply the Competition Act as though it were intended to have such effects.

(v) *'Decisions'*

Section 60(6) states that the term 'decision' as used in section 60(2)(b) and (3) includes (but, by implication, is not limited to) decisions by the European Court of Justice or the European Commission on the interpretation of *any* provision of Community law. It is not limited to provisions of EC law relating to competition matters. Thus it would include decisions relating to broad principles of law such as proportionality, and is further reason for the conclusion that such underlying principles of EC law apply to the operation of the UK prohibitions (see paragraph 3.58(iv) below for further consideration of these principles).

Section 60(6) also indicates that the term 'decision' includes a decision as to the civil liability of an undertaking for harm caused by its infringement of Community law. This provision is to take account of case law arising from the fact that Articles 81 and 82 (formerly Articles 85 and 86) have direct effect, ie give individuals private rights (damages and injunctions) to enforce them before UK courts.

(vi) *'Statements' of the European Commission*

The reference to 'statements' in section 60(3) indicates that, in addition to having regard to European Commission decisions, which are clearly Community law, a broader range of Commission measures must be taken account of. The Commission produces a range of Notices, Communications and Guidelines on matters such as the method of setting fines, co-operation with national competition authorities and national courts, and the application of the competition rules in particular sectors (for example, telecommunications). Commission Notices also explain the application of certain block exemption regulations.[80] The term covers statements which have the authority of the Commission as a whole, and so is likely to include statements published in the Commission's *Annual Report on Competition Policy*.[81] The Commission may also publish Notices on individual cases prior to making a decision or, in some cases, issuing a comfort letter; the latter are considered further in paragraph 3.74–3.76 below.[82]

It could be argued in the context of section 60 that there is a distinction between, on the one hand, Commission decisions which are 'Community law'[83] and therefore subject to the consistency requirement of section 60(1) and, on the other hand, Commission statements which of themselves are not. If so, it follows that any effect of the limitation of section 60(1) to questions of competition on the interpretation of section 60(3) does not extend

---

[80] See, eg, Commission Notice concerning Regs 1983/83 and 1984/83 of 22 June 1983 [1984] OJ C101/2 as amended by [1992] OJ C121/2.

[81] See OFT, n 4 above, para 2.1.

[82] A so-called 'Article 19(3) Notice'.

[83] European Communities Act 1972 s 2(1).

to Commission statements. However, this distinction is difficult to draw in practice because statements of the Commission govern the consequent treatment of questions arising in Community law. In any event, from the wording of section 60 it is doubtful that the obligation as regards European Commission 'statements' can be limited in this way: section 60(3) states that, 'in addition' to other obligations, the UK institutions must have regard to relevant statements of the Commission (without specifying that these must be statements of Community law); and, although it is arguable that all of section 60 must be read subject to the purposes in section 60(1), section 60(1) relates to ensuring consistency with the way 'questions arising in Community law' are treated without specifying that for such purposes the measures by which those questions are treated (such as Commission statements) must *themselves* be Community law.

Conclusion on Section 60

The detailed analysis of section 60 attempted above demonstrates above all that **3.55** this key provision of the Competition Act raises a number of difficult issues of interpretation. In part this arises from what is, in the context of UK statute, a unique and innovative provision. In many cases section 60 will no doubt successfully provide a bridge to EC competition law, and a link which will allow case law under the Act to evolve in tandem. However, in the initial period of the Act's operation it seems likely that a number of significant issues of interpretation will need to be resolved, and that the actions of the UK authorities in applying the Act will be subject to review.

To give but one example, the OFT has indicated in its guidelines on the Chapter **3.56** I prohibition a considerably higher '*de minimis*' threshold—below which it will generally view agreements as giving rise to no 'appreciable' restriction of competition, with the result that they are considered not to infringe the Chapter I prohibition[84]—than the European Commission has set out in its Notice on Agreements of Minor Importance,[85] which is a statement of the European Commission to which regard should be had under section 60(3). Moreover, the OFT's view is arguably inconsistent with the jurisprudence of the European Court establishing the doctrine of appreciability, with which section 60(2) requires consistency.[86] An

---

[84] See OFT, n 4 above, paras 2.18 to 2.22: the OFT's view is that generally there will be no appreciable effect on competition where the combined market share of the participating undertakings does not exceed 25%, subject to exceptions such as where the agreements involve price-fixing—see Ch 4 paras 4.49–4.55.

[85] Commission Notice on agreements of minor importance which do not fall under Art 85(1) [now Art 81(1)] of the Treaty establishing the European Community; C 97/C 372/04 [1997] OJ C372/13 of 9 Dec 1997. The Commission's thresholds are 5% for horizontal agreements and 10% for vertical agreements, also subject to exceptions.

[86] Case C–5/69 *Völk v Vervaeke* [1969] ECR 295; Case C–22/71 *Béguelin Import v GL Import Export* [1971] ECR 949.

issue like this seems ripe for review before, at the very least, the appeal tribunal of the Competition Commission—for example, following a challenge to an OFT negative clearance decision by an aggrieved third party.

Major Effects of Section 60 in Practice

3.57 In practical terms, there are four aspects of the obligations entailed in section 60 which deserve particular consideration:

- the extent to which consistency is required between the UK and EC procedural rules;
- the extent to which the obligations for consistency require a UK authority to take account of the European Single Market and other non-competition issues which have underpinned the development of EC competition case law;
- the treatment of EC comfort letters; and
- the extent to which Article 234 (formerly Article 177) references to the European Court will be permissible.

Each of these issues is considered in the following sections.

G. The Effect of Section 60: Procedural Issues

3.58 The procedures under which the European Commission operates Articles 81 and 82 (formerly Articles 85 and 86) are contained in Regulation 17 as amended,[87] supplemented by the jurisprudence of the European Court in interpreting that Regulation. As regards procedures for the operation of the Chapter I and II prohibitions, section 51 gives the OFT the power to produce Procedural Rules,[88] and the OFT has published a draft of these.[89] One of the most significant questions arising from section 60 is the extent to which the UK authorities are obliged to follow procedures operated at EC level. The view of the Government and the OFT is essentially that the UK is free to diverge from the EC model in its procedures under the Act. The OFT's draft Procedural Rules state:

---

[87] Reg 17 implementing Arts 85 and 86 [now Arts 81 and 82] of the Treaty, 6 Feb 1962, [1959–1962], OJ Spec Ed 87. See also specific regs dealing with particular sectors, namely: Reg 26 [1959–1962], OJ Spec Ed 129 for agriculture; Reg 1017/68 [1968] (I) OJ Spec Ed 302 for rail, road and inland waterway transport; Reg 4056/86 [1986] OJ L378/4 for maritime transport; Reg 3975/87 [1987] OJ L374/1 for air transport; Reg 4064/89 [1990] OJ L257/13 for mergers. See also Reg 27 [1959–1962], OJ Spec Ed 132 dealing with notification procedure and Reg 99/63 [1963–4], OJ Spec Ed 47 for organisation of hearings and Reg 3385/94 (replacing Reg 27 [1994] OJ L377/28).

[88] Sch 9 sets out matters which the Procedural Rules may cover. (As regards notifications, there are also a number of provisions in the Act itself—for Chapter I notifications, in ss 12 to 16 and Sch 5; and for Chapter II notifications, in ss 20 to 24 and Sch 6. Notification procedures under the Act and their differences from the EC rules are considered in more detail in Ch 12.

[89] OFT, n 59 above.

Section 60 of the Act sets out certain principles to provide for the UK authorities to handle cases in such a way as to ensure consistency with EC law. The obligation to ensure consistency only reaches to the extent that this is possible having regard to any relevant differences. Section 60 does not require the UK authorities to follow the procedural practices of the EC Commission. The Director General of Fair Trading's procedural rules therefore do not need to be consistent with the procedural practices of the EC Commission.[90]

However, as considered below, it is not at all clear that the position is as straight-forward as this, since behind the Commission's practice under Regulation 17 lie more general principles of procedure arising under the EC Treaty and the European Court (ones with which the UK institutions should act consistently). **3.59**

(i) *A relevant difference?*

The reasoning of the OFT is presumably that the divergence between its Procedural Rules and those under Regulation 17 which the European Commission operates is a 'relevant difference' for the purpose of section 60(1). Section 60(1) in fact refers to relevant differences 'between the provisions concerned' which, on the part of the UK, means Part I of the Act. It might therefore be argued that, for there to be a relevant difference within the meaning of this subsection, the UK provision must appear within Part I, ie on the face of the Act and, since the Procedural Rules do not, section 60 cannot be interpreted to allow the separation of EC and UK procedure. However, since the basis of the OFT's Procedural Rules is the enabling power in section 51, it can equally be argued that there is a provision within Part I of the Act.

(ii) *Determining a question under Part I of the Act?*

A further point made by the Government during the passage of what was then the Competition Bill through the House of Lords is that the *making* of the procedural rules (as opposed to their subsequent operation) does not give rise to section 60 consistency requirements because it does not involve the determining a question arising under Part I of the Act for the purposes of section 60(2). Indeed, if the making of the Procedural Rules did fall within the ambit of section 60(2), the possibility of creating the 'relevant difference' between the two systems as a basis for divergence from EC practice in their subsequent application (see (i) above) would never arise.

This argument ignores the possibility that an appeal on a point of procedure may be put to the appeal tribunal of the Competition Commission[91] as a basis for disputing a decision and that, in reviewing that point and any relevant Procedural Rule, the Competition Commission arguably would be

---

[90] OFT n 59 above; para 4.

[91] S 46(1) stipulates that parties may appeal against or 'with respect to' an OFT decision, which gives scope for appeals on procedural issues.

determining a question under Part I. If so, the limitation of section 60(2) to Part I questions would in this situation be no bar to the application of EC consistency obligations in the operation of UK procedure. However, the appeal tribunal would presumably by then be able to rely on the requirement to take into account 'relevant differences' as the basis for making a distinction.

(iii) *A question of competition?*

Another argument in support of restricting the UK authorities' obligations for consistency with the EC rules arises from the limitation of the application of section 60(1) to 'questions of competition'. However, as explained in paragraph 3.50(ii) above, the following subsections of section 60 do not contain this limitation. Moreover, it is difficult in practice to separate issues of procedure from matters relating purely to competition. It is relevant that section 60(2) requires consistency with the 'principles' laid down by the EC Treaty in the European Court; these principles concern such matters as proportionality and fairness which can relate as much to procedural questions as to the substantive determination of a case by the Court or the Commission. Thus the requirement to be consistent with such principles would appear to be deprived of much of its practical relevance if it did not apply in a procedural context.

(iv) *High level principles*

The difficulty in isolating purely procedural matters was recognised by the Government during the passage of the Competition Bill through the House of Lords, where Lord Simon argued

> it is not always possible completely to separate substance and procedure . . . The very fact that Articles 85 and 86 [now Articles 81 and 82] now have an internal dynamic means that they have to be understood in the context of the general principles which apply to them as part of Community law. These, which one might call high level principles, may impinge on the meaning and effect of the prohibitions as a question of law. They range from the principle of legal certainty, which carries with it the proposition that contracts should not lightly be set aside, to the principle of fairness in administrative action. They can perhaps best be summarised as the necessary underpinning of the rule of law, and in this context, law means the whole system of Community law.[92]

Thus the Government has sought to make a distinction between, on the one hand 'high level principles' underlying the operation of Articles 81 and 82 (formerly Articles 85 and 86) and, on the other, purely procedural rules by which they are put into practice. These high level principles can be taken to include the EC concepts of legal certainty, fairness, non-discrimination, objectivity and proportionality.[93] The Government also recognised at an ear-

---

[92] Lord Simon of Highbury, *Hansard,* HL vol 586 no 116 col 1363 (5 Mar 1998).

[93] There has in fact been limited recognition of the concept of proportionality in UK judicial review jurisprudence: see, eg, *Sedley J in R v Manchester Metropolitan University, ex parte Nolan,* 14 July 1993, *The Independent,* 15 July 1993.

lier stage of the Competition Bill in Parliament that the right against self-incrimination as developed by the ECJ would be available for individuals subject to investigation by the OFT.[94]

However, Lord Simon went on qualify this

> some procedures, for example 'Access to the file', are derived from ECJ/CFI judgments drawing on the high level principles, but these judgments were given in the context of the particular procedures adopted by the [European] Commission. This is shown by the fact that they are not applied in the same way in other areas of Community administrative action. The same would be true of the Director [OFT]'s rules.[95]

On the face of it, a distinction between high level principles and purely procedural requirements, as evidenced by the extent to which they are applied across the whole ambit of EC administrative action, might appear clear; but in practice this distinction would seem more difficult to maintain. For example, at EC level provision is made under Article 19 of Regulation 17 for formal oral hearings involving the parties concerned and third persons prior to the taking of infringement, negative clearance or exemption decisions by the European Commission, whereas at UK level the Procedural Rules provide (in Rule 14) simply for an opportunity to make oral representations, and this is available only for the parties themselves where the OFT proposes to take an infringement decision. The view of the OFT is presumably that its more limited procedural provision is sufficient to satisfy the high level principle of fairness arising through section 60 and the right to a fair hearing which that entails, and that there is no need to replicate the extensive European Commission procedure (a major purpose of which is to involve the national authorities of the Member States).[96]

Nevertheless, as the Government's statement recognises, European Court judgments draw on high level principles but apply them in the context of specific European Commission procedures. Consequently, when analysing decisions of the European Court with a view to considering the procedural obligations which apply arise on the UK authorities as a result of section 60, it is not always easy to identify the threshold between high level principles themselves and their application in the specific procedural context of Regulation 17.

---

[94] Lord Simon of Highbury, *Hansard,* HL vol 583 no 69 col 960 (25 Nov 1997). However, it is arguable that these principles, as set out in Case 347/87 *Orkem v Commission* [1989] ECR 3283, still fall short of requirements arising under the European Convention on Human Rights—see Ch 14 para 14.75.

[95] Ibid, col 1364.

[96] The right to a fair hearing is also guaranteed by Art 6(1) of the European Convention on Human Rights.

3.60 The uncertainties considered above in establishing the procedural obligations of the UK authorities seem set to be one of the most sensitive areas in the initial period of the Act's operation. Welcome clarification may come from the appeal tribunal of the Competition Commission following review of alleged procedural impropriety by the OFT, or indeed through the application of more general principles of judicial review law.

H. The Effect of Section 60: Non-Competition Issues

Single Market Issues

3.61 It is well recognised that a major policy objective behind the application of the EC competition rules is the achievement of a European Single Market in order to allow goods and services to move freely within the European Union. However, there exists a well documented tension between the achievement of this objective and reaching decisions which stand up to economic analysis in terms of competition alone. To some extent, EC competition law has been used to achieve what might be considered an industrial policy or political objective, and many leading EC cases reflect this.[97]

3.62 Thus, for example, the European Commission and the European Court have taken an extremely firm stance in support of 'parallel' trade, ie imports and exports between EU Member States. However, whilst restraints on parallel imports are clearly inimical to the achievement of the Single Market, it is not always clear from the decisions of the Commission or the judgments of the European Court that they appreciably restrict competition. A report prepared for the Department of Trade and Industry[98] found that, as regards vertical agreements, the European Commission, in fining companies for violation of Article 81 (formerly Article 85), was overwhelmingly concerned with Single Market issues. Similarly, in its Article 81 prohibition decisions, Single Market issues were considered to be of particular significance.

3.63 The prevalence of Single Market and other non-competition issues in EC case law and the question of their import as a result of clause 60 are clearly another issue of considerable importance. It is arguable that by focusing more closely on solely the economic impact of particular practices, the Act could be applied in a way which achieved greater economic efficiency than if non-economic policy goals (which, as in the case of the Single Market objective, may be inappropriate in the domestic context) are taken into account.

---

[97] Eg, joined Cases 56 and 58/64 *Consten SARL & Grundig-Verkaufs-GmbH v EEC Commission* [1966] ECR 299.

[98] Whish, R., and Bishop, W., *The Treatment of Vertical Agreements under the Competition Bill: A Report for the Competition Bill Team of the Department of Trade and Industry* (1998).

The Government addressed this issue during the legislative passage of the Act **3.64** through Parliament, but its views were not entirely clear. In the House of Lords, Lord Simon stated that single market objectives should not be relevant to the application of the Act:

> . . . the Community objective of ensuring a common internal market for 15 differ-
> ent national states simply does not make sense in a purely domestic context.
> Therefore, those applying the prohibitions must be able to produce a sensible trans-
> lation of the EC rules into the domestic system. This explains the reference to
> consistency between questions arising in relation to 'competition within the UK'
> which correspond to those arising in Community law in relation to 'competition
> within the Community'.[99]

It added at a later date that 'single market objectives would not be relevant to the domestic prohibition system'.[100]

But a slightly different view was expressed by the Government subsequently, at **3.65** the Committee stage in the House of Commons:

> Importing EC jurisprudence extends not only to the substantive law but to the prin-
> ciples developed under EC law. Such principles are part and parcel of the prohibi-
> tions. The fact that single market objectives will not be relevant for many agreements
> which come within the scope of the Chapter I prohibition does not mean that the
> European Commission and the UK prohibitions are different. For example, it does
> not mean that single market considerations must be dissected out of an EU decision
> before applying clause 60.
>
> Under each prohibition, what is important is whether the agreement can be said
> to have the object or effect of restricting, preventing or distorting competition. As a
> general rule, agreements which seek to divide markets on national lines raise serious
> competition concerns. This is because barriers to trade still exist between Member
> States.[101]

Section 60 itself can be interpreted in two ways. A literal reading of section 60(2) **3.66** suggests that EC case law should be imported in its entirety when determining issues arising under the Act; questions arising under Part I of the Act are required to be dealt with in a way which is not inconsistent with the treatment of corre-sponding questions arising in Community law. Since there is here no attempt to exclude the role of Single Market issues as they affect EC competition analysis, the implication is that the relevant authorities and courts should not do so.

An alternative view is that Single Market issues are not relevant to the OFT or UK **3.67** courts:

- First, although section 60(2) has a broad meaning, it contains important qual-ifications. It aims to ensure consistency with corresponding questions, 'so far as

---

[99] Lord Simon of Highbury; *Hansard*, HL vol 583, no 69, col 961 (25 Nov 1997).
[100] Lord Simon of Highbury; *Hansard*, HL vol 586, no 116, col 1365, (5 Mar 1998).
[101] Nigel Griffiths, MP, *Hansard*, Standing Cttee G, 14th sitting, col 545 (18 June 1998).

possible'. The inclusion of these words implies that there will be cases in which the application of EC law should be qualified—otherwise the words would add no meaning to the provision.

Moreover, the consistency obligation is subject to the further qualification that regard must be had to 'any relevant differences between the provisions concerned'.

Both of these might be considered to imply that, since not all aspects of EC law need to be imported into the interpretation of the UK prohibitions, the Single Market aspects can be ignored. The long title of the Competition Act— 'an Act to make provision about competition and abuse of a dominant position'—may strengthen the case that Single Market objectives are a 'relevant difference' justifying departure from the consistency obligation.[102]

However it could be argued that this means that there can only be a departure from the consistency principle where there are actually express differences in the EC and UK provisions themselves, which there may not be since the Act contains provisions that are virtually identical to Articles 81(1) and 81(3) (formerly Articles 85(1) and 85(3)) and there is nothing else on the face of the Act indicating that the Single Market and other non-competition concerns taken into account at EC level should not be followed in the UK.

- Secondly, section 60(1), the 'purpose' provision, cannot be overlooked and, as described in paragraph 3.50(ii) above, it is arguably narrower in scope than section 60(2): it attempts to ensure that questions arising under Part I of the Act in relation to competition within the UK are treated in a manner consistent with the treatment of corresponding questions arising in Community law 'in relation to competition within the Community'. This suggests that principles from EC case law will be admitted in so far as they address related UK issues of what affects competition *per se* (which is not the same as EC findings that a practice breaches the competition rules because it restricts the development of the single market, rather than in itself undermining competition).

- Thirdly, the view of the OFT is that EC Single Market objectives are not relevant to the domestic prohibition system.[103] This, combined with statements of the Government during the passage of the Competition Bill through the House of Lords, increase the likelihood of the UK courts accepting that the broader objective of EC law need not be taken into account.

3.68 However, this conclusion is not particularly satisfactory. It is undermined in practice by the difficulty, should it even be considered desirable, of separating elements in EC cases relating to the achievement of a Single Market from those relating

---

[102] A court may look at the long title in interpreting an Act—it is not necessarily a reliable guide to interpretation but should not be ignored, see F. A. R. Bennion, *Statutory Interpretation: A Code* (3rd edn, London: Butterworths, 1997) s 245.

[103] Office of Fair Trading, n 4 above, para 2.2.

purely to competition. A close reading of the EC judgments suggests that even where such policy objectives are couched in terms of economic analysis (or more likely, a more general notion of fairness), some judgments nonetheless *appear* to be driven by a desire to achieve an outcome consistent with Single Market goals.

The exclusion from the Chapter I prohibition for vertical agreements, which are **3.69** perhaps the most significant category of agreements in respect of which treatment at EC level has been influenced by non-competition concerns, will go a long way to reducing difficulties caused by this issue. Indeed, this is a policy objective behind the exclusion. Nevertheless, it seems likely that much debate will be entered into concerning the precise economic rationale of Commission decisions and European Court judgments where the furtherance of the single market objective is discernible.

Chapter I Exemption Criteria

In the light of the reasoning above as to the concern of section 60(1) with ques- **3.70** tions of competition, it is worth considering the exemption criteria under both Article 81 (formerly Article 85) and the Chapter I prohibition, since the counter-vailing economic benefits these criteria take into account are not limited to effects on competition. Rather, Article 81(3) (formerly Article 85(3)) and section 9 of the Act look to assess improvements of production or distribution and promotion of technical or economic progress to the benefit of consumers.

A report commissioned by the Government indicates that, at EC level, when **3.71** granting exemptions under Article 81(3) (formerly Article 85(3)) or issuing comfort letters, the European Commission has taken a broad range of matters into account including benefits to the environment, benefits to health and social benefits (broad objectives declared elsewhere in the EC Treaty).[104] Although the UK authorities will probably wish to take a similar approach in practice, it is arguable that under section 60 they will have no obligation to follow the Commission in taking into account such broader objectives. In fact, it can be anticipated that any divergence is as likely as not to come from a desire for a broader approach in which factors such as environmental benefits are given more weight, rather than a narrower approach in which these factors are played down.

---

[104] Whish R., *Exemption Criteria under Article 85(3) EC: A Study of the Case-law, of the European Court of Justice, the Court of First Instance and the Decisional Practice of the European Commission* (1998).

I. The Effect of Section 60: EC Comfort Letters

Status of EC Comfort Letters

3.72 An EC 'comfort letter' is a written piece of guidance from the European Commission, as an alternative to a formal negative clearance or exemption decision, stating that the Commission is prepared to consider its file on the particular matter closed (unless new facts come to light). Thus, for example, the European Commission may state that it takes the view that the agreement infringes Article 81(1) (formerly Article 85(1)) but would benefit from an Article 81(3) (formerly Article 85(3)) exemption. The European Commission most often concludes notification cases by means of a comfort letter. However, section 60 does not explicitly address the question of the weight, if any, that is to be attached to EC comfort letters in the operation of the Chapter I and II prohibitions.

3.73 Where a comfort letter has been issued, even though there is no formal European Commission decision, a national competition authority that took a contrary view to the Commission's as set out in its letter would run the risk that the Commission would subsequently make a decision granting an Article 81(3) (formerly Article 85(3)) exemption and, therefore, in accordance with the principles described above, the European Commission's decision would prevail. In the light of this, as a matter of practice the European Commission requests national authorities to consult it before deciding to adopt a different decision under national law.[105]

Status of Article 19(3) Comfort Letters

3.74 In some cases the European Commission invites third party consultation prior to its conclusion of a case by means of a notice published in the EC Official Journal, based on the procedure in Article 19(3) of Regulation 17 for publishing a notice prior to a negative clearance or individual exemption decision. It is worth considering whether EC comfort letters involving this more formal procedure amount to a 'decision' or a 'statement' of the European Commission to which the UK authorities must have regard under section 60(3).

3.75 The Commission itself has made it clear that Article 19(3) comfort letters do not have the status of decisions; they merely state that the European Commission 'does not consider it necessary to pursue the formal procedure through to the adoption of a decision under Article 85(3) [now Article 81(3)]'.[106]

---

[105] Co-operation Notice, n 2 above, para 21.
[106] European Commission Notice on procedures concerning notifications pursuant to Art 4 of Council Reg 17, [1983] OJ C295/6.

The OFT has, however, given some indication that it considers Article 19(3)   **3.76**
Notices to be statements of the European Commission for the purposes of section
60(3). An earlier draft of the OFT's guidelines drew a distinction between comfort letters preceded by a notice in the EC Official Journal under Article 19(3) of
Regulation 17, and other comfort letters—viewing the former type as, if not
Commission decisions, statements of the Commission within the meaning of section 60(3).[107] Further support for the suggestion that a comfort letter should be
considered a 'statement' can be found in the fact that the European Commission's
Competition Directorate (DG IV) has recently begun to publish lists of comfort
letters provided on its Internet website.

OFT Treatment of Comfort Letters in Practice

The OFT's declared policy with regard to the treatment of EC comfort letters is   **3.77**
likely to mean that an issue over their status may not arise in practice. In its guidelines on the Chapter I prohibition, the OFT has indicated that, as a general rule,
it will not depart from the European Commission's assessment of an agreement,
subject to three exceptions:[108]

(a) where the agreement raises particular concerns in relation to competition in
     the UK which raises concerns that do not exist in other EU Member States.
     To allay any concerns that this introduces unnecessary uncertainty, the OFT
     has stated that: '[i]t will be rare, however, for an agreement to have such a suf-
     ficiently serious and distinct effect on UK competition';

(b) where the notifying parties have received a 'discomfort' letter—ie a comfort
     letter indicating that the European Commission considers the agreement to
     infringe Article 81 (formerly Article 85) and not merit exemption, but as a
     matter of internal priorities is taking no further action; or

(c) where the agreement falls outside the scope of Article 81(1) (formerly Article
     85(1)) on the ground that there is not an appreciable effect on trade between
     EU Member States.

Since section 60(3) stipulates only that the OFT need 'have regard' to such deci-   **3.78**
sions or statements, the OFT's policy in practice of departing from the
Commission's assessment only in these limited circumstances seems unlikely to
exceed the margin of its scope for divergence afforded by that wording.

  See Chapter 12 paragraph 12.68(iv) for further explanation of the OFT's policy with regard to EC comfort letters.

---

[107] Office of Fair Trading, consultation draft dated 12 May 1998, Competition Act 1998 'EC
comfort letters', para 2.
[108] Office of Fair Trading, n 4 above, para 7.12.

J. The Effect of Section 60: Article 234 (formerly Article 177) References

Are Article 234 (formerly Article 177) References Possible?

3.79 Strictly, national courts only have the power to *apply* EC law. The *interpretation* of EC law falls within the sole jurisdiction of the European Court. However, where, in the context of national proceedings, EC law is relied upon and a question arises as to its proper interpretation, Article 234 (formerly Article 177) of the EC Treaty allows national courts to ask the ECJ for a ruling on how particular provisions of EC law should be interpreted.

3.80 Although the Article 234 (formerly Article 177) reference procedure provides the interface between the UK courts and the European Court, the procedure does not serve an appeal function. After the request is made, the ECJ issues a ruling on the question of law that is sent back to the national court, and the national court then applies that ruling to the facts of the case. The ECJ does not decide the actual case (although it has come perilously close on some occasions)—that is a matter for the national court.

3.81 An important question arising because of section 60—the purpose of which is to ensure that national law is interpreted in accordance with EC law—is whether, and if so under what circumstances, it would be appropriate or possible for a national court or tribunal to refer a question to the ECJ using the Article 234 (formerly Article 177) procedure. This is recognised as desirable, and even essential, if section 60 is successfully to harness UK competition law to the EC system, in order to ensure that the domestic system can evolve in a way which is continually aligned with EC law. If Article 234 references were not possible, the direction of Competition Act case law in the hands of the OFT and the UK courts would in time diverge from the flow of decisions and judgments at EC level.

3.82 The starting point is that the ECJ has jurisdiction under the Article 234 (formerly Article 177) procedure to consider questions of EC law only. The text of Article 234(1)(a) (formerly Article 177(1)(a)) refers to the ECJ answering questions related to 'the interpretation of this Treaty'. It has in the past not been straightforward for national courts to obtain Article 234 rulings on issues which were not clearly questions relating to the interpretation of the Treaty. For example, in one case[109] the ECJ refused to give a preliminary ruling on an Article 234 reference from the Court of Appeal on an issue that arose under a UK statute[110] that was equivalent to a provision in the Brussels Convention on Jurisdiction and Judgments. That case concerned a

---

[109] Case C–346/93 *Kleinwort Benson Ltd v City of Glasgow District Council* [1995] ECR I–615.
[110] Civil Jurisdictions and Judgments Act 1982.

domestic issue relating to the allocation of jurisdiction between the English and Scottish courts. However, in other cases the ECJ has taken a broader view. For instance, in *Massam Dzodzi v Belgian State* the Court held:[111]

> It does not appear either from the wording of Article 177 [now Article 234] or from the aim of the procedure introduced by that article that the authors of the Treaty intended to exclude from the jurisdiction of the Court requests for a preliminary ruling on a Community provision in the specific case where the national law of a Member State refers to the content of that provision in order to determine rules applicable to a situation which is purely internal to that State.[112]

The position was clarified in *Bernd Gilog v Hauptzollamt Frankfurt am Main-**3.83** Ost*,[113] where the European Court held:

> Consequently, where questions submitted by national courts concern the inter-pretation of a provision of Community law, the Court is, in principle, obliged to give a ruling . . . Neither the wording of Article 177 [now Article 234] nor the aim of the procedure established by that article indicates that the Treaty makers intended to exclude from the jurisdiction of the Court requests for a preliminary ruling on a Community provision where the domestic law of a Member State refers to that Community provision in order to determine the rules applicable to a situation which is purely internal to that State . . .
>
> A reference by a national court can be rejected only if it appears that the procedure laid down by Article 177 [now Article 234] of the Treaty has been misused and a rul-ing from the Court elicited by means of a contrived dispute, or it is obvious that Community law cannot apply, either directly or indirectly, to the circumstances of the case referred to the Court.[114]

More recently, in *Oscar Bronner v Mediaprint*,[115] the European Court specifically **3.84** considered a question of competition law which arose from the application of Austria's national competition legislation which, like the UK's Competition Act, mirrors EC competition law. The Court has clearly stated that where the applica-tion of national law requires an interpretation of EC law in relation to the same situation, the national court may make an Article 234 (formerly Article 177) ref-erence 'when it considers that a conflict between Community law and national law is capable of arising'.[116] The Court was prepared to make a ruling on this even without determining whether the case had an effect on trade between EU Member States.[117]

It seems clear from the above that the ECJ will accept jurisdiction to answer ques- **3.85** tions on *EC* law which arise under the Competition Act, ie because of section 60.

---

[111] Joined Cases C–297/88 and C–197/89 [1990] ECR I–3763.
[112] Para 36.
[113] Case C–130/95, judgment of 17 July 1997.
[114] Paras 21 and 22 respectively.
[115] Case C–7/97, judgment of 26 Nov 1998.
[116] Para 20.
[117] Para 21.

However, since the decision on whether to invoke the Article 234 (formerly Article 177) procedure is one which can only be made by the UK authorities, the authorities will, indirectly, have some influence over the amount of specific direction which is given by the ECJ over the way case law in respect of the Act develops.

Which UK Authorities can Make Article 234 (formerly Article 177) References?

3.86 Article 234 (formerly Article 177) indicates that any court or tribunal of an EU Member State may request a ruling from the ECJ. It is clear that both the Court of Appeal and the appeal tribunal of the Competition Commission will have the power to make such a reference. Regarding the latter, the Government's view in Parliament was that

> it will be recognised as having the same importance and status as the High Court . . . I have no doubt that the European Court of Justice will see the tribunal in the same light . . . Article 177 [now Article 234] of the EC Treaty expressly refers to references from tribunals as well as Courts.[118]

The Government has also indicated that it hopes the OFT will be regarded as a court or tribunal capable of making Article 234 (formerly Article 177) references.[119]

3.87 The case law of the ECJ suggests that while it is clear that the appeal tribunal will have power to make an Article 234 (formerly Article 177) reference, it is by no means clear that the OFT would have a similar power.[120] The cases suggests that the following criteria must be satisfied if a body is to be classified as a 'court or tribunal', within the meaning of Article 234 of the EC Treaty: (i) the body must be established by law; (ii) the body must be permanent; (iii) its jurisdiction must be compulsory; (iv) its procedure must be *inter partes*; (v) it must apply rules of law and (vi) it must be independent.

3.88 It is clear that the Director General of Fair Trading (it is the DGFT rather than the OFT which is the relevant authority for the purposes of the Act) is an office established by law with a permanent existence. The requirement that the body has compulsory jurisdiction means that its determinations must be binding. Again, this criterion is satisfied in the case of the DGFT. Unlike the appeal tribunal, it is more difficult to classify the proceedings of the DGFT as '*inter partes*'. The DGFT is the investigator, prosecutor and judge. However, it was held by the ECJ in the *Dorsch Consultant* case that 'the requirement that the procedure before the

---

[118] Lord Simon of Highbury, Third Reading of the Competition Bill; *Hansard*, HL, vol 583, no 64, col 444 (17 Nov 1997).

[119] Lord Simon of Highbury, Third Reading of the Competition Bill, *Hansard*, HL, vol 583, no 69, col 963 (25 Nov 1997).

hearing body concerned must be inter partes is not an absolute criterion'.[121] In that case the parties were required to be heard by the relevant body before a determination was made and that was considered to be sufficient. The rules of procedure require that the DGFT considers representations made by the parties and the parties be given the opportunity for an oral hearing.[122] As regards the final two criteria, the DGFT in determining cases applies rules of law as laid down in the Act and he is clearly independent.

Thus, although there is room for uncertainty, there is at least a good argument **3.89** that the Director General of Fair Trading is a 'court or tribunal' capable of making an Article 234 (formerly Article 177) reference.

---

[120] See Case 61/65 *Vaassen-Göbbels* [1996] ECR 377; Case C–393/92 *Almelo and others* [1994] ECR I–1477; Joined Cases C–74/95 and C–129/95 *Criminal Proceedings v X* [1996] ECR I–6609; opinion of Léger AG, Case C–44/96 *Mannesmann and Lagenbau Austria AG and others v Strohal Rotationsdruck GmbH* [1998] ECR I–73; Case C–54/96 *Dorsch Consult Ingenieurgeselleshaft mbH v Bundesbaugesellschaft Berlin mbH* [1997] ECR 1–4961.

[121] n 120 above, para 31.

[122] OFT (OFT 411), R 14(1)(b).

PART II

RESTRICTIVE AGREEMENTS:
THE CHAPTER I PROHIBITION

4

THE CHAPTER I PROHIBITION—KEY CONCEPTS

A. Overview

The Chapter I prohibition is the new UK legislative instrument for the control **4.01** of agreements and arrangements which are restrictive of competition, including cartels. It is laid down in Chapter I of the Competition Act 1998, and its principal terms are set out in section 2 of the Act. It replaces the Restrictive Trade Practices Act 1976 (RTPA) and the Resale Prices Act 1976 (RPA), which are repealed.[1]

---

[1] Competition Act 1998 s 1. This section also repeals: the Restrictive Trade Practices Act 1977, which had removed certain financing agreements from the scope of the RTPA; and the Restrictive Practices Court Act 1976, which had provided for the question of the Restrictive Practices Court for the enforcement of the RTPA and the RPA.

Framework of the Chapter I Prohibition

4.02 Under the Chapter I prohibition, certain agreements and arrangements are **prohibited** by section 2 of the Competition Act, unless they are **excluded** in accordance with section 3 or **exempt** in accordance with sections 4 to 11.

(i) **Prohibition:** Section 2 *prohibits*:

- any of the following kinds of agreement or arrangements:
    - an agreement between undertakings,[2] or
    - a concerted practice,[3] or
    - a decision by an association of undertakings,[4]
- if that agreement or arrangement meets all of the following criteria:
    - it has as its object or effect[5] the prevention, restriction or distortion of competition[6] within the United Kingdom (or a part of it),[7] and
    - it may affect trade within the United Kingdom (or a part of it),[8] and
    - it is, or is intended to be, implemented in the United Kingdom (or a part of it),[9] and
    - the effects are appreciable rather than '*de minimis*', which in most cases will be where the parties' combined market shares exceed 25 per cent.[10]

The key concepts in this prohibition are examined in this chapter.

(ii) **Exclusions:** In accordance with section 3, certain types of agreement and arrangement are *excluded* from the Chapter I prohibition. This means that they are outside the scope of the prohibition altogether. Exclusions are designated either in the Act itself or by subsequent orders made by the Secretary of State.
Exclusions are examined in Chapter 5 of this book.

(iii) **Exemptions:** In accordance with sections 4 to 11, an agreement which falls within the scope of the Chapter I prohibition may nevertheless be *exempt* from it. An agreement is exempt from the Chapter I prohibition if:

- it already benefits from an EC block or individual exemption, under Article 81(3) (formerly Article 85(3)) of the EC Treaty;[11] or

---

[2] For explanation see below, paras 4.09–4.17.
[3] See paras 4.18–4.22.
[4] See paras 4.23–4.26.
[5] See paras 4.39–4.45.
[6] See paras 4.27–4.38.
[7] See paras 4.58–4.59.
[8] See paras 4.60–4.62.
[9] See paras 4.62–4.64.
[10] See paras 4.46–4.55.
[11] Or if it would benefit from an EC block exemption apart from the fact that it does not affect trade between Member States. As a result of the Treaty of Amsterdam, Art 85(3) is renumbered Art 81(3).

- it benefits from a UK block exemption order made by the Secretary of State, or a UK individual exemption specifically granted by the OFT in respect of that agreement or arrangement. UK block and individual exemptions may only be granted if they satisfy the criteria in section 9.

The criteria for UK exemptions, under section 9, replicate the criteria for EC exemptions in Article 81(3) (formerly Article 85(3)): broadly, that the agreement or arrangement brings economic benefits which offset its anti-competitive effects.

Exemptions are examined in Chapter 6 of this book.

(iv) The **consequences of infringing** the Chapter I prohibition include: the infringing contractual provisions being void and unenforceable in a court in the UK; the parties being liable in court to third parties who have sustained losses or damage as a result of the infringement; and the possibility of the OFT ordering the parties to modify or terminate the agreement or arrangement, and/or imposing penalties (fines) for the infringement.

The consequences of infringement are examined in Chapter 10 of this book.

(v) An agreement may be **notified** to the OFT with a view to obtaining a decision or guidance on whether it infringes the Chapter I prohibition and, if it does, whether it merits exemption. The procedures for notification are examined in Chapter 12 of this book.

Relation with EC Law—the Chapter I Prohibition and Article 81 (formerly Article 85) of the EC Treaty

There is no sharp dividing line between, on the one hand, the jurisdiction of the Chapter I prohibition and, on the other hand, the jurisdiction of the equivalent EC prohibition on restrictive agreements and arrangements in Article 81 (formerly Article 85) of the EC Treaty.[12] An agreement may be subject to both prohibitions, for example where it affects trade and competition within the UK and at the same time may affect trade between EU Member States, and this will be the case for many agreements. However, in practice the regulatory burdens of this duplication are considerably reduced by the fact that the terms and practical application of the Chapter I prohibition are closely aligned with those under Article 81 (see below under the next heading)—as well as by various provisions in the Competition Act specifically designed to reduce the burdens, such as automatic UK exemption for agreements which benefit from EC exemption (called 'parallel exemption') and immunity from UK penalties for notification being valid regardless of whether the agreement is notified to the UK or the EC authorities.

4.03

---

[12] As a result of the Treaty of Amsterdam, Art 85 is renumbered Art 81.

Alignment with Article 81 (formerly Article 85)

4.04 The terms of the Chapter I prohibition, in section 2 of the Act, and the criteria for exemption in section 9, essentially replicate the wording of Article 81 (formerly Article 85) (except, of course, as to the relevant territory for jurisdictional purposes). Moreover, under section 60 of the Act, the UK courts and competition authorities are required to construe the Chapter I prohibition so as to ensure that there is no inconsistency with the principles for applying Article 81 as laid down by the European Court of Justice,[13] and also having regard to European Commission decisions and statements on Article 81.

4.05 Alignment is further strengthened by the fact that the consequences of infringing the Chapter I prohibition are broadly the same as the consequences of infringing Article 81 (formerly Article 85), and that many of the procedures (eg notifications and block exemptions) are similar.

4.06 However, the Chapter I prohibition differs from Article 81 (formerly Article 85) in a number of important respects, including:

(i)   The concept of 'exclusions' from the Chapter I prohibition: there is no equivalent concept under Article 81. The provisions for exclusions allow the UK authorities to make the scope of the Chapter I prohibition narrower than that of Article 81. For example, co-operative joint ventures which are subject to UK merger control will normally be excluded from the Chapter I prohibition, whereas they may be subject to Article 81. A more fundamental exclusion, not included in the Act itself but contemplated by the government for the future, would be in relation to 'vertical agreements' (other than price-fixing agreements); if these were to be excluded from the Chapter I prohibition that would represent a radical divergence from Article 81.

(ii) The possibility of UK block exemptions: these would grant automatic exemption from the Chapter I prohibition to categories of agreement not already covered by the EC block exemptions.

(iii) Under the Chapter I prohibition, it is the OFT which carries out the functions that are carried out under Article 81 by the European Commission.

(iv) Under the Chapter I prohibition, parties may submit confidential notifications to the OFT for 'guidance' on whether an agreement is likely to infringe the Chapter I prohibition or to be exempted. There is no equivalent procedure in respect of Article 81. (Both the Chapter I prohibition and Article 81 enable parties to notify for formal decision on whether there is an infringement and whether exemption is merited, but these involve third parties being made aware of the agreement.)

---

[13] Including the Court of First Instance (CFI).

The broader context of the relation between the Competition Act and EC law is examined in Chapter 3 of this book.

Relation with the Chapter II Prohibition

Both the Chapter I prohibition and the Chapter II prohibition (examined in Part III of this book) prohibit anti-competitive conduct in the UK. The main differences between them are that: **4.07**

(i)   The Chapter I prohibition only applies if there are two or more parties—ie it applies to bilateral or multilateral arrangements, and not to purely unilateral conduct.[14] By contrast the Chapter II prohibition can (and usually does) apply to purely unilateral conduct.

(ii) The Chapter II prohibition only applies if the anti-competitive conduct is carried out by a party (or parties) which has a dominant market position. By contrast, the Chapter I prohibition applies even if the parties are not dominant in any market.

(iii) There is a possibility of exemption from the Chapter I prohibition, where (broadly) there are economic benefits which offset the anti-competitive effect. There is no such possibility of exemption from the Chapter II prohibition.

(iv) A number of arrangements benefit from exclusion from the Chapter I prohibition but not from the Chapter II prohibition.[15] These include exclusions which the Secretary of State may add under section 3(3) of the Act.

Nevertheless, there is some overlap between the Chapter I and Chapter II prohibitions, and certain anti-competitive conduct may be subject to both prohibitions—for example, agreements in which a dominant supplier imposes a minimum purchase requirement on a business customer.[16] While such conduct could be exempted under the Chapter I prohibition, there is no exemption from the Chapter II prohibition.[17] **4.08**

---

[14] Except in the case of decisions by associations of undertakings, which are unilateral conduct on behalf of the various parties who are members of the association—see paras 4.23–4.26.

[15] See Ch 5 for exclusions from the Chapter I prohibition, and Ch 8 from the Chapter II prohibition.

[16] Note, however, that such an agreement would not be subject to the Chapter I prohibition if, as is contemplated, vertical agreements are to be excluded from the Chapter I prohibition. See Ch 5 paras 5.81–5.95 below.

[17] See Ch 6 paras 6.59–6.60 below.

B. Agreements Between Undertakings

4.09 The main type of arrangement which may come within the scope of the Chapter I prohibition is an 'agreement between undertakings'. There are two key concepts here: first, there must be an 'agreement' between parties, implying two or more parties rather than merely unilateral conduct (this agreement need not be a legally binding contract); and secondly, the agreement must be made *between* 'undertakings', rather than only within a single undertaking, or between an undertaking and a party which is not an undertaking.

4.10 The meanings of 'agreements' and of 'between undertakings' are examined in turn in the following paragraphs.

'Agreements'

4.11 The term 'agreements' under the Chapter I prohibition and under Article 81 (formerly Article 85) has a meaning which encompasses more than just formal legally binding contracts. (Indeed, it is similar to the concept of an 'agreement' under the old RTPA.) An 'agreement' can be an informal arrangement, whether or not legally binding, and need not necessarily be set out in writing: it may be an oral arrangement or even an unspoken understanding.[18] Even if it is in writing, it may be set out in one document, or in a series of documents comprising one overall arrangement— for example, several related contracts, as well as non-binding side letters and memoranda of understanding, which collectively constitute a single transaction.

4.12 This broad definition of 'agreement' may perhaps be best understood by considering the reason for it. If non-binding and unwritten arrangements did not come within the ambit of competition law, it would be easy for companies to escape the controls of competition law when arranging not to compete against each other— simply by choosing not to commit their arrangement to writing. This would make a nonsense of the purpose of competition law. It can be just as damaging to the operation of competition in an economy (and hence to the protection of consumers) if salesmen reach an informal 'gentleman's agreement' in the pub that they will not try to win orders from each other's customers, or if company directors chat on the golf-course about their proposed pricing policies, as it is if companies sign formal contracts limiting competition between them. Indeed, in practice the most seriously anti-competitive arrangements, such as price-fixing or market-sharing cartels, are *not* laid down in legal contracts, and *are* often made in secret—precisely because the participating companies hope thereby to escape detection by the competition authorities.[19]

---

[18] Although the absence of writing may present evidential problems in proving the existence of the 'agreement'.

[19] It is for this reason that competition authorities, such as the OFT and the European Commission, are given such strong powers of investigation. See Ch 14 below.

The term 'agreement' is not explicitly defined in the Competition Act but, in **4.13** accordance with section 60, it is to be interpreted consistently with the EC law interpretation of the term under Article 81 (formerly Article 85). On the basis of EC law cases, the following guidance can be drawn about what is, and what is not, an 'agreement':

(i) A legally binding contract is an 'agreement' (or part of an 'agreement'—see (v) below).

(ii) A non-contractual and non-binding written arrangement can be an 'agreement':

- It need not be embodied in a formal document, but may be in informal notes or correspondence. In one case, a series of internal memoranda, a telex message and some letters were held by the European Commission to constitute an 'agreement'.[20]

- The elements of a legally binding contract, such as consideration (mutuality of obligations), need not be present. When a Japanese ball-bearings trade association agreed with a French ball-bearings trade association that it would not sell ball-bearings into France at lower prices than those charged by the French trade association's members, the European Commission decided that this was an 'agreement', even though only one party (the Japanese trade association) had made a promise or accepted an obligation, and there was no reciprocal obligation from the French trade association.[21]

(iii) There may be an 'agreement' by virtue of a tacit understanding, even though it has not been explicitly written or spoken. For instance, when the German electrical goods manufacturer AEG consistently refused to appoint new dealers to stock its products, having already appointed a number of dealers, this was not regarded as a purely unilateral act by AEG; an 'agreement' between AEG and the existing dealers was inferred (it was in the interests of the existing dealers that they be protected against competition from new dealers).[22]

(iv) The rules of a trade association or other collective body of businesses may be an 'agreement'. Thus, for example, the European Commission has held that the rules and regulations of the London Sugar Futures Markets Limited, which administered a futures market in London for sugar, were to be considered as 'agreements' within the meaning of Article 81 (formerly Article 85).[23]

---

[20] *National Panasonic* (UK) [1982] OJ L354/28.
[21] *Franco-Japanese Ballbearings Agreement* [1974] OJ L343/19.
[22] Case 107/82, *AEG-Telefunken v Commission* [1983] ECR 3151.
[23] *London Sugar Futures Market* [1985] OJ L369/25.

(v)   An 'agreement' may arise out of a series of contracts, even if they are entered into over a period of time, rather than just from a single contract. Thus, for example, an 'agreement' was held to arise from an overall master framework agreement, followed by a series of more detailed sub-agreements implementing it, even though not all the participants were party to every single sub-agreement.[24]

(vi) However, there will not be an 'agreement' if the arrangement is *purely* unilateral. There must be some kind of consensus or arrangement to which at least two undertakings assent (see below on undertakings). The English Court of Appeal, applying Article 81 (formerly Article 85), has held that where a motor vehicle importer purely unilaterally terminated a dealership agreement, the notice of termination was not an 'agreement'; there was no consensus with the dealer (although provisions for termination in a dealership agreement would constitute an 'agreement').[25] On the other hand, the authorities may be willing to deem the existence of a consensus between the parties. The OFT has said that, where the assent of a party is secured only under pressure from the other party, there may still be an agreement between them.[26] The European Commission, in its 1996 decision *ADALAT*, held that a manufacturer's unilateral refusal to supply its wholesalers with the full quantities of goods which they had ordered (because it feared that the higher quantities would be used as parallel exports) constituted an agreement between the manufacturer and each wholesaler—on the grounds that it arose in commercial relations between manufacturer and wholesaler and that each wholesaler, by 'adapting' to the manufacturer's intentions when placing its order, thereby 'complied' with them; it is uncertain whether this radical interpretation of 'compliance' and consensus will be upheld by the European Courts, but the Court of First Instance suspended interim measures which had been imposed by the Commission in the case, stating that the Commission's decision 'leaves uncertainties as to the criteria for distinguishing the unilateral from the contractual' which should be resolved in substantive proceedings before the Court.[27]

'Between Undertakings'

4.14   It is not sufficient that there should be an agreement or arrangement between at least two parties. It must be the case that there are at least two 'undertakings' which are party to the agreement.

---

[24]   *Polypropylene Cartel* [1986] OJ L230/1.

[25]   *Richard Cound v BMW (GB)*, CA, 10 May 1995 [1997] Eu LR 277.

[26]   Office of Fair Trading, Competition Act 1998: The Chapter I Prohibition', (OFT 401) para 2.8. In such a case, however, the 'victim' of the pressure is likely to be subject to lower or no penalties.

[27]   *ADALAT*, Commission decision, [1996] OJ L201; Case T–41/96R *Bayer v Commission* (CFI judgment suspending interim measures) [1996] ECR–II 381.

There is no explicit definition of 'undertaking' in the Competition Act. When the   **4.15**
legislation was first presented to Parliament, in October 1997, it was prefaced
with an explanatory memorandum which stated:

> . . . a number of terms in the Bill such as 'undertaking' are not defined. Their mean-
> ing will be that given by EC law.[28]

The cases under EC law yield the following principles for determining whether a   **4.16**
party is an 'undertaking':

(i)   The party must be a **business**, not an individual consumer[29] or a non-
      commercial organisation.

    (a)   The business may nevertheless be state-owned. The European
      Commission has stated that, as far as EC law is concerned, including com-
      petition law, 'the position of nationalised firms is . . . no different from that
      of private firms',[30] and British Telecom was held by the European Court of
      Justice to be an undertaking even before it was privatised.[31]

    (b)   The body need not be profit-making to be an 'undertaking'—but it must
      have commercial objectives. A society which collected payments for per-
      forming rights was an undertaking, even though it only took for itself
      administrative expenses rather than profits.[32] Similarly, a non-profit
      making mutual insurance or friendly society is also likely to be regarded
      as an 'undertaking'. However, a body called Eurocontrol, which provided
      air traffic control services, was not an 'undertaking' because its function
      was to give effect to co-operation between various governments in air
      traffic control, even though in the course of doing so it collected route
      charges.[33]

(ii) An 'undertaking' is an **autonomous economic unit**, and this is not the same
      as a company.

    (a)   A company *may* be an undertaking, but only if it is a self-standing
      autonomous economic unit. If it is part of a group of companies, it is
      more likely that the group, rather than any of the individual member
      companies (parent or subsidiary) will be the 'undertaking' (see (b)
      below).

    (b)   A group of companies is regarded as collectively constituting a single
      'undertaking' where—as is normally the case—the member companies

---

[28]   Competition Bill [HL], HL Bill 33 52/1, 15 Oct 1997.
[29]   But an individual businessman may be an undertaking. See (ii)(d) below.
[30]   European Commission answer to Written Question in the European Parliament, WQ
1152/82 [1982] OJ C339/15.
[31]   Case 41/83 *British Telecommunications* [1985] ECR 873.
[32]   *Interpar v GVL* [1981] OJ L370/49.
[33]   Case C–364/92 *SAT Fluggesellschaft v Eurocontrol* [1994] I ECR 43.

together form an economic unit within which the subsidiaries do not have real autonomy in determining their line of conduct on the market (in the words of the European Court of Justice).[34]

This is of particular importance in the context of agreements between a parent and its subsidiaries. The Parker Pen company had agreements with its subsidiaries in various Member States under which the subsidiaries agreed to restrict distribution of Parker Pen products to their allocated territories, rather than competing against each other. The European Court held that these arrangements could not infringe Article 81 (formerly Article 85) because there was no agreement between undertakings; all the parties were part of the same single undertaking, because together they formed one economic unit, and each subsidiary 'although having a separate legal personality, does not freely determine its conduct on the market but carries out the instructions given to it directly or indirectly by the parent company by which it is wholly controlled'.[35]

By contrast, when a subsidiary had a distribution system which was independent of, and different from, those of its fellow subsidiaries in a conglomerate group, the subsidiary was regarded as constituting a separate 'undertaking'.[36]

(c) An unincorporated economic unit may be an 'undertaking'. In order to qualify as an 'undertaking' an autonomous economic unit need not be a legal company; it could be a firm, or a partnership, or an agricultural cooperative,[37] or even a football governing body.[38]

(d) An individual (a 'natural person') may be an undertaking if that individual can be described as an economic unit. Someone who is purely a consumer, or a shareholder in a company, is not an undertaking. (Agreements between a business and a consumer cannot infringe Article 81 (formerly Article 85) or the Chapter I prohibition.) However, if the person carries on economic activities in his or her own right, he or she may constitute an undertaking—for example, if the person is a scientist or inventor who commercially licenses or assigns technology,[39] or a self-employed or freelance consultant,[40] or a freelance performer or artiste.[41]

The individual's commercial activity will need to be continuing if he or she is to be regarded as an 'undertaking'. A person does not become an

---

[34] Case 16/74 *Centrafarm v Winthrop* [1974] ECR 1183, para 32.
[35] Case C–73/95P *VIHO Europe v Commission* [1996] I ECR 5457, para 51.
[36] Case 75/84 *Metro v Commission* [1986] ECR 3021.
[37] OFT n 26 above, para 2.5.
[38] *1990 World Cup Tickets* [1992] OJ L136/31.
[39] *AOIP v Beyrard* [1976] OJ L6/8.
[40] *Reuter v BASF* [1976] OJ L254/40.
[41] *UNITEL* [1978] OJ L157/39, [1978] 3 CMLR 306.

undertaking simply by entering into a one-off profit making activity in his or her own right, such as selling goods in a car-boot sale.

Although EC law cases on the meaning of 'undertaking' will necessarily have primacy in the interpretation of the term for the purposes of the Chapter I prohibition, if there is no analogous EC case law in a particular circumstance, it may be helpful to have regard to cases on the meaning of 'enterprise' under the UK Fair Trading Act 1973, as the concepts are broadly similar.   **4.17**

C. Concerted Practices

Even if bilateral or multilateral anti-competitive conduct falls short of an 'agreement', it may still come within the ambit of the Chapter I prohibition or of Article 81 (formerly Article 85) if it constitutes a 'concerted practice'.   **4.18**

A concerted practice occurs where two or more undertakings knowingly but tacitly co-operate with each other rather than fully competing. The word 'knowingly' is crucial here. Although undertakings may be held to be engaged in a concerted practice even if they have not reached an 'agreement' (on its broad definition), they will not be held to have done so merely because their commercial policies (eg as to price rises or falls) move simultaneously or in parallel. These are very fine distinctions, but essentially there must be a degree of **deliberate or conscious co-ordination**.   **4.19**

In *ICI v Commission*, the European Court of Justice—finding that there was a concerted practice when there had been three uniform price increases for aniline dyes throughout the European industry—stated that a concerted practice is: **4.20**

> a form of co-ordination between undertakings which, without going so far as to amount to an agreement properly so called, knowingly substitutes a practical co-operation between them for the risks of competition.[42]

However, the mere fact of the three price rises being simultaneous was *not* sufficient to establish a concerted practice. Such parallelism can be explained, for example, in terms of normal competitive responses to market conditions and may, indeed, be indicative of a highly competitive market in which players do not price above the level which the market will bear, for fear of losing sales to their competitors.   **4.21**

Therefore, in order to establish a concerted practice, evidence of conscious co-ordination is needed in addition to the fact of simultaneous or parallel behaviour. Such evidence is likely to be in the form of: **4.22**

---

[42] Cases 48–49, 51–57/69 *ICI v Commission* [1972] ECR 619, para 64.

(i) The price behaviour on the part of one undertaking (eg a price rise) following the communication to that undertaking of an intention by a competing undertaking to behave in a similar way (eg by raising prices). That communication need not be direct, and could be in the form of a public announcement or of signals being passed through common customers or suppliers.

(ii) The parallel behaviour being wholly inexplicable in terms of independent responses to normal market conditions. The European Court applies this evidential criterion very strictly, and in the *Wood Pulp* case annulled a European Commission finding of a concerted practice, on the grounds that there were alternative explanations for the parallel pricing behaviour.[43]

Examples of factors which the OFT may consider in establishing whether there is a concerted practice are: 'whether the parties knowingly enter into practical cooperation; whether behaviour in the market is influenced as a result of direct or indirect contact between undertakings; whether parallel behaviour is a result of contact between undertakings which leads to conditions of competition which do not correspond to normal conditions of the market; the structure of the relevant market and the nature of the product involved; the number of undertakings in the market, and where there are only a few undertakings whether they have similar cost structures and outputs'.[44]

D. Decisions by Associations of Undertakings

4.23 'Decisions by associations of undertakings' are the third category of arrangement—in addition to 'agreements between undertakings' as broadly defined and 'concerted practices'—which come within the ambit of the Chapter I prohibition, and also of Article 81 (formerly Article 85) of the EC Treaty.

4.24 Although the application of the Chapter I prohibition and of Article 81 (formerly Article 85) is generally limited to bilateral and multilateral arrangements, and does not generally extend to unilateral acts,[45] the provision for 'decisions by associations of undertakings' is a partial exception. The 'decision' is taken by or on behalf of a single body, and to that extent is unilateral, requiring no agreement or arrangement with any other body or party. Nevertheless, it is considered appropriate that these should be dealt with along with agreements and concerted practices, because the apparently unilateral decision is taken on behalf of a number of undertakings, and accordingly may be deemed to be the expression of an arrangement between a number of undertakings.

---

[43] Case C–89/85 *Ahlstrom v EC Commission* [1993] I ECR 1307.

[44] OFT, n 26 above, para 2.13.

[45] Unilateral anti-competitive acts are dealt with under the Chap II prohibition and Art 82 (formerly Art 86) EC, in circumstances where the party concerned has a dominant position on the relevant market.

'Association of Undertakings'

This expression is generally taken to refer to trade associations. However, it may **4.25** also extend to statutory professional bodies.[46]

'Decision'

The concept of a 'decision', like the concept of 'agreement', extends to acts which **4.26** are non-binding as well as those which are binding. Thus, for example, non-mandatory recommendations of a trade association have been held by the European Court of Justice to count as 'decisions' where the recommendations are in practice complied with voluntarily, and this compliance has a 'profound influence on competition in the market'.[47]

E. Prevention, Restriction or Distortion of Competition

This is the key element of the Chapter I prohibition. It is because an arrangement **4.27** is anti-competitive that the legislation seeks to prohibit it. Arrangements which come within the ambit of the Chapter I prohibition are only offensive, and therefore prohibited, where their object or effect[48] is 'the prevention, restriction or distortion of competition'.

Chapter 7 of this book offers *practical* examples of the kinds of arrangement which **4.28** are regarded as preventing, restricting or distorting competition—and which are therefore subject to the prohibition (unless excluded or exempted). The following paragraphs briefly outline the *conceptual* framework.

'Competition'

The protection of competition in the economy is (as its name implies) the central **4.29** objective of the Competition Act 1998. Competition is the state of affairs where a number of suppliers of the same type of product or service vie with each other to supply that product or service to a customer or a group of customers (the customer or group of customers being called the 'relevant market' for that type of product or service). We are familiar with competition in many sectors of the economy. There is, for example, competition in the retail supply of groceries, with Sainsbury, Tesco, Asda, Safeway, etc vying with each other (and, to a lesser extent, with corner shops) to supply groceries to customers. It is possible, however, to have a complete absence of competition, with only a single supplier (a 'monopolist') of a type of product or service to a group of customers, such that those

---

[46] *Consiglio Nazionale degli Spedizionieri Doganali* [1993] OJ L203/27.
[47] Case 96–102 etc/82 *IAZ International Belgium v Commission* [1983] ECR 3369, para 20.
[48] See paras 4.39–4.45 below.

customers have no choice between suppliers. In the United Kingdom, for instance, most customers can obtain their domestic water supplies from only one supplier (the local water company), and have no choice. The local water company enjoys a monopoly in respect of that group of companies (ie a 100 per cent share of that market). Until very recently, in the UK, there was no competition, either, in the supply of electricity or of telephone services. It is even possible for an absence of competition across virtually an entire economy; in Russia under Communist rule, most types of product and service were available from just one supplier, the State.

4.30 The Competition Act seeks to protect competition in the UK economy, and the Chapter I prohibition is intended to do this specifically by prohibiting agreements which prevent, restrict or distort competition.

4.31 But why is this? Why is it worth protecting competition, and prohibiting arrangements which impede competition? **It is worth identifying the standard justifications for competition—in order to be able to identify, and demonstrate in submissions to competition authorities, the ways in which a particular arrangement is beneficial and pro-competitive, or detrimental and anti-competitive.**

4.32 The government, in introducing its draft of the Bill which has become the Competition Act, justified it in these terms:[49]

> Effective and fair competition is essential to ensure *value* and *choice* for customers. In the global marketplace, competition provides a spur to British companies to *innovate and invest. Competitiveness* both at home and *in overseas markets* is enhanced by competition in the domestic market. So competition is good for business as well.[50]

This statement embodies four standard reasons for preferring competition in an economy to the absence or restriction of competition. First, competition allows consumers greater *value*: where businesses compete against each other to supply a product of a specific type to customers, each business knows that if it supplies the product at too high a price, or with poor quality, it will suffer a decline in its sales of that product, because customers will switch to a competing supplier who may sell at a lower price or with better quality. The existence of competition therefore acts as a constraint or deterrent to excessive pricing, and a spur or incentive to better quality. (Without competition, the supplier would have no deterrent to higher pricing, and no incentive to improved quality, because the supplier would know that its customers could not desert it for another supplier.) This combination of incentive and deterrent ensures value.

---

[49] Or of comparable (or interchangeable, or substitutable) products or services.

[50] 'A prohibition approach to anti-competitive agreements and abuse of dominant position: draft Bill', Department of Trade and Industry, Aug 1997, foreword by Margaret Beckett, President of the Board of Trade (page 1). Emphasis added.

Secondly, competition brings *choice*, which is a good thing for consumers *in itself*   **4.33**
(as well as by virtue of its function of incentivising better value for consumers).
Consumers generally enjoy being able to exercise choices in their purchases, rather
than feeling limited in their range of options. This is partly because people enjoy
the sensation of being a sovereign chooser, and partly because minor differences
between products of the same type mean that, the greater the choice there is, the
more individual tastes can be reflected. Consumers prefer, for instance, to buy a
car which is of a colour which accords with their taste, rather than being told: 'you
can have any colour so long as it's black'.

Thirdly, the fear of losing customers to competitors acts as an incentive to indi-   **4.34**
vidual suppliers to *innovate and invest*. As already noted competition and the fear
of losing customers are deterrents to excessive prices and spurs to maintaining
quality. But they have a more positive, active role. Suppliers in a state of competition do not wish merely to avoid losing their existing customers to their competitors, but wish to improve their revenues by gaining new customers from their
competitors. In order to do this, they need constantly to be improving their product, both as to price and to quality. They can do this by innovation and investment
in new methods of production and supply—which, by increasing the efficiency of
the process, may have a downward pressure on price and, by enabling the product
or service to have new or enhanced features, may improve the quality. It is competition leading to innovation which has ensured that, over the years, the real
price of personal computers has steadily fallen, and the quality (in terms of
increased functions, speed of performance, size of memory, etc.) has steadily
improved. Innovation and investment cost money, and companies would have
no incentive to spend that money in the absence of competition: they would have
virtually all the customers they could ever have whether or not they invested, and
therefore no prospect of gaining customers and revenue by incurring the expenditure on innovation and investment.

Fourthly, the government statement refers to 'the global marketplace' and '*com-*   **4.35**
petitiveness . . . in overseas markets'. The result of competition in the UK economy
encouraging British companies to keep a downward pressure on price, to maintain quality and to invest and innovate is that the products and services supplied
by those British companies become more attractive to people all over the world.
Consequently, people in other parts of the world will have more reason to buy the
British companies' products or services, boosting exports by British companies—
which is now fashionably called the 'competitiveness' of British companies worldwide.

In addition to these four reasons implicit in the government's statement, there are   **4.36**
other important reasons to protect and promote competition, and to prefer competition to the absence of competition. One of the most frequently cited is that

competition improves '*allocative efficiency*' in the economy. The idea here is, broadly, that it is a more sensible and more efficient use of the resources in an economy (people's labour, money, land, physical capital, etc.) if those resources are deployed for purposes where they are wanted. The opposite is wasteful: resources being deployed for a purpose, and that purpose not being wanted. There is, for example, plenty of purpose in investing money, labour, etc. in the manufacture of computer video games, because lots of people want to buy computer video games; there is little point in investing money, labour, etc. in the production and supply of hula-hoops, because there is no longer a great deal of demand for hula-hoops. If resources are directed to purposes where there is demand, that is a productive use of the resources in the economy, and it is therefore allocatively efficient (people want the product, the businesses achieve sales and perhaps grow, the businesses can employ people and pay them well, and so on). On the other hand, if resources are directed into areas where there is no demand, that is the very opposite—wastefulness or allocative inefficiency; the businesses doing it cannot achieve sales, and therefore become unprofitable and perhaps insolvent, those investing the money receive low returns on their investment or maybe even make a loss on their investment, the labour that is devoted yields low wages or ends in redundancy and unemployment. It is considered that *allocative efficiency is best achieved through competition*, because it is in a state of competition that companies (and hence investors) receive the best signals as to what products and services people want at any one time. In a state of competition, if a company starts to lose business to its competitors, it thereby learns that people want products and services as supplied by its competitors rather than as supplied by itself, and therefore the company will not waste any further resources continuing to supply products and services in the way which people no longer want. When this process is replicated across the whole economy, resources in the economy are allocated in the most efficient way. By contrast, in the absence of competition, with consumers having little choice but to buy from the one supplier, the supplier has a much poorer idea of what people really want, and resources in the economy are largely wasted.

4.37 So far, this discussion has referred to the crude categories of: (i) the existence of competition and (ii) the absence of competition. In practice, there are varying degrees of competition. Many sectors of the economy, while not being completely monopolistic, are close to it. In the supply of domestic telephone services, for example, in the UK, BT faces some competition, but has traditionally enjoyed a strongly dominant position (as at 1995, it supplied about 90 per cent of residential telephone lines[51]). At the other end of the scale, there may be a high degree of competition but it will usually fall short of 'perfect competition'. A state of perfect

---

[51] OFTEL, 'UK Telecommunications Industry Market Information', Jan 1997, Table 4.

competition arises where suppliers' pricing and other decisions are completely constrained by fear of losing customers to competitors, because there are no significant barriers to the entry of potential new suppliers into the market, and customers make their buying decisions rationally and in complete knowledge of the available options and the best value. In practice, such a situation is wholly unrealistic, and competition authorities are generally concerned only with the protection of '**workable competition**'—ie where there is a reasonably unrestricted choice of suppliers, there are not unduly high artificial entry barriers. This has been the explicit view of the European Commission in applying Article 81 (formerly Article 85) in certain circumstances (such as when permitting 'restructuring agreements' where companies in an industry facing recession agree to co-ordinate reductions in capacity and production, with a view to enabling the industry to 'slim down', become more efficient and, hence, survive[52]); indeed, the criteria for exemption from the Article 81 and Chapter I prohibitions provide that an agreement may be authorised provided that it does not allow the parties 'the possibility of *eliminating* competition in respect of *a substantial part of* the products in question' (emphasis added). By the same token, **the Chapter I prohibition is directed against arrangements which prevent, restrict or distort *workable* competition.**

'Prevention, Restriction or Distortion'

The three terms are three different degrees of impediment to competition, in decreasing order.   **4.38**

- An arrangement which **prevents** competition is one where the impediment is absolute. An example might be an agreement between two competing suppliers of cars, where one accepts an obligation not to sell any cars to customers in Greater London, and the other accepts an obligation not to sell any cars to any customers in the rest of England. Both parties are absolutely prevented from selling cars in each other's territory.

- An agreement **restricts** competition where parties accept obligations to limit the degree to which they compete, without preventing competition altogether—for example, where each one says it will not actively promote its products in the other's territory (eg by advertising, or opening a branch, etc.).

- The **distortion** of competition is the lowest level of impediment, and its inclusion in the wording indicates that the Chapter I prohibition (and Article 81 (formerly Article 85)) extends even to *indirect* impediments to competition. This may be where the parties to an arrangement do not actually accept obligations preventing them or limiting them from competing, but the effect of their arrangement is that competition does not operate as fully in the market as it would otherwise have

---

[52] Whish, R., *Competition Law* (3rd edn, Butterworths, London, 1993), 10–11 and 456–9.

done. An example would be where the effect of arrangements is that some parties are given an artificial and unfair competitive advantage over others.[53]

F. Object or Effect

4.39   In order to be caught by the Chapter I prohibition, the prevention, restriction or distortion of competition needs only to be *either* the object of the arrangement *or* the effect of the arrangement, and not necessarily both. Therefore, an arrangement may be prohibited if the prevention, restriction or distortion of competition is:

- the object or intention of the arrangement—without any need to show that it actually occurred; or
- the unintended effect or consequence of the arrangement—without any need to show that the parties wished to achieve this.

'Object'

4.40   The European Court of Justice has held that:

> there is no need to take account of the concrete effects of an agreement once it appears that it has as its object the prevention, restriction or distortion of competition.[54]

On this basis, various types of agreement have been held to fall within the prohibition *by their very nature*, including horizontal agreements to fix prices or partition markets, and vertical agreements to impose export bans or restrict the purchaser's freedom to deal with the contract goods. Collusive tendering—whereby undertakings agree to collaborate in their response to an invitation to tender (concealing this fact from the tenderer) may be a practical instance of an agreement which is anti-competitive in object even if not in effect.

4.41   However, the practical importance of this can be limited, and in 1992 the Court of First Instance overruled the European Commission's view that written evidence of a horizontal price-fixing and market-sharing agreement was sufficient to constitute an infringement, without any need to investigate the structure of the market.[55]

4.42   In any event, some investigation of effects is necessary in order to assess whether the agreement has an 'appreciable' (rather than '*de minimis*') effect—which, as described in paragraphs 4.46–4.55 below, is one of the criteria for determining whether the prohibition applies.

---

[53]   See, eg, the levy on export traffic in the *French Inland Waterway Charter Traffic: EATE Levy Case* [1985] OJ L219/35; upheld in Case 272/85 *ANTIB v Commission* [1987] ECR 2201.
[54]   Cases 56 and 58/64 *Consten and Grundig v Commission* [1966] ECR 299, 342.
[55]   Cases T–68/89 etc. *Società Italiano Vetro v Commission* [1992] II ECR 1403, para 159.

'Effect'

The fact that an arrangement can be prohibited under the Chapter I prohibi- **4.43**
tion—and under Article 81 (formerly Article 85)—merely because its *effect* is
restrictive of competition—even if its intention is not in any way restrictive—is
one of the most significant conceptual differences between the new UK legislation
and the previous Restrictive Trade Practices Act. Under the new legislation, by
contrast with the RTPA, **it is not sufficient to examine the terms of the agreement to see whether they are in themselves 'restrictions'; one needs to have
regard to the overall economic context of the arrangement, and therefore its
likely effects.**

This means that, by contrast with the RTPA, it is perfectly possible for the same **4.44**
provision in an agreement to be innocuous where that agreement occurs in one set
of economic circumstances, but to be restrictive and prohibited where it occurs in
another economic context. Thus, for example, a ten-year agreement to supply a
specific quantity of a product—with no other restrictive provision (such as exclusivity)—would not be caught under the old RTPA, but *could* be caught under the
Chapter I prohibition. In some circumstances, that ten-year supply agreement
might have the effect of making it more difficult for other parties to compete in
the market (by foreclosing them), whereas in other markets it may have no adverse
effect on competition whatever. The question arises where there is sustained collaboration between competitors, or a supply agreement of significant size and
duration, and the effects need to be assessed having regard to **external circumstances**, rather than just the terms of the agreement—in particular:

• the market shares of the parties in the sectors where they operate (this in turn
  depends on establishing the correct definition, in terms of geography and product, of the relevant market: see Chapter 8, paras 8.09 to 8.51 below);

• the number of actual and potential competitors in the markets concerned;

• the extent to which there are other similar agreements operating across the market (a 'network' of 'parallel' agreements), such that the particular agreement
  under consideration contributes to a cumulative anti-competitive effect.[56]

A further consequence of regard being had to unintended effects is that the **4.45**
Chapter I prohibition may apply even if an anti-competitive agreement has been
formally abandoned by the parties, but its effects endure.[57]

---

[56] See Case T–7/93 *Langnese-Iglo v Commission* [1995] II ECR 1533, para 94. An appeal against
this judgment was dismissed by the European Court of Justice in Case C–279/95P *Langnese-Iglo v
Commission* (judgment of 1 October 1998).
[57] Case 51/75 *EMI Records v CBS* [1976] ECR 811, para 30.

G. Appreciability and '*De Minimis*'

4.46   The Chapter I prohibition only applies where the effects of the agreement or arrangement are 'appreciable'—that is, not where the effects are minimal or '*de minimis*'. There is no explicit provision in the legislation excluding non-appreciable/'*de minimis*' agreements or arrangements, although there is, in section 40, a provision for limited immunity from OFT penalties for so-called 'small agreements' which infringe the prohibition ('small agreements' being determined by reference to the parties' turnover[58]). Nevertheless, it is a long-established principle of EC law under Article 81 (formerly Article 85), as developed by both the European Court of Justice and the European Commission, that *de minimis* agreements fall outside the scope of Article 81; and, by virtue of section 60 of the UK Competition Act, the Chapter I prohibition is to be interpreted in the light of such EC legal principles. The UK government has said:

> . . . the European Court of Justice . . . has interpreted Article 85(1) [now Article 81(1)] as requiring an appreciable effect on competition. The UK domestic prohibition is therefore also to be interpreted as catching only those agreements which have an appreciable effect on competition.[59]

4.47   There are two principal reasons for placing non-appreciable/'*de minimis*' agreements and arrangements outside the scope of the Chapter I prohibition or of Article 81 (formerly Article 85). The first is, simply, the notion that if the effects on competition are only minimal, it is unnecessary and wasteful to apply the full rigours of the law, backed up by a panoply of investigative powers and sanctions, to the arrangement in question. This is simply a question of the law having a sense of proportion. In addition, there is a specific policy reason: namely, that small and medium-sized enterprises should be encouraged to develop—in the interests of social diversity and inclusiveness, economic growth and, indeed, competition—and therefore that they should be protected from excessive regulatory burdens. Thus, the European Commission's 1986 Notice on agreements of minor importance, defining the *de minimis* agreements in respect of which the Commission would not apply Article 81, specifically stated that its aim was 'to facilitate co-operation between small and medium-sized undertakings'.[60] Similarly, the UK government, when it introduced a first draft of the Competition Act in 1997,

---

[58]   See below, Ch 10, paras 10.61–10.63. Note that a 'small agreement', as defined in s 38, is one which infringes the Chap I prohibition but its parties are protected from some of the consequences of that infringement (ie from OFT penalties in certain circumstances). By contrast, an agreement or arrangement which is non-appreciable/'*de minimis*' does not infringe the Chapter I prohibition at all.

[59]   'A prohibition approach to anti-competitive agreements and abuse of dominant position: draft Bill', Department of Trade and Industry, Aug 1997, para 2.5.

[60]   [1986] OJ C231/2. The 1986 Notice has been superseded by the 1997 Notice, which does not repeat this statement.

stated its intention 'to ensure that SMEs are not unduly burdened by the operation of the prohibition'.[61]

What is '*De Minimis*'?—EC Case Law

When is an agreement or arrangement non-appreciable and, therefore, '*de minimis*'—such that it is altogether outside the scope of the Chapter I prohibition? On the basis of section 60 of the Competition Act, regard should be had to principles established by the European Court and the European Commission. Guidance from individual cases decided by the European Commission or the European Court has been relatively vague. Appreciability will depend on a combination of factors, including the size of the undertakings concerned (SMEs are more likely to enjoy protection), their market shares in the markets affected by the agreement or arrangement, and the size of those affected markets. Agreements involving the world's largest toy manufacturer were held to be appreciable, rather than '*de minimis*', in spite of the fact that the market shares on the affected markets were less than 10 per cent, because of the size of that toy manufacturer.[62] By contrast, even where there were high market shares, the fact that the market segment was so narrow, was sufficient to allow the agreements concerned to be regarded as '*de minimis*'.[63] **4.48**

What is '*De Minimis*'?—the OFT's Practice

The OFT takes the view that an agreement will not normally be *de minimis* if the combined market share of the parties (including the corporate groups to which they belong) is no more than 25 per cent—except for where there is price-fixing, market-sharing, resale price maintenance or a 'network' of similar agreements on the market. This view is expressed in the OFT's guidelines on the Chapter I prohibition.[64] The OFT's guidelines also express the view that any agreement which does not have an appreciable effect on competition should not normally be notified to the OFT.[65] **4.49**

The OFT's basic criterion is that: **4.50**

> an agreement will have no appreciable effect on competition if the parties' combined share of the relevant market does not exceed 25 per cent, although there will be circumstances in which this is not the case.[66]

---

[61] 'A prohibition approach to anti-competitive agreements and abuse of dominant position: draft Bill', Department of Trade and Industry, Aug 1997, para 6.9. This was, however, offered as a reason for the immunity from penalties for 'small agreements', rather than in the context of '*de minimis*'.

[62] *Duffy Group v Quaker Oats (Fisher Price)* [1988] OJ L49/19.

[63] *Charles Jourdan* [1989] OJ L35/31.

[64] OFT n 26 above, paras 2.18–2.22.

[65] Ibid, para 2.18.

[66] Ibid, para 2.19.

In assessing the market share of a party, the OFT will take into account the activities of, broadly speaking, the corporate group to which the party belongs—that is, the party itself, undertakings which the party controls, undertakings which control the party and any other undertakings which are controlled by those parties.[67]

4.51 The exceptions fall into two categories. First, there are those agreements which the OFT does not regard as *de minimis* at all. Those are:

- price-fixing agreements;
- market-sharing agreements;
- resale price maintenance; and
- agreements where there is a 'network' of similar agreements which have a cumulative effect on the market in question.

The OFT takes the view that any of these agreements is 'capable of having appreciable effect' even below the 25 per cent threshold.[68]

4.52 Secondly, the OFT may find that an agreement is *de minimis* even about the 25 per cent threshold—having regard, for example, to low barriers to entry or to the countervailing purchasing power of buyers on the market.[69]

4.53 However, a practical difficulty arises from the fact that the European Commission's most recent guidance on the concept of appreciability/*de minimis* in the context of Article 81 (formerly Article 85)—which was published in 1997[70]—places the threshold at just 5 per cent for horizontal agreements and 10 per cent for vertical agreements—ie much lower than the threshold under the OFT guidance. Consequently, for an agreement where the parties' combined market share is below 25 per cent but above the European Commission's thresholds, and where the agreement may affect trade between EU Member States, it is possible that the European Commission will regard it as falling within the Article 81 prohibition, even if the OFT regards it as falling outside the Chapter I prohibition. It may be necessary to notify such agreements to the European Commission.[71]

4.54 But difficulties may also arise even where there is no effect on trade between EU Member States—ie where only the UK Chapter I prohibition is relevant, and

---

[67] OFT n 26, para 2.22.
[68] Ibid, para 2.20.
[69] Ibid, para 2.21.
[70] Commission Notice on agreements of minor importance [1997] OJ C372/13.
[71] However, para 19 of the Notice provides that, even if the parties are *above* the market share thresholds, the agreement will still generally be regarded as '*de minimis*' if the parties are all small and medium-sized enterprises as defined in Commission Recommendation 96/280 ([1996] OJ L107/4): that is, each has fewer than 250 employees and either an annual turnover not exceeding 40 million euros or a balance-sheet total not exceeding 27 million euros.

there is no concern about Article 81 (formerly Article 85) EC. As a matter of law, there must be doubt whether the OFT's 25 per cent threshold is legal, having regard to the OFT's obligations under section 60 of the Act to ensure no inconsistency with EC law principles as laid down by the European Court and to have regard to European Commission statements. This can have quite significant practical implications—for example, in the case of a restrictive agreement where the parties have combined market shares of 20 per cent. In spite of the OFT's view that such an agreement would be *de minimis*, it may be open to parties **who wish to challenge the agreement's validity** under the Chapter I prohibition to take the following steps:

- A party to the agreement, faced with legal proceedings by another party to enforce a particular provision, could raise the defence that the provision is void for infringement of the Chapter I prohibition—the court, applying the prohibition in accordance with section 60, need not be bound by the OFT's view that the 20 per cent market share renders the agreement *de minimis* (and thereby outside the prohibition).

- A third party 'victim' of the restrictive agreement may take legal proceedings for damages and/or an injunction—again, the court may well not consider that the agreement is *de minimis*.

- A third party 'victim' might also lodge a complaint with the OFT. Presumably, the OFT would reject the complaint on the grounds that the agreement was *de minimis*, but the complainant could then appeal to the Competition Commission, and ultimately to the Court of Appeal. Again, the Competition Commission and the Court of Appeal might well consider that section 60 entails that an agreement with this level of market shares is not *de minimis*.

4.55 Finally, from the point of view of the parties to the agreement **who wish to be protected from the Chapter I prohibition**, it is not clear that the OFT is right to advise that agreements which meet its definition of *de minimis* 'should not be notified' to the OFT.[72] The risks (outlined above) that the agreement could still be challenged in the courts or at the Competition Commission may make it prudent for a party ot notify for exemption as the only way of protection against such a challenge. Moreover, for the parties, the assessment of market shares (necessary in order to determine whether their agreement is *de minimis*) is by no means straightforward. There is, first, the difficulty (and considerable work involved) in knowing what the parties' market shares actually are, which requires a knowledge of the overall size of the market as well as of the parties' own sales figures. Secondly, the question of what constitutes the relevant market is often controversial, in terms of both product and geographical market definitions, and it may be that the 25 per

---

[72] OFT, n 26 above, para 2.18.

cent threshold is exceeded on some market definitions but not on others. Faced with this situation, parties may wish to argue that their agreement is *de minimis*, but in order to be comfortable that it is *de minimis* and that the OFT will not take action against them, it will often be prudent to put their arguments to the OFT (by way of a notification and/or informal discussions). While it is of course true that the problem of market definition arises at whatever level the *de minimis* threshold is set, in reality it is going to arise for a much larger number of agreements when the threshold is set at 25 per cent than when it is set at 5 per cent, since a much larger number of agreements are likely to be *potentially capable* of coming below the higher threshold. For all these reasons, it is by no means clear that the OFT's decision to set the *de minimis* threshold at 25 per cent will have the deregulatory effect which is presumably intended.

H. UK Territorial Link

4.56 Because the Chapter I prohibition is a provision of *national* competition law, it is obviously necessary to limit its application to those agreements and arrangements which have some form of territorial link with the United Kingdom. As a matter of international comity, countries seek to avoid the exercise of extra-territorial jurisdiction, which can be characterised as interference in the internal affairs of other countries.

The old Restrictive Trade Practices Act limited jurisdiction by requiring that at least two parties to the restrictive agreement must be persons 'carrying on business . . . in the United Kingdom'. The Chapter I prohibition, by contrast, has three territorial criteria (reflecting the wording and principles of Article 81 (formerly Article 85)), all of which must be satisfied in order for the Chapter I prohibition to apply:

(i) the object or effect must be the prevention, restriction or distortion of '**competition within the United Kingdom**' or a part of the United Kingdom; and

(ii) the agreement '**may affect trade within the United Kingdom**' or a part of the United Kingdom; and

(iii) the agreement or arrangement '**is, or is intended to be, implemented in the United Kingdom**' or a part of the United Kingdom.

4.57 In spite of these territorial requirements, the Chapter I prohibition may still apply even if the agreement relates to:

• goods exported out of the United Kingdom—see paragraphs 4.58–4.59 below; or

• agreements between parties located outside the United Kingdom—see paragraphs 4.62–4.64 below.

The 'United Kingdom' includes Great Britain (and its subsidiary islands) and Northern Ireland, but excludes the Channel Islands and the Isle of Man.[73]

Competition within the United Kingdom

Under section 2(1)(b), the Chapter I prohibition will only apply if the object or effect of the arrangement is the prevention, restriction or distortion of 'competition within the United Kingdom'. **4.58**

EC case law on the interpretation of Article 81 (formerly Article 85) (where the equivalent provision is 'competition within the common market') makes clear that competition within a territory may be prevented, restricted or distorted even if the arrangements relate to exports going out of that territory. This may be the case where, for example: **4.59**

- there is an economically realistic prospect that the goods will be reimported into the territory, so that the impact of the restriction is felt by consumers within the territory; or
- the arrangement regarding exports operates to the competitive advantage of certain domestic manufacturers or suppliers over others—for example, by making it harder for certain domestic producers to participate in exports, indirectly affecting their commercial position and hence their ability to compete on the domestic market. An example of this has been seen in relation to maritime transport agreements under Article 81 (formerly Article 85) where, in relation to shipping routes going to destinations outside the territory, certain ship owners based within the territory have been given privileged access over others or have agreed, through liner conference arrangements, to limit competition between themselves on those extra-territorial routes.[74]

Affecting Trade within the United Kingdom

Under section 2(1)(a), the Chapter I prohibition only applies to agreements and arrangements if they 'may affect trade within the United Kingdom'. To some extent this requirement is superfluous—if an agreement prevents, restricts or distorts competition within the United Kingdom, by definition it must affect trade within the United Kingdom[75]—and it results largely from the desire of those drafting the UK legislation to mirror the wording of Article 81 (formerly Article 85) as closely as possible. In Article 81, there is an equivalent provision to the effect that the Article 81 prohibition only applies if the agreement or arrangement **4.60**

---

[73] OFT, n 26 above, para 2.15.

[74] See *French–West African Shipowners' Committees* [1992] OJ L134; Case T–24/93 *Compagnie Maritime Belge Transports v Commission* [1996] II ECR 1201, paras 195–198 and 202.

[75] The OFT says that 'in practice it is very unlikely that an agreement which affects competition in the UK does not also affect trade in the UK'. OFT, n 26 above, para 2.16.

'may affect trade between Member States' of the European Union. In the context of Article 81, the requirement is not superfluous at all: the crucial word is 'between', and the point is that the EC law prohibition only applies if the agreement has some kind of effect on trade *between different* countries in the EU, rather than its effects being confined *purely* within a Member State. That is to say: the provision is designed to limit EC jurisdiction to agreements with *international* effects, while those with *purely national* effects are left to national competition law.[76] Thus, a cartel which has effects confined purely to one Member State will be restrictive of 'competition within the common market', but perhaps may not 'affect trade between Member States'. By contrast, in the context of the Chapter I prohibition, similar considerations do not apply: if an agreement is restrictive of 'competition within the United Kingdom', then by definition it may affect 'trade within the United Kingdom'.

4.61 Nevertheless, it is worth noting a number of points about this requirement:

(i) Section 2(1)(a) requires that there be a potential *effect* on trade within the United Kingdom—whereas section 2(1)(b) requires only that the restriction on competition within the United Kingdom should be the *object or effect*. It is perhaps here that one might argue that section 2(1)(a) is not entirely superfluous: it is conceivable that there might be an agreement which has as its object, but not its effect, a restriction of competition in the UK—and such an agreement will only be caught by the Chapter I prohibition if one can demonstrate that there is at least a potential effect on trade within the United Kingdom (see above, paragraphs 4.39–4.45).

(ii) The term 'trade' should not be construed too narrowly. It has been held, in the context of Article 81 (formerly Article 85), that the term 'trade' does not preclude the application of the competition rules to the liberal professions[77] or to sporting activities.[78]

(iii) The effect on trade within the United Kingdom may be *indirect*. The definition could extend, for example, to (a) an agreement concerning transport services to or from the UK, because it 'might affect the amount of trade which passed through a particular part, or it might affect trade in transport services sold within the UK', and (b) an agreement relating to exports out of

---

[76] Emphasis should be laid on the word 'purely' in this context. Art 81 (formerly Art 85) applies if the effect on trade between Member States is indirect as well as direct, and if it is potential as well as actual. An agreement may affect trade between Member States, and thus come within Art 81, even if all the parties are in just one Member State.

[77] European Commission, *XXVth Report on Competition Policy*, EC Commission, Brussels (1995), point 88.

[78] Case C–415/93 *Union Royale Belge des Sociétés de Football Association v Bosman* [1995] I ECR 4921; Opinion of Lenz AG, para 261.

the UK (such as an export cartel), 'because of the possibility of parallel imports into the UK'.[79]

Implemented in the United Kingdom

Section 2(3) provides that the Chapter I prohibition applies only if the agreement **4.62** or arrangement 'is, or is intended to be, implemented in the United Kingdom' or a part of it. The point here is that where the agreement is implemented entirely outside the United Kingdom, the Chapter I prohibition will not apply. However, the Chapter I prohibition may apply if the parties are all outside the United Kingdom, but their agreement is implemented within it.

The use of the term 'implemented' reflects the judgment of the European Court **4.63** of Justice in the *Woodpulp* case,[80] which considered the question whether agreements by parties situated outside the territory of the common market (the EU) could be subject to the Article 81 (formerly Article 85) prohibition, with the European Commission thereby exercising jurisdiction outside the territory of the EU, on the basis that those agreements had effects on competition within the common market (the EU). The European Court of Justice held that jurisdiction could be exercised if the agreement between the undertakings outside the territory was being 'implemented' within the territory, and that this was indeed the case where manufacturers outside the territory were fixing prices and exchanging confidential commercial information in respect of supplies into the territory.

It follows that the requirement in section 2(3) is likely to be met even if the under- **4.64** takings are located outside the United Kingdom, in so far as their restrictive agreement relates to supplies which they are making into the United Kingdom.

'Part' of the United Kingdom

Section 2(7) states that, in the context of the Chapter I prohibition: **4.65**

'the United Kingdom' means, in relation to an agreement which operates or is intended to operate only in a part of the United Kingdom, that part.

This means that the Chapter I prohibition can apply even if the effect on trade, or the restriction of competition, or the implementation, is confined to just a part of the United Kingdom. It is significant that the Competition Act does not require this to be a 'substantial part' of the United Kingdom (in this respect, it differs from the wording of the merger provisions of the Fair Trading Act 1973, but is similar to the wording of that Act's monopoly provisions: see Chapter 17 below). The

---

[79] The OFT took this view in its draft guidelines, OFT 236, draft 30 July 1998. This was an earlier draft of the guidelines on the Chapter I prohibition. The point was removed from subsequent versions.

[80] Cases 114, 125–129/85 *Ahlström v Commission (Woodpulp)* [1988] ECR 5193.

Chapter I prohibition may therefore apply even if the agreement relates only to a very small or insignificant part of the United Kingdom (subject to the requirement that the effects of the agreement should be appreciable and not '*de minimis*': see paragraphs 4.46–4.52 above).

5

EXCLUSIONS AND SPECIAL TREATMENT

A. The Concepts of 'Exclusions' and 'Special Treatment'

5.01 The Competition Act 1998 makes a radical departure from EC competition law by introducing two new concepts—(i) 'exclusions', and (ii) 'special treatment'— giving protection to agreements which would otherwise fall fully within the Chapter I prohibition.[1] There are no equivalent concepts in Article 81 (formerly Article 85) of the EC Treaty.[2]

5.02 It is important to distinguish these concepts from 'exemptions' (for which there is an equivalent concept under Article 81 (formerly Article 85) EC).[3] The distinction may be summarised as follows:

- An *excluded* agreement is one which is deemed not to come within the Chapter I prohibition at all.

- An agreement granted *special treatment* is one which benefits from an order made under section 50 of the Act protecting it from the Chapter I prohibition, whether by exclusion or exemption or otherwise.

- An agreement granted *exemption* is one which falls within the Chapter I prohibition, but which has offsetting economic benefits that justify disapplication of the prohibition.

5.03 This chapter examines the main types of agreement which can benefit from exclusion or special treatment. Agreements benefiting from exemption are considered in Chapter 6 below.

Excluded Agreements under Section 3

5.04 Under section 3 of the Competition Act, read with Schedules 1 to 4, the main types of agreement which are excluded from the Chapter I prohibition are:

- Mergers and concentrations (including concentrative joint ventures)— *Schedule 1 and section 3(2)*;

- Services of general economic interest, of the type covered by Article 86(2) (formerly Article 90(2)) of the EC Treaty[4]—*Schedule 3 paragraph 4*;

- Agreements which received 'section 21(2) clearance' under the old Restrictive Trade Practices Act—*Schedule 3 paragraph 2*;

- Compliance with planning obligations and other legal requirements— *Schedule 3 paragraphs 1 and 5*;

---

[1] There are also exclusions from the Chapter II prohibition, and special treatment may apply to agreements under the Chapter II prohibition. Note, however, that there can be no exemptions from the Chapter II prohibition. See Ch 8 below.

[2] As a result of the Treaty of Amsterdam, which amended the EC Treaty with effect from 1 May 1999, Article 85 is now renumbered Article 81.

[3] Exemptions are considered in Ch 6 below.

[4] As a result of the Treaty of Amsterdam, Art 90(2) is renumbered Art 86(2).

- Agreements relating to coal and steel which would be covered by the ECSC Treaty[5]—*Schedule 3 paragraph 8*;

- Rules of non-UK financial markets which are 'EEA regulated markets'—*Schedule 3 paragraph 3*;

- Certain agricultural products agreements—*Schedule 3 paragraph 9*;

- Agreements which are subject to similar competition scrutiny under other UK legislation—*Schedule 2*;

- Other general exclusions to be created by the Secretary of State:

  - 'Innocuous' agreements—*section 3(3) and (4)*;

  - Exclusions required by public policy—*Schedule 3 paragraph 7*;

  - Agreements fulfilling the UK's international obligations—*Schedule 3 paragraph 6*;

  - Rules of professional bodies—*Schedule 4*.

Each of these categories of excluded agreement is considered, in turn, in **Sections B to J** below.

Many of the exclusions apply 'to the extent to which' an agreement satisfies the relevant criteria. The effect of this is that not all the provisions in an agreement may fall within the relevant exclusion. Section 59(2) makes clear how the Chapter I prohibition should be applied to agreements which are only partly excluded. This provision concerns agreements which contain, in addition to the provisions benefiting from exclusion, other provisions which may infringe the Chapter I prohibition 'for other reasons'. It stipulates that, in assessing whether such an agreement infringes the Chapter I prohibition, there is no requirement to disregard the provisions to which the exclusion relates. *All* the provisions of the agreement—including the provisions to which the exclusion relates—need to be taken into account. **5.05**

In addition, it should be noted that a number of the exclusions are subject to 'clawback' provisions, whereby the OFT has the power to withdraw the exclusion—ie to direct in writing that an agreement which normally would benefit from an exclusion should, instead, be subject to the Chapter I prohibition. Although the precise terms of the 'clawback' provisions vary according to the particular exclusion, in broad terms the OFT may withdraw an exclusion either if it considers that an agreement would infringe the prohibition and would not merit unconditional exemption or if the parties have unreasonably refused to comply with an OFT request for information. **5.06**

---

[5] European Coal and Steel Community (ECSC) Treaty of 1951, also called the Treaty of Paris.

Special Treatment under Section 50

5.07 Section 50 of the Act provides that vertical agreements and land agreements which would otherwise fall within the Chapter I prohibition may benefit from 'special treatment' by which they would be protected from the prohibition. The government is proposing to issue orders under section 50, one in respect of vertical agreements and the other in respect of land agreements; these are due to come into force before March 2000.

5.08 Section 50 does not itself grant special treatment—but merely empowers the Secretary of State to do so by way of a subsequent order. Such an order could take a variety of forms, and section 50 provides that special treatment could be granted by way of exclusions or exemptions 'or otherwise'.

5.09 The types of agreement to which a special treatment order may apply are:

• Vertical agreements;

• Land agreements.

These two categories are considered individually in paragraphs 5.69–5.80 below. Section 50 provides that a special treatment order may apply to such agreements in general, or any prescribed description of such agreements. The definition of 'vertical agreements' and 'land agreements' is to be prescribed in the order.

5.10 An order made under section 50 may also empower the OFT to 'claw back' (ie withdraw) the benefit of the special treatment, by providing that in prescribed circumstances the special treatment is not to apply (or is to apply in a particular way) in relation to an individual agreement. This is likely to be where the OFT either considers that an agreement would infringe the prohibition and would not be likely to merit individual exemption, or where a party has failed without reasonable excuse to respond to an OFT request for information within 7 working days. Before exercising its 'clawback' powers, the OFT must first consult the parties to the agreement.[6] Once the OFT has done so, it must publish the 'claw back' direction in the OFT's register of decisions.

5.11 The government has published drafts of orders to be issued by the Secretary of State under section 50. These will each grant exclusion from the Chapter I prohibition—one in respect of vertical agreements (but not resale price maintenance or intellectual property licences), and the other in respect of certain land agreements. Each of these orders will include powers for the OFT to 'claw back' the exclusion. They are due to come into force before the Chapter I prohibition takes effect in March 2000. See sections K and L below for further details.

---

[6] Office of Fair Trading, Formal Consultation Draft, 'Competition Act 1998: The Draft Procedural Rules proposed by the Director General of Fair Trading', (OFT 411), R 22(4). 'Consulting' a person involves the sending of a written notice to that person, stating the action proposed and the reasons for it and inviting written representations from that person within a specified period (R 27).

B. Mergers and Concentrations—Schedule 1 and Section 3(2)

Outside the new Competition Act, there are provisions in both UK and EC law **5.12** for examining the anti-competitive effects of mergers and concentrations (including full takeovers, private acquisitions of shares or of businesses and certain joint ventures). These provisions are to be found both in the EC Merger Regulation[7] and in the merger provisions of the Fair Trading Act 1973 (FTA).

Because of this, it was felt that such mergers and concentrations should not also **5.13** have to be examined under the Chapter I prohibition. Indeed, such a requirement would create a superfluous regulatory burden on businesses, and the possibility of 'double jeopardy'.

Schedule 1 of the Act therefore excludes from the Chapter I prohibition most **5.14** kinds of merger and concentration.

Concentrations Covered by the EC Merger Regulation

There is an exclusion for agreements which are subject to the exclusive jurisdiction **5.15** of the European Commission under the EC Merger Regulation.

The Act states[8] that the Chapter I prohibition does not apply to any agreement, if **5.16** that agreement (either on its own or together with another agreement) gives rise to:

(i)   a '**concentration**'

(ii) with a '**Community dimension**';

(iii) where the European Commission would have **exclusive jurisdiction** over it under the EC Merger Regulation.

A concentration with a Community dimension is defined by reference to Articles **5.17** 1 and 3 of the EC Merger Regulation. First, a '**concentration**' includes any acquisition of sole control or joint control over another business. It therefore includes—in terms of sole control—full takeovers, acquisitions of businesses, acquisitions of a majority interest in a company and, in certain cases, acquisitions of a minority interest in a company where the acquiring shareholder is highly likely in practice to achieve a majority in shareholders' meetings (for example, because the remaining shares are widely dispersed).[9]

In addition, the term 'concentration' includes acquisitions of joint control **5.18** resulting from the formation of joint ventures; however, not every joint venture

---

[7]   Council Reg (EEC) 4064/89 of 21 Dec 1989, as amended by Council Reg (EC) 1310/97 of 30 June 1997.

[8]   Sch 1 para 6(1) and (3).

[9]   See the European Commission's Notice on the concept of a concentration [1998] OJ C66/5, especially para 14.

conferring joint control is a concentration. The formation of a joint venture (JV) will only be a concentration (a 'concentrative JV') if the parent companies must reach agreement on major decisions concerning the JV, while the JV is one which will have all the functions of an autonomous economic entity.[10]

5.19 Secondly, in order to benefit from the exclusion, the concentration must have a '**Community dimension**'. (It is generally only concentrations with a Community dimension which are examined under the EC Merger Regulation.[11]) A concentration is defined as having a Community dimension where the parties to the concentration (the 'undertakings concerned') meet the turnover criteria laid down in Article 1(2) and (3) of the EC Merger Regulation.[12]

5.20 There is also a third criterion which must be satisfied before this exclusion can apply. The Act specifies not only that there must be a concentration with a Community dimension, but also that it must be one where, under the EC Merger Regulation, the European Commission has '**exclusive jurisdiction** in the matter'. The general rule is that the European Commission has exclusive jurisdiction over any concentration with a Community dimension.[13] However, there are excep-

---

[10] For more details on this see the Commission Notice on the concept of a concentration [1998] OJ C66/5, paras 18 to 38; and the Commission Notice on the concept of full-function joint ventures [1998] OJ C66/1.

[11] However, there is an exception in Art 22(3) of the EC Merger Regulation under which Member States may request that the Commission examines concentrations even if they do not have a Community dimension (if the concentration would significantly impede competition within the requesting Member States and affects trade between Member States). In practice this exception is rarely invoked.

[12] The turnover criteria laid down in Art 1(2) and (3) are as follows. A concentration has a Community dimension if: (i) the combined worldwide turnover of all the undertakings concerned exceeds 5,000 million euros; (ii) the individual EU-wide turnover of at least two of the undertakings concerned exceeds 250 million euros; and (iii) it is not the case that more than two-thirds of the EU-wide turnover of each undertaking concerned is achieved in the same single Member State. Even if the foregoing criteria are not met, the concentration will have a Community dimension if: (i) the combined worldwide turnover of the undertakings concerned exceeds 2,500 million euros; (ii) the individual EU-wide turnover of at least two of the undertakings concerned exceeds 100 million euros; (iii) in each of at least three Member States, the combined turnover of all the undertakings concerned exceeds 100 million euros; (iv) in each of those same three Member States, the individual turnover of at least two undertakings concerned exceeds 25 million Euros; and (v) it is not the case that more than two-thirds of the EU-wide turnover of each undertaking concerned is achieved in the same single Member State.

There are special rules for identifying the 'undertakings concerned' in a concentration: where the concentration is a straightforward acquisition, the undertakings concerned are, on the one hand, the corporate group which is making the acquisition and, on the other, the business being acquired and its subsidiaries (but not the vendor company or any subsidiaries which are being retained by the vendor company); in other transactions, such as joint ventures, the rules are more complex. Art 5 of the EC Merger Regulation provides rules for calculating the turnover of each undertaking concerned. These are elaborated in the Commission Notice on calculation of turnover [1998] OJ C66/25. In broad terms, the turnover of an undertaking concerned is calculated as the total turnover of the corporate group to which it belongs. There are special provisions for calculating the turnover of banks, insurance undertakings and other financial institutions.

[13] Art 21(1) and (2) of the EC Merger Reg.

tions, and it is likely that the exclusion will not apply if any of these exceptions is invoked. The most relevant exception here is the provision that Member States may, in parallel with European Commission jurisdiction under the EC Merger Regulation, take appropriate measures in respect of the transaction to protect 'legitimate interests' other than competition. These 'legitimate interests' are defined as: 'public security' (ie defence and related concerns); 'plurality of the media' (eg rules to ensure that media ownership does not become too concentrated); 'prudential rules' (ie financial services supervision); and any other public interest concerns which may be recognised by the European Commission at the request of a Member State (the regulation of utility companies in the UK is likely to be regarded as such a legitimate interest).[14] It seems clear that, where there is a concentration with a Community dimension, if there are 'legitimate interests' to protect, the exclusion will not apply, and the Chapter I prohibition may be invoked, at least for the protection of those legitimate interests. (The other exception to the Commission's exclusive jurisdiction over concentrations with a Community dimension is where the Commission, at the request of a Member State, 'refers back' a concentration to that Member State's national authorities on the grounds of its effect on competition on a distinct market within that Member State. In practice, however, while such concentrations may not be excluded by virtue of being concentrations with a Community dimension, they are likely to be excluded by virtue of being merger situations under the FTA—see paragraphs 5.21–5.27 below.)

Merger Situations under the FTA

Schedule 1 also grants an exclusion for '**merger situations**', as defined in the merger provisions of the Fair Trading Act 1973 (FTA). Any merger situation may benefit from this exclusion—not just those which meet the thresholds for being 'qualifying' mergers. However, the OFT has 'clawback' powers to withdraw the exclusion in certain circumstances.   **5.21**

The concept of 'merger situation' in the FTA is broadly defined. It encompasses all full takeovers, full acquisitions of businesses[15] and all acquisitions of majority voting interests in a company—all of which are deemed acquisitions of a **controlling interest**. But it also extends to the acquisition of lower levels of control—including the acquisition of an ability to exercise **material influence** (which, where other shareholdings are widely dispersed, may be a voting interest as low as 15 per cent) or of the **ability to exercise control** (an interest which is higher than material influence, but short of a majority shareholding—such as where, because of a wide dispersal of shareholdings, the acquiring shareholder in practice can secure the   **5.22**

---

[14] Art 21(3) of the EC Merger Reg.
[15] Provided that the business is an 'enterprise', rather than just bare assets without any goodwill at all.

passing of ordinary resolutions at shareholders' meetings of the target company).
The formation of a joint venture may also be a merger situation, if its effect is that
one or more parents acquire at least material influence over a pre-existing business
or enterprise.

5.23   Schedule 1 paragraph 1 to the Competition Act makes clear that an agreement
will be excluded from the Chapter I prohibition if (either on its own or together
with another agreement) it results in *any* of these kinds of merger situations, or if
carried out would do so. Indeed, it goes further: whereas the FTA says only that
the acquisition of the ability to exercise material influence or the ability to exercise
control *may* be regarded as a merger situation, and that a move from the ability to
exercise material influence or the ability to exercise control to a full controlling
interest *may* be treated as a merger situation, the new Competition Act makes
clear that the exclusion definitely *does* apply in any of these cases.

5.24   The FTA allows the UK competition authorities to examine only 'qualifying'
mergers—defined as being those merger situations where either the gross value
of the assets taken over exceeds £70 million, or, in respect of any product or service which the merging businesses both supply (or which they both consume) in
the UK, their combined share of such supply (or consumption) is at least 25 per
cent. However, **the exclusion from the Chapter I prohibition, in Schedule 1,
paragraph 1, applies whether or not the merger situation is a 'qualifying
merger'.**

5.25   The OFT has 'clawback' powers to **withdraw the exclusion from certain merger
situations.** The merger situations at risk are, broadly speaking, those which are
not full acquisitions or takeovers (ie merger situations which are acquisitions of
material influence or of ability to exercise control, such as joint ventures) and
which have not been either cleared by the Secretary of State or referred to the
Competition Commission and found to be qualifying mergers.

5.26   The rules on withdrawing the exclusion are set out in paragraphs 4 and 5 of
Schedule 1.[16] These provide that the OFT may withdraw the exclusion from the
Chapter I prohibition by way of a written direction stating that the exclusion will
be withdrawn after a certain date (which must not be earlier than the date of the
direction itself). The OFT may only do so if:

- *either* the following criteria are all met:

  (i)   the OFT considers that the agreement will infringe the Chapter I prohibi-
        tion; and

  (ii) the OFT considers that it is not likely to grant an unconditional UK indi-
        vidual exemption in respect of the agreement;[17] and

---

[16]   Also in OFT, n 6 above, R 22.
[17]   See Ch 6 of this book, paras 6.38–6.58 on UK individual exemptions.

(iii) the agreement is not a 'protected agreement' (see below);

- *or* the OFT, considering whether to withdraw the exclusion, has sent a written notice to a party to the merger agreement requesting information, and the party has failed (without reasonable exercise) to comply with the request within seven working days.

Before withdrawing the exclusion, the OFT must first consult the parties to the agreement (by sending them a written notice). Once the OFT has done so, it must publish the withdrawal direction in the OFT's register of decisions.

'Protected agreements' are those in respect of which the exclusion may not be **5.27** withdrawn. They are agreements relating to merger situations where:

- the Secretary of State has made a decision to clear the merger situation, rather than refer it to the Competition Commission;

- the Secretary of State has referred the merger to the Competition Commission, and the Competition Commission has decided that it is a qualifying merger;

- the merger situation exists by virtue of a full controlling interest, rather than an acquisition of material influence or ability to exercise control (for example, where the merger situation is a full acquisition or takeover but not the formation of a joint venture or the acquisition of a minority interest);

- the merger situation is a water merger which has been referred to the Competition Commission under the special provisions for water mergers in the Water Industry Act 1991.

Restrictions 'Ancillary' to Mergers and Concentrations

Many agreements which result in mergers and concentrations include '**ancillary**' **5.28** restrictions. These are restrictions which are directly related and necessary to the implementation of the concentration or merger. Such ancillary restrictions include, for example, restrictive covenants in a sale of business agreement under which the vendor agrees not to compete against the business sold.

The exclusions from the Chapter I prohibition discussed in paragraphs 5.15–5.27 **5.29** above—ie for agreements resulting in concentrations and mergers—also extend to ancillary restrictions.

- The exclusion in Schedule 1, paragraph 6, for concentrations under the EC Merger Regulation, does not specifically refer to ancillary restrictions. It only speaks of agreements which would give rise to a 'concentration'. However, the EC Merger Regulation is stated to apply also to 'restrictions directly related and necessary to the implementation of the concentration'.[18] The exclusion in Schedule 1 para 6 may therefore be read as extending to such restrictions.

---

[18] Recital 25 to the EC Merger Reg.

- The exclusion in Schedule 1, paragraph 1, for merger situations within the meaning of the FTA, is expressly stated to extend to any provision 'directly related and necessary to the implementation of the merger provisions'.[19] This express statement is necessary because (by contrast with the concept of a concentration under the EC Merger Regulation) it is *not* implicit in the FTA's definition of a merger situation.

5.30 The European Commission has issued a useful Notice regarding restrictions ancillary to concentrations, to assist interpretation of the concept of 'restrictions which are directly related and necessary to the implementation' of a concentration. Since exactly the same form of words is used for the exclusion for FTA merger situations, in Schedule 1, paragraph 1, the European Commission Notice may be regarded as a valuable guide to interpretation of the concept in the FTA merger context as well. Indeed, the OFT has indicated that its approach will follow that set out in the European Commission Notice; nevertheless, if a party to a merger which is being notified to the OFT under the UK merger control rules has doubts on whether or not a restriction is ancillary, it should alert the OFT to this when making the merger notification.[20] In broad terms, restrictions will be regarded as 'directly related and necessary to the implementation' of a concentration or merger situation to the extent that they can be justified as necessary to give the purchaser of the business the full value of what that purchaser has acquired— ie a business operating as a going concern—but no more. Thus, for example:

- In the case of restrictive covenants by which a vendor agrees not to compete against a business sold, they may be of such geographical scope and duration as is necessary to give full effect to the value of the business transferred; the Commission Notice points out, as a rough rule of thumb, that 'a period of five years has been recognised as appropriate when the transfer of the undertaking includes the goodwill and know-how and a period of two years when it includes only the goodwill'.

- The exclusion will extend to technology and intellectual property licences which the vendor of the business grants to the acquirer on an exclusive or restrictive basis, in so far as this is necessary to enable the acquirer to have the full use of the assets transferred.

- The exclusion may also cover supply agreements between the vendor and the acquirer of the business to replace internal arrangements within the vendor's previously integrated business; these may be for such transitional period as is necessary to replace the relationship of dependency with autonomy on the mar-

---

[19] Sch 1 para 1(2).

[20] Particularly since the Competition Act 1998 s 60(3) requires that the UK authorities and courts, in applying the Chapter I prohibition, must 'have regard to any relevant . . . statement of the [European] Commission'. Office of Fair Trading, Draft, 'Competition Act 1998: Exclusion for Mergers and Ancillary Restrictions' (OFT 416), paras 4.3 and 4.19.

ket. The exclusion will not normally apply, however, if the agreements include exclusivity provisions.

- In the case of joint ventures, non-competition covenants by the parents, aimed at giving the JV autonomy on the market, will be regarded as necessary to the formation of the JV.

Powers to Amend Merger Exclusions

Under section 3(2) of the Competition Act, the Secretary of State may at any time **5.31** by order amend Schedule 1—the exclusion for mergers and concentrations—so as to add new exclusions, or remove or amend existing exclusions. Under section 3(5), such an order may provide for removal of the benefit of exclusion from a particular agreement.

C. Services of General Economic Interest—Schedule 3, Paragraph 4

Schedule 3, paragraph 4 provides that the Chapter I prohibition does not apply **5.32** to:

> an undertaking entrusted with the operation of services of general economic interest or having the character of a revenue-producing monopoly in so far as the prohibition would obstruct the performance, in law or in fact, of the particular tasks assigned to that undertaking.

This exclusion essentially replicates the words of Article 86(2) (formerly Article 90(2)) of the EC Treaty,[21] and therefore needs to be interpreted in accordance with the interpretation of Article 86(2).[22]

The policy reason behind this exclusion—and behind the provisions of Article **5.33** 86(2) (formerly Article 90(2))—is that it is thought desirable, in the wider public interest, that certain businesses providing services of general economic interest should be protected from competition. A classic example is the universal letter-delivery service provided by the Post Office: it is considered desirable, in the public interest, that there should be a service enabling inhabitants of the UK to send letters to each other, regardless of where in the country they live, and enabling them to do so at the same price (a universal charge). Such a service entails that letters are delivered on unprofitable routes (eg from and to remote rural areas) as well as on profitable routes (eg within the West End of London). If the Post Office were

---

[21] The main difference is that Art 86(2) also stipulates that, if an undertaking is to benefit from the disapplication of the EC competition rules, 'the development of trade must not be affected to such an extent as would be contrary to the interests of the Community'. Prior to the amendments introduced under the 1997 Treaty of Amsterdam, Art 86(2) had been numberd Art (90(2)).

[22] See s 60(2) of the Act, and Ch 3 of this book.

to be exposed to commercial competition in respect of its letter-delivery service, that competition would almost certainly be in respect of the profitable routes only: no one would want to compete for loss-making business. Such competitors would (in the jargon) 'cream skim' the most profitable routes, undercutting the Post Office's universal charge on those routes, and thus taking all the Post Office's profitable business, while the Post Office would be left with only the unprofitable routes. The effect would be to make the Post Office's business commercially unviable. Similar examples arise in the provision of utility services (whether by nationalised or privatised companies), where it is obviously more profitable to supply gas, electricity or water in densely-populated urban areas (with more customers, and hence more revenue, per mile of cable or pipeline) than in rural areas.

5.34 Nevertheless, the policy interest in protecting such services of 'general economic interest' must be balanced against the danger that an excessively broad exclusion would allow the companies concerned to restrict competition in other markets which can and should be competitive (for example, if a utility company enters a naturally competitive market, such as the retail selling of electrical gas cookers, etc). Therefore the scope of the exclusion must be—and is—narrowly circumscribed.

5.35 In order for the exclusion to apply, two conditions must be satisfied:

(i)   the party seeking to benefit from the exclusion must be an **undertaking** of the type defined in Schedule 3, paragraph 4; and

(ii) it must be established that applying the prohibition would **obstruct the performance** of the tasks assigned to that undertaking.

Each of these conditions is dealt with below.

An Undertaking to Which the Exclusion Applies

5.36 The undertaking must be *either* one which is 'entrusted with the operation of services of general economic interest' *or* one 'having the character of a revenue-producing monopoly'.

5.37 'Services of general economic interest' have been held in EC law to be those which do not relate only to private interests and are universally available within a State. The provision of utility services, such as electricity, water and public telephony, have all been held to fall within this definition, along with the basic letter-delivery service and television broadcasting—but less universal services, such as banking or the provisions of port services, are outside it. It is not enough that the undertaking should *provide* services of general economic interest; it must be *entrusted* with the provision of such services—and this means it must be the case that the undertaking provides the service *pursuant to* a law or act of a public authority, and not merely that provision of those services has *subsequently* been approved by public authorities.[23]

Yet even if an undertaking is not 'entrusted with the operation of services of general economic interest', it may still benefit from the exclusion if it has 'the character of a revenue-producing monopoly'. It seems at least arguable, for example, that the National Lottery would fall within this category.　**5.38**

Obstructing the Performance of its Tasks

The exclusion will only apply to the undertakings described above *in so far as* the application of the prohibition would 'obstruct the performance, in law or in fact, of the particular tasks assigned to that undertaking'. The European Court of Justice has ruled that this will only be the case to the extent that a restriction on competition:　**5.39**

> is *necessary* in order to allow the holder of the exclusive right to perform its task of general interest and in particular to have the benefit of economically acceptable conditions.[24]

The European Court of Justice made this statement in the context of a case where the Belgian authorities were seeking to prosecute an individual for infringing the national Post Office's monopoly on letter deliveries. The individual had sought to 'cream skim' by competing against the national Post Office in the collection and distribution of mail within the city of Liège, and the Belgian national court dealing with the prosecution had referred various relevant questions of EC law to the European Court. The European Court held that the introduction of competition would only obstruct the performance of the particular tasks assigned to the Belgian Post Office if it 'compromised the economic equilibrium of the service of general economic interest'—which would be the case in respect of services for which the undertaking was 'bound for economic reasons to offset losses in the unprofitable sectors against profits in the more profitable sectors' while the potential competitor concentrated only on the economically profitable operations. This would not be the case, however, 'as regards specific services dissociable from the service of general interest' (eg additional services not traditionally offered by a postal service).

The European Court, which had been asked only to comment on the legal principles involved, did not specifically identify which services could and could not be protected from competition. However, it seems likely that the exclusion will only apply in respect of the services traditionally reserved to the undertaking (the basic mail service, the supply of gas or water, etc) or in respect of other services where competition would threaten the viability of the traditional service.　**5.40**

---

[23] *Uniform Eurocheques* [1985] OJ L35/43.
[24] Case C–320/91 *Corbeau* [1993] I ECR 2533, paras 16 to 19.

D. Agreements which Received 'Section 21(2) Clearance' under the RTPA—Schedule 3, Paragraph 2

5.41 Under section 21(2) of the old Restrictive Trade Practices Act 1976 (RTPA), agreements which were notified to the OFT were assessed for their impact on competition. If, on the OFT's advice, the Secretary of State considered that restrictions in such an agreement were 'not of such significance as to call for investigation by the Restrictive Practices Court'—ie considered that they had no significant effect on competition in the UK—the Secretary of State would direct the OFT not to take any further proceedings in respect of the agreement. In short, the agreement would be cleared, and the parties would be informed that the agreement had received 'section 21(2) clearance'.

5.42 The Competition Act excludes from the Chapter I prohibition any agreement which benefits from a 'section 21(2) clearance' immediately before the new prohibition comes into force (ie as at 29 February 2000).[25]

Where there is a variation to an agreement benefiting from 'section 21(2) clearance', then, provided that the variation has been duly notified to the OFT under the RTPA,[26] the exclusion will cover the agreement as varied.[27] However, if a 'material variation' is made to the agreement after that time, it will cease to benefit from the exclusion. The OFT interprets a 'material' variation as one which gives rise to an appreciable adverse effect on competition within the meaning of the Chapter I prohibition:

> In the case of a typical commercial agreement, minor adjustments to the parties' trading relationship such as a change in delivery dates, mode of transportation, credit terms or manner of payment would not be caught by the test. On the other hand, variations to such an agreement involving the conversion of a joint marketing area into partitioned markets, or the addition of a significant competitor as a party to the agreement, are likely to be considered material.[28]

5.43 The OFT has 'clawback' powers to withdraw the exclusion. The rules for doing this are similar to those which apply for withdrawing the exclusion from certain merger situations. The OFT may withdraw the exclusion by way of a written direction stating that the exclusion will be withdrawn after a certain date (which must not be earlier than the date of the direction itself).[29] The OFT may only do so if:

---

[25] Competition Act 1998 s 3(1)(c), read with Sch 3 para 2(1).

[26] In accordance with the requirements of ss 24(2)(b) and 27(1)(c), read with reg 5 of the Registration of Restrictive Trading Agreements Regs 1984 SI 1984/392. See Ch 11, para 11.46 to 11.51 below.

[27] Office of Fair Trading, Competition Act 1998: 'Transitional Arrangements', (OFT 406, para 4.15.

[28] Ibid, para 4.16.

[29] Ibid, read with Sch 3, para 2(2).

- *either* the following criteria are both met:
  - (i) the OFT considers that the agreement will infringe the Chapter I prohibition; and
  - (ii) the OFT considers that it is not likely to grant an unconditional UK individual exemption in respect of the agreement;
- *or* the OFT, considering whether to withdraw the exclusion, has sent a written notice to a party to the agreement requesting information, and the party has failed (without reasonable excuse) to comply with the request within seven working days.[30]

Before withdrawing the exclusion, the OFT must consult the parties to the agreement. Once the OFT has done so, it must publish the withdrawal direction in the OFT's register of decisions.[31]

E. Compliance with Planning Obligations and Other Legal Requirements—Schedule 3, Paragraphs 1 and 5

There are automatic exclusions, in Schedule 3, read with section 3(1)(c) of the Act, for: **5.44**

- any agreement, to the extent to which it is a planning obligation; and
- any agreement or decision made in order to comply with a legal requirement, and any concerted practice followed in order to comply with a legal requirement.

Planning Obligations—Schedule 3, Paragraph 1

Schedule 3, paragraph 1(1), excludes from the Chapter I prohibition any agreement to the extent to which it is a planning obligation, an exclusion defined by reference to the Town and Country Planning Act 1990 (and the equivalent Scottish and Northern Irish legislation). The Secretary of State may, however, make an order amending or removing this exclusion, under section 3(3)(b)(ii) of the Act. **5.45**

The exclusion relates to obligations imposed by a planning authority in an agreement made under section 75 or section 246 of the Town and Country Planning Act 1990 (or under the equivalent Scottish and Northern Irish provisions). Such an agreement is made by the planning authority with a person interested in land (including, in the case of Crown land, with the Crown Estate Commissioners or the relevant government department) which restricts or regulates the use or development of that land, and which is enforceable by the planning authority against the person interested in the land and that person's successors in title. 'Planning **5.46**

---

[30] Ibid, read with Sch 3, para 2(3) to (9).
[31] OFT, n 6, R22. See n 6 above on the meaning of 'consult'.

obligations', as defined in sections 106 and 299A of the Town and Country Planning Act, are restrictions and obligations regulating the use of land.

Legal Requirements—Schedule 3, Paragraph 5

5.47 There are sound policy reasons for excluding agreements, decisions or concerted practices made or followed in order to comply with legal requirements: it would make no sense for the law to prohibit parties from doing something which the law expressly required.

5.48 Schedule 3, paragraph 5(1), excludes from the Chapter I prohibition agreements or decisions made in order to comply with a legal requirement, as well as concerted practices followed for that purpose.

5.49 The term 'legal requirement' is defined in paragraph 5 of Schedule 3 as any requirement:

(a) imposed by or under an enactment in force in the UK; or

(b) imposed by or under the EC Treaty or the EEA Agreement[32] which has legal effect in the UK without further enactment; or

(c) imposed by or under the law in force in another EU Member State which has legal effect in the UK.

5.50 The expression 'without further enactment' in (b) entails that provisions in directives will not be regarded as 'legal requirements', since a directive generally obliges a Member State to introduce legislation by way of further national enactment, except arguably in so far as such a provision has direct effect.[33]

5.51 There is no exact equivalent in EC competition law of the exclusion for compliance with legal requirements. However, it is a general principle of EC competition law that agreements will be outside the ambit of Article 81 (formerly Article 85) if the undertakings were *obliged* by a Member State's laws or governments to enter into them—or if the agreements were *imposed* by a Member State—but not merely if they were authorised, encouraged or supported by a Member State or its government; thus, in the *Zinc producer group* price-fixing case, the European Commission stated that:

---

[32] The EEA Agreement applies throughout the European Economic Area (EEA). This is a territory comprising all the EU Member States together with Norway, Iceland and Liechtenstein. The EEA Agreement applies many of the provisions in the EC Treaty to the territory of the EEA including, principally, those on free movement of goods, services, persons and capital, state aids and competition, and is designed to establish a single market across the entire territory of the EEA.

[33] A provision of a directive is capable of having direct effect if it is sufficiently specific and unconditional; the direct effect of a provision in a directive confers rights on individuals and companies against the Member State, and against the State's government and other 'emanations' of the State.

the fact that Member State authorities had knowledge of, participated in or approved price-fixing agreements does not protect them [the agreements] from the application of the [EC] competition rules.[34]

It is likely, in accordance with the obligation to interpret the new Competition Act in accordance with EC principles, that the exclusion in Schedule 3, paragraph 5, will be applied in a similarly limited way.

F. Coal and Steel Agreements—Schedule 3, Paragraph 8

There is a complete exclusion from the Chapter I and Chapter II prohibitions for **5.52** any agreement which relates to a coal or steel product, to the extent that the ECSC Treaty (the European Coal and Steel Community Treaty, also called the Treaty of Paris) gives the European Commission exclusive jurisdiction over such an agreement.

The ECSC Treaty applies to coal and steel products as listed in Annex 1 to the **5.53** Treaty. It is the precursor to the EC Treaty, and the EC Treaty does not apply to the coal and steel products covered by the ECSC Treaty.

There is, in Article 65 of the ECSC Treaty, a prohibition on restrictive agree- **5.54** ments. The European Commission has exclusive jurisdiction to rule on whether any agreement infringes the prohibition.

The exclusion will cease to have effect, and so the Chapter I prohibition will start **5.55** to apply to such coal and steel agreements, when the ECSC Treaty expires. The ECSC Treaty is due to expire in 2002 (after which time coal and steel are likely to be brought under the EC Treaty).

G. Rules of Non-UK Financial Markets which are 'EEA Regulated Markets'—Schedule 3, Paragraph 3

An exclusion is granted by Schedule 3, paragraph 3, read with section 3(1)(c), for **5.56** the rules, guidance and trading practices of certain non-UK financial markets in the EEA. (The EEA, or European Economic Area, comprises the Member States of the European Union together with Norway, Iceland and Liechtenstein. The rules of UK financial markets may benefit from exclusion under Schedule 2, paragraph 1.[35])

---

[34] *Zinc Producer Group* [1984] OJ L220/27, para 74.
[35] See below, paras 5.66–5.68.

5.57 The regulated markets benefiting from the exclusion are termed '**EEA regulated markets**'. These are defined as any market listed by an EEA State other than the UK under Article 16 of Council Directive 93/22/EC[36] which operates without a requirement that a dealer on the market should be physically present either on a trading floor or in the EEA State where that market provides trading facilities.

5.58 Under the exclusion, the Chapter I prohibition does not apply to:

- any agreement relating to rules made or guidance issued by an EEA regulated market;

- any decision made by an EEA regulated market, to the extent that the decision relates to any of the market's regulating provisions (ie its rules, guidance, or practices, or the trading practices of its members);

- any practices of an EEA regulated market;

- any practices which are trading practices of the members of an EEA regulated market, in relation to an EEA regulated market; or

- any agreement to which the parties are or include an EEA regulated market, or a person subject to its rules, to the extent that the agreement's provisions are required or contemplated by the regulating provisions of that market (ie by its rules, guidance or practices, or by the trading practices of its members in relation to the market).

H. Certain Agricultural Products Agreements—Schedule 3, Paragraph 9

5.59 The exclusion in Schedule 3, paragraph 9, read with section 3(1)(c), is intended to replicate in UK law the exception from the Article 81 (formerly Article 85) prohibition which applies in EC law. That EC law exception appears in Article 2(1) of Council Regulation 26/62,[37] and extends to any of the following:

- agreements, decisions or practices which form an integral part of a '**national market organisation**';

- agreements, decisions or practices which are necessary for the attainment of **the objectives set out in Article 33 (formerly Article 39) of the EC Treaty**; or

- agreements, decisions or practices of farmers, farmers' associations or associations of such associations belonging to a single EU Member State, which concern the production or sale of agricultural products or the use of joint facilities

---

[36] Under Art 16, the list must be published in the Official Journal at least once a year. See, eg, [1997] OJ C203/4 and [1998] OJ C111/21.

[37] [1962] OJ Spec Ed 129.

for the storage, treatment or processing of agricultural products, and under which there is no obligation to charge identical prices.

These three categories of arrangement are expressly excluded from the Chapter I prohibition by paragraph 9(1) of Schedule 3—subject to the possibility of withdrawal by the European Commission or the OFT (see paras 5.62 to 5.65 below).

'National Market Organisation'

A 'national market organisation' has been defined by the European Commission   **5.60**
as:

> a totality of legal devices placing the regulation of the market in the products in question under the control of the public authority, with a view to ensuring the realisation of the objectives of Article 39 [of the EC Treaty, now Article 33].[38]

This definition was in the context of a case where it was held that even a series of private-law bodies, which regulated the French new potato market, could constitute a 'national market organisation' and thus benefit from the disapplication of the Article 81 (formerly Article 85) prohibition. This was because their constitution and their relevant decisions and agreements were all placed under the control of the French public authority.

For 'realisation of the objectives' of Article 33 (formerly Article 39), see the next paragraph.

'Objectives Set Out in Article 33 (formerly Article 39) of the EC Treaty'

Article 33 (formerly Article 39) of the EC Treaty states the objectives of the EU's   **5.61**
common agricultural policy. These are:

- increasing agricultural productivity;

- thus ensuring a fair standard of living for the agricultural community;

- stabilising markets;

- assuring the availability of supplies; and

- ensuring that supplies reach consumers at reasonable prices.

The European Commission has held that an exclusive dealing arrangement in favour of producers will not generally be regarded as a means of attaining the objectives of Article 33,[39] but that a long-term purchase contract to supply African and Caribbean cane sugar to the EU does fall within those objectives.[40]

---

[38] *New Potatoes* [1987] OJ L159/2. As a result of the Treaty of Amsterdam, which amended the EC Treaty with effect from 1 May 1999, Article 39 of the EC Treaty is now renumbered Article 33.
[39] *Bloemenveilingen Aalsmeer* [1988] OJ L262/27.
[40] *Cane Sugar* [1980] OJ L39/64.

Withdrawal by the European Commission

5.62   Regulation 26 gives the European Commission the power to determine, by decision, whether an agreement fulfils the conditions (set out above) under which it may benefit from the exception from the Article 81 (formerly Article 85) prohibition.

5.63   Under Schedule 3, paragraph 9(2), to the Competition Act, if the European Commission determines that an agreement does not fulfil those conditions—and therefore cannot benefit from the exception from the Article 81 prohibition—the agreement will automatically cease to benefit from the exclusion from the Chapter I prohibition as well.

Withdrawal by the OFT

5.64   Schedule 3, paragraph 9(3) to (8) provides for 'clawback' or withdrawal of the exclusion by the OFT.

5.65   The OFT may withdraw the exclusion by way of a written direction stating that the exclusion will be withdrawn after a certain date (which must not be earlier than the date of the direction itself). The OFT may only do so if:

- *either* the OFT considers that an agreement is likely, or is intended, substantially and unjustifiably to prevent, restrict or distort competition in relation to an agricultural product;

- *or* the OFT, considering whether to withdraw the exclusion, has sent a written notice to a party to the agreement requesting information within a certain period, and the party has failed (without reasonable excuse) to comply with the request within seven working days.

Before withdrawing the exclusion, the OFT must consult the parties to the agreement. Once the OFT has done so, it must publish the withdrawal direction in the OFT's register of decisions.[41]

I. Agreements Examined Under Other UK Legislation— Schedule 2

5.66

In order to avoid unnecessary duplication, agreements which are subject to competition scrutiny under other UK enactments, similar to the Chapter I prohibition, are excluded from the Chapter I prohibition by Schedule 2, read with section 3(1)(b). Such agreements had previously been outside the ambit of the RTPA.

5.67

This exclusion applies in respect of certain agreements of the following types:

---

[41]   OFT, n 6 above, R22. See n 6 above on the meaning of 'consult'.

(i) **the Financial Services Act 1986**: certain agreements constituting, or implementing the rules or guidance of recognised self-regulating organisations, recognised investment exchanges and recognised clearing houses—as well as certain decisions of such bodies; certain trading practices of such bodies and their members; and agreements constituting, or implementing the rules of, a recognised professional body, which the Treasury has declared not to be anti-competitive or to be necessary for investor protection[42] (see also the exclusions for similar regulated financial markets in other EEA countries under Schedule 3, paragraph 3—see paragraphs 5.56–5.58 above);

(ii) **the Companies Act 1989**: agreements constituting, or implementing the rules or guidance of, recognised bodies supervising the auditing profession;[43]

(iii) **the Broadcasting Act 1990**: certain agreements relating to ITV (Channel 3 independent television) as regards networking arrangements and news provision;[44]

(iv) **the Environment Act 1995**: certain arrangements made in the context of the 'producer responsibility' recycling programme, where the Secretary of State has issued regulations for exclusion or modification of the Chapter I prohibition.[45]

5.68 By contrast, in the case of the regulated UK utility sectors (telecommunications, gas, electricity, water and railways), the Chapter I prohibition is not excluded, and the relevant sector regulator has powers to apply the Chapter I prohibition concurrently with the OFT. This is provided for in section 54 of the Act, read with Schedule 10. (There are, however, longer transitional periods in which certain gas, electricity and railways agreements enjoy a period of special protection from the prohibition.) See Chapter 19 below.

J. General Exclusions to be Granted by the Secretary of State

5.69 There are various other provisions for further exclusions which are not automatically granted by the Act, but which may be subsequently granted by the Secretary of State.

---

[42] See Sch 2, para 1, which amends ss 125 to 127 of the Financial Services Act 1986, for full details. A similar exclusion is intended in the proposed Financial Services and Markets Bill, which (when introduced to Parliament) would replace the Financial Services Act 1986.

[43] See Sch 2, para 2, which amends Sch 14, para 9, to the Companies Act 1989, for full details. There are equivalent provisions for Northern Ireland in Sch 3, para 3, which amends the Companies (Northern Ireland) Order 1990, SI 1990/593 NI 5.

[44] See for full details Sch 2, para 4, which amends s 194A of the Broadcasting Act 1990, and para 5.

[45] See for full details Sch 2, paras 6 and 7, which amend s 94 of the Environment Act 1995 and insert a new s 94A.

'Innocuous' Agreements—Section 3(3), (4) and (5)

5.70 The Secretary of State is empowered to make an order to add further exclusions to the list of general exclusions in Schedule 3 to the Act. The Secretary of State may only do this if it appears to him that agreements falling within the additional exclusion:

(i) *either* do not in general have an adverse effect on competition;

(ii) *or* are best considered under the Chapter II prohibition or under the Fair Trading Act 1973 (which includes the provisions on scale monopolies and complex monopolies[46] as well as the UK merger control rules).

Such an order may provide for removal of the benefit of the exclusion from a particular agreement.

5.71 If the Secretary of State has made an order adding a case in this way, he may also by order amend or remove such a case.

Exclusions Required by Public Policy—Section 3(6) and Schedule 3, Paragraph 7

5.72 The Secretary of State may also make orders excluding agreements from the Chapter I prohibition if he is satisfied that there are 'exceptional and compelling reasons of public policy' for the Chapter I prohibition not to apply to such agreements.

5.73 Any order make under this provision may apply either to a particular agreement or to agreements of a particular description. Exclusions made under such an order may be limited so that they apply only in circumstances specified under the order. The order may also operate retrospectively, such that the Chapter I prohibition is deemed never to have applied to the agreement or agreements.

Agreements Fulfilling the UK's International Obligations—Section 3(6) and Schedule 3, Paragraph 6

5.74 The Secretary of State may also make orders to exclude agreements from the Chapter I prohibition if he is satisfied that it would be appropriate 'in order to avoid a conflict between provisions of [Part I of the Act—the provisions on the Chapter I and II prohibitions] and an international obligation of the United Kingdom'. International civil aviation arrangements count as 'international obligations' for these purposes.

5.75 As with the 'public policy' exclusion, such an order may apply to a particular agreement or to agreements of a particular description. It may be limited to cir-

---

[46] See Chs 17 and 18 below.

cumstances specified in the order. It may also be retrospective, such that it is deemed never to have applied in relation to the agreement or agreements.

Rules of Professional Bodies—Schedule 4

The rules of professional bodies (such as the Law Society, the Institute of Chartered Accountants, and so on) are capable of being agreements or arrangements restrictive of competition, in that they may limit entry into the profession concerned (through qualification requirements) or restrict the way in which the services are performed (through limitation on fees or fee structures or on advertising). However, Schedule 4 to the Act, read with section 3(1)(d), allows the Secretary of State to exclude professional rules from the Chapter I prohibition in respect of the professional services listed in Part II of Schedule 4—being legal, medical, dental, ophthalmic, veterinary, nursing, midwifery, physiotherapy, chiropody, architectural, accounting and auditing, insolvency, patent agency, Parliamentary agency, surveying, engineering, educational and religious professional services. **5.76**

These services were excluded altogether from the old Restrictive Trade Practices Act (RTPA)—although it had been possible (and remains possible) to investigate them under the monopoly provisions of the Fair Trading Act (FTA). By contrast, in the 1989 White Paper which first proposed the new prohibition, the Government took the view that these professional services should be included within the scope of the new prohibition, and the rules could then be assessed on a case-by-case basis and, where appropriate, be amended.[47] **5.77**

In the end, the new Act has struck a middle course between the leniency of the old RTPA towards the professions, and the uncompromising radicalism of the 1989 White Paper proposals. Under Schedule 4, rules of the bodies regulating the relevant professional services are not automatically excluded—but it is open to the Secretary of State, in response to an application by such a body, to include its rules on a list of 'designated professional rules' which are thereby excluded. The OFT must maintain the list, and copies of the professional rules on it, and these must be open to public inspection. 'Rules' for this purpose include regulations, codes of practice and statements of principle.[47a] **5.78**

The OFT must keep the rules under review, and must advise the Secretary of State if it considers that certain professional rules (whether in their entirety or in part) should be added from the list or removed from it. **5.79**

---

[47] White Paper, *Opening Markets: New Policy on Restrictive Trade Practices*, Cm 727, July 1989, Annex E.

[47a] Office of Fair Trading, 'Competition Act 1998: Trade Associations, Professions and Self-Regulated Bodies', (OFT 408), para 6.2.

5.80 The problems raised by constant alterations to the rules are solved by an explicit provision that, where a rule is altered, it does not thereby automatically cease to be a 'designated professional rule'—but the professional body concerned must then notify the Secretary of State and the OFT of the alteration 'as soon as is reasonably practicable'.

K. 'Vertical' Agreements—Special Treatment

5.81 One of the most important differences from EC competition law is the power to grant special treatment for 'vertical' agreements under section 50. The government is proposing to make a special treatment order, under section 50, under which **most vertical agreements will be excluded from the Chapter I prohibition**. The exclusion order will not, however, extend to price-fixing agreements (eg resale price maintenance) or to intellectual property licences. See paragraph 5.92(ii) and (v) below.

Context

5.82 'Vertical' agreements are agreements made between parties who are at different levels in a chain of supply. Thus, for example, a 'vertical' agreement is one between a manufacturer and a distributor, or between a wholesaler and a retailer, or between a licensor and a licensee of intellectual property rights. They are to be contrasted with 'horizontal' agreements—ie agreements made between parties who are at the same level of supply and are, therefore, competitors of each other (such as agreements between two or more manufacturers, or agreements between two or more wholesalers).

5.83 Developments in economic theory since 1957—when the EC Treaty, and Article 81 (formerly Article 85), first came into effect—have cast doubt on whether restrictions in vertical agreements are as damaging to competition as restrictions in horizontal agreements, and therefore on whether they should be subject to the same prohibition. Horizontally restrictive agreements, by which competitors agree to limit their activities on the market where they compete against each other, are by definition restrictive of competition. However, the position is less obvious with vertically restrictive agreements. By way of example, it is worth considering an exclusivity agreement under which, say, a **chemical company** which has developed a new colour to be used as an ingredient in paint enters into a supply agreement with a **paint manufacturer**, under which the chemical company agrees to supply the new ingredient to that paint manufacturer, and to accept a restriction whereby it will not supply the ingredients to any other paint manufacturer. This kind of exclusive supply agreement would normally be prohibited under Article 81,[48] and would need to

---

[48] Assuming that it is an agreement which may affect trade between Member States.

be notified (to the European Commission) in order to be exempted from the Article 81 prohibition; the same would be true under the new Chapter I prohibition in the UK if it fully replicated Article 81. However, it is by no means obvious that such an exclusive supply agreement would really have anti-competitive economic effects. On the contrary, it might be pro-competitive:

- It is widely thought, for example, that exclusivity agreements lead to efficiencies in the chain of supply and distribution. If this is so, in the example of the new paint colour, the process of manufacturing and marketing the paint with the new colour will be carried on more efficiently with exclusivity than without exclusivity. That, in turn, will make the paint a more competitive product on the marketplace, inducing rival suppliers of paint to increase the efficiency with which they manufacture and market their products (because if they do not, they will lose market share). Thus the exclusivity, far from restricting competition, acts as a spur to increased competition, leading to increased efficiency through-out the market, and therefore a downward pressure on prices and an upward pressure on quality overall. The exclusivity has had the effect of removing com-petition between downstream suppliers of that particular chemical company's paint colour (that is, it has reduced '*intra*-brand' competition), but in doing so it has increased the prospects for competition between different companies' products on the market ('*inter*-brand' competition).

- There may also be a further pro-competitive effect of the exclusivity: the paint manufacturer may not have been willing to take the commercial risk of buying the new paint colour from the chemical company and introducing that colour into its paints—unless he could be assured that, if the risk paid off and the new colour proved popular among customers, he would yield the full benefit by being the only paint manufacturer on the market who would be selling paints with that new colour (and would not have to share the profits with competing manufacturers). In short, the exclusivity would act as an incentive for the paint manufacturer to agree to market the chemical company's new colour. The con-clusion which economists draw from this is that such exclusivity agreements act as an incentive to the marketing of new products, and therefore as a way of encouraging innovation, choice and (hence) competition.

However, even those who argue that exclusivity agreements can have pro-competitive effects, readily concede that this is not always the case. In particular, vertically restrictive agreements can have anti-competitive effects which outweigh any pro-competitive advantages if they result in significant *foreclosure*. Every exclusivity agreement has some foreclosure effect. Thus—to return to the exam-ple of the exclusive supply agreement between the chemical company and the paint manufacturer—the effect of the exclusivity is that all the other paint manu-facturers are foreclosed from having access to that chemical company's paint colour. But this foreclosure only matters, in competition terms, in so far as the **5.84** effect is to make it harder for rival paint manufacturers to compete on the market against the manufacturer which benefits from the exclusivity. That will be the case to the extent that the product to which the competing paint manufacturers are denied access (in this case, the chemical company's colour) represents a significant share of the relevant market. To the extent that competing paint manufacturers are able to acquire comparable (and hence competing) paint colours from other chemical companies, they are not significantly foreclosed by the exclusivity; to the extent that they do *not* have access to comparable products from other chemical companies, because the chemical company which has granted the exclusivity (and to whose colour these competing paint manufacturers are denied access) has a large share of the market, there *is* significant foreclosure. It follows that, as a broad principle, vertical exclusivity agreements are likely to be more anti-competitive to the extent that the party granting the exclusivity accounts for a high share of the market in the product for which the exclusivity is granted, so foreclosing access to that product by competitors on the market of the party to which exclusivity has been granted (and thereby hindering their ability to compete).[49]

5.85   The implications of these economic arguments are that exclusivity agreements are only really damaging to competition when one of the parties has market power or a dominant market position. If that is so, it has been argued, those anti-competitive effects can already adequately be dealt with using a prohibition on abuse of a dominant position, as in Article 82 (formerly Article 86) of the EC Treaty or the new Chapter II prohibition. There is no need for vertically restrictive agreements also to be controlled by a prohibition on all restrictive agreements, such as Article 81 (formerly Article 85) or the new Chapter I prohibition.

The EC Approach

5.86   In the context of EC competition law, the European Commission has acknowledged the implications of much of the economic thinking on vertical agreements which has developed since 1957, most recently in its 1998 Communication on Vertical Restraints, which states: '[i]t is only where inter-brand competition is weak and market power exists that it becomes important to control vertical agreements'. However, the European Commission feels that it may not be possible to rely solely on a prohibition on abuse of a dominant position, such as in Article 82 (formerly Article 86) of the EC Treaty, because 'most economists would agree that there exists market power below the level of dominance as defined by the Court of

---

[49] There is also significant foreclosure where, for a particular product, there are a large number of parallel exclusivity agreements, each of which is with a supplier which might not itself have a high market share, but which cumulatively tie up a large share of the market in the product— foreclosing potential new entrants from access to the product. This is sometimes called the 'network' effect.

Justice'.[50] Accordingly the Commission's approach has been to seek a way of relaxing the application of Article 81 (formerly Article 85) to vertical agreements, while not removing it altogether.

The European Commission had previously taken steps to reflect this thinking, **5.87** and now proposes further steps:

- The European Commission has tried to give more favourable treatment to vertical agreements by raising the threshold for treating vertical agreements as *de minimis* (and hence outside the prohibition). The Commission, in its 1997 Notice on agreements of minor importance, raised the *de minimis* threshold from a 5 per cent market share to a 10 per cent market share (while keeping the threshold at 5 per cent for horizontal agreements).[51] This move is clearly of only marginal benefit. However, the Commission could not go further, because it would then depart from the legal interpretation of *de minimis* (non-appreciability) which had been established by the European Court of Justice. In any case, strictly speaking, the Commission's Notice only protects vertical agreements from action for infringements of Article 81 (formerly Article 85) which might be taken by the Commission; it offers no protection against action in national courts.

- For many years, EC block exemption regulations have been in place which automatically exempt certain vertical agreements from the prohibition in Article 81 (formerly Article 85). Categories of vertical agreement which now benefit from EC block exemptions include exclusive distribution agreements, exclusive purchasing agreements, exclusive licences of technology, and franchise agreements.

  Now the Commission is proposing a wider block exemption to cover all vertical agreements, except those which include specifically prohibited provisions and those exceeding specified market share thresholds.[52]

  However, block exemptions can never provide a complete solution to the problem, first because each block exemption regulation specifies formalistic criteria which an agreement must satisfy if it is to benefit from the exemption (and not every agreement will satisfy those criteria), and secondly because a block exemption should only be granted if it is clear that the agreements covered by it meet all the conditions for exemption laid down in Article 81(3) (formerly Article 85(3)) of the Treaty (it is not sufficient that they are not significantly anti-competitive).

---

[50] European Commission Communication on the application of the Community competition rules to vertical restraints [1998] OJ C365/3, S I, para 2, and S III, para 1. This follows the Commission's Green Paper on Vertical Restraints in EC Competition Policy, COM(96)721 adopted by the European Commission on 22 Jan 1997.

[51] Commission Notice on agreements of minor importance [1997] OJ C372/13.

[52] Commission Communication on the application of the EC competition rules to vertical restraints, n 50 above, section V.

5.88 In EC competition law, there is therefore limited scope for taking any further steps to protect vertically restrictive agreements from the prohibition in Article 81 (formerly Article 85) of the EC Treaty. Until and unless Article 81 is itself changed, which requires amendment of the Treaty by all the Member States, it is impossible to remove vertical agreements altogether from the scope of the EC prohibition on restrictive agreements (and control them only through the EC prohibition on abuse of a dominant position, in Article 82 (formerly Article 86)). In short, without amendment of the Treaty, EC competition law is largely tied to the economic thinking of 1957 in respect of vertical agreements.

5.89 By contrast UK competition law is starting afresh—and the enactment of new legislation has presented an opportunity to reflect recent economic thinking in devising the scope of prohibitions under that legislation.

The Government's Proposals for Vertical Agreements under UK Competition Law

5.90 The UK government, in framing the scope of the new prohibitions under the Competition Act, was conscious of:

> the prevailing view among economists . . . that vertical agreements do not normally give rise to competition concerns, except where one of the parties holds market power or there exists a large network of agreements.[53]

5.91 Accordingly, the government is proposing to issue a special treatment order under section 50, which will grant exclusion to most vertical agreements (but not to intellectual property licences or to resale price maintenance—see below). The Department of Trade and Industry published a draft of the exclusion order in February 1999, and it is intended that the order will be made before March 2000 when the Chapter I prohibition comes into effect.

5.92 The main points of the order are as follows:

(i) To the extent that an agreement is a 'vertical agreement', it is to be **excluded from the Chapter I prohibition**—unless either it has been 'clawed back' by the OFT (see (iii) below) or it is one of the exceptions specified in the order (see (iv) and (v) below).

(ii) 'Vertical agreements' are to be defined in the same way as in the proposed new EC block exemption for vertical agreements. As at February 1999, the working definition was: 'an agreement (a) between two or more undertakings, each operating at a different stage of the economic process for the purposes of that agreement, and (b) in respect of the supply or purchase, or both, of goods for resale or processing or in respect of the marketing of services'.

---

[53] Ian McCartney, Minister of State at the Department of Trade and Industry, *Hansard*, HC vol 315, no 202, col 1191. Regarding 'networks' of agreements, see n 49 above.

Intellectual property licences do not fall within this definition, as they are not agreements for the supply or purchase of goods or services.

(iii) The OFT will be empowered to '**claw back**' (that is, withdraw) the exclusion. The grounds on which it may exercise such clawback powers are similar to those for other exclusions—ie where:

(a) *either* the OFT considers that the vertical agreement would (if it were not for the exclusion) infringe the Chapter I prohibition and that it is not likely to grant an unconditional UK individual exemption in respect of the vertical agreement;

(b) *or* the OFT, when considering whether or not to withdraw the exclusion, has sent a written notice to a party to the land agreement requesting information, and the party has failed (without reasonable excuse) to comply with the request within seven working days.

The Chapter I prohibition will only apply to an agreement which would otherwise benefit from the exclusion order *after* the OFT has exercised its clawback powers. The clawback is not retroactive.

(iv) There is an automatic **exception** from the exclusion order where, following an OFT clawback of a vertical agreement, the same parties enter into another vertical agreement which includes restrictions or obligations 'to the like object or effect' as those in respect of which the OFT clawback was exercised.

(v) There is also an automatic **exception** from the benefit of the exclusion order for resale price maintenance agreements—that is, for any agreement which 'directly or indirectly' has the object or effect of

(a) fixing resale prices or minimum resale prices, or

(b) fixing maximum resale prices or recommended resale prices which have the same effect as fixed resale prices or fixed minimum resale prices.

5.93 The order excludes an agreement from the Chapter I prohibition '*to the extent*' that it is a vertical agreement. This concept, which must be read with section 59(2), is more fully explained in paragraph 5.05 above. In practice, it means that if the vertical agreement is part of a wider agreement or arrangement which includes, for example, horizontal restrictions, it is only the vertical restrictions which benefit from the exclusion. Moreover, by virtue of section 59(2) of the Competition Act, when the authorities assess the entire agreement/arrangement under the Chapter I prohibition, they must view it in its entirety, not disregarding those provisions to which the exclusion relates (although those provisions in themselves remain excluded).

5.94 The order does not grant exclusion from the Chapter II prohibition, and it is possible that vertical restraints imposed by parties with a dominant position may infringe the Chapter II prohibition. (This, however, is subject to the possibility that the agreements in question may benefit from an individual exemption, whether granted by the OFT or the European Commission; as explained in Chapter 6 of this book, paragraph 6.59, the legal position appears to be that an individual exemption protects an agreement from being regarded as an abuse of a dominant position, but a block exemption offers no such protection.)

5.95 In addition, it will still be possible for the UK authorities to investigate vertical agreements under the monopoly provisions of the Fair Trading Act 1973. In particular, the complex monopoly provision may be applied to investigate an entire market sector where there is a 'network' of vertically restrictive agreements which, in combination, have a foreclosure effect across that market sector.

L. Land Agreements—Special Treatment

5.96 The government, in proposing the Competition Act, recognised that EC case law would be of little assistance in assessing whether the Chapter I prohibition applies to land agreements, because of 'the general expectation that restrictions in land agreements are unlikely to affect trade between member states—and hence to fall foul of Article 85' [now Article 81].[54]

5.97 The government considers that most land agreements, so far as they relate to the creation or transfer of an interest in land, are unlikely to have an appreciable effect on competition.[55]

5.98 The government has therefore proposed making an order under section 50 which will exclude certain land agreements from the Chapter I prohibition. A draft of the order was published by the Department of Trade and Industry in February 1999, and the intention is that the order should be in place before March 2000 when the Chapter I prohibition comes into effect.

5.99 The main features of the government's proposex **exclusion order for land agreements** are as follows:

(i) To the extent that an agreement is a 'land agreement', it is to be **excluded from the Chapter I prohibition**—unless either the exclusion is 'clawed back' by the OFT (see (iv) below) or the obligation or restriction in the land agreement is one of the exceptions specified in the order (see (v) and (vi) below).

(ii) A 'land agreement' is to mean any 'agreement between undertakings which creates, alters, transfers or terminates, an *interest in land*, or an agreement to enter into such an agreement', as well as obligations and restrictions in such an agreement. All land transfers and leases will therefore be 'land agree-

---

[54] Nigel Griffiths, Minister for Competition and Consumer Affairs, in Standing Committee G (seventeenth sitting, 25 June 1998), *House of Commons Official Report* col 633.
[55] Ibid.

ments', but the government's view is that licences will not. Consequently, licences (such as licences granted by a department store to the boutiques on its premises or, increasingly, licences granting occupation rights in industrial units) will not come within the exclusion order.

(iii) An obligation or restriction in a land agreement will benefit from the exclusion if:

(a) it is accepted by a party 'in his capacity as holder of an interest' in the relevant land, and is for the benefit of another party 'in his capacity as holder of an interest' in the relevant land; or

(b) it corresponds to such an obligation or restriction accepted by a party to the land agreement 'in his capacity as holder of an interest' in the relevant land, but relates to the imposition of such an obligation or restriction in respect of other land in which a party has an interest.

The intended effect is that restrictions and obligations imposed for the benefit of one party's interest in the land should be excluded, but not those imposed in order to benefit that party in some other separate capacity—as a trader or competitor, for example. (The government has abandoned an earlier proposal that any restriction on the terms of trading on land would not have benefited from the exclusion order.) Thus:

• Restrictions in leases in a shopping centre or shopping parade, which limit the trading activities of the tenant retailers (eg so that there is only one pharmacy, one supermarket, and so on) are intended to come within the exclusion order. The government takes the view that they benefit the interest of the landlord in his capacity as landlord, since they are necessary to attract tenants to lease premises (retailers will not lease premises in the shopping centre if they fear direct competition). According to the government, this is also the case even if the landlord himself has a retail business in the shopping centre.

• Where the landlord is an insurance company, an obligation in a lease that the tenant should insure the property *through* the landlord/insurance company (who may place it with another insurance company) is intended to come within the exclusion order—because it is imposed in order to enable the landlord to be certain that the premises are properly insured, and therefore to protect the landlord's interest as a landlord of the premises. However, an obligation to the tenant to insure the property *with* the landlord/insurance company is imposed in order to enhance the latter's business as insurer, and would not come within the exclusion order.

• However, other exclusive purchasing obligations in leases, such as beer ties and petrol 'solus' agreements, will not come within the exclusion, because they fall within the exception in (vi) below.

(iv) The OFT will be empowered to '**claw back**' the exclusion. As with the exclusion order for vertical agreements (and various of the statutory exclusions in the Competition Act), the grounds on which it may exercise such clawback powers are where:

(a) *either* the OFT considers that the land agreement would (if it were not for the exclusion) infringe the Chapter I prohibition and that it is not likely to grant an unconditional UK individual exemption in respect of the land agreement;

(b) *or* the OFT, when considering whether or not to withdraw the exclusion, has sent a written notice to a party to the land agreement requesting information, and the party has failed (without reasonable excuse) to comply with the request within seven working days.

Again, the clawback is not retroactive, and the Chapter I prohibition will only apply after it has been exercised.

(v) There is an automatic **exception** from the exclusion order where, following an OFT clawback of a land agreement, the same parties enter into another land agreement which includes restrictions or obligations 'to the like object or effect' as those in respect of which the OFT clawback was exercised.

(vi) There is also an automatic **exception** from the exclusion order for any obligation or restriction which takes effect between undertakings 'each operating at a different stage of the economic process for the purposes of that agreement . . . [which] is in respect of the supply or purchase, or both, of goods for resale or processing or in respect of the marketing of services'. The intention behind this exception is that most vertical restrictions in land agreements should not benefit from the exclusion order—for example, exclusive purchasing obligations imposed by a brewery on its public house tenants (beer ties) or by an oil company on its petrol station tenants ('solus' petrol agreements). These may, however, come within the exclusion order for vertical agreements (see paragraph 5.92) or by way of parallel exemption from one of the EC block exemptions (see Chapter 6 below).

5.100 The order excludes an agreement from the Chapter I prohibition '*to the extent*' that it is a land agreement. As explained in the context of the exclusion order for vertical agreements, where the same formula is used (see paragraph 5.93 above), this means that if the land agreement is part of a wider agreement or arrangement, it is only the restrictions and obligations specifically excluded by the order which benefit from the exclusion. Moreover, by virtue of section 59(2) of the Competition Act, when the authorities assess the wider agreement/arrangement under the Chapter I prohibition, they must view it in its entirety, not disregarding those provisions to which the exclusion order relates (although this does not remove the benefit of exclusion from those provisions themselves).

The exclusion offers no protection against the Chapter II prohibition on abuses of **5.101**
a dominant position. Care therefore needs to be taken where one of the parties
may have a dominant position in a relevant market (see Chapters 8 and 9 of this
book).

M. Notification to the OFT?

Exclusions (whether they are contained in the text of the Act itself, or in a subse- **5.102**
quent order made by the Secretary of State) apply automatically. There is no need
to notify the UK authorities in order to be granted an exclusion.

Nevertheless, the Act makes clear that, in cases of uncertainty, it is possible to sub- **5.103**
mit a notification to the OFT for a decision, and that the OFT may then make a
decision stating whether or not the agreement is excluded from the Chapter I prohibition.[56] In addition, if the parties to an excluded agreement receive notice from
the OFT that an exclusion is to be withdrawn ('clawed back'), they may choose to
notify the OFT seeking exemption for the agreement although this is likely to be
a conditional exemption.

Notifications are considered more fully in Chapter 12 below.

---

[56] S 14(2)(b).

6

EXEMPTIONS

A. Overview

6.01   Section 4 of the Competition Act provides that certain agreements which would otherwise infringe the Chapter I prohibition may be **exempted** from the prohibition. This mirrors Article 81(3) (formerly Article 85(3)) of the EC Treaty, which provides that agreements which would otherwise infringe the Article 81 (formerly Article 85) prohibition (formerly the Article 85 prohibition) may be exempted from the prohibition.

6.02   An exemption is not the same as an exclusion. Whereas an *excluded* agreement is wholly outside the scope of the prohibition, *exemptions* apply to agreements which fall within the scope of the prohibition—but which, broadly speaking, bring economic benefits which offset their anti-competitive effects. The criteria for exemption from the Chapter I prohibition are the same as those for exemption from the Article 81 (formerly Article 85) prohibition.

There are three ways of obtaining exemption from the Chapter I prohibition: **6.03**

(i)   **Parallel exemption**: if an agreement benefits from an EC exemption (ie an exemption from the Article 81 prohibition, under Article 81(3), whether an individual exemption or block exemption), it is automatically exempt from the Chapter I prohibition—*Competition Act, section 10.*

(ii) **UK block exemption**: the Secretary of State may make 'block exemption' orders in respect of specific categories of agreement, and any agreement covered by such a block exemption order will be *automatically* exempt if it meets the conditions specified in the order (these are in addition to the existing EC block exemptions)—*Competition Act, section 6.*

(iii) **UK individual exemption**: the OFT may grant an exemption to a particular agreement which has been *notified* to it, by way of an individual exemption decision, if the OFT, having assessed the agreement, takes the view that it meets the criteria for exemption—*Competition Act, section 4.*

This chapter examines all three types of exemption, but first considers the concept of an exemption.

B. The Concept of 'Exemptions'

Block Exemptions and Individual Exemptions

Agreements which fall within the ambit of the Chapter I prohibition are prohib-   **6.04**
ited (and give rise to the liabilities and risks of sanctions described in chapter 10) *unless and until* they are exempted.

- If the agreement is covered by a **block** exemption—whether an EC block exemption, which has effect by way of the 'parallel exemption' provision, or by a UK block exemption—the agreement is automatically exempt from the Chapter I prohibition, and is deemed always to have been exempted.

- If there is no block exemption, the agreement may nevertheless be exempted from the Chapter I prohibition by an **individual** exemption—whether an EC individual exemption, which has effect by way of the 'parallel' exemption provision, or a UK individual exemption. However, the agreement will only be exempt from the Chapter I prohibition if: (i) one or more of the parties has notified it to the relevant competition authority (the European Commission for EC individual exemption and the OFT for UK individual exemption); (ii) that competition authority, having assessed the agreement, is satisfied that it meets the criteria for exemptions; and (iii) the competition authority specifically grants an individual exemption in respect of the agreement. Until and unless the individual exemption is eventually *granted* by the European Commission or the OFT, the agreement may be considered to infringe the prohibition.[1] A difference between EC and UK individual exemptions is that an EC individual exemption from the European Commission (and hence a parallel exemption) may be retroactive, but cannot apply earlier than the date of notification to the European Commission[2]—whereas a UK individual exemption granted by the OFT may be retroactive without any limit (ie it may apply even earlier than the date of notification).[3]

The Criteria for Exemption—Section 9

6.05 The criteria which must be satisfied in order for an individual exemption to be granted—and, indeed, in order for a block exemption to be promulgated—are the same for both Article 81 (formerly Article 85) of the EC Treaty and the Chapter I prohibition. They are set out in Article 81(3) (formerly Article 85(3)) of the EC Treaty, and replicated in section 9 of the Competition Act 1998. Because the language of the Act reflects that of Article 81, section 9 must be interpreted in accordance with judgments of the European Court of Justice, and having regard to decisions of the European Commission, on Article 81(3).[4]

6.06 The criteria for exemption from the Article 85 prohibition and the Chapter I prohibition, are as follows. An agreement may be exempted if:

(i)   it contributes to improving production or distribution, or promoting technical or economic progress; *and*

(ii) it allows consumers a fair share of the resulting benefit; *and*

(iii) the restrictions in it are indispensable to the attainment of those objectives; *and*

(iv) it does not afford the undertakings concerned the possibility of eliminating competition in respect of a substantial part of the products in question.

All of these criteria must be met if the agreement is to be exempted. The way in which they have been applied in practice is considered below, in paragraphs 6.47–6.58.

---

[1] Except that, if the agreement has been notified to the European Commission or the OFT for an individual exemption, the parties enjoy immunity from penalties (ie fines) by that authority in respect of the period from notification until the decision on whether to exempt: Council Reg (EEC) 17, art 15(5)(a), for EC individual exemptions; Competition Act 1998, s 14(4) for UK individual exemptions.

[2] Council Reg (EEC) 17, art 6(1).

[3] Competition Act 1998 s 4(5). See also Office of Fair Trading, 'Competition Act 1998: The Chapter II Prohibition' (OFT 401), para 7.5.

[4] As a result of s 60(2) and (3) of the Act.

C. 'Parallel Exemption'—Section 10

An agreement which already has an EC exemption under Article 81(3) (formerly **6.07** Article 85(3))—whether an EC block exemption or an EC individual exemption—is automatically exempt from the Chapter I prohibition in UK law for so long as the EC exemption applies. This is called 'parallel exemption' and is provided for in section 10 of the Competition Act.

The concept of 'parallel exemption' goes a long way towards relieving businesses **6.08** of the burden of having to notify agreements to both the European Commission and the OFT, and of the risks of 'double jeopardy'. Once an agreement has received an exemption from the European Commission, there is no need to seek a separate exemption from the OFT.

In addition, the provision for 'parallel exemption' resolves (or, at least, avoids) an **6.09** issue of long-standing dispute between the United Kingdom and the European Commission: the European Commission has always maintained that, if it has exempted an agreement under Article 81(3) (formerly Article 85(3)), individual Member States are not entitled to prohibit that agreement under their own national competition laws. The UK has never accepted that argument, and has maintained that it is entitled under its national competition laws to prohibit agreements even if the European Commission has exempted them under Article 81(3) (the so-called 'double barrier' theory). Without explicitly retreating from its position, the UK has, by virtue of the parallel exemption provision, ensured that in practice it will not challenge the Commission's position.[5]

Parallel Exemption—EC Block Exemptions

Section 10(1)(a) sets out one type of parallel exemption. It states that an agreement **6.10** is automatically exempt from the Chapter I prohibition *if* it is exempt from the prohibition in Article 81 EC by virtue of a regulation adopted by the European Commission or the Council—that is, by virtue of an EC **block exemption**.

There are a number of EC block exemptions. An agreement will only benefit from the block exemption if it satisfies all the conditions laid down in the relevant block **6.11** exemption regulation. These conditions typically include:

(i) a list of restrictive provisions which may be included in an agreement without depriving that agreement of the benefit of the block exemption—the so-called '**white list**'; and

---

[5] At least not under the Chapter I prohibition. There remains the possibility that, under the monopoly provisions of the Fair Trading Act 1973 for example, the UK would prohibit conduct which had been exempted by the European Commission under Art 81(3).

(ii) another list setting out restrictive provisions, *none of which* may be included in the agreement if it is to enjoy the benefit of the block exemption—the '**black list**'.

6.12 At the date the Competition Act was enacted, there were a number of EC block exemptions in place.[6] These covered the following categories of agreement:[7]

(a) **Exclusive distribution agreements—Commission Regulation (EEC) 1983/83:**[6] This block exemption applies to agreements between just two parties—a supplier of goods, and a distributor/reseller to whom the supplier sells the contract goods for resale—under which the supplier agrees that, within a specified contract territory which is the whole or part of the EU, he will supply the contract goods (or certain of them) only to that distributor/reseller—ie the supplier appoints the other party as his exclusive distributor within the contract territory. The exclusivity, which might otherwise be prohibited as restrictive of competition, is automatically exempt, provided that it meets the conditions in the Regulation:

- Under the white list, such exclusive distribution agreements may benefit from the block exemption even if the agreement restricts the supplier himself from supplying the contract goods directly to users in the contract territory, or obliges the exclusive distributor to purchase complete ranges of goods or minimum quantities from the supplier, or restricts the exclusive distributor from '*actively*' seeking customers of the contract goods outside the contact territory.

- However, under the black list, the block exemption will not apply if, among other things, the supplier and the distributor are competing manufacturers of the contract goods, and either they enter into a reciprocal exclusive distribution agreement between themselves, or they enter into a non-exclusive distribution agreement between themselves and each has an annual turnover above 100 million euros; or if the agreement restricts the distributor from '*passive*' sales outside the contract territory, such as accepting orders; or if users in the contract territory have no alternative sources of obtaining the contract goods from distributors who are located outside the contract territory.

---

[6] However, note that the parallel exemption applies to agreements which are covered by an EC block exemption *at the relevant time*, whether or not the EC block exemption was in place at the time when the Competition Act was enacted.

[7] In this list only the principal features of the EC block exemptions are described. It is essential to check an agreement carefully against the full terms of the relevant block exemption regulation to ensure that it will benefit from that block exemption.

[8] [1983] OJ L173/1, amended by Commission Reg (EC) 1582/97 [1997] OJ L214/27, extending it to 31 Dec 1999.

(b) **Exclusive purchasing agreements—Commission Regulation (EEC) 1984/83:**[9] This block exemption applies to agreements for the sale of goods between two parties, the supplier of goods and a reseller of those contract goods, under which the reseller is subject to an 'exclusive purchasing' restriction—that is, an obligation to buy the contract goods for resale only from that supplier, or from a third party appointed by the supplier to sell the contract goods.

- Under the white list, such exclusive purchasing agreements may still benefit from the block exemption even if the reseller is obliged not to manufacture or distribute goods which compete with the contract goods and/or if it is obliged to purchase minimum quantities of the contract goods, and if the supplier is obliged not to distribute the contract goods in the reseller's principal sales area and at the reseller's level of distribution.

- However, under the black list, the benefit of the block exemption is lost if, among other conditions, the parties are competing manufacturers of the contract goods and either they enter into a reciprocal exclusive purchasing agreement between themselves, or they enter into a non-reciprocal exclusive purchasing agreement between themselves and each has an annual turnover above 100 million euros; or if the agreement is concluded for a period of more than five years or for an indefinite period.

There are special provisions in the exclusive purchasing block exemption for exclusive purchasing agreements binding public houses in respect of beer and other drinks,[10] and in respect of 'solus' exclusive purchasing agreements between petrol stations and petrol suppliers.

(c) **Motor vehicle selective distribution agreements—Commission Regulation (EEC) 1475/95:**[11] This block exemption applies to agreements or arrangements between two parties—generally a motor vehicle manufacturer and a dealer—under which the manufacturer agrees to supply new motor vehicles and spare parts, for resale within a defined territory within the EU, exclusively to that dealer or 'selectively' only to that dealer and a specified number of other undertakings within the distribution system.

- Under the white list, the block exemption continues to apply if the agreement or arrangement contains an obligation on the manufacturer not to sell the contract goods to final consumers, nor to provide servicing of the contract goods to final users, in the contract territory. It also continues to

---

[9] [1983] OJ L173/5, amended by Commission Reg (EC) 1582/97 [1997] OJ L214/27, extending it to 31 Dec 1999.

[10] In the UK, these must be read alongside the Supply of Beer (Loan Ties, Licensed Premises and Wholesale Premises) Order 1989 SI 1989/2258, especially art 2(3)(b); and the Supply of Beer (Tied Estate) Order 1989 SI 1989/2390, especially art 5(2)(b).

[11] [1995] OJ L145/25.

apply where the dealer agrees not to manufacture products competing with the contract goods; or not to sell new motor vehicles offered by other manufacturers except on separate sales premises and through a different company; or not to sell spare parts which compete with the contract goods without matching them in quality, or to use them for repair or maintenance of the contract goods; or not to maintain branches or solicit customers of the contract goods outside the contract territory, or not to entrust third parties with distribution or servicing of the contract goods outside the contract territory; or if the dealer is obliged to comply with minimum standards of distribution, sales and after-sales servicing (provided that the contract is for a minimum of five years or, if indefinite, has a minimum notice period of two years).

- However, under the black list, the block exemption will not apply, for example, if both parties are motor vehicle manufacturers; or if the manufacturer or supplier restricts the dealer's freedom to determine prices and discounts of the contract goods; or if the dealer is restricted from obtaining from third parties spare parts which compete with the contract goods and are of matching quality.

(d) **Franchising agreements—Commission Regulation (EEC) 4087/88:**[12] This block exemption applies to agreements under which one party, the franchisor, grants another party, the franchisee, the right to exploit intellectual property rights (such as trademarks, shop signs, copyrights, know-how or patents) for the purposes of marketing specified goods and/or services to end users—ie at retail level. The block exemption applies if either the franchisor grants the franchisee exclusive or sole rights within a defined area of the EU, or the franchisee agrees to be bound by certain specified restrictions on where it may exploit the franchisor on its right to manufacture, sell or supply goods competing with the franchise goods. The block exemption does not, however, apply if the parties are competing producers of goods or providers of services which are the subject matter of the franchise agreement, or if the franchisee is restricted from obtaining the franchise goods from other franchisees.

(e) **Technology transfer agreements (patent licences and know-how licences)—Commission Regulation (EC) 240/96:**[13] This block exemption applies to technology licencing agreements—whether pure patent licences, or pure know-how licences, or mixed patent/know-how licences—made between two parties which include one or more of the following obligations: (i) restrictions on the licensor licensing others in the licensee's territory or exploiting the licensed technology there itself; or (ii) restrictions on the licensee exploiting the licensed technology in the territory of the licensor, and

---

[12] [1988] OJ L359/46.
[13] [1996] OJ L31/2.

on manufacturing and 'actively' selling in other licensees' territories; or (iii) restrictions on 'passive' sales by the licensee in other licensees' territories; or (iv) obligations on the licensee to use only the licensor's trademark or 'get-up' on the licensed product; or (v) quantitative restrictions on the licensee's production and obligations to sell the licensed product only as part of the licensee's own products. The maximum permitted durations of these restrictions are:

- for patent licences: as long as the licensed product is protected by patents in the territory of the party receiving the benefit of the restriction;

- for know-how licences: ten years from the date when one of the licensees first puts the licensed product on any market in the EU (or, in the case of the obligations in (iv) and (v) above, during the lifetime of the agreement for as long as the know-how remains secret and substantial);

- for mixed patents/know-how licences: either ten years from the date when one of the licensees first puts the licensed product on any market in the EU; or, if longer, for the duration of the necessary patents which protect the licensed technology in each territory.

However, as an exception to the above, the maximum period for the obligations in (iii)—ie restrictions on passive sales by the licensee—is five years from the date when one of the licensees first puts the licensed product on any market in the EU.

In addition to these basic requirements, the block exemption Regulation contains a number of conditions designed to ensure that the terms of the licence are not excessively restrictive. It also sets out circumstances in which the European Commission is entitled to withdraw the block exemption from licences which would otherwise satisfy its terms, including in particular where the licensee's market share of the licensed product (and substitutes) exceeds 40 per cent.

(f) **Research and development agreements—Commission Regulation (EEC) 418/85:**[14] This block exemption applies to agreements between undertakings for joint research and development of products or processes or for joint exploitation of the results of research and development jointly carried out by the same undertakings.

- Under the white list, the block exemption extends to obligations not to enter research and development agreements with third parties in the field, or to carry out such research and development independently.

- However, under the black list, the block exemption does not apply where the parties are competing manufacturers and their combined market shares

---

[14] [1985] OJ L53/5; as amended by Commission Regs (EEC) 151/93 [1993] OJ L21/89, and (EC) 2236/97 [1997] OJ L306/12 extending it to 31 Dec 2000.

of the products which the research and development is designed to improve or replace exceeds 20 per cent in the EU or a substantial part of the EU.

The block exemption only applies for a limited period—in most cases, for the duration of the research and development programme and, where there is joint exploitation, for five years from the first marketing of the contract products within the EU.

(g) **Specialisation agreements—Commission Regulation (EEC) 417/85:**[15] This exempts reciprocal agreements between manufacturers under which they agree that they will not themselves *manufacture* certain products, or that they will only *manufacture* certain products jointly. The block exemption only applies where the parties' market shares are small: their combined market share of the products covered by the agreement must not exceed 20 per cent, and their aggregate turnover must not exceed 1,000 million euros.

(h) **Agreements in the insurance sector—Commission Regulation (EEC) 3932/92:**[16] This applies to agreements between undertakings in the insurance sector, and rules of trade associations in the insurance sector, involving the establishment of common risk-premium tariffs, or the establishment of standard policy conditions, or the common coverage of certain types of risk, or the establishment of common rules on the testing and acceptance of security devices. However, the exemption does not apply if, in the case of calculation of risk premiums or policy conditions, the parties agree only to use the standard risk premiums or policy conditions established under their agreement.

(i) **Maritime transport:** Since the 1980s, when the European Commission began applying Article 81 (formerly Article 85) in the maritime transport sector, a series of block exemptions have been issued in respect of specific types of activity in the sector. These include block exemptions for certain types of 'liner conference' (ie the operation of a uniform or common freight rate between vessel-operating carriers of cargo), in Council Regulation (EEC) 4056/86,[17] and of liner consortia (ie technical, operational and commercial agreements between two or more vessel-operating carriers providing international cargo shipping, for example by joint operation of the services, joint marketing, joint use of port terminals, etc), in Commission Regulation (EC) 870/95.[18]

(j) **Air transport:** Since the European Commission began applying Article 81 (formerly Article 85) in the air transport sector, in the late 1980s, there have been a number of block exemptions, covering agreements on such matters as

---

[15] [1985] OJ L53/1; as amended by Commission Regs (EEC) 151/93 [1993] OJ L21/8, and (EC) 2236/97 [1997] OJ L306/12 extending it to 31 Dec 2000.
[16] [1992] OJ L398/7.
[17] [1986] OJ L378/4.
[18] [1985] OJ L89/7.

ground handling services, computer reservations systems, joint planning of capacity, tariff consultation, slot allocation—principally in Commission Regulation (EC) 1617/93,[19] amended by Commission Regulation (EC) 1523/96,[20] and Commission Regulation (EC) 3652/93.[21]

EC Block Exemptions—Vertical Agreements

The first five block exemptions listed above all relate to 'vertical' agreements—ie   **6.13** agreements between parties which are not competitors of each other, but are at different levels in a chain of supply (such as between a manufacturer and a distributor, or between a franchisor and a franchisee, or between a licensor and a licensee). The European Commission has proposed, in its 1998 Communication on Vertical Restraints, that the various block exemptions covering vertical agreements should be replaced by a single block exemption, which would put greater emphasis on the market shares of the parties. In addition, as explained in Chapter 5 above, the government is proposing to introduce a 'special treatment' order under section 50 of the Act granting exclusion to vertical agreements, other than price-fixing agreements or intellectual property licences. If this is done, it will not be necessary to rely on the terms of the EC block exemptions in order for such agreements to escape the application of the Chapter I prohibition.[22]

EC Block Exemptions—No Effect on Trade between Member States

Section 10(2) of the Competition Act states: **6.14**

> An agreement is exempt from the Chapter I prohibition if it does not affect trade between Member States but otherwise falls within a category of agreement which is exempt from the Community prohibition [Article 81 (formerly Article 85)] by virtue of a [block exemption] Regulation.

This provision is necessary to remove an anomaly which might otherwise exist— in the case of agreements which 'do not affect trade between Member States'. The issue is as follows. An agreement which does not affect trade between EU Member States cannot come within the ambit of Article 81 (formerly Article 85) of the EC Treaty, because Article 81 only applies to agreements 'which may affect trade between Member States'. Therefore, if such an agreement cannot come within Article 81, it cannot be exempted under Article 81(3) (formerly Article 85(3)), which entails that it cannot be exempted under an EC block exemption. If the Competition Act had stated that 'parallel exemption' applied only to agreements which actually *are* exempted under an EC block exemption, the consequence

---

[19] [1993] OJ L155/18.

[20] [1996] OJ L190/11.

[21] [1993] OJ L333/37.

[22] However, if the vertical agreements also fall within the ambit of Art 81 EC Treaty, because they may appreciably affect trade between Member States, it will still be necessary to have regard to the terms of the EC block exemptions.

would be that an agreement would benefit from parallel exemption if it did (or may) affect trade between EU Member States—whereas an identical agreement would not benefit from parallel exemption if it did not affect trade between Member States.

6.15 This anomaly would be undesirable, because it would mean that companies would need to work out whether the agreement did affect trade between Member States before they could be sure that they benefited from parallel exemption. Moreover, it would have the perverse consequence that the less economically significant agreements (which are less likely to have an effect on trade between EU Member States) would be the ones which would be denied the benefit of parallel exemption, and subjected to the full rigours of the Chapter I prohibition.

6.16 Section 10(2) removes this anomaly by stipulating that, even if an agreement does not affect trade between Member States (and therefore cannot actually benefit from an EC block exemption), it will nevertheless benefit from parallel exemption if it would '*otherwise*' (ie in all other respects) fall within an EC block exemption.

EC Block Exemptions—Opposition Procedure

6.17 Section 10(1)(c) of the Competition Act extends the scope of parallel exemptions to agreements notified under the 'appropriate opposition or objection procedure'.

6.18 The 'opposition procedure' is used in a number of block exemption regulations, including those for franchising agreements (Regulation 4087/88) and technology transfer agreements (Regulation 240/96). It applies to agreements which fulfil the criteria of the particular block exemption regulation but which, in addition, contain one or more clauses which are restrictive of competition but which are neither specifically permitted in the regulation's 'white list' nor specifically prohibited in its 'black list'; such restrictive clauses are often called 'grey' clauses. Where an agreement contains a 'grey' clause, it will not be *automatically* exempt by virtue of the block exemption. Instead, under the opposition procedure, in order to be exempted the agreement must be notified to the European Commission. However, if the agreement is notified, and if the Commission does not expressly oppose exemption within a period of time specified in the block exemption regulation (normally four or six months), the agreement will then be *deemed* exempt.

6.19 The 'objection procedure' operates in a similar way. There is an objection procedure in, for example, Regulation 4056/86 on maritime transport. This provides that maritime agreements which fall within Article 81 (formerly Article 85) of the EC Treaty, and which are not covered by a block exemption, must be notified to the European Commission, following which the Commission must publish a summary of the notification as soon as possible; if the European Commission does not, within 90 days of publication, inform the applicants that there are serious doubts about the granting of an exemption, the notified agreement will be deemed exempt.

The UK Competition Act makes specific provision, in section 10(1)(c), for agree- **6.20**
ments which have been notified to the European Commission under an opposition or objection procedure. Such notified agreements will benefit from parallel
exemption if:

- the time limit for the European Commission to oppose or object to the agreement has expired, and the European Commission has not opposed or objected
  to it within that time limit; or
- the European Commission has opposed or objected to the agreement, but has
  withdrawn its opposition or objection.

Parallel Exemption—EC Individual Exemptions

Section 10(1)(b) sets out the other main type of parallel exemption. It provides **6.21**
that an agreement is automatically exempt from the Chapter I prohibition *if* it is
exempt from the prohibition in Article 81 (formerly Article 85) EC by virtue of
the European Commission having specifically granted an exemption for that
agreement—that is, if the European Commission has granted an EC **individual
exemption**.

EC individual exemptions are granted by the European Commission to agree- **6.22**
ments which fall within the ambit of Article 81 (formerly Article 85) of the EC
Treaty, but satisfy the criteria for exemption in Article 81(3) (formerly Article
85(3)).[23] In order to obtain an individual exemption from the European
Commission, the parties to the agreement must submit a detailed notification to
the Commission, submitting copies of the agreement and answering the detailed
questions about the agreement, the parties' businesses and the relevant markets
which are set out in the Commission's 'Form A/B'. (If the agreement benefits from
an EC block exemption, there is no need to seek an EC individual exemption.)

The procedures for obtaining an EC individual exemption are laid down in **6.23**
Council Regulation 17/62.[24] There is no time limit within which an agreement
must be notified to the European Commission, but individual exemptions can
only have effect in respect of the period after the date of notification. Individual
exemptions are issued for a specified period, and may be subject to conditions and
obligations. They may be revoked if there is a change in material facts, or if the
parties breach any of the obligations or conditions, or if the exemption was based
on incorrect information or induced by deceit, or where the parties 'abuse' the
exemption.

After an agreement is notified, there is no guaranteed time limit within which the **6.24**
Commission must decide whether or not to grant an individual exemption. The

---

[23] See paras 6.04–6.06 above.
[24] Council Reg (EEC) 17 [1962] OJ Spec Ed 87.

European Commission's heavy case load is such that, in practice, many notified agreements never receive a formal decision; the Commission will either issue an informal 'comfort letter' to the effect that it does not propose to take adverse action in respect of the notified agreement or, very frequently, the Commission will simply refrain from taking any action (and the agreement will expire after a number of years, whereupon the Commission will close its file). Even though notification does not, therefore, guarantee a decision on exemption, it does have the benefit of automatically protecting the parties from European Commission fines for having infringed Article 81 (formerly Article 85) by entering into the agreement (in respect of the period from notification until any decision is issued by the Commission).

6.25 In terms of the Chapter I prohibition, the main advantage of 'parallel exemption' for agreements which benefit from an EC individual exemption, is that the parties are spared the need of having to submit notifications to both the European Commission and the UK authorities. By notifying the European Commission, and obtaining an individual exemption, they are automatically exempt from the Chapter I prohibition, without having to notify separately in the UK. (In addition, under section 40 of the Competition Act, where an agreement is immune from European Commission fines by virtue of having been notified to the Commission, it is also immune from penalties under the Chapter I prohibition.[25]) The OFT takes the view, therefore, that in cases where there is clearly an effect on trade between EU Member States (such that Article 81 (formerly Article 85), as well as the Chapter I prohibition, may apply), 'there are several advantages in notifying agreements to the EC Commission under Article 85 [now Article 81]'; and that notifications to both the Commission and the OFT would be 'undesirable in terms of compliance costs for undertakings and the duplication of effort by competition authorities'.[26]

Duration of Parallel Exemption

6.26 Parallel exemption from the Chapter I prohibition cannot last longer than the EC exemption on which it is based (and may be shorter, if the OFT chooses to cancel the parallel exemption). This applies for EC block exemptions as well as for EC individual exemptions.

6.27 Section 10(4) of the Competition Act states that a parallel exemption takes effect on the date on which the relevant EC exemption takes effect. The parallel exemption ceases to have effect if:

- the EC exemption ceases to have effect; or

---

[25] See Ch 10 below on penalties and immunity from penalties.
[26] OFT, n 3 above, paras 7.1–7.13. See paras 6.39–6.43 below.

- the OFT cancels the parallel exemption; or
- the parallel exemption is deemed to be cancelled, because it was made subject to a condition imposed by the OFT, and that condition has been breached.

Parallel Exemption—OFT Conditions and 'Clawback'

Section 10(5) provides that, even where there is an EC exemption, the OFT may:　**6.28**

- make the parallel exemption in the UK subject to conditions or obligations (which it may add to, vary or remove); or
- cancel (or 'claw back') the parallel exemption in the UK.

The OFT has said that it may impose such conditions or obligations, or 'claw back' the exemption, where the agreement concerned 'has produced, or may produce, significantly adverse effects on a market in the United Kingdom or part of it'.[27]

If the OFT decides to cancel a parallel exemption, or to impose conditions or obligations on it (or add to, vary or remove them), it must first consult each party to the agreement, and also the public. Consultation of the public involves publishing the proposal in the OFT's register of decisions under the Competition Act, and also sending written notice to any interested third parties.[28]

'Section 11 Exemption'

Section 11 of the Competition Act provides for the Secretary of State to make a　**6.29**
regulation automatically exempting agreements from the Chapter I prohibition where they are subject to *national authorities' decisions under EC competition law*. Such a 'section 11 exemption' may be granted by the Secretary of State in respect of agreements which are subject to 'a ruling . . . given by virtue of Article 88 [now Article 84]of the [EC] Treaty on the question whether or not agreements of a particular kind are prohibited by Article 85 [now Article 81]'.

Rulings about whether an agreement is prohibited under Article 81 of the Treaty　**6.30**
may, under Article 84 (formerly Article 88), be made *by Member States* (as opposed to by the European Commission). Article 84 will apply for so long as there is no EC regulation or directive giving effect to Articles 81 and 82 in respect of a particular kind of agreement. Thus, while Council Regulation 17 gives effect to Articles 81 and 82 in respect of most sectors of the economy, and separate regulations for maritime and air transport give effect to Articles 81 and 82 in those sectors, there remain a number of residual sectors, mainly in relation to transport (for example, air transport between the EU and airports in non-Member States, and international maritime tramp vessel services) in respect of which there are no

---

[27] Ibid, para 4.7.
[28] Office of Fair Trading, Formal Consultation Draft, 'Draft Procedural Rules', OFT 411, R21.

EC regulations to give effect to Articles 81 and 82—and therefore Member States may make rulings on the application of Articles 81 and 82, by virtue of Article 84. Where Article 84 applies, it is for the Member State who give their competition authorities the powers to make rulings on Articles 81 and 82; and in 1986, for the first time, the United Kingdom enacted secondary legislation enabling the UK competition authorities to make rulings under Articles 81 and 82 in those areas,[29] including granting Article 81(3) exemptions—powers which have been exercised by the OFT and the Secretary of State in connection with the British Airways/American Airlines transatlantic alliance.[30]

6.31 The effect of section 11 is that, if the UK competition authorities have made a ruling, under Article 84, about whether Article 81 applies to agreements of a particular kind, those agreements may nevertheless be assessed under the Chapter I prohibition. If an Article 81(3) exemption has been granted by the UK authorities under Article 84, there cannot be a parallel exemption from the Chapter I prohibition, since the parallel exemption provisions only apply to Article 81(3) exemptions granted by the European Commission. However, section 11 provides that the UK Secretary of State is entitled to issue a regulation specifically exempting from the Chapter I prohibition agreements of this kind (eg agreements which the UK authorities are exempting under Article 81(3)). This would constitute the granting of a 'section 11 exemption'.

D. UK Block Exemption—Section 6

6.32 Just as there are EC block exemptions which automatically exempt categories of agreement from Article 85, and so likewise the Competition Act provides for UK block exemptions which automatically exempt categories of agreement from the Chapter I prohibition. Section 6 of the Competition Act provides that the Secretary of State may, on the recommendation of the OFT, make any block exemption order to exempt a category of agreement from the Chapter I prohibition. (Of course, where agreements are the subject of an EC block exemption, they will in any case be exempt from the Chapter I prohibition by virtue of parallel exemption.[31] UK block exemptions are therefore likely to be granted in respect of categories of agreement which are not already covered by EC block exemptions.)

---

[29] EC Competition Law (Arts 88 and 89) Enforcement Regulations 1996, SI 1996/2199. Articles 88 and 89 have, as a result of the Treaty of Amsterdam, now been renumbered Articles 84 and 85 respectively.

[30] See advice by the OFT to the Secretary of State, 31 July 1998, published by the Department of Trade and Industry, 6 Aug 1998.

[31] See paras 6.10–6.20 above.

Substance of a UK Block Exemption

An agreement is exempt from the Chapter I prohibition if it falls within a category **6.33** specified in a block exemption order,[32] subject to any condition or obligations imposed by the order.[33]

The block exemption order may provide that: **6.34**

- if an agreement breaches a condition in the order, the agreement automatically loses the benefit of the UK block exemption (this is equivalent to the 'black list' in EC block exemptions);
- if an agreement does not comply with an obligation imposed by the order, the OFT may by written notice deprive it of the benefit of the block exemption;
- the OFT may in specified circumstances withdraw the benefit of the block exemption from a particular agreement;
- if an agreement does not qualify for the block exemption but satisfies specified criteria, it may treated as exempt if it is notified to the OFT and, at the end of a specified period of time following notification, the OFT has not given written notice to the party that it opposes exemption (this is the same as the 'opposition procedure' in EC block exemptions[34]).

The UK block exemption order may provide that the block exemption has retroactive effect—that is, it takes effect from a date earlier than that on the date when the order was made.[35]

The UK block exemption may be time-limited—that is, a block exemption order **6.35** may provide that it is to cease to have effect at the end of a specified period.[36]

Procedure for the Making of a UK Block Exemption

The procedures for the making of UK block exemptions are set out in section 6(1) **6.36** and (2), and section 8, of the Competition Act.

Before the Secretary of State may make a block exemption order, the following **6.37** procedural steps must have occurred:

(i) The OFT must identify a particular category of agreements which are likely, in its opinion, to be agreements which satisfy the criteria for exemption in section 9 (these are the same as the Article 81(3) criteria, and are listed in paragraph 6.06 above).

---

[32] Competition Act 1998, s 6(3).
[33] S 6(5).
[34] S 7. See above, paras 6.17–6.20 for the opposition procedure in EC block exemptions.
[35] S 8(6).
[36] S 6(7).

(ii) The OFT must then publish a proposal that it will recommend to the Secretary of State that this category of agreements should be subject to a UK block exemption, and publication must be in such a way as the OFT thinks most suitable for bringing it to the attention of those likely to be affected.

(iii) The OFT must consider representations made to it.

(iv) The OFT then recommends that the Secretary of State makes a block exemption order in respect of that category of agreement.

Following this procedure, the Secretary of State may make an order giving effect to the OFT's recommendation. The Secretary of State has discretion to make the block exemption order either in the form recommended by the OFT, or subject to such modifications as the Secretary of State considers appropriate; if the latter, the Secretary of State must inform the OFT of the proposed modifications and take into account any comments made by the OFT. The Secretary of State has powers to vary or revoke a block exemption order. The Secretary of State may do so on the recommendation of the OFT (in which case the same procedure must be followed as for the making of a block exemption order), or on the Secretary of State's own initiative (in which case the Secretary of State must first inform the OFT of the proposed variation or revocation and take into account any comments made by the OFT).

E. UK Individual Exemption—Section 4

6.38 In much the same way as an EC individual exemption may be granted by the European Commission in respect of a particular agreement, on notification by the parties, so too a UK individual exemption may be granted by the OFT. Section 4(1) of the Competition Act provides that the OFT 'may grant an exemption from the Chapter I prohibition with respect to a particular agreement'—that is, may grant a UK individual exemption—if:

(a) a party to the agreement has requested an exemption by submitting a 'notification for a decision' to the OFT under section 14;

(b) the agreement satisfies the criteria for exemption in section 9.

Each of (a) and (b) is considered in turn below in, respectively, paragraphs 6.39–6.43 and 6.44–6.58.

Obtaining a UK Individual Exemption by Notification

6.39 Section 4(1) states that the OFT may only grant a UK individual exemption if a request for an exemption has been made by party to the agreement submitting a 'notification for a decision' to the OFT, under section 14. The procedure for submitting notifications is described more fully in Chapter 12 below.

When is it Appropriate to Notify the OFT?

Before submitting a notification to the OFT, parties to an agreement will need to **6.40** consider whether it is necessary to do so. **The following paragraphs summarise the practical circumstances when it will be appropriate to submit a notification to the OFT for a UK individual exemption (and/or to the European Commission for an EC individual exemption); more detailed analysis may be found in Chapter 12 on notifications, paragraphs 12.62–12.89.**

(i) **Where the agreement is covered by an EC block exemption:** Notification to the OFT (or to the European Commission) is unnecessary: the parallel exemption provisions mean that the block exemption protects from the Chapter I prohibition, even if there is no effect on trade between Member States (subject to the relatively small risk of the OFT withdrawing the parallel exemption (see para 6.28)).

(ii) **Where the agreement is excluded by virtue of Schedules 1 to 4 or an exclusion order made under section 50, or is covered by a UK block exemption made under section 6:**[37] There is no need to notify the OFT for an individual exemption; but if there may be an appreciable effect on trade between EU Member States such that Article 81 (formerly Article 85) EC may apply, notification to the European Commission may be advisable.

(iii) **Where the agreement has received an EC individual exemption from the European Commission:** Notification to the OFT is unnecessary, because of the parallel exemption provisions (see (i) above).

(iv) **Where the agreement has received a 'comfort letter' from the European Commission:** Where the European Commission does not issue a formal exemption decision but instead an informal 'comfort letter' stating that the Commission will not take action in respect of the agreement under Article 81 (formerly Article 85), this does not legally work as a parallel exemption— but because the OFT normally 'will not depart from' the European Commission's assessment in the comfort letter, normally no notification to the OFT is necessary. The exceptions to this are where the agreement raises particular concerns about competition in the UK, or where the comfort letter reflects only the fact that the Commission has higher priorities or lacks jurisdiction, rather than a substantive assessment of the agreement's effects on competition.[38]

---

[37] Or the agreement is exempted by virtue of regulations made under s 11, or an order made under s 50 providing for exemption (rather than exclusion) or otherwise providing that prescribed provisions in the Act will not apply. Note, however, that the Act does allow for the possibility of notification to determine whether these exclusions or automatic exemptions apply; ss 13 and 14.

[38] OFT, n 3 above, para 7.12.

(v) **Where the parties have notified the European Commission for an EC individual exemption, but have not yet been granted an EC individual exemption**: The OFT takes the view that it is unnecessary to notify the OFT as well.

(vi) **Where the agreement has not been notified to the European Commission (and is not covered by a block exemption or an exclusion)**: The OFT takes the view that notifications to both the OFT and the European Commission are normally 'undesirable'.[39]

- If the answer is clearly that the agreement *may not* affect trade between EU Member States, notification should be to the OFT and not to the European Commission.

- If the answer is clearly that the agreement *may* affect trade between EU Member States, the OFT sees 'several advantages' in notifying the European Commission rather than the OFT—but notifications to both may be appropriate, for example if the agreement raises particular concerns in connection with UK markets or policy such that the OFT is likely to take an interest even if there is an effect on trade between Member States.[40]

- If the answer is unclear, the parties have the opportunity to consult the OFT's officials 'as to the more appropriate authority to notify'.[41]

Obtaining a UK Individual Exemption from the OFT

6.41 A notification for a decision to the OFT, under section 14 of the Competition Act may—if the OFT considers that the criteria for exemption are satisfied (see paragraphs 6.44–6.58 below)—result in a decision by the OFT to grant a UK individual exemption in respect of that agreement. The OFT must specify the length of time for which the UK individual exemption will have effect,[42] and this period may begin earlier than the date on which the UK individual exemption is granted.[43] This means that the UK individual exemption may have retroactive effect and, unlike an EC individual exemption, this retroactive effect may be to a date earlier than the date of notification. The OFT may make the UK individual exemption subject to conditions or obligations;[44] breach of a condition automatically cancels the exemption, and failure to comply with an obligation entitles the OFT, by written notice, to cancel the exemption or to add to, vary or remove any condition or obligation.[45]

---

[39] OFT, n 3 above, para 7.1.
[40] Ibid, paras 7.4 and 7.10.
[41] Ibid, para 7.6
[42] Competition Act 1998, s 4(3)(b) and (4).
[43] S 4(5). See nn 2 and 3 above.
[44] S 4(3)(a).
[45] S 5(3) and (4).

The UK individual exemption is binding for the duration specified, until and **6.42**
unless:

- the OFT has reasonable grounds for believing that there has been 'a material
  change of circumstance' since it was granted; or

- the OFT has a reasonable suspicion that the information on which it based its
  decision to grant the individual exemption was 'incomplete, false or misleading
  in a material particular'.[46]

In either case, the OFT may, by written notice, cancel the exemption, or add to,
vary or remove any condition or obligation in it. Before doing so, the OFT must
'consult' both the party who received the individual exemption and the public
(the latter involves publication in the OFT's register of decisions and written
notice to interested third parties).[47]

The duration of an individual exemption may be extended on request. The
request must be made by way of a formal application to the OFT, using the 'Form
N'. The application must be submitted between three and 12 months before the
expiry of the individual exemption. Before granting an extension to an individual
exemption, the OFT must consult the public (by publishing a notice in the OFT's
register of decisions and by written notice to interested third parties). The decision on whether or not to grant the extension must be notified in writing to the
applicant and published (on the OFT's register of decisions and through written
notice to interested third parties).[48]

As an alternative to notifying for a decision under section 14, the parties to an **6.43**
agreement may submit a notification for guidance, under section 13. This is likely
to be a quicker procedure. It results in a statement from the OFT on whether or
not the agreement is likely to infringe the Chapter I prohibition and, if it is,
whether it is likely to be exempt from the prohibition. The effect of guidance that
an agreement is likely to be exempt is that the OFT will take no further action
against the agreement under the Chapter I prohibition, until and unless:

(i)   it has reasonable grounds for believing that there has been a material change
      of circumstance since it granted the guidance; or

(ii) it has a reasonable suspicion that the information on which the guidance was
      based was incomplete, false or misleading in a material particular; or

(iii) one of the parties has applied for a decision under section 14; or

(iv) a third party has submitted a complaint to the OFT.[49]

---

[46] S 5(1) and (2).
[47] OFT, n 28 above, R 20.
[48] Competition Act 1998 s 4(6). OFT, n 28 above, R 19.
[49] Ss 13 and 15.

Both an individual exemption decision, and guidance that an agreement is likely to benefit from exemption, have the effect that parties to the agreement are immune[50] from penalties (fines) for infringing the Chapter I prohibition. In addition, there is immunity from penalties in respect of the period from the date of notification until the decision or guidance is issued by the OFT.[51]

Satisfying the Criteria for a UK Individual Exemption

6.44 Section 4(1) provides that the OFT may only grant an exemption from the Chapter I prohibition if the agreement is one satisfying the criteria for exemption in section 9. These criteria, which replicate the criteria for EC exemption in Article 81(3) (formerly Article 85(3)), are that:

(i) the agreement must contribute to improving production or distribution,[52] or promoting technical or economic progress; *and*

(ii) the agreement must allow consumers a fair share of the resulting benefit; *and*

(iii) the restrictions in the agreement must be indispensable to the attainment of those objectives; *and*

(iv) the agreement must not afford the undertakings concerned (ie the parties) the possibility of eliminating competition in respect of a substantial part of the products in question.

All the criteria must be satisfied if the agreement is to be exempted, and the onus for demonstrating that they are satisfied rests with the parties—although OFT staff will discuss with parties any modifications to an agreement which would enable the criteria to be satisfied.[53] Each of the criteria is considered below, in paragraphs 6.48–6.58.

6.45 Because the wording of section 9, in respect of UK exemptions, mirrors the wording of Article 81(3) (formerly Article 85(3)) in respect of EC exemptions, the UK authorities, in applying the criteria, will have to act to ensure that there is no inconsistency with European Court of Justice judgments on Article 85(3) and will have to have regard to European Commission decisions under Article 85(3).[54] Accordingly, past European Court judgments and European Commission decisions on Article 85(3) provide useful guidance on how the UK authorities will apply the section 9 exemption criteria under the Competition Act.

---

[50] This immunity may in certain circumstances be removed—ss 16(4) and 15(4), respectively. See Ch 10, para 10.68 below for details.

[51] Ss 14(4) and 13(4), respectively.

[52] Note that this is the only difference from the Art 81(3) (formerly Art 85(3)) criteria. Art 81(3) refers to improving production or distribution of goods, whereas the less restrictive wording of s 9 is intended to make clear that exemption may be granted for improvements in the provision of services too.

[53] OFT, n 3 above, para 4.10.

[54] By virtue of the requirements in s 60(2) and (3) of the Competition Act. See Ch 3 above.

Before considering the exemption criteria individually, it is worth noting various **6.46** general features of the way the EC authorities have applied Article 81(3) (formerly Article 85(3)).

General Features of Exemption Policy

The underlying purpose behind exemption policy may be discerned when the cri- **6.47** teria are viewed as a whole. In broad terms, **an agreement which would otherwise be prohibited for restricting competition, will be exempted if it brings economic or technical benefits for consumers which *outweigh* the restrictive effects.** The EC authorities have applied this 'balancing test' in numerous cases; and, although these many cases were decided on their own particular merits, and therefore do not yield simple definitive conclusions about exemption policy, a few very general features may be noted:

- Agreements are more likely to be exempted in so far as they are 'upstream' in the value chain—at the level of manufacturing or, even more, at the level of research and development. Agreements which restrict competition at these levels may be exempted where they result in new products or more efficient manufacturing processes.

- Agreements relating to distribution—particularly where they are 'vertical' agreements—may be exempted where they facilitate the entry of new products on to the market, or improve the efficiency of distribution.

- The most seriously anti-competitive infringements are extremely unlikely to benefit for exemption—in particular where competitors reach 'horizontal' agreements (or cartels) to fix prices or to share markets or to engage in joint selling or tendering.

- It is a matter of EU policy that agreements which reinforce barriers to trade between EU Member States (and thus impede the development of the EU as a single market) are particularly offensive—and therefore that horizontal or vertical agreements which contain export bans or give absolute territorial protection from parallel imports, should not normally benefit from exemption. Although this consideration is obviously not so fundamental to national competition policy, it seems likely that the UK's obligations under the EC Treaty to 'abstain from any measure which could jeopardise the attainment of the objectives of the EC Treaty' entail that UK individual exemptions could not be granted in such cases either.[55]

---

[55] But see Ch 7, paras 7.79 to 7.120 on how vertical agreements are likely in practice to be treated. On applying single market objectives in the context of the Chapter I prohibition, the Minister of State, Nigel Griffiths MP, told the House of Commons Standing Committee in June 1998 that 'single market considerations' could play a part and that 'as a general rule, agreements which seek to divide markets along national lines raise serious competition concerns' (Standing Committee G, 18 June 1998, *House of Commons official report*, col 545); see also Ch 3 above.

Contributing to Improving Production or Distribution, or Promoting Technical or Economic Progress

6.48 It will normally be possible to demonstrate that an agreement contributes to improving production if, in the case of a horizontal agreement between producers, it results in a new product which could not have been developed by the parties separately 'as effectively, economically or quickly' as by the parties jointly.[56] Lower costs through longer production runs or more efficient production, and improvements in the quality or range of products or services, are examples of this. Certain vertical agreements may also be shown to contribute to improving production—for example where, by guaranteeing the producer sales revenue, they enable the producer to use its production capacity more efficiently.[57]

6.49 An agreement may contribute to **improving distribution** in a variety of ways. Typically, horizontal co-operation may result in lower costs from longer delivery runs or changes in methods of distribution. An exclusive or long-term vertical supply agreement improves distribution by giving the parties a greater degree of certainty about their revenue streams and, hence, an incentive to concentrate their efforts (in terms of delivery, marketing, promotion and service support) more fully on the contract goods.[58]

6.50 An agreement contributes to **promoting technical progress** not only where it involves co-operation leading to the development of a new and technically-improved product,[59] but also in the context of vertical agreements to license technology which create commercial incentives to disseminate new technology (in the case of the licensor) and to invest in new processes (in the case of the licensee).[60] Environmental benefits have been regarded as significant by the European Commission in this context, and as almost *per se* beneficial to consumers even if they suffer economic loss in the short run, but on the balancing test will not justify exemption if they result from agreements which prevent market entry or involve multilateral price-fixing.[61]

6.51 An agreement will be said to contribute to **promoting economic progress** even if it does not meet any of the three preceding conditions, if it permits the rationali-

---

[56] *GEC/Weir* [1997] OJ L327/26.

[57] *Carlsberg* [1984] OJ L207/26.

[58] These considerations are apparent in the recitals to the exclusive distribution block exemption (Commission Reg (EEC) 1983/83 [1983] OJ L173/1, recital (6)) and the exclusive purchasing block exemption (Commission Reg (EEC) 1984/83 [1983] OJ L173/5, recital (6)).

[59] European Commission, *XXIVth Report on Competition Policy* (EC Commission, Brussels, 1994), point 155.

[60] See the technology transfer block exemption, Commission Reg (EC) 240/96 [1996] OJ L31/2, recital (12).

[61] For more details see European Commission Directorate-General for Competition (DG IV), 'Competition Policy and the Environment—Note by the European Union', May 1995 (DEFFE/CLP(95)31).

sation or restructuring of an industry where it is necessary because of overcapacity—for example, the agreement between Dutch brick producers in the early 1990s aimed at co-ordinating production, reductions and plant closures.[62] Agreements in service sectors (such as transport and financial services) may also secure exemption under this criterion where they result in efficiency improvements which cannot be characterised as enhancing production, distribution or technical progress. Social objectives, such as the safeguarding or promotion of employment, may also fall within this criterion.[63]

The OFT considers that, in the 'balancing test' any alleged benefits must '*be sufficient to outweigh*' an agreement's restrictive effects if it is to merit individual exemption.[64]

Allowing Consumers a Fair Share of the Resulting Benefit

The mere fact that an agreement contributes to improvements in production or distribution, or technical or economic progress, does not entitle the agreement to exemption *unless* it allows consumers a fair share of the resulting benefit. Thus, for example, if an agreement results in efficiency gains, but the producers pocket the profits of these efficiency gains for themselves, without passing them on to the consumer, there can be no exemption. In a recent series of European Commission cases about exclusive purchasing agreements in the ice cream industry which had the effect of denying a new entrant (Mars ice cream) access to many retail outlets, the Commission held that any benefits resulting from the exclusivity would be denied to consumers who needed to have a choice of ice cream brands in each separate retail outlet (they were unlikely to shop around from one outlet to another).[65] Nevertheless, once parties to an agreement can show that there is a benefit (in production, distribution, technical or economic terms), it is usually possible to demonstrate that consumers will receive a fair share. Evidence that there is sufficient competition in the market to prevent the producers from pocketing the efficiency profits for themselves is often sufficient. But even where consumers suffer a short-term detriment as a result of diminishing competition, exemption may be granted if it can be shown that in the long-term consumers will benefit (for example, where industries are saved by being restructured; this, again, was the case in the recent restructuring of the Dutch brick industry[66]).

6.52

---

[62] *Stichting Baksteen* [1994] OJ L131/15.

[63] See, eg, Case 26/76 *Metro v Commission I* [1977] ECR 1875, para 29. See also the discussion in Whish, R., 'Exemption Criteria under Art 85(3) EC', a study prepared in 1998 for the government in the context of the (then) Competition Bill, para 6.1.

[64] OFT, n 3 above, para 4.10.

[65] *Langnese-Iglo* [1983] OJ L183/19 and *Schöller Lebensmittel* [1993] OJ L183/1.

[66] *Stichting Baksteen* [1994] OJ L131/15.

6.53 Finally, it should be noted that both the European Commission and the OFT take the view that 'consumers' for this purpose does not merely refer to end-users, but may include industrial customers of the parties.[67]

Restrictions Indispensable to the Attainment of those Objectives

6.54 The stipulation in section 9(b)(i) that exemption will only be granted if the agreement

> does not impose on the undertakings concerned restrictions which are not indispensable to the attainment of those objectives

is the key element of the 'balancing test' involved in assessing whether exemption should be granted. Once economic benefits for the consumer have been identified, these will only be regarded as outweighing—and hence justifying—the restrictive effects of the agreement *to the extent that those restrictive effects are indispensable or necessary to attaining the benefits*. If the restrictions go beyond what is necessary for attaining those objectives (ie if, in the balance, they start to outweigh the benefits, exemption ceases to be justified).

6.55 There are no hard-and-fast rules for determining which restrictions are, and which are not, 'indispensable' for these purposes. The general principle is that the parties to the agreement should adopt the least restrictive solution consistent with achieving the aims of the agreement in question. Thus, in the context of the equivalent provision in Article 81(3) (formerly Article 85(3)) of the EC Treaty, a joint venture between Dutch fertiliser suppliers for the joint selling of nitrogen fertiliser was not indispensable, and thus not exempted, because the parties were able to sell the products individually 'without being placed at a competitive disadvantage'.[68] By contrast, where it was *only* feasible to develop a high-technology product (coolants for nuclear reactors) through a joint venture (JV) between competitors involving joint development, production and selling, and 'a more independent and looser form of co-operation' such as 'cross-licensing of know-how or a specialisation agreement' would have been inadequate, the JV was exempted.[69]

6.56 The European Commission has taken the view that:

- In horizontal co-operation agreements, such as joint ventures, once the co-operation agreement itself has been shown to be beneficial, additional restrictions are acceptable in so far as 'they cannot be dissociated from it without jeopardising its existence', provided that their 'duration, subject matter and geographical field of application do not exceed what the creation and operation of the JV [or co-operation] normally requires'. By contrast, restrictions going

---

[67] *Rockwell/Iveco* [1983] OJ L224/19, where the parties supplied axles to motor vehicle manufacturers.

[68] *CSV (Centraal Stikstof Verkoopkantoor)* [1976] OJ L192/27, para I.

[69] *GEC/Weir* [1977] OJ L327/26.

beyond the object of the co-operation—including restrictions relating to quantities, prices or customers, and export bans—will not normally be regarded as indispensable.[70]

• In vertically restrictive agreements (such as exclusive distribution, exclusive purchasing, franchising, long-term supply, etc.), restrictions will generally be regarded as indispensable to the extent that they are necessary to protect either party's investment in the arrangement, and this may include limited territorial protection. However, restrictions are not generally indispensable if they limit a reseller's choice of customers or freedom to determine prices and conditions of sale, or if they lead to absolute territorial protection and impediments to parallel imports. The duration of the restrictions, moreover, should not go beyond what is necessary to achieving the benefits. An indication of the kinds of restrictions which generally will and will not be regarded as indispensable may be obtained by examining, respectively, the white lists and the black lists of the five main EC block exemptions on vertical agreements (see paragraph 6.12 above, (a) to (e)).

Not Affording the Parties the Possibility of Substantially Eliminating Competition

The fourth and final criterion for exemption is intended to ensure that no agreement should be exempted, however beneficial, if it substantially eliminates competition.[71] The European Commission has regarded this as being the case where a joint venture created barriers to entry so protecting a virtual monopoly in one national market,[72] and where an exclusive purchasing agreement created barriers to entry protecting a virtual duopoly.[73] The OFT takes the view that the parties must be able to show that there will continue to be effective competition in the market or markets for the goods or services with which the agreement is concerned.[74] **6.57**

Nevertheless, this criterion will only fail to be satisfied if the agreement affords the parties 'the possibility of *eliminating* competition in respect of a *substantial* part of the products in question'. In recent years, two co-operative joint venture agreements have been exempted even though, in each case, competition was removed between parties who together held market shares above 50 per cent.[75] **6.58**

---

[70] Commission Notice concerning the assessment of joint ventures [1993] OJ C43/2, paras 65, 66, 71 and 75.

[71] See, eg, recitals to the exclusive distribution block exemption (Commission Regulation (EEC) 1983/83 [1983] OJ L173/1, recitals (8) and (11)), the exclusive purchasing block exemption (Commission Reg (EEC) 1984/83 [1983] OJ L173/5, recitals (8) and (11)), the franchising block exemption (Commission Reg (EEC) 4087/88 [1988] OJ L359/46, recitals (9) and (10)) and the technology transfer block exemption (Commission Reg (EC) 240/96 [1996] OJ L31/2, recitals (16) and (17)).

[72] *WANO Schwarzpulver* [1978] OJ L322/26.

[73] *Langnese-Iglo* [1983] OJ L183/19 and *Schöller Lebensmittel* [1993] OJ L183/1.

[74] OFT, n 3 above, para 4.16.

[75] *Philips/Osram* [1994] OJ L378/37, where there was plenty of potential competition inside and outside the EU to constrain market power, and *Asahi/St Gobain* [1994] OJ L354/87.

F. Exemptions and the Chapter II Prohibition

6.59 As explained in this chapter, the Competition Act offers the possibility of exemption from the Chapter I prohibition. There is no equivalent possibility of exemption from the Chapter II prohibition. Similarly, under the EC Treaty, there is the possibility of exemption from the prohibition in Article 81 (formerly Article 85), but not from that in Article 82 (formerly Article 86).

6.60 What is less clear, however, is whether the same agreement or arrangement which is exempted from Chapter I prohibition may still be prohibited under the Chapter II prohibition. The government has said that the two prohibitions 'essentially . . . will have the same relationships to each other as do Articles 85 and 86 [now Articles 81 and 82]'.[76] This issue was considered by the European Court of First Instance in the *Tetra Pak I* case.[77] In that case, Tetra Pak, which had a dominant market position in milk packaging machines, acquired (as a result of purchasing a company) an exclusive licence to a patented process which was a potential competitor of its own packaging process. Because Tetra Pak already had a dominant position, and by virtue of acquiring the exclusive licence was enabled to impede the emergence of a competing process, this would normally have been a clear case of an abuse of a dominant position, in breach of Article 82 (and, similarly, would have infringed the Chapter II prohibition). However, Tetra Pak's enjoyment of the exclusive patent licence satisfied the criteria for benefiting from the EC block exemption for exclusive patent licences (the predecessor to the current technology transfer block exemption). The question therefore was: why should Tetra Pak's acquisition of the exclusive licence be prohibited, under Article 82, when it had been expressly authorised under the block exemption? The European Commission took the view that, in spite of the block exemption, Tetra Pak would have to renounce the exclusivity, and the Court of First Instance upheld this view:

- The Court of First Instance stated that, if an agreement benefits from a *block* exemption, it may nevertheless be prohibited as an abuse of a dominant position.

- However, the Court of First Instance also indicated that, if the agreement had received an *individual* exemption, the agreement could not then be regarded as an abuse of a dominant position. Nevertheless, the UK Government says that the OFT cannot grant an individual exemption if, in doing so, it 'would be exempting something that appears to be prohibited under the Chapter II prohibition'.[78]

---

[76] Lord Simon of Highbury, Minister at the Department of Trade and Industry, *Hansard* (HL), vol 585, no 99, col 956 (9 Feb 1998).
[77] Case T–51/89, *Tetra Pak Rausing SA v Commission* [1990] II ECR 309.
[78] Lord Simon of Highbury, n 76 above.

The OFT has endorsed this view; agreements benefitting from a (UK or EC) block exemption can be an abuse under the Chapter II prohibition; but those benefitting from a UK individual exemption, or a parallel exemption resulting from an EC individual exemption, cannot be examined under the Chapter I prohibition.[79]

---

[79] Office of Fair Trading, 'Competition Act 1998: The Chapter II prohibition (OFT 402), para 2.7.

7

COMMERCIAL AGREEMENTS SUBJECT TO THE CHAPTER I PROHIBITION

A. Overview

The purpose of this chapter is to identify typical commercial agreements and arrange-   **7.01**
ments where, in practice, the Chapter I prohibition is likely to be an issue. The chapter examines, in turn, various commercial situations, and gives guidance on the likely
application of the Chapter I prohibition to each of these. Because the Chapter I prohibition is to be applied having regard to the principles by which Article 81 (formerly
Article 85) of the EC Treaty has been applied,[1] EC case law (in the form of European
Court of Justice judgments and European Commission decisions) is cited.

The commercial agreements and arrangements that are considered below are   **7.02**
listed in the table of contents at the top of this chapter. Any single agreement may
contain more than one of these types of arrangement and, where this is the case,
the various different arrangements will need to be considered together, rather than
in isolation.

Under section 50 of the Competition Act, the government may by order grant   **7.03**
'special treatment' to 'vertical' agreements, protecting them wholly or partly from
the Chapter I prohibition. Pursuant to this power, the government has proposed
the issue of a section 50 order which will grant automatic exclusion from the
Chapter I prohibition to all 'vertical' agreements other than resale price maintenance and intellectual property licences—but subject to the possibility of the
OFT 'clawing back' the exclusion from particular agreements. The types of
arrangement identified in (L) to (Q) of the table of contents above are likely to
benefit from the exclusion.

It is important to bear in mind that, while this chapter seeks to assist in identify-   **7.04**
ing likely areas of concern, in cases where these do arise it will be prudent to seek
professional legal advice.

B. Price-Fixing between Competitors

Arrangements which involve competitors agreeing on, or co-ordinating, the   **7.05**
prices which they will charge are among the most serious infringements. They will
attract the highest penalties (fines); and agreements which contain them will not
benefit from exemption.

One of the 'Most Serious Infringements'

In the context of Article 81 (formerly Article 85) of the EC Treaty, the European   **7.06**
Commission's 1998 guidelines on fines put price cartels in the category of 'very

---

[1] Competition Act, 1998 s 60. As a result of the Treaty of Amsterdam, which amended the EC
Treaty with effect from 1 May 1999, Article 85 of the EC Treaty is now renumbered Article 81.

serious infringements', which would attract the highest levels of fines.[2] Certainly, the European Commission has in recent years imposed extremely high fines (of millions of ECU (now euros) on each undertaking) in cases of participation in price cartels or other price-fixing arrangements between competitors—most notably, during the 1990s, in the *Steel Beams*,[3] *Cartonboard*[4] and *Cement*[5] cases (although all three cases have been the subject of appeals to the European Court). An indication of the seriousness with which price-fixing is regarded relative to other infringements is provided by the Commission decision in the *SCK and FNK* case,[6] where a trade association was found to have infringed Article 81 (formerly Article 85) through price-fixing by its members, and a requirement that its members must not hire from non-affiliated suppliers: the fine for price-fixing was 11.5 million ECU, whereas the fine for the other infringement was just 300,000 ECU.

Different Types of 'Agreement'

7.07 Price-fixing will be severely condemned whatever form the 'agreement' or arrangement takes. Formal, organised price cartels will constitute serious infringements, as will less systematic contracts or written or oral arrangements between two or more suppliers. In addition, mere recommendations as to the prices to be set (for example, by a trade association) will be regarded as serious violations, as was the case under Article 81 (formerly Article 85) when a Netherlands trade association of freight forwarders circulated recommended tariff increases to its members.[7] So, too, will concerted practices between competitors, where these can be established (that is, where there is evidence that, without fully agreeing on prices, competitors have knowingly co-ordinated prices or price movements—see above, Chapter 4, paragraphs 4.18–4.22).

Different Types of 'Price-fixing'

7.08 Price-fixing arrangements will be a serious violation regardless of whether the prices are agreed in respect of supplies to all customers, or to a particular market or market segment (such as London, rather than the whole of the UK), or even to a specific customer.

7.09 An arrangement will be regarded as price-fixing whether it involves agreeing not to supply the product below a certain price,[8] or whether it involves more indirect

---

[2] Commission Guidelines on the method of setting fines imposed pursuant to Art 15(2) of Reg 17 and Art 65(5) of the ECSC Treaty, [1998] OJ C9/3. Fines exceeding 20 million ECU (now euros) are regarded as likely for undertakings who participate in such infringements.

[3] [1994] OJ L116/1. This case was not under Art 81 (formerly Art 85) EC, but under the equivalent provision of the ECSC Treaty.

[4] [1994] OJ L243/1.

[5] [1994] OJ L343/1.

[6] [1996] OJ L312/79.

[7] *Fenex* [1996] OJ L181/28.

[8] *Welded Steel Mesh* [1989] OJ L260/1.

arrangements to manipulate or stabilise prices. Ensuring that price increases are co-ordinated (ie move simultaneously at regular intervals) is also regarded as price-fixing.[9]

It is no defence that prices were previously, or to a lesser extent, fixed by the State **7.10**
or by national or international law. If there is any element of *voluntary* price-fixing on the part of the undertakings themselves, that will constitute an infringement.[10]

An agreement between *purchasers* to fix the prices at which they buy goods may also **7.11**
be regarded as infringing the Chapter I prohibition. When the users of industrial timber in Belgium agreed between themselves that they would not buy timber above a fixed maximum price, the European Commission required the agreement to be abandoned as an infringement of Article 81 (formerly Article 85).[11]

C. Market Sharing

Market sharing agreements and arrangements involve undertakings allocating **7.12**
amongst themselves geographical territories, product sectors or classes of customer—and agreeing to refrain from competing on each other's allocated 'patch'. The effect is seriously restrictive of competition, because whereas in the absence of the agreement the parties would be competing against each other in each market, the agreement entails that each one will, in its allocated patch, enjoy a monopoly or at least be protected from full competition.

Market-sharing is, along with price-fixing, categorised by the Commission as **7.13**
among the 'most serious infringements',[12] and attracts the highest fines. Thus, in 1991, the Commission imposed fines of 7 million ECU each (at that time, an unprecedentedly high fine for a breach of Article 81 (formerly Article 85)) on the chemical companies ICI and Solvay, in respect of an agreement between them that Solvay would confine its soda ash activities to Europe and ICI would confine its soda ash activities to other territories—the *Soda Ash* case.[13] Similarly, the high fines imposed in the *Cement* case[14] reflected the Commission's view that there had been

---

[9] *Cartonboard* [1994] OJ L243/1.
[10] Cases T–39 and 40/92 *CB and Europay v Commission* [1994] II ECR 49. See also *Steel Beams* [1994] OJ L116/1.
[11] *Belgian Industrial Timber*, European Commission, *Vth Report on Competition Policy* (EC Commission, Brussels, 1975), point 36. See also Office of Fair Trading, 'Competition Act 1998: The Chapter I Prohibition', (OFT 401), para 3.15.
[12] See Commission Guidelines, n 2 above.
[13] *Soda Ash–Solvay/ICI* [1991] OJ L152/1. The CFI subsequently annulled the Commission's decision, but purely on procedural grounds (Case T–30/91 *Solvay v Commission* [1995] II ECR 1775 and Case T–36/91 *ICI v Commission* [1995] II ECR 1847).
[14] See n 5 above.

market-sharing as well as price-fixing, with the European Cement Association (CEMBUREAU) seeking to maintain a 'home market rule' among its members.

7.14 As with price-fixing, market-sharing arrangements will be condemned whether they are by way of a formal cartel, or a contract between parties, or a non-binding written or oral agreement, or even a tacit understanding. The *Soda Ash* case is an example of market-sharing by tacit understanding; prior to 1962, Solvay and ICI had operated a formal written agreement not to compete in soda ash supplies in each other's territory—but in subsequent years the parties, having formally terminated the agreement, nevertheless continued in practice to maintain their rigid market separation; the practical continuance of the arrangement after 1962, even in the absence of any written agreement, was held nevertheless to infringe Article 81 (formerly Article 85).

7.15 Occasionally, however, the sharing of product markets (eg where parties agree to specialise in the manufacture of certain products in a range, or certain components in a product) may merit exemption if it enables longer production runs and greater efficiency.[15]

7.16 Sharing of sources of supply—that is, where undertakings agree not to compete against each other in the purchase of raw materials or other inputs (for example, not competing for rights to exploit an oil field or mining areas)—will be treated similarly to market-sharing.

7.17 One potential difference between the application of Article 81 and that of the new Chapter I prohibition may arise in this context. EC competition law is aimed not only at the protection of competition, but also at the creation of an integrated single or common market throughout the territory of the European Union. Market-sharing arrangements which impede the development of an integrated single market—by allocating markets geographically on the basis of national boundaries—are therefore viewed with particular severity under Article 81. Naturally, UK competition law is less concerned with this objective of EU integration, and is therefore unlikely to have the same emphasis (ie treating geographical market-sharing by national boundary so severely). Nevertheless, the government has indicated that, in its view, 'as a general rule, agreements which seek to divide markets along national lines raise serious competition concerns'.[16] Moreover, it is incumbent on the United Kingdom, as on any other Member State, to abstain from any measures which could jeopardise the attainment of the objectives of the EC Treaty and, since those objectives include the completion of the single or common market, it will not

---

[15] OFT, n 11 above para 3.11.
[16] Nigel Griffiths, Minister for Competition and Consumer Affairs in Standing Committee G, Parliamentary Debates of the House of Commons Official Report Standing Committee, 18 June 1998, col 545.

be open to the UK competition authorities actually to condone or authorise agreements which have the effect of partitioning the EU as between Member States (although such agreements are, in any case, likely to be examined under Article 81 as well as under the Chapter I prohibition).

D. Agreements between Competitors to Limit Production ('Quota Fixing')

It is restrictive of competition for competitors to agree between themselves that they **7.18** will each limit their production output, or even their production capacity (for example, by closing down factories or production lines). Such an arrangement, often called 'quota-fixing' (because the parties agree not to exceed an allotted quota of production or capacity), ensures that the overall level of supply in the market is controlled and that there are no surpluses or gluts, with the effect that, on ordinary principles of supply-and-demand, prices in the market are higher than they would otherwise be. This restrictive effect on competition can be reinforced if there is a formalised arrangement by which the parties agree that, if they exceed their quota, they will pay a penalty, and that the amount paid in penalties is shared out among those who fail to reach their quotas; this negates the commercial incentive to increase output or sales and, therefore, the incentive to compete.[17]

It is not an infringement at all for an undertaking to take a genuinely *independent* **7.19** decision to cut its production or capacity, based on its own forecast of the demand. Reducing production or capacity only constitutes an infringement if it results from an agreement or concerted practice between two or more undertakings.

'Crisis cartels' and 'restructuring agreements': There are certain limited circum- **7.20** stances in which it may be possible to obtain an exemption for agreements to limit production or capacity. These arise where economic conditions are such that there is excess capacity throughout an industry, such that it is unprofitable to retain existing capacity levels and, unless capacity is reduced in a planned or co-ordinated way, there are likely to be insolvencies, unemployment and severe damage to the industry (with a danger that the industry might not exist once the economic crisis has past). Production or capacity limitation agreements made in such circumstances—often called 'crisis cartels' or 'restructuring agreements'—would only receive exemption if it could be shown that consumers will benefit in the long term from the co-ordinated reductions (because the industry, or individual companies, will thereby be enabled to survive, preserving a competitive choice for

---

[17] Such a penalty system operated in the roofing felt cartel: Case 246/86 *Belasco v Commission* [1989] ECR 2117.

Ò

consumers), and that the limitations in the agreements go no further than is indispensable to achieving these objectives. Exemptions would normally be granted only for a limited period—ie until the economic recession passes. In 1994, the European Commission granted an exemption for five years to an agreement between sixteen major brick manufacturers in the Netherlands, under which they co-ordinated plant closures and formed a common fund to compensate for the cost of closures, with a view to resolving an overcapacity crisis in the Dutch brick industry; the exemption was granted on the condition that parties must not divulge to each other data in respect of their individual outputs and deliveries, and that they should not set quotas on production.[18]

7.21 It should be emphasised that the circumstances when crisis cartels and restructuring agreements are deemed to merit exemption will be rare. The OFT has noted that 'customers are most unlikely to see any benefits from this type of agreement'.[19]

E. Information Exchange

7.22 The exchange or passing of business information between competitors can be, but is not always, an anti-competitive agreement infringing the Chapter I prohibition.

7.23 The concern about an exchange of business information is that it 'blunts' competition on a market in that, by making businesses aware of the commercial conditions faced by their competitors, it makes the behaviour of their competitors on the market more predictable, and thereby facilitates the co-ordination of commercial behaviour between competitors. Consequently, an information exchange can achieve the effect of price-fixing or quota-fixing between competing undertakings, even without there actually being an agreement on prices or production limits. Thus, for example, an exchange of price information between competitors can lead to identical prices, and an exchange of information between competitors about their future production plans (such as whether to close production facilities or invest in new capacity) can lead to the co-ordination of output.

7.24 The crucial issue, therefore, is the extent to which an exchange of business information replaces the inherent uncertainties of market competition with predictability enabling co-ordination between competitors. The European Commission has condemned information exchanges where they have:

> replaced the normal risks of competition by practical co-operation, resulting in conditions of competition differing from those obtaining in a normal market situation . . . [and establishing] . . . a system of solidarity and mutual influence designed to co-ordinate business activities.[20]

---

[18] *Stichting Baksteen* [1994] OJ L131/15.
[19] OFT, n 11 above, para 5.11.
[20] *COBELPA/VNP* [1977] OJ C242/10.

In practice, this means that information exchanges are more likely to be regarded as infringing the prohibition if the following conditions are met:

(i)   the information exchanged is confidential to an individual business (allowing that business's commercial conduct to be predictable);

(ii)   the information exchanged is shared only among the parties to the agreement, rather than being placed in the public domain;

(iii) the parties to the exchange of information represent a significant proportion of the market (so that the information exchange is significantly affecting competition on the market);

(iv)   competition is already muted on the market; and

(v)   the information exchange is not purely in the interests of consumers.

Each of these conditions is considered in the following paragraphs.

Information which is Confidential to the Business

The types of business information whose exchange raises concerns are those   **7.25**
which enable a business's commercial behaviour to be better understood by its competitors, and hence better predicted—for example, as to prices and discounts, quantities of goods produced and sold, plans to increase or reduce production or capacity, market shares, and so on. In broad terms, they are the classes of information which an undertaking would normally regard as a business secret or as commercially sensitive. An exchange of *price* information is viewed with particular disfavour—including information on prices charged or on the elements of a pricing policy (such as discounts, costs, terms of trade, and rates and dates of price changes).[21] The exchange of *non-price* information is generally less problematic—an exchange of information on output and sales, in the view of the OFT, 'should not affect competition provided that it is sufficiently historic and cannot influence future competitive market behaviour',[22] or if it is market research or general industry studies relating to 'opinion and experience' in the sector.[23]

The exchange of these kinds of information will generally be condemned in so far   **7.26**
as it is information about an *individual* undertaking. By contrast, the dissemination of *aggregated* statistical material through a central body, such as a national trade association or government agency—allowing each individual undertaking to compare its own figures with the total industry figures, but not to see how individual competitors are performing—will generally be permitted.[24] However, the

---

[21] OFT, n 11 above, para 3.21.
[22] Ibid, para 3.24.
[23] Ibid, para 3.23.
[24] *European Wastepaper Information Service*, European Commission, *XVIIIth Report on Competition Policy* (EC Commission, Brussels, 1998), point 63.

mere fact that information is aggregated is not a defence if there are only a few undertakings participating in the aggregation, so that in practice it is easy to identify the individual market information of each participant; for example, where a French statistical body published sales and production figures of only three producers, it was easy for each one to deduce the market share of the other two, and therefore for all three to co-ordinate their competitive behaviour.[25] As a broad rule of thumb, at least four different undertakings should be involved in any aggregation of statistical information in order to avoid the risk that participants would be able to identify each other's individual market information.

7.27 Finally, the exchange of out-of-date or 'historic' market information—even where the information is of the kind which normally causes concerns—is less likely to be prohibited, because it ceases to be a relevant or useful guide to predicting an undertaking's future commercial behaviour. Sales figures which were one year old have been regarded as historic, and their exchange therefore is not a cause for concern.[26]

Not Placed in the Public Domain

7.28 The OFT takes the view that the exchange of information is more likely to be regarded as restrictive of competition if it is limited to the participants, rather than being put into the public domain.[27]

A Significant Proportion of the Market

7.29 The exchange of information between competitors, facilitating co-ordination of their competitive behaviour, will only appreciably restrict competition in the market to the extent that the participating undertakings represent a significant segment or proportion of the market. In the most serious recent case of information exchange under Article 81—between major suppliers of tractors in the UK—the participating undertakings represented 88 per cent of the UK tractor market.[28]

Muted Competition on the Market

7.30 An information exchange is more likely to have an appreciable effect on competition in the market if competition is already muted on that market. The OFT takes the view that the effect is more likely to be appreciable 'the smaller the number of undertakings operating in the market'.[29]

---

[25] *Peroxygen Products* [1985] OJ L35/1.
[26] *UK Agricultural Tractor Registration Exchange* [1992] OJ L68/19 (at 29). See also OFT, n 11 above, paras 3.22 and 3.24.
[27] Ibid.
[28] Ibid.
[29] OFT, n 11 above, para 3.19.

Thus, exchange of information has not been regarded as restrictive of competition **7.31** where the participants face strong competition from others on the market, or where barriers to entry are low. In one case, the European Commission has held that even the exchange of information on sales volumes and market shares, relating to individual undertakings and confidential to those undertakings, was acceptable because the market was not oligopolistic.[30]

Benefits to Consumers

If the information exchange can be shown to be purely for the benefit of con- **7.32** sumers, there is a prospect of its being held to be outside the prohibition, or at least exempted. An example would be where the information being exchanged is to enable co-ordination of a manufacturing standard so as to allow inter-compatibility—particularly, for instance, in the case of technological products such as computer hardware and software[31] or video and audio products, or in the context of setting industry standards in financial services such as insurance.

F. Trade Associations and Standards Bodies

Almost by definition, the operation of trade associations and standards bodies **7.33** raises issues under the Chapter I prohibition (and under Article 81 (formerly Article 85) EC), because they are organisations in which competitors co-operate with each other. Indeed, as noted in Chapter 4 above, 'decisions by associations of undertakings' (whether rules or non-binding recommendations) are specifically covered by the prohibition, no less than agreements *between* undertakings—with the consequence that an 'association of undertakings, no less than an individual undertaking, can itself be liable for infringements (including the possibility of penalties being imposed).

Nevertheless, trade associations and standards bodies are not in themselves pro- **7.34** hibited. They are not *necessarily* restrictive of competition; the co-operation can be used simply to promote the common interests of the industry concerned to the government and the general public, to enhance quality or service standards to the benefit of consumers, and/or to provide useful advice and services to members of the industry. Indeed, the OFT has specifically recognised that trade associations are 'clearly useful to members' and that they may also be 'beneficial in increasing the efficiency of the market system'.[32] But because they are *potentially* restrictive of competition, they are viewed with suspicion by competition authorities, and the

---

[30] *Eudim* [1996] OJ C111/8.
[31] *X Open Group* [1987] OJ L35/6.
[32] Office of Fair Trading, 'Competition Act 1998: Trade Associations, Professions and Self-Regulating Bodies', (OFT 408), para 5.2.

nature and extent of co-operation is closely circumscribed, such that it must not become restrictive of competition.

Admission to Membership

7.35   Competition law is concerned to ensure that a trade association, which (like any club) grants membership to some and denies it to others, does not thereby operate as a disguised way of granting competitive privileges to certain players in the market, while excluding others, such as small competitors and new entrants.

7.36   While a trade association is not obliged to admit to membership every applicant, its criteria for granting membership must be objective and qualitative (for example, based on technical standards which are relevant to the reputation of the industry).[33] In one case under Article 81 (formerly Article 85), a Netherlands trade association of dealers in bicycles made it a criterion of membership that the members should have certain levels of stock and operate from certain types of premises; these were held to be unnecessary criteria which merely excluded smaller competitors, and had the effect of restricting competition.[34]

7.37   In addition, membership criteria need to be applied in an open and non-discriminatory way. Membership rules are more likely to be acceptable if any refusal of a membership application is supported by reasons and can be challenged in an appeals procedure.[35]

Trade Association Activities

7.38   It is, of course, strictly prohibited for a trade association to be used as a forum for reaching agreement or exchanging commercially sensitive information on, for example, prices, market opportunities, production and sales. This applies as much to informal discussions in the 'margins' of trade association meetings, as well as to the formal sessions.

7.39   The trade association itself may issue rules, requirements or non-binding recommendations (such as codes of conduct) on how its members should act. These will be treated either as 'decisions by associations of undertakings' or as 'agreements' between the members to abide by the rules, requirements or recommendations;[35a] as such, they are capable of infringing the Chapter I prohibition. However, they will only actually infringe the prohibition if they restrict competition, for example by requiring or recommending that members should not undercut each other on price or 'poach' each other's customers;[36] rules and recommendations which are

---

[33]   *Retel 1988* [1991] OJ C121/2.
[34]   *Centraal Bureau voor de Rijwielhandel* [1978] OJ L20/18.
[35]   *London Sugar Futures Market* [1985] OJ L369/25.
[35a] OFT, n[32] above, para 2.1.
[36]   *IFTRA Rules* [1975] OJ L228/3; *Glass Containers* [1974] L160/1.

simply designed to raise performance standards or protect consumers, and have no anti-competitive effect, will not themselves be problematic.

Standards Bodies: Technical Standards and Quality Marks

Care must be taken that the setting of industry-wide technical standards, often **7.40** supported by a certification such as a 'quality mark' is not restrictive of competition. In most cases, co-operation in these respects will be acceptable—provided that:

(i)   the parties are free, if they so choose, to make or market products which do not conform to the agreed standards (although obviously on the understanding that any non-conforming products will not be entitled to the 'quality mark');[37]

(ii) the standards are not used to blunt competition by impeding the manufacture of differentiated products (where there is no objective qualitative reason for opposing the differentiation) or by imposing standard pricing;

(iii) the standards (and, where applicable, the criteria for the quality mark) can be objectively justified—for example, as necessary for consumer safety, environmental protection, and so on; and

(iv) any accreditation (by quality mark, etc) is granted in a non-discriminatory way, rather than with a view to excluding certain actual or potential competitors (eg foreign competitors).[38]

The OFT has said that where accreditation is 'available to all manufacturers that meet objective quality requirements, a scheme is less likely to breach the Chapter I prohibition'.[39]

Standard Terms and Conditions

Adoption of standardised terms and conditions will normally be permitted— **7.41** provided that (i) the participants remain free to use their own terms and conditions or to modify the recommended terms, and (ii) the terms do not contain provisions relating to prices, rebates or conditions of sale.[40]

---

[37] See *APB* [1990] OJ L18/35, where a pharmaceutical standards body was allowed to insist that products would only bear the quality mark if sold through pharmacies rather than other retail outlets, but not that they should only be sold through pharmacies.

[38] *Central Heating* [1972] JO L264/22, where a Belgian quality mark system in which non-Belgian equipment did not receive accreditation, was prohibited.

[39] OFT, n [32] above, para 3.20.

[40] Commission Notice on agreements, decisions and concerted practices in the field of co-operation between enterprises [1968] JO C75/3.

Exchange of Information

7.42 Trade associations may also organise the exchange of information among their members. This issue is addressed in paragraphs 7.22–7.32 above.

G. Collusive Tendering and Joint Bidding

7.43 Large organisations which wish to procure major equipment or works—for example, an airline wishing to purchase an aircraft, or a government or local authority wishing to have a road built—will often issue an invitation to companies to tender proposals for supplying the equipment or works before giving the contract to one of the businesses. Competing companies will then normally submit tenders, each one setting out the price at which it will supply the equipment or do the work, as well as other details (such as quality specifications, times for delivery or completion, and so on). The purpose of such competitive tendering is, of course, that the procuring organisation should enjoy the benefits of competition by obtaining the product or works at the best available price and quality.[41]

7.44 It is, therefore, restrictive of competition if some of the undertakings which might have competed against each other to submit tenders instead decide to co-operate. However, two different forms of co-operation need to be distinguished in this context, as they are viewed very differently by competition law:

(i) collusive tendering—which is strictly prohibited, and will never benefit from exemption; and

(ii) joint bidding or tendering, which may be exempted.

7.45 **Collusive tendering** (or 'bid-rigging') occurs where the potential competing bidders decide to co-operate *without telling the procuring organisation*. Thus, for example, they may agree amongst themselves that they will not submit tenders below a certain price, or indeed that some of them will not submit tenders at all, thereby allowing the others a free rein (this is usually part of a more elaborate long-term arrangement whereby competing firms take it in turns to submit tenders for successive contracts, ensuring that they are not competing against each other for any one contract). In these cases, the procuring organisation, which is seeking the benefits of competition through the competitive tender, is being deceived into accepting a more limited choice as a result of an agreement between the potential competitors. Any such agreement, arrangement or collusion by the potential competitors is regarded as an extremely serious infringement, and will virtually never be exempted.

---

[41] Indeed, under various EC public procurement directives, implemented in the UK by regulations, public authorities and utility companies are obliged to invite competing tenders.

Joint bidding, by contrast, occurs where two or more potentially competing ten- **7.46**
derers *openly* submit a joint bid to the procuring organisation, rather than individually submitting bids. Although this involves the individual companies
collaborating rather than competing against each other for the contract, it will not
necessarily be regarded as restrictive of competition. The principles governing the
assessment of joint bidding were set out in a 1968 Notice on co-operation issued
by the European Commission.[42] This said that where consortia between competing enterprises are set up solely 'for the joint execution of orders':

- it will not be restrictive of competition if the participating enterprises could not
  execute the specific order by themselves—for example, because of lack of experience, specialised knowledge, capacity or financial resources; thus, major
  equipment and works contracts, such as to acquire defence equipment, or to
  have the Channel Tunnel built, are simply too big for any one contractor to
  undertake alone (whether because no single contractor could afford the investment, or because no single contractor could afford the risk);
- it would not be restrictive of competition if the enterprises could not 'make an
  attractive offer' other than by setting up the consortium;
- it *would* be a restraint of competition if the enterprises agreed to work only in
  the framework of the consortium, and thus restricted themselves from working
  outside the consortium.

Where these criteria do not clearly take the joint bidding outside the prohibition,
or the co-operation is of such a significant scale that it would be risky to rely on
them, it may be prudent to notify for exemption. An exemption would be granted
on the same criteria that exemptions are granted for other joint ventures where
competitors agree to collaborate with each other: namely, that, by collaborating,
they are able to supply equipment or produce work of a better standard or quality
than they would have been able to provide individually, or indeed that they would
not have been able to undertake the contract individually. In other words, there is
a chance of exemption if the collaboration is seen as the 'indispensable' way of
achieving the works, which bring economic or technical improvements in a way
beneficial to consumers.

H. Collective Boycotts

Collective boycotts occur where a number of undertakings agree between them- **7.47**
selves that they will not deal or trade with a particular business. This is restrictive
of competition when, as is usually the case, the refusal to deal is designed to
prevent the boycotted business from competing against the participants in the

---

[42] Commission Notice, n 40 above, para II.5.

175

boycott or from undermining anti-competitive arrangements or conduct practised by those participants. Such collective boycotts are considered to be a serious infringement.

7.48 An example under Article 81 (formerly Article 85) EC was the Belgian wallpaper case, in which manufacturers of wallpaper in Belgium agreed between themselves that they would refuse to supply wallpaper to a wholesaler who was trying to sell the wallpaper at prices below those which the manufacturers wanted to maintain. The European Commission described the refusal to supply as 'one of the most serious infringements of the rules of competition' and imposed substantial fines on the participants.[43]

I. Joint Ventures (JVs)

7.49 The assessment of joint ventures is among the most complex areas of competition law. This reflects the fact that the concept of a 'joint venture' embraces a wide variety of different types of arrangement, ranging from 'structural' JVs in which businesses merge to form a new full-function autonomous undertaking (although the JV partners still operate as separate businesses in other markets) to much looser and more *ad hoc* arrangements in which independent undertakings co-operate with each other for certain limited purposes.

7.50 The complexity is increased by the fact that, even before assessing whether the JV should be permitted or prohibited, it is necessary first to establish the **type of competition law** under which the assessment must be made. Some JVs are assessed under merger control rules (broadly speaking, the more 'structural' kind), while others are assessed under the prohibitions on restrictive agreements (generally those JVs where undertakings which remain independent co-operate with rather than compete against each other), and some are assessed under both types of law. This complexity is exacerbated by the issue of whether the applicable competition law is EC or national (or both). Once these questions have been resolved, one can begin the **substantive assessment** of whether the JV is likely to be prohibited or permitted. In this, there are no simple or hard-and-fast rules; and the wide variety in the commercial nature of JVs (for example, research-and-development JVs or product manufacturing JVs), each with its own particular economic and commercial context, entails that each needs to be assessed on its own merits.

7.51 This complexity can be beneficial to parties planning a JV. It is often possible to construct the JV arrangements so that they are subject to one kind of competition law rather than another, which may have favourable implications in terms of pro-

---

[43] *Papiers Peints de Belgique* [1974] OJ L237/3. See also OFT, n 11 above, para 3.16.

cedure (ie number of necessary notifications and speed of decision-making) and sometimes also in terms of the likely outcome of the substantive assessment.

In this section, therefore, while it is clearly impossible to set out definitive rules on **7.52** the application of the Chapter I prohibition to JVs, the main questions which will need to be addressed are identified—first, in terms of which type of competition law will be applied (ie whether the Chapter I prohibition applies at all); and, secondly, with regard to how the substantive assessment is likely to be approached under the Chapter I prohibition.

Which Type of Competition Law—Can the JV be Assessed under the Chapter I Prohibition?

The matrix below sets out the basic rules for determining what type of competi- **7.53** tion law applies to a JV. In order to apply the matrix, it is necessary to ask the following questions about the JV:

(i) *Is it a 'full-function' JV?* This is a concept in EC competition law. Broadly, a JV will be 'full-function' if it performs on a lasting basis all the functions of an autonomous economic entity.[44] This will normally be the case where the JV has access to the market itself, rather than merely serving its parents (except for a short start-up period of maximum three years), and provided that it is not established for just a short finite duration and it is given sufficient resources to operate on a lasting basis.[45]

(ii) *Is there co-ordination of competitive behaviour?* This will be the case if the JV, whether full-function or not, has as its object or effect the co-ordination of the competitive behaviour of undertakings that remain independent.[46] In practice, a JV is likely to be regarded as leading to co-ordination: where both parties retain significant activities on the same product market as the JV, or (although less certainly) on upstream, downstream or closely related neighbouring markets; or if there is already a network of co-operative links between both parents.[47]

(iii) *Is there a Community dimension?* The concept of a 'Community dimension' is embodied in the EC Merger Regulation. There is a 'Community dimension' if:

---

[44] EC Merger Reg (Council Reg (EEC) 4064/89 on the control of concentrations between undertakings [1989] OJ L257, as amended by Council Regulation (EC) 1310/97 [1997] OJ L180/1), Art 3(2).

[45] Commission Notice on the concept of full-function joint ventures [1998] OJ C66/1.

[46] EC Merger Reg, Art 22(1).

[47] Ibid, Art 2(5).

the parties to the joint venture (the 'undertakings concerned') meet the turnover criteria laid down in art 1(2) and (3) of the EC Merger Regulation.[48]

The Matrix

This Matrix sets out the basic rules for identifying which kind of competition law applies to a JV in each of five broad categories.

Full function + no co-ordination + Community dimension

* EC Merger Regulation applies;[49]
* Article 81 EC is not applied by the European Commission;[50]
* UK merger control does not apply;[51]
* Chapter I prohibition is excluded.[52]

Full function + co-ordination + Community dimension

* EC Merger Regulation applies;[53]
* Article 81 EC may apply;[54]

---

[48] The turnover criteria laid down in Art 1(2) and (3) are as follows. There is a Community dimension if: the combined worldwide turnover of all the undertakings concerned exceeds 5,000 million euros; (ii) the individual EU-wide turnover of at least two of the undertakings concerned exceeds 250 million euros; and (iii) it is not the case that more than two-thirds of the EU-wide turnover of each undertaking concerned is achieved in the same single Member State. Even if the foregoing criteria are not met, there is a Community dimension if: (i) the combined worldwide turnover of the undertakings concerned exceeds 2,500 million euros; (ii) the individual EU-wide turnover of at least two of the undertakings concerned exceeds 100 million euros; (iii) in each of at least three Member States, the combined turnover of all the undertakings concerned exceeds 100 million euros; (iv) in each of those same three Member States, the individual turnover of at least two undertakings concerned exceeds 25 million euros; and (v) it is not the case that more than two-thirds of the EU-wide turnover of each undertaking concerned is achieved in the same single Member State.

There are special rules for identifying the 'undertakings concerned' in a concentration: if the JV is a pre-existing business, the 'undertakings concerned' are each of the parents and the business acquired; if the JV is a new business, the 'undertakings concerned' are each of the parents. Art 5 of the EC Merger Reg provides rules for calculating the turnover of each undertaking concerned. These are elaborated in the European Commission Notice on the calculation of turnover (94/C 385/04). In broad terms, the turnover of an undertaking concerned is calculated as the total turnover of the corporate group to which it belongs. There are special provisions for calculating the turnover of banks, insurance undertakings and other financial institutions.

[49] EC Merger Reg, Arts 1 and 3(2).

[50] Ibid, Arts 3(2) and 22(1).

[51] Ibid, Art 21(2).

[52] Competition Act 1998, Sch 1, para 6. This is subject to the exceptional cases, set out in Arts 21(3) and 9 of the EC Merger Reg, where the Commission does not have exclusive jurisdiction over concentrations with a Community dimension; see Ch 5, para 5.20.

[53] EC Merger Reg, Arts 1 and 3(2).

[54] EC Merger Reg, Arts 2(4), 3(2) and 22(1). If the co-ordination is a direct effect of the creation of the JV, the assessment under Art 81 is made in the context of the EC Merger Regulation procedure (Commission Notice, n 45 above, para 16).

- UK merger control does not apply;[55]
- Chapter I prohibition is excluded.[56]

Full function + no co-ordination + no Community dimension

- EC Merger Regulation does not apply;[57]
- Article 81 EC is not applied by the European Commission;[58]
- UK merger control applies if forming the JV involves one or both parents acquiring 'material influence' over a pre-existing business;[59]
- Chapter I prohibition may apply if:
  (i) UK merger control does not apply, or
  (ii) UK merger control does apply, but the Secretary of State has not expressly cleared the merger or referred it to the Competition Commission *and* the OFT considers that forming the JV is likely to infringe the Chapter I prohibition and unlikely to merit unconditional individual exemption.[60]

Full function + co-ordination + no Community dimension

- EC Merger Regulation does not apply;[61]
- Article 81 EC may apply;[62]
- UK merger control applies if forming the JV involves one or both parents acquiring 'material influence' over a pre-existing business;
- Chapter I prohibition applies if:
  (i) UK merger control does not apply, or
  (ii) UK merger control does apply, but the Secretary of State has not expressly cleared the merger or referred it to the Competition Commission *and*

---

[55] EC Merger Reg, Art 21(2).

[56] Competition Act 1998, Sch 1, para 6. This is subject to the exceptional cases, set out in arts 21(3) and 9 of the EC Merger Reg, where the Commission does not have exclusive jurisdiction over concentrations with a Community dimension.

[57] EC Merger Reg, Art 1.

[58] Ibid, Art 22(1). In theory, the Commission could apply Art 81 EC using its residual powers under Art 85 EC (which was previously Art 89 EC), but has said that it will generally not do so where the combined worldwide turnover is below 2,000 million euros and the individual EU-wide turnover is below 100 million euros, or where the national competition authorities could deal with the case (see statement on *British Airways/Dan Air* IP(92)1048).

[59] See Ch 5, para 5.22. Material influence may arise from a voting shareholding as low as 15 per cent, especially where other shareholdings are widely dispersed.

[60] Competition Act 1998, Sch 1, paras 1, 4 and 5. In practice it will be rare that a JV which does not lead to co-ordination of competitive behaviour would be likely to infringe the Chapter I prohibition.

[61] EC Merger Reg, Art 1.

[62] Ibid, Art 22(1).

the OFT considers that forming the JV is likely to infringe the Chapter I prohibition and unlikely to merit unconditional individual exemption.[63]

Not full function (all cases)

- EC Merger Regulation does not apply;[64]
- Article 81 EC may apply;
- UK merger control applies if the JV involves one or more parents acquiring 'material influence' over a pre-existing business (this is unlikely if the JV is not full function).
- Chapter I prohibition applies if:
    (i)   UK merger control does not apply, or
    (ii) UK merger control does apply, but the Secretary of State has not expressly cleared the merger or referred it to the Competition Commission *and* the OFT considers that forming the JV is likely to infringe the Chapter I prohibition and unlikely to merit unconditional individual exemption.[65]

Substantive Assessment under the Chapter I Prohibition

7.54   If the formation of the JV falls to be assessed under the Chapter I prohibition, or indeed under Article 81 EC—see the above Matrix—the substantive assessment will be in three stages:

(i)   *Does the formation of the JV fall within an EC block exemption?* If there is an applicable EC block exemption, and the agreements constituting the JV fully meet its criteria, neither Article 81 EC nor the Chapter I prohibition will apply to the JV. The most relevant EC block exemptions are those for research and development agreements (Regulation 418/85) and specialisation agreements (Regulation 417/85).[66] In addition, if there are any applicable UK block exemptions, and the formation of the JV fully meets their conditions, the Chapter I prohibition will not apply (although Article 81 EC may still apply).

If there is no applicable block exemption, it is necessary to answer questions (ii) and (iii).

(ii) *Does the formation of the JV restrict competition?* There is a considerable body of case law under Article 81 EC on the circumstances in which the formation of a JV is restrictive of competition. The general principles from this case law

---

[63]   Competition Act 1998, Sch 1, paras 1, 4 and 5.
[64]   EC Merger Reg, Art 3(2).
[65]   Competition Act 1998, Sch 1, paras 1, 4 and 5.
[66]   See Ch 6, paras 6.10–6.20 above.

were distilled into a European Commission Notice on co-operative joint ventures in 1993.[67] The following main points may be noted:

- The formation of a JV is more likely to be restrictive of competition if the parents are actual or potential competitors of each other, or where the JV is a competitor, supplier or customer of one or more parents and there is a division of geographical or product markets as between the JV and the parent.

- In either of the circumstances listed above, the restriction on competition will be regarded as appreciable to the extent that the parties have significant market shares in the affected markets and/or the agreements constituting the JV include provisions which are further restrictive of competition or which limit market access by third parties.

- Where the same parents operate a network of JVs between themselves, this is more likely to be regarded as restrictive.

- JVs are more likely to be restrictive to the extent that they are at a downstream level of supply (eg sales to end-users) and less in so far as they are at an upstream level of supply (eg research and development).

(iii) *Does the JV merit individual exemption?* The JV will be assessed according to the criteria for exemption described in Chapter 6 paragraphs 6.44–6.58 above. In particular, the restrictive effects of a JV are less likely to be regarded as 'indispensable' to its benefits (and therefore the JV is less likely to merit exemption) if either of the parents alone is in a position to fulfil the tasks assigned to the JV. Moreover, in the assessment of whether a JV should be exempted, particular regard will be had to whether the JV eliminates competition on a substantial part of the market.[68]

The practical consequences are, in broad terms, that:

- sales JVs have very little prospect of exemption;

- research and development JVs have a good prospect of exemption if they can be shown as necessary to achieve the objectives of the research and development;

- production/manufacturing JVs may benefit from exemption, especially if they result in a new product, or a product more efficiently manufactured.

---

[67] Commission Notice on the assessment of co-operative joint ventures pursuant to Art 85 [now renumbered Art 81] [1993] OJ C43/2.

[68] EC Merger Reg, Art 2(5).

J. Non-Competition Clauses (Restrictive Covenants)

7.55 An agreement between undertakings under which one of the parties agrees or covenants not to compete against the other is clearly an agreement which has as its 'object or effect the prevention . . . of competition'. Normally, therefore, such an agreement will fall within the Chapter I prohibition.

7.56 However, there are certain specific circumstances in which such non-competition clauses (also called 'restrictive covenants') escape the application of the Chapter I prohibition (and of Article 81 (formerly Article 85 EC))—whether because they are excluded or because they fall within a block exemption.

7.57 As a general rule, non-competition clauses will be permitted if they are necessary to give full effect to a transaction which in itself is approved—either because it is an acquisition or joint venture which has been cleared under the merger control rules, or because it is an agreement (exclusive distribution, exclusive purchasing or franchising) which satisfies the criteria of a block exemption regulation. In those circumstances, the *extent* of the non-competition covenant is crucial—it is allowed *only in so far as* it is necessary to give effect to the permitted transaction, and if it is more extensive (in duration or geographic scope) it will not be allowed.

Non-competition Clauses Benefiting from Exclusion

7.58 As described in Chapter 5 of this book,[69] the exclusion from the Chapter I prohibition which is in Schedule 1—for merger situations under the UK Fair Trading Act, and for 'concentrations with a Community dimension' under the EC Merger Regulation—also applies to non-competition clauses and restrictive covenants which are:

> 'directly related and necessary to the implementation of' the transaction.[70]

Such restrictions are also called 'ancillary' restrictions.

7.59 The kinds of transaction which will benefit from the exclusion are:

- takeovers;
- acquisitions of majority shareholdings;
- acquisitions of significant minority shareholdings which confer either 'sole control' within the meaning of the EC Merger Regulation, or 'ability to control' or 'ability to exercise material influence' under the UK Fair Trading Act 1973;
- full-function joint ventures which have a Community dimension;[71] or

---

[69] See Ch 5, paras 5.28–5.30.
[70] Competition Act 1998, Sch 1, para 1(2); Sch 1, para 6 (read with EC Merger Reg, recital 25).
[71] See above, paras 7.49–7.54. See also Office of Fair Trading, Draft, 'Competition Act 1998: Exclusion for Mergers and Ancillary Restrictions' (OFT 416).

- joint ventures which constitute 'merger situations' under the UK Fair Trading Act 1973—ie in which at least one of the parents acquires at least 'ability to exercise material influence' over a joint venture which was a pre-existing enterprise.

In relation to any of these transactions, the following kinds of non-competition **7.60** clause will be regarded as ancillary, and therefore excluded from the Chapter I prohibition. However, any non-competition clause in the context of one of these transactions which is either *outside* the following categories, or *more extensive* than described below, will be subject to the Chapter I prohibition:

(i) Non-competition clauses in a takeover, acquisition of shareholding or acquisition of business under which the vendor(s) agrees not to compete— provided that:

   – the only parties accepting a non-competition clause are the vendor(s), its subsidiaries and/or its commercial agents;

   – the only products or services covered by the non-competition clause are those which form the activity of the business which is transferred (not any business retained by the vendor);

   – the duration of the non-competition clause is no longer than five years if goodwill and know-how have been transferred, and no longer than two years if goodwill alone has been transferred (although these periods may be longer if the parties can demonstrate that customer loyalty will persist longer than these periods); and

   – the geographical area covered by the non-competition clause must be no wider than that in which the relevant products or services were sold by the transferred business before the transaction.[72]

(ii) Non-competition clauses in a joint venture under which the parents agree not to compete against the joint venture—provided that:

   – the non-competition clauses only cover the product and geographical market assigned to the joint venture;

   – the parents are withdrawing on a lasting basis from the market assigned to the joint venture.[73]

The non-competition clauses permitted by this exclusion may include covenants not to compete with the transferred business, not to solicit that business's customers, not to solicit that business's employees,[74] or not to use certain trademarks of the transferred or joint venture business.[75]

---

[72] Ancillary Restrictions Notice (Commission Notice regarding restrictions ancillary to concentrations [1990] OJ C203/5), paras III.A.1 to 6.

[73] Ibid, para V.A.

[74] *Solvay–Laporte/Interox* (EC Merger Regulation) Case IV/M.197 [1992] OJ C165.

[75] *Linde/Fiat* (EC Merger Regulation) Case IV/M.256 [1992] OJ C258.

Non-competition Clauses in Joint Ventures not Benefiting from Exclusion

7.61   Certain joint ventures do not benefit from the exclusion in Schedule 1 to the Competition Act 1998—namely, those which are neither full-function joint ventures with a Community dimension nor 'merger situations' under the Fair Trading Act. An example would be a new full-function joint venture business which did not have a Community dimension.

7.62   In such cases, non-competition covenants by the parents will normally be outside the Chapter I prohibition if the joint venture itself benefits from (individual or block) exemption. This will generally be where the covenant is regarded as necessary in order for the joint venture to succeed in its activities, provided that those activities can be regarded as innovative and beneficial to the consumer.[76]

Non-competition Clauses Benefiting from Block Exemptions

7.63   In certain EC block exemptions for vertical supply agreements, it is automatically permissible for the appointed distributor or reseller or franchisee to be obliged not to compete against the upstream manufacturer or supplier (provided that the agreement satisfies all the other conditions specified in the block exemption Regulation). Thus:

(i)   in an exclusive distribution agreement, the distributor may be obliged not to manufacture or distribute goods which compete with the contract goods— provided that this obligation does not extend beyond the duration of the agreement;[77]

(ii)   in an exclusive purchasing agreement, the reseller may be obliged not to manufacture or distribute goods which compete with the contract goods— provided that the obligation does not extend beyond the period of the agreement;[78] and

(iii) in a franchising agreement, the franchisee may be obliged not to manufacture, sell or use goods competing with the franchisor's goods which are the subject-matter of the franchise.[79]

K. Resale Price Maintenance

7.64   Resale price maintenance occurs where a supplier requires that downstream resellers of its products (such as distributors or retailers) should only resell those

---

[76]   See, eg, *Mitchell-Cotts/Sofiltra* [1987] OJ L41/31.
[77]   Commission Reg (EEC) 1983/83, Art 2(2)(a).
[78]   Commission Reg (EEC) 1984/83, Art 2(3).
[79]   Commission Reg (EEC) 4087/88, Art 2(e).

products at a price, or within a range of prices, fixed by the supplier. It may occur where the supplier has fixed the price or price range on its own initiative ('individual resale price maintenance'), or where the supplier has done so in the context of an agreement or arrangement with other suppliers ('collective resale price maintenance').

The fixing of a minimum resale price (whether individually or collectively) has **7.65** been prohibited in the UK under the Resale Prices Act 1976; individual resale price maintenance did not fall within the Restrictive Trade Practices Act 1976.

Under the new Chapter I prohibition, resale price maintenance is prohibited, **7.66** whether it is individual or collective, and whether the fixed price is a minimum or a maximum.[80]

Although most 'vertical' agreements are likely to be protected from the Chapter I **7.67** prohibition by a special treatment order under section 50 of the Competition Act, the government has made clear that vertical price-fixing agreements (ie resale price maintenance) would not benefit from this.[81]

Moreover, resale price maintenance agreements cannot benefit from the limited **7.68** immunity from penalties for 'small agreements' which is granted by section 39 of the Competition Act.[82]

Traditionally it had been thought that resale price maintenance should be permit- **7.69** ted in the retailing of books and of over-the-counter pharmaceutical medicines, and for many years both these categories enjoyed protection from the prohibition in the Resale Prices Act.

- The protection for books was, however, removed a couple of years ago, and it is unlikely that books will enjoy protection under the Chapter I prohibition.

- The protection for over-the-counter pharmaceutical medicines remains in place in 1998. It is the last remaining exemption from the prohibition in the Resale Prices Act, and the government does not think it will be overturned. Accordingly, the Chapter I prohibition will not apply to resale price mainte-nance for over-the-counter pharmaceutical medicines for a transitional period of five years—ie until March 2005.[83] Beyond that date the government intends that the full rigours of the Chapter I prohibition should apply.[84]

---

[80] *Hennessy/Henkell* [1980] OJ L383/11 (at 16).
[81] See Ch 5, 5.92(v); see also 'A prohibition approach to anti-competitive agreements and abuse of dominant position: draft Bill', Department of Trade and Industry, Aug 1997, paras 3.8 and 3.9; and the statement by Nigel Griffiths MP, Minister for Competition and Consumer Affairs, in Standing Committee G (17th sitting, 25 June 1998), *Parliamentary Debates of the House of Commons official report*, col 631.
[82] Competition Act 1998, s 39(1)(b).
[83] Competition Act 1998, Sch 13, para 24.
[84] Nigel Beard MP, *Hansard*, HC vol 315, 8 July 1998, col 1110.

L. Tying

7.70 A tying clause in a supply or sales agreement is one in which the supplier states that it will only sell a product to the purchaser provided that the purchaser also buys from that supplier another product. Thus, for example, a computer hardware manufacturer would be engaged in 'tying' if it sold its computer hardware to purchasers on the condition that they also bought their software from that manufacturer.

7.71 Although tying is in principle capable of coming within the Chapter I prohibition, it is likely to benefit from the proposed exclusion order for vertical agreements (see Ch 5, paras 5.90 to 5.95, in any event in practice tying will be regarded as restrictive of competition only if the supplier has a dominant market position in the product which the purchaser *wants* to buy (rather than the one which the purchaser is forced to buy by the tying obligation)—and in that case it can be dealt with under the Chapter II prohibition.

7.72 The possibility of tying falling within the Chapter I prohibition is made clear by section 2(2)(e) of the Competition Act, which identifies an example of the application of the Chapter I prohibition:

> Agreements, decisions or practices which . . . make the conclusion of contracts subject to acceptance by the other parties of supplementary obligations which, by their nature or according to commercial usage, have no connection with the subject of such contracts.

In practice, however, it is thought that a tying obligation does not really restrict competition unless the purchaser is economically dependent on the supplier for the product which it *wants*, in which case the purchaser has little choice but to buy the products being forced on it. Generally, however, this will only be the case where the supplier has a dominant position in the market for the product which the purchaser wants. If that is so, the tying can be challenged as an abuse of a dominant position, infringing the Chapter II prohibition (and usually is dealt with in this way): see, for example, the *Tetra Pak II* EC case, in which purchasers of Tetra Pak packaging machines were obliged to use only Tetra Pak cartons in those machines, and this was held to be an abuse of a dominant position infringing Article 82 (formerly Article 86) EC.[85] The proposed exclusion order for vertical agreements under section 50 does not exclude the application of the Chapter II prohibition.

7.73 Nevertheless, under the exclusive purchasing EC block exemption (which disapplies the Chapter I prohibition under the 'parallel exemption' rules[86]), the benefit of the block exemption will be lost if the supplier engages in tying—that is, if:

---

[85] *Tetra Pak II* [1992] OJ L72/1.
[86] See Ch 6, paras 6.07–6.28.

the exclusive purchasing obligation is agreed for more than one type of goods where these are neither by their nature nor according to commercial usage, connected to each other.[87]

In any event, it will be noted that there is no infringement if the products being 'tied' are products which in practice 'by their nature or according to commercial usage' are *connected* with each other. Nevertheless, the 'connection' defence is fairly limited—and it will not justify the tying of computer hardware with software, or of vehicle repair services with sales of lubricants.

M. Loyalty Rebates

Loyalty rebates are discounts given by a supplier to customers who buy exclusively, **7.74** or mainly, or in large volumes, from that supplier—where the discount cannot be justified in terms of the genuine cost savings involved in bulk selling (through economies of scale, transport and delivery costs, etc).

The position regarding loyalty rebates is very similar to that for tying clauses (see the **7.75** previous paragraph). In principle, loyalty rebates are capable of being addressed under the Chapter I prohibition, and section 2(2)(d) of the Competition Act makes clear that the prohibition applies to agreements and practices which

apply dissimilar conditions to equivalent transactions with other trading parties, thereby placing them at a competitive disadvantage.

In practice, however, loyalty rebates are regarded as restrictive of competition only where the supplier has a dominant position, in that they make it difficult for competitors of the dominant supplier to operate in the market. Where the supplier is dominant, loyalty rebates can be addressed under the Chapter II prohibition, rather than the Chapter I prohibition. A loyalty rebate in an agreement is likely to be excluded from the Chapter I prohibition—but not from the Chapter II prohibition—as a result of the proposed exclusion order for vertical agreements under section 50 (see Ch 5, paras 5.90 to 5.93).

N. 'Most Favoured Customer' Clauses and 'English' Clauses

'Most favoured customer' clauses and 'English' clauses are provisions in agree- **7.76** ments between suppliers and purchasers (or between licensors and licensees) under which the purchaser (or licensee) is offered an assurance that it is receiving the best available price:

---

[87] Commission Reg (EEC) 1984/83, Art 3(c).

- Under a 'most favoured customer' clause,[88] the supplier is obliged to supply to the purchaser at a price (or on terms) *at least as favourable as the price which that supplier offers to its other customers.*

- Under an 'English' clause—which is usually found in a supply agreement under which the purchaser is obliged to purchase a minimum quantity from the supplier, or exclusively from the supplier—the purchaser is entitled to obtain the contract products from another supplier if the other supplier offers a better price (or better terms) than the contract supplier.

Although these clauses appear to be pro-competitive, in that they encourage the supplier to reduce prices, they can give rise to problems.

7.77 Most favoured customer clauses were regarded as restrictive under the Restrictive Trade Practices Act 1976,[89] since they limit the freedom of the supplier in respect of the prices it charges to other customers. Under the Chapter I prohibition, reflecting Article 81 of the EC Treaty, the position is less clear. The EC block exemption for technology transfer agreements (intellectual property licences),[90] specifically states that:

> an obligation on the licensor to grant the licensee any more favourable terms that the licensor may grant to another undertaking after the agreement is entered into

is generally not restrictive of competition. However, if the purchaser benefiting from the 'most favoured customer' clause has a strong bargaining position, or even market power compared with its competitors, the clause could distort competition by placing the customer at an unfair competitive advantage over its actual and potential competitors, foreclosing competition from them—both by ensuring that it receives the most favourable price, and by making it aware of the terms on which its competitors are able to obtain supplies. In such circumstances, there may be an infringement of the Chapter I prohibition, and there is a risk also of infringing the Chapter II prohibition .

7.78 'English' clauses become problematic in so far as they enable the supplier to know the prices and terms which competing suppliers are offering. On the other hand, to some extent English clauses mitigate the worst effects of exclusive purchasing agreements (see paragraphs 7.79–7.84 below), and the EC block exemption for exclusive purchasing agreements protects:

---

[88] Most favoured customer clauses are sometimes also called 'most favoured nation' or 'MFN' clauses.

[89] Office of Fair Trading press release, 'Agreement on the Televising of Horse Racing taken to Restrictive Practices Court', 2 Aug 1990.

[90] Commission Reg (EC) 240/96, Art 2(1)(10). See Ch 6 of this book, para 6.12(e).

clauses which allow the reseller [purchaser] to obtain the contract goods from other suppliers, should these sell them more cheaply or on more favourable terms than the other party [the contract supplier].[91]

However, in two individual cases, the European Commission has objected to English clauses in the context of exclusive purchasing or minimum quantity agreements, on the grounds that they give the supplier valuable access to information on offers made by competitors, and in one of these cases the Commission only allowed the clause on the basis that the contract supplier must not be given the identity of the competing supplier offering better terms.[92] Where the contract supplier has a dominant position, English clauses are likely to cause greater concern, on the ground that they make it harder for rival suppliers to compete, and this may raise issues under both the Chapter I and Chapter II prohibitions.[93]

O. Exclusive Purchasing and Minimum Percentage Obligations

An exclusive purchasing obligation in a contract is a requirement on the purchaser   **7.79**
to buy the contract goods only from the contract supplier, and not from any other supplier. A minimum percentage obligation is an obligation on the purchaser to purchase at least a specified percentage of its requirements of the contract products from the contract supplier, and therefore no more than the remaining percentage of its requirements of those products from any other supplier.

Both types of obligations are capable of restricting competition, and of infringing   **7.80**
the Chapter I prohibition, to the extent that they foreclose competing suppliers from access to the market where the purchaser operates, and thereby distort competition. However, they are likely to benefit from the proposed exclusion order for vertical agreements under section 50 (see Ch 5, para 5.90 to 5.95).

In any event, not every exclusive purchasing contract or minimum percentage   **7.81**
obligation will fall within the Chapter I prohibition; those where the foreclosure effect is minimal will not do so because there is then no appreciable effect on competition. **There is more likely to be foreclosure, and hence an appreciable effect on competition, to the extent that the exclusive purchasing or minimum percentage obligation closes off a significant segment of the market to rival suppliers.** This will be the case where the purchaser represents a significant share of the market, or where there are networks of similar agreements covering the whole market. In addition, where the supplier has a high share of the market on which it

---

[91] Exclusivity Notice (Commission Notice of 22 June 1983 on the exclusive distribution and exclusive purchasing block exemptions [1984] OJ C101/2), para 35.

[92] *BP Kemi-DDSF* [1979] OJ L286/32; *European Gas Producers*, European Commission, XIXth Report on Competition Policy (EC Commission, Brussels, 1989), point 62.

[93] Case 85/76 *Hoffmann-La Roche v Commission* [1979] ECR 461.

operates, the exclusive purchasing agreement may be seen as reinforcing its market strength against those of actual and potential competitors, particularly where there are relatively high barriers to entry; this may also be regarded as an abuse of a dominant position, to be considered under the Chapter II prohibition.

7.82 In addition, certain exclusive purchasing and minimum purchase obligations can have beneficial effects which merit exemption (see the criteria for exemption in Chapter 6, paragraphs 6.44–6.58). For this reason, there is an EC block exemption for certain exclusive purchasing agreements which, because of the parallel exemption provisions in the Competition Act 1998, automatically exempts the covered agreements from the Chapter I prohibition as well as from Article 81 of the EC Treaty.

7.83 The EC exclusive purchasing block exemption is summarised in Chapter 6, paragraph 6.12(b). However, not every agreement can benefit from the block exemption. In order to do so, it is necessary to satisfy all the conditions in the block exemption regulation,[94] and not every agreement will do so. In particular, the block exemption will only apply if the following criteria are all met.

(i) There must be no more than two parties to the exclusive purchasing agreement—the supplier and the purchaser.[95] Nevertheless, several undertakings forming a single economic unit will count as just one party.[96] Moreover, the block exemption still applies if the supplier enters into different exclusive purchasing agreements covering the same goods with several purchasers.[97]

(ii) The purchaser must be a reseller of the contract goods; it is not sufficient that the purchaser uses the contract goods as components for manufacture into a different product, or transforms or processes them into other goods.[98]

(iii) The agreement must be fully exclusive. The block exemption 'only covers agreements whereby the reseller agrees to purchase all his requirements for the contract goods from the other party. If the purchasing obligation relates to only part of such requirements, the block exemption does not apply'.[99] In one case where a reseller was obliged to purchase 90 per cent of its requirements of the contract goods from the supplier, this was held to fall outside the block exemption.[100]

---

[94] Commission Reg (EEC) 1984/83.
[95] Ibid, Art 1.
[96] Exclusivity Notice, n 91 above, para 13.
[97] Ibid, para 14.
[98] Commission Reg (EEC) 1984/83, Art 1; Exclusivity Notice, n 91 above, para 9.
[99] Ibid, para 35.
[100] European Commission, *XVIIth Report on Competition Policy* (EC Commission, Brussels, 1987), point 29.

(iv) The agreement must be for a fixed period (and not of indefinite duration), and that period must be no more than five years.[101]

The block exemption also has special provisions automatically exempting exclusive purchasing agreements which bind **public houses** in respect of beer and other drinks, and 'solus' exclusive purchasing agreements between **petrol stations** and petrol suppliers.

If the exclusive purchasing block exemption does not apply, it may still be possible   **7.84** to apply for an individual exemption, from either the OFT or the European Commission.[102] In those cases, the applicants clearly have to argue that the criteria for exemption, in section 9 of the Competition Act (also in Article 81(3) of the EC Treaty) are fully satisfied by the agreement.[103] In particular, it is necessary to show that the agreement:

• benefits consumers by making sales and supplies more efficient and thereby reducing costs and prices, and/or by introducing a new product or competitor to the market which would not have had the incentive to enter the market without the guarantee afforded by the exclusivity or minimum percentage obligation; and

• the agreement does not tie up an excessive share of the market, so that competition is not substantially eliminated. The authorities will have regard to the market shares of both the supplier and the purchaser, as well as competitive conditions such as barriers to entry and the existence of other exclusivity agreements on the same market. In one EC decision, the fact that the three purchasers which were subject to the exclusive purchasing obligation accounted for about 30 per cent of distribution of contract goods in the relevant market, was held to preclude individual exemption.[104] Similarly, where the two dominant suppliers of ice cream bars in Germany imposed exclusive purchasing obligations on retailers, this was held to make it difficult for a potential new entrant (Mars ice creams) to enter the market.[105]

P. Long-Term Supply Contracts

A major difference between the old Restrictive Trade Practices Act and the new   **7.85** Chapter I prohibition arises in the context of long-term supply agreements. Under the RTPA, an *exclusive* purchasing obligation (ie an obligation on the

---

[101] Commission Reg (EEC) 1984/83, Art 3(d).
[102] See Ch 6 of this book.
[103] See Ch 6, paras 6.44–6.58.
[104] *Spices* [1978] OJ L53/20.
[105] *Schöller* [1993] OJ L183/1; and *Langnese-Iglo* [1993] OJ L183/19. Both Commission decisions were upheld by the Court of First Instance.

purchaser to buy the contract goods from no other supplier than the contract supplier) or a minimum *percentage* obligation (ie an obligation on the purchaser not to buy more than a certain percentage of its requirements from any supplier other than the contract supplier) were both regarded as restrictions, because they literally limited the purchaser's freedom as to the persons from whom it could purchase. By contrast, an obligation on the purchaser simply to buy a specified *quantity* of the product, and to do so over a specified period of time, was not regarded as a restriction under the RTPA—because it did not literally fetter the freedom of the purchaser to buy additional quantities from any other supplier.

7.86 The Chapter I prohibition takes a different approach. It has regard not to the literal form of the obligation, but to its practical economic effect. Although an exclusive purchasing obligation or a percentage requirement always risks infringing the Chapter I prohibition, a fixed-quantity obligation over a long period *can also be dangerous*, if in practice it entails that the purchaser will not in fact buy the goods from any competing supplier over a long period of time. Where this is the case, the practical effect is that competing suppliers are foreclosed from supplying the contract purchaser and, particularly where the contract purchaser represents a major segment of the market, this foreclosure appreciably distorts competition. The European Commission has said that:

> when a purchasing obligation of a longer duration is entered into, the relationship of supply is frozen and the role of offer and demand is eliminated to the disadvantage of *inter alia* new competitors who are thereby prevented from supplying this customer and old competitors who in the meantime may have become more competitive than the actual supplier.[106]

Long-term supply contracts always need to be assessed in the particular economic context of the affected markets. However, the following general guidelines may be of assistance:

- A fixed quantity obligation is always less dangerous than an exclusive purchasing obligation or a percentage obligation (unless the exclusive purchasing obligation falls within the exclusive purchasing block exemption).

- A fixed-quantity obligation over a long term is more likely to raise problems to the extent that:
  - the purchaser represents a significant segment of the market;
  - the supplier has market power;
  - the fixed or minimum quantity represents all or most of the purchaser's likely requirements of the product;
  - the duration of the obligation is longer than normal in the industry;

---

[106] *BP Kemi–DDSF* [1979] OJ L286/32.

– the quantity and duration cannot be justified as the minimum necessary to make it worthwhile for the supplier to supply the products to the purchaser (for certain supply agreements, involving a high degree of investment—for example, in gas or electricity infrastructure—such a justification may legitimise a long-term purchasing obligation).

Most long-term supply contracts, however, are likely to benefit from the proposed exclusion order for vertical agreements under section 50 (see Ch 5, paras 5.90 to 5.95).

Q. Exclusive Distribution and Agency Agreements

Exclusive distribution obligations are the converse of exclusive purchasing obligations: in agreements between a supplier and a purchaser/reseller, the supplier appoints that purchaser/reseller as its only distributor of the contract goods in a defined territory, and agrees not to appoint any other purchaser/reseller in that territory (and not to distribute the goods itself in that territory[107]). **7.87**

As with exclusive purchasing obligations, the Chapter I prohibition will not always apply. It will not apply to the extent that the proposed section 50 exclusion order for vertical agreement applies (see Ch 5, paras 5.90 to 5.95). Even if the exclusion order does not cover the agreement, the Chapter I prohibition will not apply if the relationship between the supplier and distributor is one of genuine commercial 'agency' (see paragraphs 7.89–7.91). It will not apply if there is no appreciable effect on competition, which depends on the extent of foreclosure (paragraph 7.92). There will be automatic exemption if the exclusive distributorship meets the terms of the EC exclusive distribution block exemption (paragraph 7.93). Finally, it may be possible to apply for individual exemption (paragraph 7.94). **7.88**

Exclusive Agency

Since the Chapter I prohibition can only apply to agreements 'between undertakings'—implying that there must be two separate parties to the agreement—an exclusive agency agreement is generally regarded as outside the scope of the prohibition, on the basis that the agent which carries out the distribution is integrated with the supplier, rather than being a separate undertaking. **7.89**

Therefore, where the exclusive distributor genuinely acts as an agent of the supplier, rather than as a separate principal, the Chapter I prohibition will not apply. **7.90**

---

[107] If there is no restriction on the supplier itself distributing the goods in the territory, but only a restriction on the supplier appointing other distributors there, this is usually described as a 'sole distributorship' rather than an 'exclusive distributorship'.

7.91   The concept of 'agent' is, however, narrowly defined. It is not possible to avoid the Chapter I prohibition simply by describing an independent distributor as an 'agent'. The European Commission set out its definition of agency in a Notice in 1962, which technically has not been superseded. However, the Commission's thinking on the concept of agency has developed considerably since 1962, and is best reflected in a draft Notice on commercial agency agreements issued by the Commission in 1990, but as yet not finalised.[108] This says that a distributor is only an agent if he is:

> a self-employed intermediary who has continuing authority to negotiate, or to negotiate and conclude—either in his own name or in the name of the principal—the sale or the purchase . . . of goods or services . . . on behalf of . . . the principal.

The Commission's view, as expressed in the 1990 draft Notice, is that this will only be the case where the agent is integrated into the principal's distribution system and cannot be required to adopt a totally autonomous commercial behaviour. In general, this will be where:

- the business of the commercial agent under the relevant agency agreement accounts for at least one-third of its activity; and
- the commercial agent does not carry product ranges which compete with those of the supplier, or otherwise carry on outside interests which would interfere with the subject matter of the agency agreement.

Appreciable Effect on Competition—Foreclosure

7.92   As in the case of exclusive purchasing agreements, exclusive distribution agreements only fall within the Chapter I prohibition (and within Article 81 EC) if they are appreciably restrictive of competition. This is more likely to be the case in so far as these following circumstances apply:

- the supplier accounts for a significant share of the market in the contract goods, such that potential competitors to the appointed distributor are foreclosed from operating effectively on the market, and consumers are deprived of choice and competition in the outlet where they buy a popular brand of the goods in question;
- the appointed exclusive distributor accounts for a significant market share in distribution of the goods of that type, so that the exclusivity reinforces its competitive position, thereby making it harder for actual and potential competitors to operate (in these circumstances, there may also be an abuse of a dominant position under the Chapter II prohibition);
- barriers to market entry are high; and
- the market is characterised by a 'network' of parallel exclusivity agreements.

---

[108]   Preliminary draft Commission Notice on commercial agency agreements (IV/484/90).

EC Block Exemption for Exclusive Distribution

Under the parallel exemption provisions of the Competition Act,[109] an exclusive **7.93** distribution agreement will be automatically exempt from the Chapter I prohibition (as well as from Article 81 of the EC Treaty) if it comes within the terms of the EC block exemption for exclusive distribution.[110] In order to benefit from this, the agreement must fully meet all the conditions specified in the block exemption regulation, and this will not be the case with every exclusive distribution agreement. In particular, the block exemption will only apply if the following conditions are all satisfied.

(i) There must only be two parties to the agreement—the supplier and the distributor. Nevertheless, as explained above, several undertakings forming one economic unit will count as just one party, and the supplier does not lose the benefit of the block exemption if it enters into its different exclusive distribution agreements covering the same goods with several distributors.[111]

(ii) The exclusivity appointment must relate to a defined contract territory, which may be the whole or part of the EU.[112]

(iii) Only one distributor may be appointed in the contract territory in respect of the contract goods. If there are two or more distributors in the territory, the rules on selective distribution apply (see paragraphs 7.95–7.99 below).

(iv) The distributor must be allowed to engage in 'passive' sales to customers in another exclusive distributor's contract territory (for example, responding to unsolicited orders), although the distributor may be restricted from engaging in 'active marketing' of the contract goods to customers outside the contract territory (eg seeking customers, establishing branches and maintaining distribution depots).[113]

(v) Customers in the contract territory must be able to obtain the contract goods from alternative sources of supply outside the contract territory; this has been held to preclude the supplier from agreeing not to supply distributors outside the contract territory on the grounds that it suspects that those distributors will resell into the contract territory by way of 'parallel imports'.[114]

Applying for Individual Exemption

Even if an exclusive distribution agreement falls within the ambit of the Chapter **7.94** I prohibition, and does not satisfy the terms of the block exemption, it may still be

---

[109] See Ch 6, paras 6.07–6.28.
[110] Commission Reg (EEC) 1983/83. See Ch 6, para 6.12(a).
[111] Commission Reg (EEC) 1983/83, Art 1; Exclusivity Notice, n 91 above, paras 13 and 14.
[112] Commission Reg (EEC) 1983/83, Art 1.
[113] Ibid, Art 2(2).
[114] European Commission, *XXVIIIth Report on Competition Policy* (EC Commission, Brussels, 1988), point 21.

possible to obtain exemption by applying for an individual exemption either to the OFT or to the European Commission. In order to obtain an individual exemption, the applicant will need to argue that the criteria for exemption, as set out in section 9 of the Competition Act (and in Article 81(3) of the EC Treaty), apply to the exclusive distribution agreement.[115] In particular, the applicant would need to demonstrate that:

- the agreement will make distribution more efficient, reducing costs and the prices paid by consumers, and/or the agreement encourages a new product or a new competitor to enter the market (either a competitor who has never previously supplied that product, or one who has only supplied it outside the UK) in that no one would take the risk of distributing the product unless guaranteed exclusivity; and

- competition is not substantially eliminated in respect of the contract goods—having regard to the market shares of the supplier and the distributor, barriers to entry and the existence of parallel agreements.

In practice, an exclusive distribution agreement is more likely to be granted exemption to the extent that it generally tracks the principles set out in the EC block exemption.

R. Selective Distribution

7.95 A selective distribution system is one where a manufacturer appoints a limited number of distributors or dealers in a contract territory, refusing admission to others. Such systems are common in various economic sectors, including sales of good quality hi-fi equipment (where a particular manufacturer may appoint only a limited number of 'authorised dealers') and in motor car selling (where the manufacturer will appoint a limited number of garages as its dealers).

7.96 In principle, a selective distribution agreement is capable of restricting competition, by limiting the number of competitors at the distribution/dealership level.

7.97 In practice, under EC law, selective distribution agreements have been regarded as acceptable (and even falling outside Article 81 altogether), if there is an objective qualitative justification for including only certain dealers and excluding others—for example, where the product requires retail outlets which have staff who are technically qualified to provide quality pre- and after-sales service (as with computer equipment or hi-fi), or where the product requires retail outlets whose prestige reflects the prestige of the branded product, as with certain perfumes.[116] These

---

[115] See Ch 6, paras 6.44–6.58.
[116] *Yves Saint Laurent* [1992] OJ L12/24; *Givenchy* [1992] OJ L236/11.

qualitative criteria must be objectively necessary, and spurious criteria will not be acceptable—as where a skin product company insisted on selling its goods only through pharmacies.[117] There must be no quantitative limit.[118] Moreover, the criteria must be applied in an open and non-discriminatory way; in other words, every dealer meeting the criteria must be admitted to the system.

However, even where a selective distribution system satisfies these conditions, it **7.98** may nevertheless be prohibited if the market is such that there is no room for other forms of distribution.[119] Each selective distribution agreement needs to be assessed on its own particular circumstances; it may be outside the Chapter I prohibition altogether, or alternatively it may require notification for exemption.

Selective distribution in motor vehicles is addressed under the block exemption for motor vehicle selective distribution agreements.[120] **7.99**

S. Intellectual Property Licences

The licensing of intellectual property rights raises complex issues in competition **7.100** law. Intellectual property rights may attach to technology, to the invention or improvement of products, to creative works and to processes—and may take the form of patents, know-how (ie technology that, although not patented, is secret, substantial and identified), copyright (including in respect of computer software), trade marks, design rights, or any mixture of these.

It is recognised that competition in an economy is enhanced if there is technolog- **7.101** ical and creative innovation; and that, in order to encourage such innovation, there must be appropriate commercial rewards both for the inventors or creators themselves, and also for those who take the risk of exploiting the new technology or creation (eg through manufacturing or marketing). In practice, people are generally only likely to invest in an invention or creation if they are themselves given exclusive rights to exploit their invention or creation—that is, ownership of an intellectual property right—or if they can be assured of a revenue stream from someone else who is willing to exploit the right—that is, a licensee of their intellectual property right. Moreover, the licensee is generally only willing to take the commercial risk of exploiting the new technology or creation if it is granted some form of exclusive right to do so—that is, an exclusive licence of the intellectual property right.

---

[117] *Vichy* [1991] OJ L75/57.
[118] *Hasselblad* [1982] OJ L161/18.
[119] Case 75/84 *Metro v Commission (no. 2)* [1986] ECR 3021.
[120] Commission Reg 1475/95. See Ch 6 of this book, para 6.12(c).

7.102 Competition law needs to strike a balance between respecting the exclusivity of intellectual property rights and licences, so as to incentivise pro-competitive innovation, and at the same time ensuring that the exclusivity is not so extensive that it unnecessarily precludes competition which might otherwise exist.

7.103 As a result, any licence of intellectual property rights is subject to a web of special rules designed to achieve this balance. In terms of the prohibitions on restrictive agreements (in the UK Chapter I prohibition and in Article 81 of the EC Treaty), the rules do not only relate to provisions which give exclusivity to licensees, but also to other kinds of provision which may restrict competition, including:

- provisions protecting the licensor from competition;
- provisions intended to protect other licensees from competition;
- production limits on the licensee;
- limits on the 'fields of use' for which the licensee can exploit the licensed intellectual property;
- restrictions on either party's freedom to determine prices and discounts;
- restrictions on the licensee sub-licensing or assigning the licence;
- minimum quality obligations on the licensee;
- post-termination restrictions on the licensee;
- obligations on the licensee to 'grant back' licences of improvements made by the licensee;
- confidentiality obligations on the licensee;
- royalty payments obligations on the licensee;
- obligations on the licensee as regards branding, trade marks, names, etc. on the licensed product;
- 'no challenge' obligations on the licensee, and other obligations and provisions intended to protect the validity of the licensor's intellectual property rights;
- obligations on the licensee to use its 'best endeavours' in manufacturing and marketing the licensed products.

7.104 **In assessing whether a particular licence agreement relating to intellectual property rights (patents, know-how, copyright, trade marks, design rights, or a mixture) is lawful under the Chapter I prohibition, the following questions need to be asked:**

(i) *Is the licence covered by an exclusion from the Chapter I prohibition?*
  If so, the licence is altogether outside the scope of the Chapter I prohibition, until and unless the OFT 'claws back' the exclusion. However, if the licence may have an appreciable effect on trade between EU Member States, it still needs to be assessed in terms of the prohibition in Article 81 of the EC Treaty.

(ii) If (i) does not apply: *is the licence non-restrictive, by virtue of being an 'open' licence?*
If so, neither the Article 81 prohibition nor the Chapter I prohibition applies to the licence. However, care needs to be taken, as the concept of an 'open' licence is fairly narrowly circumscribed.

(iii) If (ii) does not apply: *does the licence benefit from an EC block exemption?*
If so, it is automatically exempt from the Article 81 prohibition and, by virtue of the parallel exemption provisions, from the Chapter I prohibition.

(iv) If (iii) does not apply: *is the licence capable of receiving individual exemption?*
In order to receive individual exemption, the licence needs to be notified either to the European Commission (which grants an EC individual exemption that, by virtue of the parallel exemption provisions, automatically exempts the licence from the Chapter I prohibition) or to the OFT (which can grant exemption only from the Chapter I prohibition—useful where there is no likely effect on trade between EU Member States).

In the following paragraphs, each of these questions is considered in turn. In addition, consideration is given to: **7.105**

- the need to ensure that there is no abuse of a dominant position which could constitute an infringement of the Chapter II prohibition and perhaps Article 82 of the EC Treaty;
- the impact of section 70 of the Competition Act, which repeals sections 44 and 45 of the Patents Act 1977.

Is the Licence Excluded from the Chapter I Prohibition?

Under section 50 of the Competition Act, the government may make an order giving 'special treatment' to vertical agreements, protecting them wholly or partly from the Chapter I prohibition. One possibility is that they be excluded altogether from the Chapter I prohibition. **7.106**

At the time of writing, it seems unlikely that intellectual property licences will benefit from the exclusion order proposed under section 50. In the House of Commons Standing Committee which considered the legislation, the then Minister for Competition said, as regards 'licences of pure intellectual property rights': **7.107**

> We do not believe that there is a need to cover such agreements with the special treatment proposed. Licensing of intellectual property rights has been subject to Article 85 [now Article 81] in the UK for more than 25 years. A licence to use intellectual property rights, as such, is not restrictive—it grants a freedom.[121]

---

[121] Nigel Griffiths MP, Minister for Competition and Consumer Affairs, in Standing Committee G (17th sitting, 25 June 1998), *Parliamentary Debates of the House of Commons official report*, col 632. See also Ch 5 above, para 5.92(ii).

Although this seems to suggest that intellectual property licences would not benefit from exclusion under a section 50 order, the reasoning given is that the government takes the view that there is no *need* to do so, because such licences are not restrictive at all. Since intellectual property licences have been held to fall within Article 81 of the EC Treaty, and therefore are capable of falling within the Chapter I prohibition, this appears to be somewhat baffling logic. It remains to be seen whether, on further reflection, Ministers will conclude that intellectual property licences should be subject to a section 50 order.

7.108 Even if intellectual property licences are not excluded from the Chapter I prohibition by virtue of a section 50 order, they may benefit from one of the other exclusions. For example, if the licence is granted in the context of a merger, it may benefit from the exclusion for mergers and concentrations in Schedule 1 to the Competition Act.[122]

7.109 The significance of benefiting from an exclusion is that the intellectual property licence is outside the Chapter I prohibition, and that there is no need to notify it or be concerned as to whether it complies with a block exemption.

7.110 However, the OFT may claw back the exclusion at a later date (for example, if the licence would otherwise infringe the Chapter I prohibition and the OFT does not consider that it merits exemption). Moreover, while the exclusion protects the licence from the UK Chapter I prohibition, it offers no protection against the prohibition in Article 81 of the EC Treaty, which could apply if the licence may appreciably effect trade between EU Member States. Therefore, if there may be such an effect on trade between Member States, care needs to be taken that the licence does not infringe Article 81, or that it is exempted from Article 81.

Is the Licence Non-restrictive, by Virtue of Being an 'Open' Licence?

7.111 A body of case law under Article 81 (formerly Article 85) of the EC Treaty has held that, in certain circumstances, the exclusive licensing of intellectual property rights is not restrictive of competition and therefore outside the prohibition altogether. This body of case law—proceeding from the European Court of Justice's *Nungesser* judgment[123] (which concerned the licensing of plant breeders' rights in maize seed) and developed in European Commission cases—is applicable to the interpretation of the Chapter I prohibition, by virtue of section 60 of the Competition Act 1998.[124]

---

[122] See Ch 5, paras 5.12–5.31.

[123] Case 258/78 *Nungesser v Commission* [1982] ECR 2015, at para 58.

[124] S 60 provides that the Chapter I prohibition must be applied consistently with ECJ judgments on the application of Art 81 EC, and having regard to European Commission decisions and statements. See Ch 3 above.

The case law provides that an exclusive licence of intellectual property rights will **7.112** be regarded as an 'open' licence, and hence not restrictive of competition (and outside the prohibition), provided that:

- the licensee is not given 'absolute territorial protection'—ie is not protected from competition by other licensees or parallel importers;

- the exclusivity is indispensable to launching the products on the relevant market, because of the 'newness' of the products concerned or the amount of investment involved;

- the exclusivity is not for an excessive length of time (ie a period longer than is indispensable to launching the products on the relevant market).[125]

If the exclusivity satisfies these conditions it will generally be regarded as outside the prohibitions in Article 81 and the Chapter I prohibition. However, parties need to be cautious in relying on these principles, given that their scope is circumscribed by the above conditions, and that the imprecise nature of those conditions means that an exclusivity provision would need to satisfy them unequivocally.

Moreover, even if the *exclusivity* falls outside the prohibitions the licence could **7.113** still be subject to the prohibitions if it contains *other* provisions which are restrictive of competition (for example, those listed in paragraph 7.103 above). In general, such provisions will not be regarded as restrictive of competition if they are entirely of the type listed in article 2(1) of the technology transfer block exemption, in Commission Regulation (EC) 240/96[126]—although if the licensee has a strong position on the market for the licensed product (and equivalent products), for example a market share above 40 per cent, this cannot be relied on.

Does the Licence Benefit from an EC Block Exemption?

If the licence agreement benefits from an EC block exemption then, by virtue of the **7.114** 'parallel exemption' provisions, it is automatically exempt from the Chapter I prohibition—whether or not it may affect trade between EU Member States (until and unless the EC exemption ceases to have effect, or the OFT cancels the parallel exemption).[127] In order to benefit from an EC block exemption, the licence in question must satisfy all the criteria in the relevant EC block exemption regulation.

The most relevant block exemption regulation is the technology transfer block **7.115** exemption, in Commission Regulation (EC) 240/96.[128] Information on this

---

[125] See, eg, the European Commission's statement on *Knoll/Hille-Form*, European Commission, *XIIIth Report on Competition Policy* (EC Commission, Brussels, 1983), point 144.
[126] [1996] OJ L31/2.
[127] See Ch 6, paras 6.07–6.28.
[128] [1996] OJ L31/2.

block exemption is set out in chapter 6 of this book, paragraph 6.12(e). However, it only applies to licences:

- of patents (defined as extending to patent applications, utility models, supplementary protection certificates for medicinal products, and plant breeder's certificates); or

- of know-how (defined as a body of technical information that is secret, substantial and identified in any appropriate form); or

- of a mixture of patents and know-how.

The technology transfer block exemption does not apply to licences of other intellectual property rights, such as copyright (eg in computer software licences) or trade marks. These may require to be notified for an individual exemption—see paragraphs 7.117–7.119 below.

7.116 Other block exemptions which may be relevant if the technology transfer block exemption does not apply include those for:

(i) franchising agreements—Commission Regulation (EEC) 4087/88;[129] and

(ii) research and development agreements—Commission Regulation (EEC) 418/85.[130]

Is the Licence Capable of Receiving Individual Exemption?

7.117 If the licence is likely to fall within the Chapter I prohibition, and does not benefit from exclusion or an EC block exemption, it may be possible to obtain individual exemption—by notifying it either to the European Commission or to the OFT. An exemption granted by the European Commission will protect the agreement both from Article 81 EC and, by virtue of 'parallel exemption', from the Chapter I prohibition—whereas an exemption granted by the OFT will protect it only from the Chapter I prohibition (the latter is therefore generally appropriate only in cases where it is clear that there may not be any appreciable effect on trade between EU Member States and/or there are special issues relating to UK markets or policy).

7.118 In order to qualify for individual exemption, the licence will need to satisfy the criteria set out in Article 81(3) of the EC Treaty, which are the same as those set out in section 9 of the Competition Act; these are explained in Chapter 6 above, paragraphs 6.44–6.58.

7.119 Although each case is examined on its own merits, in general a licence (eg of software or other copyright, or of a trademark) is most likely to be exempted if its pro-

---

[129] [1988] OJ L359/46—see above, Ch 6, para 6.12(d).
[130] [1985] OJ L53/5; as amended by Commission Regs (EEC) 151/93 [1993] OJ L21/89, and (EC) 2236/97 [1997] OJ L306/12 extending it to 31 Dec 2000. See Ch 6, para 6.12(f).

visions would—if it were a know-how licence—satisfy the technology transfer block exemption.

Intellectual Property Licences and the Chapter II Prohibition

Where either the licensee or the licensor may be said to hold a dominant position **7.120** in its market, care needs to taken that the licence provisions do not constitute an abuse of that dominant position, thereby giving rise to an infringement of the Chapter II prohibition (and, if there may be an effect on trade between Member States, of Article 82 (formerly Article 86) of the EC Treaty). These issues are more fully explained in Chapters 8 and 9 of this book, and in particular Chapter 9, paragraphs 9.81 to 9.82.

It is worth bearing in mind, in particular, that an intellectual property right may **7.121** be held to constitute an 'essential facility' to competing in certain markets, and therefore *per se* a dominant position, such that refusal to license the right to others may be an abuse of that dominant position; this was the case, for example, with regard to the copyright which broadcasting companies owned in their programme information in the *Magill* case.[131]

Repeal of Sections 44 and 45 of the Patents Act 1977

Section 70 of the Competition Act provides that sections 44 and 45 of the Patents **7.122** Act 1977 shall cease to have effect.

Sections 44 and 45 of the Patents Act 1977 were deterrents to some of the more **7.123** anti-competitive effects of patent agreements and licences, providing that:

(i)   in the case of section 44—where a patent licence 'tied' the licensee to buying products other than the patented product from the licensor, such provision was void and, moreover, the licensor would not then be able to succeed in proceedings for infringement of that patent;[132]

(ii) in the case of section 45—once the patent or patents protecting the licensed product cease to be in force, either party could terminate the licence on three months' written notice, or could apply to a court to vary the terms and conditions of the licence.

The repeal of these provisions presumably reflects the government's view that the Chapter I and Chapter II prohibitions now provide adequate safeguards against anti-competitive licences, so rendering sections 44 and 45 of the Patents Act superfluous.

---

[131] Cases C–241–242/91P *RTE and ITP v Commission* [1995] ECR I–743.
[132] Unless the licensee had been offered a reasonable alternative without the tie condition and the tie could be ended on three months' notice.

PART III

ABUSE OF DOMINANT POSITION: THE
CHAPTER II PROHIBITION

ABUSE OF DOMINANT POSITIONS, MONOPOLIES
AND THEIR REGULATION

8

THE CHAPTER II PROHIBITION—KEY CONCEPTS

A. Overview

The Chapter II prohibition is the new legislative instrument for the control of **8.01** conduct which amounts to an abuse of a dominant position in a UK market.[1] It is laid down in Chapter II of the Competition Act 1998, and its principal terms are set out in section 18 of the Act. It replaces the anti-competitive practices provisions of the Competition Act 1980, and relegates the monopoly provisions of the Fair Trading Act 1973 to a largely residual role.[2]

---

[1] Competition Act 1998 s 18(1). A 'dominant position' on a market is often also termed 'market power', although the UK and EC authorities have recently indicated that a dominant position involves a higher, or 'substantial', level of market power. See Office of Fair Trading, 'Competition Act 1998: The Chapter II Prohibition' (OFT 402), para 3.9. The European Commission has also pointed out that most economists would agree that it is possible for market power to exist below the level of a dominant position. See Communication of the Commission on the application of the Community competition rules to vertical restraints (98/C 365/03), OJ C365/3 of 26 Nov. 1998, Section III, para 1.

[2] See Chs 17 and 18 below on the monopoly provisions of the Fair Trading Act 1973.

8.02 **Prohibition**: the Chapter II prohibition *prohibits* conduct in which all the following elements are present:

- an abuse[3]
- by one or more undertakings[4]
- of a dominant position[5]
- where the dominant position is enjoyed within the United Kingdom and
- where there is an effect on trade within the United Kingdom.[6]

The United Kingdom means either the whole of the United Kingdom or any part of it.[7] Thus, where a market is purely local, for example the operating area for a bus service, the Chapter II prohibition may apply to the behaviour of a party holding a dominant position in such market.

8.03 **Exclusions**: mergers and concentrations are *excluded* from the Chapter II prohibition and there are also a number of general exclusions from it.[8] By contrast with the Chapter I prohibition, there is no provision for *exemption* from the Chapter II prohibition.

8.04 The **consequences of infringing** the Chapter II prohibition are similar to those for the Chapter I prohibition. The undertaking (or undertakings) found to have abused a dominant position is liable in any UK court to third parties who have sustained losses or damage as a result of the infringement; any contractual provision which constitutes an infringing abuse is void and unenforceable in a UK court; the OFT may order cessation or modification of the conduct to bring the infringement to an end; and the OFT may impose penalties (fines) for the infringement.

8.05 An undertaking which is engaged in conduct which it considers may infringe the Chapter II prohibition may **notify** the OFT of such conduct and the OFT may give guidance or make a decision whether the conduct is likely to infringe the prohibition.[9] Where the OFT gives guidance that the conduct is unlikely to infringe the Chapter II prohibition it may take no further action with respect to such conduct unless: there has been a material change in circumstances; or the original information on which the guidance was given was incomplete, false or misleading; or a complaint has been made.[10]

---

[3] For explanation see below, para 8.95–8.108.
[4] See para 8.80–8.89.
[5] See para 8.52–8.79.
[6] See next para, and also Ch 4 paras 4.60–4.61.
[7] S 18(3).
[8] S 19(1)(b), Sch 3.
[9] Ss 21(1) and 22(1).
[10] S 23(2).

No penalty may be imposed in relation to conduct[11] in respect of which guidance **8.06** has been given unless the OFT gives written notice that it is removing the immunity. Such notice may be given where: the OFT considers that there are reasonable grounds for believing there has been a material change in circumstances, the OFT has a reasonable suspicion that the original information on which the guidance was given was incomplete, false or misleading, or a complaint has been made and if the OFT considers it likely that the conduct will infringe the Chapter II prohibition.[12] Where the information given to the OFT was incomplete, false or misleading the removal of immunity may be retrospective to a date earlier than the date on which the notice is given by the OFT.[13]

In the case of a decision, where the OFT has determined that the conduct does not **8.07** infringe the Chapter II prohibition it may take no further action with respect to such conduct unless it has reasonable grounds for believing that there has been a material change of circumstances since the decision was given or there is reasonable suspicion that the information on which the decision was based was incomplete, false or misleading in a material particular.[14] No penalty may be imposed where such a decision has been given. However, the OFT may give written notice of withdrawal of the immunity where it has reasonable grounds for believing that there has been a material change of circumstances since the date of the decision or it has reasonable suspicion that the information on which the decision was based was incomplete, false or misleading in a material particular, and the OFT considers it likely that the conduct would infringe the prohibition.[15] If the OFT has reasonable suspicion that information on which the decision was based, and which was provided to it by an undertaking engaging in the conduct, was incomplete, false or misleading in a material respect the removal of immunity may be retrospective.[16]

B. Relation with Article 82 (formerly Article 86) of the EC Treaty

The Chapter II prohibition is in many respects identical to that contained in **8.08** Article 82 (formerly Article 86)[17] of the EC Treaty. Thus, in accordance with the obligation to treat questions arising under the UK Act in a manner consistent with the treatment of corresponding questions arising in European Community law,[18]

---

[11] S 23(3).
[12] S 23(4).
[13] S 23(5).
[14] Ss 24(1)–(2).
[15] Ss 24(3)–(4).
[16] S 24(5).
[17] By virtue of the Treaty of Amsterdam, which amends the EC Treaty, Art 86 is renumbered Art 82.
[18] See Ch 3 paras 3.47–3.57.

guidance on the interpretation of the key concepts of dominance and abuse can be obtained from a review of the decisions and practices of the ECJ and the European Commission. However, a number of differences between the UK provision and Article 86 should be noted:

- Article 82 (formerly Article 86) refers to an abuse of 'a dominant position within the common market'. The Chapter II prohibition refers to abuse of a dominant position within the United Kingdom 'in a market'. Thus, although the dominant position must exist in the United Kingdom, the market may be a market which extends beyond the UK. The Government has made it clear that there must be dominance in a relevant market and that although this market must include the UK, it is not necessary that the market is entirely contained within the UK.[19] The reference to 'a market' also makes it clear that, unlike the jurisdictional tests for merger control and monopoly references under the Fair Trading Act 1973, the existence of dominance in an economic market (as opposed to a 'reference market' under the 1973 Act) is required.[20]

- Article 82 (formerly Article 86) requires that the abuse must 'affect trade between Member States'. As would be expected, under the Act the abuse must 'affect trade within the United Kingdom'.[21]

- The Act, in giving examples of abusive behaviour, refers to 'conduct' which may constitute an abuse.[22] Article 82 (formerly Article 86), in setting out examples of abuse, does not use the term 'conduct'. It is unlikely that this is a substantive difference between the two provisions. Section 18(2) merely gives examples of abusive behaviour, it is not a definitive list of behaviour that would be abusive. It has been suggested that the reference to 'conduct' has the effect of excluding omissions from the scope of the provision.[23] However, the examples set out in section 18(2) clearly include negative as well as positive behaviour, for example, 'limiting production'.[24] In any event, a failure to act, for example a failure to supply when requested to do so, can be said to fall within the definition of 'conduct', at least when the failure to act takes the form of a refusal to deal with another party or a failure to respond to requests from another party.

- Article 82 (formerly Article 86) refers to an undertaking holding 'a dominant position within the common market [ie EU] or in a *substantial* part of it'. By contrast there is no geographic substantiality test in relation to the Chapter II prohibition. The United Kingdom is defined as 'the United Kingdom or any part of it'. This is a significant difference between the two sets of provisions. In many cases,

---

[19] See Lord Simon of Highbury, *Hansard*, HL vol 586, col 1336 (5 Mar 1998).
[20] See para 8.16 and 8.17 below.
[21] See Ch 3 paras 3.28–3.33 for more details.
[22] S 18(2).
[23] See Ch 3 para 3.27.
[24] S 18(2)(b).

one of the difficulties in establishing an infringement of Article 82 is the need to demonstrate that the dominant position is enjoyed in a substantial part of the common market. Under the UK provision, it is possible to envisage an undertaking that enjoys a dominant position in a small but distinct geographic market, for example a private hospital with a local catchment area, or a local bus or train service, being dominant in respect of its local market. Such undertaking would thus fall within the scope of the Chapter II prohibition.

• There are a number of exclusions from the Chapter II prohibition.[25] These are set out in Schedule 1 relating to mergers and concentrations and the general exclusions are set out in Schedule 3. The Secretary of State can add to this list of general exclusions. These exclusions include compliance with legal requirements, such as UK legal enactments.[26] The concept of the supremacy of EC law means that compliance with national legal requirements would not necessarily be a defence if a party has abused a dominant position under Article 82 (formerly Article 86).[27] There is also a public policy exception[28] under the Act under which the Secretary of State may, for exceptional and compelling reasons of public policy, make an order that the Chapter II prohibition will not apply in particular circumstances. There is no equivalent provision under EC law. Article 86(2) (formerly Article 90(2)) of the EC Treaty does provide for an exception to the competition rules in relation to certain undertakings entrusted with certain public service obligations and revenue producing monopolies, where the rules obstruct the performance of the tasks assigned to the undertaking and a similar provision is included in Schedule 3.[29] Article 86(2) has been very narrowly interpreted by both the European Commission and the ECJ.[30] However, the public policy exclusion in paragraph 7 of Schedule 3 is broader than Article 86(2). It is not restricted to a limited range of undertakings and it applies whenever the Secretary of State is satisfied that exceptional and compelling public policy reasons exist. Lastly, there are also specific exclusions for conduct which relates to a coal or steel products where the European Coal and Steel Treaty gives the European Commission exclusive jurisdiction[31] and the Secretary of State may order that the Chapter II prohibition will not apply in a specific situation so as to avoid conflict with international obligations.[32]

As with Article 82 (formerly Article 86) Article 86, there is no power to grant exemptions from the prohibition of abuse of a dominant position.

---

[25] See Ch 5.

[26] Sch 3, para 5, see paras 5.47–5.51 ibid.

[27] See Joined Cases 43 and 63/82 *Vereniging ter Bevordering van het Vlaamse Boekwezen & Vereeniging ter Bevordering van de Belangen des Boekhandels v EC Commission* [1984] ECR 19.

[28] Sch 3, para 7, see paras 5.72–5.73 ibid.

[29] Sch 3 para 4, see paras 5.32–5.40 ibid.

[30] See, eg, Case C–320/91 *re: Corbeau* [1993] ECR I–2533.

[31] Sch 3, para 8, see paras 5.52–5.55 ibid.

[32] Sch 3, para 6, see paras 5.74–5.75 ibid.

C. Market Definition

The Significance of Market Definition

8.09 The concept of a 'dominant position' on a market is intimately connected with the definition of the relevant market. Market power does not exist in a vacuum but in the context of the appropriate market. Thus, the definition of the relevant market is a critical step in establishing whether an undertaking is dominant. It will be relevant in determining market shares and the extent to which there are barriers to market entry. Market definition is also important in determining whether otherwise abusive behaviour is considered to be 'conduct of minor significance' and thus benefits from an immunity from fines.[33] Failure by the OFT to define the relevant market correctly in a particular case may lead to its decision being overturned.[34]

8.10 Regard must be had to both the relevant product market and the relevant geographic market.

8.11 A simple example of the significance of product market definition is as follows:

> A company sells 75 per cent of all bananas sold in the United Kingdom. However, it sells only 40 per cent of all soft fruit sold in the United Kingdom and 10 per cent of all fruit sold. If the relevant market is that for bananas, the company is almost certainly dominant. If the market is that for all fruit (or, even broader, all foodstuffs) it is most unlikely to be dominant. If the appropriate market is that for soft fruits it may be dominant.

8.12 The following hypothetical example illustrates the significance of the definition of the geographic market:

> Private hospital A is located in the city of Liverpool. It is the only private hospital in Liverpool. Thus, if the relevant geographic market is the city of Liverpool (and on the assumption that 'private hospitals' are the relevant product market), private hospital A will enjoy a 100 per cent share of the local market for private hospitals. If, however, the geographic market is wider, for example the north west of England, private hospital A will enjoy only a 40 per cent share, and if the market is even broader, say all of the United Kingdom, it would have only a very small share. Thus, at one extreme, if the market is defined as Liverpool, private hospital A is clearly dominant. At the other extreme, if the market is defined as the whole of the UK, it will clearly not be dominant.

---

[33] S 40(2).
[34] Case 6/72 *Europemballage Corp and Continental Can Co Inc v EEC Commission* [1973] ECR 215.

In some cases, particularly in relation to transport markets, the product market   **8.13**
will be defined in terms of geographic location. For example, hypothetical Airline
A provides a service between Heathrow and Edinburgh. If the product market is
airline services between Heathrow and Edinburgh it enjoys a 70 per cent market
share. If, however, the product market is airline services between all London airports—encompassing Heathrow, Gatwick, Stansted, City and Luton—and
Edinburgh, Airline A's market share is much smaller. This is a separate question
from the geographic market question. Thus, once it is determined that the product market is, say, routes between all London airports and Edinburgh, a separate
geographic issue is whether a significant number of passengers served by such
routes may also use other routes, say between Birmingham and Edinburgh, which
means that the Birmingham–Edinburgh service is, at least in part, serving the
same geographic market as the London–Edinburgh service.

Defining Markets

There is no simple test to identify a relevant market. There is a range of criteria   **8.14**
that the competition authorities take into account, some of which carry greater
weight than others, and the significance of particular criteria may vary from case
to case. Decisions of the European Commission under Articles 81 and 82 (formerly Articles 85 and 86) and, more recently, under the EC Merger Regulation
provide some guidance on how the UK authorities are likely to define markets
under the Act. However, it is not possible to follow precedent strictly in relation
to market definition. Competitive conditions may change over time, particularly
in respect of products subject to rapid technological change; or the previous cases
may relate to an area of the EU where conditions are very different from the UK.
The context of the competition matter under consideration will have a bearing on
how the market is defined. Thus, market definition in relation to a merger
between suppliers of a particular product may not be identical to the definition
adopted if a particular abuse by the supplier of such product is being considered.[35]

The European Commission has published a Notice on market definition.[36] The   **8.15**
Notice seeks to provide guidance on how the European Commission applies the
concept of relevant product and geographic market in its enforcement of
European Community competition law. In accordance with their obligation to
ensure consistency between EC law and practice and the application of the Act,[37]
the OFT and the appeal tribunal of the Competition Commission may be
expected to adopt the principles laid down in the Notice and by European

---

[35] Office of Fair Trading, 'Competition Act 1998: Market Definition' (OFT 403), paras
5.15–5.20.
[36] Commission Notice on the definition of the relevant market for the purposes of Community
competition law, adopted 3 Oct 1997 [1997] OJ C372/5.
[37] See Ch 3 paras 3.28–3.37.

Commission practice. The approach of the United States competition authorities in defining markets is also of relevance. In a number of cases, products and services that will be subject to scrutiny under the Act will have previously been subject to review by the US authorities. Even where this is not the case, guidelines on market definition issued by the Federal Trade Commission and the Department of Justice[38] are widely respected by economists and officials as laying down a practical guide to market definition in a variety of circumstances.[39] The OFT has also published its own guidelines on market definition under the Act which draws on the European Commission Notice and US guidelines.[40]

8.16 Some guidance may also be obtained from the practice of the OFT and the MMC (the predecessor of the Competition Commission) in relation to market definition under other legislation—in particular the merger control and monopoly provisions of the Fair Trading Act 1973. However, it is necessary to view such practices with caution. For the purposes of monopoly enquiries it is necessary to define the 'reference market' within which the monopoly situation is believed to exist. Similarly, where a merger reference is made in the United Kingdom on the basis of the 'market share' test a reference market must be defined for jurisdictional purposes in order to determine whether the merging enterprises enjoy a 25 per cent share of the market. The Fair Trading Act requires that such 'market' is a 'description of goods or services'. This need not conform to an economic definition of the relevant market.

8.17 There is little doubt that the definition of the reference market has influenced the MMC's analysis of the economic market.[41] The concept of the reference market will continue to be used for monopoly inquiries (see Chapter 17 below) and for merger investigations, and this may influence the approach of OFT officials and the Competition Commission. Existing UK precedents may therefore continue to be of some value, although they should always be considered in the context of the provisions of the Act, EC law and the OFT market definition guidelines.

The Relevant Product Market

8.18 The identification of the relevant product market is not an abstract exercise but a tool to help to determine whether an undertaking holds a dominant position. It is therefore necessary to examine the conditions of competition, supply and

---

[38] US Department of Justice and Federal Trade Commission, *Horizontal Merger Guidelines*, issued 1992, revised 1997.

[39] See, eg, National Economic Research Association, Inc., *Market Definition in UK Competition Policy*, OFT Research Paper 1, Feb 1992.

[40] OFT, n 35 above.

[41] See, eg, MMC reports on *William Cook*, CM 1196, Aug 1990, and *Rhone Poulenc/Monsanto*, CM 826, Oct 1989.

demand on the market in question.[42] Where a product is capable of different uses there is no obligation to define the markets separately according to the use to which the product is put. It depends on the circumstances in each case whether a product with several potential uses constitutes a single relevant market or several.[43]

Products or services may be considered to be part of the same market if they can   **8.19**
be substituted for each other, that is, if they can be regarded as interchangeable.

The OFT has in the past stated: **8.20**

> [A] market is usually identified . . . by considering the characteristics of the product or service itself and its users in relation to any substitutes that may be available . . . [44]

Form N,[45] which is to be used for notifications for guidance or decisions under the Chapter I or Chapter II prohibitions, states:

> a relevant product market comprises all those products and/or services regarded by the consumer of the product or service as inter-changeable or substitutable by reason of their characteristics, prices or intended use[46]

The starting point for an analysis of substitutability is to consider the particular   **8.21**
products or services that are supplied by the firm (or parties) that is being investigated. The OFT proposes applying a 'hypothetical monopolist test' to such products by asking the question:

> whether a hypothetical monopolist of these products would maximise its profits by consistently charging higher prices than it would if it faced competition?[47]

The application of this test requires a consideration of potential substitutes for the relevant products or services. If the hypothetical monopolist increased prices above a competitive level, would consumers switch to substitute products? If they would, the substitute products can be added to the potential market and the test can be applied again with a further set of alternative products. Eventually a group of products is identified from which consumers would not switch even if there were a price rise. This will normally be the market definition used by the OFT. In the case of an oligopolistic market, the test would be applied looking at the group of hypothetical oligopolists rather than a single monopolist.

---

[42] Case C–333/94P Opinion of Ruiz-Jarabo Colomer AG, *Tetra Pak International SA v EC Commission* [1996] ECR I–5951.

[43] See Case IV/34.621 *Irish Sugar plc* [1997] OJ L258/1 where white granulated sugar was divided into two separate markets—industrial sugar and retail sugar. Each involved the same basic product but were differentiated by the usage to which the products were put; the volumes sold and the types of customer.

[44] OFT, *Monopolies and Anti-Competitive Practice: A Guide to the Provisions of the Fair Trading Act 1973 and the Competition Act 1980* (London: OFT, 1995).

[45] Office of Fair Trading, Formal Consultation Draft, 'Form for notifications for guidance or decision under Chapters I and II of the Competition Act 1998' (OFT 409), Part 2 para 6.

[46] Ibid, Part 2, para 6.

[47] OFT, n 35 above, para 2.8.

Substitutability may be considered from the demand and supply side.

Demand Substitution

8.22 The European Commission's Notice recognises the US methodology as one way of determining the relevant market and the OFT guidelines state that this will normally be the approach followed by the OFT.[48] The US guidelines have the advantage of laying down a practical test for identifying the market known as the 'SSNIP' test (Small but Significant and Non-transitory Increase in Price). The US guidelines state:

> A market is defined as a product or group of products and a geographic area in which it is produced or sold such that a hypothetical, profit-maximising firm, not subject to price regulation, that was the only present and future producer or seller of those products in that area likely would impose at least a 'small but significant and non transitory' increase in price, assuming the terms of sale of all other products are held constant.

8.23 A 5 to 10 per cent price increase is usually considered 'small but significant'. The assumption is that if product A competes with product B a permanent 5 to 10 per cent increase in the price of product A would lead consumers to switch from product A to product B thus demonstrating that the two products are substitutable. If the application of the test shows that products A and B are substitutable for each other, the exercise is repeated with product C and, if C is considered to be substitutable, A, B and C, are tested as against D until the relevant group of products is identified.

8.24 Substitutes do not have to be physically or technically identical products to be part of the same market. Thus, for example, matches and disposable lighters have been considered to be in the same market because consumers view them as close substitutes.[49] Similarly, products with different prices may nevertheless be substituted because, if the lower priced product became more expensive, consumers may switch to the higher priced product. If a 5 to 10 per cent price rise would have such an effect the products may be part of the same market.

8.25 The European Commission's Notice sets out an example of how demand substitution analysis may work by seeking to apply the US test to a hypothetical merger between soft drink manufacturers. In such cases an issue is whether soft drinks with different flavours belong to the same market. The question to address is whether consumers of flavour A would switch to other flavours when confronted with a permanent price increase of 5 per cent to 10 per cent for flavour A. If a sufficient number of consumers would switch to, say, flavour B in such circumstances to such an extent that the increase in the price for flavour A would not be profitable for its manufacturer because of resulting loss of sales, then the market would

---

[48] OFT, n 35 above, para 3.2.
[49] MMC report, *Matches and Disposable Lighters*, Cm 1854, Mar 1992.

comprise at least flavours A and B. A similar analysis would then have to be made as between flavours A and B, on the one hand, and C, on the other hand, until an appropriate group of products is identified.

While this provides a theoretical basis for analysis and appears to lay down a prac- **8.26** tical test, it gives rise to a number of difficulties in practice, not the least of which is that, in the absence of empirical evidence of the effect of such price movements, there is considerable scope for debate as to how far price movements of this kind would lead to consumers switching between products.

There are a number of criticisms of the US test. These criticisms were described in **8.27** an OFT Research Paper[50] as:

- there is nothing precise about the 5 per cent figure. In some cases other price differences may be more appropriate;

- the approach gives rise to particular problems in abuse of market power cases where a dominant player may have priced up to its profit maximising level, so that a further 5 per cent rise would be unprofitable. These will lead to wider market definitions than if the 5 per cent rise is based on a competitive price level. The fact that the relevant undertaking has made excessive profits may be taken as evidence that the price level is uncompetitive. In such a case the OFT would have to give greater weight to factors other than the hypothetical monopolist test in defining the relevant market;[51]

- how should the price rise be measured? The US guidelines suggest that the test should be applied to the gross price charged for the relevant product. However, this could give rise to inconsistent treatment between resellers and agents. It may be more appropriate to apply the 5 per cent price rise to the value added by the relevant firm, for example, the retailer's gross margin and the agent's commission. The OFT has indicated that it will normally apply the test to the selling price but, where appropriate, compensate for differences between the 'value added' and the selling price by retaining some flexibility in the size of the price differential;[52]

- how long should be allowed for market responses to the movement in price? The OFT guidelines suggest a rule of thumb of one year, although this period may differ from case to case.[53] Shorter or longer responses would lead to different market definitions.[54]

---

[50] See n 39 above.
[51] OFT, n 35 above, paras 5.13–5.14.
[52] Ibid, para 3.2.
[53] Ibid, para 3.5.
[54] In Case 333/94 P *Tetra Pak International SA v Commission of the European Communities* [1996] ECR I–5951 the judgment of the CFI was challenged before the ECJ on the ground, *inter alia*, that the CFI took into account only short term interchangeability when deciding whether there was sufficient product substitutability for the purpose of market definition. The ECJ did not consider this point in any detail, confining itself to stating that, contrary to Tetra Pak's submission, the CFI did not confine itself to examining short-term substitutability.

8.28 In practice the European Commission has adopted a flexible approach to demand side substitutability analysis. Criteria identified in the European Commission's Notice and OFT draft market definition guidelines include:

- Evidence of substitution in the recent past is of great significance, where such evidence is available. Thus, where there has been a relative change of price the consumer reaction to such change will be of critical importance in assessing substitutability, for example, in *Chiquita*[55] the European Commission regarded published research by the Food and Agriculture Organisation as significant for the purpose of defining the market for bananas. The research showed that 'the prices or available quantities of other fruits have very little influence on the prices and availability of bananas'.[56]

- There are quantitative tests specifically designed for the purpose of delineating markets. These tests measure factors such as elasticity and cross-elasticity of demand and similarities of price movements and level over time. Where these tests are capable of standing up to detailed scrutiny they will be taken into account.[57]

- The views of customers and competitors are also important. The European Commission, as a matter of routine, will contact major customers and competitors of the company being investigated and, in addition to seeking views on the substantive competition issues will seek views on market definition, including views as to likely customer reaction to a hypothetical 5 per cent movement in price. The OFT has indicated that it will often interview customers and competitors.[58] The views of third parties have had a significant impact on European Commission decisions, for example, in the merger between Aérospatiale and Alenia/de Havilland[59] the fact that the 'overwhelming majority' of competitors and customers contacted by the European Commission agreed with the European Commission's market classification was considered to be an important factor in a product market definition that was critical to the outcome in that case. This is a more difficult exercise where there are many millions of consumers, for example, for soft drinks, although even in such cases the views of distributors or retailers such as supermarkets, will be of value.

- Consumer surveys may be of particular value in the case of consumer goods where there are many ultimate purchasers of the product. A distinction is drawn between studies produced by the parties in the normal course of their business and used for their own internal purposes, for example, pricing and marketing decisions, and studies carried out specifically for the purpose of the competition

---

[55] *Chiquita*, Commission decision of 17 Dec 1975 [1976] OJ L95/1.
[56] OFT, n 35 above, para 3.6.
[57] Ibid, para 3.6.
[58] Ibid, para 3.6.
[59] Case IV/M.053 *Aérospatiale/Alenia/De Havilland* [1991] OJ L334/42.

law procedure. The former are likely to carry more weight. The latter, in the words of the European Commission's Notice, 'will usually be scrutinised with utmost care'.

- Barriers and costs associated with switching to possible substitutes are taken into account. These may take a variety of forms, for example: regulatory barriers; technical restrictions; constraints in downstream markets making access to such markets difficult; high cost of capital investment; the location of customers; uncertainty about quality and reputation of unknown suppliers etc. These factors may, for example, mean that products with very similar functions—such as gas and electricity—are not effectively substitutable for each other. The OFT considers such evidence to be a significant factor in determining whether substitution takes place.[60]

- If there are distinct groups of customers with specific and separate requirements with no significant scope for trade between the customers then even apparently identical products may be considered to be in separate markets. Thus, a distinction is often drawn between original equipment suppliers and the suppliers of replacement parts.[61]

- Product substitution may be possible for some customers but not for others; for example, there may be health or dietary reasons why certain consumers of particular foodstuffs cannot switch to other foodstuffs even though such switching is possible for other consumers. The former group of consumers are regarded as 'captive'. The key issue is whether substitution by the non-captive consumers will prevent the supplier charging prices above competitive levels. If it would, then the existence of a captive group of consumers is not relevant for market definition purposes. In some cases a supplier will be in a position to distinguish between the captive and non-captive groups charging higher prices to the former; for example, in relation to air transport services, business users may place a premium on time and therefore would not regard train services as an acceptable substitute to airline services. Leisure users may be less time sensitive and may regard trains as an alternative. In such a case there may be more than one market—a leisure market and a business market—for an apparently identical service.[62]

Supply Substitution

Products which are not fully substitutable on the demand side may nevertheless **8.29** be considered to be substitutes because it is very easy for producers to switch from producing one product to producing the other. This would prevent a hypothetical monopoly supplier from charging higher prices because, if it were to do so,

---

[60] OFT, n 35 above, para 3.6.

[61] See, eg, Case IV/M.043, *CEAC/Magneti-Marelli* [1991] OJ L222/38; Case IV/M.012, *Varta/Bosch* [1991] OJ L320/26; Case IV/M.134, *Mannesmann/Boge* [1993] OJ L114/34.

[62] OFT, n 35 above, paras 3.7–3.8.

alternative suppliers could easily enter the market. A very significant ease of switching is required. The European Commission's Notice states:

> Supply-side substitutability may be taken into account when defining markets in those situations in which its effects are equivalent to those of demand substitution in terms of effectiveness and immediacy. This requires that suppliers are able to switch production to the relevant products and market them in the short-term without incurring significant costs or risks in response to small and permanent changes in relative prices.

8.30   The OFT will include supply-side substitutes within the market definition only when it is clear that substitution would take place quickly. This is defined in the OFT draft market definition guidelines as normally being less than one year, although the period will vary depending on the product.[63]

8.31   The physical ease of switching production is only one factor that is taken into account. Also relevant is the extent to which it would be possible rapidly to establish a new brand or distribution network.[64] If there is any serious doubt on this point such substitutes will not be included.

8.32   The overriding test, however, is the same as when considering demand substitutability: would the supply side substitution under consideration be sufficient to prevent the hypothetical monopolist in the supply of one product from setting prices independently of the supply-linked substitute?[65]

8.33   The classic example of supply side substitutability is in relation to shoes. On the demand side, size 12 shoes are of course not substitutable for size 8 shoes. However, a producer of size 8 shoes could easily switch production to size 12 shoes and thus size 8 and size 12 shoes may be considered to be part of the same market.

8.34   The European Commission Notice and the OFT guidelines[66] give the example of paper. Paper may be found in different qualities, for example, standard writing paper and high quality paper for art books. Such different qualities are not substitutable on the demand side. However, paper plants can manufacture the different qualities and switch production between qualities at minimal cost and in a short time frame. Paper manufacturers are therefore able to compete for orders of various qualities and adapt their manufacturing capabilities accordingly. Thus, the various qualities of paper constitute a single relevant market.

8.35   Supply side substitution must be distinguished from potential competition. The latter exists where a party which is not yet in a market has the financial, technical and other abilities to enter if conditions are suitable. Potential competition is

---

[63] OFT, n 35 above, para 3.16.
[64] Ibid, para 3.17.
[65] OFT, Research Paper 1; see n 39 above.
[66] OFT, n 35 above, para 3.14.

relevant to a later stage of the analysis than that of relevant product market definition in determining whether a player is dominant in that market. A critical question in distinguishing supply side substitutability from potential competition is the degree of investment in additional resources (or adaptation of existing resources including marketing resources) that is required to switch between products and the time required in order to switch.

Evidence of supply side substitutability may be provided from the following sources:[67]

8.36

- a questionnaire to potential suppliers to determine whether substitution is technically possible; how much it would cost and how long it would take. The OFT guidelines consider the key question to be whether it would be economic to switch production given a small (ie 5–10 per cent) price increase;

- the OFT may ask firms whether they have spare capacity or are free to switch production; this may not be possible, for example, because of capacity constraints or difficulties in obtaining raw materials;

- the views of customers may be sought on whether they would acquire the relevant product from a new supplier.

The Relevant Geographic Market

The relevant geographic market is defined in Form N as follows:

8.37

> The relevant geographic market is the area in which undertakings concerned are involved in the supply of products or services in which the conditions of competition are appreciably different from neighbouring areas.[68]

This requires consideration of demand and supply side factors, including the scope for imports. The OFT guidelines[69] indicate that retailing markets are more likely to be defined on the demand side while wholesaling and manufacturing markets are more likely to be defined on the supply side.

The OFT's starting point is normally to look at the area which is supplied by the relevant parties and then consider whether consumers would switch to suppliers in neighbouring areas in response to a small price increase. If there is significant scope for such substitution it would prevent the companies from increasing prices and the next area is added to the geographical market definition.

8.38

In practice, an appropriate starting point is the actual conditions of competition in different areas. If there are significant differences in market shares or prices in different areas this suggests that each such area may constitute a separate

8.39

---

[67] Ibid, para 3.20.
[68] OFT, n 45 above, Part 2, para 6.
[69] OFT, n 35 above, para 4.2.

geographic market.[70] However, such differences are by no means conclusive evidence of the existence of separate geographic markets. They may be accounted for, for example, by historic factors which do not present a material barrier to entry for players from other areas. Thus, if prices rose, players from neighbouring areas would have no difficulty in moving into the area in which the price increase was implemented. On the other hand, if there are local factors making such entry difficult (for example, the need to obtain regulatory clearances or licences, or local customer preferences), or if the cost of moving into the neighbouring area was a significant impediment to entry (for example, the need to set up local production or marketing facilities at significant cost), then the two areas may be considered to be separate geographic markets.

8.40 The factors to be taken into account in determining if an area constitutes a distinct geographic market include:

- The ability for firms in one area to supply customers in neighbouring areas within one year:[71] If significant sums will need to be spent on advertising or marketing, or if distribution channels are foreclosed, substitution is unlikely to be possible.

- Past evidence of diversion of orders to other areas: This involves consideration of whether such diversion has taken place and, where it has, the conditions under which it took place. Thus, if prices in area A rose by, say, 5 per cent relative to the same product in area B, but there was no diversion of orders from area A to area B, this would suggest that each area is a separate geographic market. If there was such a diversion but only for a very limited group of customers, for example only those with businesses in both area A and area B, this again would suggest that each area is a separate market.

- Demand characteristics such as local preferences for particular brands, language, culture or local convenience: Certain of these factors are more likely to constitute a barrier to trade in goods between the United Kingdom and other countries than between areas within the United Kingdom. However, some factors may be a barrier to trade between different localities. Thus, private consumers may be unlikely to be prepared to open an account with a branch of a bank (other than a telephone banking service), or use a private hospital for routine surgery, outside their locality. Similarly, there may be local preferences for certain brands or types, for example types of beer, which would make it difficult for distributors in one area to sell into another area.

---

[70] See Case IV/34.621, *Irish Sugar plc* [1997] OJ L258/1 in which important price differences between the Republic of Ireland and Northern Ireland was a factor indicating that the two geographic markets were separate.

[71] OFT, n 35 above, para 4.7.

- Views of customers and competitors on the boundaries of the geographic market: These will be of value, although such surveys are subject to the same limitations as similar surveys relating to product markets.

- Current geographic patterns of purchase: These will not be decisive[72] but may be relevant in supporting other evidence of separate markets. The position was explained by Sir Leon Brittan (who was the EC Competition Commissioner at the time) in the context of a merger case:

  > The *CEAC/Magneti-Marelli* (IV/M.23) case provides a good example of this problem. No legislation exists preventing the import and sale of batteries into France. Thus, one might expect the geographic reference market to be wider than a single Member State. However, when the Commission examined this problem it discovered that due to the existence of consumer brand loyalty and the lack of a cross-border distribution and marketing infrastructure, imports would not be likely to enter France in response to an increase in demand. More likely, the price would increase. The market was thus considered national.[73]

- Evidence of significant imports: Such evidence may indicate that the market is international, but this is not necessarily so, for example, where imports come from subsidiaries of domestic suppliers or there are import quotas.[74] A lack of imports is not necessarily evidence that the market is not international: an increase in prices domestically may encourage import penetration.[75]

- Switching costs associated with the diversion of orders to companies located in other areas: Transport costs are particularly important in this regard. Such costs must normally be considered relative to the price of the relevant product.[76] Thus, a product such as cement, which can only be transported a limited distance, can only be sold in a local area. Similarly, low value products, such as beverage containers, which have to be transported in large quantities may have a more limited geographic market particularly if they are used in the context of 'just in time' production delivery requirements.

Chains of Substitution

Products that are not direct substitutes may nevertheless be considered to be part **8.41**
of the same market if they are linked by a 'chain of substitution'. Such a chain may exist at either the product or a geographic level.

At the product level the OFT's guidelines use the example of motor vehicles in **8.42**
order to illustrate what is meant by a 'chain of substitution'.[77] A large Mercedes

---

[72] Ibid, para 4.9.
[73] Address to the Centre for European Policy Studies, Brussels, 25 Oct 1991.
[74] OFT, n 35 above, para 4.9.
[75] Ibid, para 4.10.
[76] Ibid, para 4.8.
[77] Ibid, paras 3.9–3.10.

Benz is unlikely to be a direct substitute for a Volkswagen Polo. If the price of a Volkswagen rose, customers would be more likely to switch to a Fiat or Ford rather than a large Mercedes. However, if the price of all small cars rose, customers might switch from these cars to a slightly larger car, for example, a Ford Escort-sized car, because of the narrowing of the price differential. These cars might then be included in the same market as the smaller cars. If the price of the Escort-sized cars increased those customers might switch to the smaller cars or slightly larger cars, for example, a Ford Mondeo-sized car. Similarly, if the price of the Mondeo-sized car increased, customers might switch to the next size up or down. Thus a chain of substitution might link cars from the Polo to the Mercedes. In practice, while such a chain might link a group of products it is unlikely to link the whole range of products. It is therefore unlikely that the Polo and the Mercedes would be considered to be part of the same market. This is because there may be a break in the chain, for example, between the family-sized cars and luxury cars. In any event, the OFT does not consider these issues in a vacuum but in the context of the actual supply and demand situation. Thus if a particular firm monopolises part of the chain, the purchasers in that part of the chain may have no, or limited, alternative sources of supply. Therefore, the hypothetical monopolist in relation to that part of the chain would be free to raise prices.[78]

8.43 Chains of substitution may also operate at a geographic level. Thus, for example, a supermarket will generally have a local catchment area. Hence, a supermarket store in Birmingham would not be considered to be substitutable for a supermarket store in Glasgow. However, in such a case, there is likely to be a geographic chain linking, say, Birmingham and Glasgow. Thus there will be a group of consumers who are able to use either the Birmingham store or one a little further north, and similarly there will be a group of consumers who are in a position to use either the store that is further north or another store and so on, thus geographically linking stores with local catchment areas across the country. In this way outlets with a predominantly local consumer base may nevertheless form part of a national geographic market. Of course, the position would be different if there were a store where there was no geographic overlap or where the geographic overlap was not significant, for example, a store serving a remote or island community.

Transport Markets

8.44 Defining the relevant market in relation to transport can give rise to particular difficulties. As explained in paragraphs 8.37 to 8.40 above, the market must be defined in geographic terms and, in the context of a transport case, this may mean, for example, that airline services between Edinburgh and Heathrow may or may not be part of a market including all flights between Edinburgh and the various

---

[78] Office of Fair Trading, n 35 above, paras 3.11–3.12.

London airports. In some cases there may be substitutability between different routes. This issue has been considered by the European Commission in relation to a number of concentrations in the air transport sector.[79] The cases indicate that routes may be substitutable depending on:

- the distance of the routes—the longer the distance the more likely they are to be substitutable. Thus Glasgow–London may not be substitutable for Edinburgh–London, but Glasgow–New York may be substitutable for Edinburgh–New York;

- the points served by different routes—the closer such points are together the more likely they are to be substitutable. Thus Belfast City–London may be substitutable for Belfast International–London but not for Dublin–London; and

- the frequency on individual routes—the less the frequency the greater the likelihood of substitutability. Thus, if Manchester–London and Leeds/Bradford–London each have two flights a day the two routes may be substitutable. If each has, say, six flights a day it is unlikely that consumers would regard them as alternatives.

On the question of substitutability between different airports in the same city, the **8.45** European Commission took the view in *British Airways/TAT* that Heathrow and Gatwick airports were substitutable for each other, and therefore flights between Heathrow and Lyon were part of the same market as flights between Gatwick and Lyon. However, it is necessary to consider this market definition in the context of a merger. It does not follow that the same definition would be used for the purposes of an analysis in relation to the Chapter II prohibition.[80]

A further factor delineating transport markets is the availability of connections. **8.46** Thus, for example, it may be that for flights between Edinburgh and London the availability of onward connections with particular airlines or to particular destinations is important for particular travellers. Thus, for example, in *British Midland v Aer Lingus*,[81] concerning the refusal by Aer Lingus to interline with British Midland on the London Heathrow–Dublin route, the European Commission stated:

> Even though air travel between Dublin and other London airports than Heathrow could sometimes be substituted to [sic] travel to Heathrow, that is not so for a large

---

[79] Case IV/M *Delta/PanAm* [1991] OJ C289/14; Case IV/M *Air France/Sabena* [1992] OJ C272/5; Case IV/M.259 *British Airways/TAT* [1992] OJ C326/16; Case T–2/93 *Air France v Commission* [1994] ECR II–323; Case IV/M 278 *British Airways/Dan Air*, on appeal Case T–3/93 *Air France v EC Commission* [1994] 2 CEC 376..

[80] See Office of Fair Trading, n 35 above, paras 5.18–5.20 and *British Midland/Aer Lingus* (n 81 below) where Heathrow–Dublin was considered to be the relevant market in an Art 82 (formerly Art 86) case.

[81] *British Midland/Aer Lingus*, Commission decision 92/213 of 26 Feb 1992 [1992] OJ L96/34; [1993] 4 CMLR 596, para 1.4.

number of travellers. In particular business travellers traditionally prefer Heathrow, among other reasons because other London airports are not served as frequently as Heathrow, and because they do not offer a similar range of connections and therefore will be less suited to onward travel beyond London.

The availability of onward connections with airlines which share frequent traveller programmes may be a particular incentive for some travellers to use a particular route; for example, Heathrow has more connections than any of the other London airports and the European Commission expressed concern about the combination of the frequent traveller programmes of British Airways and American airlines when it examined the proposed link between these airlines.[82]

8.47 On a more localised level, time-related markets may exist in relation to travel on particular routes. Thus, if a railway company operates services between Cambridge and London, the passengers using its services early in the morning and in the evening are likely to be commuters travelling to work. For these travellers, the timing of the service is vital. However, for passengers prepared to travel at other times of the day there may be a number of possible services which they could use. For off-peak travellers, bus and coach services between Cambridge and London may be a viable alternative. Thus services between Cambridge and London during peak hours may form a distinct market from the off-peak services, although the starting and finishing points and mode of transport are exactly the same. This is often reflected in the difference between peak and off-peak fares. By defining the market on a temporal basis, the availability of competition on a particular route may vary during the course of the day as well as varying between weekday and weekend travellers.

8.48 Similarly, train services may compete with air services (or coach services may compete with train services) for leisure travellers who do not regard speed as a priority. Business travellers who are more time constrained may not regard a train service as a suitable alternative to an airline service or a coach as an alternative to a train.

Secondary Product Markets

8.49 Secondary products are products that are purchased only if a customer has brought another product (the primary product). Thus, for example, a printer is the primary product and toner and paper for it are secondary products. Similarly, a car is a primary product and car spare parts are secondary products.

8.50 The secondary product may be part of a separate market from the primary product, for example, in the case of cars and car tyres. In other cases the secondary product will be part of the same market as the primary product; for example, an aircraft engine manufacturer may have a monopoly of the provision of spare parts

---

[82] Commission Notice concerning the alliance between British Airways and American Airlines [1998] OJ C239/10.

to the engine that it supplies. Purchasers of aircraft engines will take into account the relative cost of spare parts when deciding which engine to purchase.

The OFT identifies three possible market definitions for secondary products:[83]   **8.51**

(a) a single market, including both the primary and secondary products (for example cars plus their spare parts);

(b) multiple markets, where there is one market for the primary product and separate markets for secondary products for each primary product brand (for example, Ford spare parts, Fiat spare parts etc); or

(c) dual markets, one for all brands of primary products and one for all brands of secondary products, for example, a market for new cars and a separate market for spare parts for all cars.

If customers take account of the whole-life cost of the product before purchasing, the secondary product is likely to be part of the same market as the primary product. Relevant factors include the proportion of the primary product's price represented by the secondary product (the higher the proportion the more likely customers are to have regard to whole-life cost); the size of the purchaser; information available to customers on costs, servicing and reliability of the secondary product; and predictability as to how often spare parts or servicing will be required.[84]

D. Dominance

Background

Dominance may be enjoyed by either a single undertaking or jointly by a group of   **8.52**
two or more undertakings. Joint (or collective) dominance is considered in paragraphs 8.80 to 8.89 below.

Dominance may be enjoyed by a party as a seller or supplier of goods or services   **8.53**
or as a purchaser of such goods or services.[85]

The Act does not define what constitutes a 'dominant position' other than by ref-   **8.54**
erence to geographic scope, that is, the dominant position must be enjoyed within the United Kingdom.[86] Guidance on what may constitute a dominant position must be obtained from the case law and practice under European Community law and the OFT guidelines.[87]

---

[83] Office of Fair Trading, n 35 above, para 5.6.

[84] Ibid, para 5.8.

[85] For an example of dominant purchasers see Case T–57/91 *National Assn of Licensed Opencast Operators and Ors v British Coal Corporation* [1993] 4 CMLR 615.

[86] S 18(3).

[87] See in particular: Office of Fair Trading 'Competition Act 1998: The Chapter II prohibition' (OFT 402), and Office of Fair Trading, Formal Consultation Draft, Competition Act 1998; 'Assessment of Market Power' (OFT 415) 14 Jan 1999 ('The Market Power Guidelines').

8.55   The ECJ has defined the concept of a dominant position as:

> A position of economic strength enjoyed by an undertaking which enables it to prevent effective competition being maintained on the relevant market by giving it the power to behave to an appreciable extent independently of its competitors, customers and ultimately of its consumers.[88]

The key characteristic of a dominant position is the ability of an undertaking to act to a large extent independently of the competition. Thus, an undertaking which is compelled by the pressure of its competitors' price reductions to lower its own prices would generally not be dominant.[89]

8.56   Dominance does not mean the complete absence of competition. Thus, the fact that some competitors may operate on the relevant market does not exclude the possibility of a firm being dominant. The Court has stated as follows:

> an undertaking does not have to have eliminated all opportunity for competition in order to be in a dominant position.

It is the ability to contain competition, not the ability to ignore it, which is characteristic of dominance.[90]

8.57   Relevant factors in determining whether an undertaking is constrained by competitors include the strength of existing competitors, evidenced, in particular, by market shares; the scope for potential competition, which is determined by the strength of any barriers to entry to the relevant market; and other constraints such as strong buyer-power from customers.[91]

Acquiring Dominance

8.58   There are four means by which firms may achieve a dominant position:[92]

(a)   The firm may be granted market power by a public authority: In the UK the process of market liberalisation and privatisation has meant that in most cases industries that are capable of benefiting from competition are not subject to restrictions on competition imposed by the state. However it does remain the case that there are certain 'natural monopolies', for example, the electricity distribution networks and water pipelines. In such cases external regulation will usual provide the means of regulating the market behaviour of the monopolist, and in most cases the external regulator will, in addition to any powers under the relevant licence, concurrently enforce the Chapter II pro-

---

[88]   Case 27/76 *United Brands Co. & Anor v EC Commission* [1978] ECR 207.

[89]   Case 85/76 *Hoffmann-La Roche & Co. AG v EC Commission* [1979] ECR 461; Case 332/81 *Michelin v EC Commission* [1983] ECR 3461.

[90]   See J. Temple Lang, 'Some Aspects of Abuse of Dominant Positions in European Community Antitrust Law' (1979) 3 *Fordham Intl LF*.

[91]   Office of Fair Trading, 'The Chapter II prohibition' n 87 above, para 3.11.

[92]   D. Hay, 'Oxford Review of Economic Policy', Vol 9, No 2.

hibition.[93] The process of privatisation may result in the granting of market power to the privatised entity even where there are no long-term barriers to entry. Thus, the Rail Regulator found that the three rolling stock companies which had acquired passenger rail rolling stock at the time of rail privatisation had a 'likelihood of a dominant position', and in order to deal with this possibility the Regulator requested the preparation of a code of conduct that would provide a framework of behavioural standards. Departures from the code would be investigated as potential abuses under the Act.[94]

(b) Achieving dominance by 'skill, foresight and industry': Dominance arises because the relevant undertaking has been a successful competitor. Once the undertaking has acquired a dominant position behaviour that was acceptable in pursuit of market strength may be unacceptable if used as a means of retaining or extending market power.

(c) Acquiring dominance as a result of anti-competitive behaviour such as predatory pricing: As will be discussed below, such behaviour is not prohibited when engaged in by a non-dominant firm.[95] However, such behaviour if engaged in by a dominant player with the effect of sustaining a dominant position or acquiring a dominant position on a related market would be considered to be abusive.

(d) Acquiring a dominant position by merger: Mergers are subject to separate control under the Fair Trading Act 1973 and the EC Merger Regulation.[96]

Significance of Market Shares

The Relevance of Market Shares

The most important factor (although not the only factor) in assessing dominance **8.59** is a company's market share. Apart from the absolute size of market share, it is also necessary to consider its relative size as compared to the company's competitors; the extent to which market share fluctuates over time; and the nature of the relevant market.

The holder of a complete monopoly is obviously in a dominant position. This cat- **8.60** egory includes state created monopolies.[97] Similarly a monopoly manufacturer of spare parts, where the only alternative source of such parts is cannibalising old machines, enjoys a clear dominant position.[98]

---

[93] See Ch 19.

[94] Office of the Rail Regulator, *Review of the Rolling Stock Market*, May 1998.

[95] Indeed, it is arguable that a non-dominant firm cannot over the medium term price below cost because it would be driven out of business.

[96] Reg 4064/89 [1989] OJ L395/1.

[97] Joined Cases 6 and 7/73 *Istituto Chemioterapico Italiano SpA and Commercial Solvents Corporation v EC Commission* [1974] ECR 223.

[98] Case 22/78 *Hugin Kassaregister AB & Anor v EC Commission* [1979] ECR 1869.

8.61   Very large market shares approaching 100 per cent are almost conclusive evidence of dominance.[99]

8.62   Any market share over 50 per cent will, in the absence of evidence to the contrary, be evidence of a dominant position, particularly if such a market share has been held for a long time and has not fluctuated materially over time. Thus, in *AKZO* a market share of 57 per cent gave rise to dominance.[100]

8.63   Market shares below 50 per cent may in certain circumstances, when taken together with other factors, give rise to a position of dominance, although the OFT has stated that market shares of below 40 per cent will be unlikely to give rise to a finding of dominance unless there is strong evidence to the contrary, for example, if competitors are very weak.[101]

8.64   The relative market shares of competitors are important. Where there is a significant difference between the market share of the largest player on the market and those of its main competitors this will be considered relevant. Thus, in the *United Brands* case,[102] United Brands was considered to be dominant with a market share of 45 per cent where the nearest competitors had a market share several times smaller. Similarly, Tetra Pak[103] was found to be dominant on the market for non-aseptic packaging because it had a market share of 55 per cent while its two main competitors had shares of 27 per cent and 11 per cent. By contrast, where two or more firms have large but similar market shares they may not be considered to be dominant. In *Metaleurop*[104] firms with shares of 20 and 30 per cent were considered not to be dominant because of the presence of other major players.

8.65   In some sectors there are a limited number of contracts awarded each year, and therefore market shares may fluctuate significantly depending on which firm has been awarded contracts at a particular time. Similarly, in a developing market, for example a high tech market, market shares may rise and fall rapidly as new products are introduced. In such cases a consideration of market shares over time is a more useful guide to market power than a snapshot of market share in a particular year.[105]

---

[99]   *BBI/Boosey & Hawkes*, Commission decision 87/500 of 29 July 1987 [1987] OJ L286/36, and Joined Cases 40–48, 50, 54–56, 111, 113 and 114/73 *Suiker Unie v EC Commission* [1975] ECR 1663.

[100]   Case 62/86 *AKZO Chemie BV v EC Commission* [1991] ECR I–3359.

[101]   Office of Fair Trading, 'The Chapter II prohibition' n 87 above, para 3.13.

[102]   See n 88 above.

[103]   *Tetra Pak II*, Commission decision 92/163 of 24 July 1991 [1992] OJ L72/1.

[104]   *Metaleurop SA*, Commission decision 90/363 of 26 June 1990 [1990] OJ L179/41.

[105]   Office of Fair Trading, n 87 above, 'Assessment of Market Power' (OFT 415), 14Jan 1999, para 4.2.

The following general guidelines may therefore be laid down in relation to market **8.66**
shares:

- if a market share exceeds 50 per cent a player will be dominant other than in exceptional circumstances;
- if the market share is between 40 and 50 per cent a player will normally be considered to be dominant unless circumstances suggest otherwise;
- if a market share is below 40 per cent a player will rarely be dominant but exceptionally may be if other strong relevant factors are present.

The significance of market definition must be considered in this regard. The competition authorities do not define markets in a vacuum. By narrowing or extending a relevant market definition there can be a significant impact on relevant market shares. Thus, for example, an undertaking producing and selling cola drinks may have a share of 60 per cent of the sale of all cola drinks, but only 20 per cent of the sale of all carbonated soft drinks. The decision whether the relevant market is for cola drinks or carbonated soft drinks is therefore critical in deciding whether there is dominance. In cases where there are a number of plausible market definitions, market shares may be considered on the basis of alternative definitions, although if the alternatives give rise to different conclusions on the question whether an undertaking is dominant the OFT will ultimately have to decide which definition is the most relevant. In cases where, regardless of definition, the outcome would be the same, the OFT may not reach a final view on market share.[106]

Measuring Market Share

Market share may be assessed on the basis of the value of sales or the volume of **8.67**
sales. The OFT prefers measurements by value.[107] However, volume measurements may be appropriate in some circumstances, for example, where there are no industry-wide figures available in relation to value of sales or where volume gives a better indication of market conditions, for example, passenger volumes may be a useful measure in the transport sector.

The OFT, in conducting an investigation, may survey relevant parties in the market **8.68**
in order to obtain a view of total market size if reliable public information is not available. This option is not available to the parties themselves. Indeed, an exchange of sales information between competitors may itself infringe the Chapter I or Chapter II prohibition. It will therefore often be the case that when the parties are preparing a submission to the OFT they will only have limited market information, and they are more likely to have information on volume shares than on shares by value. In such cases, it is obviously appropriate to submit the

---

[106] Ibid, paras 4.7–4.8.
[107] Ibid, para 4.5.

best information available indicating how far it is thought market shares by value would diverge from the volume figures. Sources of information, apart from the parties' own estimates, include third party surveys of the relevant sector, for example, analyst reports and trade association statistics.

8.69 Market shares by value are measured on the basis of sales (rather than costs of production). The sale that is relevant is that from the undertaking to its direct customers rather than the sales to end users. Thus, for example, an undertaking which sells to wholesalers which then sell on to ultimate consumers will take account of the cost of its sales to wholesalers rather than the prices charged to the ultimate consumer.[108]

8.70 In cases where an international market is being considered, the OFT may look at a range of exchange rates over a period of time, particularly in situations where exchange rate fluctuations make a material difference to market share calculations.[109]

8.71 Where there are undertakings on a market which produce for their own consumption, the question arises whether own-production should be taken into account in assessing the overall size in the market. This would normally only be done where it is possible for the undertaking to switch relatively easily from internal production to external sales. Where, for example, all of the internal capacity is required in order to meet internal requirements the undertaking's internal capacity would not be taken in to account.[110]

8.72 Imports are of course taken into account in assessing the UK market size (just as exports would normally be discounted).[111]

Barriers to Entry

8.73 The second most important factor in assessing dominance, after market shares, is the extent to which the undertaking faces, or may face, competition from new entrants or existing smaller players who can increase their market significance.

8.74 If a party has a large market share, but the market is not difficult to enter, the undertaking will be constrained from increasing prices by the fear that, if it does so, competitors will enter the market. Thus, the existence and extent of barriers to entry, and barriers to expansion once the market has been entered, is important.[112]

---

[108] Office of Fair Trading, n 87 above, 'Assessment of Market Power' para 4.6.
[109] Ibid, para 4.6.
[110] Ibid, para 4.6.
[111] Ibid, para 4.6.
[112] Office of Fair Trading, 'The Chapter II prohibition', n 87 above, paras 3.14–3.16.

Factors that may indicate the existence of such barriers include: regulatory restric-   **8.75**
tions such as licensing requirements, particularly if the number of licences are
rationed;[113] technological advantages enjoyed by an incumbent player;[114] a mature
market, with the consequence that new entrants can only obtain market share
from existing players;[115] the need to make significant investments to enter the
market which cannot be recovered on exit (high 'sunk' costs),[116] for example,
investment in specialist machinery, or in establishing a brand this is a particular
problem if the existing players have already recovered much of the cost of the initial investment and therefore it would be difficult for a new player to recover costs
from revenues it is able to earn operating in the market; the reputation of the existing player for predatory behaviour (which may deter entry); the existence of exclusivity agreements (which may deny a new entrant access to a distribution
network); economies of scale requiring entry on a large scale to compete on a cost
effective basis and inability to get access on equal terms to a key asset, for example,
slots at an airport.

The assessment of the significance of barriers to entry is difficult. One test that is   **8.76**
often applied is the cost to a new undertaking of obtaining, say, a 5 per cent market share. The relevant costs include not just production costs but also the cost of
establishing a market presence and an effective distribution network. Evidence of
successful entry in the past is also important (as is evidence of unsuccessful
attempts at entry). A further factor is the time that it would take to establish an
effective market presence. Successful entry is more likely in a growing market than
in one which is static, because new entry would be less likely to have a significant
impact on prices and profits.[117]

Buyer Power

In some markets the potential market power of a seller (or a buyer) is counterbal-   **8.77**
anced by the power of a buyer (or seller). The test is whether, in the absence of the
buyer, prices would have been higher.[118] Thus, buyer power is more likely to be
significant in counteracting potential market dominance where the seller has only
a very limited choice of buyers, but buyers have a broader choice of sellers. If, for

---

[113] *Napier Brown/British Sugar*, Commission decision 88/518 [1988] OJ L284/41.
[114] *Tetra Pak I*, Commission decision 88/501 [1988] OJ L272/27.
[115] *Eurofix-Bauco Hilti*, Commission decision 88/138 [1998] OJ L65/19.
[116] Office of Fair Trading, n. 108 above, paras 5.12–5.17 distinguish between endogenous costs
and exogenous costs. Exogenous costs are determined solely by the technology of a particular industry; thus, for example, it is necessary to invest heavily in plant to be a player in the steel industry.
Endogenous costs are determined by the behaviour of the incumbent undertakings, for example, the
non-recoverable components of spending on advertising and on research and development.
Endogenous costs are therefore determined by the incumbent undertakings which are able to raise
entry barriers, for example, by increased expenditure on advertising.
[117] Ibid, paras 5.26–5.31.
[118] Office of Fair Trading, n. 108 above, paras 6.1–6.2.

example, the purchaser is tied in to a supplier through a long-term contract or switching costs would otherwise be high, for example, because plant is especially adapted to produce the buyer's product, buyer power may not be of sufficient significance to counteract other indications of dominance.

8.78 Countervailing buyer power may not counteract stronger seller power where the buyer also has market power as a seller in a downstream market. In such a case it may simply be able to pass on excessive prices charged by the seller to the consumer and therefore have no incentive to exert pressure on the supplier.

Other factors Indicating Dominance

8.79 The ECJ, in *United Brands*, held that 'in general a dominant position derives from a combination of several factors which taken separately are not necessarily determinative'. The following factors, in combination with significant market shares, have, in appropriate circumstances, been considered to provide evidence of dominance:

- Vertical integration[119]
- The ability to maintain market share in a period of market downturn[120]
- Economic dependence of customers on the relevant firm[121]
- The ability to repulse attacks from competitors[122]
- The ability to eliminate or seriously to weaken existing competitors[123]
- The ability 'if not to determine, at least to have an appreciable influence on the conditions under which the competition will develop, and in any case to act largely in disregard of it so long as [the competitors' conduct] does not operate to its detriment'[124]
- Significant influence over the technical know-how associated with the product market
- The possession of a significantly more advanced commercial/marketing organisation than competitors[125]
- The ability to maintain market share while consistently charging a price premium over currently available substitutes, or a traditional role as the 'price leader' in the market[126]

---

[119] *Soda Ash-Solvay*, Commission decision 91/297 of 19 Dec 1990 [1991] OJ L152/1.
[120] *ECS/AKZO*, Commission decision of 14 Dec 1985 [1985] OJ L374/1.
[121] Case 226/84 *British Leyland v EC Commission* [1986] ECR 3263.
[122] *ECS/AKZO*, Commission decision 85/609 of 14 Dec 1985 [1985] OJ L374/1; *Italian Flat Glass* [1989] OJ L 33/44; Case 27/76 *United Brands Co. & Anor v EC Commission* [1978] ECR 207.
[123] *ECS/AKZO* n 122 above.
[124] Case 85/76 *Hoffmann-La Roche v EC Commission* [1979] ECR 461.
[125] *ECS/AKZO* n 122 above; Case 85/76 *Hoffmann-La Roche v EC Commission* [1979] ECR 461.
[126] *Soda Ash-Solvay* n 119 above.

- A marked customer preference for a particular brand, or the especially close per-ceived identification of the manufacture of a brand with the activities and/or ethos of customers[127]

- Competitors' perceptions that an undertaking is dominant or their reluctance to compete aggressively for its customers[128]

- Protection against imports by anti-dumping duties or other forms of duties[129]

- The fragmentation of competition, for example, as a result of limited product ranges of competitors or limited geographic range of competitors[130]

- The inability of competitors to use the same competitive methods as the dom-inant undertaking, for instance because they lack the resources necessary for capital investment, limited sources of supply, introducing essential logistics sys-tems, making economies of scale, or large scale marketing initiatives[131]

- Structure of demand in the market, for instance, where there were 5,000 pur-chasers for a product (bulk vitamins) but 25 per cent of sales were made to just 22 large firms.[132]

Joint (Collective) Dominance

The Chapter II prohibition applies to conduct 'on the part of one or more **8.80** undertakings'. A group of undertakings may be jointly (or collectively) dominant on a particular market even though individually no one undertaking in the group is solely dominant.

In order to give rise to collective dominance it is not sufficient that the parties **8.81** engage in parallel behaviour.[133] There must be a link of some kind between the parties. The question is whether a relationship of a kind that would give rise to an agreement or concerted practice for the purposes of the Chapter I prohibition and Article 81(1) (formerly Article 85(1)) is sufficient, or whether something more is required or indeed if a connection that falls short of a relationship that would infringe the Chapter I prohibition may also give rise to joint dominance in some circumstances.

The circumstances in which undertakings may be jointly dominant have been **8.82** clarified by the European Commission, the Court of First Instance and the ECJ in a number of recent cases.

---

[127] *BBI/Boosey & Hawkes*, Commission decision 87/500 of 29 July 1987 [1987] OJ L286/36.
[128] *Soda Ash-Solvay*, n 119 above.
[129] Ibid.
[130] *ECS/AKZO*, n 122 above.
[131] Case 27/76 *United Brands Co. & Anor v EC Commission* [1978] ECR 207.
[132] Case 85/76 *Hoffmann-La Roche v EC Commission* [1979] ECR 461.
[133] Although this would be sufficient grounds on which to base a complex monopoly investiga-tion under the Fair Trading Act 1973: see Ch 17.

8.83 In *Società Italiana Vetro*[134] the Court of First Instance had to consider an appeal from the European Commission in *Italian Flat Glass*.[135] Three producers of flat glass had been engaged in price-fixing and quota allocation agreements. These agreements were found to infringe Article 81(1) (formerly Article 85(1)) and the European Commission held, on the same facts as those giving rise to the Article 81(1) infringement, that there was also an infringement of Article 82 (formerly Article 86). The agreement between the producers meant that they presented themselves to the market as a single entity; their business decisions were to a large extent interdependent and they had exchanged products between themselves, thereby giving rise to a degree of production interdependence. These arrangements led to a collectively dominant position. The Court of First Instance did not accept the European Commission's decision to the extent that the European Commission found that the agreements that constituted the infringement of Article 85(1) were, of themselves, sufficient to give rise to joint dominance just because the parties collectively held a large market share. However, the Court of First Instance accepted that it could be the case that there could be economic links between parties which could give rise to joint dominance, for example, agreements or licences which give rise to a technological lead giving the parties the opportunity to act independently of competitors and customers.

8.84 In *Almelo*[136] the ECJ held that for 'a collective dominant position to exist, the undertakings . . . must be linked in such a way that they adopt the same conduct on the market'. In *French-West African Shipowners Committees*[137] the European Commission found that shipowners who were members of a committee were jointly dominant because there were structural links between the parties in that ownership of some members was common and that the shipowners shared out business between themselves and controlled cargo landing, so that there was no competition between the parties.

8.85 Similarly, in *Port of Rødby*[138] two ferry companies which operated on a particular route were jointly dominant because they fixed common rates, co-ordinated timetables and jointly marketed their resources.

8.86 Recently in *France v Commission*[139] the test applied by the Court of First Instance in the context of a concentration was whether the concentration would 'lead to a situation in which effective competition in the relevant market is significantly impeded by the undertakings involved in the concentration and one or more

---

[134] Joined Cases T–68/89, T–77/89 and T–78/89 *Società Italiana Vetro SpA, Fabbrica Pisana SpA and PPG Vernante Pennitalia SpA v EC Commission* [1992] ECR II–1403.
[135] Commission decision of 7 Dece 1988 [1989] OJ L33/44.
[136] Case C–393/92 *Almelo* [1994] ECR I–1477, paras 41–42.
[137] Commission decision of 1 Apr 1992 [1992] OJ L134/1.
[138] Commission decision of 21 Dec 1993 [1994] OJ L55/52.
[139] Joined Cases C–68/94 and C–30/95 *France and Others v EC Commission* [1998] ECR I–1375.

other undertakings which together, in particular because of factors giving rise to a connection between them, are able to adopt a common policy on the market and to act to a considerable extent independently of their competitors, their customers and also of consumers'.

The European Court of Justice is presently considering the scope of the concept **8.87** of joint dominance in the context of the *Cewal*[140] case. The case concerns the finding by the European Commission of an abuse of a joint dominant position by members of a shipping conference line (Cewal) operating between Zaïre and certain Northern European ports. The European Commission and the Court of First Instance found that the parties had enjoyed a collectively dominant position which they had abused. The finding of joint dominance and abuse (as well as the fines imposed) is being challenged before the ECJ. One of the issues is the extent to which behaviour which gives rise to an agreement or concerted practice for the purposes of Article 81 (formerly Article 85) can also establish the 'economic links' required in order to give rise to collective dominance for the purposes of Article 82 (formerly Article 86). Advocate General Fennelly was of the view that, although concerted behaviour alone does not satisfy the test of collective dominance, it is possible to rely on evidence of an infringement of Article 81 in order to establish collective dominance.

The cases suggest that the 'economic links' or 'factors giving rise to a connection **8.88** between' the parties can take many forms, for example, the use of model conditions of supply drawn up by a common trade association (*Almelo*); cross-shareholdings, common directorships or even family links with economic consequences and the pursuit of a common market strategy or sales policy.[141]

In most of these cases the relevant behaviour which constituted joint dominance **8.89** (with the exception of cross-ownership) would also constitute the behaviour that gave rise to an abuse and such behaviour would in most cases also infringe the Chapter I prohibition.

Essential Facilities

An undertaking may be considered to be dominant on a market through the own- **8.90** ership of an 'essential facility'. An essential facility is a facility such as an infrastructure, or an intellectual property right, which a competitor would not be able

---

[140] Joined Cases C–395/96P and C–396/96P *Compagnie Maritime Belge BV and Dafra-Lines v Commission of the European Communities*, opinion of Fennelly AG delivered on 29 Oct 1998; Commission Decision 93/83 EC of 23 Dec 1992 and decision of the CFI in Joined Cases T–24/93, T–25/93, T–26/93 and T–28/93 *Compagnie Maritime Belge Transport and Others v EC Commission* [1996] ECR II–1201.

[141] Case 30/87 *Bodson v Pompes Funèbres des Régions Libérés* [1988] ECR 2479 and Joined Cases 40/73–48/73, 50/73, 54/73–56/73, 111/73 and 113/73 to 114/73 *Sukier Unie and Onrs v EC Commission* [1975] ECR 1663.

to replicate and without access to which that competitor would be unable to compete effectively on the market.

8.91 The European Commission has considered ports to be essential facilities[142] where access to the port is necessary to operate on a particular shipping market and there are no feasible alternatives, and in other EU Member States this doctrine has been applied to postal services,[143] the rail network,[144] energy production and distribution,[145] tramway and bus services.[146]

8.92 In the *European Night Services* case (ENS)[147] the CFI took a narrow view of the concept of an essential facility. It held that a product or service cannot be considered necessary or essential unless there is no real or potential substitute.[148]

8.93 The ECJ considered the doctrine of essential facilities for the first time in the recent case of *Oscar Bronner v Mediaprint*.[149] Advocate General Jacobs set out the factors to be taken into account in determining whether something could be considered an essential facility:

> An essential facility can be a product such as a raw material or a service, including provision of access to a place such as a harbour or airport or to a distribution system such as a telecommunications network . . .
>
> In deciding whether a facility is essential the Commission seeks to estimate the extent of the handicap and whether it is permanent or merely temporary. The test to be applied has been described by one commentator as 'whether the handicap resulting from the denial of access is one that can reasonably be expected to make competitors' activities in the market in question either impossible or permanently, seriously and unavoidably uneconomic'.[150] The test to be applied is an objective one,

---

[142] *B&I Line plc v Sealink Harbours Ltd and Sealink Stena Ltd*, Commission decision of 11 June 1992 [1992] 5 CMLR 255 and *Sea Container v Stena Sealink*, Commission decision 94/19/EC of 21 Dec 1993 relating to a proceeding pursuant to Art 86 [now Art 82] of the EC Treaty (*Sea Containers v Stena Sealink*—interim measures) [1994] OJ L15/18

[143] Finnish case: *Postitoimintalaki* 29 Oct 1993/907 para 4.2 referred to by Jacobs AG in Case C–7/97 *Oscar Bronner GmbH & Co KG v Mediaprint Zeitungs- und Zeitschriftenverlag GmbH & Co KG and others* (pending case), para 53.

[144] *Eisenbahnbeforderungsgesetz* 1998, BGB1. 180/1988 para 3, referred to by Jacobs AG in Case C–7/97 *Oscar Bronner GimbH & Co KG v Mediaprint Zeitungs- und Zeitschriftenverlag GmbH & Co. KG and others* para 53.

[145] *Elektrizitätswirtschaftsgesetz* 1975 BGBI. 260/175 paras 6 and 8, referred to by Jacobs AG in Case C–7/97 *Oscar Bronner GimbH & Co KG v Mediaprint Zeitungs- und Zeitschriftenverlag GmbH & Co. KG and others* para 53.

[146] *Kraftfahrlinienverkehrsgesetz* 1952, BGBI 84/1952 para 8(2), referred to by Jacobs AG in Case C–7/97 *Oscar Bronner GmbH & Co. KG v Mediaprint Zeitungs- und Zeitschriftenverlag GmbH & Co KG and others* para 53.

[147] Judgment of the CFI, 15 Sept 1998 in Joined Cases T–374/94, T–375/94, T–384/94 and T–388/94, *European Night Services Ltd and others v Commission*.

[148] Para 209.

[149] Opinion of Jacobs AG, Case C–7/97 *Oscar Bronner GmbH & Co KG v Mediaprint Zeitungs- und Zeitschriftenverlag GmbH & Co KG and others* [1999] 4 CMLR 112, at paras 50 and 51.

[150] J. Temple Lang: 'Defining Legitimate Competition: Companies' Duties to Supply Competitors, and Access to Essential Facilities' (1995) 18 *Fordham International Law Journal*, 437.

concerning competitors in general. Thus a particular competitor cannot plead that it is particularly vulnerable.

See Ch 9, paragraphs 9.61 to 9.78 for details on how the concept of 'essential **8.94** facilities' has been applied in practice.

E. Abuse

General

The concept of abuse has been defined by the ECJ as follows: **8.95**

> ... the behaviour of an undertaking in a dominant position which is such as to influence the structure of a market where, as a result of the very presence of the undertaking in question, the degree of competition is weakened and which, through recourse to methods different from those which condition normal competition in products and services on the basis of the transactions of commercial operators, has the effect of hindering the maintenance of the degree of competition still existing on the market or the growth of that competition.[151]

The Act sets out examples of conduct that may constitute an abuse.[152] These **8.96** include:

- directly or indirectly imposing unfair purchase or selling prices or other unfair trading conditions;
- limiting production, markets or technical development to the prejudice of consumers;
- applying dissimilar conditions to equivalent transactions with other trading parties, thereby placing them at a competitive disadvantage;
- making the conclusions of contracts subject to acceptance by other parties of unconnected supplementary obligations.

This list of conduct is not exhaustive. Conduct that is not described in the list may nevertheless give rise to an abuse.

Conduct for which there is objective justification is not abusive; thus, for exam- **8.97** ple, a dominant company can refuse to supply a customer that it believes to be uncreditworthy. Although if there are other more proportionate measures that the supplier could reasonably have taken, for example cash sales, then it may be abusive for it to refuse supply.

An undertaking in a dominant position is entitled to take reasonable steps to pro- **8.98** tect its commercial interests when they are attacked. However, if the purpose of

---

[151] Case 85/76 *Hoffmann-La Roche & Co AG v EC Commission* [1979] ECR 461.
[152] S 18(2).

such behaviour is to strengthen its dominant position it is not allowed. Thus, where a dominant undertaking is party to an agreement and insists on strict enforceability of the agreement in order to remove a competitor from the market, Article 82 (formerly Article 86) is infringed.[153]

Intent

8.99 The competition authorities are primarily concerned with the effect of the behaviour rather than whether the dominant undertaking intended to cause harm. To that extent evidence of intent is irrelevant. However one of the tests that has sometimes been applied in distinguishing between behaviour that constitutes normal competitive conduct (and thus does not give rise to an abuse) and abusive behaviour is the purpose of the behaviour. Thus, in *AKZO/ECS*[154] the ECJ held that where a dominant undertaking prices at above its average variable costs but below its average total costs it may be guilty of predatory pricing where the objective of the undertaking is to eliminate a competitor. Further, it may be the case that even pricing above the average cost level with the intention of eliminating a competitor is abusive.[155]

Relations between Dominance and Abuse

8.100 The existence of dominance does not have to be the cause of the abuse. Thus, conduct that is common to both a dominant and a non-dominant company may be abusive when engaged in by the dominant company.

8.101 Section 18 of the Act does not contain any indication as to the relationship between the dominant position and its abuse. In this regard it is similar to Article 82 (formerly Article 86). It is possible to identify the following categories of relationship between the dominant position and the abuse:[156]

(a) the dominant position and the abuse are confined to the same market;

(b) the abuse takes place on the dominated market but its effects are felt on another market on which the undertaking does not hold a dominant position;

(c) the abuse is committed on a market on which the undertaking does not hold a dominant position in order to strengthen its position on the dominated market;

---

[153] Cases T24–26 and 28/93 *Compagnie Maritime Belge Transports SA and Others v EC Commission* [1996] ECR II–1201.

[154] [1985] OJ L374/1 and Case C–62/86 *AKZO Chemie BV v EC Commission III* [1991] ECR I–3359.

[155] See the Opinion of Fennelly AG in *Cewal* n 140 above.

[156] Opinion of Ruiz-Jarabo Colomer AG in Case C–333/94P *Tetra Pak International SA v EC Commission* [1996] ECR I–5951.

(d) the abuse takes place on a market separate from, but related to and connected with, the market dominated by the undertaking;

(e) the dominant position and the abuse are on different and unrelated markets.

The typical situation is set out at (a) and is not problematic. At the other extreme, the ECJ has held that the application of Article 82 presupposes a link between the dominant position and the alleged abusive conduct, which is normally not present where the abuse arises in relation to a market other than the dominated market and produces effects on that other market other than in special circumstances.[157]

There are precedents for applying Article 82 (formerly Article 86) to the circum-   **8.102** stances described in (b), (c) and (d) above. In the case of (b), for example, an undertaking which holds a dominant position on the market for a raw material and which refuses to supply that raw material to a competitor or potential competitor on a downstream market, with the effect that the dominant undertaking's position on the downstream market is strengthened, may infringe Article 82.[158]

In the case of category (c), the abuse is committed on a market on which the   **8.103** undertaking does not hold its dominant position in order to strengthen its position on the dominated market. Thus, for example, where a dominant undertaking, which also operates on a market other than the dominated market, gives preferential terms to customers on the non-dominated market if such customers purchase the product in respect of the market on which the undertaking holds the dominant position, with the effect that that dominant position is strengthened because competitors find it more difficult to enter the dominated market, this will infringe Article 82 (formerly Article 86).[159]

There is no general prohibition restraining the behaviour of a dominant company   **8.104** in relation to activities on markets which have no connection with the market on which it is dominant. However, it was held in the *Tetra Pak* case[160] that where special circumstances exist and there are close associative links between the two markets, Article 82 (formerly Article 86) may apply.

In *Tetra Pak II* the company was dominant on the market for aseptic packaging. It   **8.105** was alleged to have conducted itself on the market for non-aseptic packaging in a way which amounted to an abuse. The CoFI upheld the European Commission's decision that the company's position on the aseptic packaging market allowed it

---

[157] Case C–333/94P *Tetra Pak International SA v EC Commission*, [1996] ECR I–5951, para 27.

[158] Joined Cases 6/73 and 7/73 *Istituto Chemioterapico Italiano SpA and Commercial Solvents Corporation v EC Commission* [1974] ECR 223; Case 311/84 *Centre Belge d'Études de Marché v CLT and IBB* [1985] ECR 3261.

[159] Case T–65/89 *BPB Industries and British Gypsum v EC Commission* [1993] ECR II–389 upheld in Case C–310/93P, *BPB Industries plc v EC Commission* [1995] ECR I–865.

[160] Case C–333/94P *Tetra Pak International SA v EC Commission* [1996] ECR I–5951.

to act abusively on the non-aseptic market.[161] The CFI held that there must be 'associative links' between the two markets (situation (d) envisaged above). These links existed and gave the company a 'freedom of conduct compared with the other economic operators in the non-aseptic markets'. This aspect of the decision was upheld by the ECJ.[162] It held that the application of Article 82 (formerly Article 86) required a link between the dominant position and the abuse. In the case where a company was dominant on one market and engaged in abusive conduct on another market Article 82 would only apply if special circumstances existed. This was the case in *Tetra Pak* because the company's market power on the aseptic market gave it a favoured status on the non-aseptic market. The factors that were relevant in establishing such a favoured status included the fact that customers were common for both the aseptic and non-aseptic products and the fact that Tetra Pak and its main competitors were present on both sets of markets. Given its almost complete domination of the aseptic market with nearly a 90 per cent market share. Tetra Pak could count on a favoured position on the non-aseptic market.

8.106 It has been suggested by the English court that the prohibition on the abuse of a dominant position may even apply if the dominant position and the abuse are on different and unrelated markets and there is no link (situation (e) above). In *Heathrow Airport Limited v Forte (UK) and others*[163] Lawrence Collins QC had to consider a situation where Forte leased premises from Heathrow Airport for the purpose of supplying light catering services to airlines. Forte considered that the rent charged by Heathrow was excessive, unfair and discriminatory and was exacted as a result of an abuse of a dominant position by Heathrow, thus infringing Article 82 (formerly Article 86) of the EC Treaty. Heathrow Airport did not operate in the flight catering services market and Forte did not operate in the markets in which Heathrow Airport operated. Lawrence Collins QC considered a number of European Commission decisions indicating that Article 82 would apply to cases in which an undertaking in a dominant position discriminates against its partners for reasons other than its own interests.[164] In these cases there had been a link between the market in which the dominant undertaking operated and the undertaking to which it was giving a preference. Thus, for example, in the *Irish Continental Group* case, the Chamber of Commerce which controlled the French port of Roscoff, which refused an Irish ferry company access to begin services, had an interest in Britanny Ferries which operated a service that would have been in competition with the Irish ferry company. Similarly, in the *Zaventem Airport* case the Belgian state (acting through its intermediary, the airport author-

---

[161] Case T–83/91 *Tetra Pak International SA v EC Commission* [1994] ECR II–755.
[162] Case C–333/94P *Tetra Pak International SA v EC Commission* [1996] ECR I–5951.
[163] [1998] Eu LR 98.
[164] See *Irish Continental Group v CCI Morlaix* [1995] 5 CMLR 177; *Re Zaventem Airport Landing Fees: British Midland v Belgium* [1996] 4 CMLR 232.

ity) was giving preferential treatment to its national airline. Nevertheless, Lawrence Collins QC held:

> that consequently, until the European Court has considered this question of principle, it is certainly arguable that there can be an abuse of a dominant position even if the competition which is affected is not competition with the undertaking in the dominant position. It is no objection to the defence under Article 86 [now Article 82] that [Heathrow Airport] is not operating in the market for catering supplies. Refusal by an airport authority of access to a market, or discriminatory treatment, may amount to an abuse if the other conditions are fulfilled.

It may be that Lawrence Collins QC's views are of relevance in the context of **8.107** access to an essential facility[165] (although it is difficult to see how the criteria required for establishing the existence of an essential facility applied in the context of Heathrow Airport and catering facilities). However, even in relation to essential facilities the general view is that the dominant undertaking that controls the essential facility must have an interest in the downstream market to which it is denying or restricting access in order to give rise to a claim under Article 82 (formerly Article 86) (or the Chapter II prohibition).

It would appear, therefore, that if the dominant position and the abuse are on dif- **8.108** ferent and unrelated markets (situation (e) above), in the absence of special circumstances and the type of 'associated links' envisaged in the Tetra Pak case, the prohibition on the abuse of a dominant position would not apply.

---

[165] See paras 8.90–8.94 above.

9

TYPES OF CONDUCT CONTROLLED BY THE CHAPTER II PROHIBITION

A. Overview

9.01 The purpose of this chapter is to identify various types of commercial conduct where, in practice, the Chapter II prohibition is likely to be an issue. (In the same way, Chapter 7 of this book identifies typical commercial agreements and arrangements where the Chapter I prohibition is likely to be an issue.)

An undertaking (business) needs to avoid the types of conduct covered by the **9.02** Chapter II prohibition (as described in this chapter) if *either* by itself it has a dominant position on a relevant market in all or part of the UK, *or* it has sufficient 'links' with other undertakings and they jointly have a dominant position on such a market (see *paragraph 9.05 below*).

The specific kinds of commercial conduct which are considered in this chapter are **9.03** listed in the table of contents at the top of the chapter as C to L.

It is important to bear in mind that, while this chapter seeks to assist in identifying likely areas of concern, in cases where these do arise it will be prudent to seek professional legal advice.

This chapter deals, in turn, with the main kinds of conduct which are likely to **9.04** constitute 'abuses of a dominant position' and, therefore, to infringe the Chapter II prohibition. By way of guidance, regard is had to EC case law on the equivalent prohibition in Article 82 (formerly Article 86) of the EC Treaty (in the form of European Court of Justice (ECJ) judgments and European Commission decisions), since the Chapter II prohibition has to be applied in the light of the principles laid down by that EC case law.[1]

Who is Subject to the Prohibition?

Conduct is prohibited under the Chapter II prohibition only if it is carried out by **9.05** an undertaking which has a dominant position in the whole or part of the United Kingdom.

- An 'undertaking' means, broadly speaking, a business. It must be an 'autonomous economic entity', but does not have to be a company.[2]

- By contrast with the Chapter I prohibition, the undertaking does not need to be a party to an agreement or arrangement with other undertakings.

- An undertaking may be subject to the Chapter II prohibition *even if it is not party to any agreement or arrangement with other undertakings.* This is in complete contrast with the Chapter I prohibition; purely unilateral conduct by an undertaking may be prohibited under the Chapter II prohibition.

- However, the only kinds of undertaking subject to the Chapter II prohibition are those which have a *dominant position* on a market in the whole or part of the United Kingdom. The question whether undertakings have a dominant position depends on the correct definition of the relevant market in which they operate (in terms of both product definition and geographical definition); these issues are discussed in Chapter 8 above, paragraphs 8.09–8.51.

---

[1] Competition Act 1998 s 60. See Ch 3 above for an explanation of how this works.
[2] For an explanation of the term 'undertaking', see Ch 4 paras 4.15–4.17.

- The dominant position may be held by one undertaking or, sometimes, by several undertakings who together enjoy *joint dominance* on a market.[3] In order for undertakings to be jointly dominant, there must, according to the European Court of Justice, be economic or structural links between them (eg agreements or licences or common ownership or intentionally common conduct on such matters as pricing), although the European Commission has indicated its view that 'the kind of interdependence which often comes about in oligopolistic situations' (such as in the mobile telephony market) may be sufficient.[4] The concept of joint (or 'collective') dominance is more fully considered in Chapter 8 of this book, paragraphs 8.80–8.89.

What Kind of Conduct is Prohibited?

9.06 The mere fact of holding a dominant position (solely or jointly) does not in itself infringe the Chapter II prohibition. **Infringement occurs only when there is conduct which *abuses* the dominant position.** Conduct which constitutes an abuse of a dominant position may take many forms (the most common of which are identified in this chapter), but broadly falls within two conceptual categories:

(i)   Where the dominant undertaking behaves *exploitatively in its trading relations with customers or suppliers* which are economically dependent on it. This will be the case if it tries to extract from them trading benefits which it would not have reaped if there had been normal and healthy competition.[5] This will usually be the case in the context of the prices and other trading terms which the dominant undertaking imposes in its dealings with its customers; however, a dominant undertaking may also be in a position to exploit individual suppliers who are economically dependent on it (for example, a farmer may be economically dependent on the major supermarket which it supplies).

(ii)   Where a dominant undertaking engages in 'unfair commercial practices . . . intended to *eliminate, discipline or deter smaller competitors*'.[6] The indirect effect of this kind of *exclusionary* or structural abuse is, ultimately, the same as that of exploitative abuse: by reducing the ability of rival undertakings to compete, the dominant undertaking thereby limits the range of competitive choice available to customers (and, therefore, deprives customers of the benefits of wide competition in terms of price, quality standards, etc).

---

[3] Cases T–68/89, T–77/89 and T–78/89 *Società Italiana Vetro v Commission* [1992] ECR II–1403. See also Opinion of Fennelly AG in Cases C–395/96P and C–396/96P *Compagnie Maritime Belge v Commission*, 29 Oct 1998, paras 15–47.

[4] Commission Notice on the application of competition rules to access agreements in the telecommunications sector [1998] OJ C265/2.

[5] Case 27/76 *United Brands v Commission* [1978] ECR 207.

[6] *ECS/AKZO*, Commission decision of 14 Dec 1985 [1985] OJ L374/11.

General Principles: How Should a Dominant Undertaking Behave?

This means that businesses ('undertakings') which enjoy a dominant market posi- **9.07**
tion have to be particularly careful to ensure that their conduct is beyond
reproach. In the recent case of *Compagnie Maritime Belge*,[7] the European Court of
First Instance (CFI) stated that the prohibition imposes a special duty on firms in
a dominant position not to allow their conduct to impair genuine undistorted
competition in the common market, and that in principle this duty covers all conduct that affects the growth or maintenance of competition in a market where
competition has been weakened by the presence of a dominant firm. **Dominant
undertakings may take reasonable steps to protect their interests, but may not
set out to strengthen their dominant position.**

The concept of proportionality is important in this context. It is applicable in **9.08**
particular to cases where it is necessary to decide whether any given behaviour is
abusive or is no more than a proper commercial response to a competitive threat
from another market player: even a dominant firm may defend its interests by
'counter-attacking' a competitor, but not if its actual purpose is the strengthening
or abuse of its dominance (*United Brands*,[8] in which United Brands's refusal to
supply was held to be disproportionate and, hence, abusive). By the same token,
it is acceptable to respond vigorously to the entry of a new competitor on the market, but it is not acceptable to aim to drive that new competitor out of the market
altogether.[9] Again, while an undertaking may legitimately aim to 'avoid subsidis-
ing' a competitor, it may not seek to do so by cutting all supplies to a customer
who deals with that competitor rather than by, for instance, terminating some
special deal with that customer.[10]

An undertaking with a dominant position must not infringe the prohibition even **9.09**
if its compliance can only be secured at the cost of terminating a part of its business altogether. Thus, in *Decca*[11] the European Commission responded to Racal
Decca's argument that it could provide the DNS transmission service only if it
could be sure of obtaining a price covering the costs of the service and a reasonable
profit by stating that 'no undertaking has the right to ensure the continuation of
its business by means which infringe existing laws, inter alia, competition law.
Therefore, the criticised behaviour remains unlawful even if there were no other
alternatives to those of ceasing to supply and abandoning the market for DNS

---

[7] Cases T–24/93, T–25/93, T–26/93, T–28/93 *Compagnie Maritime Belge Transports and others v Commission* [1996] ECR II–1201 (appeal pending).

[8] Case 27/76 *United Brands v Commission* [1978] ECR 207.

[9] Cases T–24/93, T–25/93, T–26/93, T–28/93 *Compagnie Maritime Belge Transports and others v Commission* [1996] ECR II–1201 (appeal pending).

[10] *BBI/Boosey and Hawkes: Interim Measures*, Commission decision of 29 July 1987) [1987] OJ
L286/36.

[11] *Decca*, Commission decision of 21 Dec 1988 [1989] OJ L43/27.

transmissions'. (In any event, on the particular facts of the *Decca* case, it was considered that there *were* alternatives open to Racal Decca.)

B. Abusive Conduct—The Statutory List

9.10 Section 18(2) of the Competition Act 1998 provides a list of the types of conduct which 'may, in particular, constitute an abuse'. This list, which mirrors the wording of Article 82 (formerly Article 86) of the EC Treaty, is as follows:

(a) the imposition of unfair prices, terms or conditions;

(b) limiting production, markets or technical development to the prejudice of consumers;

(c) applying dissimilar conditions to equivalent transactions with other trading parties, thereby placing them at a competitive disadvantage;

(d) making the conclusion of contracts subject to the acceptance of supplementary obligations unconnected to the subject of the contracts.

This list is non-exhaustive, and conduct may constitute an abuse even if it is not on the list. The remainder of this chapter gives a more detailed account of the main types of conduct which are regarded as abusive.

C. Pricing Abuses

Excessive Pricing

9.11 The OFT has said that:

> Perhaps the most obvious form of abuse is where a dominant undertaking charges prices higher than it would do if it faced effective competition.[12]

However, the OFT has expressed caution about finding excessive prices to be an abuse.[13] This caution reflects the enormous difficulties in establishing that a price is in fact 'excessive'—ie clearly higher than it would be in a competitive market.

9.12 It is well-established in EC case law that excessive pricing can constitute an abuse of a dominant position. In the *General Motors*[14] case, the European Commission held that charging unfairly high prices is an abuse; although the European Commission's decision imposing a fine was later annulled by the ECJ, the principle was upheld by the ECJ.

---

[12] Office of Fair Trading, 'Competition Act 1998: The Chapter II Prohibition', (OFT 402), para 4.7.

[13] Ibid, paras 4.8–4.13.

[14] *General Motors Continental NV*, Commission decision of 19 Dec 1974 [1975] OJ L29/14.

In *United Brands*,[15] the ECJ stated that 'charging a price which is excessive because it has no reasonable relation to the economic value of the product supplied [is] . . . an abuse'. In general, the measure of what is excessive is what is or is not 'objectively justified'.[16] Examples from EC cases have included: charging a base rental for a machine in some countries which was higher than the purchase price in others;[17] making the financial loss to a leaseholder too great for him to consider early termination of lease; and charging prices which were excessive in relation to the economic value of the service provided—except where the price was set at such a level as a result of initial miscalculation or inexperience, and was afterwards lowered.[18] It is possible for prices to be regarded as excessive even if the dominant undertaking is not making excessive profits if, for example, its costs are higher than those of firms providing the same service elsewhere.[19]

9.13

On the basis of ECJ judgments and European Commission decisions, it is possible to identify criteria for determining whether a price charged by a dominant undertaking is excessive and, therefore, an abuse. The main possible criteria are:

9.14

(i)   That the selling price is disproportionately higher than the costs, yielding very high profits (particularly when compared with other competitors in the market).[20] However, as the OFT has pointed out, a high price-to-cost ratio need not be indicative of abusive conduct; it may, for example, reflect a good record of efficiency, or be a natural feature of markets with a high rate of innovation (reflecting returns on innovation and incentives to further innovation). The OFT takes the view that, to be an abuse, the price-to-cost ratio 'would have to be *persistently* excessive without stimulating new entry or innovation' with profits which '*significantly* and persistently exceeded . . . cost of capital'.[21]

(ii) That the prices charged by the dominant undertaking (or by the jointly dominant undertakings) significantly exceed those charged for the identical product or service on another geographic market, where that other geographic market is a fully competitive market (ie there are no dominant players in that market[22]).

---

[15]   Case 27/76 *United Brands v Commission* [1978] ECR 207 para 250.

[16]   Case 40/70 *Sirena v Eda* [1971] ECR 69.

[17]   *Tetra Pak II*, Commission decision of 24 July 1991 [1992] OJ L72/1; upheld on appeal in Case T–83/91 *Tetra Pak v Commission (II)* [1994] ECR II–755, and Case C–333/94P *Tetra Pak v Commission* [1996] ECR I–5951.

[18]   Cases 6 & 7/73 *Istituto Chemioterapico Italiano and Commercial Solvents Corporation v Commission* [1974] ECR 233.

[19]   Case 110/88 *Lucazeau v SACEM* [1989] ECR 2811.

[20]   This is the test in Case 27/76 *United Brands v Commission* [1978] ECR 207.

[21]   OFT, n 12 above, paras 4.9 and 4.10.

[22]   Case 30/87 *Bodson v Pompes Funèbres* [1988] ECR 2479. See also Commission Notice on the application of competition rules to access agreements in the telecommunications sector [1988] OJ C265/2, paras 105–109.

(iii) That the prices are higher than they would be on the basis of pricing principles set out in EC legislation (such as legislation on interconnection pricing in telecommunications[23]).

9.15 Within the UK, the national competition authorities have developed experience of investigating excessive pricing prior to the entry in force of the Competition Act 1998—in particular, under the anti-competitive practices provisions of the Competition Act 1980 (now repealed), under the monopoly provisions of the Fair Trading Act 1973 and in the context of challenges to regulators' proposed price caps in the privatised utilities. In the case of these investigations, the MMC (Monopolies and Mergers Commission, forerunner to the Competition Commission) has frequently examined the level of a company's profits on the basis of rate of return on capital. Where profit margins do not exceed 20 per cent, the MMC has generally refrained from alleging excessive pricing. In the *Chlordiazepoxide and Diazepam*[24] report, the MMC criticised profits of over 70 per cent. Indeed, profits of only 25 per cent were condemned by the MMC in its report on *Certain Industrial and Medical Gases*[25] (although it was relevant in this case that the dominant company met a low risk stable demand for its product). However, in cases where manufacturers are perceived as operating particularly efficiently, profits of over 40 per cent (and in the *Soluble Coffee*[26] report profits of over 100 per cent) were not regarded as operating against the public interest.

9.16 The OFT now says that, in applying the Chapter II prohibition:

> Excessive prices are likely to be regarded as an abuse only in markets where an undertaking is so dominant, and new entry so unlikely, that it is clear that high profits will not stimulate successful new entry or innovation within a reasonable period.[27]

Discriminatory Pricing

9.17 As noted above, section 18(2)(c) of the Competition Act, and Article 82(c) EC, specifically provide that an abuse may arise where a dominant undertaking is

> applying dissimilar conditions to equivalent transactions with other trading parties, thereby placing them at a competitive disadvantage.[28]

As a result, **where a supplier charges different prices to different sets of customers, and the prices cannot be objectively justified (eg in terms of different transport costs), this has been held to constitute an abuse.** Charging a higher

---

[23] Commission Notice on the application of competition rules to access agreements in the telecommunications sector [1988] OJ C265/2, paras 105–109.

[24] MMC report, *Chlordiazepoxide and Diazepam* (complex monopoly), HC 177, Apr 1973.

[25] MMC report, *Certain Industrial and Medical Gases* (complex monopoly), HCP 13 (1956–67).

[26] MMC report, *Soluble Coffee* (complex monopoly), Cm 1459, Mar 1991.

[27] OFT, n 12 above, para 4.12.

[28] See para 9.10 above.

price to customers who also buy from the dominant undertaking's actual or potential competitors is a particularly flagrant example of anti-competitive price discrimination, and is regarded as an abuse.[29] In addition, under EC competition law, there has been concern where dominant undertakings have discriminated in favour of customers of their own nationality as against customers of other nationalities[30] (nationality discrimination is a particular concern in EC law, which seeks to complete a single market in the EU through the reduction of barriers to trading between different EU Member States).

In this context, the following points have arisen: 9.18

- Illegitimate discriminatory pricing has been held to occur, for example, where a shipping port levied port duties on some of the ferry companies which used its port, while exempting others from the duties.[31]

- It is justifiable to set different prices as between customers in different geographic areas, if the transport costs are different—but the price differences must not be *greater than* is justified by the relevant differences in transport costs.[32]

- However, it is permissible to discriminate in favour of regular customers, to the detriment of occasional customers (even if the occasional customers had previously been regular, and had become occasional through no policy of their own).[33]

- Another circumstance where differential pricing may be permissible arises in industries with relatively high fixed costs and low marginal costs—for example, 'network' industries such as telecommunications, electricity, railways, etc. If an undertaking in a network industry sets prices simply in order to recover marginal costs (the cost of supplying each additional unit of output), this will lead to a lack of profitability, because the undertaking might then never be able to recover its enormous fixed costs. It may therefore be more efficient to set higher prices for customers with a higher willingness to pay, thereby enabling the recovery of fixed costs; this may be regarded as an acceptable form of price differentiation.[34]

The OFT is likely to consider price discrimination to constitute an abuse only if there is evidence that the prices are 'excessive' (see paragraphs 9.11 to 9.16 above) or that it is being used to exclude competitors.[35]

---

[29] Case C–62/86 *AKZO v Commission* [1991] ECR I–3359.
[30] *Brussels Airport*, Commission decision of 2 June 1995 [1995] OJ L216/8; Case 27/76 *United Brands v Commission* [1978] ECR 207.
[31] Case C–242/95 *GT-Link v De Danske Statsbaner* [1997] ECR I–4449.
[32] *Tetra Pak II*, Commission decision of 24 July 1991 [1992] OJ L72/1; upheld on appeal in Case T–83/91 *Tetra Pak v Commission (II)* [1994] ECR 755, and Case C–333/94P *Tetra Pak v Commission* [1996] ECR I–5951.
[33] Case 85/76 *Hoffmann-La Roche v Commission* [1979] ECR 461.
[34] OFT, n 12 above, para 4.15.
[35] Ibid, para 4.16.

9.19 In addition, **it is price discrimination, and an abuse, if the dominant supplier charges the *same* price to *different* customers, even though the costs of supply are different**. Thus, for example, a policy of uniform delivered prices throughout the country could be discriminatory if there are significant differences in transport costs.[36]

9.20 An area of uncertainty is whether it is an abuse for a dominant supplier to charge a more favourable price **in supplying its own group companies than in supplying outside customers which compete against its own group companies**. The wording in paragraph (c) of Article 82, and of section 18(2), refers to 'applying dissimilar conditions to equivalent transactions *with other trading parties*'; and it has traditionally been thought that this means that it is only an abuse to discriminate as between different external customers (which are all 'other trading parties'), rather than discriminating as between intra-group supplies and external customers. However, two recent cases in the ECJ have created the suggestion that price discrimination may fall within paragraph (c) even where the only differentiation is between intra-group supplies and external customers:

- In *Deutsche Bahn*[37] the CFI held that there was price discrimination, within the meaning of paragraph (c), where one container shipping company, Transfracht (a subsidiary of the German state railway Deutsche Bahn), was charging higher prices than a competitor, Intercontainer, and this difference was attributable to Deutsche Bahn. However, the case is not a clear precedent. Deutsche Bahn had not itself charged Intercontainer higher prices than it had charged its own subsidiary Transfracht (on the contrary, it had charged Intercontainer lower prices); the difference in the price charged by the two container companies was simply 'attributable' to Deutsche Bahn because Deutsche Bahn, as a participant in the consortium which ran Intercontainer, had vetoed Intercontainer's price changes.

- In *GT-Link*,[38] the ECJ held that it could be price discrimination, within the meaning of paragraph (c), if a shipping port was exempting its own ferry services from port levies, while charging those port levies to competing ferry services. However, the value of this case as precedent is weakened by the fact that it was left to the national court to determine whether this was in fact abusive price discrimination,[39] and also because (as noted above) the port owner was discriminating in favour of some of its customers *as well as* in favour of its own port services.

---

[36] OFT, n12 above, para 4.14.

[37] Case T–229/94 *Deutsche Bahn v Commission* [1997] ECR II–1689.

[38] Case C–242/95 *GT-Link v De Danske Statsbaner* [1997] ECR I–4449.

[39] The ECJ was ruling on a question of law referred to it by the national court under Article 234 (which was then numbered Article 177) of the EC Treaty.

In any event, price discrimination in favour of intra-group companies may still constitute an abuse of a dominant position if it relates to the provision of access to an 'essential facility': see paragraphs 9.61–9.78 below.

Predatory Pricing—ie Illegitimate Below-cost Pricing

9.21 Whereas it can be an abuse of a dominant position to charge prices which are *too high* (see paragraph 9.11 above), it may also be an abuse to charge prices which are *too low*.

Charging prices which are too high—excessive pricing—is regarded as an abuse on the grounds that it is exploitative of customers.

9.22 Charging prices which are too low (ie prices which are below cost) may be an abuse on the grounds that it is exclusionary, being aimed at eliminating smaller competitors from the market—that is, where the smaller competitors cannot charge prices which are as low as those charged by the dominant company, and therefore are disabled from retaining customers and remaining in the market. This situation is known as 'predatory' pricing. Obviously, not all low pricing by a dominant undertaking is predatory and (hence) abusive. A dominant undertaking may be able to sell at lower prices than any of its competitors simply because it is more efficient—for example, through economies of scale, investment in automated processes, and so on. This will be the beneficial outcome of a competitive market—and it is no part of the role of competition law to prevent this.

9.23 Low pricing becomes predatory, and therefore illegitimate, when the pricing cannot be explained simply by efficiencies consistent with competing profitably in a competitive market—but is clearly unprofitable, and only explicable as a device to impede non-dominant competitors from participating in the market. Where this is the case, the long-term result will be that competition is reduced in the market, there is no competitive spur to efficiency, and prices ultimately rise to levels higher than they would be in a competitive market. **A clear test for determining whether low pricing by a dominant undertaking is predatory or legitimate was established by the ECJ in the** *AKZO* **case,**[40] **as follows:**

(i) **Prices which are below average variable costs must be presumed abusive.** Variable costs are those which vary according to the quantities produced; if prices are below average variable costs, each additional unit of production sold at that price involves further losses. As the European Court of Justice noted in *AKZO*, the only interest which a dominant undertaking could have in pricing at such levels is that of eliminating competitors. (The OFT considers that, once either of these tests is satisfied by a dominant undertaking,

---

[40] Case C–62/86 *AKZO v Commission* [1991] ECR I–3359; followed in Case C–333/94 *Tetra Pak v Commission (II)* [1996] ECR I–5951. See also: OFT, n 12 above, paras 4.18 to 4.30.

there is an abuse without any further need for the OFT to establish that the undertaking actually could recoup its losses by higher prices.[41])

(ii) **Prices which are above average variable costs, but below average total costs (fixed costs plus variable costs), are regarded as predatory *if* it can be established that the intention was to eliminate a competitor.** Where a dominant undertaking sells at prices below average total costs, it is clearly doing so at a loss. However, the intention to eliminate a competitor is not the *only* possible explanation for doing so (each additional item produced and sold at this prices does not exacerbate the loss, and indeed may contribute towards recouping the investment in fixed costs), and therefore pricing between average total and average variable costs will be illegitimate only if there is further extrinsic evidence that the intention was to eliminate a competitor. Such evidence may be found, for example, in documents which the OFT or the European Commission obtains when it carries out an investigation (see Chapter 14 below); or in price-cutting which is clearly targeted at a new entrant rather than occurring across-the-board; or in evidence that the dominant party is, in the short term, making losses (or lower profits) as a result of the price-cutting.[42]

9.24 For 'network' industries (such as telecommunications or railways), where there are relatively large fixed costs, the European Commission considers that the *AKZO* test does not provide a sufficient safeguard. In such industries, where there are relatively low costs of producing an additional 'unit of production' (eg the supply of a telephone call), pricing will virtually never be below average variable costs. Given this, the Commission thinks that pricing in network industries should still be presumed to be predatory (without the need to provide extrinsic evidence of intention to eliminate a competitor) if, while being above average variable costs, it is below 'the total costs which are incremental to the provision of the service'.[43]

Price Cutting

9.25 In some cases a reduction in prices by a dominant undertaking (or group of dominant undertakings) with the purpose of eliminating a competitor will be considered to be abusive even if the prices following the reduction are above average total costs.[44] In *Cewal* the CFI held that the practice of a group of dominant shipping lines of using 'fighting ships' that were designed to eliminate competition of by an

---

[41] OFT (n 12 above), paras 4.29 to 4.30.

[42] The OFT also appears to think that prices which are below 'long-run avoidable costs', but above average variable costs may be evidence of predation ('long-run avoidable costs' exclude sunk costs and costs shared in common with other activities). See OFT, n 12 above, paras 4.23 to 4.28.

[43] Commission Notice on the application of competition rules to access agreements in the telecommunications sector [1998] OJ C265/2 paras 110 to 116.

[44] Joined Cases T–24/93, T–25/93, T–26/93 and T–28/03 *Compagnie Maritime Belge Transports and others v Commission* [1996] ECR II–1201 (the '*Cewal*' Case).

independent competitor infringed Article 82 (formerly Article 86). The practice employed comprised designating certain Cewal vessels as fighting ships. Special 'fighting rates' were fixed and these vessels were utilised on sailing dates closest to the sailing dates of the competitor. The jointly fixed fighting rates were lower than the rates normally charged by Cewal and, according to the European Commission, were determined not on the basis of costs but solely in order for the rates to be the same or lower than the prices advertised by the competitor. Advocate General Finnelly, in his Opinion to the ECJ[45] stated that it was significant that the ECJ in *AKZO* did not expressly restrict its definition of predatory pricing to cases where there was below-cost pricing. All that the ECJ did in *AKZO* was identify *two types* of predatory pricing contrary to Article 82. While it was the case that normally non-discriminatory price cuts by a dominant undertaking which do not entail below-cost sales should not be regarded as being anti-competitive, different considerations may apply where a dominant undertaking implements a policy of selective price cutting with a demonstrable aim of eliminating all competition. This is particularly the case in relation to markets such as maritime transport where costs may be an unreliable guide to the reasonableness of competitive strategies adopted by dominant firms and where, once a ship has been designated to sail on a particular day, the cost of transporting an additional container shipped as a result of the reduced-rate offer may be close to zero. A particular feature which also appeared to be relevant to the Advocate General in *Cewal* was that Cewal did not merely enjoy a dominant position but a *de facto* monopoly. What was also clear in *Cewal* was that the dominant undertakings shared the resulting loss of revenue between themselves, and it was clear that once the new competitor was eliminated prices would return to their previous level. The Advocate General concluded:

> Article 86 [now renumbered Article 82] cannot be interpreted as permitting monopolists or quasi-monopolists to exploit the very significant market power which their superdominance confers so as to preclude the emergence of either a new or additional competitor. Where an undertaking, or group of undertakings whose conducts must be assessed collectively, enjoys a position of such overwhelming dominance verging on monopoly, comparable to that which existed in the present case at the moment when [the new entrant] entered the relevant market, it would not be consonant with the particularly onerous special obligation affecting such a dominant undertaking not to impair further the structure of the feeble existing competition for them to react, even to aggressive price competition from a new entrant, with a policy of targeted, selective price cuts designed to eliminate that competitor. Contrary to the assertion of the appellants, the mere fact that such prices are not pitched at a level that is actually (or can be shown to be) below total average (or long-run marginal) costs does not, to my mind, render legitimate the application of such a pricing policy.[46]

---

[45] Joined Cases C–395/96P and C–396/96P, *Compagnie Maritime Belge NV and Dafra-Lines v Commission*, Opinion of Finnelly AG delivered on 29 Oct 1998.

[46] Ibid., para 137.

Rebates and Discounts which are Abusive

9.26   Dominant undertakings need to exercise particular care in their policies for granting rebates and discounts to customers. In particular, they must be able to justify the grant of rebates as reflecting genuine costs savings, rather than an intention to eliminate a competitor; otherwise the rebates will be regarded as abuses. (Indeed, even where rebates and discounts do reflect genuine cost savings, they may nevertheless constitute an abuse if the desire to eliminate a competitor can be shown to underlie them.[47])

- **Loyalty or fidelity rebates** are discounts which a supplier gives to its customers if they buy exclusively, or mainly, or in large volumes, from that supplier. In order to avoid infringing the prohibition, the supplier must be able to show that the discount can be justified in terms of the genuine costs savings arising from selling in large quantities—through economies of scale, proportionately lower transport and delivery costs, and so on.

- **'Top-slice' discounting** occurs where a supplier gives a particularly large discount to a customer for the 'top slice' or remaining proportion of that customer's requirement above the core tonnage which the customer would purchase from it irrespective of rebates. Where the customer would normally purchase this top slice from a third party, the top-slice discounting ensures that the supplier protects its profit margins in respect of the core tonnage, while inducing the customer not to go elsewhere for any of its requirements. This makes it particularly difficult for a competing non-dominant supplier to operate in the market, since in order to win even the small amount of business represented by the top slice, the competing supplier would almost certainly have to sell unprofitably. Consequently, such 'top-slice' discounting by a dominant undertaking will raise a very strong presumption that it is an abuse.[48]

- **Granting discounts to some customers, but not to others**, will constitute abusive price discrimination, unless the differences can be justified by objective differences in supplying the customer (eg differences in transport costs). See paragraphs 9.17 and 9.18 above.

Because discounting generally arises in the context of supply agreements, it may also infringe the Chapter I prohibition (and Article 81 of the EC Treaty).

---

[47] *Soda Ash/Solvay*, Commission decision of 19 Dec 1990 [1991] OJ L152/21.
[48] Ibid.

D. Exploitative or Harsh Trading Terms

Excessive pricing is not the only way in which a dominant undertaking might **9.27** abuse its market power by exploiting the customers who are economically dependent on it. The dominant undertaking could, in addition, impose unfavourable conditions on the customer—and where these terms are more unfavourable than would obtain in a competitive market (ie in the absence of dominance), this will constitute an abuse, infringing the prohibition. Examples from EC case law have included:

- leases of machinery, in which the customers (lessees) were prohibited from altering the machinery in any way, from transferring the leases, from sub-letting the machines, from doing any work with them on commission for third parties, or from obtaining repair, maintenance or spare parts from anyone other than the lessor/supplier;[49]

- intellectual property licences which obliged the licensee to pay royalties even for works unprotected by the right, or which excluded the licensee's right of recourse to the courts to settle disputes.[50]

E. Discriminatory Trading Terms

The provision in paragraph (c) of section 18(2) of the Competition Act, and in **9.28** Article 82 (formerly Article 86) EC, that it may be an abuse where the undertaking is '*applying dissimilar conditions to equivalent transactions with other trading parties, thereby placing them at a competitive disadvantage*' is relevant where the discrimination relates to terms and conditions, as well as where it relates to price.[51]

However, there are two aspects of this on which EC case law is unclear: **9.29**

(i) whether discrimination in favour of the supplier's own group companies, and against external customers, is prohibited by this—see paragraph 9.20 above; and

(ii) whether discrimination against parties who are *not actually customers, but who would like to be customers*, is prohibited. Examples might be where a dominant undertaking refuses to supply such potential customers, or imposes terms of supply so that they cannot realistically become customers. Traditionally, it had been thought that the reference in paragraph (c) to 'transactions with other trading parties' necessarily entailed actual transactions

---

[49] *Tetra Pak II*, n 17 above.
[50] *Gema I*, Commission decision of 2 June 1971 [1971] OJ L134/15.
[51] For discrimination as to price, see paras 9.17 to 9.24 above.

with actual trading parties. However, the possibility that it might also apply to potential customers has been raised by the CFI's judgment in *Tiercé Ladbroke*,[52] which considered whether the refusal to supply television feed of French horse races to Belgian betting shops, at the same time as such television feed was being supplied to betting shops in Germany, constituted discrimination in breach of Article 82 EC. The CFI found that this refusal did not fall within paragraph (c). However, the Court reached this conclusion on the ground that the Belgian betting shops were in a separate market from the German betting shops; significantly *it did not say that the fact that the Belgian betting shops were only potential competitors ruled out the application of paragraph (c)*. In any event, discriminatory refusal to supply, or the discriminatory imposition of impediments to supply, may be prohibited under the case law applicable to refusals to supply or license (paragraphs 9.47–9.60 below) or on restrictions of access to 'essential facilities' (paragraphs 9.61–9.75).

F. Vertical Restraints in Supply Agreements

9.30 'Vertical restraints' may, if they are imposed by a dominant undertaking, infringe the Chapter II prohibition (and Article 82 EC). Vertical restraints are restrictions on competition imposed as between parties at different levels of supply—for example, by a supplier or a dealer in a supply agreement, or by a licensor on a licensee in an intellectual property licence.

9.31 In principle, vertical restraints are also capable of infringing the Chapter I prohibition (and Article 81 EC), but **the risks are greater under the Chapter II prohibition**, having regard to the following considerations:

(i) The **special treatment order** which the Government is proposing to give under section 50 is likely to grant vertical agreements exclusion from the Chapter I prohibition, but not from the Chapter II prohibition—*see Chapter 5 paragraphs 5.90–5.93.*

(ii) Agreements which are protected from the Chapter I prohibition, and from Article 81, by **block exemptions** (eg the EC block exemptions for exclusive distribution, exclusive purchasing, or technology transfer) are *not* automatically protected from the Chapter II prohibition or from Article 82[53]—*see Chapter 6 paragraphs 6.59–6.60.*

(iii) However, an agreement which has received an **individual exemption** under Article 81 or the Chapter I prohibition *is* protected from the Chapter II pro-

---

[52] Case T–504/93 *Tiercé Ladbroke v Commission* [1997] ECR II–923.
[53] Case T–51/89 *Tetra Pak Rausing v Commission* [1990] ECR II–309. See also OFT, n 12 above, para 2.7.

hibition (and, if the individual exemption was granted under Article 81(3), from Article 82)[54]—*see Chapter 6, paragraphs 6.59–6.60.*[55]

Types of Vertical Restraint which may Infringe the Chapter II Prohibition

Where the Chapter I prohibition does not apply to a supply agreement containing vertical restraints—for example, because the agreement is excluded under a 'special treatment' order, or because it benefits from individual exemption—the Chapter II prohibition may nevertheless apply to vertical restraints when they involve a dominant undertaking.[56] **9.32**

The most likely examples of agreements which might be at risk are:[57] **9.33**

(i) **Exclusive or selective dealing**—comprising:

- **Exclusive purchasing agreements**—these are supply contracts in which the supplier obliges the purchaser (who may be a distributor or retailer) to buy the contract products only from itself, and not from any competing supplier.[58] Recent cases where the European Commission has applied Article 82 to exclusive purchasing agreements have included *BBI/Boosey and Hawkes*,[59] when the supplier insisted that its customer should cease dealings with a competing supplier; and *Nordian*,[60] in which the Commission only abandoned Article 82 proceedings against a Canadian company which was a supplier of an ingredient for radio pharmaceuticals, once the Canadian company agreed not to implement exclusive purchasing clauses in its sales contracts with European customers (the effect of these clauses had been to prevent the development of the only European competitor in the market).

- **Exclusive distribution or reselling agreements**—these are supply agreements in which the supplier agrees not to appoint anyone other than the contract purchaser as distributor or reseller of its goods in the contract territory.[61]

- **Selective distribution systems**—These are a weaker form of exclusive distribution agreement, in which the supplier appoints only a limited number of distributors or retailers in the contract territory.[62]

---

[54] Ibid.

[55] However, the UK Government considers that the OFT cannot grant an individual exemption if, in doing so, it would be exempting something that appears to be prohibited under the Chapter II prohibition: Lord Simon of Highbury, Minister at the Department of Trade and Industry, *Hansard* (HL), vol 585, no 99, col 956, 9 Feb 1998.

[56] OFT, n 12 above, para 4.33.

[57] Ibid, para 4.35.

[58] See Ch 7, paras 7.79–7.84 above for a fuller explanation of exclusive purchasing agreements.

[59] [1987] OJ L286/36 (European Commission interim measures decision).

[60] European Commission press release IP/98/647, 9 July 1998.

[61] See Ch 7, para 7.87–7.94 above for a fuller explanation of exclusive distribution agreements.

[62] See Ch 7, paras 7.95–7.99 above for a fuller explanation of selective distribution systems.

(ii) **Minimum percentage purchasing obligations**—these are akin to exclusive purchasing agreements, but whereas in an exclusive purchasing agreement the purchaser is obliged to buy 100 per cent of its requirements of the contract goods from the supplier, in these the obligation relates to a lesser percentage.[63] Although they are to some extent less restrictive of competition than full exclusive purchasing agreements, in that they allow competing suppliers *at least some* access to the contract purchaser, they may be less easy to justify (see paragraph 9.34 below).

(iii) **Franchise fees** and other fixed charges imposed on a purchaser for the right to buy or stock the supplier's products—these are imposed by the supplier to create an artificial incentive to purchase a relatively high quantity of products from that supplier.

(iv) **Long-term supply agreements**—these are agreements which, while they do not actually prevent the purchaser from buying the contract products from competing suppliers, impose a purchase obligation of such lengthy duration, and covering such a high quantity, that in practice competing suppliers are foreclosed from access to the purchaser.[64]

(v) **Prohibitions on resale**—these are supply agreements in which the supplier prohibits the purchaser (or even the purchaser's customers) from reselling the contract products. These kinds of restriction have been held to be abuses of a dominant position, infringing Article 82.[65]

(vi) **Resale price maintenance**—this is where a supplier imposes on the purchaser (a distributor or retailer) an obligation not to resell the contract products below a certain minimum price. It should be noted that, under the Chapter I prohibition, this kind of vertical restraint will not benefit from exclusion under a 'special treatment' order.[66]

'Objective Justification'

9.34 Although there is no possibility of exemption from the Chapter II prohibition, it may be possible to argue that the vertical restraint is outside the Chapter II prohibition, on the grounds that it can be objectively justified. The OFT has indicated possible justifications—in particular, the legitimate wish to prevent competitors

---

[63] See Ch 7, paras 7.79–7.84 above for a fuller explanation of minimum percentage obligations.

[64] See Ch 7, paras 7.85–7.86 above for a fuller explanation of long-term supply contracts and their possible foreclosure effects. For an example of long-term supply agreements being considered under Art 82 (formerly Art 86), see the *Soda Ash–ICI* and *Soda Ash–Solvay* cases [1991] OJ L152/21 (the Commission decisions were overturned by the CFI, but on procedural rather than substantive grounds).

[65] Case 102/77 *Hoffmann-La Roche v Centrafarm* [1970] ECR 1139; see also Case 40/73 *Suiker Unie v Commission* [1975] ECR 1663.

[66] See Ch 7, paras 7.64–7.69, for a fuller explanation of resale price maintenance.

'free-riding' on an investment (where such free-riding would remove the incentive to invest) and the achievement of economies of scale. Thus:

- It may be legitimate for a motor car manufacturer or a hi-fi manufacturer to limit its supplies only to those car or hi-fi dealers who agree to provide pre-sales service such as demonstrations of the motor cars or hi-fi equipment. Such selection prevents rival retailers from free-riding on the demonstration services by offering the products to customers at cheaper prices (after those customers have already benefited from the demonstration of the product elsewhere). The selection will be legitimate only if it is done in accordance with criteria which are necessary, objective, transparent and applied in a non-discriminatory way.

- It may be acceptable for a supplier to impose an exclusive purchasing obligation on dealers if the supplier provides staff training, technical support, equipment, and so on, since otherwise competing suppliers could 'free ride' on that investment if they were allowed to supply the contract product to the dealers to whom such support and equipment had been supplied.

- The imposition of selective distribution may be legitimate to achieve economies of scale in distribution.

- The imposition of franchise fees or other non-linear prices, which create barriers to entry by a retailer's competitors, may be legitimate to reduce the risks retailers incur from stocking the contract product.

- The imposition of *maximum* resale price caps may be a legitimate way of preventing resellers exploiting market power.

In any event, the OFT will accept these justifications only to the extent that the restrictive effects on competition are indispensable to achieving them, and proportionate to the putative benefits.[67]

G. Tying and Full-Line Forcing

Paragraph (d) of section 18(2) of the Competition Act—and also of Article 82— **9.35** provides that conduct may constitute an abuse of a dominant position if it consists in:

> making the conclusion of contracts subject to acceptance by the other parties of supplementary obligations which, by their nature or according to commercial usage, have no connection with the subject of the contracts.

The practices of tying and full-line forcing may, therefore, constitute abuses.

(i) **Tying** occurs when a supplier stipulates that it will only sell a product to a purchaser provided that the purchaser also buys another product from that

---

[67] OFT, n 12 above, paras 4.42–4.46.

supplier. Thus, for example, a computer hardware manufacturer is engaged in 'tying' if it sells its hardware to purchasers on the condition that they also buy their software from that manufacturer; and a supplier of photocopiers is engaged in 'tying' if it supplies its photocopiers on the condition that the person supplied (whether a purchaser or a lessee) also acquires maintenance and repair services from the supplier.

(ii) **Full-line forcing** is an extreme form of tying, where the stipulation imposed by the supplier is that, if a purchaser buys any one of that supplier's products, it must also buy that supplier's full product range (or, alternatively, that the purchaser will pay more for one product unless it buys the full product range).

Examples of Tying which may Infringe the Chapter II Prohibition

9.36   Cases where tying has been held to constitute an abuse of a dominant position, under Article 82 EC, have included:

- *Hilti*[68]—a supplier of powered nail guns required its customers also to purchase the nails and cartridge strips from itself.

- *Tetra Pak II*[69]—the dominant supplier of carton filling machines required its customers also to buy the cartons, the spare parts for repairing the machines, and the maintenance service, from itself.

- *Télémarketing*[70]—a dominant broadcasting company required its advertisers also to use its associated tele-sales business, thereby eliminating all competition on the tele-sales market.

- *Digital*[71]—a supplier of computer hardware and software allowed its customers to buy these products separately, but gave them a considerable discount if they bought them together as a single 'package'. The European Commission insisted that the price of buying them as a single package must not be less than 90 per cent of the sum of the list prices of each component individually.

'Objective Justification'

9.37   There are various possible ways in which tying may be justified. However, the scope for such justifications is fairly narrow and, on the EC law principle of 'proportionality', the tying must be no more than is indispensable for the alleged justification.[72]

---

[68]   Case T–30/89 *Hilti v Commission* [1991] ECR II–1439.
[69]   Case T–83/91 *Tetra Pak v Commission (II)* [1994] ECR II–755; Case C–333/94P *Tetra Pak v Commission* [1996] ECR I–5951.
[70]   Case 311/84 *CBEM v CLT and IPB* [1985] ECR 3261.
[71]   European Commission press release IP/97/868, 10 Oct 1997.
[72]   European Commission decision in *Tetra Pak II* [1992] OJ L72/1. See n 17 above for the citations of the appeals in this case (the Commission decision was upheld on appeal).

By way of example: 9.38

(i)   The wording in paragraph (d) of Article 82, and of section 18(2) of the Competition Act, deems tying to be an abuse only where the products being tied 'by their nature or according to commercial usage, have no connection'. There is scope for some argument whether separate products are 'connected' in such a way as to legitimise tying. For instance, shoelaces are almost certainly sufficiently connected with shoes for it to be legitimate to sell them together. However, the competition authorities will generally be reluctant to permit tying on these grounds. Indeed, the European Commission has recently indicated that it will expect separate products to be untied or 'unbundled', even if their sale had previously been tied or bundled, wherever it is or becomes feasible to sell them separately.[73]

(ii) A supplier of a product might produce technical arguments to the effect that it is in the interests of the customers' health or safety that they should buy spare parts, associated products or maintenance services from the supplier of the main product. However, such arguments were rejected in the *Hilti* and *Tetra Pak II* cases, on the ground that the relevant health and safety requirements were adequately protected as a result of general legal obligations.

(iii) In *Tetra Pak II*, the dominant supplier also sought to argue that, in order that its maintenance obligations under the product guarantee could be performed effectively, maintenance and repair services on the product should only be provided by itself. However, this was rejected where the tying of the maintenance and repair services endured beyond the guarantee period.

(iv) The OFT has said that the imposition of tying or full-line forcing may be a legitimate way of achieving economies of scope in production and distribution.[74]

H. Extending a Dominant Position

As already noted, the mere *creation* of a dominant position does not itself infringe   9.39
the Chapter II prohibition or Article 82 (formerly Article 86). Only the *abuse* of a dominant position constitutes an infringement.

However, it has been held that the *extension* of a dominant position may be an   9.40
abuse, without the need to demonstrate any further anti-competitive conduct. The following are examples.

---

[73] See Commission Notice on the application of competition rules to access agreements in the telecommunications sector, n 4 above, para 103; applying Case C–333/94 *Tetra Pak v Commission* [1996] ECR I–5951.

[74] OFT, n 12 above, para 4.46.

Mergers and Acquisitions

9.41 Technically, it may be an abuse for a dominant undertaking to strengthen its dominance by acquiring a competitor on that market[75] (or the technology of such a competitor, where that technology is essential to competing on the market).[76]

9.42 In practice, this is unlikely to be of much importance, because the acquisition is likely to constitute either a 'merger situation' within the meaning of UK merger control,[77] or a 'concentration' within the meaning of the EC Merger Regulation,[78] or both:

- There is an absolute exclusion from the Chapter II prohibition for any conduct which results either in a 'merger situation' or in a 'concentration' with a Community dimension (and which therefore falls under the EC Merger Regulation),[79] or for any conduct which is directly related and necessary to the attainment of such a merger situation or concentration. Virtually every acquisition or merger will benefit from this exclusion from the Chapter II prohibition—with the possible exception of certain acquisitions of technology.

- Article 82 EC will generally not be applied by the European Commission to any 'concentration', whether or not it has a Community dimension (such that it can be examined under the EC Merger Regulation).[80] Again, virtually every merger and acquisition benefits from this.

Extension (and Exercise) of a Statutory Monopoly

9.43 In recent years, there has been a series of EC cases in which Article 86 has been applied to the outcome of State action to extend (or, in some cases, apparently merely to create) a statutory monopoly; Article 82 of the EC Treaty (formerly Article 86), read with Article 86(1) (formerly Article 90(1)), entails that Member States may not take measures which would give rise to an abuse of a dominant position.

9.44 This does not mean that the extension, or creation, of statutory monopoly can *always* be challenged under Article 82 or the Chapter II prohibition. EC law pro-

---

[75] Case 6/72 *Europemballage Corp and Continental Can Co Inc v Commission* [1973] ECR 215.

[76] *Tetra Pak I* [1988] OJ L272/27, upheld on appeal in Case T–51/89 *Tetra Pak Rausing v Commission* [1990] ECR II–309.

[77] That is, a situation where enterprises 'cease to be distinct' within the meaning of the Fair Trading Act 1973 s 65(1). See above, Ch 5 paras 5.21–5.23.

[78] A 'concentration' is defined in Art 3 of the EC Merger Reg (Council Reg (EEC) 4064/89 on the control of concentrations between undertakings [1989] OJ L257, as amended by Council Reg (EC) 1310/97 [1997] OJ L180/1). See above, Ch 5 paras 5.17–5.18.

[79] For the meaning of 'Community dimension', see Ch 5 para 5.19.

[80] EC Merger Reg, Art 22(1). In theory, the European Commission could exercise its residual powers under Art 85 EC (formerly Art 89) to apply Art 82 to concentrations, but is unlikely to do so.

vides that undertakings which have 'the character of a revenue-producing monopoly' (or which are 'entrusted with the operation of services of general economic interest') are *only* subject to the competition rules in so far as this 'does not obstruct the performance . . . of the particular tasks assigned to them';[81] there is a virtually identical provision in the UK Competition Act, which is relevant for the Chapter II prohibition.[82]

It follows that **the *extension* of a statutory monopoly may infringe the prohibition if it gives the undertaking concerned more protection than is necessary for performing its particular tasks**—for example, if a post office is given monopoly rights which go beyond those necessary for enabling it to fulfil its 'universal service obligation' (ie to deliver mail from and to every address in the country). Thus, it has been held to be an abuse, infringing Article 82, when a monopoly public telephone network had its monopoly rights extended by being given the power to approve or veto other suppliers of telephone apparatus—thereby extending the undertaking's monopoly from the area of the tasks assigned to it (ie providing a public telephone network) to a different, ancillary market (ie the supply of telephone apparatus).[83] Two significant consequences flow from this case:

(i) There can be an abuse of a dominant position even where the dominant position is held in one market, and the abuse occurs in a separate, although ancillary, market.[84]

(ii) In the case, the ECJ held that it is an abuse, infringing the prohibition, if a dominant undertaking **reserves for itself, without any objective justification, an ancillary activity** which could be carried out by a third-party competitor on a neighbouring market, with the aim of eliminating competition on that market.

Both these principles have been of importance in the development of the cases on access to 'essential facilities', as described in paragraphs 9.61–9.78 below.

In addition, there is the suggestion from the European Court that **it may be an abuse for a State to *create* a statutory monopoly, or at least for the undertaking to *exercise* such statutory monopoly, in the absence of an 'objective justification'.** Thus, when the German State granted monopoly rights to an employment recruiting agency, the exercise of those monopoly rights (ie preventing private enterprises from offering services of the same kind) was held to be an abuse, where the monopoly undertaking was manifestly incapable of satisfying demand in the market.[85]

9.45

9.46

---

81 Art 86(2) EC (formerly Art 90(2)).
82 Competition Act 1998 Sch 3, para 4. See above, Ch 5, paras 5.32–5.40.
83 Case C–18/88 *RTT v GB-Inno-BM* [1991] ECR I–5941.
84 This has been explicitly recognised by the OFT for the purposes of the Chapter II prohibition: see OFT, n 12 above, paras 4.51 and 4.52.
85 Case 41/90 *Höfner & Elsner v Macrotron* [1991] ECR I–1979.

I. Refusals to Supply or License

9.47   Undertakings which hold a dominant position may be *obliged* to supply products to other parties, or even to license intellectual property rights to other parties, even though they do not wish to. The refusal to supply, or to license, may be an abuse of their dominant position.

9.48   The following paragraphs consider the rules in respect of:

(i)   refusal to supply an existing customer;

(ii)   refusal to supply a potential customer;

(iii) refusal to license intellectual property rights.

Refusal to Supply an Existing Customer

9.49   It is well established that a dominant undertaking cannot, in normal circumstances, refuse to continue supplying goods to an existing customer. This was stated most forcefully in the *United Brands* case, where the ECJ held that it was an abuse of a dominant position for United Brand to terminate supplies of bananas to Olesen, a Danish banana ripener. The European Court's judgment began with the words:

> it is advisable to assert positively from the outset that an undertaking that is in a dominant position for the purpose of marketing a product . . . cannot stop supplying a long-standing customer who abides by normal commercial practice, if the orders placed by this customer are in no way out of the ordinary. Such conduct . . . would limit markets to the prejudice of consumers and . . . might in the end eliminate a trading party from the relevant market.[86]

9.50   There can be an 'objective justification' for a refusal to supply, but, in accordance with the EC law principle of 'proportionality', the refusal must be indispensable to the alleged justification. In *United Brands*, the dominant undertaking justified its termination of supplies to Olesen, on the ground that Olesen had failed to take proper care in ripening and distributing its bananas. The Court held that, while a dominant firm was entitled to defend its legitimate commercial interests, in this case the extreme remedy of terminating supplies was not justified by Olesen's conduct. By contrast, in *Leyland Daf*,[87] the English Court of Appeal, applying Article 82 EC,[88] held that it was an objective justification for a vehicle manufacturer to refuse to supply parts to a customer unless and until that customer paid in full.

---

[86] Case 27/76 *United Brands v Commission* [1978] ECR 207 at 292.
[87] *Leyland Daf v Automotive Products* [1994] 1 BCLC 245, English Court of Appeal.
[88] Art 82 EC has 'direct effect', so that it can be applied in litigation in the national courts of EU Member States.

Refusal to Supply a Potential Customer

It appears from the case law of the European Court of Justice that it may be an **9.51** abuse for a dominant undertaking to refuse supplies to a potential customer where:

- the dominant supplier is able to control supply of the product, and the potential customer wishes to manufacture derivatives;

- the dominant supplier's product is 'essential' for the exercise of the potential customer's activity; or

- the dominant supplier's product is a new product, and the refusal to supply prevents its introduction, in spite of clear potential demand.

These principles are drawn, in particular, from two cases of the ECJ.

The first, *Commercial Solvents*, was decided before *United Brands* and, indeed, **9.52** was precedent for the *United Brands* judgment. Like *United Brands*, the *Commercial Solvents* case concerned the termination of supplies to an existing customer. However, the reasoning in the judgment was expressed in much broader terms, suggesting that it could apply to refusals to supply a potential customer. In the case, Commercial Solvents, the Italian subsidiary of a US corporation, was found to have abused its dominant position as the sole EC supplier of an essential raw material for an anti-tuberculosis drug, when it terminated supplies of that raw material to an Italian drug manufacturer, Zoja. The motive of Commercial Solvents was that, having begun to manufacture the drug itself, it wanted to eliminate competition. The European Court's judgment held that:

> . . . an undertaking being in a dominant position as regards the production of raw material and therefore able to control the supply to manufacturers of derivatives, cannot just because it decides to start manufacturing these derivatives (in competition with its former customers) act in such a way as to eliminate their competition.[89]

This principle, by contrast with the principle enunciated in *United Brands*, does not seem to depend on the customer being an existing, rather than just a potential, customer.

The CFI implicitly acknowledged the extension of the principle to cover poten- **9.53** tial customers in the *Tiercé Ladbroke* case. In *Tiercé Ladbroke* (considered in paragraph 9.29 above), there was a refusal, on the part of the suppliers of video feed of French horse races, to provide this video feed to betting shops in Belgium. The CFI held that this was not an abuse of a dominant position, mainly because the national markets concerned were separate (the French market was separate from the Belgian market). However, the CFI indicated that, if this had not been

---

[89] Cases 6 and 7/73 *Commercial Solvents v Commission* [1974] ECR 223 at 250.

the case, it *might* have found that the refusal to supply constituted an abuse of a dominant position (although on the particular facts it would not have done so):

> The refusal to supply the applicant could not fall within the prohibition . . . unless it concerned a product or service which was either *essential for the exercise of the activity in question in that there was no real or potential substitute* or was *a new product whose introduction was prevented, despite specific, constant and regular potential demand on the part of the consumers*.[90]

Significantly, the CFI did not consider that the fact that the Belgian betting shops were only potential, rather than existing, customers was an impediment to a finding that there was an abuse of a dominant position.

9.54 Equally significant is the CFI's use of the term 'essential'—with its implicit endorsement of the developing doctrine of access to essential facilities (see paragraphs 9.61–9.78 below).

Refusal to License Intellectual Property Rights

9.55 If a dominant supplier is in certain circumstances obliged to supply goods to potential customers, is it also the case that a dominant holder of intellectual property (IP) rights is similarly obliged to license those rights? In answering this question, competition law has had to balance the legitimate interests conferred by IP rights with the need to ensure that competition in ancillary markets is not eliminated.

9.56 The answer—developed primarily in two judgments of the ECJ, *Volvo v Veng*[91] and *Magill*[92]—is that **there is no general obligation on dominant firms to license intellectual property rights, but such an obligation can arise in certain 'exceptional' circumstances.**

9.57 *Volvo v Veng* concerned a refusal by a car manufacturer to license the registered industrial design of one of its components to a manufacturer of spares parts which wanted to import imitations of the protected design. The ECJ held that this was *not* an abuse of a dominant position. On the contrary, it was the very essence of the registered design that it should protect the manufacturer from imports of imitation products. However, the ECJ left open the possibility that, in exceptional circumstances, it might be an abuse of a dominant position to refuse to license IP rights, for example where the holder of the IP rights:

- arbitrarily refused to supply spare parts to independent repairers;
- fixed prices for spares at an unfair level; or
- decided no longer to produce spare parts for a particular model of car, even though that model was in widespread use.

---

[90] Case T–504/93 *Tiercé Ladbroke v Commission* [1997] ECR II–923 at 969, emphasis added.
[91] Case 238/87 *Volvo v Veng* [1988] ECR 6211.

Magill concerned the refusal by broadcasting companies, which owned the copy-   **9.58**
right in programme information about their broadcasts, which they used for publishing weekly programme guides,[93] to license the copyright in that programme
information to someone who wished to publish a competing programme guide.
The ECJ held that this refusal to license was an abuse of a dominant position—
the broadcasters were abusing the IP rights which they enjoyed by virtue of their
dominant position in the broadcasting market, so as to eliminate potential competition on an ancillary downstream market (ie that of publishing weekly programme guides). The ECJ accepted (as it had in *Volvo v Veng*) that, as a rule, it is
not an abuse for dominant undertakings to license their intellectual property
rights to competitors—but that it may be an abuse in 'exceptional circumstances',
and those exceptional circumstances applied in the *Magill* case because:

- the licence was necessary for the appearance of a new product (ie a competing
  weekly programme guide);

- there was nothing inherent in the activities concerned which provided an objective justification for a refusal to license;

- by denying access to the basic information which was the 'indispensable . . . raw
  material' for the production of a competing programme guide, the broadcasters were reserving to themselves a secondary, ancillary market.

It is not entirely clear from the Court's judgment whether *all* the circumstances
have to be satisfied for the refusal to constitute an abuse, or whether just one
would suffice.

In truth, while both *Volvo v Veng* and *Magill* recognise that a refusal to license   **9.59**
could be an abuse in exceptional circumstances, it is difficult to reconcile the contrary rulings which were made on the facts of the two cases. In *Volvo v Veng*, a
refusal to license which would eliminate a potential competitor was permitted,
whereas in *Magill* such a refusal was prohibited. Perhaps the facts of the two cases
are distinguishable, in that the refusal to license in *Volvo v Veng* protected the IP
right-holder from competition on its own main market (ie the manufacture of the
cars themselves), whereas the refusal in *Magill* protected the IP right-holders from
competition on a secondary, ancillary and derivative market (ie the downstream
market of publishing weekly programme guides).

In this way, *Magill* can be seen as building on the case law prohibiting a dominant   **9.60**
undertaking from reserving to itself an ancillary market.[94] As such, it paves the

---

[92] Cases C–241 and 242/91P *RTE and ITP v Commission* [1995] ECR I–743.

[93] Such as *Radio Times* and *TV Times*. At the time the case began, *Radio Times*, a BBC publication, contained only BBC programme information, and *TV Times*, issued by Independent
Television Publications, contained only ITV programme information.

[94] See above, para 9.45, and in particular *RTT v GB-Inno-BM*, n 83 above.

way for the ECJ's acceptance of the doctrine on access to essential facilities, which is considered in the following paragraphs.[95]

J. Restrictions on Access to Essential Facilities

Essential Facilities—the Practical Problem

9.61 The developing case law on restricting access to essential facilities arises out of a real practical problem, which has been made manifest in recent years as competition has begun to be sought in 'network' industries such as public transport, telecommunications and the supply of gas and electricity.

9.62 The problem is this. In many of these network industries, the supplier of the relevant service has historically also owned the 'upstream' network or infrastructure which is essential to the provision of the service. Typically, in the case of each service, both have been owned by a single monopolist (usually state-owned). Thus, for instance, the telecommunications company has provided the service to customers and also owned the telephone lines; the gas company has supplied consumers with gas and also owned the pipelines; the bus company has provided bus services to passengers and also owned the bus stations; the state shipping line has ferried passengers and also owned the port; and so on. The result of this historic situation is that, when efforts are made to introduce competition in the provision of the service, any potential new competitor faces an overwhelming barrier to entry: the potential entrant will not be able to compete with the incumbent (and hitherto monopolistic) supplier of the relevant service unless it can enjoy access, on reasonable terms, to the network and infrastructure facilities which are essential to providing the service. Unless a new gas supplier can use the existing pipelines at reasonable rates, unless a competing telephone company can use the telephone lines at reasonable rates, unless a rival bus company can use the bus station on reasonable terms, unless a rival shipping company can use the port on reasonable terms, unless there is reasonable access to the essential facility upstream, the possibility of competition on the downstream market is eliminated.

---

[95] However, an English Patent Court judgment in 1998, *Philips Electronics v Ingman* (Ch D (Pat Ct), unreported) has interpreted *Volvo v Veng* and *Magill* much more narrowly, and expressly rebutted the propositions that refusal to license IP rights might be an abuse of a dominant position, and that IP rights might constitute an 'essential facility'. In the judgment, Laddie J rejected the claim that it was an abuse of a dominant position, infringing Art 82 (formerly Art 86), for Philips Electronics to charge high royalties for the licensing of its patent rights to a compact disc manufacturer (those rights being necessary for entering the compact disc production market). He held that *Volvo v Veng* showed that there could not be a 'market' in IP rights (and hence, presumably, there could not be a dominant position through control of IP rights), whereas *Magill* was distinguishable in that the broadcasters' dominant position was in products (advance weekly programme listings) rather than in any IP rights.

Of course, it is theoretically possible for the potential entrant to compete by build- **9.63**
ing its own rival infrastructure. But in many cases the costs of doing so are pro-
hibitive and, in terms of the economic needs of society as a whole, it would be
exceptionally wasteful to have duplicate gas pipelines, duplicate electricity networks, duplicate bus stations, and so on.

In reality, the owners of the essential facilities are unlikely *voluntarily* to allow their **9.64**
potential downstream competitors access to those facilities. The essential facility
is, after all, their property. Why should they let others use their property for the
purpose of depriving them of some of their customers?

The question arises: should the owners of essential facilities (such as pipelines, **9.65**
ports and other infrastructure) be *obliged* to grant access to those essential facilities on reasonable terms? On the one hand, the requirements of competition law
might suggest that, indeed, they should. After all, without such an obligation, it is
virtually impossible for competition to develop on these markets.

The difficulty is that, if the owners of essential facilities are obliged to give their **9.66**
competitors access to those facilities, they fail to recoup their investment in the
facilities (while the new competitors 'free-ride' on that investment). The danger is
that, as a result, there will be a significant disincentive to investment in infrastructure and networks—to the detriment of the consumers who are supposed to
benefit from increased competition.

Competition law therefore has to balance the desirability of encouraging compe- **9.67**
tition in network industries, as against the need to preserve sufficient incentives
for investing in networks and infrastructure.

What is the Essential Facilities Doctrine?

The view of the European Commission

In a series of decisions in recent years, the European Commission has begun devel- **9.68**
oping a doctrine that **it is an abuse of a dominant position, and therefore prohibited, unreasonably to restrict access to an essential facility**. In 1992, the
European Commission stated that:

> the owner of an essential facility which uses its power in one market to strengthen its
> position on another related market, in particular, by granting its competitors access
> to that related market on less favourable terms than those of its own services,
> infringes Article 86 [now renumbered Article 82] where a competitive disadvantage
> is imposed upon its competitor without objective justification.[96]

The case concerned access by a shipping company to a seaport owned by a rival **9.69**
shipping company. The European Commission has applied the doctrine to other

---

[96] *Sealink/B&I–Holyhead: interim measures* [1992] 5 CMLR 255, para 41.

seaport cases,[97] access to airport facilities,[98] and access to telecommunications networks.[99]

9.70 The European Commission's view of limiting access to essential facilities as an abuse of a dominant position seems to rely on the following propositions:

(i)   The ownership of an essential facility confers a 'dominant position' on its owner. For this to be the case, access to the facility must be generally essential to the ability to compete, such that refusal of access makes competition either impossible or seriously and unavoidably uneconomic.[100]

(ii) The dominant position is abused by unreasonably restricting access to competitors of the owner's downstream activities, in any of the following ways:

• refusing access completely;

• granting access, but doing so only at a price which is unreasonable or which discriminates against the potential new entrant;[101]

• delaying (unduly and inexplicably or unjustifiably) in responding to a request for access;[102]

• failing to take moderate or reasonable steps to accommodate the commercial requirements of a new entrant, where such steps would have been taken by an essential facility owner which was independent of any of the competitors[103] (in the case of a seaport, the consequent obligation might involve moving the incumbent's slots or developing the harbour in such a way as to make it economically feasible for the new entrant to compete).

(iii) An 'objective justification' may be a defence to an allegation of infringement, but such justification must be 'compelling'—for instance, unavailability of capacity to provide access, or lack of consumer demand.[104]

The View of the OFT

9.71 The OFT's draft guidelines on the Chapter II prohibition recognise the concept of an essential facility, but apparently only in the context of *refusals* of access (rather than any *restriction* of access):

---

[97]   *Port of Rødby* [1994] OJ L55/52.

[98]   *Brussels Airport* [1995] OJ L216/8.

[99]   European Commission Notice on the application of competition rules to access agreements in the telecommunications sector [1998] OJ C265/2.

[100]   Ibid, para 91(a). See also Ch 8 paras 8.90–8.94.

[101]   Ibid, para 97. See also the European Commission decision in *Alpha Flight Services/Aéroports de Paris* [1998] OJ L230/10.

[102]   Ibid, para 95.

[103]   *Sea Containers v Stena Sealink* [1994] OJ L15/8.

[104]   Even lack of capacity may not be sufficient justification, and the European Commission has suggested that the incumbent may be obliged to 'ration' capacity between itself and the new entrant. See European Commission Notice on the application of competition rules to access agreements in the telecommunications sector, n 99 above, para 96.

A facility can be viewed as essential if access to it is indispensable in order to compete on the market and duplication is impossible or extremely difficult owing to physical, geographical or legal constraints (or is highly undesirable for reasons of public policy). In general, ownership of an essential facility confers a dominant position (unless there are a number of competing facilities within the same relevant market). The refusal of access may then constitute an abuse. Potential examples include: ports, bus stations, utility distribution networks and some telecommunications networks.[105]

'Essential Facilities' in Other Jurisdictions

The doctrine of essential facilities has developed out of US law under which free- **9.72**
dom to deal or not to deal is regarded as a fundamental aspect of freedom of trade. The US essential facilities doctrine has been developed by the courts to require a company with monopoly power to contract with a competitor where five conditions are met.[106] The first condition is that an essential facility is controlled by a monopolist (ie a facility access to which is indispensable in order to compete on the market with the company which controls it—for example, railroad bridges serving a particular town,[107] a local telecommunications network[108] a local electricity network[109]). The second condition is that it would be practically or reasonably impossible to duplicate the facility. It is not sufficient that duplication would merely be difficult or expensive, but absolute impossibility is not required.[110] The third requirement is that a competitor is denied use of the facility or refusal to contract or refusal to contract on reasonable terms.[111] The fourth condition is that it is feasible for the facility to be provided. Finally, there must be no legitimate business reason for refusing access to the facility eg legitimate technical or commercial reasons[112] or possibly on grounds of efficiency.[113] In individual Member States of the EU, the essential facilities doctrine has been applied to postal services,[114] the rail network,[115] energy production and distribution,[116] tramway and bus services.[117]

---

[105] OFT, n 12 above, para 4.50.

[106] *MCI Communications v AT&T*, 708 F 2d 1081 (7th Cir 1983), 464 US 891 (1983).

[107] *United States v Terminal Railroad Associations of St Louis*, 224 US 383 (1912).

[108] *MCI Communications v AT&T*, 708 F 2d 1081 (7th Cir 1983), 464 US 891 (1983).

[109] *Other Tail Power Co v United States*, 410 US 366 (1973).

[110] *Fishman v Estate of Wirty*, 807 F 2d 520 (7th Cir 1986).

[111] *Eastman Kodak Co v Southern Photo Materials Co*, 273 US 359 (1927).

[112] *Byars v Bluff City News Co*, 609 F 2d 843 (6th Cir 1979).

[113] Bork, R., 'The Antitrust Paradox' (New York, Free Press, 1979, reprint 1993), 346. *Aspen Skiing Co v Aspen Highlands Skiing Corp*, 427 US 585 (1985).

[114] Finnish law on postal services, *Postitoimintalaki* 29 Oct 1993/907 para 4.2 (referred to by Jacobs AG in Case C–7/97 *Oscar Bronner v Mediaprint*, judgment of 26 Nov 1998).

[115] Austrian law on rail networks, *Eisenbahnforderungsgesetz* 1998, BGB1. 180/1988 para 3 (referred to by Jacobs AG in Case C–7/97 *Oscar Bronner v Mediaprint*, above).

[116] Austrian law on electricity, *Elektrizitätswirtschaftsgesetz* 1975 BGBI. 260/175 paras 6 and 8 (referred to by Jacobs AG in Case C–7/97 *Oscar Bronner v Mediaprint*, n 114 above).

[117] Austrian law on tramway and bus services, *Kraftfahrlinienverkehrsgesetz* 1952, BGBI 84/1952 para 8(2) (referred to by Jacobs AG in Case C–7/97 *Oscar Bronner v Mediaprint*).

Legality of the 'Essential Facilities' Doctrine

9.73 In applying the Chapter II prohibition, the UK competition authorities are obliged to ensure that there is no inconsistency with principles laid down in ECJ judgments. They need only 'have regard to' European Commission decisions and statements.[118]

9.74 Consequently, although the European Commission has been active in developing the doctrine of access to essential facilities, it is necessary to see how well-founded that doctrine is in the legal principles enunciated by the ECJ.

9.75 An analysis of the European Court's legal principles shows that **there is some recognition of an obligation of access to essential facilities, but it is much more tentative than the European Commission's decisions and statements would suggest.**

9.76 Until recently, ECJ case law on Article 82 (formerly Article 86) did *not* seem to leave room for a doctrine under which it is an abuse for an owner of an essential facility unreasonably to restrict access to that essential facility. As already noted:

- An outright *refusal* to supply existing customers (and probably potential customers) has been recognised as an abuse (the *United Brands, Commercial Solvents* and *Tiercé Ladbroke* judgments).[119]

- An outright *refusal* to license intellectual property has been recognised as an abuse only in 'exceptional' circumstances (the *Volvo v Veng* and *Magill* judgments)[120]—and the reluctance to interfere with intellectual property rights might be regarded as implying an even greater reluctance to require owners of physical property to cede their property rights to others.

- Imposing *discriminatory terms* has been regarded as an abuse—but generally only when there is an existing rather than merely a potential trading relationship between the parties (subject possibly to statements in the *Tiercé Ladbroke* judgment),[121] and generally only where the discrimination was in favour of an external customer rather than the downstream activities of the dominant undertaking itself (subject perhaps to the judgment in *Deutsche Bahn*).[122] Both of these limitations appear to be inconsistent with the 'essential facilities' doctrine as developed by the European Commission.

9.77 However, more recent judgments in the European Court have suggested a recognition of some form of essential facilities doctrine, albeit somewhat narrower in scope than that enunciated by the European Commission.

---

[118] Competition Act 1998 s 60. See Ch 3 above.

[119] See above, paras 9.49–9.50 .

[120] See above, paras. 9.55–9.60.

[121] See above, paras 9.28–9.29.

[122] See above, para 9.20.

- The first explicit statement by the ECJ of the concept of 'essential facility' has come in the case of *Oscar Bronner v Mediaprint*. The Advocate General's Opinion in the case had been that the principles in *Magill* could be extended beyond intellectual property licensing, and could be applied to require a dominant newspaper publisher to grant a competitor access to its distribution network, 'whether understood as an application of the essential facilities doctrine, or, more traditionally, as a response to a refusal to supply goods or services'.[123] In its judgment, the ECJ rejected the claim that the newspaper publisher was abusing its dominant position when it refused to grant the competitor access to its network—but accepted that the relevant question was whether the refusal of access 'deprives that competitor of a means of distribution judged *essential* for the sale of its newspaper'.[124] The ECJ thought that, in order for there to be an abuse, the following conditions must all be met:

  - the refusal would be 'likely to eliminate all competition' in the market of the party requesting access;

  - the refusal is 'incapable of being objectively justified'; and

  - access is 'indispensable' to the competitor's ability to carry on the business 'in as much as there is no actual or potential substitute' for the facility (this last criterion is only satisfied if it is 'not economically viable' for the requesting party to establish a rival facility, whether alone or in collaboration with others; the fact that the requesting party would on its own be too small is not itself enough to establish economic unviability).[125]

- In another case decided around the same time, the CFI has explicitly recognised the concept of an essential facility. In the *European Night Services* case,[126] the Court considered whether locomotives owned by a consortium of European railway operators were 'necessary or essential facilities . . . [ie] essential for [the consortium's] competitors, in the sense that without them they would be unable to penetrate the relevant market or to continue operating on it'; the Court concluded that in fact they were not.

Finally, the 1997 *Tiercé Ladbroke* judgment,[127] in which the refusal to supply **9.78** video feed was held *not* to be an abuse, raises intriguing questions for the essential facilities doctrine. In the case, although the CFI did not use the term 'essential

---

[123] Opinion of Jacobs AG in Case C–7/97 *Oscar Bronner v Mediaprint*, 28 May 1998. The Advocate General is an official of the Court who presents a legal assessment of the case for the judges, prior to judgment. His Opinion, although not binding precedent, has considerable persuasive weight, particularly in the absence of a judgment on the issue.

[124] Case C–7/97 *Oscar Bronner v Mediaprint*, judgment of 26 Nov 1998, para 37; emphasis added.

[125] Case C–7/97 *Oscar Bronner v Mediaprint*, judgment of 26 Nov 1998, paras 41, and 45–47.

[126] Cases T–374/94, *European Night Services Ltd and Others v Commission* and others, judgment of 15 Sept 1998, para 212.

[127] See n 52 above.

facility', it did say that the prohibition would not apply unless it concerned a product which was either 'essential for the exercise of the activity in question in that there was no real or potential substitute' or a new product whose introduction was thereby prevented. Significantly, the possibility that the prohibition might apply was held to exist *in spite of the fact* that the owner of the 'essential' product was not itself a competitor on the downstream market. Conceivably, this leaves the way open for a wider extension of the doctrine.

K. Unfair or Disproportionate Behaviour to Competitors

9.79 Dominant undertakings are under an obligation to ensure that any commercial response by them to a competitive threat from another market player is proportional, objectively justified, and not aimed at *excluding* those competitors from the market.

9.80 This obviously limits the manner in which dominant undertakings may respond to competition, and certain practices have been held to be prohibited, including:

- direct threats to a competitor;[128]
- buying up a competitor's products in bulk to eliminate competition;[129]
- buying up competing firms who threaten dominance because of technological developments;[130]
- altering transmission signals so as to cause unlicensed receivers made by a competitor to malfunction.[131]

L. Intellectual Property Rights—Special Considerations

9.81 The OFT has made clear that, even though intellectual property rights (IPRs) are arguably monopolistic in nature, it is anxious to ensure that the Chapter II prohibition does not inflict undue burdens on holders of such rights. The OFT has said:

> even where an undertaking is dominant, the legitimate exercise of an IPR is unlikely to be considered abusive. The role of IPRs in encouraging creative and innovative activity is recognised. It is, however, possible that the way in which an IPR is exercised may give rise to concern if it goes beyond the legitimate exploitation of the IPR—if it is used to leverage market power from one market to another, for example.[132]

---

[128] *AKZO v Commission*, n 29 above.
[129] *Tetra Pak II*, n 17 above.
[130] Ibid.
[131] *Decca*, n 11 above.
[132] OFT, n 12 above, para 4.4.

The main issues which the Chapter II prohibition raises for holders of intellectual **9.82** property rights are, as discussed in the preceding paragraphs:

- imposition of excessively high royalty payments on the licensee (*see paragraphs 9.11–9.16*)

- imposition of exploitative or harsh terms on the licensee (*paragraph 9.27*);

- vertical restraints in the licence agreement, including exclusivity obligations, and limitations on resales including resale price maintenance—where the licensor clearly has a dominant market position, the technology transfer block exemption will not in itself be of assistance, although it will be a guide to individual exemption policy and an individual exemption will be sufficient protection from the Chapter II prohibition (*paragraphs 9.30–9.34*);

- acquisition of competing technology—in practice, this is unlikely to be a problem, particularly if the acquisition constitutes a 'merger situation' or a 'concentration' (*paragraphs 9.41–9.42*);

- a refusal to license—in exceptional circumstances, such as where the refusal eliminates competition on a downstream market (*paragraphs 9.55–9.60*).

PART IV

CONSEQUENCES OF INFRINGING
THE PROHIBITIONS

10

CONSEQUENCES OF INFRINGEMENT

A. Overview

It is fundamental to the policy behind the new Competition Act that the conse- **10.01**
quences of anti-competitive agreements and conduct should be much more severe
than under the old UK competition law. On the day the new legislation was introduced before Parliament, in October 1997, Margaret Beckett, the then Secretary
of State for Trade and Industry, described it as:

providing a strong deterrent against cartels and abuses of market power . . . Stiff penalties for firms which breach the prohibition will reduce anti-competitive behaviour in the economy.[1]

As a result of these 'stiff penalties', it is particularly important for businesses to comply with the new UK legislation, and not to engage in anti-competitive agreements or conduct which would infringe either the Chapter I or the Chapter II prohibition. It is intended that these penalties will be effective in deterring anti-competitive practices in the UK, to the overall benefit of the national economy. More specifically, for the 'victims' of anti-competitive practices (whether they are customers or suppliers or competitors), there is added protection, not only by virtue of the increased deterrence, but through direct remedies, such as the right to obtain damages or injunctive relief in the courts, and the right to obtain from the OFT 'interim measures' to prevent anti-competitive practices from doing irrevocable damage while they are in the process of being investigated.

10.02 However, although these penalties are new in the context of national competition law, they will be familiar to any UK business which has come within the jurisdiction of EC competition law. The main consequences of infringing the Chapter I and Chapter II prohibitions—described in detail in this chapter—are essentially the same as the consequences of infringing Articles 81 and 82 (formerly Articles 85 and 86) of the EC Treaty:

(a) In court—**voidness and unenforceability** of any contractual provisions which infringe the prohibitions;

(b) In court—**liability to third parties** for losses which such third parties sustain as a result of the infringement, by way of damages and/or injunctive relief;

(c) OFT action—**directions to terminate or modify** the infringement;

(d) OFT action—imposition of **penalties (fines)** on the infringing parties;

(e) OFT action—directions to impose **interim measures** in respect of the infringement.

10.03 Each of these consequences is dealt with, in turn, in paragraphs 10.04–10.84 below. Because the Competition Act provisions setting out these consequences closely reflect the equivalent provisions for the consequences of infringing Articles 81 and 82 (formerly Articles 85 and 86) of the EC Treaty, they are to be interpreted in line with European Court judgments on those equivalent EC provisions, and having regard to relevant European Commission decisions and statements.[2]

---

[1] Department of Trade and Industry press release, 'Competition Bill to Benefit Consumers and Business', P/67/662, 16 Oct 1997.

[2] By virtue of s 60(2) and (3). See Ch 3 above.

A key element in enabling a company to avoid infringements of the prohibitions—and also, if infringement occurs, to mitigate the penalties—is the establishment and maintenance of an effective in-house competition **compliance programme**. This subject is addressed in paragraphs 10.47–10.54 below, and in more detail in Chapter 15.

B. In Court—Voidness and Unenforceability

Section 2(4) of the Act provides that: **10.04**

> Any agreement or decision which is prohibited by subsection (1) [ie by the Chapter I prohibition] is void.

This replicates Article 81(2) (formerly Article 85(2)) of the EC Treaty which states that any agreements or decisions prohibited under Article 81 shall be automatically void.

There is no equivalent provision stating that infringements of the Chapter II pro- **10.05** hibition are void. Similarly, there is no provision in the EC Treaty stating that infringements of the Article 82 prohibition (formerly the Article 86 prohibition) are void. However, it is thought as a matter of EC law that infringements of Article 82 do give rise to voidness;[3] and this will also be true of infringements of the Chapter II prohibition.

The Concept of Voidness

This consequence of infringement relates to **contractual provisions**. Many **10.06** infringements of the Chapter I prohibition will arise by virtue of contracts (although some will arise by virtue of non-binding agreements or concerted practices); and certain infringements of the Chapter II prohibition will also arise by virtue of contracts (for example, a dominant supplier who enters contracts with its customers under which it imposes 'tying' obligations, may thereby be found to be abusing its dominant position). A contractual provision is normally enforceable in court. The effect of voidness is that it is unenforceable in court. Therefore, if A enters into a contract with B, and B breaches a term of the contract, it is open to A to sue B in court for breach of contract; however, if the contractual term infringes either the Chapter I or the Chapter II prohibition, B can raise the defence that it is not in breach of contract, because the contractual provision was void and therefore cannot be enforced by A.

---

[3] Case 127/73 *BRT v SABAM* [1974] ECR 51, para 14; Case 66/86 *Ahmed Saeed Flugreisen v Zentrale zur Bekämpfung Unlauteren Wettbewerbs* [1989] ECR 803, para 45. See also: Livingston, D., *Competition Law and Practice* (London, FT Law & Tax, 1995), para 27.10; and Whish, R., *Competition Law* (3rd edn, London, Butterworths, 1993), 324.

10.07   The voidness exists only while the prohibited economic effects are being generated by the agreement. If a contractual clause which was void under the Chapter I prohibition then ceases to infringe the prohibition—for example, because the parties' market shares subsequently decline, rendering the effects '*de minimis*'; or because an exclusivity agreement is assigned by one of the parties to another undertaking, removing its appreciable foreclosure effect—the contractual clause thereby loses its voidness and becomes valid.[4]

10.08   Voidness, raising a defence to enforcement proceedings, is the only consequence in court as between the parties themselves. The parties cannot use an infringement of the prohibitions as a 'sword' to seek damages (see paragraphs 10.24–10.25 below).

What is Void—the Entire Contract or Just the Infringing Clause?

10.09   Very often, where there is an infringement of one (or more) of the prohibitions, it will be the case that only a part of the contract breaches the prohibition—for example, if there is an exclusive dealing contract, it may be that only the clause granting exclusivity is in breach of the prohibition, while the other clauses (as to the appointment of the dealer, the quantity and quality of goods to be supplied, payment, and so on) are perfectly lawful.

10.10   In such cases, the question arises whether section 2(4), which says that '*any* agreement . . . which is prohibited . . . is void' means that the entire contract is void, or only that the particular clauses which infringe the prohibition are void. A draft of the new UK legislation, published by the government in August 1997, used different wording from that which currently appears in section 2(4). It said, instead:

> Any *provision of* an agreement or decision which causes the agreement or decision to infringe the prohibition imposed by subsection (1) [the Chapter I prohibition] is void.[5]

This clearly signalled an intention that only the infringing provisions, rather than the entire contract, should be void and unenforceable. The change from that draft to the current wording of section 2(4) might be interpreted as suggesting a change of policy intention, and a decision that the entire contract, rather than just the infringing provision, ought to be rendered void. However, it is understood[6] that the

---

[4]   *Passmore v Morland and others*, Court of Appeal (judgment of 2 February 1999) [1999] NPC 14. The judgment related to contractual voidness under Art 81(2) EC (which at that time was numbered Art 85(2)), but it should also apply to voidness under the Chapter I prohibition. (Chadwick LJ said: '. . . the nullity imposed by Article 85(2) has the same temporaneous or transient effect as the probition in Article 85(1). It follows that if, as a result of a change of circumstances, the prohibition no longer applies as between the parties to the agreement, then the agreement between them ceases to be void.')

[5]   'A prohibition approach to anti-competitive agreements and abuse of dominant position: draft Bill', Department of Trade and Industry, Aug 1997, cl 2(4), emphasis added.

[6]   Private information.

change of wording was *not* motivated by such a change of policy intention, but was merely intended to ensure that section 2(4) should conform with the equivalent EC competition law provision, in Article 81(2) (formerly Article 85(2))—which refers to the agreement, rather than a provision in the agreement, being void.

The interpretation of Article 81(2) is therefore crucial here. The European Court **10.11** of Justice has held that **voidness affects only the individual elements of the agreement which are prohibited, although it is a matter for each Member State's national law whether the void provisions are severable from the rest of the contract or instead render the rest of the contract void.**[7]

In the United Kingdom, the courts have considered whether, as a matter of **10.12** national law, the provisions which are void for infringing Article 81 are severable from the rest of the contract or instead render the whole contract void. The courts have held that the void provisions may be severed from the rest of the contract, leaving the other provisions valid—unless the effect of severing the prohibited provisions would be that the remaining contract:

- could be said to fail for lack of consideration;
- would be 'so changed in its character as not to be the sort of contract that the parties intended to enter into at all';
- would be without 'the heart and soul' of the original agreement.[8]

In practice, in two major English Court of Appeal cases, this has meant that a minimum royalties provision in a patent licence agreement remained valid even though other provisions in the agreement were void for infringing Article 81; but a motor vehicle selective distribution agreement, in which the dealer's main obligations were void for infringing Article 81, such that its only real valid obligation was the obligation to pay for the manufacturer's cars and parts, was thereby rendered void in its entirety.

Recovering Payments Already Made

Finally, there remains the question of what happens when a party has already **10.13** made payments under a contract which is subsequently declared void for infringing Article 81 or the Chapter I prohibition: is the party entitled to recover the monies which it has paid?

This has long been a controversial issue, but it seems to have been resolved by a **10.14** Court of Appeal judgment in 1998[9] which held that, since a contractual provision

---

[7] Case 56/65 *Société La Technique Minière v Maschinenbau Ulm* [1996] ECR 235; and Case 319/82 *Société de Vente de Ciments et Bétons de l'Est v Kerpen & Kerpen* [1983] ECR 4173.
[8] *Chemidus Wavin v TERI* [1977] FSR 181 [1978] 3 CMLR 514 at 520, CA; and *Richard Cound Limited v BMW (G.B.) Limited* [1997] EuLR 301, CA.
[9] *Gibbs Mews v Gemmell,* [1998] EuLR 588, CA.

which infringes Article 81 is illegal, a party to the contract cannot claim restitution for losses caused to it as a result, even if that party was in some sense a 'victim' of the provision. This principle would also apply to the Chapter I prohibition. On the facts of the case, the Court of Appeal held that there was no infringement, and so technically its statements on the point are merely obiter dicta, but they are strongly expressed and likely to be regarded as authoritative.

C. In Court—Liability to Third Parties

10.15 There is no *express* provision in the Competition Act that parties which infringe the Chapter I or Chapter II prohibition are liable in court to third parties. There are, however, provisions of the Act which strongly *imply* the existence of such liability, including in particular:

- section 55(3)(b), regarding confidentiality, which refers to information 'made with a view to the institution of, or otherwise for the purposes of, *civil proceedings brought under* or in connection with *this Part* [ie the Chapter I and Chapter II prohibitions]';[10]

- section 58(2), which refers to 'proceedings in respect of an alleged infringement of the Chapter I prohibition or of the Chapter II prohibition . . . which are brought otherwise than by the Director [OFT]'; and

- section 60(6)(b), which makes clear that court decisions must ensure no inconsistency with decisions of the European Court as to 'any corresponding question arising in Community law' including as to 'the civil liability of an undertaking for harm caused by its infringement of Community law' (which seems to imply that there is corresponding civil liability for harm caused by infringements of the Chapter I and Chapter II prohibitions).

10.16   In any event, the rule that the Act should be interpreted in accordance with the EC principles[11] also suggests this, since infringements of Articles 81 and 82 of the EC Treaty (formerly Articles 85 and 86 respectively) do give rise to liability to third parties in national courts. Moreover, during the passage of the legislation through Parliament government ministers made clear that this was indeed the intention of ministers. In October 1997, Lord Simon, Minister at the Department of Trade and Industry said:

> we are including provisions to facilitate rights of private action in the courts for damages.[12]

---

[10] Emphasis added.
[11] Competition Act 1998, s 60(2) and (3).
[12] *Hansard*, HL, vol 582, no. 55, col 1148 (30 Oct 1997).

A month later his Ministerial colleague Lord Haskel said:

> third parties have a right of private action. Our clear intention in framing this Bill is that third parties may seek injunctions or damages in the courts if they have been adversely affected by the action of undertakings in breach of the prohibitions. This is an important element of the regime. There is no need to make explicit provision in the Bill to achieve that result. Third party rights of action under the domestic regime are to be the same as those under Articles 85 and 86 [now Articles 81 and 82].[13]

As a matter of English law, following the judgment in *Pepper v Hart*, such **10.17** Ministerial statements may now be used for statutory interpretation.[14] (Lord Haskel's statement, however, leaves room for one point of doubt, as a result of its final sentence with its statement that rights of action are to be the same as under Articles 81 and 82. While there is no doubt that third parties can claim injunctive relief in UK courts under Articles 81 and 82, some commentators take the view that it is still not absolutely certain that they can claim damages.[15])

Third Parties Claiming Injunctive Relief

When parties participate in anti-competitive agreements which infringe the **10.18** Chapter I prohibition, or engage in abuse of a dominant position in breach of the Chapter II prohibition, third parties who suffer loss as a result (such as customers, suppliers or competitors) are entitled to seek injunctive relief in the courts—that is, a court order that the infringement should cease. This has clearly been established in the English courts in the context of the EC competition prohibitions. Thus, for example, when a brewery operated tenancy agreements in its tied pubs which had the effect of excluding from those pubs amusement machines supplied by third parties, one such third-party supplier of amusement machines obtained an injunction preventing the brewery company from excluding its machines, on the grounds that this element of the tenancy agreement infringed Article 81.[16]

In principle, third parties may also obtain interlocutory injunctions—that is, **10.19** injunctions which prohibit an agreement or conduct which is the subject of court proceedings, pending the final resolution of those proceedings. However, in practice there are strong arguments against granting interlocutory injunctions in competition cases. This is often because it is difficult to show that the 'balance of

---

[13] Lord Haskel, Government Whip, *Hansard*, HL, vol 583, no. 69, col 955 and 956 (25 Nov 1997).

[14] In *Pepper v Hart* [1993] AC 593, the HL established that 'reference to Parliamentary material should be permitted as an aid to the construction of legislation which is ambiguous or obscure or the literal meaning of which leads to an absurdity . . . where such material clearly discloses the mischief aimed at or the legislative intention lying behind the ambiguous or obscure words'. In the case of statements to Parliament, this will normally be 'the statement of the Minister or other promoter of the Bill' (*per* Lord Browne-Wilkinson at 634).

[15] This issue is discussed more fully in paras 10.21–10.23 below.

[16] *Cutsforth v Mansfield Inns* [1986] 1 WLR 558, QBD.

convenience' favours ordering parties to cease their commercial arrangements or conduct for the sake of third parties claiming to be harmed by such arrangements or conduct. In addition, difficulties are created by the fact that the third party seeking to obtain an interlocutory injunction—the plaintiff—is required to give a 'cross-undertaking in damages', ie guaranteeing that damages will be paid to the defendant parties if the plaintiff loses the main proceedings, to compensate the defendant parties for losses which they sustain as result of the interlocutory injunction: courts find it very difficult to quantify the level of such losses where they result from an order to cease commercial conduct.[17]

10.20   Consequently, third parties seeking interlocutory relief against an alleged infringement may find it easier to request administrative 'interim measures' from the OFT (see paragraphs 10.75–10.84 below).

Third Parties Claiming Damages

10.21   The government, in devising the Competition Act 1998, has made clear its policy intention that third parties who suffer losses as a result of infringement of the Chapter I or Chapter II prohibitions should be able to seek damages as well as injunctive relief. On the day the legislation was introduced before Parliament, the senior sponsoring minister, Margaret Beckett, then Secretary of State for Trade and Industry, said:

> Consumers and competitors who suffer will have a right to damages.[18]

Mrs Beckett's statement was not made to Parliament, and so is not authoritative for purposes of statutory interpretation (applying the rule in *Pepper v Hart*). However, Lord Haskel's statement to the House of Lords (cited above) is authoritative, saying that 'third parties may seek injunctions or damages in the courts' if adversely affected by a breach of the new prohibitions, but then complicating matters by adding that third party rights of action are to be 'the same as those under Articles 85 and 86 [now Articles 81 and 82]'.[19]

10.22   The complication is that it is not absolutely certain that third parties *do* in fact have a right to damages in the English courts under Articles 81 and 82. By contrast with injunctive relief, it has never been conclusively established in the English courts that damages are available to third parties for losses sustained as a result of infringing Articles 81 and 82. When the House of Lords considered whether an injunction should be granted in the case of *Garden Cottage Foods v Milk Marketing Board*,[20] Lord Diplock stated that any cause of action for an

---

[17] See, eg, the judgment of Aldous J in *Macarthy PLC v UniChem Limited* (27 July 1989).
[18] Department of Trade and Industry press release, n 1 above.
[19] See n 13 above.
[20] [1984] AC 130, 144–5 and 152.

infringement of Article 82 would sound in damages, but this statement was obiter dictum and Lord Wilberforce disagreed. Similarly, when the Court of Appeal considered the legality under the EC free movement rules of an import ban, in the *Bourgoin* case,[21] Parker and Nourse LJJ both explicitly endorsed Lord Diplock's view that damages may be obtained in a court action for breach of Article 82 but, again, these remarks were obiter dicta. In 1998, the Court of Appeal in *Gibbs Mew v Gemmell*[22] cited an Advocate General's Opinion in a previous European Court of Justice case as 'further support . . . for the view that it is third party competitors who are intended to be protected by provisions' such as Article 81 and who can recover damages for losses suffered as a result of infringement of those provisions; but, again, these remarks are, strictly speaking, just obiter.

Commentators are divided on this point.[23] However, government intentions are **10.23** so clearly in favour of third party damages for breach of the Chapter I and Chapter II prohibitions that it seems highly unlikely that a court would rule that damages were unavailable. Moreover, once it is clarified that they are available in British courts under the UK prohibitions, it is virtually certain that they would be available under Articles 81 and 82 as well.

Damages Cannot be Claimed by the Parties Themselves

While infringements of the prohibitions may entitle third parties to claim dam- **10.24** ages in the courts, *the parties themselves* are not entitled to such remedies from each other. (As noted above, each party may use infringements as a defence to enforcement action by the other, however.)

This seems to follow from the Court of Appeal's judgment in *Gibbs Mew v* **10.25** *Gemmell*[24] where it was held, obiter dictum, that parties to an agreement which infringed Article 81 (formerly Article 85) could not seek damages or restrictions as a result, because English law does not allow a party to an illegal agreement to claim damages or restrictions for loss caused by being a party to the illegal agreement. The same reasoning would undoubtedly apply in respect of the Chapter I and Chapter II prohibitions.

---

[21] *Bourgoin SA v Ministry of Agriculture* [1986] QB 716, CA, 1086 and 1089.
[22] [1998] EuLR 588, CA.
[23] See, eg Smith, MR, 'Private Enforcement in National Courts' (issue 29, up to date to 1 Jan 1998), in Freeman, P., and Whish, R., *Butterworths Competition Law*, vol 3, division XI, paras 170, 189 and 190: '[i]t is almost, though not absolutely, certain that a remedy in damages is available to a party who can establish that he has suffered loss as a result of breach of Article 85 or 86 [now Articles 81 and 82]'. Contrast, however, Green, N., and Robertson, A,. *Commercial Agreements and Competition Law* (2nd edn, London, Kluwer, 1997), para 7.102: 'it is now established that an action for damages will lie for breach of Articles 85 and 86 EC [now Articles 81 and 82].'
[24] [1998] EuLR 588, CA.

Third Parties Citing Infringements as a Defence

10.26   As discussed in paragraphs 10.04–10.14 above, a party to a contract who is sued for breach of contract may cite infringement of the competition prohibitions as a defence in the court proceedings.

10.27   A more difficult issue arises about whether third parties who are sued in the courts may also raise as a defence the fact that the plaintive is infringing the competition prohibitions. The issue has arisen in the English courts in the context of litigation to enforce intellectual property (IP) rights against third parties, where the third parties have raised the defence that the plaintiff seeking to enforce the intellectual property rights is infringing Article 82 (formerly Article 86). In the Court of Appeal, it was held in the *Chiron* case that third parties may not rely on competition infringements as a defence to IP enforcement actions, except in 'extraordinary cases', because those third parties had other remedies available in respect of the alleged competition infringements. However, in that case, the third party defendant was not claiming that the attempt to enforce the IP right was *in itself* an infringement.[25]

10.28   By contrast, in certain cases, the attempt to enforce an IP right may itself be an abuse of a dominant position, infringing Article 82 and the Chapter II prohibition.[26] These might be among the 'extraordinary cases' referred to by the Court of Appeal in *Chiron*; indeed, in an obiter dictum in an earlier case in 1984, Oliver LJ in the Court of Appeal had said that, in proceedings for breach of copyright, the plaintiff (who held a dominant position) was seeking to compel the defendant 'to enter into an agreement which would, if entered into, constitute an abuse under Article 86 [now Article 82], so that the relief claimed is thus itself an abuse'.[27] In such circumstances, it is at least arguable that the English court should not grant relief which is itself an infringement of the competition rules, and therefore that it is appropriate for the defendant to rely on the infringement as a defence to the IP enforcement proceedings.

Third Party Rights Outside the Courts

10.29   In the context of this survey of the remedies available to third parties in courts, it is worth briefly referring to the administrative remedies available to third parties for breach of the Chapter I and Chapter II prohibitions—ie through approaches to the OFT:

- Third parties may submit complaints to the OFT, alleging that an agreement infringes the Chapter I prohibition or that conduct infringes the Chapter II

---

[25]   *Chiron Corp. v Murex Diagnostics Ltd (No 2)* [1994] FSR 187, [1994] 1 CMLR 410.

[26]   See, eg, the ECJ's judgment in the *Magill* case: Cases C–241 and 242/91P *RTE and ITP v Commission* [1995] I ECR 743, para 50.

[27]   *British Leyland v Armstrong* [1984] 3 CMLR 102, CA.

prohibition; this is implicit in, respectively, sections 15(2)(d) and 23(2)(c) of the Act. If such complaints give the OFT a 'reasonable suspicion' of an infringement, it may commence a formal investigation under section 25. A complaint may have this effect even if the OFT has already given the parties guidance that there is no infringement. *See Chapter 13 below for details of OFT investigations induced by complaints.*

• Even if the OFT has made a formal decision that there is no infringement, or granting exemption, there is a right for third parties who have a sufficient interest in the decision—and also for representatives of such third parties, such as consumer groups—to appeal to the OFT requesting withdrawal or variation of the decision, under section 47. *See Chapter 16 below on appeals.*

• Third parties may also, as part of a complaint to the OFT, request the OFT to impose 'interim measures' to require termination or modification of an agreement or conduct which is alleged to infringe the prohibition, pending full investigation, under section 34. *See paragraphs 10.75–10.84 below on interim measures.*

In addition, similar remedies are available to third parties from the European Commission, if the third parties can show that the alleged infringements also come within the jurisdiction of Articles 81 or 82 (formerly Articles 85 or 86) of the EC Treaty.

D. OFT Action—Directions to Terminate or Modify

Sections 32 and 33 of the Act allow the OFT to make 'directions' requiring termination or modification of, respectively, an agreement infringing the Chapter I prohibition or conduct infringing the Chapter II prohibition. **10.30**

Basis and Content of Directions

Before the OFT can issue directions under section 32 or 33, the OFT must have made a decision that an agreement infringes the Chapter I prohibition or that conduct infringes the Chapter II prohibition. Such decisions (which are made under section 31 and are given in writing to the persons likely to be affected), will have been the outcome of either (a) the parties having requested a decision on their agreement or conduct by way of notification to the OFT (under section 14 or 22),[28] or (b) the OFT having conducted an investigation into the agreement or conduct on its own initiative or as a result of a complaint from a third party (under section 25).[29] **10.31**

---

[28] See Ch 12 below.
[29] See Chs 13 and 14 below.

10.32 The OFT has wide discretion, under sections 32 and 33, to give such directions as it 'considers appropriate to bring the infringement to an end'. In particular, such directions may include provisions:

(a) requiring the parties to modify the agreement or conduct in question; or

(b) requiring the parties to cease the agreement or conduct in question.

10.33 This discretion is wider than the equivalent *express* powers of the European Commission, which provide only for orders to terminate infringements of Article 81 or 82.[30] (In practice, however, the European Commission can require modifications as a condition of approving an agreement or conduct.) Moreover, OFT directions may also require positive action—eg to report back periodically to the OFT.[31]

The direction need not be addressed to the infringing party and may, for example, be addressed to its parent company or to an individual.[32]

The OFT's direction must be given in writing. Under the OFT's draft Procedural Rules (made under Schedule 9 paragraph 14), the OFT must, at the same time as issuing a direction, inform the addressee in writing of the facts on which the direction is based and the OFT's reasons for giving the direction, and must publish the direction by means of an entry in the OFT's register of decisions under the prohibitions.[33]

Breach of Directions

10.34 Section 34 empowers the OFT to take enforcement action in court in respect of breaches of any directions to terminate or modify.

10.35 If a person fails, without reasonable excuse, to comply with a direction under section 32 or section 33, the OFT may apply to the court for an order.

10.36 The court order may require the person in breach of the direction to make good its default within a specified time. If the direction required anything to be done in the management or administration of an undertaking (ie a business), the order may require that undertaking or any of its officers to do it.

10.37 Under the court order, the person in breach (or the officer of an undertaking responsible for the breach) may be required to pay the costs of obtaining the order.

If a person then fails to comply with the court order, this is contempt of court, which carries criminal sanctions of fines or imprisonment.

---

[30] Council Reg (EEC) 17 [1962] OJ Spec Ed 87, Art 3.

[31] Office of Fair Trading, 'Competition Act 1998: Enforcement' (OFT 407), para 2.3

[32] Ibid, para 2.2.

[33] Office of Fair Trading, Formal Consultation Draft, 'Competiton Act 1998: The Draft Procedural Rules proposed by the Director General of Fair Trading', (OFT 411), Rr 17(1)(a) and (2).

Appeals Against Directions

Any undertaking receiving a direction under section 32 or 33 may appeal against **10.38** it to the Competition Commission (appeal tribunal).[34] A further appeal against the Competition Commission's decision may be made to the Court of Appeal (or, in Scotland, the Court of Session), but only on a point of law.[35] Third parties have no right of appeal in respect of directions under section 32 or 33.[36]

The making of an appeal does not suspend the effect of a direction,[37] but the rules of the Competition Commission (appeal tribunal) may provide that it can make an interim order to suspend the effect of a direction.[37a]

E. OFT Action—Penalties (Fines)

Under the Competition Act, the UK competition authorities for the first time **10.39** have powers to impose fines—which the Act calls 'penalties'—for infringements of competition law. By contrast, under EC competition law, the European Commission has long had powers to impose fines of up to 10 per cent of turnover on parties which infringe Articles 81 or 82 (formerly Articles 85 or 86).[38]

The power to impose penalties is subject to various immunities, as described in **10.40** paragraphs 10.60–10.74 below.

The main provisions for the imposition of penalties under the new UK **10.41** Competition Act are set out in section 36(1) and (2):

- Penalties may be imposed if the OFT has made a *decision* that there has been an infringement of the Chapter I prohibition or the Chapter II prohibition. (It is not a prerequisite that the OFT should have given a *direction* to terminate or modify the infringing agreement or conduct.[39])

- The requirement to pay the penalty is imposed by the OFT.

- The penalty is imposed on an 'undertaking' (ie a business). Where there is a trade association, the association and/or its members may be liable.[40]

- In the case of an infringement of the Chapter I prohibition, the penalty may be imposed on any undertaking which is a party to the infringing agreement. (Although in principle all the parties to the agreement which are within the

---

[34] Competition Act 1998, s 46(1), (2) and (3).
[35] S 49(1).
[36] See n 66 below.
[37] S 46(4).
[37a] OFT, n 31 above, para 2.7.
[38] Council Reg (EEC) 17 [1962] OJ Spec Ed 87, Art 15(2).
[39] See paras 10.30–10.38 above.
[40] OFT, n 31 above, para 4.45.

jurisdiction will be liable to the penalty, in practice this need not necessarily be the case: it is possible, for example, that if one party is the 'victim', it will not be subject to a penalty. In addition, as explained in paragraphs 10.52–10.54, 'whistle blowers', who reveal to the OFT the existence of a cartel of which they are members, are likely to be rewarded with a reduced penalty.)

- In the case of an infringement of the Chapter II prohibition, the penalty may be imposed on 'the undertaking concerned'—that is, the undertaking whose conduct constitutes the abuse of a dominant position.

- A penalty may be imposed jointly and severally on a parent company and a subsidiary where they are within the same undertaking. It may also be imposed on companies which take over the infringing undertaking or on successor undertakings although, so far as possible, liability will follow responsibility for actions (thus where an infringing undertaking is subsequently sold by its parent, the parent may still be liable following the sale).[41]

The extent to which the imposition of penalties by the OFT must conform with EC fining practice, because of section 60 of the Act, is uncertain. When the legislation was being considered by Parliament, government ministers expressed the view that section 60 would not apply to 'purely procedural matters', but would apply in respect of 'high level principles' which have a bearing on procedure, such as principles of fairness and legal certainty. They also regarded penalties as an aspect of procedures.[42] It is clear that the UK authorities will follow broad EC law principles on fining—such as having regard to the gravity and duration of infringements (see paragraph 10.46 below)—but it is likely that they will not feel constrained to follow European Commission practice in every detail. However, since the distinction between principles and details is not always clear-cut, much will remain speculative until there is actual practical experience through cases under the Competition Act.

Penalties Only Payable for 'Intentional or Negligent' Infringements

10.42 Section 36(3), mirroring EC law on fines,[43] provides that an undertaking may only be subject to a penalty if it has infringed the Chapter I or Chapter II prohibition 'intentionally or negligently'.

10.43 Applying EC law principles sheds some light on the meaning of 'intentionally or negligently'. The OFT has also indicated what its approach will be:

---

[41] OFT, n 31 above, paras 4.43 and 4.44.

[42] Lord Simon of Highbury, Minister at the Department of Trade and Industry, *Hansard*, HL, vol 586, no 116, cols 1363 to 1365 (5 Mar 1998).

[43] Council Reg (EEC) 17 [1962] OJ Spec Ed 87, Art 15(2).

- The intention or negligence need not be on the part of the undertaking's senior management; it may arise if any person authorised to act on behalf of the undertaking has such intention or negligence.[44]

- If the undertaking was subject to court orders or undertakings under the old UK legislation (the Restrictive Trade Practices Act or the resale Prices Act), in respect of similar anti-competitive activities, the OFT may regard this as evidence of intention or negligence.[45]

- The intention or negligence relates to the facts, not the law; ignorance of the law (ie ignorance that the practice is an infringement) is not a defence.[46]

- A finding of intention is possible if the object of the agreement or conduct was to restrict competition, or if the undertaking was willing or prepared to carry out the actions knowing that they were or were reasonably likely to restrict competition, or that the undertaking 'could not have been unaware' that the object was restrictive. Internal documents or evidence of deliberate concealment may be used as evidence of this.[47]

- If a type of agreement or conduct has never previously been condemned, the OFT takes the view that this does not absolve the undertaking from negligence. However, in such cases the European Commission's practice has been to impose nil or very small fines.[48]

- Clear infringements may raise a presumption of intention or negligence. For instance, the defence that it was a 'mere oversight' when invoices were issued with the words '*exports prohibited*' has not been accepted.[49]

- If an undertaking has participated in the infringement under pressure, this may still be consistent with a finding of intention or negligence; however, a penalty may be reduced, depending on the circumstances.[50]

Level of Penalties

The Act itself specifies only two criteria for the level of penalties to be imposed: **10.44**

(i)   no penalty may exceed 10 per cent of the turnover of the undertaking on which it is imposed;[51] and

---

[44] Case 100/80 *Musique Diffusion Française v Commission* [1983] ECR 1825. See also OFT, n 31 above, para 4.3.

[45] OFT, n 31 above, para 4.4.

[46] Case 19/77 *Miller v Commission* [1978] ECR 131. See also OFT, n 31 above, para 4.7.

[47] Ibid, paras 4.6 and 4.8.

[48] Ibid, para 4.3.8. *Vegetable Parchment* [1978] OJ L70/54.

[49] Case C–277/87 *Sandoz v Commission* [1990] ECR 45.

[50] OFT, n 31 above, para 4.11.

[51] This has been specified as 10% of its UK turnover. S 36(8), read with OFT, n 31 above, para 4.1.

(ii) the amount of the penalty must take into account any penalty or fine already imposed by the European Commission or by the authorities of another EU Member State in respect of the same agreement or conduct.[52] (The Act does not make it absolutely clear whether this means that the UK penalty should be reduced by the amount of any penalties or fines already paid to such other authorities, which seems likely; or alternatively the very opposite: that the level of the UK penalty should reflect the same kind of assessment as made by the other authorities, in which case, the higher the fine paid to the European Commission or another Member State authority, the higher would be the UK penalty. However the OFT takes the view that it means the former.[53]) In practice it will be rare that the same agreement or conduct is considered by both the European Commission and the OFT and, where this is the case, it may be that there is a materially different factor for the two authorities (eg a particular impact on UK markets or policy) which could lessen the extent to which the OFT has regard to the Commission fine. Fines imposed by non-EU authorities need not be taken into account at all.

In addition, however, the OFT must issue **guidance** about the appropriate amount of penalties, and more detailed criteria are set out in that guidance. The guidance must be published, and the OFT may at any time alter the guidance, in which case it must publish the altered guidance. Before publishing any guidance, the OFT must obtain the approval of the Secretary of State and must consult any relevant utility sector regulator.[54]

10.45 Although the guidance is not legally binding, the OFT must have regard to the current published guidance when setting the amount of a penalty. Similarly, in considering any appeal against the penalty, the Competition Commission or the Court of Appeal must have regard to the current published guidance.

10.46 Although at the time of writing (December 1998), this guidance has not yet been published, the OFT has indicated that it will have regard to the following factors:

- the **gravity** of the infringement—see (i) below;
- the **duration** of the infringement, which may result in the penalty being increased—see (ii) below;
- any **aggravating or mitigating circumstances**, which may result in an increase or decrease of the level—see, for example, paragraphs 10.47–10.59 below; and
- **objective factors** such as any economic or financial benefits which the parties have derived from the agreement (together with the fact that the amount must not exceed 10 per cent of the undertaking's UK turnover.[55]

---

[52] S 38(9).
[53] OFT, n 31 above, para 4.40.
[54] See Ch 19 below on utility regulation.
[55] OFT, n 31 above, para 4.33.

The obligation to have regard to gravity and duration reflects the requirements in the EC Regulation which grants the European Commission its fining power. In this connection, the following points should be noted:

(i) With regard to the **gravity** of the infringement, the following points emerge from the EC cases. An infringement will be regarded as grave, and hence meriting a higher fine, to the extent that:

    – the agreement is particularly restrictive (for example, price-fixing and market sharing);

    – the abuse of a dominant position is particularly anti-competitive: for example, where an undertaking with a particularly high market share acts to eliminate a small competitor;

    – the parties have high market shares or are particularly large businesses;

    – the undertaking concerned made financial gains from the infringement;

    – the infringement is deliberate or a repeat offence'

    – the undertaking concerned led, or instigated, the infringement'

    – the undertaking concerned has been unco-operative with the competition authorities in their investigation of the infringement.

In 1998 the European Commission issued guidelines on the method by which it sets fines.[56] In these it specified the kinds of infringement which would be regarded as most grave, and hence attracting most fines. Those most relevant for UK purposes are:

    • *very serious infringements* (attracting the highest fines)—horizontal restrictions such as price cartels and market-sharing quotas, and clear-cut abuse of a dominant position by undertakings holding a virtual monopoly;

    • *serious infringements* (attracting significant fines)—other horizontal restrictions, with a wide market impact, and other abuses of a dominant position (refusals to supply, discrimination, exclusion, loyalty discounts made by dominant firms in order to shut competitors out of the market, etc);

    • *minor infringements* (attracting small fines)—restrictions, generally in vertical agreements, with limited market impact.

(ii) As regards the EC principle that fines will be higher to the extent that the infringement is of long **duration**, the 1998 European Commission Notice states that, if the infringement lasts longer than one year, the fine should rise by 50 per cent, with an extra 10 per cent for every year after five years.

Finally it should be noted that, in the view of the Inland Revenue, penalties imposed under the Competition Act will not be tax deductible—ie may not be deducted in computing trading profits for tax purposes.[56a]

---

[56] [1998] OJ C9/3.
[56a] OFT, n 31 above, para 4.13.

Reductions in the Level of Penalties

10.47 It is likely that an undertaking will benefit from a reduction in penalties for infringements if it can demonstrate either of the following mitigating circumstances:

(i)   it had actively implemented an **effective compliance programme**; or

(ii) it was the '**whistle blower**' on a secret cartel, where that cartel is the basis of the infringement.

Implementing an Effective Compliance Programme

10.48 The OFT is anxious to encourage businesses to implement effective in-house 'compliance programmes'. Such programmes—which are usually run by in-house counsel or company secretaries, working closely with external competition lawyers—are *primarily* designed to ensure that the business does not infringe the prohibitions. This is done partly by establishing a compliance programme and procedures appropriate to the company, generally set out in a compliance manual. These should set out the company's commitment to compliance, the basic competition rules *as they apply to the business activities of the company concerned*, and the consequences of infringement both for the company and for individual employees (including disciplinary consequences within the company). The manual should be supplemented with effective training (through seminars tailored to the needs of the staff or management concerned) and evaluation (through continual monitoring and regular audits, and procedures to put right any infringements uncovered).

10.49 A compliance programme is likely to be effective (and will only be regarded by the OFT as effective) only if it has the clear and visible support of senior management.

10.50 In a speech in May 1998[57] the head of the OFT, John Bridgeman, Director General of Fair Trading, said that, if a company does implement and maintain an effective compliance programme, this will not only help to avoid infringements, but may also result in a reduction of OFT penalties if an infringement does then occur:

> Occasionally compliance programmes will fail and despite them an infringement may take place. Even then, the mere fact that a compliance programme has been implemented may be of benefit. Although my policy on penalties is still being formulated, it is highly likely that I will take into account the efforts made by the business concerned to ensure compliance when considering the level of financial penalty that should be imposed. However, just having a programme is unlikely to be suffi-

---

[57] Bridgeman, J., 'The New UK Competition Legislation: the View from the Director General of Fair Trading', OFT speech 98/11, delivered at Norton Rose IIR conference on Competition Law Compliance, 19 May 1998.

[58] OFT, n 31 above, para 4.35.

cient to mitigate a penalty if it has not been effectively implemented, evaluated and regularly audited.

Since then, the OFT has given some indications of the grounds on which a com-   **10.51**
pliance programme would serve to reduce a penalty. The OFT has said that the parties will need to show that:

- the programme has been actively implemented;
- the programme has the visible and continuing support of, and is observed by, senior management;
- there are appropriate compliance policy and procedures in place;
- there is active and continuing training for employees at all levels who may be involved in activities affected by competition law; and
- the programme is evaluated, with formal audits being carried out at regular intervals to ensure that it is delivering its objectives.[58]

Full details of how to establish a compliance programme are set out in Chapter 15 below.

Blowing the Whistle on a Secret Cartel

The European Commission published a Notice in 1996 stating that a participant   **10.52**
in a secret cartel (which had fixed prices, production or sales quotas, or shared markets, or banned imports and exports) may expect a significant reduction in fines, or even exemption from fines, if it were to alert the European Commission to the existence of the cartel and co-operate in the subsequent investigation.

The level of reduction in fines enjoyed by that 'whistle blower' would vary accord-   **10.53**
ing to how early it alerted the European Commission: the sooner the whistle is blown, the greater the reduction.[59]

The OFT has said that it 'intends to operate a similar policy', such that an under-   **10.54**
taking which (i) comes forward with information and (ii) co-operates with an OFT investigation into a cartel, may be granted a reduction in the level of penalty which would otherwise have been imposed on that undertaking.[60]

Procedures Relating to Penalties

If the OFT requires an undertaking to pay a penalty, it must give written notice of   **10.55**
this.[61] The written notice must specify a date before which the penalty must be paid; this date must not be earlier than the time within which the undertaking concerned may appeal against the penalty.[62]

---

[59] Commission Notice on the non-imposition or reduction of fines in cartel cases [1996] OJ C207/4.
[60] OFT, n 31 above, para 4.39.
[61] Competition Act 1998, s 36(6)(a).
[62] S 36(6)(b) and (7).

10.56 Under the OFT's procedural rules, when requiring payment of a penalty the OFT must inform the person concerned in writing of the facts on which the penalty is based and the reasons for imposing it.[63]

10.57 Any undertaking on which the penalty is imposed may appeal to the Competition Commission as to the fact of its imposition or its amount.[64] A further appeal against the Competition Commission's decision may be made to the Court of Appeal, either on a point of law or as to the amount of a penalty.[65] Third parties have no right to appeal in respect of penalties.[66]

10.58 Where an appeal is made against the imposition or amount of a penalty, this suspends the effect of the decision imposing the penalty.[67]

10.59 If an undertaking fails to pay in full the penalty required by the OFT, within the date specified in the OFT's written notice, the OFT may take legal proceedings to recover the outstanding amount as a civil debt. However, such proceedings may not be taken until the period for making an appeal has expired without an appeal having been made or, if an appeal has been made, until that appeal has been determined.[68]

Immunities from Penalties

10.60 There are a number of circumstances in which an undertaking which would otherwise be liable for a penalty is immune from penalties. These are:

- for '**small agreements**' which infringe the Chapter I prohibition—*see paragraphs 10.61–10.63 below*;

- for '**conduct of minor significance**' which infringes the Chapter II prohibition—*paragraphs 10.64–10.66 below*;

- where there has been a **favourable OFT decision or guidance** in respect of the agreement or conduct—*paragraphs 10.67–10.68*;

- for **agreements notified to the OFT** which infringe the Chapter I prohibition, in respect of the period between the date of notification and the date of an OFT decision or guidance—*paragraphs 10.69–10.71*;

- for **agreements notified to the European Commission** which infringe the Chapter I prohibition, in respect of the period between the date of notification

---

[63] OFT, n 33 above, R 17(1)(b).
[64] Competition Act 1998, ss 46(1), (2) and (3)(g).
[65] S 49(1). In Scotland, the appeal is to the Court of Session.
[66] OFT, n 31 above, para 4.47. S 47(1), which provides for third party appeals, identifies the decisions against which a third party appeal may be made as those in paras (a) to (f) of s 46(3). Decisions on penalties are in s 46(3)(g). However, other decisions may in future be 'prescribed' as appealable by third parties.
[67] S 46(4).
[68] S 37.

and the date when the European Commission determines the matter—*paragraphs 10.72–10.74*.

Each of these is examined in the following paragraphs.

'Small Agreements'—Chapter I Prohibition

Under section 39 of the Act an undertaking is immune from a penalty for infringing the Chapter I prohibition if it is a party to a 'small agreement'. In addition, an undertaking is immune from the penalty if it acted on the 'reasonable assumption' that section 39 gave it immunity in respect of the agreement.[69]   **10.61**

The **definition** of 'small agreement' is not set out in the Act itself, but in secondary legislation. However, the Act specifies that: **10.62**

- The criteria by which the secondary legislation may define small agreements may include (a) the parties' combined turnover and (b) the share of the market affected by the agreement. The OFT has indicated that the threshold will be based on the parties' UK turnover.[70]

- The Act specifies that 'price fixing agreements' can never be small agreements. A 'price fixing agreement' is defined in section 39(9) as an agreement which, in object or effect, restricts the freedom of a party to the agreement to determine the prices to be charged to third parties for the product or services covered by the agreement.[71]

Immunity for small agreements may be **withdrawn**. The OFT may make a decision withdrawing the immunity if it has investigated a small agreement and, as a result, considers that the agreement is likely to infringe the Chapter I prohibition. The OFT must give written notice of the withdrawal to each party whose immunity is withdrawn. The date of the withdrawal must be after the date on which the decision (not the notice) is made, and must be set having regard to the amount of time which the parties are likely to require in order to ensure that the agreement does not further infringe the Chapter I prohibition.[72]   **10.63**

'Conduct of Minor Significance'—Chapter II Prohibition

Under section 40 of the Act, an undertaking is immune from penalties for infringing the Chapter II prohibition if its conduct is 'conduct of minor significance'. In addition, an undertaking is immune if it acted on the 'reasonable assumption' that section 40 gave it immunity in respect of its conduct.[73]   **10.64**

---

[69] S 36(4).
[70] S 39(2). See also Office of Fair Trading, 'Competition Act 1998: The Chapter I prohibition' (OFT 401), para 6.3.
[71] S 39(1)(b) and (9).
[72] S 39(4) to (8).
[73] S 36(5).

10.65   As in the case of small agreements, the **definition** of 'conduct of minor significance' is not set out in the Act itself, but in secondary legislation. However, the Act
provides that the criteria for defining conduct of minor significance may include
the turnover of the person whose conduct it is and/or the share of the market
affected by the conduct. The OFT has indicated that the threshold will relate only
to the turnover of the dominant undertaking.[74]

10.66   There are provisions for the OFT to **withdraw** immunity for conduct of minor
significance. These are the same as the provisions for withdrawing immunity for
small agreements (as described in paragraphs 10.61–10.63 above).[75]

Favourable Decisions or Guidance—Chapter I and Chapter II Prohibitions

10.67   There is immunity from penalties whenever, following a notification by the parties, the OFT has issued a favourable decision or guidance—that is, a decision or
guidance, in respect of either the Chapter I prohibition or the Chapter II prohibition, that the matter notified does not give rise to an infringement (including
where this is because it is, or is likely to be, exempted from the Chapter I prohibition).[76]

10.68   Under the Act, the same rules regarding immunity from penalties in this context
apply regardless of whether it is a decision or guidance, and regardless of whether
it is the Chapter I or the Chapter II prohibition. The basic immunity is given
under:

- section 16(3) for decisions that the Chapter I prohibition is not infringed;
- section 15(3) for guidance that the Chapter I prohibition is unlikely to be
  infringed;
- section 24(3) for a decision that the Chapter II prohibition is not infringed; and
- section 23(3) for guidance that the Chapter II prohibition is unlikely to be
  infringed.

In each case, however, the OFT may **remove** the immunity where the OFT
decides to take further action in respect of the matter notified, which it may do in
any of the following circumstances:[77]

(i)   if it has reasonable grounds for believing that there has been a material
      change of circumstance since it gave its decision or guidance;

(ii) if it has reasonable suspicion that the information on which it based its deci-
      sion or guidance was materially incomplete, false or misleading;

---

[74] S 40(2). See also Office of Fair Trading, 'Competition Act 1998: The Chapter II prohibition'
(OFT 402), para 2.8.
[75] S 40(4) to (8).
[76] See Ch 12 below on the procedures for notification to the OFT for a decision or guidance.
[77] Subss (4) and (5) of ss 16, 15, 24 and 23.

(iii) (in the case of guidance) if a third party has made a complaint to the OFT; or

(iv) (in the case of guidance under the Chapter I prohibition) if one of the parties to the agreement has submitted a notification for a decision.

Even where any of these circumstances applies, the OFT may only remove the immunity if it (a) considers it likely that the agreement or conduct will infringe the prohibition *and* (b) gives written notice to the party which submitted the notification that the immunity is to be removed. The notice must specify a date on which the immunity will be removed (which, where the OFT has acted because of materially incomplete, false or misleading information, may be a date before the date of the notice).

Agreements Notified to the OFT—Chapter I Prohibition Only

There is provisional immunity from penalties for any agreement which is notified **10.69** to the OFT for a decision or for guidance in respect of the Chapter I prohibition.

This provisional immunity, which mirrors similar provisional immunity under **10.70** Article 81 (formerly Article 85) of the EC Treaty,[78] protects an agreement from penalties in respect of any infringement which occurs during the period (a) beginning with the date of notification and (b) ending with the date on which the application for a decision or guidance is determined.[79] However, if the OFT has issued the parties with a provisional decision that an agreement is likely to infringe the Chapter I prohibition and that an exemption would not be appropriate, provisional immunity from penalties is deemed never to have applied to the agreement.[79a]

There is no equivalent provisional immunity in respect of the Chapter II prohibi- **10.71** tion.

Agreements Notified to the European Commission—Chapter I Prohibition Only

Under section 41 of the Act, where an agreement has been notified to the **10.72** European Commission with a view to obtaining an exemption from the Article 81 (formerly Article 85) prohibition, under Article 81(3) (formerly Article 85(3)), the agreement is protected by provisional immunity from OFT penalties in respect of any infringement of the Chapter I prohibition which occurs after notification to the Commission but before the Commission has determined the matter (including by way of comfort letter[80]).

In such circumstances, there is in any case immunity from European Commission **10.73** fines under Article 81,[81] and this parallel immunity from OFT penalties is

---

[78] Council Reg (EEC) 17 [1962] OJ Spec Ed 87, Art 15(5)(a).
[79] Competition Act 1998, ss 14(4) and 13(4).
[79a] OFT, n 31 above, para 4.26.
[80] OFT, n 31 above, para 4.19.
[81] Council Reg (EEC) 17 [1962] OJ Spec Ed 87, Art 15(5)(a).

designed to ensure that parties which notify the European Commission do not also have to notify the OFT in respect of the same agreement if they wish to be assured of immunity from penalties and fines.

10.74 If the European Commission withdraws the benefit of provisional immunity from its fines under Article 81, from that date the parallel immunity from OFT penalties, under section 41, is also lost.

F. OFT Action—Interim Measures

10.75 Section 35 of the Competition Act makes express provision for the OFT to impose 'interim measures' to terminate or modify an agreement or conduct which may infringe the Chapter I or Chapter II prohibitions, in circumstances where the OFT has not yet completed its investigation into whether there is an infringement.

10.76 This provision is a central feature of the new legislation. In EC competition law, by contrast, there is no legislation expressly providing for interim measures— although since the 1980s the European Commission has imposed interim measures in respect of suspected infringements of Articles 81 and 82 (formerly Articles 85 and 86), deriving its authority from judgments of the European Court of Justice.[82]

10.77 The policy intention underlying the new Competition Act's provision for interim measures was graphically illustrated in October 1997, while the legislation was being formulated, in a speech given by Nigel Griffiths, then a junior government minister responsible for competition policy:

> A good example is the small bus company which finds itself being driven to the wall by a large operator deliberately setting fares at anti-competitive levels. After driving the poor rival out of business, the larger company can increase fares and earn profits. The present Fair Trading Act [ie the old legislation] operates like a policeman after the burglar has cleaned the householder out. Labour's new Bill [ie the new legislation] gives powers to the Office of Fair Trading to take more immediate action against the abuse.[83]

In other words, interim measures are necessary to stop the burglar before he has cleaned the householder out.

The Content of Interim Measures

10.78 The OFT's direction to impose interim measures may provide for such measures as it 'considers appropriate' to bring to an end the suspected infringement of the

---

[82] In particular, Case 792/79R *Camera Care v Commission* [1980] ECR 119.
[83] Department of Trade and Industry press release, 'Griffiths tells Conference about New Competition Policy', P/97/638, 8 Oct 1997.

Chapter I or Chapter II prohibition—including requiring the party concerned to terminate the agreement or conduct, or to modify it.[84]

Accordingly, the directions which the OFT may make by way of interim measures are as wide as the directions which it may make following a decision that there has actually been an infringement. **10.79**

When May the OFT Impose Interim Measures?

Section 35 (1) to (5) lays down the criteria which must be satisfied in order for the OFT to be able to impose interim measures. It must be the case that all the following criteria are met: **10.80**

(i)   The OFT has a 'reasonable suspicion' that either the Chapter I or the Chapter II prohibition has been infringed, but the OFT has not yet completed its investigation into the matter. The OFT has said that the existence of a 'reasonable suspicion' will depend on its own judgment and on the information available; it may, for example, arise where there are copies of secret agreements provided by disaffected members of a cartel, statements from employees or ex-employees, a complaint supported by evidence, or economic evidence (eg of price movements).[85]

(ii)   The OFT considers that it is necessary to act 'as a matter of urgency'.

(iii) The aim of the interim measures is:

   • *either* to 'prevent serious, irreparable damage' to a particular person or category of person;

   • *or* to 'protect the public interest'.

   The OFT has envisaged examples of 'serious, irreparable damage' to a person as being where, as a result of the anti-competitive agreement or conduct, a smaller undertaking is being put out of business or is suffering considerable competitive disadvantage; and the OFT sees the need to 'protect the public interest' as arising, for instance, where damage is being caused to an industry.[86] Apart from the OFT's examples, regard should be had to EC case law when interpreting this criterion, applying section 60 of the Competition Act, since the criterion reflects EC jurisprudence on interim measures.[87]

(iv) The OFT has given advance written notice to the person against whom the interim measures would be ordered, indicating the nature of the proposed direction and the OFT's reasons for wishing to give it.

---

[84] Competition Act 1998, s 35(6) and (7).
[85] OFT, n 31 above, para 3.4.
[86] Ibid, paras 3.5 and 3.6.
[87] Case T–44/90 *La Cinq v Commission* [1992] ECR II–1.

(v)   The person against whom the interim measures would be ordered has had an opportunity to make representations in response to the written notice.

10.81   An application for interim measures (by a complainant) should provide as much evidence as possible to demonstrate that the alleged infringement is causing serious, irreparable damage, and should indicate as precisely as possible the nature of the interim measures being sought.[88]

10.82   When the OFT is proposing to make an interim measures direction, it must, if so requested by the addressee of the interim measures, give the addressee an opportunity to inspect the documents in the OFT's file relating to the proposed directions. However, the OFT may withhold any document if it considers the document to be confidential or internal to the OFT.[89]

10.83   The OFT must publish interim measures directions in its register of decisions under the prohibitions.[90] The OFT will also publish them on the Internet and perhaps in appropriate trade journals.[91]

10.84   A breach of a direction for interim measures, where these have been imposed for a suspected infringement of the Chapter I or Chapter II prohibition, carries the same consequences as for a breach of directions to terminate or modify (as described in pargraphs 10.34–10.37 above).[92]

G. Relation Between Court Proceedings (Private Litigation) and OFT Action

10.85   As this chapter has shown, alleged infringements of the Chapter I prohibition may be the subject both of court proceedings (ie private litigation) and also of investigations by the OFT. In addition, the same agreements or conduct may be the subject of investigation by the European Commission under Article 81 or 82 (formerly Article 85 or 86).

10.86   Difficulties may arise if an agreement or conduct is or has been the subject both of court proceedings *and* of proceedings as it is before the OFT (or, indeed, before the European Commission). To what extent, first, is a court bound by **prior decisions of the OFT** under the Chapter I or Chapter II prohibition? Secondly, is it appropriate that a court should reach a judgment that an agreement infringes the Chapter I prohibition (and possibly also Article 81), and award damages against the parties, while at the same time that agreement is the **subject of a notification**

---

[88]   OFT, n 31 above, para 3.7.

[89]   OFT, n 33 above, R 18.

[90]   OFT, n 33 above, R 17(2).

[91]   OFT, n 31 above, para 3.12.

[92]   Competition Act 1998, s 35(6) and (7).

to the OFT (or to the European Commission) with a view to obtaining exemption?

The Competition Act contains relatively little guidance to assist in resolving these difficulties—although, in section 58(3), it envisages that rules of court may make provision in respect of assistance to be given by the OFT in court proceedings under the Chapter I or Chapter II prohibition. Pending the issuance of such rules (or of any further rules, advice or information which the OFT may publish under sections 51 and 52 of the Act), it may be appropriate **to have regard by analogy to the EC law position**—that is, the case law and guidance on the relation between national court proceedings and European Commission proceedings under Articles 81 and 82 (formerly Articles 85 and 86) EC. However, the value of the analogy is to some extent limited by the fact that the EC law in this area is in large part based on the doctrine of the supremacy of Community law over inconsistent national law and, in particular, on the need to avoid conflict between *EC* and *national* institutions (eg between the European Commission and the national courts); this issue is clearly less relevant to the relation between the courts and the OFT, both of which are national institutions.   **10.87**

Nevertheless, the requirements of section 60 of the Competition Act—under which the courts, in determining questions under the UK prohibitions, must ensure no inconsistency with EC Treaty and European Court principles in determining any corresponding question in EC law, and in addition must have regard to any relevant statement or decision of the European Commission—may be grounds for having regard to EC case law in this area, and also to the European Commission's Notice on co-operation between national courts and the Commission in the application of Articles 85 and 86 (now Articles 81 and 82).[93]   **10.88**

The following paragraphs consider—on the basis of the currently available guidance (including, by analogy, the relegant EC law)—a number of practical situations where the relation between court proceedings and OFT action is likely to be an issue.   **10.89**

Court Proceedings After a *Prior* Finding by the OFT

(i) **Prior individual exemption decision**: The Competition Act section 58(1) provides that the OFT's findings of fact are binding. However, this is subject to a number of exceptions: (a) where the time for bringing an appeal against the OFT has not yet expired; (b) where the decision is the subject of an appeal to the Competition Commission (appeal tribunal); (c) where the Competition Commission has ruled on an appeal and not confirmed the OFT's finding of fact; (d) where the OFT has decided to take further action in   **10.90**

---

[93] Commission Notice on co-operation between national courts and the Commission in applying Articles 85 and 86 (now Articles 81 and 82) of the EEC Treaty [1993] OJ C39/6.

respect of the case on the grounds of a material change of circumstance or a reasonable suspicion that the information on which the decision was based was materially incomplete, false or misleading; or (e) where the court directs otherwise.

Apart from this, EC case law suggests that individual exemption decisions by the European Commission are binding on national courts; so too are EC block exemptions.[94] Both of these operate, through the 'parallel exemption' provisions of the Competition Act, as automatic exemptions from the Chapter I prohibition. By analogy, UK individual exemption decisions by the OFT (and UK block exemptions) ought also to be regarded as binding, although this is not established.[95]

(ii) **Prior decision finding an infringement**: As noted above, the OFT's findings of fact are binding (subject to the exceptions described in (i) above).

Apart from that, European Commission decisions finding an infringement of Article 81 or 82 (formerly Article 85 or 86) EC are not regarded as being formally binding on national courts, but as providing national courts with significant information which may be taken into account by the courts to enable them to reach a judgment.[96]

By analogy, OFT infringement decisions may perhaps be expected to have the same effect, although this has yet to be established.

(iii) **Prior negative clearance decision by the OFT**: These are likely to be treated as having a similar effect to infringement decisions (as in (ii) above).

A negative clearance decision is a statement that the agreement or conduct falls *outside* the ambit of the Chapter I or Chapter II prohibition respectively (or Article 81 or Article 82 respectively)—unlike an exemption decision which means that, although an agreement comes within the ambit of the Chapter I prohibition (or of Article 81), it has offsetting economic benefits which merit disapplication of the prohibition from that agreement.

Negative clearance decisions, in EC law, do not have the binding force of exemption decisions as described in (i) above. Instead, negative clearance decisions are to be treated as having a similar effect as infringement decisions—except that Advocate General van Gerven in the European Court of Justice took the view that EC negative clearance decisions perhaps ought to be treated as having lesser significance than EC infringement decisions.[97]

---

[94] Commission Notice on co-operation between national courts and the Commission in applying Articles 85 and 86 (now Articles 81 and 82) of the EEC Treaty [1993] OJ C39/6, para 24(a). Opinion of Van Gerven AG in Case C–128/92 *Banks v British Coal Corporation* [1994] ECR I–1209 at para 59.

[95] See Kon, S., and Maxwell, A., 'Enforcement in National Courts of the EC and New UK Competition Rules: Obstacles to Effective Enforcement' [1998] ECLR 443 at 453: 'analogies with enforcement of Commission Decisions by domestic courts may be of only limited assistance'.

[96] Commission Notice (n 93), para 20. Opinion of Van Gerven AG (n 94) at para 60.

[97] Commission Notice (n 93), para 20. Opinion of Van Gerven AG (n 94) at para 60.

However, an EC negative clearance decision is likely to be taken into account in court proceedings under the UK prohibitions only if it is given on the grounds of a substantive competition analysis rather than for jurisdictional reasons (ie for the reason that there is not an appreciable effect on trade between EU Member States).

(iv) **Prior 'comfort letter'/administrative letter:** The European Commission often deals with cases by way of an informal comfort letter (or administrative letter) rather than a formal decision. It is quite likely that the OFT will, for reasons of convenience, resort to a similar device.

An OFT comfort letter or administrative letter would not be a decision, and therefore a finding of fact set out in the comfort letter will not be binding on the courts by virtue of Competition Act section 58.

Under EC law, European Commission comfort letters are treated as not formally binding, but as constituting a factor which the courts take into account.[98] However, an EC comfort letter is likely to be such a factor in court proceedings under the UK prohibitions only if it was given on the basis of a substantive competition assessment—but not if it was given on the grounds that the European Commission does not have jurisdiction (ie because of insufficient effect on trade between EU Member States) or that the European Commission has other internal priorities.

(v) **Prior OFT guidance:** Findings of fact in OFT guidance are not binding on the parties under Competition Act section 58, as guidance is not a decision.

Since there is no European Commission equivalent to OFT guidance, EC law can offer little assistance by way of analogy. However, it is submitted that guidance should be treated in a similar way to EC comfort letters or administrative letters: ie they are taken into account but are not binding on the courts. Although guidance has a more formal status than a comfort letter, and is likely to be more fully reasoned, guidance shares the fundamental characteristic with comfort letters that it is granted without third parties having an opportunity to comment, and on this ground guidance ought not to be regarded as any more determinative in court proceedings.

Notifications being Assessed *During* Court Proceedings

Even if there has been no *prior* finding by the OFT, there may be OFT proceedings *in progress* at the time of the court proceedings. This is likely to be where a notification was made before the court proceedings, but has not yet been determined, or where a notification is submitted after the court proceedings have been initiated (eg where the defendant in court proceedings wishes to seek an **10.91**

---

[98] Commission Notice (n 93), paras 20 and 24(a). Opinion of Van Gerven AG (n 94), at para 60.

exemption for the agreement being litigated, which would then defeat the plaintiff's claim). In this latter case, the rules and procedures, as currently envisaged, **give every incentive for a party who is alleged in court proceedings to have infringed the Chapter I prohibition, then to submit a notification for exemption.** In particular:

- the OFT has said that, if an agreement is challenged in the UK courts on the basis that it infringes the Chapter I prohibition, the OFT will endeavour to give priority to such cases if notified—and, if the OFT concludes that the agreement merits exemption, the exemption is likely to be granted with retroactive effect (there is no limit on the OFT's power to grant an exemption from the Chapter I prohibition with retroactive effect; unlike an exemption under Article 81 (formerly Article 85), it can be backdated to before the date of notification);[99]

- the government has expressed the view that OFT proceedings should not be suspended while court proceedings are in progress (and, when the Competition Bill was progressing through Parliament, the government was not silling to accept an amendment which would have had this effect);[100]

- it is likely to be possible for court proceedings to be 'stayed' while OFT proceedings are in progress, by analogy with the position as regards EC competition law (as applied by the European Court and national courts in the UK)—see below.

10.92   The question of when court proceedings should be stayed until after a notification has been dealt with has arisen in the context of EC law—ie the question whether national court proceedings on the application of Articles 81 and 82 should be stayed while the European Commission is considering a notification. Statements of the position in the context of EC law have appeared in the European Commission's Notice on co-operation between national courts and the Commission,[101] and in the European Court of Justice's judgment in the *Delimitis* case.[102] Statements on the requirements of English legal rules in this EC law context (ie staying Article 81 court proceedings pending the outcome of European Commission proceedings) were made in the judgment of the Court of Appeal in the 1995 *MTV* case.[103] The analogy with EC law is not strictly relevant in the context of the Competition Act, because (as noted above) the rules setting out the relation between national court proceedings and European Commission decisions largely relate to questions of the supremacy of Community law over con-

---

[99]   OFT, n 70 above, para 7.13.

[100]   Lord Simon of Highbury, Minister in the Department of Trade and Industry, *Hansard*, HL, vol 585, no 99, col 986 (9 Feb 1998).

[101]   See n 93.

[102]   Case C–234/89 *Delimitis* [1991] ECR I–935.

[103]   *MTV Europe v BMG Records* (UK) Ltd [1997] 1 CMLR 867.

flicting national law. Nevertheless, a leading practitioner of EC and competition litigation in the UK has said that:

> in a purely national situation . . . the court might consider it better for the OFT to reach a position on the notification which could then be the subject of independent challenge through the appeal process than risking a different assessment in the civil litigation.[104]

Notwithstanding these caveats about the analogy with the EC law position, the rules on staying national court proceedings under Articles 81 and 82 EC while the European Commission is considering a notification are as follows: **10.93**

(i) **Where the agreement clearly infringes the prohibitions and may on no account merit exemption:** The European Court in *Delimitis* took the view that the national court may continue the proceeding and give judgment.[105] The English Court of Appeal in *MTV* endorsed this view.[106]

(ii) **Where the agreement or conduct is clearly outside the ambit of the prohibitions:** The European Court took the view that the national court may continue the proceedings and give judgment.[107] The English Court of Appeal in *MTV* endorsed this position.[108]

(iii) **Where the outcome of the notification is unclear, and an exemption may be granted, the European Court provides that the national court may decide to stay the proceedings:**[109] The English Court of Appeal in *MTV* emphasised that there is no obligation on the national courts to stay the proceedings, but only to ensure that a premature judgment in the action should not conflict with a later ruling by the European Commission. On this basis, the Court of Appeal refused to overrule the decision of the lower court that, in order to achieve this, it was sufficient to direct that the action should not be set down until one month after the Commission had published its decision.[110]

Where a national court is considering a question of EC law, it may refer that question to the European Court of Justice under Article 234 (formerly Article 177) of the EC Treaty.[111] Because the Chapter I and Chapter II prohibitions are to be interpreted by courts so as to ensure no inconsistency with the principles laid down by the EC Treaty and the European Court of Justice, under section 60(2), **10.94**

---

[104] Flynn, J., 'Using the Courts: Strategic Overview', delivered at Norton Rose IIR conference on Competition Law Compliance, 19 May 1998.

[105] *Delimitis* (n 102), at para 47.

[106] *MTV* (n 103), at 878.

[107] *Delimitis* (n 102), para 47.

[108] *MTV* (n 103), at 879.

[109] *Delimitis* (n 102), para 52.

[110] *MTV* (n 103), at 879 and 880.

[111] As a result of the amendments to the EC Treaty introduced by the Treaty of Amsterdam Art 177 became Article 234.

it is almost certainly open to courts in the UK, when assessing cases under the Chapter I and Chapter II prohibitions, to make an Article 234 reference (formerly Article 177 reference) to the European Court of Justice.[112]

---

[112] See Ch 3 above, paras 3.79–3.89. This is confirmed by the European Court of Justice in Case C–7/97 *Oscar Bronner v Mediaprint* (judgment of 26 Nov 1998).

PART V

TRANSITIONAL PROVISIONS

11

TRANSITIONAL PROVISIONS

'Transitional periods' and 'continuing proceedings' are relevant for the treatment, under the Chapter I prohibition, of all agreements made before the starting date on 1 March 2000—whether they are made before the enactment date (B) or during the interim period (C). They are dealt with fully in **11.29–11.38**.

Utilities agreements, in the electricity, gas and railways sectors may benefit from special rules in respect of their treatment under the Chapter I prohibition—whether made before or after the starting date. See **11.33(iii)** and **11.52–11.53**, and **Chapter 19, 19.34–19.38**.

A. Overview

11.01 The Chapter I prohibition does not only apply to new agreements, but also to pre-existing agreements which were already in place prior to the enactment of the Competition Act 1998 on 9 November 1998.

11.02 This does not mean, however, that parties to pre-existing agreements become *immediately* subject to the Chapter I prohibition. In the Act, Schedule 13, read with section 74(2), lays down transitional provisions which give parties to most pre-existing agreements a period of time before they become subject to the Chapter I prohibition—a sixteen-month 'interim period' from enactment of the Competition Act to the 'starting date' (the date when the Act comes into force, 1 March 2000), plus, in most cases, a further 'transitional period' of one or five years after the starting date. During this period, parties have the chance to check and, if necessary, to modify or terminate their agreements to ensure that they do not infringe the Chapter I prohibition.

11.03 Schedule 13 also deals with the extent to which the old UK laws on restrictive agreements—the Restrictive Trade Practices Act 1976 (RTPA) and the Resale Prices Act 1976 (RPA)—continue to apply to pre-existing agreements.

11.04 Finally, Schedule 13 makes provision for the way in which, during the sixteen-month 'interim period' between the enactment of the Competition Act and the starting date, pre-existing agreements *and* new agreements are to be treated, both under the old laws and under the new Chapter I prohibition.

11.05 *The Chapter II prohibition is not covered by the transitional provisions in Schedule 13. The Chapter II prohibition comes into force on the same date as the Chapter I prohibition—the 'starting date', 1 March 2000. This gives businesses which may have a dominant market position sixteen months (from enactment to starting date) to ensure that their activities will not infringe the Chapter II prohibition when it comes into force. After that time, the Chapter II prohibition enters into full force and effect, with no additional 'transitional period'. By contrast with the Chapter I prohibition, there will be no possibility of obtaining, in advance of the starting date, 'early guidance' from the OFT on the application of the Chapter II prohibition to particular conduct. After the starting date, the authorities will no longer be able to carry out investigations under the Competition Act 1980, but the monopoly provisions of the Fair Trading Act 1973 will still apply.*[1]

Key Dates

11.06 The transitional provisions in Schedule 13 revolve around a number of key dates, as follows.

> **Enactment date:** the date on which the Competition Act received Royal Assent and was thereby enacted—**9 November 1998**.
>
> **Interim period:** the sixteen-month period from the 'enactment date' up to the 'starting date'—from **9 November 1998 to 29 February 2000** (inclusive). (This should not be confused with 'transitional periods'—see below.)

---

[1] See below, Chs 17 and 18 of this book.

Starting date: the date, sixteen months after the enactment date, when the Chapter I prohibition comes into force (the Chapter II prohibition comes into force on the same date)[2]—**1 March 2000**.

Transitional period: a period *after* the starting date during which pre-existing agreements (ie agreements which were in place at the starting date) are not subject to the Chapter I prohibition. The length of the transitional period depends on the type of agreement; it is generally one year, but may be up to five years (details are given in paragraph 11.24–11.38 below). New agreements made after the starting date do not benefit from any transitional period—**1 March 2000 to 28 February 2001 (or, in some cases, to 28 February 2005)**.

The Basic Rules Summarised

Different rules apply to agreements depending on when the agreement is 'made' (ie signed)—namely: **11.07**

(i)   agreements made before the enactment date;

(ii)   agreements made during the interim period (that is, between the enactment date and the starting date);

(iii)   agreements made after the starting date.

The basic rules for these categories of agreement can be summarised as follows. **11.08**

(i)   *Agreements made before the enactment date*

- Chapter I prohibition
  - During the interim period,[3] the Chapter I prohibition does not apply at all.
  - After the starting date,[4] the Chapter I prohibition does apply; but agreements which received RTPA section 21(2) clearance are excluded, and most other agreements are not subject to the Chapter I prohibition for a 'transitional period' of one or five years, or during 'continuing proceedings' in the Restrictive Practices Court. (There is no equivalent protection from the Chapter II prohibition.)
- RTPA
  - During the interim period,[5] the RTPA fully operates (including notification obligation even for agreements made less than three months before enactment date).

---

[2] The starting date is set by an order of the Secretary of State made under s 76(3) of the Act. The provisions of Sch 13 come into force immediately on the enactment date (by virtue of s 76(2)).

[3] See para 11.10 below for details.

[4] See paras 11.11–11.12.

[5] See paras 11.13–11.15.

- After the starting date,[6] despite repeal of RTPA, voidness and third-party liability continue in respect of existing registrable agreements which were not duly notified (or which were found by the Restrictive Practices Court to be contrary to the public interest). Most orders of the Restrictive Practices Court cease to apply, and most proceedings before the Restrictive Practices Court cease.[7]

(ii) *Agreements made during the interim period (ie between the enactment date and the starting date)*

- Chapter I prohibition

  - During the interim period,[8] the Chapter I prohibition does not apply, but parties to agreements made during the interim period can apply to the OFT for 'early guidance' on whether the agreement is likely to infringe the Chapter I prohibition when it comes into force. (There is no possibility of early guidance under the Chapter II prohibition.)

  - After the starting date,[9] the Chapter I prohibition does apply; but most agreements which were made during the interim period are not subject to the Chapter I prohibition for a 'transitional period' of one or five years, or during 'continuing proceedings' in the Restrictive Practices Court. (There is no equivalent protection from the Chapter II prohibition.)

- RTPA

  - During the interim period,[10] the RTPA applies in a 'weak' form. Registrable agreements which are 'made' during the interim period are not subject to the notification requirement unless they are price-fixing agreements.[11] However, the OFT may still use its RTPA powers of scrutiny and action against any registrable agreement, where it considers that the agreement raises serious competition concerns. No agree-

---

[6] See paras 11.16–11.18.

[7] In broad terms, proceedings relating to *enforcement* under the RTPA cease at the starting date. The proceedings which survive are of two types: first, proceedings relating to a *substantive competition assessment* of the agreement—these are called 'continuing proceedings' and their outcome determines whether the agreement will benefit from a transitional period under the Chapter I prohibition—and, secondly, proceedings needed to *facilitate the transition* from old to new legislation (RTPA s 3 proceedings in respect of interim orders in relation to substantive proceedings, which are needed because the authorities want the right to restrain anti-competitive agreements during continuing proceedings when they are not subject to the Chapter I prohibition, and RTPA s 26 proceedings relating to registrability under the RTPA since businesses need to know whether provisions are valid or void for non-notification of a registrable agreement).

[8] See paras 11.19–11.27.

[9] See paras 11.28–11.38.

[10] See paras 11.39–11.43.

[11] However, this 'non-notifiability' does not benefit variations made during the interim period to registrable agreements which had been made before the enactment date: see paras 11.46–11.51 below.

ment made in the interim period will be eligible for section 21(2) clearance.

- After the starting date,[12] despite the repeal of the RTPA, voidness and third-party liability continue in respect of existing registrable agreements which were not duly notified (or which were found by the Restrictive Practices Court to be contrary to the public interest). However, price-fixing registrable agreements made within three months before the starting date are not void under the RTPA if they are not notified—but, unless they are notified *before* the starting date, they lose the benefit of a one-year transitional period under the Chapter I prohibition.

  Most orders of the Restrictive Practices Court cease to apply, and most proceedings before the Restrictive Practices Court cease.[13]

(iii) *Agreements made after the starting date*

- Chapter I prohibition[14]
  - The Chapter I prohibition fully applies with immediate effect (except for certain agreements in the electricity, gas and railway sectors which are made in the first five years after the starting date).

- RTPA
  - The RTPA does not apply at all to agreements made after the starting date.

In the remainder of this chapter, these provisions are explained in more detail. The **11.09** UK authorities have recognised that the provisions of Schedule 13 are extremely complex, and paragraph 3 of Schedule 13 entitles the OFT to 'publish advice and information explaining provisions of this Schedule to persons who are likely to be affected by them'. In fact, the OFT has issued an excellent guide to the provisions.[15] In addition, the Department of Trade and Industry has taken the unusual step of publishing its own guide to Schedule 13, which deals with each paragraph of the Schedule in sequence, and is a useful aid to interpreting the individual paragraphs.[16]

---

[12] See paras 11.44–11.45.
[13] See n 7 above.
[14] See paras 11.52–11.53 below.
[15] Office of Fair Trading, 'Competition Act 1998: Transitional Arrangements' (OFT 406).
[16] Department of Trade and Industry, 'A Guide to the New Transitionals Schedule in the Competition Bill', June 1998.

B. Agreements Made Before the Enactment Date
(9 November 1998)

Treatment under the Chapter I Prohibition

Treatment During the Interim Period

11.10 During the sixteen-month interim period (between the enactment date and the starting date), the Chapter I prohibition has not yet come into force, and therefore does not apply at all to agreements which were made before the enactment date. There is no possibility of notifying for 'early guidance' on the application of the Chapter I prohibition to agreements made during the interim period (see paragraphs 11.20–11.27 below).

Treatment After the Starting Date

11.11 From the starting date onwards, the Chapter I prohibition enters into full force and effect. As at that date, *in principle* it applies to all agreements, pre-existing agreements as well as new agreements.

11.12 However, agreements made (ie signed) before the enactment date are likely to benefit from one of the exceptions to this principle—such that either they do not become subject to the Chapter I prohibition at all, or they only become subject to it at a later date. These exceptions to the principle apply if an agreement falls within any of the following categories:

- **The agreement received 'section 21(2) clearance' under the RTPA**: a significant number of agreements made before the enactment date are likely to have received section 21(2) clearance under the RTPA. All such agreements are permanently outside the Chapter I prohibition, by virtue of an exclusion in Schedule 3—provided that:

  (i) the section 21(2) clearance is in place as at the starting date,

  (ii) there is no subsequent 'material variation' to the agreement, and

  (iii) the OFT does not subsequently exercise its powers to 'claw back' the exclusion.

  Details of this exclusion are given in Chapter 5 paragraphs 5.41–5.43 of this book.

- **The agreement qualifies for a 'transitional period'**: even if an agreement is not permanently excluded by section 21(2) clearance, it is likely to qualify for a 'transitional period'. This means that the application of the Chapter I prohibition is postponed, and does not start until the end of the transitional period. In general, the transitional period is one year from the starting date, but it may be as long as five years. However, there is no transitional period for agreements to the extent that they were void or unlawful under the RTPA or the RPA. The rules are set out in paragraphs 11.29–11.34 below.

- **The agreement is the subject of 'continuing proceedings' in the Restrictive Practices Court, under either the RTPA or the RPA**: certain pre-existing agreements which, as at the starting date, are the subject of 'continuing proceedings' in the Restrictive Practices Court will not be subject to the Chapter I prohibition until after the continuing proceedings have ceased. When the continuing proceedings cease, the agreement concerned either becomes immediately subject to the Chapter I prohibition or enjoys the benefit of a subsequent transitional period (generally of five years), depending on the substantive outcome of the continuing proceedings. Details are set out in paragraphs 11.35–11.38 below.

Treatment under the RTPA and the RPA

Treatment During the Interim Period

Agreements which were made before the enactment date are fully subject to the RTPA and the RPA throughout the interim period (ie up to the starting date). **11.13**

Consequently, any agreement 'made' (ie signed) before the enactment date will, if it is a registrable agreement under the RTPA, need to be notified to the OFT within the statutory time limit under the RTPA, which is normally within three months of being made (subject to the exception for non-notifiable agreements in RTPA, section 27A).[17] **11.14**

This obligation to notify pre-existing registrable agreements applies even to agreements which are made less than three months before the enactment date, such that the deadline for notification falls in the interim period. Such an agreement must be notified to the OFT in accordance with the normal requirements of the RTPA, and does not benefit from the special non-notifiability provisions that apply to agreements made during the interim period (which are considered in paragraphs 11.40–11.41 below).[18] Moreover, in these cases, the OFT has indicated that it will not normally exercise its discretion under RTPA, section 35(1) to extend the time limit for notification 'other than in the most exceptional circumstances'.[19] **11.15**

Treatment After the Starting Date

As at the starting date, both the RTPA and the RPA are repealed, by virtue of an order made under section 1 of the Competition Act 1998.[20] (The repeal has effect **11.16**

---

[17] This is also true of variations which give rise to a notification obligation under RTPA, s 24, read with the Registration of Restrictive Trading Agreements Regs 1984, SI 1984/392, reg 5.
[18] OFT, n 15 above, para 2.2.
[19] Ibid, para 2.4.
[20] Competition Act 1998, s 76(3).

after the starting date even in respect of agreements which, after the starting date, continue to enjoy the benefit of a transitional period during which they are protected from the Chapter I prohibition as well.) However, in spite of the repeal, certain important consequences of the RTPA and the RPA continue to have effect; most importantly, **voidness and third-party liability endure after the repeal in respect of restrictions in pre-existing agreements which were registrable but not duly notified**—details are set out in paragraph 11.18 below.

11.17 The main implications of the repeal of the RTPA and the RPA are that:

(a) Most orders of the Restrictive Practices Court cease to have effect, namely:

- Restraining orders where restrictions in a registrable agreement have been held to operate against the public interest, under RTPA, section 2(2);

- Restraining orders where the OFT has taken action in respect of a registrable agreement which has not been duly notified to the OFT, under RTPA, section 35(3);

- Orders requiring parties to a registrable agreement to be examined on oath by the OFT, following the issue of a 'section 36 notice' to the party, under RTPA, section 37;

- Orders for an injunction or other relief following proceedings brought by the Crown in respect of the operation of unlawful (collective or individual) resale price maintenance, under RPA, section 25(2).[21]

However, 'interim orders' under RTPA, section 3 continue in force after the starting date, and moreover new interim orders can be made after the starting date, as explained in paragraphs (vii) and (viii) below.

(b) Ministerial and administrative approval orders under the RTPA cease to have effect—namely those for: agreements important to the national economy under s29(1); agreements holding down prices under section 30(1); wholesale co-operative societies under section 32; and agricultural, forestry and fisheries associations under section 33.[22]

(c) Certain proceedings which are before the Restrictive Practices Court at the starting date (ie in respect of an application which is made before the starting date, but not yet determined as at that date) cease. These are generally proceedings which relate merely to *enforcement* under the RTPA or the RPA, and include:[23]

---

[21] Competition Act 1998, Sch 13, para 9(1).

[22] Sch 13, para 9(1) and (2).

[23] The proceedings which do not cease are those involving a *substantive competition assessment*, which are called 'continuing proceedings', (see (vi) below, and also proceedings necessary to *facilitate the transition* from the old regime to the new (see (vii) to (ix) below).

- Applications for a restraining order in respect of restrictions in a registrable agreement on the grounds that they are against the public interest (under RTPA, section 2(2)), and applications to discharge or vary such an order (under RTPA, section 4(1));[24]

- Applications for a restraining order in respect of registrable agreements which have not been duly notified (under RTPA, section 35(3));

- Applications for an order entitling the OFT to examine on oath a party to a registrable agreement, following the issue of a 'section 36 notice' (under RTPA, section 37(1));

- Applications for an order to declare that restrictions in a registrable agreement, which is already unlawful under a Fair Trading Act order, is contrary to the public interest (under RTPA, section 40(1));

- Applications relating to orders already in force under section 18(2) of the Restrictive Trade Practices Act of 1956 (under RTPA, Schedule 4 paragraph 5);

- Applications by the Crown for an order restraining resale price maintenance (under RPA, section 25(2)).[25]

Nevertheless, even after the starting date, the Restrictive Practices Court will still have the power to make a costs order in relation to any proceedings (whether or not such proceedings have ceased by virtue of the starting date).[26] In addition, certain proceedings before the Restrictive Practices Court will be able to continue after the starting date, as explained in paragraphs (vi) to (ix) below.

However, in spite of the repeal, some of the most important consequences of the RTPA and the RPA *persist* in respect of pre-existing agreements made before the starting date (including agreements made before the enactment date). In particular: **11.18**

(i)   Under the RTPA, if a pre-existing registrable agreement had not been duly notified to the OFT within the statutory time limit:

- The right of third parties to bring civil proceedings where they sustained losses as a result (as breach of statutory duty), under RTPA, section 35(2), continues indefinitely. However, this is only in so far as that right relates to any period before the starting date (or, where there are 'continuing proceedings', to any period before the determination of the proceedings: see paragraphs 11.35–11.38 below)—which means that, where a third

---

[24] But applications for a declaration that restrictions are against the public interest (under RTPA, s 1(3)) will continue.
[25] Sch 13, para 8(1) and (2).
[26] Sch 13, para 8(3).

party takes civil proceedings for damages for losses which it has sustained as a result of non-notification of a registrable agreement, *the damages will be limited to losses sustained in the period before the starting date* (or before the determination of any 'continuing proceedings').[27]

- The voidness of the relevant restrictions in the agreement, under RTPA, section 35(1)(a), continues indefinitely.[28]

(ii) Under the RTPA, if the parties to a pre-existing registrable agreement had, before notifying it to the OFT, given effect to restrictions in it, or enforced or purported to enforce those restrictions:

- The right of third parties to bring civil proceedings where they sustained losses as a result, under RTPA, section 27ZA, continues indefinitely. However, as with the equivalent right for unnotified registrable agreements, this is only in respect of losses sustained before the starting date (or before the determination of any 'continuing proceedings').[29]

(iii) Under the RTPA, if the Restrictive Practices Court declared a registrable agreement to be contrary to the public interest:

- The voidness of the relevant restrictions in the agreement, under RTPA, section 2(1), continues indefinitely.[30]

(iv) Under the RPA, if parties operated unlawful collective resale price maintenance,[31] or maintained minimum resale prices by agreement or through the withholding of supplies.[32]

- The right of third parties to bring civil proceedings where they sustained losses as a result, under RPA, section 25, continues indefinitely. However,

---

[27] Sch 13, para 13(1).

[28] This, at least, is the view of the OFT as stated in para 6.9 of its guidelines on the 'Transitional Arrangements', n 15 above. However, the Competition Act itself, including Sch 13, is silent on the point. The view of the OFT and the government seems to be that there is no need for the Act to provide for this expressly, since as a matter of general law the voidness of contractual provisions survives the repeal of the legislation which gave rise to the voidness. This view is presumably based on s 16(1) of the Interpretation Act 1978, as applied in cases such as *Coates v Diment* [1951] 1 All ER 890. But there must be some doubt about this view, for the following reasons. S 16(1) of the Interpretation Act 1978 only applies 'unless the contrary intention appears', and the fact that the Competition Act 1998 is silent on the question of continuing voidness, but expressly provides for third-party liability (which s 16(1) of the Interpretation Act 1978 also provides for), may be regarded as evidence of 'contrary intention' in the Competition Act 1998. Moreover, a recent Court of Appeal judgment has held that, as a matter of English law, a contractual provision that was void for infringement of Art 81 EC (formerly Art 85), may subsequently become valid where Art 81 ceases to apply as a result of changing economic effects (*Passmore v Morland and others* [1998] EuLR 588): while this case is distinguishable, in that it did not relate to Art 81 ceasing to apply because of *repeal*, it could cast doubt on the proposition that a contractual provision that was void under RTPA, s 35(1)(a) does not subsequently become valid where RTPA, s 35 ceases to apply. It would be preferable if this point were to be clarified.

[29] Competition Act 1998 Sch 13, para 13(1).

[30] See n 28 above.

[31] Contrary to RPA, s1 or s 2.

[32] Contrary to RPA, s 9 or s 11.

as with the RTPA, this is only in respect of losses sustained in the period before the starting date (or before the determination of any 'continuing proceedings').[33]

- Void resale price maintenance provisions in contracts (under RPA, section 9(1)), continue to be void.[34]

(v)   The OFT's 'register' of registrable agreements, under the RTPA, will continue to be maintained after the starting date. This is intended to allow parties to check the status of pre-existing agreements, which may have an impact on their validity under the Chapter I prohibition (for example: if an agreement received 'section 21(2) clearance', it is excluded from the Chapter I prohibition; if an agreement was never notified under the RTPA but should have been, the relevant restrictions will not receive the benefit of any transitional period). Moreover, the OFT will continue to have statutory duties to file certain agreements on the register—namely: those few registrable agreements made during the interim period which are notifiable and are notified to the OFT but which are not entered on the register before the starting date (ie price fixing agreements);[35] agreements which are subject to proceedings under the RTPA which do not cease on the starting date by virtue of the RTPA's repeal;[36] and agreements on which a court has given directions to the OFT after the starting date as to whether the agreement is registrable and/or notifiable.[37] Existing rights of confidentiality in the register's 'special section', and existing regulations concerning notification and the maintenance of the register, remain in force, subject to any modifications which may be prescribed.[38]

However, it is the OFT's intention that, although the public will have full access to the register for an initial period after the starting date, subsequently regulations will be made reducing access to the register.[39]

(vi)   The RTPA and the RPA will continue to apply to any agreement after the starting date, for so long as that agreement is protected from the Chapter I prohibition because of 'continuing proceedings' before the Restrictive Practices Court.[40]

---

[33] Competition Act 1998, Sch 13, para 13(2).
[34] See n 28 above.
[35] See para 11.40 below.
[36] See paras (vi) to (ix) below.
[37] A registrable agreement under the RTPA normally needed to be notified to the OFT under RTPA, s 24. However, certain registrable agreements are non-notifiable, by virtue either of an order under RTPA, s 27A or of the Competition Act 1998, Sch 13, para 5 (as to which, see paras 11.40–11.41 below).
[38] The provisions on the continuing register are set out in the Competition Act, Sch 13, para 10.
[39] OFT, n 15 above, para 7.2.
[40] Competition Act 1998, Sch 13, para 14(4).

The term 'continuing proceedings' is defined as proceedings before the Restrictive Practices Court under the RTPA or the RPA, in respect of an application which was made before the starting date, but which had not yet been determined by the time of the starting date—but does not include proceedings for interim measures under RTPA, section 3 or proceedings to rectify the OFT register under RTPA, section 26.[41] In practical terms, the category of 'continuing proceedings' encompasses those Restrictive Practices Court proceedings which involve a *substantive competition assessment* of the agreement—namely applications either (a) for a declaration that restrictions are against the public interest, under RTPA, section 1(3),[42] or (b) for or in respect of an order that a class of goods should or should not be exempted from the rules on resale price maintenance, under RPA, section 14 (ie, in practice, the review of the exemption order for over-the-counter pharmaceutical products).

The concept of 'continuing proceedings' is significant because of their impact on the application of the Chapter I prohibition to the agreement concerned. The outcome of the continuing proceedings (in effect, the outcome of the substantive competition assessment) determines whether the restrictive provisions benefit from a five-year transitional period or from no transitional period at all. Details are set out in paragraph 11.38 below.

(vii) Where an 'interim order' has been sought by the OFT in the Restrictive Practices Court, under RTPA, section 3, and the application was made before the starting date but not yet determined by the starting date, the RTPA continues to apply in relation to the application.[43]

(viii) New 'interim orders' may be sought by the OFT in the Restrictive Practices Court even after the starting date, where they relate to RTPA proceedings brought by the OFT in the Restrictive Practices Court to have restrictions in a registrable agreement declared contrary to the public interest, and those proceedings were commenced before the starting date but not yet determined by the starting date.[44]

---

[41] Sch 13, para 15.

[42] However, an application for a *restraining order* on the ground that restrictions are against the public interest, under RTPA, s 2(2), would not continue and would cease at the starting date—see para (c) of 11.17 above.

[43] Competition Act 1998, Sch 13, para 11(1)(a).

[44] Sch 13, para 11(1)(b). This provision is necessary because the RTPA proceedings in the Restrictive Practices Court are 'continuing proceedings' and therefore, as explained in paras 11.35–11.38 below, the Chapter I prohibition will not apply to the agreement concerned even after the starting date while the proceedings are in progress. Since the agreement may be significantly anti-competitive, but not subject to the Chapter I prohibition, RTPA powers are needed even after the starting date to enable the OFT to restrain it.

(ix)   Where there is an application in the Restrictive Practices Court under RTPA, section 26—either for rectification of the OFT's register, or for a declaration on whether an agreement is registrable and/or notifiable—the RTPA continues to apply in relation to the application if it was made before the starting date but not determined by the time of the starting date.[45]

C.   Agreeements Made During the Interim Period (From 9 November 1998 to 29 February 2000 Inclusive)

Treatment under the Chapter I Prohibition

Treatment During the Interim Period

Agreements which are made (ie signed) during the sixteen-month interim period are not subject to the Chapter I prohibition during the interim period (and only become subject to it on or after the starting date—see paragraphs 11.28–11.38 below).   **11.19**

However, in anticipation of the starting date, parties to agreements made during the interim period (but not before then) may, even before the starting date, apply to the OFT for '**early guidance**' on whether the agreement is likely to infringe the Chapter I prohibition (and, where appropriate, on whether it is likely to be exempt).   **11.20**

There is, however, no possibility of obtaining 'early guidance' in relation to the Chapter II prohibition.   **11.21**

The provisions for obtaining early guidance are set out in Schedule 13, paragraph 7. This provides that an application for early guidance, made during the interim period, will be treated in the same way as a proper notification for guidance (ie one made after the Chapter I prohibition has come into force) under sections 13 and 15 of the Act.[46] That is, a party to the agreement will be able, during the interim period, to seek early guidance by notifying the agreement to the OFT.   **11.22**

The application for early guidance must be made in accordance with the OFT's directions on early guidance, which were issued in November 1998.[47] These appear in Appendix 2 to this book. The key points are: **11.23**

(i)   Notification is by way of a **Form EG** submitted to the OFT. A copy of the Form EG is in Appendix 3 to this book.

---

[45] Sch 13, para 12(1).

[46] On the procedures and effects of a notification for guidance, see Ch 12, paras 12.06–12.13, and Ch 10 paras 10.67 to 10.71.

[47] Sch 13, para 7(2). Office of Fair Trading, 'Competition Act 1998: Early Guidance Directions', OFT 412.

(ii)   In general, a Form EG should only be submitted if Article 81 EC (formerly Article 85) is unlikely to apply (ie where it is not the case that the arrangement may appreciably affect trade between Member States of the EU).

(iii)   The **information** to be provided is as prescribed in the Form EG. In broad terms, it should describe: the arrangements, the parties, the relevant product and geographic markets, the parties' position on those markets, the state of competition in those markets, arguments as to why the parties believe that the arrangement merits either negative clearance (ie a statement that the Chapter I prohibition does not apply at all) or exemption, and grounds for believing that any transitional periods apply (see paragraphs 11.29–11.34 below).

(iv)   However, the OFT may **dispense** with the obligation to submit some of the information required, if the OFT considers it 'unnecessary' for examination of the case. In practice, parties should approach the OFT informally in advance to agree on which information requirements may be dispensed with.

(v)   The information in the Form EG must be **correct and complete**; the inclusion of false or misleading information entails that this obligation has not been complied with.

(vi)   If, following submission of the Form EG, there are **material changes** in the facts contained in it of which the applicant knows, or ought reasonably to know, the applicant must communicate this to the OFT voluntarily and without delay (or, where the applicant has been informed that a utility sector regulator is dealing with the application, to that regulator—see Chapter 19 below).

(vii)   The Form EG must be submitted to the OFT in the original version, plus two copies. If the applicant believes that a utility sector regulator has concurrent jurisdiction (see Chapter 19), the applicant must submit a further copy *to the OFT* for each relevant utility sector regulator.

(viii) Documents submitted with the Form EG (for example, the agreement which is the subject of the application) must be supplied in the original form (or as a certified true copy), and with two extra copies.

(ix)   **Utilities**: If the OFT considers that a utility sector regulator may have concurrent jurisdiction to give guidance, the OFT must as soon as practicable send a copy of the application to that regulator, and inform the applicant in writing that it has done so. If the sector regulator then does exercise jurisdiction, the applicant must be informed in writing of that fact.

(x)   **Confidential information**: If the applicant considers that any information contained in the application is confidential, the applicant should set that information out in a separate Annex marked 'confidential information' and explain why it should be treated as such. Information is confidential if its disclosure would or might significantly harm the legitimate business interests of the undertaking to which it relates, or if it relates to the private affairs of an individual and its disclosure would or might significantly harm that individual's interests.

(xi)   **Other parties**: Parties may make joint applications, and may nominate a joint representative to submit and receive documents on behalf of some or all of them. Alternatively, if the application is not made jointly, the applicant must take all reasonable steps to notify the other parties to the agreement in writing that the application has been made and, when the applicant receives acknowledgement of receipt from the OFT, notify the other parties accordingly within seven working days.

The application takes effect on the day on which the Form EG and accompanying documents are received by the OFT; if they are submitted after 6.00 pm, they are treated as having been received on the next working day. If the information is incomplete in a material respect, the OFT must without delay inform the applicant in writing of that; the application is then only effective on the date when the complete information is received by the OFT (or, if a utility sector regulator has jurisdiction, by that regulator), but if the OFT or the utility sector regulator has not informed the applicant that the application is incomplete within a month, the application is deemed to have been effective on the date it was received.   **11.24**

Once the OFT has determined the application, the OFT must give guidance in writing, together with the facts and reasons, to the applicant 'without delay'.   **11.25**

The OFT may subsequently withdraw guidance, but must first consult the person to whom the guidance was given, and may only then withdraw the guidance by giving written notice stating the reasons for the withdrawal.   **11.26**

In response to an application for early guidance, the OFT will seek to give early guidance prior to the starting date. If the OFT fails to give early guidance before the starting date, it may, in respect of the notification for early guidance, give proper 'guidance' (ie under sections 13 and 15 of the Act) on or after the starting date. Either way, the guidance given will, after the starting date, have effect in the same way as guidance given under sections 13 and 15—namely, that where the guidance is favourable (indicating that the agreement is likely to be either outside the Chapter I prohibition or exempt), the parties will be protected from penalties and from action by the OFT against the agreement.[48] Moreover, where an application for early guidance is made but not determined before the starting date, the   **11.27**

---

[48] Unless and until there is a complaint by a third party, or a material change of circumstances, or an application for a formal decision, or grounds to believe that the application was materially incomplete, false or misleading.

notification will have the same effect as notification for full guidance under section 13: the parties to the notified agreement benefit from provisional immunity from penalties until guidance is given.

Treatment After the Starting Date

11.28 From the starting date, the Chapter I prohibition comes into full force and effect, in respect of all agreements (whether made before enactment, during the interim period, or after the starting date)—except that **most agreements which are made (ie signed) during the interim period only become subject to the Chapter I prohibition at a later date, on either of the following grounds:**

- where the agreement qualifies for a 'transitional period', or
- where the agreement is the subject of 'continuing proceedings' in the Restrictive Practices Court, under the RTPA or the RPA.[49]

The rules for both 'transitional periods' and 'continuing proceedings', which are fairly complex, are as follows.

Transitional Periods

11.29 The rules on transitional periods apply equally to all agreements which are made (ie signed) before the starting date. That is, transitional periods are available equally to agreements made during the sixteen-month interim period and to agreements made before the enactment date.[50]

11.30 **The Chapter I prohibition does not apply to an agreement to the extent to which there is a transitional period for the agreement.[51]**

11.31 The expression '*to the extent to which*' is important in this context. An agreement is protected from the Chapter I prohibition *to the extent* that there is a transitional period. Moreover, as shown below, different transitional periods may apply to an agreement *to the extent* that it meets certain criteria. This means that some provisions in an agreement may benefit from a transitional period, while others may not, and also that some provisions may benefit from longer transitional periods than others. The result is that, at any point after the starting date, it could be that the Chapter I prohibition applies to some provisions of an agreement, but not to all. Where this is the case, and the OFT needs to assess whether there is an infringement of the Chapter I prohibition, the effect of paragraph 1(5) of Schedule 13 is that the OFT must have regard to the agreement as an integral

---

[49] The position is therefore the same as for pre-existing agreements made before the enactment date, as described in paras 11.11–11.12 above, except that agreements made during the interim period cannot receive 's 21(2) clearance' under the RTPA (by virtue of Sch 13, para 6(b)).

[50] However, many agreements made before the enactment date will be altogether excluded from the Chapter I prohibition, by virtue of having s 21(2) clearance (see para 11.12 above). Agreements made during the interim period cannot have s 21(2) clearance.

[51] Competition Act 1998, Sch 13, para 19(2).

whole, rather than as if the protected provisions did not exist (this does not mean that the protected provisions *lose* their protection, but only that the remaining provisions should not be considered artificially out of the context of the overall agreement).[52]

During the transitional period, even though the Chapter I prohibition does not apply to a particular agreement, it will be possible to notify the agreement to the OFT with a view to obtaining an advance decision or guidance in respect of that agreement (under sections 13 to 16 of the Act); in doing so, the notifying party should indicate in paragraph 11 in Part 2 of the Form N the duration of any transitional period considered relevant, by reference to Schedule 13.[53] In addition, if the parties have received notice that the transitional period is to be terminated (see paragraph 11.34 below), they may notify the agreement for an exemption, although this is likely to be a conditional exemption. **11.32**

In general, any agreement made before the starting date has a transitional period of one year from the starting date. However, some have no transitional period, and some have a transitional period of five years. The OFT may issue a direction to extend the transitional period for a particular agreement, or to terminate it. Where, as at the starting date, there are 'continuing proceedings' in the Restrictive Practices Court, under the RTPA or the RPA, and they result in a favourable outcome for the parties, any transitional periods available only start at the end of the continuing proceedings (rather than at the starting date). **11.33**

(i) **Transitional period of one year—Chapter I prohibition applies from 1 March 2001:**[54] The general rule is that agreements made before the starting date have a transitional period of one year.[55] This is subject only to the exceptions described below.

The one-year transitional period also applies to those few agreements which are made in the final three months of the interim period, and which are both registrable and notifiable (ie because they are price-fixing agreements) under the RTPA, *provided* that they are duly notified to the OFT (under the RTPA) before the starting date and that no attempt was made to operate the relevant restrictions before notification.[56]

---

[52] This is similar to s 59 of the Competition Act as regards excluded provisions in an agreement; see Ch 5, para 5.05. See also, on the expression 'to the extent to which', OFT, n 15 above, paras 4.5 and 4.6.

[53] Pursuant to an order under Sch 13, para 19(3).

[54] Or, in the case of 'continuing proceedings' with a favourable outcome for the parties, one year after the end of the continuing proceedings.

[55] Competition Act 1998, Sch 13, para 19(1). See also OFT, n 15 above, para 5.15.

[56] Sch 13, para 25(3). This also applies to variations of agreements, where they are variations which would normally need to be notified under RTPA, s 24 and the Registration of Restrictive Trading Regulations 1984, SI 1984/392, reg 5. See para 11.51 below on variations. See also the last part of (ii) below on the position if the agreement or variation is not duly notified.

(ii) **No transitional period—Chapter I prohibition applies immediately from starting date on 1 March 2000**: There is no transitional period for an agreement, to the extent to which it is:

- void under the RTPA as at the starting date—whether this is because of failure duly to notify a registrable agreement (under RTPA, section 35(1)(a)), or a Restrictive Practices Court restraining order resulting from such failure (RTPA, section 35(3)), or a Restrictive Practices Court declaration that restrictions are against the public interest (RTPA, section 2(1)), or a Restrictive Practices Court restraining order pursuant to such a declaration (RTPA, section 2(2));[57]

- unlawful or void under the RPA, as at the starting date;[58]

- void or unlawful under the RTPA or the RPA at the end of 'continuing proceedings' in the Restrictive Practices Court, where those continuing proceedings are in progress as at the starting date[59]—the Chapter I prohibition only applies from the *end* of the continuing proceedings;

- a registrable and notifiable agreement in respect of which a party has, contrary to RTPA, section 27ZA, unlawfully tried to enforce or give effect to the relevant restrictions before notifying the agreement to the OFT;[60]

- an agreement, made in the final three months of the interim period, which is both registrable and notifiable (ie because it is a price-fixing agreement) under the RTPA, and which was not duly notified to the OFT before the starting date.[61]

(iii) **Transitional period of five years—Chapter I prohibition applies from 1 March 2005**: There is a transitional period of five years for:

- an agreement, to the extent that it contains provisions which the Restrictive Practices Court has found not to be contrary to the public interest (whether before the starting date or following continuing proceedings);[62]

---

[57] Sch 13, para 20(1)(a) and (b).

[58] Sch 13, para 20(1)(c).

[59] Sch 13, para 20(3). In practice, 'continuing proceedings' will normally be applications either (a) for a declaration that restrictions are against the public interest, under RTPA, s 1(3); or (b) for or in respect of an application that a class of goods should or should not be exempted from the provisions of the RPA, under RPA, ss 14–17 (currently, over-the-counter pharmaceutical goods benefit from this exemption).

[60] Sch 13, para 20(2).

[61] Sch 13, paras 20(3) and 25(4). See paras 11.40–11.41 on notifiable agreements made in the interim period. See also (i) above on the position if such agreements, made during the final three months of the interim period, are duly notified.

[62] Sch 13, para 23. In the case of a pre-starting date finding that provisions are not contrary to the public interest, this is subject to para 20(4) which provides that there is no transitional period where there are then continuing proceedings (eg by way of appeal) and the provisions are subsequently found to be void and unlawful.

- an agreement, to the extent that it contains provisions which relate to a class of goods exempted from the RPA under RPA, section 14 (whether before the starting date or following continuing proceedings)—in practice, these are resale price maintenance agreements relating to over-the-counter pharmaceutical products;[63]

- certain agreements which have been subject to competition scrutiny under the Financial Services Act 1986 or the Broadcasting Act 1990, where the Secretary of State has directed the OFT not to take the agreement before the Restrictive Practices Court (under section 127 of the Financial Services Act, where there are agreements which either do not significantly restrict competition or have countervailing benefits for investor protection, and under section 194A of the Broadcasting Act 1990 for agreements relating to network news provision on Channel 3 (ITV));[64]

- an agreement in the electricity and gas sectors in respect of which either (a) in respect of which the RTPA was already disapplied under the relevant sector legislation,[65] or (b) to the extent that it was a variation is made in the five years after the starting date such that the agreement becomes of a type such that, if the RTPA had not been repealed, it would have been disapplied by the relevant sector legislation[66] or (c) the Secretary of State has made a special 'transitional order';[67]

- an agreement in the railways sector in respect of which either (a) the RTPA was already disapplied under the relevant sector legislation,[68] or (b) an agreement required or approved by the Secretary of State of the Rail Regulator under the Railways Act 1993.[69]

11.34 The OFT may give directions to **extend** or to **terminate** the transitional period for any particular agreement.

- An extension may be made either on the OFT's own initiative, or following an application by one of the parties which must be made within three months

---

[63] Sch 13, para 24. In the case of a pre-starting date exemption under RPA, s 14, this too is subject to para 20(4) (see n 62).

[64] Sch 13, para 26.

[65] Sch 13, paras 28(1), 30(1), 32(1) and 34(1). The relevant sector legislation is: the Electricity Act 1989, the Gas Act 1986, the Gas (Northern Ireland) Order 1996.

[66] Sch 13, paras 28(2)–(4), 30 (2)–(4) and 32(2)–(4).

[67] Sch 13, paras 29, 31 and 33. A transitional order can apply to an agreement made after—as well as before—the starting date, and in either case expires five years after the starting date (1 Mar 2005): see paras 11.52–11.53 below. Note that, if there is a subsequent variation to such an agreement which has the effect that the RTPA would not have been disapplied or that the transitional order ceases to apply, the benefit of the transitional period is lost.

[68] Sch 13, para 34(2). The relevant sector legislation is the Railways Act 1993.

[69] Sch 3, para 34(3) and (4). Only these provisions of the agreement so required or approved benefit from the transitional period. This also applies to agreements made such in the five years after the starting date (see para 11.53 (ii) below).

before the end of the original transitional period. A one-year transitional period may be extended by up to twelve months, and any other transitional period may be extended by up to six months. Only one extension may be granted.[70]

An application for an extension must enclose the agreement and explain: (i) its purpose, (ii) the basis for considering that there is a transitional period, (iii) the need for extending the transitional period, (iv) the likely application of the prohibition to the agreement at the end of the period and any grounds for believing that an exemption is likely. It must also specify the length of the transitional period, the date of its expiry, and the period of the extension being sought. Three copies of the application and of the agreement must be submitted. The OFT will respond within two months (or an extension will be deemed to be granted, which will be the period applied for, provided that this does not exceed the maximum period of extension allowed—see above). If the OFT grants an application for extension, it must publish a notice specifying the period of extension granted. If, on the other hand, the OFT refuses an application, or grants a shorter extension than requested, this must be notified to the applicant in writing. (Normal rules for joint applications, treatment of confidential information, and the effective date of the notification apply.[71])

In practice, the OFT is likely to grant extensions only where it is the case *both* that there would not be a serious infringement of the Chapter I prohibition *and* that there are good reasons for requiring the extension (eg because the agreement is being renegotiated, or it is due to expire shortly after the end of the original transitional period, or the parties have a legitimate need for more time to prepare a notification).[72]

- A termination may be ordered by the OFT *either* if it considers that the agreement would (but for the transitional period or a relevant exclusion) infringe the Chapter I prohibition and not warrant an unconditional exemption, *or* if a party has failed, without reasonable excuse, to comply with an OFT written request for information within seven working days after the request is made. Before ordering a termination of the transitional period, the OFT must consult the parties to the agreement; this involves sending written notice to the parties concerned. After consultation, the OFT must publish the decision to terminate the transitional period in the register.[73] In practice, the OFT is likely to exercise the power to terminate a transitional period if it is concerned that the agree-

---

[70] Sch 13, para 36.

[71] Office of Fair Trading, Formal Consultation Draft, 'Competition Act 1998: The Draft Procedural Rules proposed by the Director General of Fair Trading', (OFT 411), R 24. See also Ch 12 on notifications.

[72] OFT, n 15 above, para 5.4.

[73] Sch 13, paras 37 and 38. See also Office of Fair Trading, 'Draft Procedural Rules' (n 71), rule 23. In connection with requests for information, the same rules (as to legal privilege, the provision of false or misleading information, disclosure of information, etc) apply as elsewhere in the Competition Act (Sch 13, para 1(2), read with, respectively, ss 30, 44, and 55 to 56 of the Act).

ment may have a serious adverse effect on competition, such that it is appropriate to review the agreement immediately (this may be triggered by a complaint).[74]

Continuing Proceedings

Special rules apply to agreements which, as at the starting date, are subject to 'continuing proceedings' in the Restrictive Practices Court under the RTPA or the RPA. As already described, while most Restrictive Practices Court proceedings cease at the starting date, 'continuing proceedings' are those which, broadly speaking, involve a substantive competition assessment of the agreement. For this reason, they need to continue, and they determine whether the agreement can benefit from a transitional period under the Chapter I prohibition.

11.35

In summary, the Chapter I prohibition does not apply until the continuing proceedings are brought to an end. If the outcome is unfavourable to the parties, the Chapter I prohibition applies to the relevant provisions immediately on the date when the continuing proceedings end. If the outcome is favourable to the parties, the Chapter I prohibition only applies to the relevant provisions after a transitional period of five years beginning at the date when the continuing proceedings come to an end.

11.36

'Continuing proceedings' are **defined**, in paragraph 15 of Schedule 13, as:

11.37

> proceedings in respect of an application made to the [Restrictive Practices] Court under the RTPA or the RPA, but not determined, before the starting date.

In practice, very few types of Restrictive Practices Court proceedings fall within the definition of 'continuing proceedings'. Many types of proceedings cease immediately at the starting date, as described in paragraph 11.17 above. Moreover, a further category of proceedings may continue after the starting date, but are expressly excluded from the definition of 'continuing proceedings'—these are proceedings in respect of an interim order under RTPA, section 3, for rectification of the OFT's register under RTPA, section 26, and for declaration on whether an agreement is registrable and/or notifiable under RTPA, section 26 (see above, paragraph 11.18 (vii) to (ix)).[75] Once these types of proceedings are removed, those Restrictive Practices Court proceedings which *do* fall within the definition of 'continuing proceedings' are those which involve a substantive competition assessment of the agreement, namely:

• proceedings instituted by the OFT for a declaration that restrictions are contrary to the public interest, under RTPA, section 1(3);[76]

---

[74] OFT, n 15 above, para 5.10.
[75] Sch 13, paras 11 and 12.
[76] But note that proceedings for a restraining order following such a declaration, under RTPA, s 2(1), cease at the starting date and therefore are not continuing proceedings.

- proceedings instituted by the OFT, or by the relevant suppliers of goods, for or in respect of an application that a class of goods should or should not be exempted from the rules on resale price maintenance, under RPA, sections 16 and 17;[77] and

- an appeal against the outcome of any such proceedings.

11.38 Continuing proceedings are only 'determined' at the expiry of the period in which it would have been possible to appeal against the outcome or, if an appeal is made, on the date when such an appeal is disposed of or withdrawn.[78]

The **effect** of 'continuing proceedings' is as follows:

- The Chapter I prohibition does not apply to an agreement at any time when the agreement is subject to 'continuing proceedings' under the RTPA, or *to the extent that* it is the subject of continuing proceedings under RPA, sections 16 and 17.[79]

- Where that is the case, the RTPA or the RPA continues to apply.[80]

- To the extent that the agreement is found to be void or unlawful when the proceedings are determined, there is no transitional period thereafter[81] (other provisions, not covered by the proceedings, may benefit from a transitional period, for example of one year).

- To the extent that the agreement is found not to be contrary to the public interest, or relates to a class of goods found to be exempt under RPA, section 14, there is a transitional period of five years beginning on the date when the proceedings are determined[82] (again, other provisions, not covered by the proceedings, may benefit from a one-year transitional period).

- If the Restrictive Practices Court orders the continuing proceedings to be discontinued, the Chapter I prohibition (or any applicable transitional period, usually one year) comes into immediate effect at that point.[83]

Treatment under the RTPA and the RPA

Treatment During the Interim Period

11.39 Although the RTPA and the RPA remain in force until the starting date (and therefore throughout the interim period), **the application of the RTPA to agreements made during the interim period is modified in two significant respects.**

---

[77] The only current exemption, under RPA, s 14, relates to over-the-counter pharmaceutical products.
[78] Sch 13, para 15(4) and (5).
[79] Sch 13, para 14(1) and (2).
[80] Sch 13, para 14(4).
[81] Sch 13, para 20(4).
[82] Sch 13, paras 23(2) and 24(2), read with paras 21 and 22.
[83] Sch 13, paras 18(2), 21 and 22.

First, Schedule 13 paragraph 5 provides that most agreements made during the **11.40** interim period are 'non-notifiable'—ie there is no obligation to notify them (furnish particulars of them) to the OFT.[84] The only exceptions to this are registrable agreements in which the relevant restrictions or information exchange provisions relate to prices (so-called 'price-fixing agreements')[85] and also registrable agreements which the OFT has already entered on its register.[86] (In addition, where variations to such agreements would normally need to be notified to the OFT, under RTPA, section 24 and the 1984 Regulations, these remain subject to an obligation to notify—see paragraphs 11.46–11.51 below.) In the case of these exceptional agreements which are notifiable, the three-month deadline for notification cannot be extended.[87] If the notifiable registrable agreement is made within the final three months of the interim period, such that the deadline for notification would occur after the starting date, there is no possibility of notifying under the RTPA after the starting date (because the RTPA is repealed by then): if it is notified before the starting date, the agreement benefits from a one-year transitional period; whereas if it is not notified before the starting date there are no sanctions for non-notification (in terms of voidness) but the one-year transitional period is lost.[88]

(It should be noted, however, that the benefit of non-notifiability does not apply **11.41** to *variations* made during the interim period where they vary pre-enactment registrable agreements—see paragraphs 11.46–11.51 below.)

Secondly, agreements made during the interim period will not be able to obtain **11.42** 'section 21(2) clearance'.[89] In practice, the impact of this will be limited. It will

---

[84] Sch 13, para 5.

[85] Sch 13, para 5(b) says that, in order to benefit from this non-notifiability, an agreement made in the interim period must satisfy, *inter alia*, the condition in RTPA, s 27A(1)(c). That condition is that the agreement 'is not, and has never been, a price-fixing agreement'. 'Price-fixing agreement' is defined in RTPA, s 27A(3), as any agreement which is registrable by virtue of a restriction in respect of any matter in RTPA, s 6(1)(a), s 6(1)(b) or s 11(2)(a), or by virtue of an information provision in respect of any matter in RTPA, s 7(1)(a) or s 12(2)(a). Provided that two parties accept relevant restrictions, only one party needs to accept a restriction in respect of any such matter (ie as to prices or charges) for an agreement to be treated as a price-fixing agreement.

[86] Sch 13, para 5(b) says that, in order to benefit from this non-notifiability, an agreement made in the interim period must satisfy, *inter alia*, the condition in RTPA, s 27A(1)(d). That condition is that the agreement is not an agreement in respect of which the OFT has filed particulars on the OFT register.

[87] Sch 13, para 6(c).

[88] Sch 13, paras 20(3) and 25. The view of the OFT is that no third party liability for breach of statutory duty would arise either—see OFT, n 15 above, para 2.9, but it is not clear from the wording of Sch 13, para 25(4) itself that this is the case. Note, however, that voidness and third-party liability would apply if an attempt were made to give effect to the relevant restrictions prior to notification.

[89] Sch 13, para 6(b). 'S 21(2) clearance' under the RTPA was the direction given by the Secretary of State that the restrictions in a registrable agreement, which had been notified to the OFT, were not 'of such significance' as to warrant referral to the Restrictive Practices Court; in practice, it meant that no further action was taken by the UK competition authorities in respect of that

only affect that small category of registrable agreements made in the interim period which are notifiable—and, although these agreements cannot benefit from 'section 21(2) clearance' under the RTPA, they will benefit from a one-year transitional period under the Chapter I prohibition (provided that they are notified under the RTPA before the starting date), and it will also be possible to seek from the OFT 'early guidance' as to the application of the Chapter I prohibition.[90]

11.43 Apart from these modifications, the OFT will retain powers to apply the RTPA to agreements made during the interim period, and it intends to apply those powers to seriously anti-competitive agreements; it does not want the interim period to be a hiatus between the RTPA and the Chapter I prohibition during which seriously anti-competitive agreements can escape the control of competition law. The OFT has stated[91] that it:

> intends to keep an active watch for anti-competitive agreements during the interim period and will not hesitate to call in agreements for competition scrutiny under [its] powers in section 36 of the [RTPA] if necessary. The [OFT] also has discretion to institute Restrictive Practices Court proceedings up to the starting date[92] and in urgent cases interim orders to restrain anti-competitive agreements may be obtained from the Court.[93]

Treatment After the Starting Date

11.44 The treatment under the RTPA and the RPA, after the starting date, for agreements made during the interim period is exactly the same as for agreements made before the enactment date. **See paragraphs 11.16 above for full details.**

11.45 In summary, the RTPA and the RPA are repealed as from the starting date. However, in spite of the repeal, certain important consequences of the RTPA and RPA continue to have effect. Among these, where an agreement is made during the interim period, and is both registrable and notifiable (see paragraphs

---

agreement. As a corollary of the removal of 's 21(2) clearance', there is also the removal of the concept whereby the OFT had a duty to refer an agreement to the Restrictive Practices Court unless the Secretary of State gave s 21(2) clearance; by virtue of Sch 13, para 6(a), the OFT has no such duty to refer agreements made during the interim period to the Court, but has discretion to do so.

[90] See paras 11.19–11.27.

[91] OFT, n 15 above, para 2.5.

[92] As noted in n 89 above, by virtue of Sch 13, para 6(a) the OFT will have discretion to refer agreements made during the interim period to the Restrictive Practices Court. Such referrals, made under RTPA, s 1(2)(c), are with a view to obtaining a court declaration that restrictions are 'contrary to the public interest' and void, perhaps followed by a restraining order. It will be possible for proceedings for a declaration (but not a restraining order) to continue beyond the starting date as 'continuing proceedings'.

[93] Proceedings for interim orders, under RTPA, s 3, may continue beyond the starting date; and new proceedings for interim orders may be commenced even after the starting date where they relate to substantive proceedings commenced before the starting date to have restrictions declared contrary to the public interest (see para 11.18 (vii) and (viii) above).

11.40–11.41 above), but is not duly notified, voidness and third-party liability endure beyond the repeal.[94]

'Variations' Made During the Interim Period—Treatment under the RTPA

Special care needs to be taken in respect of variations which are made during the interim period to registrable agreements under the RTPA. In particular, although most agreements which are made during the interim period are non-notifiable (see above, paragraphs 11.40–11.41), it appears that **where a registrable and notifiable agreement is then *varied* during the interim period, the variation does not benefit from non-notifiability.**   **11.46**

The RTPA's rules on variations are set out in sections 24(2)(b) and 27(1)(c) of the RTPA, read with regulation 5 of the Registration of Restrictive Trading Agreements Regulations 1984.[95] The rules, applicable for so long as the RTPA remains in force, provide that, where an agreement is registrable and notifiable under the RTPA, any variation to that agreement must be notified to the OFT within three months of the making of the variation—but this notification obligation applies only if the variation has the effect of creating a new restriction, or terminating an existing restriction, or altering the scope of an existing restriction.   **11.47**

As noted above, the RTPA remains in force until the starting date, and therefore throughout the interim period. Although most *agreements which are made during the interim period* benefit from non-notifiability by virtue of Schedule 13, paragraph 5, to the Competition Act, this benefit is not granted for *variations* made during the interim period.[96] Therefore, if during the interim period there is a variation to a registrable and notifiable agreement (which is of a type requiring to be notified under the Registration of Restrictive Trading Agreements Regulations 1984), such a variation will still need to be notified.[97] Notifiability therefore remains for the following categories of variation made during the interim period:[98]   **11.48**

(i)   a variation to a registrable (and notifiable) agreement made before the enactment date;

(ii)   a variation to an agreement, where that agreement was made during the interim period which is registrable and did not benefit from non-notifiability (ie registrable agreements in which the relevant restrictions or

---

[94] Except if the registrable agreement was a notifiable agreement made during the last three months of the interim period and not notified before the starting date—in which case voidness does not apply (Sch 13, para 25(4) and see n 88 above as regards third party liability). See also, on variations made during the interim period, paras 11.46–11.51 below.

[95] SI 1984/392.

[96] See paras 11.40–11.41 above.

[97] As above. See also OFT, n 15 above, paras 2.3 and 2.7.

[98] Under RTPA, s 24(2)(a) and (2A).

information exchange provisions relate to prices, and also registrable agreements which the OFT has already entered on its register);

(iii) a variation to an agreement which has the effect of making an agreement which is both registrable and not non-notifiable (eg where the variation creates a restriction relating to prices).

11.49 Note, however, that if the agreement is non-notifiable under Schedule 13, paragraph 5, the variation is also non-notifiable, since it is not a variation to a registrable and notifiable agreement a result of (unless the variation has the effect of making an agreement which is both registrable and not non-notifiable, eg by creating a price restriction).

11.50 It is essential that such variations which are notifiable should be duly notified to the OFT under the RTPA. If not, all the relevant restrictions in the agreement as varied are void, and give rise to third-party civil liability; this voidness and civil liability endure beyond the repeal of the RTPA at the starting date.

Variations Made During the Last Three Months of the Interim Period

11.51 As noted above, there are special provisions for agreements made during the final three months of the interim period.[99] Applying these provisions, in conjunction with the rules set out above on variations made during the interim period, the following provisions apply to variations made during the last three months of the interim period (which are variations requiring them to be notified under the RTPA):

- If such a variation is notified to the OFT before the starting date, it benefits from a one-year transitional period under the Chapter I prohibition.[100]

- If such a variation is not notified before the starting date, the one-year transitional period under the Chapter I prohibition is lost, and there may be RTPA liability to third parties, although the sanction of voidness does not apply.[101]

---

[99] These provisions are discussed in para 11.40 (n 88) and para 11.33(ii) and (iii) above.
[100] Sch 13, para 25(3). This is provided that no attempt has been made to give effect to the relevant restrictions prior to notification under the RTPA.
[101] Sch 13, para 25(3) and (4). Again, this is provided that no attempt has been made to give effect to the relevant restrictions prior to notification under the RTPA. See n 88 above as regards third party liability.

D. Agreements Made After the Starting Date (1 March 2000)

Treatment under the Chapter I Prohibition

11.52 Agreements made on or after the starting date, are fully subject to the Chapter I prohibition with immediate effect.[102] They do not benefit from any transitional period after the starting date.[103]

11.53 However, this is subject to exceptions for certain agreements in the electricity, gas and railways sectors. Such an agreement, if made or varied in the first five years after the starting date, can benefit from a transitional period lasting up to the fifth anniversary of the starting date,[104] in which case it is outside the Chapter I prohibition during that transitional period, if (in broad terms) it meets either of the following criteria:

(i) the agreement, or agreement as varied, is of a type which (if the RTPA were still in force) would have benefited from disapplication of the RTPA under the relevant sector legislation (although this is not the case for railways agreements);[105] or

(ii) the agreement is one in respect of which, in the case of electricity and gas agreements, the Secretary of State has made a special 'transitional order'[106] or, in the case of railway agreements, one which is required or approved by the Secretary of State or the Rail Regulator under the Railways Act 1993 (only those provisions so required or approved benefit from the transitional period).[107]

More details on these provisions for the electricity, gas and railways sectors are in Chapter 19.

Treatment under the RTPA and the RPA

11.54 Neither the RTPA nor the RPA applies at all to agreements made on or after the starting date. Both are repealed as at the starting date.

---

[102] Competition Act 1998, s 76(3) and Sch 13, para 1(1). The Chapter II prohibition also applies with immediate effect as of that date.

[103] Transitional periods only apply to agreements made before the starting date: Sch 13, para 19(1).

[104] The Act calls this fifth anniversary 'the end of the relevant period', and defines 'the relevant period' as the period beginning with the starting date and ending immediately before its fifth anniversary: Sch 13, para 27.

[105] Sch 13, para 28(2) to (4) for electricity, para 30(2) to (4) and para 32(2) to (4) for gas. The relevant sector legislation is: the Electricity Act 1989, the Gas Act 1986 and the Gas (Northern Ireland) Order 1996.

[106] Sch 13, paras 29, 31 and 33.

[107] Sch 13, para 34(3).

PART VI

PROCEDURES UNDER THE PROHIBITIONS

12

NOTIFICATION

A. Overview

Introduction

Agreements or conduct may be notified to the OFT with a view to obtaining **12.01** **guidance** or a **decision** on the application of the Chapter I and Chapter II prohibitions. The Act provides a structure of formal statutory procedures for the making of notifications, their treatment by the OFT and the consequences of the resulting determination of the notification: for Chapter I notifications, in sections 12 to 16 and Schedule 5; and for Chapter II notifications, in sections 20 to 24 and Schedule 6. These provisions are augmented by the Procedural Rules which the OFT has the power to make under section 51 of the Act (Schedule 9 specifies matters which the Procedural Rules may cover, although the OFT is not limited to these).[1]

12.02 This chapter sets out the relevant procedures for making a notification, reviews the effects of such a notification, and considers the advantages and disadvantages of notifying.

12.03 The procedures for notification will come into effect from 1 March 2000. Prior to that, however, it is possible for parties to agreements made between 9 November 1998 and 29 February 2000 inclusive to notify for 'early guidance' on the application of the Chapter I prohibition. (It is not possible to apply for early guidance under Chapter II, and agreements made before 9 November cannot be notified until 1 March 2000.) Early guidance applications will be governed by Schedule 13 and the procedural requirements in the OFT's Early Guidance Directions,[2] rather than those in the sections of the Act mentioned above and the Procedural Rules— see Chapter 11, paragraphs 11.19–11.27.

Differences between Guidance and Decisions

12.04 The Act distinguishes between notification for guidance[3] and notification for a decision.[4] In the case of the Chapter I prohibition, an applicant can notify for a decision whether the relevant agreement infringes the prohibition, or for an exemption decision, or guidance on whether the agreement *is likely to* infringe or be exempt. In the case of the Chapter II prohibition, for which there is no possibility of exemption, an applicant can notify only for a decision as to whether the relevant conduct infringes the prohibition or guidance on whether it *is likely to* infringe.

12.05 The principal differences between a notification for a decision and a notification for guidance are as follows:

(i)   The decision procedure involves a greater deal of publicity and third party consultation than the guidance procedure: (a) basic information concerning

---

[1] See Office of Fair Trading, Formal Consultation Draft, Competition Act 1998: 'The Procedural Rules Proposed by the Director General of Fair Trading' (OFT 411). These Rules must be approved by an order made by the Secretary of State before they come into operation.

[2] Sch 13 para 7 and Office of Fair Trading, Competition Act 1998: 'Early Guidance Directions' (OFT 412).

[3] S 13 in relation to the Chapter I prohibition and s 21 in relation to the Chapter II prohibition.

[4] Ss 14 and 22.

a decision application is published and relevant third party comment must be taken account of by the OFT, (b) third parties are consulted by the OFT prior to certain types of proposed decision, and (c) the decision itself is published. There are none of these publication or consultation obligations in relation to a notification for guidance.[5]

(ii) The circumstances in which the OFT can take further action in respect of agreements or conduct following 'positive' guidance—that an agreement is unlikely to infringe or is likely to be exempted, or that conduct is unlikely to infringe—are less limited than the circumstances in which the OFT can take further action following a favourable decision.

- Unlike a decision case, a guidance case may be re-opened in the event of a third party complaint to the OFT about the agreement or conduct in question. This is a corollary of the absence of third party consultation under the guidance procedure.

- In the case of the Chapter I prohibition, a guidance case may be re-opened if one of the parties to the agreement notifies it for a decision granting individual exemption.

(iii) The OFT has an obligation (the sanction of a court direction) to determine an application for a decision without undue delay. There is no such obligation in relation to an application for guidance.

(iv) An individual exemption decision by the OFT is likely to be regarded as binding on a court. It seems probable that guidance that an agreement is likely to be exempt will not be conclusive but will be a factor to which the court has regard. It is possible that, presented with such guidance, the court would grant a stay of proceedings pending an actual decision by the OFT. See Chapter 10, paragraphs 10.85–10.94, for further consideration of the treatment by UK courts on individual exemption applications and determinations.

These differences between the guidance and decision procedures are explained in more detail below.

B. Notification for Guidance

Making the Application

A party to an agreement who thinks that the agreement may infringe **the Chapter I prohibition** may notify the agreement to the OFT and apply for guidance.[6]   **12.06**

---

[5] However, it should be noted that the OFT has no specific statutory confidentiality obligations in relation to applications for guidance over and above its general obligations in ss 55 and 56.

[6] S 13(1).

12.07   The OFT may give the applicant guidance on whether or not the agreement is likely to infringe the Chapter I prohibition.[7] If the agreement is likely to infringe the prohibition if it is not exempt, the OFT's guidance may also indicate whether the agreement is likely to be exempt under a block exemption, a parallel exemption or a section 11 exemption,[8] or, alternatively, whether it would be likely to grant an individual exemption if asked to do so.[9] Similarly, a person who thinks that its conduct may infringe **the Chapter II prohibition** may notify the conduct to the OFT and apply for guidance.[10] The OFT may give guidance on whether or not the conduct is likely to infringe the Chapter II prohibition.[11]

12.08   In contrast to the equivalent provisions in the Act regarding a decision application, the notification provisions for guidance do not expressly mention the possibility of the OFT giving guidance that an exclusion is likely to apply but, in giving guidance that an agreement is unlikely to infringe, the OFT can be expected to specify that this is because of the effect of an exclusion where that is the case.

12.09   Once the OFT has determined the application, it must without delay give guidance to the applicant in writing, stating the facts on which the guidance has been based and the reasons for it.[12]

12.10   Notification for guidance under Chapter I provides **provisional immunity from penalties** until the outcome of the application: no financial penalty for infringement of the Chapter I prohibition (see Chapter 10, paragraphs 10.39–10.74 as regards penalties) may be imposed in respect of the agreement for the period beginning with the date of notification and ending with the date specified by notice in writing to the applicant (which cannot be earlier than the date on which the application is determined).[13] However, this immunity from penalties can be removed if, after a preliminary investigation of a guidance application under Chapter I, the OFT makes a **provisional decision** that the agreement will infringe the prohibition and that it would not be appropriate to grant an individual exemption (see paragraph 12.40 below for more details).[14]

Effect of Guidance

12.11   In cases where the OFT has given 'positive' guidance—ie that an agreement is unlikely to infringe the Chapter I prohibition or is likely to be exempt and, in the

---

[7] S 13(2).
[8] S 13(3)(a).
[9] S 13(3)(b).
[10] S 21(1).
[11] S 21(2).
[12] OFT, n 1 above, R 10.
[13] S 13(4). Provisional immunity from penalties is not available in respect of Chap II notifications.
[14] Sch 5 para 3.

case of conduct, that it is unlikely to infringe the Chapter II prohibition—that guidance provides a significant degree of legal comfort for the persons concerned.

The guidance is binding on the OFT, in that it is precluded from taking further action, except in limited circumstances. **The OFT is to take no further action with respect to the relevant agreement or conduct, unless:** **12.12**

(i) it has reasonable grounds for believing that there has been a *material change of circumstance* since guidance was given;

(ii) it has a reasonable suspicion that the guidance was based on *information which was incomplete, false or misleading* in a material particular;

(iii) a *third party complaint* has been made to the OFT about the agreement or conduct (in the case of the Chapter I prohibition, a complaint by a person who is not a party to the agreement);[15] or

(iv) if, where guidance has been given under Chapter I, there is by one of the parties to the agreement a *subsequent application for a decision.*

Where the OFT proposes to take further action in respect of an agreement or conduct following positive guidance, it must consult the person to whom guidance was given.[16]

Positive guidance also provides **immunity from penalties**, except in limited circumstances. Generally, no penalties for infringement of the prohibitions may be imposed in relation to the relevant agreement or conduct.[17] However, this immunity may be lifted by the OFT if it: **12.13**

(a) takes action in one of the circumstances described in paragraphs (i) to (iv) above;

(b) considers it likely that the agreement would infringe the Chapter I or Chapter II prohibition; and

(c) gives written notice to the person on whose application the guidance was given that the immunity is being removed as from a specified date.[18]

The lifting of immunity from penalties may be retroactive to a date earlier than that of the notice in cases where the OFT has reasonable suspicion that information on which the guidance was based was incomplete, false or misleading in a material particular, and that information was provided by a party to the agreement or a person engaging in the conduct.[19]

---

[15] Ss15(2) and 23(2).
[16] OFT, n 1 above, R 11.
[17] Ss 15(3) and 23(3).
[18] Ss 15(4) and 23(4).
[19] Ss 15(5) and 23(5).

C. Notification for a Decision

Making the Application

12.14   A party to an agreement who thinks that the agreement may infringe **the Chapter I prohibition** may notify the agreement to the OFT and apply for a decision.[20] The OFT may make a decision whether the Chapter I prohibition has been infringed and, if it has not, whether that is because of the effect of an exclusion or because the agreement is exempt from the prohibition (ie because it falls within a block exemption, a parallel exemption or a section 11 exemption).[21]

12.15   An applicant may also request that the agreement be given an individual exemption.[22] In practice most notifications will involve such a request. An individual exemption may be granted subject to conditions or obligations and for a specified period of time.[23] Where the OFT proposes to grant a conditional exemption, it must consult the applicant, specifying the proposed conditions or obligations.[24] An individual exemption may be retroactive—ie to have effect from a date earlier than that on which it was granted.[25] This date may be prior to the date of notification.[26] The OFT has indicated that it may give exemption with retroactive effect prior to the date of notification in cases where an agreement which has already received an Article 81 (formerly Article 85) comfort letter from the European Commission is challenged under the Chapter I prohibition before the UK courts, and so a party notifies the agreement to the OFT; the OFT will endeavour to treat such cases with priority.[27] It is foreseeable that such exemptions might be retroactive to the date that the EC notification was made.

12.16   A person who thinks that its conduct may infringe **the Chapter II prohibition** may notify the conduct to the OFT and apply for a decision.[28] The OFT may make a decision whether the Chapter II prohibition has been infringed and, if it has not, whether this is because of the effect of an exclusion.[29]

---

[20]   S 14(1).
[21]   S 14(2).
[22]   S 14(3).
[23]   S 4(3) and (4); see Ch 6 for further details on exemptions.
[24]   OFT, n 1 above, R 12(1)(a).
[25]   S 4(5).
[26]   This contrasts with the position under EC law under which exemption under Art 85(3) can only take effect from the date of notification—Council Regulation (EEC) 17/62, First Reg Implementing Arts 85 and 86 of the Treaty, Art 6(1).
[27]   Office of Fair Trading, Competition Act 1998: 'The Chapter I Prohibition' (OFT 401), para 7.13. The OFT has also indicated that it will endeavour to give priority to notifications in borderline cases where the parties have made a prior notification to the European Comission but it has declined jurisdiction due to the absence of an effect on trade between full Member States. Ibid, para 7.6. It can be anticipated that the OFT may also grant retroactive exemptions in these cases.
[28]   S 22(1).
[29]   S 22(2).

Procedural Safeguards for the Applicant

Where the OFT proposes to make an infringement decision, ie that either the **12.17**
Chapter I or the Chapter II prohibition has been infringed, there are three express
procedural safeguards in the Procedural Rules which aim to ensure the applicant
sufficient rights of defence: [30]

- The OFT must send the applicant a **statement of objections**—it is required to
  give written notice to the applicant stating the matters to which it has taken
  objection, the action it proposes and the reasons for doing so.

- There is an opportunity for the applicant to make **oral or written representations**—the OFT is required to inform the applicant that any such representations made to the OFT within a specified period will be considered, and give
  the applicant an opportunity to make them.

- The applicant is entitled to **access to the file**—if requested, the applicant or his
  authorised representative is to be given an opportunity to inspect the documents in the OFT's file relating to the proposed decision. (However, the OFT
  is entitled to withhold from inspection any internal document or any document which a person has stated is confidential or is so in its opinion—see paragraph 12.32 below as to the meaning of confidential information.[31])

Other procedural safeguards for the applicant arising under EC law and applying
as a result of the 'governing principles' section[32] are considered in more detail in
Chapter 3, paragraphs 3.58–3.60.

As with guidance applications, once the OFT has made a decision whether or not **12.18**
the Chapter I or Chapter II prohibition has been infringed, it must without delay
give written notice to the applicant (and any other person which it is aware is party
to the agreement or conduct), stating the facts on which the decision has been
based and the reasons for it.[33] In addition, where there has been '**undue delay**' by
the OFT in determining an application for a decision, a person aggrieved by the
OFT's failure to determine the application in accordance with the specified procedure is able to obtain court directions to secure that the application is determined without 'unnecessary further delay'.[34]

Again, as with guidance applications under the Chapter I prohibition, notifica- **12.19**
tion for a decision under the Chapter I prohibition provides **provisional immunity from penalties** until the outcome of the application: no financial penalty for

---

[30] OFT, n 1 above, R 14(1); see also Ch 14 paras 14.85–14.87.
[31] OFT, n 1 above, R 14(2).
[32] S 60.
[33] OFT, n 1 above, R 15(a)(i).
[34] Sch 5 para 7 and Sch 6 para 7; these provisions may not be brought into force by commencement order until the notification system has bedded down.

infringement of the Chapter I prohibition may be imposed in respect of the agreement for the period beginning with the date of notification and ending with the date specified by notice in writing to the applicant (which cannot be earlier than the date on which the application is determined).[35] However, the OFT may make a **provisional decision** removing the provisional immunity if, after a preliminary investigation, the OFT considers it likely that the agreement will infringe the prohibition and that it would not be appropriate to grant an individual exemption (see paragraph 12.40 below for more details).[36]

Effect of a Decision

12.20   The OFT may make a decision that an agreement or conduct does not infringe the Chapter I or Chapter II prohibition—either because it does not fall within the prohibition at all (a 'negative clearance' decision) or because an exclusion applies; or, in the case of an agreement notified under the Chapter I prohibition, because the agreement is exempted as a result of a block, parallel or section 11 exemption. The OFT may alternatively make a decision granting the agreement an individual exemption. These types of favourable decisions provide legal security for the persons concerned. The decision precludes the OFT from taking further action in relation to the agreement or conduct, except in limited circumstances. An individual exemption decision is also likely to be regarded as binding on a court and so preclude third party action (or an action by one of the parties, for example, to facilitate withdrawal from a contract).

12.21   **The OFT is to take no further action with respect to the relevant agreement or conduct, unless:**

(i)   it has reasonable grounds for believing that there has been a *material change of circumstance* since guidance was given; or

(ii)   it has a reasonable suspicion that the guidance was based on *information which was incomplete, false or misleading* in a material particular.[37]

Where the OFT proposes to take further action in respect of an agreement or conduct following a favourable decision, it must consult the person to whom the decision was given.[38]

12.22   A favourable decision also provides **immunity from penalties**, except in limited circumstances. No penalties for infringement of the prohibitions may be imposed in relation to the relevant agreement or conduct,[39] but this immunity may be lifted by the OFT if it:

---

[35] S 14(4).
[36] Sch 5 para 3.
[37] Ss 16(2) and 24(2).
[38] OFT, n 1 above, R 16(1).
[39] Ss 15(3) and 24(3).

(a) takes action in one of the circumstances described in paragraphs (i) or (ii) above;

(b) considers it likely that the agreement would infringe the Chapter I or Chapter II prohibition; and

(c) gives written notice to the person on whose application the guidance was given that the immunity is being removed as from a specified date.[40]

As with the guidance procedure, the lifting of immunity from penalties may be retrospective to a date earlier than that of the notice in cases where the OFT has reasonable suspicion that information on which the decision was based was incomplete, false or misleading in a material particular, and that information was provided by a party to the agreement or a person engaging in the conduct.[41]   **12.23**

Publication and Third Party Consultation during a Decision Case

Unlike a guidance application, an application for a decision and its subsequent determination involves at several stages of the procedure a degree of publicity and third party consultation. This is commensurate with the fact that greater legal certainty results for the parties following a favourable decision, than there arises for the parties with guidance. Where an agreement or conduct has been notified for a decision, the following obligations arise on the OFT under the Act itself and the Procedural Rules: **12.24**

(i) *On receipt of an application*, the OFT has a duty to arrange for it to be published in a way most suitable for bringing it to the attention of those likely to be affected by it, unless the OFT is satisfied that it will instead be sufficient to seek information from one or more particular persons other than the applicant.[42] To fulfil this obligation, the OFT will maintain a public register on which will be entered a summary of the nature and objectives of the agreement or conduct in question;[43] this notice will correspond to the 250 word Summary in Part 4 of Form N, the prescribed notification form. The **OFT register** will be open to public inspection at the OFT between 10am and 4pm every working day, and will also be accessible on the OFT's Internet website.[44] The OFT will also publish a weekly gazette containing summaries of notifications for decisions.[44a] Details of the notification may also be published in suitable trade or national press.[45] The OFT must then

---

[40] Ss 16(4) and 24(4).
[41] Ss 16(5) and 24(5).
[42] Sch 5 para 5(2), and Sch 6 para 5(2).
[43] OFT, n 1 above, R 7(2).
[44] OFT, n 1 above, R 7(2).
[44a] Office of Fair Trading, Competition Act 1998: 'The Major Provisions' (OFT 400), para 7.5.
[45] Office of Fair Trading, Formal Consultation Draft, 'Form N For Notification for Guidance or Decision under Chapters I and II of the Competition Act 1998' (OFT 409), part 1, para 1.4, and part 2, para 12.1(b).

take into account any representations made by persons other than the applicant.[46]

(ii) Where the OFT *proposes to make an individual exemption decision*, under the Chapter I prohibition, whether or not subject to conditions or obligations, it *must* consult the public;[47] and where it *proposes to make a decision that the Chapter I or Chapter II prohibition has not been infringed*, it *may* consult the public.[48] Public consultation involves publishing the proposal by means of an entry on the register and consulting such third parties as appear to the OFT likely to be interested.[49] The OFT will also publish the invitation to comment on its Internet website, and usually in its weekly gazette and relevant trade and national press.[49a]

(iii) When the OFT *has made a decision*, it must publish the decision, together with its reasons for making it,[50] which it does by means of an entry on the public register mentioned at (i) above.[51] Where an application for a decision does not result in one (eg the application is withdrawn or the case is closed by means of an administrative letter), the OFT will still enter an indication of its outcome on the register.[52]

(iv) Where the OFT has taken *further action following a favourable decision* under either prohibition, it will publish the decision by means of an entry on the public register.[53]

D. Notification Procedure

12.25 Notifications must be made in accordance with the Procedural Rules laid down by the OFT.[54] There are, in addition to those mentioned in the above paragraphs, a number of other procedural requirements common to both notifications for guidance and those for a decision. These are explained below.

Form of Notification

12.26 Notifications must be made to the OFT on a standard form—Form N.[55] The same form for making a notification should be used, regardless of whether the

---

[46] Sch 5 para 5(3) and Sch 6 para 5(3).
[47] OFT, n 1 above, R 12(1)(b) and (c).
[48] OFT, n 1 above, R 12(2).
[49] OFT, n 1 above, R 27(1)(c) and (i).
[49a] OFT, n 44a above, para 7.6.
[50] Sch 5 para 6, and Sch 6 para 6; OFT, n 1 above, Rr 7 and 15(b).
[51] OFT, n 1 above, Rr 7 and 27(1)(i).
[52] OFT, n 1 above, R 7.
[53] OFT, n 1 above, Rr 16(2) and 27(1)(i).
[54] Sch 5 para 2(i); Sch 6 para 2(i).
[55] Sch 5 para 3, and Sch 6 para 3; OFT, n 1 above, R 1.

notification is for guidance or a decision or whether it is in respect of the Chapter I or Chapter II prohibition.

The purpose of Form N is to provide the OFT with sufficient information to enable **12.27** it to reach a view on an application for guidance or a decision. It is necessary to supply the original plus two copies of the completed Form N.[56] Where documents are submitted as part of the Form, such as the relevant agreement in the case of notification under Chapter I, this will include three copies of the relevant agreement. If the Form N is signed by an authorised representative, such as a solicitor, rather than the applicant itself, the documents submitted should include written proof of the representative's authority to act on the applicant's behalf.[57] Documents submitted as part of Form N should be the original or certified as true copies of the original.[58] With the agreement of the OFT, the application may be made on disc or using another electronic format.[59] See paragraphs 12.36–12.37 below as regards additional copies for relevant sector regulators with concurrent jurisdiction.

Content of Notification

Information in Form N must be **correct and complete**, and for these purposes **12.28** information which is false or misleading is treated as incorrect and incomplete.[60] (The Act also contains criminal sanctions on supplying false or misleading information—see paragraphs 12.42–12.46 below.)

Where there arises a material change in the facts contained in an application of **12.29** which the applicant knows, or reasonably ought to know, this must be communicated by the applicant without delay to the OFT or, where the OFT has informed the applicant which, if any, of the sector regulators exercise concurrent jurisdiction, to the relevant sector regulator.[61]

Where the OFT finds that the Form N is incomplete in a material respect it must, **12.30** without delay, inform the applicant accordingly in writing and fix such time limit as it considers appropriate for outstanding information, including documents, to be provided (an incomplete notification will delay the effective date of application—see paragraph 12.35 below).[62]

The OFT may dispense with the obligation to submit particular information, **12.31** including any document, required on Form N if it considers that information to be unnecessary for the examination of the case.[63]

---

[56] OFT, n 1 above, R 3(2).
[57] OFT, n 1 above, R 4(1).
[58] OFT, n 1 above, R 3(1).
[59] Form N, part 1, para 1.6.
[60] OFT, n 1 above, R 4(2).
[61] OFT, n 1 above, R 5(4).
[62] OFT, n 1 above, R 5(3).
[63] OFT, n 1 above, R 4(4).

12.32 The applicant is required to set out any information in the notification which it considers to be **confidential information** in a separate annex marked 'confidential information' and explain why it should be treated as such.[64] Confidential information is:

- commercial information the disclosure of which would, or might, significantly harm the legitimate business interests of the undertaking to which it relates; or

- information relating to the private affairs of an individual the disclosure of which would, or might, significantly harm his interests.[65]

Effective Date of Application

12.33 An application has effect on the date on which it is received by the OFT; however, an application received after 6pm on a working day is treated as being received on the next working day.[66] The OFT is obliged to acknowledge receipt of the application to the applicant without delay.[67]

12.34 If the OFT has not informed the applicant that the application is incomplete within one month following the date on which the application was received, the application is deemed to become effective on the date of its receipt by the OFT.[68]

12.35 In a case where the OFT informs the applicant that the notification is incomplete in a material respect, the application does not have effect on the date on which it was originally received but on the date on which the complete information is received (unless it is received after 6pm, in which case it will be treated as received on the next working day).[69]

Notification to Sector Regulators with Concurrent Jurisdiction

12.36 Where the applicant considers that one or more sector regulators may have concurrent jurisdiction, one extra copy of Form N (including any documents) must be submitted to the OFT for each such regulator.[70] Copies should also be sent directly to the relevant regulators.[71] However, failure to send additional copies to or for relevant regulators will not make the notification incomplete.[71a]

---

[64] OFT, n 1 above, R 4(5).
[65] OFT, n 1 above, R 27(1)(b).
[66] OFT, n 1 above, R 5(1).
[67] OFT, n 1 above, R 5(2).
[68] OFT, n 1 above, R 5(5).
[69] OFT, n 1 above, R 5(3).
[70] OFT, n 1 above, R 3(3).
[71] Office of Fair Trading, Competition Act 1998: 'Concurrent Application to Regulated Industries' (OFT 405), paras 3.3 and 3.4. The OFT encourages this, and it may be to parties' advantage in terms of speed in handling the case, but there is no requirement to do so in the Procedural Rules.
[71a] Ibid.

If, following submission of an application, the OFT considers that a sector regu- **12.37**
lator has or may have concurrent jurisdiction in relation to the application it
must, as soon as practical, send a copy of the Form N to the sector regulator and
inform the applicant in writing that it has done so.[72] The OFT must inform the
applicant in writing of which regulator is to exercise jurisdiction as soon as practical (and the applicant will also be told if the application is subsequently transferred to the jurisdiction of a different regulator).[73]

See Chapter 19 for further details on the concurrent powers of the sector
regulators.

Joint Applications

Where a joint application is made, Form N must be submitted to the OFT either **12.38**
by all the applicants, or by an authorised representative, nominated in the application to submit and receive documents on behalf of all (or some) of the applicants.[74] Written proof of the joint representatives' authority to act should be
submitted with the Form N.[75]

Obligations to Inform Other Parties

A party to an agreement who makes an application under the Chapter I prohibi- **12.39**
tion must take all reasonable steps to notify all other parties to the agreement that
the application has been made and whether the application is for guidance or a
decision.[76] Similarly, under the Chapter II prohibition, where an application
relates to the conduct of two or more persons, the applicant must take all reasonable steps to notify all the other parties in the same way.[77] Such notification to
other parties shall be given in writing within seven working days of the applicant
receiving the OFT's acknowledgement of receipt of the application. The applicant is required to send to the OFT a copy of the notification to the other party.[78]

Provisional Decisions

If, after a preliminary investigation, the OFT considers it likely that the agree- **12.40**
ment or conduct will infringe the Chapter I or Chapter II prohibition and, in the
case of an agreement notified under the Chapter I prohibition, that it would not
be appropriate to grant an individual exemption, it may make a provisional decision.[79] If the OFT proposes to make a provisional decision, it must consult the

---

[72] OFT, n 1 above, R 8(1).
[73] OFT, n 1 above, R 8(2).
[74] OFT, n 1 above, R 2.
[75] OFT, n 1 above, R 4(1).
[76] Sch 5 para 2(2).
[77] Sch 6 para 2(2).
[78] OFT, n 1 above, R 6.
[79] Sch 5 para 3(l), and Sch 6 para 3(1).

applicant.[80] This obligation is less extensive than that of the OFT in cases where it proposes to make an infringement decision. In infringement cases the OFT must give written notice to the applicant and other parties to the agreement or conduct and also provide an opportunity for oral and written representations.[81] If the OFT makes a provisional decision, however, it need only give written notification of the decision to the applicant, but this should include an account of the facts on which it is based and the reasons for it.[82] A provisional decision does not affect the final determination of the application, but in the case of a notification under the Chapter I prohibition, the provisional immunity from penalties that otherwise takes effect from the date of notification is taken as *never* having applied.[83]

Fees

12.41 The OFT has the power to charge fees in respect of functions specified in the Procedural Rules,[84] and it can be anticipated that the OFT will charge a fee for making a notification.[85] Fees may be calculated by reference to turnover of the parties, and different fees can be specified in connection with different functions, so there may be different fees depending on the size of the companies involved or on whether an application is for guidance or a decision.

E. Provision of False or Misleading Information

12.42 In relation to the exercise of powers in respect of the Chapter I and Chapter II prohibitions, it is a criminal offence for a person to provide the OFT with information which is false or misleading in a material particular where that person knows that the information is false or misleading or is reckless as to whether it is.[86] This means that where Form N is signed by an authorised representative of the notifying party (or a person authorised as joint representative), such a party (eg a firm of solicitors) would risk criminal liability if the person signing knew that, or was reckless as to the fact that, the information provided was materially false or misleading.

---

[80] OFT, n 1 above, R 9(1).

[81] See para 12.17 above. At EC level the Commission will normally issue a statement of objections prior to taking a provisional decision and the applicant is given a right to reply but not necessarily to have an oral hearing. Case 8–11/66 *Cimenteries v Commission* [1967] ECR 75; Case T–19/91 *Vichy v Commission* [1992] ECR II–415.

[82] Sch 5 para 3(2)(a), and Sch 6 para 3(2); R 9(2).

[83] Sch 5 para 3(2)(b).

[84] S 53.

[85] The OFT has indicated that it will publish a separate booklet explaining its fees; OFT, n 44a above, para 10.1. The Formal Consultation Draft of the Form N also refers to fees; see Form N, part 2, para 12.2.

[86] S 44(1). See also Ch 14 paras 14.61–14.65.

It is also an offence for a person to provide such false or misleading information to another person, knowing the information to be so or reckless to the fact, where the person supplying it knows that the information is to be used for the purpose of providing information to the OFT in connection with the OFT's functions in respect of the prohibitions.[87] Thus, for example, if a notification is made by one party to an agreement and the other party to the agreement has provided the notifying party with the relevant information, such other party would be guilty of an offence if it had provided materially misleading information in the knowledge that it was to be used for the purpose of making the notification. **12.43**

These offences may create personal liability for individuals as well as applying to undertakings—see Chapter 14, paragraphs 14.49–14.50 for further details. **12.44**

A person guilty of an offence is liable on summary conviction to a fine not exceeding £5,000,[88] and on conviction on indictment to imprisonment for a term not exceeding two years or to a fine or both.[89] **12.45**

If false or misleading information is provided (regardless of whether the applicant has intentionally or recklessly been misleading) the application is not considered to be complete—see paragraph 12.28 above.[90] **12.46**

F. Contents of the Application—Form N

Form N is in four parts. Part 1 contains notes on making the application; part 2 requires the most significant information which will determine the outcome of the case; part 3 contains the acknowledgement of receipt, the top half of which should be filled in by the applicant in preparation for its completion and return by the OFT; and part 4 requests a non-confidential summary required for entry on the public register in decision cases.[91] **12.47**

Care must be taken in completing the Form, not only because of the obligations described in paragraphs 12.28 and 12.29 above, but because it is important from the applicant's point of view to achieve the most successful presentation of its case for the OFT to consider. The Form describes itself as 'essentially a check-list of the information which must be supplied to the [OFT] to enable [it] to determine a notification',[92] but in submitting the information required it is advisable to follow the numbering and structure of the Form. Where parties consider that it may not **12.48**

---

[87] S 44(2).

[88] Fines for the offences on summary conviction may be up to 'the statutory maximum', which is currently £5,000 (Interpretation Act 1978, s 5, Sch 1; Magistrates Court Act 1980, s 32).

[89] S 44(3).

[90] OFT, n 1 above, R 4(2).

[91] See para 12.24 above.

[92] Form N, part 1, para 1.1.

be necessary to provide all requested information,[93] this should be discussed with the OFT in advance of making the application. Confidential information should be placed in a separate annex,[94] identified as such with cross-references in the main body of the notification.

12.49 A copy of the Formal Consultation Draft of Form N is located in [Appendix 4]. What follows is a summary and commentary on the most important section of the Form—the substance of the notification required under part 2.

(a) Section 1 of part 2 requires information on and contact details for *the applicants and other parties* to the agreement or carrying out the conduct.

- A few lines will be sufficient to give a brief description of the relevant parties and their business activities.

- It would be usual to include in the contact details a direct line telephone number, fax number and, where available, an e-mail address.

- Partnerships, sole traders and unincorporated bodies must give the name and address of the proprietors or partners, but, for large partnerships, a partnership address should be sufficient (although this is not expressly provided for).

- Where the applicant is an authorised representative (for example, a solicitor) or a joint representative where there is more than one applicant, and so proof of authority to act needs to be provided, this would normally be in the form of a signed authorised statement by the appointing party or parties. There are practical advantages in appointing a joint representative in the case of a application by more than one party; without one, a representative of each of the parties has to be identified as authorised to submit and receive documents.

- To fulfil the obligation on the applicant to inform other parties of the application and provide details of this to the OFT, the applicant would typically state that faxes or letters containing a draft of the notification (excluding confidential information) had been or were being sent to the other parties on a specified date, and might provide the OFT with copies of such correspondence. In exceptional cases the OFT is likely to accept that it may not be possible to inform all parties of the notification—for example, where there is a standard form agreement to which there are too large a number of parties for it to be practicable.

(b) Section 2 requires information on *the purpose of the notification*: whether the application is for guidance or a decision, and whether it relates to the Chapter

---

[93] See para 31 above.
[94] See para 12.32 above.

I or the Chapter II prohibition. In the case of a Chapter I notification for an individual exemption, the applicant is able to specify the date on which it would like the exemption to take effect, if different from the date of notification, thus enabling requests for retroactive exemption (although this is only likely to be granted in more exceptional circumstances).

(c) Section 3 deals with *jurisdiction*: whether the notification relates to a utility sector for which there is concurrent jurisdiction by the relevant sector regulator; whether the agreement or conduct has been considered by the European Commission (supplying a copy of Form A/B, the EC equivalent of Form N, will alleviate unnecessary repetition of information); and whether it is subject to the jurisdiction of any other national competition authority. Previous contacts with the OFT, a sector regulator or the European Commission should also be detailed, and this would include informal discussions preliminary to the notification.

(d) Section 4 requests *details of the agreement or conduct* being notified, including copes of the relevant documents.

- The brief description asked for will provide the OFT with an overview—the following sections of part 2 of the Form allow a more thorough consideration of the market context of the parties concerned, the agreement or conduct, and its effect on competition. This section should therefore be sufficient to give the OFT a feel for the scope of the arrangements or behaviour, but there is no need to set out in great detail information covered subsequently. Technical details, for example as contained in know-how agreements, may be omitted so long as such omission is indicated.

- Where, however, there is no written version of the agreement or the conduct, eg the agreement itself is not in writing, a full description should be included in the Form N. The OFT has indicated that it will not accept notification of prospective agreements (ie those into which the parties have not yet entered) or prospective conduct.[95] Thus it will not be possible to notify agreements in draft form although the parties may wish to make informal contact with the OFT.[96]

- An identification of any provisions which may be restrictive is required. In the case of an agreement notified under Chapter I, these might typically be provisions which relate to: prices, discounts or other trading conditions; quantities of goods to be made or distributed, or services to be offered; technical development or investment; the choice of markets or sources of

---

[95] OFT, n 44a above, para 7.2. Ss 13(1) and 14(1) preclude notification of a proposed arrangement which falls short of an agreement within the meaning of s 2.

[96] This would seem a drawback to the notification procedures under the Act, limiting the usefulness of the guidance route in particular. The European Commission in practice accepts notifications of draft agreements under Art 81 (formerly Art 85).

supply—purchases from or sales to third parties; the application of similar trading terms for the supply of equipment, goods or services; whether to offer different goods or services separately or together.

(e) Section 5 requires further *information on the corporate groups* to which the parties belong, including annual reports and accounts.

(f) Section 6 requires an explanation of the *relevant product and geographic markets*. Section 7 requests specific information on *market shares*, and details of *major competitors and customers*, and other companies with which the parties may have ownership or trading links. Section 8 asks for information on *barriers to entry* into the relevant markets and the existence of *potential competition*. These three sections of the Form are critical in explaining the economic context in which the relevant agreement or conduct can be analysed.

- The parties should describe the nature of the relevant products or services and how they relate to other products or services, and the structure of the relevant market—buyers, sellers, geographical extent (which may be larger or smaller than the UK), turnover, degree of competition, ease of market entry and substitutable products and services.

- The amount of detail and degree of precision that are required in these sections will vary from case to case. As regards section 6, in many cases there will be a number of alternative credible market definitions and, to the extent that it is considered that the agreement or conduct should not give rise to competition concerns on any realistic market definition, it would be unnecessary to include extensive arguments in relation to market definition. In other cases, the market definition may be of more critical significance—for example, where the applicant has a high market share if the market is defined in one way but a lower share if it is defined in a different way—and will therefore require more detailed consideration.

- Where different market definitions have been suggested by the parties in earlier notifications, or where the parties are proposing a definition different to that used by the UK, EC or other competition authorities in other cases, it will be necessary to explain why the definition used in the other cases is not appropriate, for example, because the market has changed over time or because the context of this case is different to the other case.

- Market shares should be given by value (if available) and also by volume if volume is an appropriate measure. Where parties do not have a clear idea of total market size or the shares of competitors they should give best estimates and indicate the basis for making the estimate. Where market information contained in published studies is believed to be incorrect the reasons why this is considered to be the case should be explained.

- There is not necessarily a precise dividing line between the various topics to be reviewed in these sections. Thus, for example, as a matter of practicality, arguments relating to market definition overlap with issues relating to barriers to market entry.

- Wherever possible, arguments should be supported with hard facts and examples. Thus, for example, if it is being argued that entry into the relevant market is not difficult and relatively inexpensive, it would be helpful to include case studies of successful market entry and costings relating to the likely expenditure required to enter the market.

- Details of relevant market studies, either compiled by the parties or by independent third parties, should be supplied. Pre-existing market studies (ie not prepared specifically for the purposes of the notification) will carry more credibility.

(g) Section 9 requests the parties' reasons for seeking a decision or guidance that the Chapter I or Chapter II prohibition is *not infringed*. Thus, for example, the parties may seek to argue that the parties to an agreement are not actual or potential competitors, or that information that it has been agreed be exchanged between the parties is not confidential business information of a type that will have an impact on competition.

(h) Section 10 requires the parties to give their reasons why, in the case of a notification under the Chapter I prohibition where decision or guidance as to *individual exemption* is requested, an agreement satisfies the relevant criteria for exemption to be granted.

- The relevant benefits can normally be demonstrated by indicating the extent to which the agreement would, for example, lead to innovation or improve the efficiency of production or distribution, and how this would benefit consumers in terms of better products or more cost efficient production or distribution arrangements.

- Generally, the most significant issues which arise when seeking an individual exemption relate to the extent to which the restricted provisions are indispensable and why they do not eliminate competition. In most cases, therefore, it is in these areas that the most detailed arguments would need to be addressed. On indispensability the parties may seek to argue that without the restrictions the beneficial effects of the agreement would not be achieved. Thus, for example, in the case of a research and development agreement containing arrangements for exclusivity on sales, it might be argued that the parties would not make the necessary investment in research if they were not guaranteed a period of sales exclusivity to exploit the relevant products. It will generally be sufficient to show that there are other actual and potential competitors in the market in order to demonstrate that competition is not eliminated or to show that the relevant agreement will result in a new, better or more cost efficient product or service thus widening or improving consumer choice without removing all viable competition.

(i) Section 11 requests details of any *transitional periods* (for the duration of which the Chapter I prohibition does not apply—see Chapter 11) that the notified agreement benefits from.

(j) Finally, section 12 deals with *other miscellaneous information*, including: any reason for urgent treatment of the application (for example, if the agreement must come into force on a certain date in order to enable related commercial arrangements to be undertaken); details of trade press in which third party views could be sought on an application for a decision; and whether the parties wanted to submit further information not yet available.

G. Extension or Cancellation of Exemptions and Exclusions

Extension of Individual Exemptions

12.50 A party to an agreement in respect of which the OFT has granted a individual exemption, which will be of a specified duration, is able to apply for an extension of the period for which the exemption has effect.[97] A person who wishes to do so should apply by submitting a Form N, and the relevant rules regarding copies and content of notifications apply.[98] Such an application must be submitted no more than 12 months and not less than three months before the expiry of the exemption.[99]

12.51 If the OFT proposes to grant the application, it must consult publicly, which it will do by means of an entry on the OFT register and consultation of such third parties as appear likely to be interested.[100] Once it has made an extension decision, the OFT must give written notice to the applicant and publish the decision on the register, specifying the period of extension granted.[101]

Cancellation or Variation of Individual Exemptions

12.52 The OFT is able to cancel an individual exemption from the Chapter I prohibition, or remove a condition or obligation to which the exemption is subject, or

---

[97] S 4(6).
[98] OFT, n 1 above, R 19(1) and (4).
[99] OFT, n 1 above, R 19(2).
[100] OFT, n 1 above, Rr 19(3) and 27(1)(c) and (i).
[101] OFT, n 1 above, R 19(4).

impose additional conditions or obligations, if: (i) it has reasonable grounds for believing that there has been a material change of circumstance, or (ii) it has a reasonable suspicion that the information on which it based its exemption decision was incomplete, false or misleading in a material particular.[102]

Where the OFT proposes to cancel or vary an individual exemption in this way, it **12.53** must consult the person to whom notice of the exemption decision was given.[103] It must also consult the public, which it will do by means of an entry on the OFT public register and consultation with such third parties as appear likely to be interested.[104] Where the OFT proceeds with the decision, it must give notice to the person in question in writing, stating the facts on which the decision is based and the reasons for it, and publish the decision, which it will do by means of an entry on the register.[105]

Cancellation or Variation of Parallel Exemptions

Where an agreement benefits from a parallel exemption, the OFT is able to **12.54** impose conditions or obligations subject to which a parallel exemption is to have effect, to vary or remove any such condition or obligation, to impose additional conditions or obligations, or to cancel the exemption.[106] The OFT will exercise these powers where it finds that an agreement benefiting from a parallel exemption has produced, or may produce, significantly adverse effects on a market in the UK or part of it.[107]

Where the OFT proposes to exercise these powers, it must consult each person **12.55** who is a party to the agreement and also the public by means of an entry on the register and consultation of interested third parties.[108] If the OFT does take such action then, as with cancellation or variation of individual exemptions, it must give written notice to each of the parties to the agreement in question, giving details of the variation or cancellation, stating the facts on which the decision is based and the reasons for it, and publish the decision on the register.[109] Where the OFT cancels a parallel exemption, its decision may be retroactive, ie take effect on a date earlier than that on which notice of cancellation is given.[110]

---

[102] S 5.
[103] OFT, n 1 above, R 20(1).
[104] Ibid and R 27(1)(c) and (i).
[105] OFT, n 1 above, Rr 20(2) and 27(1)(i).
[106] S 10(5).
[107] OFT, n 1 above, R 21(1)
[108] OFT, n 1 above, Rr 21(2) and 27(1)(c) and (i).
[109] OFT, n 1 above, Rr 21(3) and (4), and 27(1)(i).
[110] S 10(6) and OFT, n 1 above, R 21(5).

Withdrawal of Exclusions

12.56 A number of the exclusions in the Act (and, it is anticipated, the orders for special treatment of vertical agreements and land agreements) provide for the benefit of the exclusion to be withdrawn by the OFT in specified circumstances. Withdrawal of exclusions and the procedural requirements for doing so are dealt with in Chapter 5.

H. Notifications in Practice—Use of Administrative Letters

12.57 The OFT has estimated that, following a period of adjustment in the initial years after the introduction of the Act, the number of Chapter I notifications it will receive annually will be around 1,000: 600 applications for guidance and around 400 for a decision.[111] However, this figure is likely to be significantly reduced—it can be anticipated by even as much as half—as a result of the planned order to be made under section 50 of the Act providing special treatment for vertical agreements under the Chapter I prohibition (most likely by way of an exclusion from the prohibition—see Chapter 5, paragraphs 5.81–5.95). The OFT expects very few notifications under the Chapter II prohibition.[112]

12.58 The OFT suspects that, if it does receive as many Chapter I notifications as this, a good proportion of them will be unnecessary in that the agreements concerned will either clearly be unlikely to have as their object or effect an appreciable effect on competition (for example, on the narrowest possible market definition), or clearly fall within the scope of an exclusion, or block or parallel exemption.[113] In such cases, rather than giving a decision or guidance, the OFT may issue a form of administrative letter equivalent to a 'comfort letter' from the European Commission, which explains that the agreement does not have an appreciable effect on competition or is covered by an exclusion, or block or parallel exemption.[114]

12.59 As explained above (see paragraphs 12.11–12.13 and 12.20–12.23), notification for guidance or a decision initiates formal statutory procedures, and favourable results following such an application provide a significant degree of legal security—from financial penalties, from subsequent adverse treatment by the OFT,

---

[111] Margaret Bloom, Director of Competition Policy, Office of Fair Trading: paper to 'The Europeanisation of UK Competition Law' conference, 10 Sept 1998 , para 10 (note that Mrs Bloom's paper expresses her personal views and not necessarily those of the OFT). By comparison 221 notifications were made to DG IV of the European Commission in 1997.

[112] Ibid.

[113] See Ch 4, paras 4.46–4.55, as regards appreciability, and Ch 6, as regards block and parallel exemptions.

[114] Margaret Bloom, n 111 above, para 10.

and in the courts. (The guidance procedure should not be confused with the OFT's informal procedure for 'confidential guidance' under the merger provisions of the Fair Trading Act 1973, which has no such statutory basis.)

An administrative letter, on the other hand, is without such formal legal basis—it **12.60** creates no express statutory obligations on the OFT. Nevertheless, an administrative letter from the OFT provides parties with a considerable degree of comfort in practice. An applicant can generally rely on the OFT not taking further action except in foreseeable circumstances such as, for example, a material change in the structure of the market. Moreover, general principles of administrative law apply, so such a letter is likely to give rise to a 'legitimate expectation' on the applicant's part which limits the OFT from taking further, contradictory action without objectively justifiable reasons (eg new information comes to light—in effect similar to the limited grounds for further action following a favourable decision or positive guidance). Although it will not offer the same degree of protection as a decision, an administrative letter has the advantage over a decision that it is not appealable to the Competition Commission by third parties who show a 'sufficient interest'.[115] Where an application had been made for individual exemption from the Chapter I prohibition, and this was dealt with by means of an administrative letter, the parties could if necessary make a subsequent application for a retroactive individual exemption (eg backdated to the time when the first notification was made) if the status of the agreement under the Chapter I prohibition was disputed by a third party.

Thus, although it is likely that applicants have a right to insist on a decision, at **12.61** least as to individual exemption, if they wish,[116] an administrative letter should prove acceptable to the applicant in many cases.

I. Whether to Notify the OFT

Notification is not compulsory. This section considers the main advantages and **12.62** disadvantages involved and some of the practical and tactical considerations that are likely to arise when deciding whether to notify.

General Advantages of Notification

The following advantages are offered by a notification: **12.63**

(i) As explained in paragraphs 12.10 and 12.19 above, notification of an agreement for guidance or a decision under Chapter I ensures *provisional*

---

[115] S 47; see Ch 16, para 16.05–16.12 regarding third party appeals.
[116] S 60; European Commission Notice on co-operation between national competition authorities and the Commission in cases falling within the scope of Art 81 or 82 (formerly Art 85 or 86) of the EC Treaty, para 38; and Case T–23/90 *Peugeot v Commission* [1991] ECR II–653, para 47.

immunity from penalties for the period from the date of notification until the application is determined. Although this provisional immunity from penalties can be withdrawn if the OFT makes a provisional decision after a preliminary investigation, if EC experience is any guide, provisional decisions are likely to be rare in practice and limited to cases where there is an overwhelming argument that the prohibition has been infringed and that there are no grounds for an exemption—for example, pure price-fixing cases.

(ii) The parties may obtain a *decision that the Chapter I or Chapter II prohibition is not infringed* (whether a negative clearance, or confirmation that an exclusion applies, or in the case of the Chapter I prohibition only, that the agreement is likely to be exempt under a block exemption, a parallel exemption or a section 11 exemption), or guidance that that is likely to be the case. Such a decision or guidance is of particular value in a situation where there is doubt whether the prohibition is being infringed and this is having a restraining effect on the applicant's business activities. In the case of an agreement notified under the Chapter I prohibition, an application seeking a decision that the prohibition was not infringed would in nearly all cases be coupled with an application for an individual exemption in the event that the former was not available.

An attempt to obtain negative clearance or confirmation that an exclusion applies is the only point of notifying conduct that may infringe the Chapter II prohibition. An applicant might seek negative clearance under the Chapter II prohibition for two reasons:

- First, in a situation where a company is uncertain whether it is dominant on a particular market (or is uncertain about market definition), the OFT's determination could clarify the company's position. The risk of such a notification is that, if the OFT considered the company to be dominant, this could act as a significant restraint on the company's commercial behaviour and, because the OFT had determined the matter, the scope for doubt or argument would be limited in the future. Even where the OFT's conclusion was that the company was not dominant, the structure of the market and the applicant's position in it (eg market share) might well change over time, in which case it would be unsafe to rely on the OFT's earlier determination.

- Secondly, a negative clearance would be of benefit in relation to the Chapter II prohibition where a company which is dominant requires clarification as to whether conduct it is embarking on is abusive.

In practice, it has been extremely unusual for a company to seek negative clearance in relation to possible Article 82 (formerly Article 86) infringements at EC level. The general view has been that the disadvantages of bringing such matters to the attention of the European Commission have out-weighed any benefits that might arise from greater clarity.

(iii) Under the Chapter I prohibition the parties may obtain an *individual exemption decision*;[117] such a decision can only be obtained if the agreement is notified. An exemption may be retroactive[118] even to a date earlier than that of notification. However, in practice, the exemption is normally likely to be backdated to the date of notification (although the OFT has indicated exceptions where it will grant an exemption retroactive to an earlier date where there has been a prior EC notification—see paragraph 12.15 above). Therefore a party which delays notification until difficulties arise—for example, where another party to the agreement seeks to challenge its validity—runs a risk that even if an exemption is ultimately granted it will provide no protection in respect of the period prior to the notification.

(iv) As explained in paragraphs 12.11 to 12.12 and 12.20–12.23 above, both guidance and a decision can provide the applicant with a considerable degree of legal security. Positive guidance or a favourable decision ensures that the OFT will take no further action with regard to the conduct or agreement, except in limited circumstances, and that there will be immunity from penalties.

(v) If civil proceedings are brought before a UK court in respect of alleged infringements of the Chapter I prohibition, the fact that a notification for individual exemption has been made (even though the OFT may not have determined the outcome at the time of the commencement of the court proceedings), or even that, although a notification has not been made, the agreement may well satisfy the Chapter I exemption criteria and so the parties wish to make an exemption notification, may persuade the court to stay the relevant proceedings until the OFT has made a determination of such an application.

See Chapter 10, paragraphs 10.85–10.94 for more detailed consideration of the treatment by UK courts of agreements or conduct which are or have been subject to scrutiny by the OFT as well.

(vi) Notification of an agreement indicates to the OFT that the parties have demonstrated good faith and a willingness to co-operate. They also become the 'first movers', ensuring that from the outset the OFT understands the issues from their perspective rather than that of a complainant.

---

[117] S 4.
[118] S 4(5).

General Disadvantages of Notification

12.64 The main disadvantages of notification are as follows:

(i) In contrast to notification under the Restrictive Trade Practices Act, which was quick and relatively straightforward, notification under the Competition Act is quite likely to be a time-consuming and, sometimes, an expensive process. A detailed form must be completed giving a broad range of information. Some of the information, particularly in relation to markets and market shares may be difficult to compile and, in complex cases, expert economic advice may be required.

(ii) There are relatively few obligations on the OFT as regards the timescale for reaching a view on the notified agreement or conduct,[119] although the OFT can be expected to introduce non-binding administrative timetables once the prohibitions come into force.[120]

(iii) The OFT may, as a result of a notification, take an interest in an arrangement, company or market sector with which it would otherwise be unfamiliar. In the case of a notification for decision, the OFT will publish limited details of the notification (see paragraph 12.24 above), so competitors or other third parties who become aware of the notification may take the opportunity to voice concerns that would not otherwise have been raised with the OFT.

(iv) Although in some cases guidance or a decision will allow parties some certainty as to the OFT's attitude when they undertake similar agreements or conduct subsequently, in practice similar but not identical future (and previous) agreements or conduct may have to be notified for the sake of consistency and because areas of sensitivity have been identified. Unhelpful precedents may be created for future notifications. An argument by the applicant on, say, market definition which is accepted by the OFT in relation to a particular agreement or conduct may be less helpful in relation to subsequent agreements or conduct.

(v) Further notifications of the actual agreement or conduct which has been notified may still be necessary, particularly in the case of an agreement, such as where following an individual exemption decision there has been a material change in circumstances[121] or where the exemption expires.[122]

---

[119] There are obligations in the Procedural Rules to communicate matters to relevant parties without delay, and in the case of a decision, the OFT may be challenged before the court if there is 'undue delay' (see para 12.18 above). There is, however, no definition of what is meant by an undue delay and this will ultimately be determined by the practice and procedure of the OFT.

[120] OFT, n 1 above, introductory para 10.

[121] S 5(1).

[122] S 4(3)(b).

In addition, it should not be overlooked that, if information provided is incomplete, false or misleading in a material particular, any guidance or decision cannot be relied upon and, if false or misleading information is provided intentionally or recklessly, the applicant may be guilty of a criminal offence (see paragraphs 12.28 and 12.42–12.46 above). Thus there is a high burden to ensure accuracy on a party seeking to notify.   **12.65**

Other Practical Considerations

It can be seen that a notification is not a mere administrative filing; it sets in course   **12.66** detailed investigations by the authorities and can have far reaching consequences for the companies concerned. Therefore, in deciding whether to notify an agreement, companies will, finally, wish to take into account a range of factors specific to the case in question:

- the commercial significance of the agreement in general and, in particular, the significance of any provisions of the agreement that may be unenforceable;

- the risk that other parties to the agreement may seek to rely on unenforceability of clauses in the event of a dispute;

- the likelihood of third parties, such as customers, suppliers or competitors, complaining to the authorities or bringing an action in the courts;

- the extent to which any possible infringement would be of sufficient seriousness to give rise to the possibility of penalties;

- the desirability of maintaining a good and open relationship with the OFT, particularly in the event of having to deal with the OFT on other matters in the future.

Lastly, it should also be borne in mind that parties will not be precluded from   **12.67** making **informal contact** with the OFT regarding agreements or conduct. A potential applicant may in some cases find it useful to seek a preliminary view from the OFT before deciding to notify (particularly in cases where a notification to the European Commission under Articles 81 or 82 (formerly Articles 85 or 86) is also being considered—see paragraphs 12.80–12.89 below). However, it can be anticipated that the OFT will be less willing to divert its resources to extensive informal contact than the European Commission, for whom the distinction between a formal application and informal discussion is less important, since the majority of cases are determined informally (by means of a comfort letter) and there is no fee to be forgone if a formal notification is not made.

When Notification to the OFT is Unnecessary

As explained above, there are a range of factors which need to be weighed in the   **12.68** balance when considering whether to notify. In the case of agreements, however, parties should also be aware that in some cases there will clearly be no need to make a notification. Indeed, the OFT would usually seek to discourage notification in such circumstances. The following paragraphs consider the circumstances likely in practice when there will be no need to submit a notification to the OFT for a UK individual exemption (and/or to the European Commission for an EC individual exemption).

(i) *Where the agreement is covered by an EC block exemption:*
Notification is normally unnecessary either to the OFT or to the European Commission, provided that all the conditions in the EC block exemption are satisfied. The agreement is automatically exempt from Article 81 (formerly Article 85) EC and, by virtue of the parallel exemption provisions,[123] from the Chapter I prohibition. Automatic exemption from the Chapter I prohibition applies even if the agreement does not affect trade between EU Member States—and so does not fall within the jurisdiction of Article 81— but nevertheless satisfies all the block exemption criteria.[124] (The OFT may cancel a parallel exemption or attach conditions to it, but where it proposes to do so the OFT consults the parties in advance,[125] and it is open to them to notify at that stage.) However, if the practice may constitute an abuse of a dominant position, the block exemption will not protect it from being challenged under either Article 82 (formerly Article 86) EC or the Chapter II prohibition.[126]

(ii) *Where the agreement is excluded by virtue of Schedules 1 to 4 or an exclusion order made under section 50, or is covered by a UK block exemption made under section 6:*[127]
There is no need to notify the OFT for an individual exemption. However, if there is an appreciable effect on trade between EU Member States such that Article 81 (formerly Article 85) EC may apply, the UK exclusions and exemptions do not offer protection against Article 81, and it may be prudent to notify the European Commission for an EC individual exemption where this may be the case. (In addition, as above, if there is an abuse of a dominant position, a UK block exemption or an exclusion from the Chapter I prohibition will not give protection against action under Article 86 or, unless it is an exclusion from the Chapter II prohibition, under the Chapter II prohibition.)

---

[123] S 10.
[124] S 10(2).
[125] S 10(5); OFT, n 1 above, R 21.
[126] See Ch 6, para 6.60 above.
[127] Or the agreement is exempted by virtue of regulations made under s 11, or an order made under s 50 providing for exemption (rather than exclusion) or otherwise that prescribed provisions in the Act will not apply. Note, however, that the Act does allow for the possibility of notification to determine whether these exclusions or automatic exemptions applies: ss 13 and 14.

(iii) *Where the agreement has received an EC individual exemption from the European Commission:*

Notification to the OFT is unnecessary. By virtue of the parallel exemption provisions,[128] the EC individual exemption has the effect that the agreement is exempt from the Chapter I prohibition as well as from Article 81 (formerly Article 85) EC. (The OFT may cancel a parallel exemption or attach conditions to it, but where it proposes to do so the OFT consults the parties in advance,[129] and it is open to the parties to notify the agreement to the OFT at that stage). The individual exemption also protects the agreement from being challenged under either Article 82 (formerly Article 86) EC or the Chapter II prohibition.[130] An EC individual exemption will also be binding on a UK court.

(iv) *Where the agreement has received a 'comfort letter' from the European Commission:*

In most cases the European Commission does not issue a formal exemption decision in respect of a notified agreement, but instead an informal 'comfort letter' stating that the Commission will not take action in respect of the agreement under Article 81 (formerly Article 85). Although such a 'comfort letter' does not give rise to parallel exemption from the Chapter I prohibition—section 10(1) of the Competition Act grants parallel exemption only where there is an applicable EC block exemption Regulation or a formal EC individual exemption decision—it will generally not be necessary to notify the agreement to the OFT, because the OFT normally 'will not depart from' the European Commission's assessment as set out in the comfort letter.[131] The exceptions to this are where:

- the agreement raises particular concerns about competition in the UK;

- the European Commission's decision not to take action against the agreement is due to the Commission having higher internal priorities but the comfort letter indicates that the agreement infringes Article 81 and would not merit exemption (a 'discomfort' letter); or

- the European Commission's decision not to take action against the agreement is based only on the fact that the Commission lacks jurisdiction (ie because the agreement may not appreciably affect trade between EU Member States) and not on a substantive assessment of the agreement's effects on competition.[132]

---

[128] S 10.
[129] S 10(5); OFT, n 1 above, R 21.
[130] See Ch 6, para 6.60.
[131] OFT, n 27 above, para 7.12.
[132] Ibid.

If the parties do notify the OFT in these circumstances, they should enclose with their notification three copies of the comfort letter received from the European Commission.[133]

(v) *Where the parties have notified the European Commission for an EC individual exemption, but have not yet been granted an EC individual exemption:*

The OFT takes the view that it is unnecessary to notify the OFT as well, since the effects of notifying the European Commission are that it confers provisional immunity both from fines under Article 81 (formerly Article 85) and from penalties under the Chapter I prohibition,[134] and also that it offers the prospect of both individual exemption from Article 81 and parallel exemption from the Chapter I prohibition. The only advantage of notifying the OFT as well would be where it is important to obtain an exemption from the Chapter I prohibition backdated to a date before that of notification (ie if the agreement had been in place for a considerable time before notification, and there may be real practical exposure to the risk that third parties who sustained losses in that pre-notification period would take legal proceedings for damages to recover their losses); a retroactive exemption in respect of the period pre-notification is possible under the Chapter I prohibition but not under Article 81,[135] but such an exemption does not protect the parties from the consequences of infringing Article 81.

If none of the above circumstances apply, it may be prudent to notify the OFT—or, where the agreement has an effect on trade between EU Member States, the European Commission (see paragraphs 12.72–12.89 below).

J. Whether to Notify the OFT for a Decision or Guidance

12.69 It is also worth considering the relative merits of the alternative procedures available for notifying under the Act. As explained in paragraph 12.01 above, both notification for guidance and notification for a decision are formal statutory procedures under the Act. Like a favourable decision, positive guidance ensures protection from further OFT action except in limited circumstances, and provides immunity from financial penalties. The OFT has, however, indicated that in certain cases it will seek to deal with notifications by means of an administrative letter similar to the comfort letters given by the European Commission (see paragraphs 12.57–12.61 above), which would offer the parties a more limited degree of protection.

---

[133] OFT, n 45 above, para 3.2.
[134] S 41.
[135] S 4(5); see Ch 6, para 6.41.

The advantages of a notification for guidance over a notification for a decision are: **12.70**

- *Confidentiality*—an application for a decision includes a significant degree of publicity and third party consultation (see paragraph 12.24 above). This is not the case with an application for guidance. Parties wishing to avoid publicity and an opportunity for third parties such as competitors to make adverse comments will find the decision route more attractive.

- *Speed*—in view of the lighter procedural requirements, determination of a guidance application is likely to be quicker than determination of a decision. This will be of benefit where parties need to obtain the OFT's determination quickly.

- *No third party appeals*—a third party showing 'sufficient interest' will be able to appeal against an OFT decision to the Competition Commission,[136] but no such third party rights exist in respect of guidance (even assuming a third party became aware of the determination).

- *Less chance of administrative letter*—it can be foreseen that there might be more chance of an application for a decision being determined by means of an administrative letter: the greater procedural requirements on the OFT in reaching a decision mean that, in very straightforward cases, there will be greater justification for closing the file informally (eg a notified agreement clearly falls within an exclusion or a parallel exemption). A decision application in cases such as this may therefore result in less legal security for the parties than a guidance application.

- *Fees*—if, as is likely, fees are charged for notifications, it is quite possible that a guidance notification will be cheaper than a decision notification, reflecting the greater use of administrative resources required in a decision case.

The advantages of an application for a decision over an application for guidance are: **12.71**

- *Protection from the OFT*—a favourable decision offers greater protection against the OFT re-opening the case than positive guidance. In particular, guidance, but not a decision, can be overturned in the event of a third party complaint.[137]

- *Protection in the courts*—an individual exemption decision is likely to be binding on a court, providing protection against third party action or in a dispute between the parties to an agreement, whereas guidance that an agreement is likely to be exempted is likely to be only a factor to which the court has regard.

---

[136] S 47 and see Ch 16 on appeals.
[137] Ss 15(2)(d) and 23(2)(c). With a decision application, third party comment will already have been taken into account.

- *Public consultation necessary*—in complex cases (for example, a notification concerning a new, high-technology market of which the OFT has no experience) it may be difficult for the OFT to give sufficiently definite guidance without wider public consultation. If this is anticipated, the applicant may find it more fruitful to apply for a decision from the outset, provided that it is prepared to countenance the resulting publicity.

K. Whether to Notify the OFT or the European Commission

Overlap between UK and EC Jurisdictions

12.72 Restrictive agreements which may affect trade within the United Kingdom fall within the Chapter I prohibition. Where they may (ie actually or potentially) also affect trade between EC Member States to an appreciable extent, they will fall under the jurisdiction of Article 81 (formerly Article 85) of the EC Treaty as well. Similarly, abusive conduct by a dominant company which may affect trade within the United Kingdom will be contrary to the Chapter II prohibition, but will also fall within the scope of the prohibition in Article 82 (formerly Article 86) of the EC Treaty if it affects trade between Member States and if the dominant position is enjoyed in a substantial part of the EU.

12.73 Where an agreement or conduct affects trade within the UK but not between Member States, the only notification that needs to be considered is an application to the OFT under the Chapter I or II prohibition. However, if there is an effect on trade both within the UK and between Member States, such that both the EC and the UK competition authorities will have jurisdiction, the issues for the parties are more complex. The parties will need to consider which authority to notify—the OFT, the European Commission or both.

12.74 The OFT has stated as regards the Chapter I prohibition that:

> The starting point in determining which is the more appropriate authority for notifications is to assess whether or not the agreement may affect trade between Member States. In practice, parties would be advised to consider fully the application of Article 85(1) [now Article 81(1)] before notifying agreements to the [OFT] under Chapter I.[138]

Similar considerations apply in respect of conduct which may fall under Article 82 (formerly Article 86) as well as the Chapter II prohibition.

---

[138] OFT, n 27 above, para 7.3.

Meaning of Effect on Trade between EU Member States

The concept of an effect on trade between EU Member States has been accorded **12.75** a wide meaning. Moreover, there is no clear dividing line between agreements that affect trade between EU Member States and those that do not.

An agreement which expressly prohibits imports or exports between EU Member **12.76** States can clearly be seen to affect trade between them. However, the Court has also held that an agreement extending over the whole territory of a Member State but no further (in the case in question, a cement price-fixing cartel in the Netherlands) by its very nature has the effect of reinforcing compartmentalisation of markets along national boundaries, and so could be considered to affect trade between Member States.[139] An effect on trade between EU Member States has also been found by the European Commission where a product was only traded in a particular region in France.[140]

In another case,[141] a joint venture between Italian undertakings to produce televi- **12.77** sion audience rating figures was found to affect trade between Member States, even though all of the television channels and advertising agencies involved were Italian, because some of the television programmes shown originated outside Italy, some of the advertising air time bought was to advertise non-Italian prod-ucts, and one of the television channels could be picked up outside Italy. A further example of particular relevance to the UK concerned an agreement relating to the supply of electricity in Scotland.[142] This was considered by the European Commission to affect trade between Member States, even though there was no direct trade in electricity between Scotland and another Member State, because an interconnector linked the French electricity grid to the grid in England and Wales and the networks were considered to be interdependent, even though the capac-ity of the interconnector was very small in the context of the electricity output of England and Wales.

Thus, parties to what is at first sight a purely national agreement must exercise **12.78** caution before determining that the agreement will not have an actual or poten-tial effect on trade between EU Member States, such that it is outside the scope of Article 81 (formerly Article 85). Similar factors apply in respect of conduct and the application of Article 82 (formerly Article 86).

Parties should therefore consider whether there is an effect on trade between EU **12.79** Member States:

---

[139] Case 8/72 *Vereeniging van Cementhandelaren v Commission* [1972] ECR 997.
[140] Case 123/83 *Bureau National Interprofessionnel du Cognac (BNIC) v Clair* [1985] ECR 391 and Case 136/86 *Bureau National Interprofessionnel du Cognac (BNIC) v Aubert* [1989] 1 CEC 363.
[141] *Auditel*, Decision 93/668, [1994] 1 CEC 2070.
[142] Case IV/33.473 *Scottish Nuclear.*

- If the answer is clearly no, any notification should be to the OFT and not to the European Commission.

- If the answer is clearly yes, it will normally be advisable to notify the European Commission rather than the OFT.

- If the answer is unclear, they have an opportunity to consult the OFT 'as to the more appropriate authority to notify'.[143]

Borderline cases where the answer is not clearly no are considered in more detail in the following paragraphs.

Overlapping Jurisdictions—Whom to Notify?

Advantages in Notifying the European Commission and not the OFT

12.80 Where an agreement or conduct does fall within the scope of Article 81 or 82 (formerly Article 85 or 86) as well as Chapter I or II, a single notification will have benefits to the parties in terms of convenience and compliance costs. The OFT has itself stated that dual notifications, ie notifications to both the UK and EC authorities, are 'undesirable in terms of the compliance costs for undertakings and the duplication of effort by competition authorities'.[144]

12.81 In such cases, it will normally be appropriate to make any notification considered necessary to the European Commission rather than the OFT, and the OFT sees 'several advantages' in doing so.[145]

12.82 The following advantages are offered by *notification to the European Commission for a negative clearance* decision under Article 81 or 82 (formerly Article 85 or 86), as compared with notification to the OFT for a decision that the Chapter I or II prohibition has not been infringed:

    (i)   A decision by the OFT that the Chapter I or Chapter II prohibition does not apply will not bind the European Commission or national competition authorities in other Member States. However, as explained in the following paragraph, a negative clearance decision by the European Commission under Article 81 or 82 (formerly Article 85 or 86) will at least in some cases effectively preclude action by the OFT under the Chapter I or Chapter II prohibition.

    (ii) Where the European Commission makes a decision granting negative clearance under Article 81 or 82 (formerly Article 85 or 86), ie a decision that the agreement or conduct does not fall within the scope of the relevant EC prohibition, the extent of protection from the Chapter I or II prohibitions will depend on the reason for negative clearance:

---

[143] OFT, n 27 above, para 7.6.
[144] Ibid, para 7.1.
[145] Ibid, para 7.4.

- Where the reason for the negative clearance is that the agreement does not contain provisions that are restrictive of competition, or that the conduct does not amount to an abuse of a dominant position, the position is likely to be that, in accordance with the obligation on the OFT to deal with matters in a manner which is consistent with the treatment of corresponding questions arising in community law (in particular its duty to have regard to any relevant European Commission decision),[146] the OFT would in most cases not find an infringement of the Chapter I or Chapter II prohibition. The same applies for the UK courts, which are also subject to such a duty. There is therefore nothing to be gained by seeking guidance or a decision from the OFT.

- If, however, negative clearance is granted by the European Commission on the ground that there is not considered to be an effect on trade between Member States, it is quite possible that the agreement or conduct in question may nevertheless affect trade within the United Kingdom, in which case the OFT or a UK court could find that it infringes one of the UK prohibitions. Where this is a concern, a notification may also need to be made to the OFT—either on receipt of the EC comfort letter, or, if the parties consider an informal negative clearance of this type to be the likely outcome of the EC notification, simultaneously with the notification to the European Commission (see paragraph 12.89 below on the OFT's policy with dual notifications).

12.83 In the case of agreements, the advantages offered by a *notification to the European Commission for individual exemption* under Article 81(3) (formerly Article 85(3)) over a notification to the OFT for exemption from the Chapter I prohibition are even greater:

(iii) A notification to the European Commission for an exemption under Article 81(3) (formerly Article 85(3)) confers provisional immunity from both fines under EC law and penalties under the Competition Act during the period from the date of notification until the European Commission determines the matter or withdraws the benefit of provisional immunity.[147] The reverse will not apply: a notification to the OFT will provide such provisional immunity from penalties for infringement of the Chapter I prohibition,[148] but not fines under Article 81 (formerly Article 85).

---

[146] S 60.

[147] S 41.

[148] Ss 13(4) and 14(4). Under the Competition Act provisional immunity from penalties is given in respect of applications under Chap I for guidance or decision that the prohibition will not apply, as well as those for exemption. This differs from the position under EC law where provisional immunity from fines is available for notifications for individual exemption under Art 81(3) (formerly Art 85(3)), but not for notifications for negative clearance under Art 81 or 82 (formerly Art 85 or 86): Council Reg (EEC) 17, n 26 above, Art 15(5).

(iv) Where the European Commission makes a formal decision granting individual exemption under Article 81(3) (formerly Article 85(3)), this will also constitute an exemption from Chapter I (a parallel exemption[149]—see Chapter 6, paragraphs 6.07–6.31).[150] However, the reverse will not apply: an individual exemption from the Chapter I prohibition will not count as an exemption under Article 81(3), and so parties would still be at risk from action by the European Commission and in UK civil court proceedings by third parties relying on Article 81 (formerly 85).[151] Similarly, where an agreement has been notified under an Article 81 opposition procedure and either the European Commission does not oppose the agreement or its opposition is withdrawn, the agreement receives the benefit of a parallel exemption from the Chapter I prohibition.[152]

(v) An Article 81(3) (formerly Article 85(3)) exemption has effect in all EC Member States. A Chapter I exemption has no such effect: it covers only the UK (and does not preclude the application of Article 81 (formerly Article 85) in the UK if the agreement or conduct also affects trade between Member States).

(vi) The OFT is able to grant retroactive exemption, ie taking effect from a date earlier than the exemption decision, including earlier than the date of notification,[153] whereas generally the European Commission can grant exemption retroactive only to the date of notification.[154] There is therefore an advantage in notifying under EC law at the earliest date possible in order to establish the date from which Article 81(3) (formerly Article 85(3)) exemption can apply. If notification under UK law is subsequently considered necessary, it will be possible for the OFT to backdate the exemption.

---

[149] S 10(1)(b).

[150] However, the OFT can, under s 10(5), revoke or vary a parallel exemption in specified circumstances.

[151] Purely national agreements, that is agreements between parties located within one Member State which 'do not relate either to imports or exports between Member States' do not need to be notified in order to be eligible for an exemption under Art 81(3) (formerly Art 85(3)) (Council Reg (EEC) 17, n 26 above, Art 4(2)). However, this provision only offers exemption from the need to notify, not protection from Art 81(1) (formerly Art 85(1)) itself, and a fine may still be imposed in relation to such an agreement if it has not been notified: Joined Cases 240–252, 261, 262, 268 and 269/82 *Stichting Sigarettenindustrie v EC Commission* [1985] ECR 3831. In view of the uncertainty as to whether an agreement would fall within this exception and the fact that the only way to be certain about obtaining an immunity from fines is to notify, this provision in practice offers little comfort to parties.

[152] S 10(1)(c).

[153] S 4(5).

[154] Council Reg (EEC) 17, n 26 above, Art 6(1). The Commission is able to grant Art 81(3) (formerly Art 85(3)) exemptions retroactive to a date earlier than notification for a limited category of agreements as defined in Art 4(2) (although its proposals for reform of the treatment of vertical restraints under Art 81 (formerly Art 85) include extending this Art 4(2) exception to vertical agreements—Proposal for a Council Reg (EC) amending Reg 17: First Reg implementing Arts 85 and 86 [now Arts 81 and 82] of the Treaty, 98/C 365/07 [1998] OJ C–365/30, Art 1), whereas the OFT can grant such exemptions to all types of agreement.

Where the European Commission concludes an Article 81 or 82 (formerly Article   **12.84** 85 or 86) notification informally by means of a *'comfort letter'* rather than a formal decision, as is often the case, this may provide the parties some advantages before the OFT depending on the nature of the comfort given (see paragraph 12.68 above on the treatment of EC comfort letters).

Cases Requiring Dual Notification

It can be seen from the preceding paragraphs that, because of the advantages   **12.85** offered by notification under EC law, it will often be more appropriate to make a notification only to the European Commission. Similar considerations apply in respect of conduct which may fall under Article 82 (formerly Article 86) and the Chapter II prohibition.

However, where it is unclear whether the effect on trade between Member States   **12.86** criterion is satisfied, it may nevertheless be desirable to make notifications to both the European Commission and the OFT.

In such cases where there may be a need to make dual notifications, the OFT has   **12.87** indicated as regards agreements that it should nevertheless not be necessary to notify both authorities at the outset. It encourages parties to consult it informally on the appropriate authority for notification.[155] It has also indicated that, in possible dual notification cases where in fact only the European Commission is notified, but the Commission declines jurisdiction due to the absence of an effect on trade between Member States, or where a civil action under the Competition Act subsequently arises in the UK courts, the OFT will endeavour to give priority to any notification the parties then consider it necessary to make under the Chapter I prohibition.[156] In those cases where agreements are subsequently challenged in the UK courts, the OFT has also indicated that, where an agreement fulfils the exemption criteria, the OFT is likely to grant exemption with retroactive effect (eg to the date on which the EC notification was made).

The OFT has provided some procedural alignment where parties do decide to   **12.88** make a dual notification. There will be no need to repeat in the Form N all the information given to the European Commission in Form A/B, but information specific to the UK market must be included to the extent not already given in Form A/B and three copies of Form A/B should be enclosed (four if a utility sector regulator has concurrent jurisdiction) in the notification to the OFT.

The OFT has also given an indication of its policy in cases where dual notifica-   **12.89** tions have been made.[157] There will be close liaison between the OFT and the European Commission, and, where it is clear that the European Commission will

---

[155] OFT, n 27 above, para 7.6.
[156] Ibid, paras 7.7 and 7.13.
[157] Ibid, paras 7.9–7.10.

deal with the agreement either by formal decision or by a comfort letter, the OFT will generally take no action until the European Commission has completed its assessment and informed the parties. However, in two circumstances the OFT will, exceptionally, proceed immediately to consider the notification it has received rather than waiting for the European Commission to complete its case:

(i) where the agreement raises particular concerns in relation to competition in the UK; or

(ii) where the OFT considers the agreement involves important legal, economic or policy developments (an example of an economically important agreement would be a large joint venture).

In the rarer cases of conduct which parties are considering whether to notify under Article 82 (formerly Article 86) and the Chapter II prohibition, it can be presumed that the OFT will adopt a similar approach.

13

COMPLAINTS AND WHISTLE-BLOWING

A. Overview

Complaints about possible infringements of the Act may be made to the OFT or, **13.01** if the alleged infringement falls within the jurisdiction of a sector regulator, to the relevant sector regulator. The purpose of the complaint is to persuade the OFT or the regulator that there are reasonable grounds for suspecting an infringement of either the Chapter I or Chapter II prohibition and thus encourage the OFT or the regulator to commence an investigation.

B. Who May Complain?

The Act does not set out a formal procedure for making a complaint, neither does **13.02** it indicate what degree of interest in the matter a complainant must show in order for its complaint to be considered.[1] The OFT has a discretion whether to conduct an investigation. It is unlikely that a complaint made by a third party with no interest in the matter complained about would be pursued by the OFT in the absence of other complaints or broader concerns. The most likely complainants are parties to an agreement that may infringe the Chapter I prohibition; suppliers, customers, licensors, licensees or distributors (or potential suppliers, customers,

---

[1] This may be compared to the position on the European Community law where a complainant must demonstrate 'a legitimate interest'; Council Reg (EEC) 17/62, First Regulation Implementing Arts 85 and 86 of the Treaty Art 3(2)(b). This has never been defined by the Court.

licensors, licensees or distributors) who consider that they have been adversely affected by a restrictive agreement or abusive behaviour; competitors who consider that conditions of competition are being restricted because of agreements or behaviour that are anti-competitive and individual consumers or consumer groups who believe that anti-competitive agreements or behaviour are having an adverse effect on the market. Complaints may be brought by groups, such as consumer groups, trade unions or trade associations. Public bodies, such as local authorities or health authorities, may complain, for example, if they suspect that suppliers have been involved in collusive tendering.

C. Timing

13.03 There is no stipulated period within which a complaint should be made. However, if the complainant seeks interim measures as well,[2] the complaint should be made as soon as possible after the complainant becomes aware of the agreement or behaviour in question; this is because one of the factors which will be taken into account when the OFT decides whether to adopt interim measures is the urgency of the situation.

D. Sector Regulator or OFT?

13.04 Complaints must be made to either a sector regulator or the OFT—not to both.[3] Where a complaint relates to issues falling within the concurrent jurisdiction of a sector regulator, the complaint will usually be dealt with by that regulator rather than the OFT.[3a] If a complaint relates to an industry that falls within the scope of a sector regulator it should therefore normally be made to that regulator. In particular, if the complaint alleges infringement of both a licence condition and the prohibitions in the Act in relation to the same subject matter, it will be considered by the sector regulator.[4] Complainants will be told as soon as possible which authority is dealing with the case, and of any subsequent changes.[4a]

---

[2] See Ch 10, paras 10.75–10.84.
[3] OFT, Competition Act 1998: 'Concurrent Application to Regulated Industries (OFT 405) para 3.5.
[3a] Office of Fair Trading, Competition Act 1995: 'The Major Provisions' (OFT 400), para 3.5.
[4] Where new information comes to light after the original complaint has been submitted it should be sent to the authority which dealt with the original complaint: ibid, para 3.5.
[4a] OFT, note [3a] above, para 3.5.

E. UK Authorities or European Commission?

Where a complaint relates to an agreement or behaviour that affects trade between **13.05** Member States of the European Community as well as affecting trade within the United Kingdom, the complainant will have a choice whether to complain to the European Commission or the OFT.

If a notification has been made by the parties to the agreement or behaviour to the **13.06** European Commission then any complaint relating to the notified arrangement or related matter should be addressed to the European Commission. This will also be the case where, for example, the European Commission has granted a clearance and a complainant wishes to raise matters that it believes were not fully disclosed to the European Commission or wishes to argue that circumstances have changed since the clearance was given.

If no notification has been made to the regulatory authorities by the parties to an **13.07** agreement or behaviour a complainant, in choosing its jurisdiction, will wish to identify the authority that is most likely to pursue the complaint. In this regard the Court of First Instance (CFI) had made it clear that the European Commission is entitled to reject a complaint which does not display sufficient Community interest to justify further investigation.[5]

The European Commission has stated that it intends to concentrate on notifica- **13.08** tions, complaints and own-initiative proceedings having particular political, economic or legal significance to the Community. Where these features are absent in a particular case, complaints should, as a rule, be handled by national courts or authorities.[6] In cases where there is a clear UK significance, for example, because the parties are all UK parties or the agreement primarily relates to the UK then, unless there are exceptional circumstances, the complaint should be directed to the OFT which would be more likely to investigate than the European Commission. Even in more marginal cases, for example, where the agreement involves non-UK parties but it has a particular impact on the UK market, it will be the case that, unless there are elements that give rise to a particular Community significance, a complaint to the OFT is more likely to result in an investigation than is a complaint to the European Commission.

It is possible that a respondent to a complaint made to the OFT may subsequently notify the relevant agreement to the European Commission. Where an agreement is notified to the European Commission seeking an exemption under Article 81(3) (formerly Article 85(3)) the CFI has held that, because the European

---

[5] Case T–24/90 *Automec Srl v EC Commission ('Automec II')* [1992] ECR II–2223.
[6] European Commission notice on co-operation between national courts and the Commission in applying Arts 85 and 86 [now Arts 81 and 82] of the EEC Treaty [1993] OJ C39/6)

Commission has exclusive powers to apply Article 81(3), the applicant has the right to obtain a decision from the European Commission on the substance of its request for an exemption.[7] A respondent to a complaint to the OFT may therefore seek to circumvent the OFT's investigation by making a notification to the European Commission. In such cases the European Commission is likely to leave the substantive investigation of whether there has been an infringement of the Chapter I prohibition to the OFT. If there has been such an infringement then, subject to the question whether there is an effect on trade between Member States, there is also likely to have been an infringement of Article 81(1) (formerly Article 85(1)). In the event that it is found that there has been an infringement, the European Commission would then decide whether to grant an exemption under Article 81(3) (formerly Article 85(3)). This would be in accordance with the principles set out in the European Commission's notice on co-operation with national competition authorities.[8]

13.09   The European Commission notice also provides, in such circumstances, for the OFT to have the power to ask the European Commission for its provisional opinion on the likelihood of the notified agreement being exempted. The European Commission has indicated that it would deliver its provisional opinion on this, in the light of a preliminary examination of the questions of fact and law involved, as quickly as possible once the complete notification is received. If the examination of a notification reveals that the agreement in question is unlikely to qualify for exemption under Article 81(3) (formerly Article 85(3)) and that its effects are mainly confined to one Member State, the opinion will state that further investigation of the matter is not a priority for the European Commission. This view will be given in writing to the national authority and the notifying parties. This letter will also state that it will be highly unlikely for the European Commission to take a decision before the national authority has taken its final decision and that the notifying parties retain their immunity from fines. The OFT should, in such cases, undertake to contact the European Commission forthwith if its investigation leads it to a conclusion which differs from the European Commission's opinion, for example, if the OFT concludes that the Chapter I prohibition would not be infringed. Thus, in effect, the European Commission would give priority to the UK investigation in relation to the Chapter I prohibition. The European Commission would only initiate proceedings, and thus take the matter out of the hands of the OFT, in exceptional circumstances, for example, where against all expectations the OFT is likely to find that there has been no infringement of the

---

[7]   Case T–23/90 *Automobiles Peugeot SA v EC Commission* [1991] ECR II–653.
[8]   European Commission notice on co-operation between national competition authorities and the European Commission in handling cases falling within the scope of Art 85 or 86 [now Art 81 or 82] EC [1997] OJ C313/3.

Chapter I prohibition or where national proceedings are unduly long and drawn-out.[9]

F. Contents of a Complaint

There is no official form for submitting a complaint but guidance as to the **13.10** information normally required has been set out by the OFT.[10]

A complaint to the OFT is more likely to trigger an investigation by it if the com- **13.11** plaint is properly substantiated. The complaint should set out some evidence indicating why there are reasonable grounds to suspect that the prohibitions have been infringed. This may include, for example, evidence relating to price movements; copies of documents, such as correspondence or press statements, suggesting that there may have been an infringement, or statements from parties who have been involved in, or have knowledge of, the alleged anti-competitive activities.

The complaint should normally state: **13.12**

(i) *the identity of the person making the complaint.* A complaint is more likely to be effectively pursued by the OFT if the identity of the complainant is disclosed. The OFT has stated that there may be practical difficulties in pursuing anonymous complaints where full information is not available and clarification cannot be sought from the applicant.[11] However, an anonymous complaint that contains strong evidence of an infringement may encourage the OFT to investigate further on its own initiative;

(ii) *relationship to the respondent and the reason for the complaint.* For example, whether the complainant is a competitor or customer of the company complained about.

(iii) *details of the complaint.* It is helpful to include as much detail as possible, for example, if an infringement of the Chapter II prohibition is being alleged an explanation of why it is considered that the relevant company is dominant (including, where available, relevant market and market share information for the undertakings concerned and competitors); and as much detail as possible about the alleged abuse, for example, the occasions on which the abusive behaviour occurred and a description of the acts that gave rise to and constituted the abusive behaviour;

(iv) *details of the harm caused.* If there is evidence of the harm caused to the complainant or others as a result of the alleged infringement it would be important to include in such evidence, for example, an indication of business lost

---

[9] European Commission, n 8 above, paras 55–63.
[10] OFT, n [3a] above, paras 8.1–8.5.
[11] OFT, n 10 above, para 8.2.

or details of the effect of the respondent's behaviour on prices or profitability. Evidence of the harm caused would, in any event, be essential if interim measures are also sought;[12]

(v) *documentary evidence.* If appropriate, copies of relevant correspondence or telephone attendance notes;

(vi) *information about the relevant market.* Where available, a market description; market values and volumes; market shares of the undertaking complained about and the complainant and major competitors and broad details of competitive conditions in the market, for example recent entry and recent exits from the market. If independent studies concerning the market exist, for example, analysis reports, they should be provided.

G. Confidentiality

13.13   In order to exercise its right of defence, the respondent will have to have all relevant details of the complaint. To the extent that confidentiality requirements requested by the complainant mean that this is not possible, it will be more difficult for the OFT to proceed with the case.

13.14   If the complainant does not wish the company complained about to know that it has made a complaint, this should be made clear to the OFT at the time that the complaint is submitted or earlier if there are earlier discussions with the OFT.[13] However, in many cases, even if the details of the complainant's name is withheld, its identify will be apparent from the content and context of the complaint.

13.15   The respondent will usually be asked to comment on the complaint and may be given copies of the complaint and relevant correspondence. In the event that the OFT proposes to make an infringement decision, the respondent has a right to examine the documents in the OFT's files, unless any document is considered to be confidential.[14] It is therefore essential that any confidential material is included in a separate annex and is clearly indicated. An explanation of why the information is considered to be confidential should be included.

13.16   The test for deciding whether information is confidential is high. It must either be:

- commercial information, the disclosure of which would, or might, significantly harm the legitimate business interests of the undertaking to which it relates;[15]

---

[12] See Ch 10, para 10.75–10.84.
[13] OFT, n 10 above, para 8.4.
[14] OFT, Formal Consultation Draft, Competition Act 1998: 'The Draft Procedural Rules Proposed by the Director General of Fair Trading' (OFT 411), Rr 14(1)(c) and 14(2)(a).
[15] S 56(3)(i) and OFT, n 14 above, R 27(1)(b)(i)

or

- information relating to the private affairs of an individual, the disclosure of which would, or might, significantly harm his interests.[16]

An indication of the extent to which the OFT may regard information as falling within the scope of the confidentiality provisions is given by its practice in relation to the treatment of applications to place details of an agreement registered under the Restrictive Trade Practices Act (RTPA) on the 'special section' of the Register.[17] Under the RTPA information may be placed on the special section, and therefore not open to public inspection, where, in the opinion of the Secretary of State, the information would 'substantially damage the legitimate business interests of any person'. It is likely that the test under the Competition Act involves a lower threshold than the test under the RTPA on a basis that 'substantial' damage is more serious than 'significant' harm. A further difference is that the RTPA refers to damage to the business interests of 'any person' whereas the Procedural Rules under the Act refer to the legitimate business interests of 'the undertaking to which [the information] relates'. In applying the RTPA test the Secretary of State has accepted, for example, that sensitive pricing information may be included in the special register provided it would cause substantial damage, that is, something greater than ordinary damage.   **13.17**

In general, it may be anticipated that information about current, or very recent, pricing or terms and conditions of trade would satisfy the significant harm test. Similarly, disclosure of information about confidential business investment plans may give rise to significant harm. Information relating to prices paid by an undertaking may also satisfy the test. A more difficult category of information is where disclosure might cause embarrassment but not harm, for example, internal discussions within a company about the merits of competitors or the likely business prospects of customers.   **13.18**

The test of confidentiality described above and set out in rule 27 is not the only test that the OFT may apply in deciding whether to withhold information on grounds of confidentiality. It may also withhold other information at the 'access to file' stage[18] which 'in the opinion of the Director' is otherwise confidential.[19]   **13.19**

The OFT is not obliged to comply with the complainant's request for confidentiality but generally, to the extent that it proposes to disclose any information that has been requested should be kept confidential, it must, if reasonably practicable, consult the complainant and the OFT has indicated that it will do this as regards information provided by a complainant in a confidential annex.[20]   **13.20**

---

[16] S 56(3)(ii) and OFT, n 14 abvove, R 27(1)(b)(ii).
[17] See RTPA, s 23(3)(a) and (b).
[18] See Ch 14, para 14.87.
[19] OFT, n 14 above, R 14(2).
[20] Ibid, para 2.5(2); OFT, n 10 above, para 8.2.

H. Involvement of the Complainant

13.21 If the OFT considers that the complaint does not reveal a possible breach of the rules, it will inform the complainant as soon as possible and the matter will be closed.[21] Generally, the OFT will provide the complainant with as much detail as possible, although this is not an automatic right.

13.22 The position of the complainant is different from that of a party to litigation before a court. If the OFT commences an investigation, the control of the investigation lies with the OFT. Thus, the fact that a complainant subsequently chooses to withdraw a complaint will not necessarily result in the proceedings coming to an end if the OFT considers that there continue to be sufficient grounds for reasonably suspecting an infringement. Indeed, to the extent that the complainant has documents or information that are necessary for the purposes of the investigation, the OFT may exercise its powers to require the complainant to produce the relevant document or provide the relevant information, and it may even conduct an investigation on the complainant's premises.

13.23 A complainant has no right to be kept informed of the progress of an investigation. The OFT has an obligation, before making a decision that the Chapter I or Chapter II prohibition has been infringed, to give written notice of the proposed decision to persons 'likely to be affected by the proposed decision' and to give such persons an opportunity to make representations.[22] The draft procedural rules require notice to be given to parties to the relevant agreement or conduct.[23] A complainant is therefore not necessarily a person likely to be affected, although in some cases, it may be, for example if the complainant is a party to an agreement that it is considered may infringe the Chapter I prohibition.

13.24 In the event that the OFT decides that the prohibitions have not been infringed, a complainant with a 'sufficient interest'[24] may make a reasoned request to the OFT in writing to withdraw or vary the decision.[25] Such an application must be made within one month of the publication of the decision. If the OFT refuses to withdraw or vary the decision following such a request, it must notify the applicant accordingly.[26] The applicant may then appeal to the Competition Commission against the decision of the OFT.[27]

---

[21] OFT, n 10 above, para 8.3.
[22] S 31(2).
[23] OFT, n 14 above, R 14.
[24] See Ch 16, paras 16.05–16.12.
[25] S 47 and OFT, n 14 above, R 26(1).
[26] S 47(4).
[27] S 47(6).

The making of such an application does not have the effect of suspending the **13.25** decision.[28]

I. Whistle-blowing

One of the difficulties faced by competition authorities—particularly in cartel **13.26** cases where a number of firms seek to agree matters such as common prices or production quotas—is proving such matters. In some cases there may be a 'smoking gun', for example, notes of meetings disclosed as a result of an on-site investigation. In others there may be economic evidence of co-ordination, although this is notoriously hard to establish. The most effective evidence is likely to come from disclosure by a party to the cartel. In some cases parties may wish to disengage themselves from the cartel but are concerned about the consequences. In such cases, an indication from the authorities that they will agree a significant reduction in fines, or even the non-imposition of fines, may encourage and support such 'whistle-blowing'. The European Commission has issued a notice indicating the circumstances in which it would exercise leniency to whistle-blowers[29] in cases relating to secret cartels aimed at fixing prices, production or sales quotas, sharing markets or banning imports or exports. The notice sets out circumstances in which the volunteering of information will lead to the non-imposition of a fine or a very substantial reduction in its amount; a substantial reduction or a significant reduction.

The OFT has indicated that it will have regard to the European Commission's **13.27** notice when imposing a penalty or deciding on the amount of a penalty for an infringement of the Chapter I prohibition.[30] There is therefore an incentive for undertakings to volunteer information relating to cartels.

The European Commission notice states that there will be non-imposition or a **13.28** very substantial reduction of at least 75 per cent where an enterprise:

(a) informs the European Commission about a secret cartel before the Commission has undertaken an investigation provided it does not otherwise have evidence to establish the cartel's existence;

(b) is the first to adduce decisive evidence of the cartel's existence;

(c) puts an end to its involvement in the cartel no later than the time of disclosure;

---

[28] S 47(7).
[29] European Commission notice on the non-imposition or reduction of fines in cartel cases, 10 July 1996 [1996] OJ C207/4.
[30] OFT, Competition Act 1998: 'Enforcement' (OFT 407), para 4.39.

(d) provides the European Commission with all relevant information and documents concerning the cartel and continues to co-operate through the investigation;

(e) has not compelled another enterprise to take part in the cartel and has not acted as an instigator or played a determining role in it.

An enterprise satisfying points (b) to (e) above, and which discloses information to the European Commission after it has ordered an on-site investigation on the premises of parties to the cartel which has failed to provide sufficient evidence to initiate proceedings, will benefit from a reduction in fine of 50 to 75 per cent.

13.29 In other cases an enterprise which co-operates may benefit from a 10 to 50 per cent reduction in fine. This may include a situation where, after proceedings are commenced, the enterprise does not substantially contest the Commission's case.

14

INVESTIGATIONS BY THE OFT AND RIGHTS OF DEFENCE

A. Overview

The Competition Act provides the OFT with extensive new powers of investigation, which mark a considerable change as compared with the previous regime. The OFT may investigate an arrangement or behaviour following notification by the parties, receipt of a complaint by another party or on its own initiative. The procedures regarding notifications are reviewed in Chapter 12, and the making of complaints is considered in Chapter 13. This chapter looks at the OFT's powers and procedures in relation to investigations.   **14.01**

14.02 For the purposes of an investigation, the OFT may:

- require the production of documents or information;
- enter premises without a warrant; and
- enter *and* search premises with a warrant.

The latter two powers to conduct on-site investigations (commonly called 'dawn raids', in cases where no advance notice is given) represent a significant departure from the previous UK regime, where no such powers existed. Each of the three broad powers is considered below, as are: the sanctions for not co-operating with an OFT investigation (criminal offences); the limitations on the OFT's investigatory powers; and the powers of investigation that the OFT is able to exercise under other relevant competition law. Some consideration is also given to the best approach to be taken in practice by parties facing an on-site investigation by the OFT.

14.03 Finally, the Act gives a number of protections to parties who are the subject of infringement proceedings. In particular, they have the right to know the OFT's case against them; the right to make written and oral representations and a right of access to the OFT's file. These 'rights of defence' are reviewed.

14.04 Where instructive, comparison is made with the powers of the European Commission when investigating under Articles 81 and 82 (formerly Articles 85 and 86). A difficult question which follows from this is the extent to which principles of EC procedure must be followed by the OFT, ie whether procedural aspects of EC law are imported into the context of investigations under the Act as a result of the obligations for consistency with EC law which arise under section 60. This issue is considered in Chapter 3 paras 3.58–3.60.

B. When Investigatory Powers Can be Used

14.05 The OFT may conduct an investigation if 'there are reasonable grounds for suspecting' that either the Chapter I or Chapter II prohibition has been infringed.[1] This is not a high threshold. Obvious examples giving rise to reasonable grounds for suspicion would be sight of copies of secret agreements given by disaffected members of a cartel (or even information from members of the cartel that such agreements exist) or statements from ex-employees. But the fact that a number of competing undertakings have identical prices, or regularly change their prices at the same time, may be enough to constitute reasonable grounds for suspecting that a restrictive arrangement exists, even though there may be other equally reasonable explanations for such similarities in behaviour. The OFT stated in a draft

---

[1] S 25.

of its guidelines on Powers of Investigation that a reference to anti-competitive behaviour in a newspaper alone will not give rise to reasonable grounds for suspecting an infringement.[2] This was deleted from the final version of the guidelines.

This starting point for the use of the investigatory powers is a lower threshold than **14.06** the triggers for exercising powers of investigation under the previous UK competition legislation. In particular, it contrasts with the grounds for action under the legislation concerning the control of anti-competitive agreements which the Competition Act is replacing—the Restrictive Trade Practices Act 1976—under which the OFT needed 'reasonable cause to believe' that a person had entered into an agreement caught by the Act in order to request information.

The OFT has indicated that it will in practice seek to obtain information through **14.07** informal inquiries, whether written or oral, in addition to—or instead of—using its investigatory powers under the Act.[3] In many cases parties may find it beneficial to co-operate with the OFT on this basis rather than triggering use of the formal powers, with the possible sanctions for non-co-operation they entail. There is also the risk that non-compliance with an informal request will lead the OFT to draw adverse implications on the question being investigated. Refusing to comply with an informal request may nevertheless be of benefit in some cases by giving the undertaking a breathing space that allows it to prepare properly for a formal investigation.

C. Production of Documents and Information

The OFT may require any person to produce a specified document or specified **14.08** information which it considers relates to any matter relevant to the investigation.[4]

The duty to produce documents or information when requested is not restricted **14.09** to the parties to the alleged anti-competitive agreement or behaviour. Competitors, suppliers or customers may be asked to supply information relating to, for example, market size and market shares or competitive conditions on the relevant market. An adviser to the alleged participants may be required to produce documents or information.[5]

This power must be exercised by written notice.[6] There is no requirement that **14.10** the notice be signed by the Director General of Fair Trading, in contrast to the

---

[2] Office of Fair Trading, Formal Consultation Draft, Competition Act 1998 'Powers of Investigation' (OFT 404), para 2.1.
[3] OFT, n 2 above, para 2.3.
[4] S 26(1).
[5] Subject to the rules on legal privilege—see paras 14.67–14.69 below.
[6] S 26(2).

provisions relating to the authorisation of entry to premises without a warrant (see paragraph 14.21 below), where the Director General's personal signature is required. The notice will specify the documents required. It must:

(i)   set out the subject matter and purpose of the investigation; and

(ii) describe the various offences that the person would be committing if he fails to comply with the obligation to produce the document, destroys or falsifies a document, or provides false or misleading information.[7]

14.11 The notice may also specify:

(iii) the time and place at which the document or any information is to be produced;

(iv) and the manner and form in which it is to be produced or provided.[8]

14.12 If the document is produced, the OFT may take copies or extracts from it and may require any present or past officer or employee to provide an explanation.[9] A person asked for such an explanation may be accompanied by a legal advisor.[10] If a document is not produced the person may be required to state, to the best of his knowledge and belief, where the document is.[11]

14.13 A 'specified document' is one which is specified, or described, in the notice (for example: 'the memorandum prepared for the marketing meeting that took place on 3 January 1999'), or it could be a document which falls within a category of documents that are specified or described in the notice (for example: 'the marketing director's desk diaries for the years 1996–1999').[12]

14.14 The term 'document' covers information recorded in any form, so including computer and e-mail records, and 'information' includes estimates and forecasts.[13] The power entitles the OFT to require the compilation of information which is not otherwise available in documentary form. Thus, the marketing director of a particular company may be asked to compile information on market shares. It may also be the case that, for example, customers of an undertaking that is being investigated may be asked to provide information concerning the occasions on which the undertaking has refused to supply or has increased prices.

14.15 The OFT has indicated that this power of investigation is the one that it will tend to rely on most frequently, but also that it will not necessarily use the power before

---

[7] S 26(3).

[8] S 26(5).

[9] S 26(6)(a) and see para 14.25(iii) below.

[10] Office of Fair Trading, Formal Consultation Draft, Competition Act 1998: 'The draft Procedural Rules proposed by the Director General of Fair Trading' (OFT 411), Rule 13(3).

[11] S 26(6)(b).

[12] S 26(4).

[13] S 59(1).

carrying out an on-site investigation—for example, it may be used for the first time after the on-site investigation to clarify facts that have emerged. There is nothing to preclude the power being used more than once in an investigation, for example, to produce further information following consideration of material provided in response to an earlier notice.[14]

Comparison with the Position under EC law

The power of the OFT to require documents and information is similar to that of the European Commission under EC law,[15] but its scope is in a number of respects wider than the EC power. **14.16**

First, the EC law power is restricted to obtaining 'all necessary information',[16] whereas the Act entitles the OFT to require any information that it 'considers relates to any matter relevant to the investigation'.[17] In practice the scope of the EC power is interpreted widely,[18] but the test in the Act is a subjective one and there are circumstances where it may be that the OFT would have the power to require information where the European Commission would not. One example is where information is required by the Commission from a third party in order to help establish whether other information it has been provided with is correct. It is arguable that such third party information is not 'necessary' to the investigation, given that the relevant information is already available to the authorities, but in an investigation under the Act there could be little doubt that this third party information related to a matter relevant to the investigation such that the OFT could require its provision. **14.17**

A second more significant difference in the scope of the respective powers is that the European Commission is restricted to obtaining information from Member States, undertakings and associations of undertakings,[19] whereas the OFT has the power to require any person to provide information, which includes an individual.[20] The Act therefore entitles the OFT to require particular employees or ex-employees to provide information. Individuals also run the risk of committing the criminal offences that arise for non-compliance (see paragraph 14.51 below). **14.18**

Thirdly, EC law provides for a two stage procedure for obtaining information. The European Commission must first make a written request, in respect of which there is no legal obligation on an undertaking to comply. It is only if the requested **14.19**

---

[14] Office of Fair Trading, n 2 above, para 3.1. The power may also be used if further information is needed following a notification for guidance or decision.

[15] Council Reg (EEC) 17 [1959–62] OJ Spec Ed 87, Art 11.

[16] Ibid, Art 11(1).

[17] S 26(1).

[18] Case T–39/90, *SEB v Commission I* [1991] ECR II–1497.

[19] See n 14 above.

[20] S 59(1).

information is not supplied within the time limit fixed by the European Commission or, if it is supplied incompletely, that the European Commission may take a decision requiring the relevant information to be supplied.[21] In contrast, the procedure under the Act is a single stage procedure imposing an immediate obligation to comply, although in practice the OFT may make an initial informal request.[22]

14.20 The European Commission's powers are also subject to the principles of proportionality and appropriateness.[23] It must only ask for documents or information that is necessary for the investigation and in a manner causing least inconvenience possible to the undertaking.[24] This procedural principle will apply in the UK (see Chapter 3 paragraphs 3.58 to 3.60 on relevant EC principles). In practice, however, it will be more difficult for an undertaking to ascertain whether the request is disproportionate to the needs of the investigation, given the wider OFT power. In view of the fact that there are express provisions in the Act to protect confidentiality, the confidentiality of the information requested will not of itself make the request disproportionate.[25]

D. Power to Enter Premises Without a Warrant

14.21 Any officer of the OFT who is authorised in writing by the Director General of Fair Trading to do so ('an investigating officer') may enter any premises in connection with an investigation.[26]

- *On-site inspection* with *notice*
  The general rule is that an investigating officer is required to give the occupier of the premises a written notice which:

  (i)   gives at least two working days' notice of intended entry;

  (ii)   indicates the subject matter and purpose of the investigation; and

  (iii) indicates the offences that would be committed if the person fails to comply, destroys or falsifies documents, or provides false or misleading information.[27]

  There is no requirement for the occupier of the premises to be suspected of infringement; for example, the occupier may be the supplier or customer of an undertaking which is suspected.

---

[21] See n 15 above, Art 11(5).

[22] See para 14.07 above.

[23] The CFI has held that 'the obligation on an enterprise to furnish information should not represent a burden for the enterprise which is disproportionate to the needs of the investigation' (Case T–39/90, *SEB v Commission* [1991] ECR II–1497).

[24] Case 36/79 *National Panasonic v Commission* [1980] ECR 2033.

[25] S 56.

[26] S 27(1).

[27] S 27(2).

- *On-site inspection* without *notice ('dawn raid')*

    The OFT does not need to give notice where it has reasonable suspicion that the premises are, or have been, occupied by a party to an agreement which is the subject of the investigation or an undertaking the conduct of which is the subject of the investigation.[28] Similarly, notice does not have to be given where the investigating officer has taken all reasonably practicable steps to give notice but has not been able to do so.[29]

    Where the investigating officer is exercising his power to enter the premises without notice, he must produce evidence of his written authorisation, and a document indicating the subject matter and purpose of the investigation and the nature of the offences that the occupier may be committing if he did not co-operate.[30]

The OFT has indicated that the investigating officer will normally arrive at premises during office hours and that he will produce evidence of his identity as well as the evidence of authorisation (which will also indicate that the occupier may request that his legal adviser is present).[31]   **14.22**

Premises can include domestic premises, but only if they are used in connection with the affairs of an undertaking (for example, where a business is run from home or, less certain, where a company officer habitually works from home or if business documents are kept there). Premises may also include any vehicle, for example, a company car.[32]   **14.23**

The investigating officer has no power to force entry when making an on-site inspection without a warrant—if he is denied entry he will have to obtain a warrant (see paragraph 14.33 below).   **14.24**

OFT's Powers During the Inspection

An investigating officer entering the premises may:[33]   **14.25**

(i)   take with him such equipment as appears to him to be necessary, for example, a laptop computer or recording equipment;

(ii)   require any person on the premises to produce any documents he considers relate to any matter relevant to the investigation;[34]

(iii) if the document is produced, require such a person 'to provide an explanation of it'. The extent of the obligation to provide an explanation is unclear.

---

[28] S 27(3)(a).
[29] S 27(3)(b).
[30] S 27(4).
[31] OFT, n 2 above, para 4.9.
[32] S 59(1).
[33] S 27(5).
[34] See para 14.17 above as regards the subjective test of relevance.

On a strict interpretation the obligation is likely to be limited to explaining matters directly related to the document—for example, the meaning of any abbreviations or shorthand in the document, or the way in which formulae or equations have been applied in a spreadsheet, or possibly how it relates to other documents referred to in the document that has been produced.

This can be contrasted with the position under EC law, where European Commission inspectors have the power to 'ask for oral explanations on the spot' during investigations.[35] This has been interpreted as giving rise to a right to ask for extensive explanations of issues arising out of the documents produced, for example, asking where data that forms the basis of calculations in a document were obtained from.[36] It is unlikely that the wider interpretation of the EC provision would be imported into the interpretation of section 27 of the Act as a result of section 60 (rather, there is a 'relevant difference' between EC law and the Act, such that the section 60 obligations do not arise). There is also a defence against self-incrimination (see paragraphs 14.70–14.75 below).

A further contrast with the EC position is that under EC law it is for the undertaking being investigated to nominate the person who will respond to the inspector's question.[37] Under the Act the inspector may require a specified person to provide an explanation. It is not clear from the wording of section 27(5) whether the person providing the document is the only person who can be required to provide an explanation or whether the inspector may require any person on the premises to provide the explanation. The common sense view would be that the explanation could be asked of a person other than the one producing the document because the person having access to the document is not necessarily the one who was responsible for compiling or receiving the document.

(iv) require any person to state where any such document is to be found.[38] This power is in addition to the obligation to produce a document at (ii) above and would be relevant where, for example, the person concerned did not have authority to enter the part of the building in which the document was stored or if the document was stored in another place, including domestic premises.

The obligations regarding documents at (ii) to (iv) above apply to any person on the premises, not just employees, and may therefore extend, for example, to a sub-contractor, such as a computer operator or a temporary secretary.

---

[35] Reg 17 (n 15 above), Art 14(1)(c).
[36] See Kerse, C. S., *EC Antitrust Procedure* (4th edn, Sweet & Maxwell, London, 1998), para 3.35.
[37] *Fabbrica Pisana* [1980] OJ L75/30.
[38] S 28(5)(c).

(v) take copies of, or extracts from, any document which is produced. There is no obligation on the occupier of the premises to produce copies of the documents, but the occupier would normally be well advised to assist in the production of copies in order to ensure that he has first hand knowledge of what documents the investigating officer has taken and to avoid unnecessarily drawing out the length of the investigation;

(vi) require any information which is held in a computer and is accessible from the premises, and which the investigating officer considers relates to any matter relevant to the investigation, to be produced in a form in which it can be taken away, *and* in which it is visible and legible.[39] Thus, the investigating officer can require a computer print-out in hard copy. However, it would not appear to include transferring information onto a floppy disc. Although this is a form in which the information can be taken away, it is not a form which is visible and legible.

In any case, for the purposes of the Act 'documents' includes documents in electronic form.[40] Thus the powers (described in (ii) to (v) above) to take possession of documents, to take copies of documents and to take steps to preserve documents apply in relation to information stored in electronic form (and therefore may include copying onto a floppy disc or a laptop computer). The power (described in (vi)) to require the production of computer information places an obligation on the occupier actively to assist the OFT in accessing information stored on a computer. It is to be noted that, although the information on a computer must be accessible from the premises, for example, from a computer terminal, there is nothing to stop the OFT requiring access to information being stored elsewhere, for example, an off-site computer database.

No Power to Search During On-site Inspections Without a Warrant

An investigating officer who enters premises under a written authorisation rather than a warrant does not have the power of search. He is dependent upon persons on the premises to whom he has made a request to produce documents or identify where documents are to be found. Thus, although he is able to take documents or computer print outs away, it appears that he does not have the right to open cupboards or filing cabinets, or access a computer system himself. This is in contrast to the position regarding on-site investigations with a warrant, where a power to search is expressly provided (see paragraph 14.36(b) below). **14.26**

However, parties who do not comply with a request to produce documents may be guilty of an offence (see paragraph 14.51 below).[41] A person asked to produce **14.27**

---

[39] S 28(5)(e).
[40] S 59(1).
[41] Ss 42–44.

a document which is in his possession or under his control must do so unless he can demonstrate it is not reasonably practicable, and likewise a person required to provide information or an explanation of a document must do so unless he can show a reasonable excuse not to.

14.28 EC law imposes a duty of active co-operation upon undertakings under investigation.[42] This means that it is unlikely to be sufficient just to show the investigating officer where the files are or to tell the investigating officer that he may have access to all the undertaking's files; the obligation is to produce the specific documents required.[43] Thus, although European Commission officials have no right of search, EC law has been described as imposing a 'duty to find' on the undertaking concerned. It is likely that a similar obligation to produce the specific documents requested by the inspector arises under the Act, since it clearly imposes a duty to produce the requested documents.

14.29 In respect of investigations under Articles 85 and 86, European Commission officials have the right to see documents *in situ* and to review all relevant files. However, there are differences between the relevant provisions of the Act and those of Regulation 17,[44] which sets out the procedure for investigations under Articles 85 and 86, that may indicate that the rights of an investigating officer under the Act are, in this respect, less extensive than those of a European Commission official. In particular, European Commission officials are authorised 'to examine the books and other business records' of the undertaking concerned,[45] whereas the Act authorises the investigating officer to require a person 'to produce any document which he considers relates to any matter relevant to the investigation'. Thus the Act clearly emphasises the obligation of the person on the premises to produce the document, with the possible implication that there is not a more extensive right for the inspector to see the documents *in situ*. This may be contrasted with the EC position where the right 'to examine' more obviously gives rise to the implication of a right to see the documents in their normal location.

14.30 An interpretation of the Act more in keeping with the position under EC law is that the right to enter premises includes a right to enter any part of the premises to which entry has been authorised and where the relevant business is conducted.

14.31 There is some authority for a wide interpretation of the term premises at EC level. In *AKZO*[46] a European Commission Decision authorised an investigation at the premises of AKZO Chemicals BV in Amersfoot and Hengelo in the Netherlands. In fact the office in which the relevant information was kept was in Arnhem.

---

[42] Case T–46/92 *Scottish Football Association v EC Commission* [1994] ECR II–1039.
[43] *Fabricca Pisana* (decision 80/334) [1980] OJ L75/30; Case 374/87, *Orkem v European Commission* [1989] ECR 3283.
[44] See n 15 above.
[45] See n 15 above Art 14(1)(a).
[46] *AKZO Chemicals BV* [1994] OJ L294/31.

AKZO refused the inspectors access to the Arnhem office on the ground that it was an office of AKZO NV (not AKZO Chemicals BV). The European Commission imposed a fine on AKZO Chemicals BV for failing to submit to the inspection. It held that when an undertaking is referred to in a Decision authorising an investigation, the investigation is not confined to the offices referred to in the Decision unless the Decision specifically restricts the geographic location. Further, to the extent that the business of AKZO Chemicals BV is carried on in the offices of AKZO NV (which was the case here) such offices are regarded as the premises of AKZO Chemicals BV.

As a matter of practice, OFT inspectors may well require sight of documents *in* **14.32** *situ* as a condition of agreeing to wait for an extended period for the arrival of lawyers (see paragraph 14.46 below regarding access to legal advice during an on-site investigation). Furthermore, if inspectors believe that the documents 'produced' to them were not complete, the undertaking being investigated would be well advised to show the investigators where the documents are normally stored so as to reduce the risk of a prosecution for obstruction for failure to produce all relevant documents or an investigation under warrant.

E. Power to Enter and Search Premises Under a Warrant

On the application of the OFT, a judge may issue a warrant if he is satisfied as to **14.33** one of the following circumstances:[47]

(i)   **failure to comply with a request for documents**: there are reasonable grounds for suspecting that there are on any premises documents, the production of which has been required under section 26 (production of specified documents or information) or section 27 (entry of premises without a warrant), and they have not been produced as required;

(ii)   **interference with documents**: there are reasonable grounds for suspecting that there are on any premises documents which the OFT has the power under section 26 to require to be produced, and that, if the documents were required to be produced, they would not be produced but would be concealed, removed, tampered with or destroyed; or

(iii)   **entry without a warrant not possible**: an investigating officer has attempted to enter premises in the exercise of his powers under section 27 but has been unable to do so, and there are reasonable grounds for suspecting that there are on the premises documents, the production of which could have been required under section 27.

---

[47] S 28(1).

14.34 The second ground for issue of a warrant is thus the only one where the OFT will be able to carry out an on-site investigation without use of one of the other two investigatory powers first.

14.35 The meaning of premises under this power is the same as that in respect of the OFT's power of entry without warrant (see paragraph 14.23 above).

OFT's Powers During the Inspection

14.36 A warrant authorises a named officer of the OFT, and any other OFT official to whom the Director General has given written authorisation to accompany the named officer, to:[48]

(a) enter the premises specified in the warrant, using such force as is reasonably necessary for the purpose. The OFT officer is able to use force only if he is prevented from entering the premises, and only such force as is reasonably necessary for the purpose of gaining entry to the premises. Force cannot be used against a person;

(b) search the premises and take copies of, or extracts from, any document appearing to be of a kind in respect of which the warrant was granted. This will enable the OFT to search particular offices, desks, and filing cabinets. The power to use force under (a) above applies only as regards the entry of premises; no ability to use force is provided in respect of the power to search. It therefore appears unlikely that, once on the premises, the OFT can use force to access, for example, locked rooms or sealed filing cabinets (although a party which refuses to open such offices or cupboards may risk an offence for obstructing the OFT—see paragraph 14.56 below);

(c) take possession of any such documents if such action appears to be necessary for preserving the documents or preventing interference with them, or if it is not reasonably practical to take copies of the documents on the premises. There is thus no right to take original documents if they are unlikely to be interfered with and suitable copying facilities are made available to the OFT officials on the premises—unless, perhaps, the volume of documents concerned is so great that it would not be reasonably practical to copy them on the premises;

(d) take any other steps which appear to be necessary for the purposes of preserving the documents or preventing interference with them. This may include, for example, sealing documents in a filing cabinet or a particular room where they have to be left overnight during a two-day inspection;

(e) require any person to provide an explanation of any document appearing to be of a kind required for the purposes of section 26 or 27 or to state where it

---

[48] S 28(2).

may be found. As with the equivalent power during entry of premises without a warrant (see paragraph 14.25(iii) above), there is no more general right to require information by means of an oral investigation on the spot;[49] and there is also a defence against self-incrimination (see paragraph 14.70 below).

(f) require any information which is held in a computer and is accessible from the premises and which the named officer considers relates to any matter relevant to the investigation, to be produced in a form in which it can be taken away and in which it is visible and legible. As with the equivalent power during entry without a warrant, this imposes an obligation on the occupier actively to assist the OFT in accessing computer information stored and, provided that the information is accessible from the premises, it may be stored on a computer located elsewhere.

14.37 As mentioned in respect of the power to enter premises without a warrant, a document for the purposes of the Act in any case extends to information recorded in any form,[50] and so the powers in (b) to (e) above include documents stored in electronic form and the power to search will extend to computer databases.

14.38 Any person entering premises by virtue of a warrant may take such equipment as appears to him to be necessary.[51] This might include lock-breaking equipment to allow entry by force, and IT equipment used to access, de-encrypt or prevent destruction of computer and e-mail records.

Documents in Respect of Which the OFT Can Take Action

14.39 The category of documents in respect of which action can be taken by the OFT as described in paragraph 14.36 above depends on the grounds under which the warrant is obtained:

- Where the warrant is granted after failure to comply with a request to produce documents, it will be those documents which were not produced.

- Where the warrant is granted after the OFT was unable to enter premises using its powers of entry to premises without warrant, it will be documents which the officer considers relate to any matter relevant to the investigation.

- Where the warrant is issued to prevent interference with documents, it will be the documents which the officer considers relate to any matter relevant to the investigation and would be concealed, removed, tampered with or destroyed; but, in addition, the warrant may also authorise appropriate action in relation to any other documents on the premises relating to the investigation where the

---

[49] As compared with investigations under Arts 85 or 86, where EC officials have power to require oral explanations on the spot—see n 15 above, Art 14(1)(c).

[50] S 59(1).

[51] S 28(4).

judge is satisfied that it is reasonable to suspect that there are also such documents on the premises.[52] This covers a situation where there are two sets of documents on the premises, the first of which it is believed will be destroyed and the second of which the OFT does not believe will be destroyed but which are nevertheless relevant to the investigation. Where a warrant is granted in relation to the first group of documents, the OFT has the same powers in relation to the second group provided that the warrant authorises such action in relation to the second group.

Any document of which possession is taken may be retained for a period of three months.[53]

The Warrant

14.40 The warrant, issued by a High Court judge,[54] must indicate the subject matter and purpose of the investigation and the nature of the offences that may be committed by a person who fails to comply with the relevant obligations, destroys or falsifies documents, or provides false or misleading information.[55] The warrant must specify the premises to be entered.[56] A warrant is in force for a period of one month beginning with the day on which it was issued.[57]

14.41 The warrant must be produced before the relevant powers are exercised,[58] and the OFT has indicated that the officer will produce evidence of his identity and present a document setting out his powers and alerting the party to the opportunity of requesting the presence of his legal adviser.[59] If there is no one at the premises when the named officer proposes to execute the warrant he must, before executing it:

(i) take such steps as are reasonable in all the circumstances to inform the occupier of the intended entry. It is not clear precisely what steps must be taken in order to comply with this obligation. The OFT has indicated that it will normally arrive at premises during office hours[60] but, if the proposed search is to take place outside business hours, the obligation would presumably extend to notifying a representative of the occupier of the intended search. If this is not possible, it is arguable that the obligation extends to delaying the entry until the start of normal business hours, unless there are reasonable grounds to

---

[52] S 28(3).
[53] S 28(7).
[54] In Scotland the relevant court is the Court of Session.
[55] S 29(1).
[56] S 28(6)(a).
[57] S 28(6).
[58] S 29(2).
[59] OFT, n 2 above, para 5.10.
[60] Ibid.

believe that the relevant documents would be interfered with. If the officer is unable to inform the occupier of the intended entry he must, when executing the warrant, leave a copy of it in a prominent place on the premises;[61] and

(ii) if the occupier is informed, afford him or his legal or other representative a reasonable opportunity to be present when the warrant is executed.[62] Generally the OFT can be expected to wait not more than an hour for a legal representative to arrive (see paragraph 14.47 below). If the occupier could reasonably arrive at the premises in a short period, but it would take longer for a legal adviser to arrive, the occupier could probably not require that entry be delayed until the legal adviser arrived, even if the occupier chose not to go to the premises within that shorter time scale.

If premises are unoccupied, or the occupier is temporarily absent, the named officer is obliged to leave the premises that he has entered by virtue of the warrant as effectively secured as he found them.[63]

14.42 The power to enter and search under warrant is therefore very wide-ranging and a wish to avoid entry under such powers will be an incentive to companies to co-operate in other circumstances with the OFT, whether informally or in relation to requests for documents or investigations commenced under the power to enter premises without warrant.

14.43 It has been suggested that the significance of the provisions permitting entry and search with a warrant can be overstated.[64] The fact that it is an offence to obstruct the officer investigating, or to fail to comply with his requirements in respect of an investigation without warrant will generally be enough to persuade the relevant undertaking to co-operate without exercise of the warrant. In any event, the OFT is likely to wish to avoid investigations under warrant as they are likely to be extremely resource-intensive. The OFT prefers co-operation to the use of its investigative powers in a trigger-happy way. However, the knowledge that such powers exist is likely to be an effective incentive to persuade firms to co-operate.

F. Access to Legal Advice During a Dawn Raid

14.44 The Act does not impose an obligation on the investigating officer to delay an on-site inspection without notice (under either section 27 or section 28) until legal advice is obtained. However, the procedural rules provide that, where the occupier

---

[61] S 29(4).

[62] S 29(3).

[63] S 28(5).

[64] Paper by George Peretz of Monckton Chambers, former in-house lawyer with the OFT, to the IIR Competition Law Compliance conference 19 May 1998, 'The Powers of the UK Authorities—Requests for Information and On-site Investigations'.

so requests, the investigating officer will wait 'a reasonable time' for the occupier's legal adviser to arrive before continuing the investigation, and if he is satisfied that any conditions he considers it appropriate to impose will be complied with.[65]

14.45 A reasonable time is defined only as 'such period of time as the officer considers is reasonable in the circumstances',[66] and the OFT has indicated that it will wait only a short time and that any delay must be kept to a strict minimum.[67] The OFT will not delay for legal advisers to arrive if the undertaking has an in-house legal adviser (presumably either already on the premises, or nearer to them than the external counsel—in which case the OFT may wait only until the in-house legal adviser arrives) or if the on-site inspection is following advance notice.[68]

14.46 The OFT has reserved the right to attach conditions when agreeing to wait for legal advisers to arrive due to the concern that any delay may allow an opportunity for evidence to be tampered with or other parties to a suspected infringement to be tipped off about the investigation. Thus, for example, the conditions could include the officer requiring a room or filing cabinets in which relevant documents are kept to be sealed pending the start of the inspection, for external e-mail to be suspended or for the officer to remain in occupation of particular offices.

14.47 Assuming that appropriate conditions to protect documents and other evidence from tampering are met, there appears to be no reason why the officer should not wait until such time as the company under investigation's specialist competition lawyers are able to arrive. However, the OFT has signalled that its practice will be to go no further than the European Commission.[69] European Commission officials generally wait no more than an hour, provided they are satisfied that in the meantime evidence will not be interfered with and that they will not be prevented from entering and remaining on the premises, and so it is likely that the OFT's investigating officer would be prepared to wait only for a similar period of fairly limited duration.

14.48 The undertaking being investigated is able to request the presence of its legal adviser at any time during the investigation,[70] but in most cases it will clearly be desirable for lawyers to be summoned at the beginning of the investigation (the investigating officer will make the undertaking aware of the option of requesting its legal adviser to be present when he arrives[71]), not least because there may be a

---

[65] See n 10 above, Rule 13(1).
[66] Ibid, R 13(2).
[67] See n 2 above, paras 4.10 and 4.11.
[68] Ibid, para 4.11.
[69] See n 2 above, para 4.10.
[70] Ibid, para 4.10; Rule 13(1) allows for this.
[71] Ibid, para 4.9.

greater likelihood that the investigating officer will not consider it reasonable to delay for legal advisors to arrive once the investigation is under way.

G. Penalties for Non-Compliance

There are a number of offences for which a person may be liable under the **14.49** Competition Act. The definition of 'person' for the purposes of these offences includes individuals as well as undertakings.[72] Thus, where an offence is committed, the individual member of a company's staff carrying out the relevant act may be personally liable. The company may be liable in addition, if the individual member of staff acted representing the company's 'directing mind and will.[73] This is likely to be the case where the individual is a director, but the class of individuals who can be said to represent a company's directing mind may also be wider than just senior management.[74] It may be difficult for the company to disclaim liability for the acts of more junior members of staff acting in the course of their employment, even if they act contrary to the company's stated policies.

In addition, where it is the case that the company is liable for an offence under the **14.50** Act, if it is proved that the offence has been committed with the consent or connivance of any director, manager, secretary or other similar officer of the company (or any person purporting to act in such capacity) or was attributable to such an officer's neglect, that person will be individually liable for the offence as well as the company.[75] The relevant offences are as follows.

Failure to Comply with a Requirement and Intentional Obstruction

A person is guilty of an offence if he *fails to comply with a requirement* imposed on **14.51** him under any of the three broad investigatory powers—section 26 (obligation to produce a document or information), section 27 (power to enter premises without a warrant) or section 28 (power to enter and search premises under a warrant).[76]

It is a defence for a person charged with such offences to prove: **14.52**

(i) that the document was not in his possession or under his control; and

(ii) that it was not reasonably practicable for him to comply with the requirement.[77]

---

[72] S 59(1).
[73] *Tesco Supermarket v Nattrass* [1971] All ER 127.
[74] *Meridian Global Funds Management Asia Ltd v Securities Commission* [1995] 3 WLR 413(PC).
[75] S 72.
[76] S 42(1).
[77] S 42(2).

14.53 For the defence to apply both these requirement must be satisfied. Thus, for example, if a secretary was asked, during an on-site inspection, to produce a particular document which she knew to be in her employer's desk drawer, she would not be in a position to claim as a defence that she did not have any right of access to the desk. If, however, the desk drawer was locked and she had no key it would be arguable that it was not reasonably practicable for her to comply with the requirement. Even in such a case, if the secretary was aware that the document had been typed on the office word processing system to which she had access, she may have an obligation to facilitate access by the OFT to the electronic version of the document.

14.54 There is an additional defence where the offence relates to a failure to provide information, or an explanation of a document, or to state where a document is to be found: it is a defence for the person to prove that he had a reasonable excuse for failing to comply with the requirement.[78]

14.55 To the extent that the OFT official concerned has failed to act in accordance with the requirements of sections 26 or 27, no offence is committed by a person who fails to comply with any requirement.[79]

14.56 A person is also guilty of an offence if he *intentionally obstructs* an officer acting in exercise of his powers under section 27, or one acting in exercise of his powers under a warrant issued under section 28.[80]

14.57 A person guilty of an offence is liable on summary conviction to a fine not exceeding £5,000,[81] and, on conviction on indictment, to an unlimited fine.[82] In the case of a person who is guilty of intentionally obstructing an officer in the exercise of his powers under a warrant (ie under section 28), he is liable on summary conviction to a fine not exceeding £5,000,[83] and on conviction on indictment, to imprisonment for a term not exceeding two years or to an unlimited fine or to both.[84]

Destroying or Falsifying Documents

14.58 A person is guilty of an offence if, having been required to produce a document under section 26, 27, or 28:

---

[78] S 42(3).
[79] S 42(4).
[80] S 42(5).
[81] Fines on summary conviction for offences under the Competition Act may be up to 'the statutory maximum', which is currently £5,000 (Interpretation Act 1978, s 5, sch 1; Magistrates Court Act 1980, s 32).
[82] S 42(6).
[83] See n 81 above.
[84] S 42(7).

(i)   he intentionally or recklessly destroys or otherwise disposes of it, falsifies it or conceals it; or

(ii) he causes or permits its destruction, disposal, falsification or concealment.[85]

A person guilty of such an offence is liably on summary conviction to a fine not exceeding £5,000,[86] and, on conviction on indictment, to imprisonment for a term not exceeding two years or to an unlimited fine or both.[87]

This offence can only be committed *after* an obligation to produce the document   **14.59**
is imposed. Thus, an undertaking that regularly destroys non-essential documents at specified intervals will not be guilty of an offence if documents relevant to an investigation have been destroyed prior to the investigation. An undertaking which discovers potentially embarrassing documents prior to the commencement of an investigation may similarly destroy such documents even outside a formal document disposal procedure. However, in the latter case the selective destruction of documents may well give rise to considerable suspicion on the part of the OFT once an investigation has commenced. In this regard, it is to be noted that the offence relating to the provision of false or misleading information[88] may be committed if an undertaking fails to disclose information relating to documents relevant to the investigation even if such documents have been destroyed. Thus, for example, even though an undertaking may have destroyed records of meetings with competitors it may commit an offence if, when asked for information, it fails to disclose that such meetings took place and that records were kept.

A person can be guilty of this offence if he 'recklessly' destroys documents, as   **14.60**
stated in (i) above. This may cover a situation where a company has a document retention policy involving the systematic destruction of documents or other records (including computer records) that do not have to be kept for specific purposes and where, having been required to produce a document, the company does not take steps to exclude the relevant documents from the scope of the document destruction regime with the result that the document is destroyed.[89]

False or Misleading Information

The third offence created under Part I of the Act is broader in that it applies in rela-   **14.61**
tion to any information provided by a person to the OFT in connection with any function of the OFT under Part I. It is not restricted to information provided in relation to section 26, 27 or 28 but includes, for example, information provided

---

[85] S 43(1).
[86] See n 81 above.
[87] S 43(2).
[88] See para 14.61 below.
[89] See para 14.64 below for further consideration of the meaning of recklessness.

in a complaint or in a notification (see Chapter 12, paragraph 12.42 as regards notifications).

14.62 A person is guilty of an offence if:

(i) he provides information which is false or misleading in a material particular, and he knows that the information is false or misleading in a material particular, or is reckless as to whether it is;[90] or

(ii) he provides any information to another person (a) knowing the information to be false or misleading in a material particular, or reckless whether it is false or misleading in a material particular, and (b) knowing that the information is to be used for the purpose of providing information to the OFT in connection with its functions under Part I of the Act.[91]

This covers a situation where, for example, one undertaking is making a notification on behalf of a number of undertakings and one of the other undertakings provides misleading information to the first knowing that the information is to be used in the notification. It also applies where, for example, a company director fails to disclose correct information to a company employee who is responding to an OFT request for information.

14.63 Information may be 'misleading' if it contains a material omission, for example, if in response to a request for information of dates of price increases, the information provided does not relate to all dates in which prices were increased.

14.64 The offence is committed if a person is reckless whether the information is false or misleading. This covers a situation where the person providing the information does not intend to mislead but takes an unjustifiable risk that the information is misleading. The offence is certainly committed where the person providing the information is aware of the risk that it is misleading and may be committed—depending on the definition of recklessness that is adopted by the courts—where, even though not aware of the existence of the risk, the person concerned fails to give any thought to the possibility of an obvious risk that the information is misleading (with the determination of obvious risk being judged from the perspective of a reasonable person, ie objectively).[92] Circumstances in which the offence may be committed recklessly include, for example, failure properly to take obvious measures to check or verify market share information or other market data.

14.65 A person guilty of an offence under these provisions is liable on summary conviction to a fine not exceeding £5,000,[93] and, on conviction on indictment,

---

[90] S 44(1).
[91] S 44(2).
[92] See *R v Caldwell* [1981] 1 All ER 961 and *R v Cunningham* [1957] 2 QB 396.
[93] See n 81 above.

to imprisonment for a term not exceeding two years or to an unlimited fine or both.[94]

H. Limits on the OFT's Powers

There are a number of limitations on the OFT's powers which a company subject to investigation should be aware of, as explained below.

14.66

Legal Privilege

There is no obligation to produce or disclose a privileged communication. This means a communication:

14.67

(i)   between a professional legal adviser and his client; or

(ii) made in connection with, or in contemplation of, legal proceedings for the purpose of those proceedings,

which in proceedings in the High Court[95] would be protected from disclosure on grounds of legal professional privilege.[96]

A 'professional legal adviser' has been interpreted in the UK courts to include an in-house lawyer as well external counsel. The definition of privileged communication is therefore broader than under EC law where privilege only attaches to written communications between an independent (that is an outside) lawyer entitled to practise in an EU Member State and any internal documents reporting the content of advice from outside counsel.[97]

14.68

As a matter of good practice businesses should keep privileged documents separate from other documents and in clearly marked files so that they are clearly identifiable in order to avoid the risk of such documents being disclosed in error, in particular, during an on-site investigation.

14.69

Privilege Against Self-incrimination

The extent to which undertakings may be required to produce information that would provide evidence establishing that the undertaking has infringed competition rules is an issue that has arisen under EC law.[98] EC law does not give rise to a right to silence in such circumstances where an infringement does not relate to a criminal matter but to an economic regulation. However, in order to preserve an

14.70

---

[94] S 44(3).
[95] Or, in Scotland, the Court of Session.
[96] S 30.
[97] Case 155/79, *AM&S Europe Limited v. EC Commission* [1982] ECR 1575.
[98] Case 27/88, *Solvay et Cie v EC Commission* [1989] ECR 3355; Case 347/87 *Orkem v EC Commission* [1989] ECR 3355.

undertaking's right of defence, the European Commission is not permitted to ask questions, the answers to which would necessarily oblige a company to admit the existence of the infringement. But this does not extend to a restriction on the right of the European Commission to require documents, even though the documents might establish the existence of an infringement, and so it is only a limited qualification on the Commission's powers.

14.71 The position under EC law is therefore that, whilst there is no obligation on a party to answer a question such as 'describe the occasions on which you met with competitor X to discuss prices', it is possible for the European Commission to ask: 'on what occasions did you meet with competitor X? What was discussed at those meetings?'

14.72 The OFT has acknowledged that these principles against self-incrimination will apply,[99] as a result of the operation of the 'governing principles' section (see Chapter 3, paragraphs 3.58–3.60 above), and that:

> the [OFT] may compel an undertaking to provide specified answers or specified information but cannot compel the provision of answers which might prove an admission on its part of the existence of an infringement which it is incumbent on the [OFT] to prove.

The OFT has, however, indicated that it will request documents or information relating to facts such as whether a particular employee attended a particular meeting.

14.73 Thus, while an undertaking may not be required to admit guilt, it may be required to answer questions that establish guilt. The limited scope of, and uncertainty surrounding, the extent of the right against self-incrimination will mean that in practice there will be few occasions on which it would be possible or sensible to seek to rely on the right.

14.74 In particular, a party wishing to take advantage of the right against self-incrimination therefore runs a risk of committing a criminal offence if it is subsequently held that the right was not relevant to the circumstances of his case, and as a result he has failed to comply with a requirement to produce information or intentionally obstructed an investigation.[100]

14.75 An excessively limited interpretation of the right against self-incrimination may well be in conflict with Article 6(1) of the European Convention on Human Rights, which provides the right to a fair hearing, including the privilege against self-incrimination.[101] Under the Human Rights Act 1998,[102] it is unlawful for

---

[99] OFT, n 2 above, para 6.3–6.4.
[100] S 42; see para 14.51 above.
[101] *Saunders v UK* (1997) 23 EHRR 313. *Funke v France* (1993) 16 EHRR 297.
[102] Human Rights Act 1998 s 6.

public authorities such as the OFT to act in any way incompatible with the Convention.

Protection of Confidential Information

Parties which are the subject of an investigation will be concerned to limit the **14.76** public disclosure of information obtained by the OFT. The OFT is subject to a general restriction on disclosure of information relating to the affairs of any individual or to any particular business of an undertaking during the lifetime of that individual or while the business is carried on, unless consent has been obtained from the person from whom the information was initially obtained and, if different, the relevant individual or business to which the information relates.[103] However, a significant exception to this requirement is where the disclosure is made for the purpose of facilitating the performance of any relevant functions of the OFT, which includes functions under Part I of the Act and any function under the Fair Trading Act 1973.[104]

There are further duties on the OFT regarding confidentiality where it is consid- **14.77** ering whether to disclose information, ie by publishing the material or otherwise making it available to third parties.[105] First, the OFT must have regard to the need for excluding, so far as is practicable, any information which it would be contrary to the public interest to disclose. Secondly, it must have regard to the need for excluding so far as practicable:

(i) commercial information, the disclosure of which would, or might, in its opinion, significantly harm the legitimate business interests of the undertaking to which it relates; and

(ii) information relating to the private affairs of an individual, disclosure of which would, or might, in its opinion, significantly harm that individual's interests.

The OFT must also consider the extent to which the disclosure is necessary for the **14.78** purposes that the OFT is proposing to make it.

The OFT has advised that, where a person supplies a document or information in response to a written notice (ie under section 26), material which is considered confidential should be clearly marked as such and put in a separate confidential annex.[106] Where documents or copies are supplied during the course of an on-site inspection, all information considered confidential should be identified as such to the OFT after the inspection (it is advisable to confirm confidentiality claims in

---

[103] S 55(1) and (2).
[104] S 55(3).
[105] S 56.
[106] OFT, n 2 above, para 6.5.

writing to the OFT). The OFT will edit documents where it proposes not to disclose such confidential information by blanking out the relevant sections or by aggregating figures.[107]

14.79 Where the OFT proposes to disclose any information submitted to it by persons who are not party to the agreement in question or who have not engaged in the investigated conduct, it will consult the person who provided it if it is practicable to do so,[108] and this will extend to information submitted by occupiers of premises visited who are not themselves suspected of an infringement but are, for example, the customers or suppliers of an undertaking which is suspected.

I. Approach to Dealing With a Dawn Raid

14.80 As a general rule, there is nothing to be gained by taking an unco-operative or aggressive approach towards the OFT officials. As explained in paragraph 14.51 above, the company, and the relevant individual, risk prosecution if such behaviour extends to failing to comply with requirements or intentional obstruction. As a practical matter, the company may learn less of the background and reasons for the investigation, and its representatives will find it more difficult to influence the OFT in ways beneficial to the company in the longer term. Adopting a careful but positive approach should put a company's representatives in a better position to monitor and to some extent influence the conduct of an investigation.

Preparing in Advance

14.81 A company which is operating in an industry sector or in particular circumstances where it believes there may be a risk of an OFT investigation may make a number of preparations in advance. In particular, it is advisable to:

(i) *nominate personnel to deal with the investigators.* The OFT has itself indicated that, when carrying out an investigation, an appropriate person should be designated as a point of contact for the OFT officer investigating.[109] For internal purposes, the senior executives who are to represent the company in dealings with the investigators should be identified in advance of any investigation. Such individuals can then be briefed in advance on the nature and the extent of the OFT's powers and on the appropriate procedures to be followed. A sufficient number of executives should be nominated to minimise the risk that no designated representative is in the office when the inspectors call. It is unwise to call on persons to play a leading role

---

[107] OFT, n 2 above, para 6.8.
[108] N 10 above, Rule 25.
[109] OFT, n 2 above, paras 4.9 and 5.10.

whose functions are peripheral to the likely areas of inquiry. A 'lead' representative should be identified, who can call on other senior managers as necessary. Personnel should be nominated at any site which is likely to be at risk of an inspection. The areas at the greatest risk are those in which marketing or sales records are maintained and where marketing or sales decisions are made;

(ii) *brief relevant employees*, for example, reception staff, on who should be contacted in the event that OFT officials arrive;

(iii) *prepare information about the company*, for example, a chart which can be made available to the investigators showing the company's management structure and identifying the roles of the senior executives. In addition, prepare introductory general remarks dealing with the company's activities and role. The purpose of this is to limit the OFT's investigation to the relevant part of the business with which the investigation is concerned. It also provides an opportunity for the company to indicate to the inspectors that it intends to adopt a co-operative approach and may enable the company to find out more at an early stage about the purpose of the investigation;

(iv) *implement a compliance programme*. Such a programme would aim to both minimise the risks of the company being subject to an investigation (by raising staff awareness of competition law issues and thus reducing the risk of an infringement) and provide in-depth instruction in dealing with OFT inspectors in the event of a raid. See Chapter 15 for more details of compliance programmes.

At the Start of the Investigation

There are a number of helpful steps that can be taken on arrival of OFT officials **14.82** and in the first stages of any inspection:

(i)   *contact the nominated executive*. When the inspectors arrive they will usually ask to speak to a senior executive. They may identify the executive by name. The receptionist should contact the named executive and (if different) the personnel nominated as explained in 14.81(i) above. While that person, or (if he or she is uncontactable or out of the office) an acceptable substitute, is being located, the receptionist should ask the inspectors to wait. The inspectors will normally be prepared to wait a few minutes (but no longer) while this is done;

(ii)   *check the identity of the inspectors*. The inspectors will carry identity cards and authorisations or copies of the relevant warrant. It is appropriate to telephone the OFT to ensure that the persons claiming to be the inspectors are indeed authorised officials of the OFT!

(iii) *establish the scope of the investigation.* The inspectors may only exercise powers in relation to documents which fall within the scope of the investigation. The scope and purpose of the investigation will be set out in the written authorisation or warrant carried by the OFT officer investigating. The company should ask to see this document and to take a copy. This is important as it will enable the company to have as clear an idea as possible about the scope of the investigation. The officials may be willing to explain the purpose of, and background to, the investigation and what sort of material will be required;

(iv) *summon legal advisers.* Alert lawyers so that they can be making their way to the company's premises. Fax them copies of the authorisation or warrant. The OFT will normally wait up to an hour for any legal advisers that the company requests to be present. Compliance with any conditions required by the officials, for example, the sealing of cupboards or filing cabinets to prevent relevant information from tampering, should be undertaken. If the investigation is under warrant and the premises are unoccupied, the officials are obliged to give a reasonable opportunity for either legal advisers or the occupier to be present;

(v) *notify other appropriate senior staff* (they may have to clear diaries) and, if necessary, any parent company or other appropriate company officer should also be notified;

(vi) *prepare a press release.* There is a risk that the fact that the investigation has taken place will become public and, to cover this eventuality and the adverse publicity, a short press statement should be prepared, but not issued unless and until details otherwise become public;

(vii) *limit the location of the investigation,* where possible. Although the inspectors will wish to see the files *in situ,* they may be prepared to work from a room allocated to them, particularly where this facilitates the reviewing, copying and listing of documents;

(viii) *nominate a note taker.* This is essential to ensure that an accurate as possible record of the course of the investigation can be prepared.

During the Investigation

14.83 Once the investigation is under way, the following steps should be taken by the relevant company personnel and, if present, the company's legal advisers:

(i) *accompany the investigator.* The OFT officials should be accompanied by a representative of the undertaking at all times, particularly if they have had to be accommodated, or are working temporarily, in an executive's office. Officials may split up, with different officials working in different locations, in which case several personnel may be required to accompany them;

(ii) *avoid volunteering unnecessary verbal explanation.* As explained above, the power of OFT officials to ask for oral explanations is limited to providing an explanation of the relevant documents (for example, asking the meaning of abbreviations) and requiring a person to state where the documents are to be found. They have no right to ask broader questions relating to the alleged infringement. To the extent that a document contains information that may be misleading and it is easy to clear up any such misleading impression, it would normally be sensible to do so. However, staff should be discouraged from engaging in unnecessary discussion with the officials. There will be opportunities for volunteering other explanation later in the case, once it is clearer what the OFT's concerns are;

(iii) *consider whether information is relevant.* As explained above, in being able to discern whether documents or information relate to any matter relevant to the investigation, the OFT has a wide power to determine what documents it wishes to examine. Nevertheless, with the aim of limiting the number of documents that the OFT takes copies of to a minimum, it may be worth arguing that certain information is not relevant to the scope of the investigation in borderline cases where this is credible.

(iv) *prepare a record of the OFT officer's statement.* A shorthand note or record of at least the official's introductory explanations and any subsequent comments they may make should be taken;

(v) *prepare copies of documents.* It will be advisable to make ready access to a photocopier and a relevant operative. Three copies of any documents the officials require should normally be taken—one for the officials, one for the company and one for its legal adviser. Each document copied should be marked to show who and where it comes from. As well as being convenient, the preparation of additional copies of documents as they are provided to the OFT is an effective way of simultaneously compiling an accurate record for the company's use. If the officials keep their own list of documents, it is helpful to ask for a copy of this as well so that it can be cross-checked against the company's list;

(vi) *provide complete documents.* Documents requested by the officials must be submitted in their entirety. If a document cannot be found or is incomplete, a note of this should be made and, if there is an obvious explanation, this should be given;

(vii) *maintain legal privilege.* It is necessary to maintain confidentiality for privileged legal advice. To the extent that a file contains both privileged and non-privileged material, the privileged material should be extracted from the file and not disclosed to the investigating officials;

(viii) *identify business secrets.* Any document containing business secrets which might harm the company's commercial interests (as opposed to privileged

419

information which can be withheld from the OFT itself) should be marked as confidential on the relevant copy. This is a means of seeking to limit the scope and extent of any disclosure to third parties. However, the company being investigated will have an opportunity once the investigation is over to review the documents which have been copied by the officials and to make any further comments in relation to confidentiality;

(ix) *prepare a record of files reviewed by inspectors.* A complete and detailed note of all files and other records examined by the officials (whether or not copies have been taken) should be kept. This will be helpful after the investigation in assessing the scope and purpose of the investigation.

After the Investigation

14.84 Finally, the following steps should be taken immediately after the on-site inspection:

(i) *review the documents inspected.* The company and its legal advisers should make an immediate and thorough review of documents taken or copied (and documents inspected but not required). If information needs to be amplified or corrected (for example, if a document which is part of a group requested by the officials has been overlooked) this should be done as quickly as possible. Similarly, it may be appropriate, if a document contains misleading or inaccurate information, to let the OFT know of this as soon as possible;

(ii) *confirm claims for confidentiality,* both as to business secrets and, where it is at issue, legal privilege.

The OFT may submit further written requests for documents and information.

J. Rights of Defence

14.85 Companies subject to investigation have the protection of procedural safeguards which will become of particular relevance during the conduct of a case following the initial investigation. These safeguards also apply where a case is opened following a notification (as opposed to a complaint or an 'own-initiative' investigation by the OFT).

14.86 Certain principles of EC case law regarding the rights of parties subject to investigation under Article 81 or 82 may also apply due to the operation of the 'governing principles' section in the Act, which creates obligations for application of the Act consistently with EC law and decision-making. In addition, as explained in paragraph 14.70–14.75 above, the European Convention on Human Rights and the Human Rights Act 1998 lay down principles with which public authorities such as the OFT must act consistently. The extent to which these safeguards—for example, proportionality and the right to a fair hearing—are imported for the benefit of parties being investigated where the express provisions of the Act and the procedural rules are more limited in that respect is by no means certain, and the issue is considered in more detail in Chapter 3, paragraph 3.58–3.60.

Whatever the exact position regarding these EC principles, there are a number of **14.87** express procedural safeguards for companies being investigated which will be of relevance following an initial investigation by the OFT (these also come into play in a case following a notification to the OFT—see Chapter 12 paragraph 12.17–12.19). Where the OFT proposes to make an infringement decision, ie that either the Chapter I or the Chapter II prohibition has been infringed, there are three express safeguards for the party subject to investigation in the procedural rules:[110]

- *statement of objections*—the OFT must give written notice to the undertaking being investigated, and any other person it is aware is a party to the agreement or conduct which the OFT considers has led to the infringement, stating the matters to which it has taken objection, the action it proposes and the reasons for doing so. Some guidance on role and function of the statement of objections may be obtained from EC law. The statement of objections is, according to the ECJ:

  > A procedural and preparatory document, intended solely for the undertakings against which the procedure is initiated with a view to enabling them to exercise effectively their right to a fair hearing.[111]

  If EC precedent is followed the OFT, in making its decision, will only be able to rely on concerns in respect of which the undertaking being investigated has been given an opportunity to respond, that is, concerns set out in the statement of directions. It is therefore not possible to introduce new issues later in the proceedings.

  Statements of objections issued by the European Commission are usually divided into two parts. The first part describes the relevant facts, including a description of the relevant market and the position of the undertakings concerned in the market and details of the facts establishing the infringement. The second part contains a legal assessment indicating why Article 81(1) or Article 82 applies, and why Article 81(3) (if appropriate) is not applicable. The basis for any proposed measures, for example fines, is also described. A statement of objections can be a very substantial document, and in more difficult or serious cases can run to several hundred pages. The statement of objections may also refer to relevant supporting documents which may be attached or which would be available for inspection by the parties.

---

[110] See n 10 above, R 14(1).
[111] Case C–62/86, *AKZO v Commission* [1991] ECR I–3359, para 29.

- *oral or written representations*—the OFT is required to inform the undertaking being investigated, and other parties to whom the statement of objections was sent, that any such representations made to the OFT within a specified period will be considered, and give those persons an opportunity to make them. Parties will generally make both a written and an oral reply. At EC level the written reply is often a substantial document in which the factual and/or legal basis of the European Commission case is disputed. The parties may, and often do, attach extensive supporting documents, where appropriate evidence may be submitted from independent experts. To the extent that the parties accept part of the OFT's case the question may arise whether this may subsequently challenge such parts before the appeals tribunal. On the basis that the appeals tribunal may fully rehear the case there appears no reason why they should not.

  The procedure is primarily a written procedure. Although there is scope to make oral representations, the purpose of such representations is to elaborate upon a written response.[112] It is likely that the oral representations will therefore not be made in the context of a formal hearing at which third parties may be present along the lines of hearings conducted in similar circumstances by the European Commission. Instead, the oral procedure will be more akin to the procedure followed by the OFT in merger cases where the parties enter into discussions with OFT officials on a relatively unstructured basis. However, in the case of procedures under the Act, it is likely that the oral procedure will be conducted by a senior OFT official who has had no previous involvement with the case, nor any direct management or supervisory responsibility for its conduct. This role is similar in many respects to that of the Hearing Officer in European Commission cases. It is likely that this will give the procedure a higher degree of formality than is currently the case in OFT merger discussions with parties.

- *access to the file*—the undertaking or other party is to be given an opportunity to inspect the documents in the OFT's file relating to the proposed decision if it so requests (although the OFT is entitled to withhold from inspection confidential information, defined as in paragraph 14.77 above).[113] In addition the OFT may refuse to allow access to information which 'in the opinion of the Director' is otherwise confidential.[114] This would appear to give the OFT a broad power to withhold information where, for example, there is concern that disclosure would reveal the identity of a confidential informant and that, by doing this, the ability of the OFT to obtain information about possible infringements would be undermined. However, this must be balanced against the respondent's right of defence. While this may not be seriously undermined

---

[112] See n 10 above, introductory para 7.
[113] Ibid; R 14(2) and R 27(1)(b).
[114] OFT, n 10 above, R 14(2).

by the non-disclosure of the name of the complainant, any more extensive failure to disclose may be viewed more seriously.

European Commission practice is, if the file is very short, to provide relevant copies to the parties. If it is longer the parties may inspect the file at the European Commission's offices. The CFI has held that access to the file is:

> 'one of the procedural guarantees intended to protect the rights of the defence and to ensure, in particular, that the right to be heard . . . can be exercised effectively.'[115]

It was held in the *Soda Ash* case[116] by the Court of First Instance that it is not for the European Commission to decide which documents may be useful for the defence. The undertakings under investigation must be given the opportunity to examine all relevant documents. Similarly, the fact that access to the file may cause an administrative burden for the European Commission was not a relevant factor. The Court held in *Soda Ash* that failure to give proper access to the file may lead to the annulment of a decision where non-disclosure of the documents in question might have influenced the course of the procedure and the content of the decision to the detriment of the applicant.[117]

On this basis, the OFT would not be able to use the lack of relevance of the particular document as the reason for refusal to disclose. However, it may be that the UK position is less strict than that under EC law. The Act provides that in considering whether to exclude information the OFT must, in addition to considering the harm that disclosure will cause, take account of 'the extent to which disclosure is necessary for the purposes, for which—the . . . Director is proposing to make the disclosure'.[118] It may therefore be the case that, to the extent that a document is of limited value to the respondent in exercising its right of defence, the OFT would be justified in adopting a broader view on the need to protect confidentiality.

K. Investigations by the OFT Under Other Legislation

European Commission On-site Investigations

National competition authorities such as the OFT are required to assist the   **14.88**
European Commission in carrying out dawn raids under EC competition law: where an undertaking opposes an investigation under Article 81 or 82 of the EC

---

[115] Cases T–10–12/92 and 15/92 *SA Cimenteries CBR and others v Commission* [1992] ECR II–1571.

[116] Cases T–30, 36 and 37/91 *Solvay and ICI v Commission* [1995] ECR II–1775.

[117] The European Commission has now issued a notice on the internal rules of procedure for processing a request for access to the file in cases pursuant to Arts 85 and 86 EC, Art 65 and 66 ECSC and Council Reg (EEC) No 4064 [1997] OJ C23/3.

[118] S 56(3)(b)

Treaty, the Member State concerned is obliged to afford the necessary assistance to Commission officials to enable them to make their investigation.[119] Previously, the OFT relied on the inherent jurisdiction of the High Court to grant an injunction requiring undertakings subject to an investigation to comply (there was no power to use force). However, the Act confers new powers on the OFT either to assist the European Commission in EC investigations in the UK or to carry them out at its request.

14.89 First, where a European Commission investigation is being, or is likely to be obstructed, the OFT is able to obtain a warrant authorising its officials and those of the European Commission to enter the relevant premises, search for books and records which the Commission officials have the power to examine, using such force as is reasonably necessary for the purpose.[120]

14.90 Secondly, the OFT is able to obtain a warrant where it is conducting an investigation under Article 81 or 82 at the request of the European Commission if the investigation is being, or is likely to be, obstructed. The warrant will authorise an OFT officer, accompanying OFT staff and European Commission officials to enter the relevant premises and to search for books and records that the authorised OFT officer has the power to examine, using such force as is reasonably necessary for the purpose.[121]

14.91 Since an investigation in these circumstances takes place under EC law, parties should be aware that the scope of protection for legally privileged communications is narrower than that in investigations under the Act: it will not include correspondence with, or advice from, in-house lawyers.

14.92 It is a criminal offence intentionally to obstruct OFT or Commission officials in the exercise of their powers under the warrant. A person guilty of such an offence is liable on summary conviction to a fine not exceeding £5,000,[122] and, on conviction on indictment, to imprisonment for a term not exceeding two years or to an unlimited fine or to both.[123]

Fair Trading Act Investigations

14.93 The Act also strengthens the OFT's powers of investigation into 'complex' and 'scale' monopolies under the Fair Trading Act 1973 in order to bring these into line with the investigatory powers under the Competition Act.[124] The OFT will be able to require the production of specified documents, estimates, forecasts,

---

[119] N 15, Art 14(6).
[120] S 62.
[121] S 63.
[122] See n 81 above.
[123] S 65.
[124] S 66, amending s 44 of the Fair Trading Act.

returns or other information from relevant producers, suppliers and recipients of goods or services in the UK. It will also be able to enter the business premises of such persons without notice and require the production of relevant documents and explanations of those documents. However, the enhanced Fair Trading Act powers of investigation do not include a power to enter and search premises under warrant.

The OFT intends to allow the occupier of premises subject to an on-site investi- **14.94**
gation under the Fair Trading Act a similar opportunity to summon legal advisors as it gives companies being investigated under the Competition Act.[125]

The Competition Act also enhances the sanctions for failing to comply with the **14.95**
new investigatory powers under the Fair Trading Act.[126] A person is guilty of an offence if he: intentionally obstructs the OFT in the exercise of investigatory powers; refuses or wilfully neglects to comply with a requirement to produce documents; or wilfully interferes with documents. On summary conviction, a person guilty of any of these offences is liable to a fine not exceeding the £5,000;[127] on conviction on indictment, a person found guilty is liable to an unlimited fine, or, in the case of neglecting to produce or interfering with documents, imprisonment for a term not exceeding two years in addition or as an alternative to the fine.

---

[125] OFT, (n 2), para 9.4.
[126] Fair Trading Act 1973, s 46, as amended by Competition Act 1998, s 67.
[127] S 46 as amended refers to 'the prescribed sum', which is currently £5,000 (Magistrates Court Act 1980, s 32).

15

COMPLIANCE PROGRAMMES

A. Overview

15.01 The impact that the Competition Act will have on the business and practices of any organisation will depend on a variety of factors, such as: the extent to which the activities of the company are already within the scope of EC competition law (Articles 81 and 82 (formerly Articles 85 and 86) EC); whether the organisation is or may be dominant on national or local markets; whether the organisation operates in a sector that is subject to particular scrutiny by the competition authorities; the size and diversity of the organisation; and the nature of the organisation's relationships with its suppliers, customers and competitors. The impact of competition law can be felt at different levels within an organisation. A company may infringe the rules as a result of activities carried out by employees below senior management level as well as because of higher level executive decisions.

15.02 The risk of infringing competition law is therefore perhaps greater than in relation to other legislation. For these reasons, the Director General of Fair Trading (head of the OFT) has strongly recommended that large and diverse businesses implement a corporate compliance programme if they do not already have one.[1] Such programmes reduce the risk of infringing the law by ensuring that relevant employees are sufficiently knowledgeable about the provisions of the law and use that knowledge to good effect. If the programme has effective monitoring or audit

---

[1] Bridgeman, 'The New UK Competition Legislation: The View from the Director General of Fair Trading', OFT speech 98/11, delivered at Norton Rose IIR conference on Competition Law Compliance, 19 May 1998.

mechanisms, it can help companies detect infringements at an early stage and thus take appropriate remedial action, as well as possibly reducing the level of any penalty imposed if there is then an infringement. Increasing awareness through compliance programmes also increases the opportunities for an organisation to use competition law as a 'sword' as well as a 'shield', by alerting personnel to possible infringements of the law by other organisations with which they deal or compete, so that appropriate enforcement action can be taken.

This chapter[2] reviews the advantages of a competition compliance programme **15.03** and considers what such a programme may consist of. It is emphasised that the type and scope of a programme will very much depend on the factors relevant to a particular company. In some cases, a detailed and comprehensive programme is required. In other cases a much more limited exercise is appropriate.

B. Benefits of a Compliance Programme

An effective compliance programme will give rise to a number of benefits, in par- **15.04** ticular:

(i)   it reduces the risk of employees infringing the competition rules and thus reduces the risk of penalties or other remedial action being invoked against the company, and of agreements being unenforceable;

(ii)   it puts senior management in control by giving them a warning of potentially unlawful conduct, so that they have the opportunity either to avoid the potential infringement or to take appropriate remedial steps;

(iii) there may be financial advantages, in that an effective compliance programme may help avoid time-consuming investigations, the possibility of a significant financial penalty, the risk of third party actions and adverse publicity;

(iv)   the awareness of possible anti-competitive conduct by competitors, suppliers or customers will be raised in the eyes of relevant employees and thus, where there is such behaviour, the organisation will be in a better position to take appropriate steps against the infringement—whether at a commercial level, by complaining to the competition authorities or by bringing private proceedings in court;

(v)   in some cases, despite the existence of an effective compliance programme, the organisation will nevertheless infringe the rules. At EC level a compliance programme that is operated effectively may be a factor leading to the

---

[2] See Lazar, E., Ensuring Compliance, European Counsel, February 1998; Preece, S., Complying with the New UK Competition Law, Chartered Secretary, May 1998; O'Meara, B., 'Corporate Antitrust Compliance Programmes' [1998] *ECLR* 59.

reduction in the level of any fine.[3] The Director General of Fair Trading has said that, in setting penalties:

> It is highly likely that I will take into account the efforts made by the business concerned to ensure compliance when considering the level of financial penalty that should be imposed. However, just having a programme is unlikely to be sufficient to mitigate a penalty if it has not been actively implemented, evaluated and regularly audited.[4]

C. Elements of an Effective Compliance Programme

15.05 The OFT has specifically indicated that it may take into account the existence of a compliance programme as a mitigating circumstance reducing the amount of any penalty, but only provided that a number of essential elements are in place.[5] The OFT has indicated that in its view there are five essential elements that it would expect to be included as a minimum in any compliance programme. These are:

- active implementation;
- support of senior management;
- appropriate compliance policy and procedures;
- training; and
- evaluation.[6]

Active Implementation

15.06 Continued, pro-active implementation of a compliance programme is a feature running through all the essential components of the programme outlined below. It is insufficient for a compliance programme to be adopted and then effectively left dormant.

---

[3] *National Panasonic (UK) Limited*, Decision 82/853 [1982] OJ L354/29; *John Deere*, Decision 85/79 [1985] OJ L35/58; *Viho/Toshiba*, Decision 91/532 [1991] 2 CEC 2; *Viho/Parker Pen*, Decision 92/426 [1992] OJ L233/25; on appeal Case C–73/95P [1996] ECR I–5457. However, the existence of a compliance programme is not identified as an 'attenuating circumstance' in the European Commission's Guidelines on the method of setting fines, (see [1998] OJ C9/3). The OFT, on the other hand, is likely to treat this as a 'mitigating factor' in setting penalties—see para 15.05 below.

[4] Bridgeman, n 1 above.

[5] The Office of Fair Trading, Competition Act 1998: 'Enforcement' (OFT 407), para 4.35.

[6] Ibid. See also Bulletin of the Canadian Competition Bureau on 'Corporate Compliance Programs', 3 July 1997.

Support of Senior Management

A compliance programme should have the visible and continuing support of **15.07** senior management and be observed by them. Such support indicates the importance that the organisation attaches to compliance and encourages more junior employees to respond positively 'by demonstrating its commitment and involvement, senior management will send a message that violations of the [competition rules] are not accepted as a legitimate business practice'.[7]

The support of senior management can be demonstrated in a number of ways— **15.08** for example, by a letter from the chairman or chief executive to employees, by an introduction to any compliance manual by the chairman or chief executive, or by the attendance of senior management at in-house seminars.

Appropriate Compliance Policy and Procedures

In many organisations a compliance policy and procedure can only be compiled **15.09** after an audit of key business areas has been conducted.[8] It is only after such an audit that the nature and extent of any areas of risk can be identified.

A typical compliance policy will have a high level statement setting out the organ- **15.10** isation's commitment to comply with the competition rules and its expectations that all staff do the same. It should also contain an overview of relevant competition rules (UK and, where appropriate, EC along with any other jurisdictions in which the business operates) and an indication of the risks and penalties of not complying, covering both risk to the organisation in terms of non-enforceability of agreements, fines and civil liabilities and risk to individuals which, under the UK legislation, relates primarily to the giving of false or misleading information.[9] It is also appropriate to give an indication of the breadth of the competition authorities' investigatory powers. This helps bring home to individuals the wide scope which the authorities have for detecting possible infringements.

Although 'off the shelf' compliance programmes are available, generally, for the **15.11** compliance policy to be meaningful to employees, it is necessary that it relates to the specific activities of the business. This may in some cases mean different compliance documents, or different sections of a compliance document, to cover various businesses within a single organisation. General statements that, for example, it is inappropriate to talk to competitors about prices will carry little weight with employees. It is much more useful to refer to the specific circumstances in which there may be scope for contact with competitors in the particular sector, for

---

[7] Bulletin of the Canadian Competition Bureau on 'Corporate Compliance Programs', 3 July 1997.
[8] See paras 15.18–15.25 below.
[9] S 44.

example, through particular trade associations or industry groups, and indicate what is acceptable and unacceptable behaviour in these contexts. Practical examples are always helpful. Behaviour that is nearly always unacceptable, for example, discussing planned price changes with competitors, needs to be clearly set out.

15.12 A policy document will often indicate the consequences for the individual if a company's compliance procedures are not complied with. This will normally involve some form of disciplinary action, the nature of which would depend on the seriousness of the infringement. Some companies require employees to sign an undertaking to act in accordance with compliance policies, and that undertaking is incorporated in the individual's contract of employment. The Director General of Fair Trading has indicated that he would 'envisage that many firms will want to consider disciplinary action against any employee who deliberately or negligently involves the company in a breach of the law'.[10] The policy will normally also contain details of relevant procedures, such as the name of persons to contact in the event of doubt whether a proposed agreement or conduct is acceptable. This will often be a member of the legal department. Alternatively it may be a senior employee in each department or location of the business.

15.13 The policy and procedures will normally be included in a compliance manual, whether in paper form or available electronically to employees. In some businesses abbreviated versions of the manual are distributed to employees. In many cases individuals are asked to sign a form confirming that they have read the compliance manual and return it to an appropriate person within the organisation.

Training

15.14 The preparation of a policy is not sufficient. The OFT's view is that it is essential for there to be active and ongoing training for employees at all levels who may be involved in activities that are touched by competition law.

15.15 Training should cover the policy and procedures described in paragraphs 15.09–15.13 above. A training programme can only be effective if the relevant employees understand the scope of the competition authorities' powers of investigation. When employees understand that, for example, jottings in the margin of an agenda during a meeting, e-mails exchanged between colleagues or records of telephone and fax transmissions may all provide evidence of anti-competitive behaviour, they are more likely to ensure that, on the assumption that they are behaving lawfully, they do not give scope for competition authorities to misunderstand their activities.

15.16 Thus a training programme should emphasise the need not to make written or electronic records that could be misinterpreted and also that, where there are

---

[10] Bridgeman, n 1 above.

records which may wrongly suggest there is an infringement, a proper explanation of why, in fact, no infringement was involved needs to be included on the relevant file. Similarly, discussions with competitors, suppliers and customers have to be unambiguous. These points are most effectively put across to employees by examples, followed up in some cases by an audit or mock 'dawn raid' (see paragraphs 15.18–15.20 below).

As mentioned above, the most effective training is geared specifically at employees in a particular part of the business and considers competition law issues in the context of those employees' activities. Different businesses use different methods of training; most use some form of seminar but this may be augmented by videos, interactive CD-ROMs etc.[11] Such training is normally available on the introduction of the new compliance policy, and then on an induction basis for new staff and to update existing staff at regular intervals. **15.17**

Evaluation

Monitoring, formal auditing and reporting mechanisms provide both employees and senior managers with evidence that there is a check on their activities and can also measure how successful the compliance programme has been in terms of avoiding infringements. An audit is often a starting point for the development of a compliance programme. Regular audits of the programme subsequently will ensure that it continues to deliver its objectives. **15.18**

There are a number of possible elements to the evaluation. At one level employees may be asked to give direct feedback on how successful particular aspects such as the training programme have been. There may also be *ad hoc* or regular audits of documents or behaviour by members of the in-house legal department or external lawyers. Some businesses have undertaken mock 'dawn raids', under which external lawyers investigate the business, or parts of the business, and where most of the staff consider that the investigation is a genuine OFT or European Commission investigation. This has been commented on favourably by OFT officials.[12] The benefit of such an activity is that it imparts a clear understanding of the sort of material that the OFT or European Commission will look for and may find of interest, and that it helps to disclose to senior management areas of possible concern within the business. **15.19**

Audits will normally focus on particularly sensitive areas such as sales and marketing, strategic planning and points of contact with competitors. In order to **15.20**

---

[11] The OFT has produced a free educational video on the Competition Act, 'Compliance matters'; larger companies may consider commissioning a bespoke educational video targeted specifically to their business.

[12] Margaret Bloom, Director of Competition Policy, Office of Fair Trading: paper to 'The Europeanisation of UK Competition Law' conference, 10 Sept 1998 (note that Mrs Bloom's paper expresses her personal views, which are not necessarily those of the OFT).

ensure that the audit or mock dawn raid is as authentic and wide-ranging as possible, all material that competition authorities may investigate should be reviewed. This includes e-mail (including 'deleted' e-mails that are accessible within the organisation), electronic and hard copy diaries, handwritten notes and memos, credit card bills, telephone and fax records, etc.

15.21 Following the audit or mock dawn raid, those conducting it should prepare a report, either in writing or orally. To the extent that areas of concern and possible infringements are discovered during the audit, these need to be brought to the attention of senior managers and appropriate remedial action then needs to be taken. The destruction of documents because they may indicate a possible infringement is not recommended, not least because such information almost invariably will come to light, for example, because third parties have corresponding documentation and records, or because disgruntled or former employees disclose them.

15.22 In such cases where there is an innocent explanation for an apparently damaging document a written record should be kept of the explanation. Thus, for example, if there is a document containing details of price rises to be announced in the future by competitors and such information was obtained by sales staff from customers in the normal course of their business, it is appropriate to include a note on the file of the source of information. This avoids the risk that during a future inspection the authorities will draw the conclusion that the information was obtained as a result of an information exchange between competitors.

15.23 Where the records show a serious infringement of the rules it may be appropriate for senior management to approach the competition authorities directly, indicating the nature of the infringement and steps to be taken (including the introduction of a compliance programme) to avoid such infringements in the future, rather than waiting for an infringement to be discovered. In most such cases of voluntary disclosure the risk of a penalty being imposed is likely to be low.

15.24 If the only competition concern is in relation to UK law, then an audit of this kind could be carried out by either in-house lawyers or external legal counsel. Professional privilege will attach to both.[13] However, if the agreements or activities of the organisation are also within the scope of EC competition law, then as regards the application of the EC law professional privilege will not attach to a document produced by in-house lawyers.[14] In any event, for an audit to be of value it should be carried out by lawyers with relevant experience of competition law, who thus have a clear idea of the type of material and practices the competition authorities are interested in.

---

[13] See Ch 14, paras 14.67–14.69.
[14] Case 155/79 *AM & S Europe Limited v EC Commission* [1982] ECR 1575 and Case T–30/89 *Hilti AG v EC Commission* [1990] ECR II–163.

Care must be taken not to give the impression that the audit is being used as a **15.25**
means of concealing evidence of a possible infringement. It has been suggested by
European Commission officials that, in some cases, a competition audit, particularly if it involves a mock dawn raid, may be taken as an indication that the organisation has concealed evidence.[15] The European Commission has particular
concerns if there is any indication that relevant documents have been removed
from the premises by the parties conducting the audit.

D. Document Retention

It is unwise and often counter-productive to engage in selective destruction of **15.26**
documents that may indicate an infringement (see paragraph 15.21 above).
Further, if a document is interfered with or destroyed once an investigation is
commenced[16] or if the OFT is misled concerning the existence or content of a
document that has been destroyed prior to the investigation,[17] the relevant company or individual may be guilty of an offence.

Many organisations will, however, have a document retention policy under which **15.27**
all documents and electronic records are systematically destroyed on a regular
basis unless their retention is required for legal or business reasons. Such 'good
housekeeping' should not give rise to concern on the part of the authorities.
Where, as part of such a document retention and destruction exercise, documents
are discovered which may indicate an infringement of the competition rules, it
may in some cases be advisable to keep such documents with a written explanation on the file of either why, as a matter of fact, the document does not evidence
infringement or, if it does, what remedial steps were taken to deal with the
infringement. Such action is particularly advisable where other copies of the relevant document may be available in other organisations or where there may be references to the document, or to meetings that the document evidences, elsewhere.

E. Acquiring a Business

A business acquisition may be subject to UK, EC or other national merger control **15.28**
laws. An examination of such rules is outside the scope of this book. However, as
part of the due diligence exercise which a purchaser of a business may undertake
prior to acquisition, it may be appropriate to review the extent of competition law
compliance by the business that is being acquired. In particular, a purchaser will

---

[15] See, eg, *Cartonboard*, IV/C/33.833 1[1994] OJ L143/1, para 23.
[16] S 43.
[17] S 44.

wish to ensure that material agreements do not infringe the Chapter I prohibition (or Article 81 (formerly Article 85)) or, if they do, that they have been exempted. Otherwise, key provisions of such agreements may be unenforceable. In addition, there is a risk of penalties under the Act (or fines under EC law) and civil (third party) liabilities in the event of previous infringements. While it may be possible for the acquirer to safeguard against such risks to some extent through obtaining warranties from the seller where these are available, the infringements may not come to light until some years after the acquisition, by which point the warranties may be of little value. In any event, in the case of continuing infringements, the extent to which the liability for such infringements rests with the previous owners of the business may be at issue.

16

APPEALS

A. Overview

Appeals may be brought by parties to whom a decision is addressed, ie parties **16.01** to an agreement or to conduct which is the subject of a decision, and in some circumstances they may be brought by third parties. Appeals are from the OFT to an appeal tribunal of the Competition Commission on the facts or law, and from an appeal tribunal to the Court of Appeal on law or on the amount of a penalty. Rules with respect to appeals and appeal tribunals are to be made by the Secretary of State after consultation with the President of the Competition Commission Appeal Tribunals. Preparation of the rules is likely to be one of the President's first priorities.

B. Appeals to the Competition Commission

Appeals by Parties Subject to an OFT Decision

Parties to an agreement in respect of which the OFT has made a decision under **16.02** the Chapter I prohibition and any person in respect of whose conduct the OFT

435

has made a decision under the Chapter II prohibition may appeal to the appeal tribunal of the Competition Commission against, or with respect to, the decision.[1]

16.03 The following OFT or sector regulator decisions may be challenged on appeal:[2]

(i)   as to whether the Chapter I prohibition is infringed;

(ii) as to whether the Chapter II prohibition is infringed;

(iii) as to whether to grant an individual exemption;

(iv) in respect of an individual exemption:

    (a) as to whether to impose any condition or obligation;

    (b) where such condition or obligation has been imposed, as to the condition or obligation;

    (c) as to the period of an individual exemption;

    (d) as to the date from which the individual exemption is to take effect;

    (e) as to whether to extend the period for which an individual exemption has effect, and as to the period of any extension;

    (f) as to the cancellation of an exemption;

(v)   as to the imposition of any penalty for infringing the Chapter I or Chapter II prohibition or as to the amount of any such penalty;

(vi) as to the withdrawal or variation of any of the decisions described in (i) to (iv) above following an application by a third party.[3]

16.04 The appeal can also be against any directions to terminate or modify agreements or conduct which have been given by the OFT or a sector regulator, or against interim measures directions. The making of an appeal does not have the effect of suspending the decision to which the appeal relates except in relation to an appeal against the imposition or the amount of a penalty, in which case the penalty only is suspended.[4]

Appeals by Third Parties

16.05 The Act also provides for the possibility of third party appeal.[5] A third party is any person other than one who is a party to an agreement in respect of which the OFT has made the decision or one who is a person in respect of whose conduct the OFT has made the decision.[6]

---

[1] S 46(1)–(2); no appeal is possible in respect of guidance (as opposed to a decision) under Chapter I or II by the OFT.

[2] S 46(3)

[3] Under s 47(1).

[4] S 46(4).

[5] Note also that where the OFT has given guidance rather than a decision, it is possible for the case to be re-opened following a complaint from a third party—ss 15(2)(d) and 23(2)(c).

[6] S 47(1).

The third party may apply to the OFT to seek the withdrawal or variation of a **16.06** decision falling within categories (i) to (iv) above (ie not in relation to the imposition or amount of a penalty) or any other decision that may be prescribed.

However, a third party may only appeal if it has a 'sufficient interest'; the OFT **16.07** may refuse to accede to a third party request if:

(a) the applicant does not have sufficient interest in the relevant decision;

(b) that, in the case of an applicant claiming to represent persons who have a sufficient interest, the applicant does not represent such persons; or

(c) that the persons represented by the applicant do not have such an interest.[7]

The Act contains no definition of what constitutes a sufficient interest or where a **16.08** person or body may properly be considered to represent a group of persons with a sufficient interest, but during its passage through Parliament the government indicated that it considered representative bodies such as the Consumers' Association or trades institutions would have a sufficient interest.[8] The term 'sufficient interest' is used to define the class of persons who have the right to be heard by the European Commission in competition cases.[9] The term has never been defined by the ECJ, but Advocate General Lenz has said that a person may have a sufficient interest 'if he has been affected by the conduct of the undertaking against which the competition proceedings have been initiated'.[10] Thus, a person who has suffered legal or economic consequences as a result of the disputed agreement or behaviour is likely to have a sufficient interest. The appeal tribunal will have to decide how material such consequences must be to give rise to such an interest. Thus, for example, a local authority which suffered loss as a result of a bidding ring involving tenderers for a contract would clearly have a sufficient interest in any appeal relating to an alleged infringement of the Chapter I prohibition by the tenderers. However, would such interest extend, for example, to individual council tax payers in the local authority's area who claim to have an interest because of the impact of the bidding ring on council costs and thus indirectly on the level of council tax?

A third party application to the OFT must be made in writing within one month **16.09** of the publication of the decision in question. It must state why the applicant believes that it has a sufficient interest in the decision and give reasons why the applicant believes that the relevant decision should be withdrawn or varied.[11] The making of an application does not suspend the effect of the relevant decision.[12]

---

[7] S 47(1).

[8] Lord Simon of Highbury; *Hansard* HL, vol 583, no 64, col 452 (17 Nov 1997).

[9] Reg 17 [1956–62] OJ Spec Ed 87.

[10] Case 53/85 *AKZO Chemie v Commission* [1986] ECR 1965.

[11] S 47(2); Office of Fair Trading, Formal Consultation Draft, 'Competition Act 1998: The Draft Procedural Rules Proposed by the Director General of Fair Trading' (OFT 411), R 26(1).

[12] S 47(7).

16.10 Provided that a sufficient interest is shown, the OFT will consider whether to accept or reject the request. If it proposes to grant the application, it will consult the person to whom notice of the decision was given by giving written notice and stating the action it proposes and the reasons for it, and informing that person that it will consider any written representations within a specified period.[13]

16.11 If the OFT proceeds to grant the application, it will give notice to that person and to the third party appellant, and also publish the decision to grant the appeal by means of an entry on the OFT register.[14] The addressee of the OFT's original decision would then have a right of appeal to the Competition Commission against the new decision as described in paragraph 16.03 above.

16.12 If the OFT decides that the third party applicant does not have a sufficient interest or that the application does not show sufficient reason why the relevant decision should be withdrawn or varied, it will notify the applicant.[15] Where the OFT has decided not to proceed because of lack of sufficient interest or insufficient reasons, the third party may then appeal to the Competition Commission against this decision.[16]

C. Procedure on Appeal to the Competition Commission

16.13 The Secretary of State is empowered to make rules providing the necessary procedure for the hearing of appeals. Part II of Schedule 8 to the Act sets out matters which must or may be provided for in the rules,[17] but there is no restriction on them covering further matters.[18] In producing the rules, the Secretary of State must consult with the President of the Competition Commission Appeal Tribunals (and such other persons as he thinks appropriate) available until the President is appointed. The Chairman of the Competition Commission has identified as basic objectives:

- full disclosure of arguments and proper opportunity for parties to comment on each other's position;
- thoroughness and rigour;
- timeliness;
- efficiency in public administration.[19]

---

[13] OFT, n 11 above, R 26(2) and R 27(1)(c).
[14] Ibid, R 26(3) and R 27(1)(i).
[15] Ss 46(3) and 47(4).
[16] S 47(6).
[17] S 48(2).
[18] S 48(4).
[19] Dr Derek Morris, 'The Role of the Competition Commission', speech to the Annual CBI Competition Conference, 11 Nov 1998.

The rules are likely to be made available in draft for public consultation in the sec- **16.14**
ond half of 1999, with a view to putting them in place in time for 1 March 2000,
the date when the Chapter I and II prohibitions come into force. The following
paragraphs explain the matters provided for in Schedule 8 which the rules are
likely to cover.

Commencing an Appeal

An appeal to the Competition Commission must be made by sending a notice of **16.15**
appeal to the Competition Commission within a specified period.[20] The notice
must set out the grounds of appeal in sufficient detail to indicate to what extent
the appellant:

(i)   contends that the disputed decision was based on an error of fact;

(ii) contends that the disputed decision was wrong in law;

(iii) is appealing against the OFT's exercise of discretion in making a decision, for
      example, in deciding to grant or not to grant an individual exemption in
      respect of the Chapter I prohibition.

The appeal tribunal may give an appellant leave to amend the grounds of appeal
identified in the notice of appeal.

The rules may make provision for: the period in which appeals may be brought; **16.16**
the form of the notice of appeal and the information which must be given in the
notice; the procedure for amending a notice of appeal; and with respect to
acknowledgement of a notice of appeal.[21]

Structure of Appeal Tribunals

The President of the Competition Commission Appeal Tribunals must constitute **16.17**
an appeal tribunal on receipt of a notice of appeal from an applicant. An appeal
tribunal will consist of a chairman, who will be either the President himself or
selected from the panel of chairmen (who will be required to have at least seven
years' legal qualification), together with two other appeal panel members.[22] See
Chapter 2 paragraphs 2.14–2.21 for further details of the structure and staffing of
the appeal panel and appeal tribunals.

---

[20] Sch 8 para 2(1). The relevant period for appeals to the CFI in relation to European
Commission decisions is two months from the date of notification or publication of the decision or
the date on which the appellant had, or should have had, sufficient notice of the terms of the decision.

[21] Sch 8 para 6.

[22] Sch 7 para 27.

Rejection of Appeals

16.18   The rules may provide for an appeal tribunal to reject an appeal if it considers that the notice of appeal reveals no valid ground of appeal, or it is satisfied that the appellant has habitually and persistently without any reasonable ground instituted vexatious proceedings or made vexatious applications in any proceedings.[23]

Pre-hearing Reviews and Security

16.19   The rules may provide for pre-hearing reviews (preliminary considerations of the proceedings) and there may also be provision for security, ie provision for ordering a party to the proceedings to pay a deposit of an amount not exceeding a specified sum if it wishes to continue participating in them.[24] Such an order may also contain provisions concerning the manner in which the amount of such a deposit is to be determined, the consequences of non-payment of the deposit and the circumstances in which the deposit may be either refunded to the payee or paid to another party.[25]

16.20   The extent to which the power to require the provision of security is exercised may significantly influence the use made of the appeal procedure. One of the great advantages of complaining to the European Commission as opposed to commencing civil proceedings before a national court is that the complainant is not required to put its funds at risk or pay the respondent's costs in the event of an adverse outcome. If the deposit requirement is used other than in exceptional circumstances, this is likely to be a deterrent to making appeal applications; parties will need to have a reasonably high degree of confidence in the likely outcome of the appeal before commencing the procedure. This may have the desirable effect of discouraging appeals which have little chance of success but are simply brought to cause inconvenience to the other side or, in the case of addressees of a decision, to defer the payment of a penalty. However, it may also discourage parties from bringing appeals in circumstances in which the appeal would have a reasonable chance of success.

Conduct of Appeals

16.21   Provisions may be made concerning the manner in which appeals are to be conducted, in particular:

(i)   whether they are to be held in private for any reason requiring the protection of confidential information;

---

[23] Sch 8 para 7.
[24] Sch 8 para 8(2)–(3).
[25] Sch 8 para 8(4).

(ii)   as to the persons entitled to appear on behalf of a party;

(iii) requiring persons to attend to give evidence and produce documents;

(iv)   enabling an appeal tribunal to refer a matter back to the OFT if it appears that the matter has not been adequately investigated;

(v)   enabling an appeal tribunal, on the application of a party or on its own initiative, to require disclosure between the parties, or the production by parties of documents or classes of documents;

(vi)   for the appointment of experts;

(vii) for the award of costs or expenses and for taxing or otherwise settling any costs or expenses.[26]

Government statements during the passage of the Competition Bill through Parliament indicated two strands of thinking as to the procedures to be established for the appeal tribunal.[27] On the one hand, it 'envisage[d] a rather user-friendly specialised tribunal'[28] whose procedures and decisions 'should promote transparency as far as possible'.[29] It stated that there are advantages in dealing with such matters in a tribunal rather than a court: 'The procedural rules by which the tribunal operates may be tailored to suit the nature of the matters it will typically deal with . . . '.[30] On the other, it envisaged 'more court-like arrangements than are appropriate for MMC inquires under the Fair Trading Act'.[31] It remains to be seen how formalised procedures of the appeal tribunal will be but, if the OFT's policy in developing its Procedural Rules is any indication, the Competition Commission may initially take a restrained approach, providing the minimum procedures necessary, and allowing for the development of further rules following experience of the system's operation over time. **16.22**

Penalties and Fees

Rules may also cover the circumstances in which an appeal tribunal may order that interest is payable and the manner in which it should be calculated. In particular, the rules may provide for compound interest to be payable if an appeal tribunal upholds the decision of the OFT to impose a penalty or does not reduce a **16.23**

---

[26] Sch 8 para (9).

[27] See Kon, S., and Maxwell, A., 'Enforcement of the EC and New UK Competition Rules [1994] ECLR 443.

[28] Statement by Lord Haskel during the Third Reading of the Competition Bill in the House of Lords, *Hansard* HL vol 586 No. 116 col 1353 (5 Mar 1998).

[29] Statement by Lord Simon of Highbury, during the Second Reading of the Competition Bill in the House of Lords, *Hansard*, HL vol 582 No 55 col 1148 30 Oct 1997.

[30] Statement by Lord Simon of Highbury during the Third Reading of the Competition Bill in the House of Lords, *Hansard*, HL vol 583 No. 64 col 444 17 Nov 1997. At col 445 he went on to say: '[t]he primary function of the tribunal will be to re-hear and review the evidence considered by the director, not to initiate its own in-depth investigations'.

[31] Ibid.

penalty which the OFT has imposed by more than a specified percentage, although in such cases interest would not be payable in respect of any period prior to the date on which the appeal had been brought.[32]

16.24 Fees may be charged with respect to specified costs of proceedings before an appeal tribunal, with the amount of such costs to be determined by the tribunal.[33]

Withdrawal of Appeal

16.25 In relation to the withdrawal of appeals, the rules may make provision:

(i) that a party which has brought an appeal may not withdraw it without the leave of the appeal tribunal or, in specified circumstances, the President or the Registrar;

(ii) for the appeal tribunal to grant leave to withdraw the appeal on such conditions as it considers appropriate;

(iii) enabling the appeal tribunal to publish any decision which it could have made had the appeal not been withdrawn;

(iv) as to the effect of withdrawal of an appeal; and

(v) as to any procedure to be followed if the parties to proceedings on an appeal agree to settle.[34]

Interim Orders

16.26 Rules may also provide for an appeal tribunal to make an interim order granting on an interim basis any remedy which the tribunal would have power to grant in its final decision. Such an order may in particular suspend the effect of a decision made by the OFT or vary the conditions or obligations attached to the exemption.[35] This is an important power. The extent to which parties seek to obtain such an interim order may depend on how far the tribunal will require the payment of a deposit (see paragraphs 16.19 and 16.20 above) as a condition of granting an interim order.

Joinder of Parties

16.27 Finally, rules may provide for a person who is not a party to proceedings on an appeal to be joined in those proceedings and for appeals to be consolidated on terms as the appeal tribunal thinks appropriate.[36] This will enable third parties who may be affected by the outcome of the appeal, for example complainants, to be joined in the proceedings.

---

[32] Sch 8 para 10.
[33] Sch 8 para 11.
[34] Sch 8 para 12.
[35] Sch 8 para 13.
[36] Sch 8 para 14.

Outcome of Proceedings

Decisions of an appeal tribunal may be taken by majority (ie two to one). The **16.28**
decision must state whether it was unanimous or taken by a majority.

The decision must be set out in a document which contains a statement of the rea- **16.29**
sons for the decision and be signed and dated by the chairman of the appeal tribunal.[37] The President of the Competition Commission Appeal Tribunals may
make appropriate arrangements for publication of the tribunal's decision.[38]
However, the obligations in relation to confidentiality which apply to the OFT
also apply to the tribunal.[39]

D. Powers of the Appeal Tribunal

An appeal tribunal is obliged to determine an application on the merits by refer- **16.30**
ence to the grounds set out in the notice of the appeal.[40] A tribunal may:

(i)   confirm or reverse the decision which is the subject of appeal;

(ii)   remit the matter to the OFT;

(iii) impose or revoke, or vary the amount of, a penalty;

(iv)   grant or cancel an individual exemption or vary any conditions or obliga-
       tions imposed in relation to the exemption by the OFT; or

(v)   make any other decision which the OFT could have made.[41]

Any decision of an appeal tribunal has the same effect and may be enforced in the
same manner, as a decision of the OFT.[42]

If an appeal tribunal upholds the OFT decision which is the subject of the appeal, **16.31**
it may nevertheless set aside any findings of fact on which the OFT's decision was
based.[43] This will allow parties taking private actions before the UK courts in
respect of infringements of the Chapter I or II prohibition to take issue with the
relevant facts (findings of fact are otherwise binding on parties).[44]

The appeal tribunal will have much broader powers than the CFI has in relation **16.32**
to EC competition law. The EC Court has a power of judicial review of European

---

[37] Sch 8 para 4(1) and (2).
[38] Sch 8 para 4(4).
[39] Sch 8 para 4(3); and s 56.
[40] Sch 8 para 3(1).
[41] Sch 8 para 3(2).
[42] Sch 8 para 3(3).
[43] Sch 8 para 3(4).
[44] S 58.

Commission decisions, but it has no general appellate role.[45] The appeal tribunal is not similarly restricted. It may undertake a formal rehearing of the case. It may then review the OFT decision in its entirety including the facts on which it is based, all relevant issues of law and the remedies.

16.33   Although the applicant can contend errors of fact before an appeal tribunal, the powers of a tribunal stop short of any investigatory powers, and so a tribunal is likely to remit cases back to the OFT where it considers that it would be more effective for the OFT to resume investigation (see Chapter 14 on the exercise of the OFT's investigatory powers). In this regard, the OFT has stated:

> The appeal tribunal will not carry out investigation work: if substantial new evidence comes to light at the appeal stage, the case will be referred back to the Director General.[46]

16.34   It is for the appellants to indicate in the notice of appeal what issues they wish the appeal tribunal to consider, and the appeal tribunal is limited to considering such issues. However, it is likely that appellants will generally draft the notice of appeal in broad terms to ensure that the appeal tribunal is able to consider the full range of possible issues, to allow for the consideration of points which only occur to the parties during the course of the appeal.

16.35   The difference in jurisdiction of appeal tribunals as compared with the CFI at EC level is demonstrated in a number of ways:

- An appeal tribunal is able to grant an individual exemption from the Chapter I prohibition, whereas the CFI has no such power in relation to Article 81(3) (formerly Article 85(3)).

- An appeal tribunal may, where it reverses a decision of the OFT, deal with the matter itself and thus impose its own decision and remedy; it may, but does not have to, remit the matter to the OFT. The CFI, on the other hand, does not have the power to substitute its own decision for that of the European Commission. Where the CFI annuls a European Commission decision, the European Commission must then consider what action, if any, to take and this may include re-opening the procedure.

- The appeal tribunal can impose or revoke a penalty or vary the amount of any penalty.

- The class of persons which can appeal the OFT's decisions is wider than the class which may appeal European Commission decisions, the former including as it does broader interest groups (ie third parties with a sufficient interest, or their representatives).

---

[45]   The Court has taken a broad view of its powers in this regard and in a number of cases it has undertaken a more detailed factual analysis of European Commission decisions.

[46]   Office of Fair Trading, 'Competition Act 1998: The Major Provisions' (OFT 400), para 14.5; and see Lord Simon's comment at n 30 above.

E. Appeals from the Competition Commission

The Act also provides for the possibility of appeal *from* an appeal tribunal of the   **16.36**
Competition Commission. Such an appeal may be on a point of law arising from
any decision of an appeal tribunal, or from any decision of an appeal tribunal as to
the amount of a penalty.[47] Thus, there is no right of appeal in relation to findings
of fact, although it may be arguable that a manifest disregard of the facts by the
appeal tribunal gives rise to an issue of law. An appeal may be made only to the
appropriate court, with leave, and at the instance of a party or the instance of a
person who has sufficient interest in the matter (ie an appropriate third party).[48]
In relation to proceedings in England and Wales, the appropriate court is the
Court of Appeal; in relation to Scotland, it is the Court of Session; and, in relation
to Northern Ireland, it is the Court of Appeal in Northern Ireland.[49]

---

[47] S 49(1).
[48] S 50(2).
[49] S 50(4).

Appeals from the Cooperation Commission

Part VII

MONOPOLY INVESTIGATIONS

17

MONOPOLY INVESTIGATIONS—FRAME-
WORK OF THE LEGISLATION

A. Overview

Under the UK's new system of competition law, anti-competitive practices will be **17.01** controlled not only by the Chapter I prohibition and the Chapter II prohibition, but also by the pre-existing legislation in the **monopoly provisions of the Fair Trading Act 1973 (FTA)**. Whereas the Competition Act 1998 repealed the Restrictive Trade Practices Act 1976, the Resale Prices Act 1976 and the provisions on anti-competitive practices in the Competition Act 1980, the monopoly provisions of the FTA are retained and, indeed, strengthened.

By contrast with the new Chapter I and Chapter II prohibitions, the FTA monop- **17.02** oly provisions do not render certain types of practice automatically unlawful. Instead, they allow the UK competition authorities to investigate conduct and, where that conduct is found to operate against the public interest, to order remedial action to be taken for the future (with no retrospective penalties or liabilities). Investigations may be made in respect of either of two types of 'monopoly situation':

(i) 'Complex monopoly situations': These are, broadly speaking, investigations into entire markets or sectors in the economy, rather than individual companies or firms, and may be conducted where, in respect of at least 25 per cent of the sector, there is conduct restrictive of competition (even without any

449

anti-competitive agreement or concerted practice). The complex monopoly provisions fill a lacuna, as neither the Chapter I prohibition nor the Chapter II prohibition is properly capable of controlling sector-wide abuses: the Chapter I prohibition controls concerted practices but that is only where there is some degree of deliberate co-ordination between the market players; while the Chapter II prohibition can control abuses by two or more firms which are jointly dominant, but the definition of joint dominance is fairly narrow.

(ii) 'Scale monopoly situations': These are investigations into conduct by any single company or enterprise which accounts for at least 25 per cent of the supply (or consumption) of a particular product or service in the UK. There is, of course, considerable overlap between the purpose of scale monopoly investigations and that of the Chapter II prohibition on abuse of a dominant position, and there was much debate whether the scale monopoly provisions should be retained in the new regime.[1] In deciding to retain the scale monopoly provisions alongside the Chapter II prohibition, the government expressed the belief that they should only be used either: (i) where 'there has already been proven abuse under the prohibition *and* the [OFT] believes there is a real prospect of future different abuses by the same firm';[2] or (ii) if the scale monopoly arises in a regulated utility sector.[3]

17.03 While retaining the FTA monopoly provisions, the Competition Act 1998 also makes a number of significant changes, as follows:

• The OFT will have new and stronger powers in connection with its initial investigations into monopoly situations. These powers will be similar, but not identical, to the powers of investigation in connection with the Chapter I prohibition and Chapter II prohibitions,[4] and will include powers (enforceable by the sanction of criminal penalties) to require UK businesses to produce relevant documents or information, and to enter business premises to obtain such documents or information.[5]

• The government is empowered to extend the scope of the monopoly provisions to cover services involving 'permitting the use of land' (eg the letting of properties).[6]

---

[1] See Ch 1 of this book, paras 1.12–1.21.

[2] 'A prohibition approach to anti-competitive agreements and abuse of dominant position: Draft Bill', Department of Trade and Industry, Aug 1997, para 6.23. See also Lord Simon of Highbury, Minister in the Department of Trade and Industry, *Hansard*, HL, vol 585, no 99, col 350.

[3] Department of Trade and Industry, 'A Fair Deal for Consumers: Modernising the Framework for Utility Regulation—the Response to Consultation', July 1998, 20.

[4] See Ch 14 for OFT powers under the Chapter I and Chapter II prohibitions.

[5] Competition Act 1998, ss 66 and 67. See Ch 18, paras 18.11–18.19 below for details.

[6] Competition Act 1998, s 68.

- Full-length investigations, which previously were conducted by the Monopolies and Mergers Commission, will now be conducted by the Competition Commission, which replaces it.[7]

In essence, in investigating a scale monopoly situation or a complex monopoly situation, the UK authorities need to ask three questions: first, whether they have **jurisdiction** to investigate—ie whether there is a scale or complex monopoly situation; secondly, whether practices on the part of the persons in whose favour the monopoly situation exists 'operate, or may be expected to operate, against the **public interest**'; and, thirdly, what action should be taken to **remedy** any effects identified as operating against the public interest. These three issues are dealt with in this chapter. Chapter 18 below addresses the procedures for applying the monopoly provisions. **17.04**

B. Jurisdiction—When Can Monopoly Investigations be Conducted?

'Complex Monopoly Situation'

An investigation into a complex monopoly situation is, essentially, designed to uncover anti-competitive practices and other market failures which occur in a particular sector of the economy, even in the absence of any restrictive agreement or collusion or dominant market position. In recent years there have been complex monopoly situations into such sectors as foreign package holidays,[8] domestic electrical goods (ranging from television sets to washing machines),[9] contact lens solutions,[10] and the retailing of recorded music (on CD, vinyl and tape).[11] **17.05**

The Competition Commission may be asked (by the OFT or by the Secretary of State[12]) to investigate a 'complex monopoly situation'. This is defined in section 11 of the FTA, read with sections 6(1)(c) and 7(1)(c), as arising where the following two conditions are both met: **17.06**

(i) Two or more persons 'whether voluntarily or not, and whether by agreement or not, **so conduct their respective affairs as in any way to prevent, restrict or distort competition**' in connection with the production or supply of goods, or the supply of services, of any description.

---

[7] Competition Act 1998, s 45(3).

[8] Monopolies and Mergers Commission report, *Foreign Package Holidays*, Cm 3813, Dec 1997.

[9] Monopolies and Mergers Commission reports, *Domestic Electrical Goods*, Cm 3675 and 3676, July 1997.

[10] Monopolies and Mergers Commission report, *Contact Lens Solutions*, Cm 2242, May 1993.

[11] Monopolies and Mergers Commission report, *The Supply of Recorded Music*, Cm 2242, June 1994.

[12] The Secretary of State may sometimes act jointly with other ministers, normally within the Department of Trade and Industry, in referring the matter to the Competition Commission.

- There must be at least two persons or companies which behave in a manner restrictive of competition, whether or not there is any collusion between them and whether or not they intend to do so.

- For the purposes of counting, companies in the same corporate group count as just one company.

- Although two is the minimum number of persons which can constitute a complex monopoly, there is no maximum number, and in the 1993 investigation into private medical services, the 12,000 consultant doctors who do private work were held collectively to constitute a complex monopoly situation.[13]

(ii) The persons or companies behaving in this manner must together account for **at least 25 per cent** of the supply (or consumption) of goods or services of that description.

- None of the individual persons or companies needs to have a dominant market position, provided that together they account for at least 25 per cent of the sector.

- The 25 per cent criterion is *not* a market share threshold; it is satisfied where the persons or companies together account for at least 25 per cent of the supply of goods or services of *any* description, whether or not that description corresponds to the correct economic definition of the relevant market.

17.07 The definitions of 'supply of goods' and 'supply of services', in section 137 of the FTA, make clear that virtually every economic sector is capable of being investigated under the complex monopoly provisions:

- 'Goods' is not specifically defined, but there are provisions as to what is included in, and excluded from, the term.
  - It specifically includes: (i) buildings and other structures; (ii) ships; (iii) aircraft; and (iv) hovercraft.
  - It specifically excludes: gas supply through pipes to tariff customers; raw cane or beet sugar; sugar beet; hops; and water.[14]
- 'Supply' of goods includes supply by way of sale, lease, hire or hire-purchase. If the goods are buildings or other structures, 'supply' includes the construction of buildings or other structures by one person for another person.
- 'Services' for these purposes extends to the supply of any matter other than goods.

---

[13] Monopolies and Mergers Commission report, *Private Medical Services*, Cm 2452, Feb 1994.
[14] Fair Trading Act 1973, s 50, read with Sch 5 Part I, and Sch 7 Part I.

- It specifically includes: (i) making arrangements for sharing telecommunications apparatus; (ii) provision of caravan sites; (iii) provision of bus stops and bus stations; (iv) the supply of railway network services and station services (ie as carried out by Railtrack); and (v) making arrangements permitting rail operators to use the Channel Tunnel (ie as carried out by Eurotunnel).

- It does not specifically extend to the supply of land, but the Competition Act 1998 provides that the Government may order the inclusion of services relating to use of land (and, for that purpose, may amend or repeal the provisions for the specific inclusion of the services identified as (ii) to (v) above).[15]

- It specifically excludes: services for the carriage of passengers or goods by national railways (ie as carried out by the train operating companies); letter postal services; the running of certain telecommunications systems; the provision of port facilities; air navigation services; and international air carriage (otherwise than by charter flight).[16]

- 'Supply' of services includes the undertaking and performance for gain or reward of engagements (whether professional or other) for services, including making services available to potential users—but does not include rendering services under an employment contract.[17]

'Scale Monopoly Situation'

Investigations into a scale monopoly situation are, essentially, designed to uncover anti-competitive practices and abuses on the part of single businesses which have a significant position in their economic sector. To this extent, the scale monopoly provisions of the FTA largely fulfil the function of the new Chapter II prohibition on abuse of a dominant position and, as noted in paragraph 17.02 above, the government has indicated that it intends that the scale monopoly provisions should only be used:

17.08

(i)   in the regulated utility sectors;[18] *or*

(ii) where an abuse of a dominant position has already been proven under the Chapter II prohibition, and the OFT believes that there is a real prospect of future different abuses by the same firm.

The government envisages that scale monopoly investigations would therefore occur only in 'exceptional circumstances'[19]. Although the Competition Act 1998 does not actually limit the power to conduct scale monopoly investigations to

---

[15] Fair Trading Act 1973, s 137(3A), inserted by Competition Act 1998, s 68.

[16] Fair Trading Act 1973, s 50, read with Sch 5, Part I, and Sch 7, Part I.

[17] Fair Trading Act 1973, s 137(3).

[18] Department of Trade and Industry, n 3 above, 20. See also: Office of Fair Trading, 'Competition Act 1998: The Major Provisions' (OFT 400), paras 13.4 and 13.5

[19] 'A prohibition approach to anti-competitive agreements and abuse of dominant position: Draft Bill'; Department of Trade and Industry, Aug 1997, para 6.23.

these situations, it is expected that the government will ensure that the OFT does not initiate scale monopoly investigations in any other circumstances by using the Secretary of State's powers:

(a) to give general directions to the OFT indicating considerations to which it should have particular regard in determining whether to initiate a monopoly investigation by the Competition Commission (FTA, section 12(2)(c)); and/or

(b) to veto an OFT decision to initiate a monopoly investigation by the Competition Commission (FTA, section 50(6)). Until now, the only instance of the Secretary of State using these veto powers was in the context of an OFT decision to initiate an investigation by the Monopolies and Mergers Commission (the predecessor to the current Competition Commission) into alleged anti-competitive practices in the operation of bus services on the Isle of Arran (an island off the western coast of Scotland); the investigation, which would have been conducted under the Competition Act 1980, now repealed, was vetoed by the then Secretary of State, Michael Heseltine, who was strongly opposed to excessive regulatory interference in business and imposed the veto on the grounds that 'the size of this case did not justify the costs and burden of an investigation into the competition issues raised'.[20]

17.09 A 'scale monopoly situation' is defined—in sections 6(1)(a) and (b), and section 7(1)(a) and (b), of the FTA—as arising where one person (or company or corporate group) accounts for at least 25 per cent of the supply or consumption of goods or services of a particular description.

• As with complex monopoly situations, the 25 per cent criterion does not necessarily relate to market share. The criterion is met where a party accounts for 25 per cent of the supply or consumption of goods or services *of any description*—regardless of whether that description is the correct definition of the relevant economic market.

• The expressions 'goods', 'supply of goods', 'services' and 'supply of services' have the same meaning as in the context of complex monopoly situations (see paragraph 17.07 above).

Territorial Requirement

17.10 The monopoly situation must relate to the supply or consumption of goods within the United Kingdom. (There are also separate provisions for monopoly investigations where there are arrangements to prevent the supply of goods or services into the United Kingdom,[21] or to restrict exports from the United Kingdom

---

[20] Department of Trade and Industry press release, 14 Feb 1994.
[21] Fair Trading Act 1973, ss 6(1)(d) and 7(1)(d).

where one person or company or corporate group accounts for at least 25 per cent of UK production of goods or services of a particular description.[22] However, to date no monopoly investigations have been carried out under these provisions.)

The 25 per cent criterion in relation to complex or scale monopoly situations may **17.11** be met in respect of supplies or consumption in only a *part* of the United Kingdom[23]—for example, where a company accounts for more than 25 per cent of the supply or consumption of goods or services in Scotland, but not in the whole of the UK.[24]

The legislation does not specify that this should be 'a *substantial* part' of the **17.12** United Kingdom (this is in contrast to the UK's merger control legislation, but in line with the Chapter I and Chapter II prohibitions), so that there could be a monopoly investigation if the 25 per cent share were satisfied just in one locality in the UK, no matter how small; this might be the case, for example, in respect of localised markets such as bus services.

C. Substantive Assessment—the Public Interest

Where a monopoly situation is established, the next step is to establish whether **17.13** any act or omission on the part of the person(s)—or companies or corporate groups—in whose favour the monopoly situation exists:

> operates, or may be expected to operate, against **the public interest**.

The expression 'the public interest' is not defined anywhere in the legislation. However, section 84(1) of the Fair Trading Act provides that, where the Competition Commission is required to investigate whether any matter operates or may be expected to operate against the public interest, it 'shall take into account all matters which appear to [it] in the particular circumstances to be relevant'. This naturally gives the Competition Commission a great deal of discretion to determine the public interest. However, section 84(1) also says that the Competition Commission 'among other things, shall have regard to the desirability' of various factors, which are identified as follows:

(a) maintaining and promoting effective competition in the supply of goods and services in the UK;

(b) promoting the interests of consumers in the UK;

(c) promoting, through competition, costs reductions, innovation and increased market entry;

---

[22] Fair Trading Act 1973, s 8.
[23] Fair Trading Act 1973, s 9.
[24] Monopolies and Mergers Commission report, *Animal Waste*, Cm 2340, Sept 1993, para 10.6.

(d) maintaining and promoting 'the balanced distribution of industry and employment' in the UK; and

(e) maintaining and promoting competitive activity on the part of UK suppliers in markets outside the UK.

In this list, which is not exhaustive, items (a) to (c) are all concerned with promoting competition in UK markets. Item (d) relates to regional, industrial and employment policy. Item (e) is concerned with export promotion.

17.14 In practice, the promotion of competition in UK markets has been the primary concern of monopoly investigations in the past.[25] This is likely to remain the case in the future: in the case of complex monopolies, the very definition of 'complex monopoly situation' entails that the public interest concern will be related to the prevention, restriction or distortion of competition (see paragraph 17.06 above); and, in the case of scale monopolies, the government has indicated its intention that the scale monopoly provisions should be used only as an adjunct to the Competition Act 1998, with a view to identifying structural remedies for anti-competitive conduct which infringes the Chapter II prohibition on abuses of a dominant position.[26]

17.15 The wide discretion in assessing the public interest which is accorded to the Competition Commission—previously named the Monopolies and Mergers Commission—has been complemented by a tendency on the Commission's part to assess each case on its own particular merits, while rarely regarding the competition analysis in previous cases as any form of precedent.[27] In this context, the examples set out below of assessments of the 'public interest' in previous complex monopoly investigations should be regarded as primarily illustrative. In particular, these examples have been selected to show practices which have been condemned as contrary to the public interest under the complex monopoly provisions, but which it would have been difficult or impossible to prohibit under either the Chapter I or the Chapter II prohibition:

• excessive pricing (*see paragraphs 17.16–17.18 below*);

• parallel pricing (*paragraphs 17.19–17.22*);

---

[25] Fair Trading Act 1973, s 49(2)(c). It should be noted, however, that it is possible to limit the scope of monopoly investigations so as to cover only certain aspects of the public interest (s 49(2)(c) and (3), or to cover only the purely factual questions whether there is a monopoly investigation, what steps are being taken to maintain it and whether any act or omission on the part of the relevant persons is attributable to the monopoly situation (s 48—see Ch 18, para 18.23 below).

[26] 'A prohibition approach to anti-competitive agreements and abuse of dominant position: draft Bill', Department of Trade and Industry, Aug 1997, para 6.22.

[27] This contrasts with the European Commission's practice under Arts 81 and 82 EC (formerly Arts 85 and 86), where previous decisions are often cited as precedent. Because of s 60 of the Competition Act 1998, the OFT will also be required to have regard to previous European Commission cases as precedent when determining questions arising under the Chapter I and Chapter II prohibitions 'in relation to competition within the United Kingdom'.

- recommended resale prices (*paragraphs 17.23–17.25*);
- parallel exclusivity (*paragraphs 17.26–17.28*), and
- lack of transparency (*paragraphs 17.29–17.30*).

Excessive Pricing

Complex monopoly investigations have examined whether the prices of products **17.16** are 'excessive' even in the absence of an agreement or concerted practice, and even where the firms concerned have not held individually dominant positions (and probably would not be regarded as 'jointly dominant' for the purposes of the Chapter II prohibition).

An example is the 1995 inquiry into the supply of *Video Games* in the UK,[28] initi- **17.17** ated in response to concerns that the sale prices of video games by the two major players, Nintendo and Sega, were excessive (particularly when compared with prices in other countries). It was accepted that there was competition between the two companies (and no evidence of collusion), and neither company could clearly be said to have a dominant position—Sega's UK market share of combined console and games software trade sales was 38 per cent, and Nintendo's was less than 25 per cent (such that Nintendo was not even a scale monopolist).[29] Nevertheless, the Monopolies and Mergers Commission concluded that a complex monopoly situation existed in favour of both Sega and Nintendo, resulting in retail prices for the largest selling format games being 'significantly higher' than in the United States.[30] The complex monopoly was found to operate against the public interest in a number of respects, including the setting of 'excess prices' for the cartridges which both companies supplied to third party publishers of their software (the publishers needed these cartridges to ensure that the software was compatible with the companies' hardware), thereby raising software prices across the whole market—as well as by various technical features and restrictions in technology licences granted to third party software publishers which had the effect of limiting market entry.[31] In assessing whether prices were excessive, regard was had in particular to two factors:

(i) comparisons of retail prices in the UK with those in the United States, France and Germany (after taking account of different indirect tax rates in those countries);[32] and

(ii) the profitability of the companies concerned—with their return on turnover being compared with those of 'a number of other major international

---

[28] Monopolies and Mergers Commission report, *Video Games*, Cm 2781, Mar 1995.
[29] Ibid, paras 2.21 and 2.22.
[30] Ibid, para 2.62.
[31] Ibid, para 2.97.
[32] Ibid, paras 2.56 to 2.62.

companies with strong brands operating in similar markets', Nintendo's profitability was found to be very near that of the most profitable, and Sega's in the middle band.[33]

Another complex monopoly investigation into allegations of excessive pricing, carried out almost contemporaneously with that into video games, related to *The Supply of Recorded Music*[34] (ie on compact discs, vinyl records and tapes) in the UK.

17.18 This found that there was a complex monopoly situation comprising the main UK retailers of recorded music (WH Smith, Our Price, HMV and Woolworths), with practices restrictive of competition, in that these companies managed to secure from the manufacturers discounts which were larger than those available to other retailers—but did not find that this prevented a competitive market in retailing.[35] As regards excessive pricing, when the prices of compact discs were compared with those in the United States, it transpired that, after taking account of different tax rates and the exchange rates, the retail price differences for recorded music as between the UK and the United States were no more than for 'a range of other goods' and, when comparisons were made between the UK and other countries, the UK generally had lower prices for compact discs.[36]

Parallel Pricing

17.19 Parallel pricing is the phenomenon where competitors' prices are broadly similar across the market (or a significant part of it), and movement in those prices (upwards or downwards) occurs roughly at the same time. This is often symptomatic of market failure, and the operation of an oligopolistic rather than a competitive market: in a competitive market, it is more likely that competitors will seek to undercut each other, and that neither prices nor price movements will be stable.[37]

17.20 Parallel pricing can be prevented under the Chapter I prohibition only where there is an 'agreement' or 'concerted practice' between the competitors to fix their prices; as described in Chapter 4 paragraphs 4.18–4.22, there needs to be at least an element of deliberateness on the part of the competitors in order to establish a concerted practice or an agreement. Moreover, parallel pricing can only be prevented under the Chapter II prohibition only if a dominant position can be

---

[33] Ibid. paras 2.52 to 2.55.
[34] Monopolies and Mergers Commission report, *The Supply of Recorded Music*, Cm 2599, June 1994.
[35] Ibid, para 2.125.
[36] Ibid, paras 2.82 and 2.89.
[37] However, similar prices across a market may instead be the result of a highly competitive market, where competitive pressures are such that all the competitors in the market set their prices at the lowest commercially viable level.

shown to be held by the parties concerned (ie joint dominance), and if there is evidence of an anti-competitive abuse of such position.

Complex monopoly situations offer the possibility of remedying the market failure represented by parallel pricing even if there is no evidence of an agreement or concerted practice, or of an abuse of a dominant position. This was the case in the 1993–94 complex monopoly investigation into *Private Medical Services*.[38] A significant proportion of the hospital consultants who supplied private medical services (nearly three-quarters of them) were found to be setting their fees broadly in line with pricing guidelines issued by the British Medical Association (the representative organisation of doctors).[39] This was held to be against the public interest, because it resulted in fees for private medical services being higher than they would otherwise have been.[40] However, there was no evidence of an agreement or concerted practice between the thousands of consultants concerned (who, together, accounted for at least 25 per cent of the total supply of private medical services, thus giving rise to the complex monopoly situation): the Monopolies and Mergers Commission reported that, in spite of some complaints that anæsthetists and pathologists fixed their charges, there was 'no evidence of widespread abuse and there has been no criticism of the activities of groups in other specialities'.[41] Moreover, none of the consultants concerned could be said to have a dominant position in the market (each one had only a very small market share), and there is no suggestion that the consultants were united by the kind of 'economic links' which would give rise to joint dominance under the Chapter II prohibition.[42]

17.21

It will not always be the case, however, that parallel pricing is found to operate against the public interest. UK petrol wholesalers were found in 1990 to have a tendency to increase prices almost simultaneously and by roughly the same amount.[43] However, this was not found to be against the public interest: this was not only because there was no evidence of collusion between the competing petrol wholesalers[44] (as noted above, there can be an adverse public interest finding even in the absence of a concerted practice), but also because there was no evidence that the wholesalers were making monopoly profits.[45] The Monopolies and Mergers Commission concluded that the market was competitive.[46] (There was, however, sufficient evidence of practices restrictive of competition to give rise to a complex

17.22

---

[38] Monopolies and Mergers Commission report, *Private Medical Services*, Cm 2452, Feb 1994.
[39] Ibid, para 11.26.
[40] Ibid, para 11.120.
[41] Ibid, para 11.64.
[42] Case T–68/89 *Società Italiano Vetro v Commission* [1992] ECR II–1403.
[43] Monopolies and Mergers Commission report, *The Supply of Petrol*, Cm 972, Feb 1990, paras 1.9 and 8.46.
[44] Ibid, para 8.52.
[45] Ibid, para 8.75.
[46] Ibid, para 8.223.

monopoly situation, such as the 'solus' tie under which petrol wholesalers impose exclusive purchasing obligations on the retailers to whom they supply petrol. This suggests that a relatively low threshold of anti-competitiveness is needed for a finding of a complex monopoly situation, but a much higher degree is needed if there is to be an adverse public interest conclusion.)

Recommended Resale Prices

17.23   Resale price maintenance—the imposition by suppliers of an *obligation* on purchasers not to resell contract goods below a minimum price—is prohibited under the Chapter I prohibition (see Chapter 7, paragraphs 7.64–7.69). However, the Chapter I prohibition does not extend to *recommended* resale prices which are not legally binding.[47]

17.24   Nevertheless, in certain market conditions non-binding recommended resale prices can have anti-competitive effects—and these can be investigated and terminated under the complex monopoly provisions, even though they are not prohibited under the Chapter I prohibition. In July 1997, the government published the reports of two complex monopoly investigations which had been initiated over two years earlier. These concerned the operation of recommended resale prices in the retailing of domestic electrical goods—both 'brown' goods such as televisions, hi-fi systems and video recorders, and 'white' goods such as washing machines, dishwashers, fridges and freezers. In both investigations, the Monopolies and Mergers Commission had found that the manufacturers of the brown and white goods who published recommended resale prices constituted a complex monopoly situation, and concluded that the use of recommended resale prices in these two sectors operated against public interest—because nearly all suppliers informed retailers of a recommended resale price, and most retailers took account of that recommended resale price in setting their own prices.[48]

17.25   To remedy the adverse effect on the public interest, it was decided to prohibit the use of recommended resale prices (RRPs) in the retailing of the domestic electrical goods concerned. The statement on this by the Secretary of State, Margaret Beckett, indicates the flexible and pragmatic way in which the complex monopoly provisions can be applied, according to the particular circumstances of the market investigated. Thus, no attempt is made to prohibit RRPs altogether, but only where a complex monopoly investigation has found them to be the cause of market failure:

---

[47] Case 161/84 *Pronuptia de Paris v Pronuptia de Paris Irmgard Schillgallis* [1986] ECR 353, para 27.
[48] Monopolies and Mergers Commission reports: *Domestic Electrical Goods: I* ('brown' goods), Cm 3675–I, July 1997, vol I, para 1.11; *Domestic Electrical Goods: II* ('white' goods), Cm 3676–I, July 1997, vol I, para 1.11.

I also propose to prohibit the use of RRPs themselves in the eight electrical goods markets, as the MMC [Monopolies and Mergers Commission] have recommended. RRPs are widely used in retailing and *I do not consider the use of RRPs generally to be a cause for concern.* I have considered carefully the comments which parties had made to MMC about the possible benefits of RRPs. The MMC believed, however, that nothing short of a prohibition on RRPs would deal effectively with the adverse effects they found. They considered that the use of RRPs is so entrenched in *the way business is conducted in these UK markets* that tackling only the associated practices, such as the ways in which pressure is put on dealers to adhere to RRPs, would be an insufficient remedy . . .

Hence my decision to prohibit the use of RRPs in these markets.[49]

Parallel Exclusivity

As already noted, exclusive purchasing agreements are automatically exempted from the Chapter I prohibition provided that they meet the criteria set out in the EC block exemption (see Chapter 6, paragraph 6.12(b)), and are likely to be excluded under the government's section 50 order for vertical agreements (see Chapter 5, paragraph 5.92). They are only caught by the Chapter II prohibition if either the supplier or the purchaser has a dominant position. **17.26**

There may, nevertheless, be cases where exclusive agreements have a significantly anti-competitive effect in a market, particularly where that market is oligopolistic and a significant proportion of the market is covered by parallel exclusivity agreements, thus making new market entry difficult and weakening the prospects for competition in that market. **17.27**

The complex monopoly provisions can be used to address this situation, where neither the Chapter I nor the Chapter II prohibition would be capable of doing so. This was the case with the complex monopoly investigation into the supply of *Carbonated Soft Drinks* in the UK, which was conducted in 1990–1.[50] The market for the supply of carbonated soft drinks could be characterised as oligopolistic, with Coca-Cola Schweppes accounting for 43 per cent of supplies and Britvic for a further 22 per cent (by value).[51] Both suppliers, in their sales to retail outlets in the 'leisure trade' (pubs, fast-food restaurants and clubs), imposed exclusive purchasing obligations in a large number of cases—nearly one-third of Coca-Cola Schweppes's sales to the leisure trade, and nearly 15 per cent of Britvic's.[52] The Monopolies and Mergers Commission's conclusions about the effects on the public interest related specifically to the market concerned: **17.28**

---

[49] Department of Trade and Industry press release P/97/512, 30 July 1997, 'Margaret Beckett acts on recommended retail prices and refusal to supply in the domestic electrical goods market'; emphasis added.

[50] Monopolies and Mergers Commission, *Carbonated Drinks*, Cm 1625, Aug 1991.

[51] Ibid, para 10.3 (Table 10.1).

[52] Ibid, para 1.19.

> In other sectors, a possible benefit of exclusive agreements might be that they lead to greater promotion and marketing of the product as a means of new entry, particularly in the case of small and medium-sized undertakings. This is not likely to be the case for carbonated drinks in the leisure trade, as only the larger manufacturers can in practice bid for the contracts . . . More generally, we note in this connection the strength of the position of [Coca-Cola Schweppes and Britvic] . . . , and the fact that such agreements cover a significant proportion of [their] . . . sales to the leisure trade.[53]

The Monopolies and Mergers Commission fully appreciated that the agreements might be covered by the EC block exemption on exclusive purchasing agreements, but believed that this did not prevent it from examining 'whether adverse effects arise from particular practices in the United Kingdom and from considering what remedial action, if any, would be appropriate'.[54] The outcome was a prohibition on exclusivity provisions in the carbonated drinks supply agreements operated by Coca-Cola Schweppes and Britvic.

Lack of Transparency

17.29 Some practices which are not in themselves restrictive of competition—and are incapable of being addressed under the Chapter I or Chapter II prohibition—may nevertheless give rise to market dysfunctions, for example by impeding the ability of consumers to make informed choices in the market. These can be investigated and remedied under the complex monopoly provisions.

17.30 A prime example occurred in the complex monopoly investigation into *Foreign Package Holidays* in 1997.[55] Three of the UK's largest travel agencies were held to constitute a complex monopoly situation as a result of various practices restrictive of competition, including selling package holidays in such a way as to give a competitive advantage to the tour operators with which they were each vertically integrated (ie the tour operator in the same corporate group as that travel agent). One of the issues considered by the Monopolies and Mergers Commission, in examining whether the complex monopoly operated against the public interest, was the fact that these major travel agents were vertically integrated with major tour operators. The conclusion was that vertical integration itself in this particular industry did not operate against the public interest, since its anti-competitive effects were 'slight' and, indeed, it resulted in 'keener' prices and more choice of foreign package holidays for consumers'.[56] Nevertheless, it was felt that the market would operate better if ownership links between the tour operator and travel agent businesses of the largest groups were made clearer to the public, so that 'a significant proportion of consumers would be prepared to shop around more, thus putting

---

[53] Monopolies and Mergers Commission, *Carbonated Drinks*, Cm 1625, Aug 1991 para 10.93.
[54] Ibid, para 10.85.
[55] Monopolies and Mergers Commission report, *Foreign Package Holidays*, Cm 3813, Dec 1997.
[56] Ibid, paras 2.193 and 2.194.

more competitive pressure on the vertically integrated travel agents'.[57] Accordingly, it was concluded that the failure to take sufficient steps to make customers aware of the vertical integration was a practice which operated against the public interest,[58] and the remedy proposed was that the travel agents concerned should permanently display the ownership links on their shop fronts.[59]

D. Remedies

The flexibility of the monopoly investigation system extends to the remedial **17.31** action which may be taken. Where a (complex or scale) monopoly investigation results in a finding that certain practices operate against the public interest, the Secretary of State has a wide range of options for remedies, giving a discretion far more extensive than that available under the Chapter I or Chapter II prohibitions where the only *remedy* (as opposed to sanction) is a requirement to 'bring the infringement to an end'.[60]

The range of remedies which may be enforced by a binding ministerial order, in **17.32** the event that a monopoly situation is found to operate against the public interest, is set out in Schedule 8 to the Fair Trading Act 1973.[61] (In addition, it is possible to secure even more wide-ranging remedies by way of undertakings—see Chapter 18, paragraphs 18.66–18.67 (using new numbering suggested for Ch 18) below.) These include the possibility of requiring businesses to alter their commercial conduct in a wide variety of ways, and in addition the option to impose *structural* remedies or changes to the business—provided that the Minister considers the action 'requisite' for the purpose of remedying or preventing adverse effects identified by the Competition Commission (formerly the Monopolies and Mergers Commission).[62] Thus, orders may be made under Schedule 8:

- prohibiting: entry into, or carrying out of, any agreement; refusals to supply; 'tying' arrangements (ie making supply conditional on the buying of other goods or the doing of any other specified matter); discriminatory pricing; discriminatory supply policies; pricing other than in accordance with published price lists; or recommended resale pricing;

---

[57] Ibid, para 2.195.
[58] Ibid, para 2.176.
[59] Ibid, para 2.199.
[60] Competition Act 1998 ss 32 and 33.
[61] Fair Trading Act 1973 s 56.
[62] Fair Trading Act 1973 s 56(2). The Competition Commission (Monopolies and Mergers Commission) must have concluded that the monopoly situation operates against the public interest before ministers may impose any remedies by order. However, there is no requirement that the remedies ordered should accord with the Commission's recommendations for remedies, and the minister has discretion to order whatever he considers a 'requisite' remedy.

- requiring the publication of: price lists; accounting information; or market information;

- imposing 'structural' prohibitions or obligations—such as prohibitions on acquisitions of companies or businesses; obligations to divide up a business, company or corporate group (including by transfers of property or shares); limitations, within an existing company, of voting rights; requirements, within a company, for business activities to be carried on separately.

17.33 In practice, the authorities have been willing to exercise their discretion to apply remedies widely. Remedies which would not be available under the Chapter I or Chapter II prohibition have been applied in accordance with the particular circumstances of the market concerned. Examples include the outcome of the following complex monopoly investigations:

(i) *The supply of beer.* A complex monopoly investigation into the supply of beer in the UK found that the system of tied pubs (ie public houses owned by, and thus vertically integrated with, brewers) limited competition in the supply of beer, and made beer prices higher than they would otherwise have been. A wide range of remedies were ordered, including **structural remedies whereby large brewery groups were required to dispose of pubs**: it was made unlawful for brewing groups which held interests in more than 2,000 licensed premises to maintain ties on more than half the premises in excess of 2,000.[63]

(ii) *Performing rights.* The Performing Right Society (PRS) was responsible for administering the royalties payable to writers of music for performances of the music in which they have a copyright. The PRS was held to constitute a scale monopoly situation, and its administrative practices were found to be inefficient. The provision in its articles of association giving it sole rights to administer the collection and payment of live performance royalties were held to operate against the public interest. Among the remedies adopted as a result was a requirement to **change the company's articles of association**, such that PRS members were entitled to self-administer their own live performance rights.[64]

(iii) *Private medical services:* The publication by the British Medical Association of recommended fees for hospital consultants to charge for private medical services was, as described in paragraph 17.21, found to operate against the

---

[63] Monopolies and Mergers Commission report, *The Supply of Beer*, Cm 651, Mar 1989; the Supply of Beer (Tied Estate) Order 1989, SI 1989/2390.
[64] Monopolies and Mergers Commission report, *Performing Rights*, Cm 3147, Feb 1996; undertakings given by Performing Right Society Limited, 27 Feb 1997 (press release, Mar 1997).

public interest. Consequently, the BMA was **prohibited from publishing fee guidelines or recommended charges.**[65]

(iv) *White salt:* The prices charges by producers of white salt were found to be excessive and contrary to the public interest. The remedy was a binding **price control**, under which prices for white salt supplies within the UK were subject to an index-linked cap.[66]

---

[65] Monopolies and Mergers Commission report, *Private Medical Services*, Cm 2452, Feb 1994; undertakings given by British Medical Association, 21 Sept 1994 (press release, 17 Nov 1994).
[66] Monopolies and Mergers Commission report, *White Salt*, Cmnd 9778, June 1986; undertakings given by Staveley Industries plc, 16 Mar 1988 (press release, 8 Apr 1988) and amended 11 June 1992.

18

MONOPOLY INVESTIGATIONS—PROCEDURE

A. Procedural Overview

18.01 The procedural framework for monopoly investigations is fundamentally different from that which applies to the Chapter I and Chapter II prohibitions. This difference reflects the fact that the monopoly provisions are, in essence, concerned with *investigation and remedy* rather than prohibition. Consequently, under the monopoly provisions (and by contrast with the Chapter I and Chapter II prohibitions):

- no conduct is **unlawful or prohibited** until *after* it has been investigated and found to be a monopoly situation which operates against the public interest (unless the party concerned chooses to give a binding 'statutory undertaking' to the authorities to cease the conduct);

- **rights of private enforcement** in the courts are very limited, and apply only *after* conduct has been investigated and found to be a monopoly situation which operates against the public interest (or after a party has chosen to give a binding 'statutory undertaking' to cease such conduct).

The Competition Authorities

There are three main competition authorities involved in monopoly investiga-   **18.02**
tions. They are:

- the **OFT** (Office of Fair Trading), whose main role is to carry out a preliminary investigation of the conduct concerned, and decide whether to make a 'monopoly reference'—ie whether the conduct should be referred to the Competition Commission for a full monopoly investigation;

- the **Competition Commission** which, after a monopoly reference is made, conducts the full monopoly investigation and then produces a detailed report setting out the outcome of its investigation (the Competition Commission takes over this function from the Monopolies and Mergers Commission, as a result of the Competition Act 1998); and

- the **Secretary of State** for Trade and Industry (and other ministers, normally in the Department of Trade and Industry), to whom the Competition Commission's report is submitted—with responsibility for publishing the report and, if the report concludes that there is a monopoly situation which operates against the public interest, taking action to remedy the adverse effects to the public interest.

Summary of the Procedural Steps

The procedures for monopoly investigations are laid down in the Fair Trading Act   **18.03**
1973 (FTA), as amended by section 7 of the Deregulation and Contracting Out Act 1994 (which provides for parties to give binding 'statutory undertakings' as an alternative to a full monopoly investigation), and by sections 66 and 67 of the Competition Act 1998 (which strengthen the OFT's powers of investigation in relation to monopoly situations). The procedural steps may be summarised as follows:

(i)   The OFT conducts a **preliminary investigation** into whether there are grounds for believing that a monopoly situation may exist—*FTA, sections 44 and 46.*

- The OFT may do so on its own initiative, or following a complaint (for example, from a customer or competitor who may have suffered as a result of conduct)—including, in the case of scale monopolies, where there has been an infringement of the Chapter II prohibition (ie an abuse of a dominant position) and the OFT believes that there is a real prospect of future infringements by the same business.

- In conducting these preliminary investigations, the OFT has powers of investigation, which have been considerably strengthened by the Competition Act 1998, including powers to require suppliers and customers of the goods or services concerned to produce documents, accounting information and other business information, as well as powers to enter their business premises and obtain and view documents there and obtain explanations of those documents; these powers are enforceable with the sanction of a fine or imprisonment for non-compliance.

- The OFT's preliminary investigation generally takes several months.

(ii) Following the preliminary investigation, if the OFT considers that there is or may be a monopoly situation, the OFT may: either make a **monopoly reference to the Competition Commission**, initiating a full monopoly investigation—*FTA, section 50*; or propose that the businesses concerned give **statutory undertakings** to the Secretary of State as an alternative to a monopoly reference if the OFT considers that these would suffice to deal with any relevant adverse effects of the monopoly situation—*FTA, sections 56A to 56G*. Two points should be noted in this context:

- It is also possible for a monopoly reference to the Competition Commission to be made by the Secretary of State and Ministers, if they think that a monopoly investigation exists or may exist—*FTA, section 51*. In practice, the Secretary of State and Ministers do not normally make monopoly references, although this was done in the exceptional circumstances of the 1993 monopoly investigation into the UK gas industry[1].

- The Secretary of State has powers, within a fortnight of the making of a monopoly reference by the OFT, to order the Competition Commission not to proceed with the investigation—that is, to veto the OFT's monopoly reference—*FTA, section50(6)*. Again, these powers are not normally exercised, although they were exercised in one case under the (now defunct) anti-competitive practices provisions of the Competition Act 1980, when the then Secretary of State felt that an inquiry into bus services on the Isle of Arran was contrary to his policy of reducing unnecessary regulatory burdens on business.[2]

---

[1] See Monopolies and Mergers Commission report, *Gas*, Cm 2314, Aug 1993, vol 1, 57–8.
[2] Department of Trade and Industry press release, 14 Feb 1994.

(iii) If a monopoly reference is made, the **Competition Commission conducts the monopoly investigation**—*FTA, sections 81 to 85*. The Competition Commission must complete the investigation and produce a report on its conclusions. This must be done within the time limit specified in the monopoly reference; there is no statutory maximum time limit, but in practice monopoly references typically specify a time limit of one year or more.

During the monopoly investigation, the Competition Commission takes written and oral evidence from the parties alleged to constitute a monopoly situation, and from interested third parties, with a view to assessing:

(a) whether there is a monopoly situation and in whose favour it exists;

(b) whether the parties in whose favour the monopoly situation exists are taking steps to maintain the monopoly situation;

(c) whether any acts or omissions on the part of such parties is attributable to the monopoly situation; and

(d) whether any facts identified in answer to the preceding questions 'operate, or may be expected to operate, against the public interest'. (Sometimes the monopoly reference will be 'limited to the facts', in which case the Competition Commission does not address question (d).)

If the Competition Commission does identify effects adverse to the public interest, it may make recommendations on how to remedy or prevent those adverse effects. At the end of the investigation, the Competition Commission must submit its report to the Secretary of State.

(iv) After receiving the Competition Commission's report, the Secretary of State must consider its conclusions and any recommendations. The **Secretary of State publishes the Competition Commission report, and announces a decision** on what action is to be taken in the light of the report's conclusions. The Secretary of State may only take action in respect of the monopoly situation if the Competition Commission has found that there is a monopoly situation and specified particular effects adverse to the public interest—*FTA, section 56*.

(v) If the Competition Commission has identified adverse effects to the public interest, **the Secretary of State may (but does not have to) make an order or accept undertakings to remedy the adverse effects**—*FTA, sections 56 and 88*. In doing so, the Secretary of State has regard to any recommendations in the Competition Commission report, and any subsequent advice from the OFT, but the Secretary of State is not bound by either.

Each of these steps is described in the following paragraphs.

B. Preliminary Investigation by the OFT

18.04 The initial stage of the monopoly procedure is a preliminary investigation conducted by the OFT, with a view to discovering whether a (complex or scale) monopoly situation may exist. In practice the OFT also examines whether there are public interest/competition concerns relating to that monopoly situation which would warrant a monopoly reference to the Competition Commission or a request for 'statutory undertakings' as an alternative to a monopoly reference.

Sources of Investigation

18.05 The OFT may commence a preliminary investigation into a possible monopoly situation as a result of any of the following:

(i) A **complaint** submitted to the OFT—for example, from a competitor or customer of the party or parties allegedly constituting the monopoly situation, where such competitor or customer is sustaining losses as a result of anti-competitive or abusive behaviour by such parties. In practice, most investigations are set in motion by complaints of this nature.[3] (The OFT's approach to handling complaints is discussed in paragraphs 18.06–18.07 below.)

(ii) On the OFT's **own initiative**: the OFT routinely monitors the national press and trade publications for information about possible monopoly situations, and this monitoring and other internal research sometimes triggers a preliminary investigation.[4]

(iii) **Following a proven infringement of the Chapter II prohibition**: the government has expressed the view that scale monopoly investigations should be used only in 'exceptional circumstances' where there has already been proven abuse of a dominant position, in breach of the Chapter II prohibition, and the OFT believes that there is a real prospect of future different abuses by the same firm.[5]

The OFT's Handling of Complaints—Initial Consideration (ie Before a Preliminary Investigation is Launched)

18.06 As noted above, the OFT is prepared to initiate a preliminary investigation under the monopoly provisions if it receives a complaint from a third party, such as a customer or competitor. It will not always do so, and first it conducts an initial consideration to establish whether there is substance in the complaint; the OFT has a

---

[3] Office of Fair Trading, *Monopolies and Anti-competitive Practices* (3/95), 25.
[4] Ibid.
[5] Department of Trade and Industry, 'A prohibition approach to anti-competitive agreements and abuse of dominant position: draft Bill', Aug 1997, para 6.23. See also Lord Simon of Highbury, Minister in the Department of Trade and Industry, *Hansard*, HL, vol 585, no 99, col 350.

target that, in 90 per cent of cases, it will reach a decision on whether to proceed to a more formal preliminary investigation within 30 working days following receipt of a complaint.[6]

The main features of the initial consideration are as follows: **18.07**

- Although the OFT is prepared to consider complaints made orally over the telephone, the OFT generally expects the complaint to be confirmed in writing.[7]

- The complaint must give as full details as possible of the conduct complained about, including any available evidence.

- The party whose conduct is complained about is contacted, and given the opportunity to respond.

- Very often, the complainant will not want its identity disclosed to the party complained about. If so, the complainant should make this clear to the OFT. The OFT may, however, feel that it cannot pursue the complaint without disclosing the complainant's identity to the party complained about—but, before any such disclosure, the OFT invariably first seeks the complainant's permission.

- At the end of the period of initial consideration, the complainant receives a letter informing it whether the OFT will proceed to a preliminary investigation, or whether the complaint has been dismissed.

- All complaints are retained on file, enabling the issue to be re-examined at a later date if appropriate.[8]

The Preliminary Investigation Itself

The OFT's preliminary investigation into whether there may be a monopoly situation (and, if so, whether there are public interest concerns which warrant a monopoly reference or undertakings as an alternative) generally lasts several months. The OFT has set itself a target that, in 75 per cent of cases, it will compete its preliminary investigation within a period of six months.[9] The preliminary investigation is generally carried out by a small team of OFT officials, including an economist and a legal adviser. **18.08**

The OFT conducts the preliminary investigation by correspondence and, if appropriate, meetings with the main interested parties: the party or parties alleged to constitute the monopoly situation, the complainant (if any), relevant trade associations, competitors, customers and any customer/user bodies.[10] **18.09**

---

[6] Office of Fair Trading, *Code of Practice on Enforcement*, Jan 1994, 9.
[7] OFT, n 3 above, 25.
[8] Ibid, 25–6.
[9] OFT, n 6 above, Jan 1994, 9.
[10] OFT, n 3 above, 26.

18.10 In order to assist the gathering of information in the course of this preliminary investigation, the OFT has significant statutory powers of investigation. These powers, which have been considerably strengthened by the Competition Act 1998, are discussed in paragraphs 18.11–18.19 below.

The OFT's Powers of Investigation

18.11 The OFT's powers of investigation, in connection with its preliminary investigation of monopoly situations, are set out in sections 44 and 45 of the Fair Trading Act 1973 (FTA), as amended by sections 66 and 67 of the Competition Act 1998.

Powers of Investigation

18.12 The OFT may exercise the powers of investigation discussed in this paragraph where all the following criteria are met:

(i) it appears to the OFT that there are grounds for believing that a monopoly situation may exist;[11] and

(ii) it appears to the OFT that there are grounds for believing that it would not be precluded from making a monopoly reference to the Competition Commission;[12] and

(iii) the OFT is exercising the powers in order to assist it to decide whether or not to make a monopoly reference to the Competition Commission, or whether or not to propose the acceptance of statutory undertakings as an alternative.[13]

18.13 When these criteria are satisfied, the OFT is empowered to impose any of the requirements listed in (a) to (c) below on any person who is:

- a producer or supplier of the goods or services in question in the United Kingdom (ie a person who is a party to the alleged monopoly situation, or a competitor of such a person), or

- a customer of the goods or services in question in the United Kingdom.[14]

18.14 The requirements which may be imposed on any such person are:

(a) On written notice from the OFT, to **produce relevant documents**—including information recorded in any form (such as on computer)[15]—which are in that person's custody and control, provided such documents are specified or fall within a category specified in the written notice (the OFT may require that the documents be produced at a time and place specified in the written

---

[11] Fair Trading Act 1973, s 44(1)(a).
[12] Ibid, s 44(1)(b).
[13] Ibid, s 44(1) and (1A).
[14] Ibid, s 44(3).
[15] Ibid, s 44(8)(b) and (c).

notice).[16] The OFT has powers to take copies of the documents, and to require explanations from the person notified, or any past or present officer or employee of that person.[17] If the document is not produced, the OFT has powers to require the person to state, to the best of its knowledge and belief, where the document is.[18]

(b) On written notice from the OFT, to give the OFT **estimates, returns or other information** specified in the notice. (The OFT written notice may specify the time, and the form and manner, on which such information must be given.[19])

(c) To allow OFT officials **entry into business premises**. The OFT may require any person there to produce relevant documents in that person's custody or control, or to give the OFT an explanation of such documents. The OFT officers will allow the person 'a short time' for the party's legal adviser to be contacted and to arrive at the premises if this is reasonable and does not unduly delay or impede the investigation.[20]

Limitations on the Powers

There are two main limitations on the powers listed above. First, no person needs **18.15** to comply with any requirement, unless the OFT official shows evidence of a written authorisation by the Director General of Fair Trading (the head of the OFT) that that official is authorised to act on behalf of the Director General in exercising these OFT powers (whether that authorisation is general or specific).[21]

Secondly, the OFT's powers of investigation do not extend to compelling any **18.16** person to produce documents or information which such person could not be compelled to produce in civil proceedings in the High Court (or, in Scotland, the Court of Session).[22] Broadly, this means that persons are protected from providing the OFT with:

- documents enjoying legal professional privilege (communications between a solicitor and a client, and certain communications in contemplation of litigation);

- 'without prejudice' communications;

- documents benefiting from 'public interest privilege'; and

- information or documents which benefit from the privilege against self-incrimination in section 14 of the Civil Evidence Act 1968 (read with section 72 of the Supreme Court Act 1981).

---

[16] Ibid, s 44(2)(a) and (4).
[17] Ibid, s 44(5)(a).
[18] Ibid, s 44(5)(b).
[19] Ibid, s 44(2)(b) and (4).
[20] Ibid, s 44(2)(c). See also Office of Fair Trading, 'Competition Act 1998: Powers of Investigation' (OFT 404), para 9.4 read with paras 4.10–4.11
[21] Ibid, s 44(7) and Sch 1, para 7.
[22] Ibid, s 44(6).

Sanctions for Non-compliance with the Powers

18.17   Section 46 of the FTA, as amended, imposes severe penalties for non-compliance with the OFT's powers of investigation as listed in paragraph 18.14 above. In particular:

(i)   refusal (or wilful neglect) to comply with an OFT requirement under the powers carries the possibility of a fine and/or imprisonment (of up to two years);[23]

(ii)   wilfully altering, suppressing or destroying a document which the OFT has required the person to produce, carries the possibility of a fine and/or imprisonment (of up to two years);[24]

(iii)   intentional obstruction of the OFT in respect of any of its powers carries the possibility of a fine.[25]

Providing False or Misleading Information

18.18   Section 93B of the Fair Trading Act 1973 makes it a criminal offence for a person to furnish any information to the OFT (or to the Competition Commission or the Secretary of State) in connection with (among other things) its monopoly investigation functions if:

• the information is false or misleading in a material particular; and

• the person furnishing the information either knows this, or is reckless as to this (ie as to its being materially false or misleading).

18.19   Under section 132, where an offence has been committed by a company, and it is proved to have been committed with the consent or connivance of—or to be attributable to any neglect by—any director, manager, company secretary or other similar officer of the company, that individual *as well as* the company is guilty of the offence, and liable to be punished accordingly.

The maximum penalty for committing the offence is a two-year term of imprisonment or a fine (or both).

C. Reference to the Competition Commission or Statutory Undertakings as an Alternative

18.20   Once the OFT has concluded its preliminary investigation, it may either:

(i)   decide not to proceed further with the case, because no major competition issues are found; or

---

[23]   Fair Trading Act 1973, s 46(4).
[24]   Ibid, s 46(8).
[25]   Ibid, s 46(7).

(ii)   make a **monopoly reference** to the Competition Commission; or

(iii) propose that the businesses concerned give **statutory undertakings** to the Secretary of State as an alternative to a monopoly reference (sometimes called undertakings 'in lieu' of a monopoly reference).

Monopoly Reference to the Competition Commission

A monopoly reference is a request by the OFT (or by the Secretary of State[26]) to the Competition Commission requiring the Competition Commission to conduct a monopoly investigation and then to submit a report on its findings to the Secretary of State. The OFT may make a (complex or scale) monopoly reference where it appears to the OFT that a monopoly situation exists or may exist in relation to the supply of goods of any description or the supply of services of any description.[27] The goods or services in question are called, respectively, the 'reference goods' or 'reference services'. **18.21**

The monopoly reference must specify the reference goods or reference services.[28] The monopoly reference asks the Commission to investigate: **18.22**

(a)   whether a monopoly situation exists in relation to the reference goods or services;[29]

and, if so:

(b)   what kind of monopoly situation it is (for example, a scale monopoly situation or a complex monopoly situation);[30]

(c)   in favour of which persons the monopoly situation exists;[31]

(d)   whether such persons are taking steps to exploit or maintain the monopoly situation (and, if so, by what uncompetitive practices or in what other way);[32]

(e)   whether any act or omission is attributable to the monopoly situation and, if so, how;[33]

(f)   whether any facts found by the Competition Commission in investigating the above issues—or any act or omission on the part of the persons constituting the monopoly situation in respect of matters in the reference—'operates, or may be expected to operate, against the public interest'.[34]

---

[26]   See para 18.03(ii) above. The Secretary of State may sometimes make the reference jointly with other ministers.

[27]   Fair Trading Act 1973, s 50(1).

[28]   Ibid, s 47(1)(a) and (b).

[29]   Ibid, s 48. See Ch 17, paras 17.05–17.12 for the definition of 'monopoly situation'.

[30]   Ibid, s 48(a).

[31]   Ibid, s 48(b).

[32]   Ibid, s 48(c).

[33]   Ibid, s 48(d).

[34]   Ibid, ss 49(1)(b) and (2)(c). See Ch 17, paras 17.13–17.30 for a discussion of how this 'public interest' test is applied.

18.23   The monopoly reference need not cover all the issues listed above, and may be limited in a number of ways:

- The Competition Commission may be asked to investigate only a complex monopoly situation.[35]

- The Competition Commission may be asked to examine a monopoly situation in only a part of the United Kingdom.[36]

- The monopoly reference may specify particular matters (relating to pricing, referred to supply and/or discrimination) to be investigated by the Competition Commission in terms of their effect on the public interest.[36a]

- The monopoly reference can exclude the question of public interest—in (f) above—altogether. In that case, it is called a 'monopoly reference limited to the facts'.[37]

- The monopoly reference may exclude the question of whether the persons in whose favour the monopoly situation exists are taking steps to exploit or maintain the monopoly situation—in (d) above.[38]

18.24   The monopoly reference may be varied by the authority which has made the monopoly reference (ie the OFT or the Secretary of State), although it is not possible to vary a monopoly reference which includes a public interest question so that it becomes a monopoly reference limited to the facts (the opposite is, however, possible).[39]

18.25   **Secretary of State's veto:** Where the OFT makes a monopoly reference, or varies a monopoly reference, it must send a copy of the reference or the variation to the Secretary of State. The Secretary of State has fourteen days in which to direct the Competition Commission not to proceed with the reference or the variation.[40] As described in paragraph 18.03(ii) above, in practice it is extremely rare for the Secretary of State to veto a monopoly reference (although the government has indicated that monopoly references might be vetoed if scale monopoly references are made for purposes other than where there has already been an infringement of the Chapter II prohibition and other infringements by the same firm are apprehended, or where the scale monopoly occurs in a regulated utility sector).

18.26   **Time limits:** the monopoly reference must specify a period within which the Competition Commission must complete its investigation and submit to the

---

[35]   Fair Trading Act 1973, s 47(2).
[36]   Ibid, s 47(1) (c). See Ch 17, paras 17.10–17.12, on monopoly situations in relation to only a part of the UK.
[36a]   Ibid, s 49(2)(i) and (3).
[37]   Ibid, s 48.
[38]   Ibid, s 49(2).
[39]   Ibid, s 52.
[40]   Ibid, ss 50(6) and 52(4).

Secretary of State its report setting out the answers to the questions in the monopoly reference.[41] (The report does not have to be *published* within this time period.) Typically, the period is about a year, although some recent monopoly investigations have been even longer. The Secretary of State may issue directions to extend the time period for completing the investigation and submitting the report (for example, where it appears to the Competition Commission that the issues are too difficult to be resolved within the time limit).[42]

Statutory Undertakings as an Alternative to ('in Lieu of') a Monopoly Reference

Where the OFT's preliminary investigation has given rise to OFT concerns that a **18.27** monopoly situation may be operating against the public interest, it is possible for the OFT to negotiate a settlement with the companies or businesses allegedly forming the monopoly situation, under which the latter will give statutory undertakings to remedy the public interest concerns, as an alternative to the time and expense involved in a full monopoly situation. Obviously, for the companies or businesses concerned there is a strategic judgement to make at this point: is it worth expending the money and management time involved in a full monopoly investigation in the hope that the Competition Commission, having fully examined the facts, may reach conclusions more favourable to that company or business than the OFT has done in its preliminary investigation (ie might conclude that there is no monopoly situation, or no adverse effects to the public interest)? If a full monopoly investigation does not offer this more optimistic prospect for the company or business, it may be worthwhile to negotiate statutory undertakings.

Such statutory undertakings are called **undertakings as an alternative to—or 'in** **18.28** **lieu of'—a monopoly reference.** The mechanism for them is set out in sections 56A to 56G of the Fair Trading Act 1973, which were inserted by the Deregulation and Contracting Out Act 1994. The OFT negotiates these statutory undertakings, but the company or business gives them to the Secretary of State. They are legally binding on the party giving them and, if they are breached, enforcement proceedings may be taken under section 93A by the Secretary of State (or, in limited circumstances, by a third party): see paragraph 18.67 below.

The OFT may propose that the Secretary of State accept statutory undertakings **18.29** 'in lieu' if the OFT:

(a) considers that a monopoly situation exists;

(b) considers that facts relating to the monopoly situation 'may now or in future operate against the public interest';

---

[41] Ibid, s 55(1).
[42] Ibid, s 55(2).

(c) would make a monopoly reference, including the question of public interest, in relation to this monopoly situation (were undertakings in lieu not to be accepted); and

(d) considers that the statutory undertakings which are proposed 'would be sufficient' to deal with the relevant adverse effects to the public interest.[43]

All the above criteria must be met in order for the statutory undertakings mechanism to be invoked.

18.30 The OFT may initiate the procedure for negotiating undertakings in lieu either by directly contacting the parties identified during its preliminary investigation as constituting the monopoly situation, or by publishing a notice (in suitable newspapers, trade journals or other media) setting out its intention to make a monopoly reference in respect of named parties and inviting anyone who wishes to offer an undertaking in lieu to notify the OFT within a specified period. Obviously, the latter procedure is more appropriate where there is a complex monopoly situation involving a large number of parties.[44]

18.31 Following these approaches by the OFT, the OFT must consider any offers of undertakings to see whether they would be sufficient to remedy the adverse effects on the public interest which have been identified. In doing so, the OFT consults the parties making the offer, and usually also any third parties who may have an interest (particularly customers or competitors).

18.32 Once it has completed these consultations, the OFT may decide that adequate statutory undertakings 'in lieu' will not be forthcoming, in which case it may still proceed with the making of a monopoly reference to the Competition Commission. If, on the other hand, the OFT considers that satisfactory undertakings have been offered, it then publishes a formal notice setting out:

• the terms of the monopoly reference which would be made;

• the terms of the proposed undertakings; and

• the OFT's reasons for believing that the proposed undertakings would be sufficient to remedy the adverse effects on the public interest.

The notice must specify a time period within which interested parties may submit their comments on the proposals.[45]

18.33 After the specified time period has expired, the OFT considers comments received and may engage in further negotiations with the parties offering the undertakings. The OFT then takes a final view—either proceeding with the monopoly reference (if the OFT does not consider that satisfactory undertakings have been offered),

---

[43] Fair Trading Act 1973, s 56A(1).
[44] OFT, n 3 above, 29.
[45] Fair Trading Act 1973 s 56B.

or recommending to the Secretary of State acceptance of the undertakings proposed.[46]

If the Secretary of State accepts the proposals, he publishes the undertakings.[47]

Once statutory undertakings have been given, the OFT must keep them under review—and advise the Secretary of State whether they have been breached, or whether they need to be varied or superseded, or whether the parties concerned can be released from them.[48] If they are breached, the remedies are as set out in paragraph 18.67 below.   **18.34**

For a period of one year after acceptance of the undertakings the OFT may not make a monopoly reference 'in the same, or substantially the same, terms' as those published in the context of the proposal for undertakings (subject to limited exceptions).[49]   **18.35**

D. Monopoly Investigation by the Competition Commission

The Competition Commission's monopoly investigation commences immediately after the monopoly reference has been made, and must be completed (and the report submitted to the Secretary of State) by the end of the time limit specified in the monopoly reference.   **18.36**

The Competition Commission

The Competition Commission was established under the Competition Act 1998. It takes over the functions of the old Monopolies and Mergers Commission, which it replaces.[50] (In addition, it has the further, separate function of being a tribunal for hearing appeals against OFT decisions under the Chapter I and Chapter II prohibitions.[51]) The main provisions regarding governance of the Competition Commission are set out in Schedule 7 to the Competition Act.   **18.37**

In connection with its functions in conducting monopoly investigations, the Competition Commission comprises: **18.38**

- a **'reporting panel' of members** of the Competition Commission, including the Competition Commission's chairman and its deputy chairmen (there must be at least one deputy chairman, and will usually be three)—the reporting panel members are not full-time officials, but are individuals of high reputation

---

[46] Ibid, s 56A(2).
[47] Ibid, s 56G.
[48] Ibid, ss 56E and 56F.
[49] Ibid, s 56D(1).
[50] Competition Act 1998, s 45(3).
[51] See Ch 16.

appointed by the government from business, the professions, trade unions and the academic world (usually professional economists);

- the **staff** of the Competition Commission—this is a body of full-time civil servants, of which the head is the Secretary to the Competition Commission (the staff will include specialist legal advisers, economists and accountants, in addition to the mainstream administrators, although some of the specialist functions are increasingly being contracted out).

18.39   The reporting panel members are responsible for the decisions made by the Competition Commission in a monopoly investigation (ie as to the responses to the questions set out in the monopoly reference), and they conduct the oral hearings which form a part of the investigation procedure. The staff provide administrative and professional support to the reporting panel members, including preparing first drafts of the Competition Commission's report.

18.40   Any single monopoly investigation is conducted by a 'group' of reporting panel members: there must be at least three reporting panel members in the group,[52] and in practice there are normally four to six. The group on any particular investigation is selected by the Competition Commission's chairman. The group is chaired either by the Competition Commission's chairman or by one of the deputy chairmen.

18.41   The group in the investigation is supported by a team from the staff, headed by a 'team leader'. The team includes a reference secretary (the main point of contact with the external parties), as well as a legal adviser, an economic adviser and an accountant from the Competition Commission's staff.

The Competition Commission's Proceedings—Written Submissions and Oral Hearings

Formal Powers to Obtain Information

18.42   The Competition Commission's formal powers to obtain information in the course of its investigations are set out in section 85 of the Fair Trading Act 1973. The Competition Commission may, by written notice, require any person to:

- provide the Competition Commission with 'estimates, returns or other information' as may be specified in the notice (and may specify a time and manner in which this must be done)—provided that the person carries on business;

- produce, at a time and place specified in the notice, any relevant documents in the person's custody or control, as specified or described in the notice;

- attend and give evidence at an oral hearing with the Competition Commission.

---

[52] Competition Act 1998, Sch 7, para 15(2).

As with the OFT's powers to require evidence or documents, these powers are subject to the limitation that no person may be compelled to give evidence or produce any document which it could not be compelled to give in proceedings before the High Court (or, in Scotland, the Court of Session).[53] Subject to this, failure to comply with a written notice from the Commission may result in contempt of court proceedings (which can lead to imprisonment); and the wilful alteration, suppression or destruction of any document required under such a notice is a criminal offence which may give rise to a fine and/or imprisonment of up to two years.[54]

In practice, it is extremely rare for the Competition Commission to have to invoke the section 85 procedures in order to obtain written or oral evidence. Parties normally provide written and oral evidence voluntarily. **18.43**

In Practice—Written Submissions

Written submissions may be made to the Competition Commission at the initiative of any person. However, in the case of the main parties (the alleged monopolists themselves, complainants, major competitors and customers in the industry, and so on), the Competition Commission will specifically invite written evidence, by sending each such party one or more letters setting out a list of questions which need to be answered. **18.44**

It is normal to respond to these questions by way of a fairly lengthy submission; although the response must provide all the information set out in the questions, it is not necessary to do so in the order in which the questions are asked, and typically a party will provide the information in the context of a detailed argument setting out its case (however, it is helpful to the Competition Commission if there is some kind of list identifying where in the submission each question is answered). It is usual for parties to engage legal advisers and, often, professional economists in the preparation of these written submissions. **18.45**

In Practice—Oral Hearings

In addition, the most important parties involved in the investigation are invited to oral hearing at the Competition Commission's headquarters (in Carey Street, London WC2). Each hearing takes place with one party only. The proceedings are 'inquisitorial'—rather than (as in the case of an English court case) 'adversarial'—and are relatively informal. **18.46**

At the hearing, the Competition Commission is represented by all (or most) of the members of the group conducting the investigation, along with the reference secretary, and other Competition Commission staff to take notes. **18.47**

---

[53] Fair Trading Act 1973, s 85(3). See above, para 18.16 for an explanation of this limitation.
[54] Ibid, s 85(7), (7A) and (6).

18.48 The party giving oral evidence should be represented by its most senior staff (usually including the chairman, chief executive and/or managing director), together with colleagues who have a specialist knowledge of the relevant markets being investigated (heads of the relevant divisions, heads of marketing, and so on); they are normally also accompanied by legal representatives.

18.49 Each hearing lasts at least half a day, and normally a full day (ending at around 4 pm). It takes place privately. The chairman of the Competition Commission group conducting the investigation asks a series of questions to the most senior representative of the party, who may then ask one of his colleagues to field the question. Other members of the Competition Commission group also usually put supplementary questions. During the hearing, a transcript is taken, and a copy of the transcript is sent to the party for factual verification.

Providing False or Misleading Information

18.50 The provisions of sections 93B and 132 of the FTA apply to information furnished to the Competition Commission in connection with its monopoly investigation functions. In broad terms, these make it a criminal offence to furnish information to the Commission which is materially false or misleading (where the person knows this to be the case or is reckless as to the fact). Directors, managers, company secretaries, etc can also be liable if the false or misleading information is provided by their company.

Details of these provisions are set out in paragraphs 18.18–18.19 above.

18.51 It is believed that there has been only one occasion where these provisions have been invoked. In 1995, the OFT pursued an allegation that one of the companies involved in the monopoly investigation into ice creams may have given false or misleading evidence to the Monopolies and Mergers Commission (the forerunner of the Competition Commission).[55]

Stages in the Competition Commission's Investigation

18.52 The investigation proceeds through a number of stages, as follow.

18.53 (i) **Collecting factual evidence**
The main purpose of the initial stage is to enable the Competition Commission to familiarise itself with the markets being investigated, and the main parties involved, and in doing so to establish whether or not there is a (complex or scale) monopoly situation. At the outset, the Competition Commission identifies the main parties, such as the parties forming the alleged monopoly situation, as well as complainants, customers, consumer bodies and major competitors. Within a day or so of the monopoly reference

---

[55] *The Economist,* 6 Jan 1996, 29.

being made, these parties will receive a questionnaire inviting a written submission on the main factual aspects, including questions on:

- the business of the party or parties forming the alleged monopoly situation;

- the business of the party receiving the questionnaire (if different);

- corporate organisation (subsidiaries, joint ventures, and so on);

- price levels and pricing policies;

- profitability;

- agreements and other arrangements with other companies;

- membership of trade associations;

- employees' membership of trade unions.

As described above, it is normal for these parties to respond with a full written submission (see above, paragraphs 18.44–18.45).

At the same time, the Competition Commission places advertisements in the press (including the relevant trade journals) with a view to inviting other interested parties to submit their views.

It is also common for the Competition Commission to make 'site visits' to the premises of the main parties (for example, the factory). Usually, all or most members of the Competition Commission group conducting the investigation attend the site visits (they generally enjoy it), as do a handful of members of the staff team, including the team leader and the reference secretary. From the Competition Commission's point of view, the purpose of the site visit is to see in practice how the reference goods or services are produced or supplied. The Competition Commission representatives also take the opportunity to elicit information from the company by way of informal questions to personnel at the site. For the company, the site visit represents an early opportunity both to establish good working relations with the Competition Commission group members, and also to make the key points in its case directly to the members at an early stage and in ways that have visual impact. It is therefore sensible for the company—and helpful to the Competition Commission representatives—if the company puts some thought into planning the day of the site visit, with an organised programme in which the Commission representatives can see various aspects of its business which are relevant to the points at issue in the investigation.

In addition, at this initial stage, the Competition Commission may hold oral hearings with parties other than the main parties. The hearings with the main parties often take place at subsequent stages.[56]

---

[56] Monopolies and Mergers Commission, *The Role of the MMC* (5th edn, Sept 1996), 10.

18.54 (ii) **Assessing the issues**

At the second stage, the Competition Commission considers the 'issues' raised by the monopoly situation, with a view to establishing whether it operates (or may operate) against the public interest.

The Competition Commission, having identified the party or parties which it considers to constitute a monopoly situation, sends each such party a letter—called the 'issues letter'—which:

- expresses the provisional view that there is a monopoly situation, and summarises the Competition Commission's understanding of the relevant facts about the market and of third party criticisms of the parties forming the alleged monopoly situation;

- identifies the public interest issues which the Competition Commission consider to arise from the monopoly situation;

- invites the addressee to comment.

Traditionally the issues letter has been confidential (like all other correspondence to or from the Competition Commission during the inquiry), but in one recent monopoly inquiry, by way of experiment, the issues letter was made public enabling third parties to comment.[57] The addressee is given about a month to respond in writing to the issues letter. This response is normally by way of a full written submission (see paragraphs 18.44–18.45 above). The Competition Commission may be sympathetic to requests to extend the deadline for responding, but such extensions will be very short.

Once the Competition Commission has had an opportunity to consider the written submissions from the main parties in response to the issues letter, each of the main parties is invited to an oral hearing, at which all the main relevant matters will be raised—both as to whether there is a monopoly situation and whether it operates against the public interest (see paragraphs 18.46–18.49 above).

18.55 (iii) **Considering possible remedies**

The Competition Commission may, in its report to the Secretary of State, recommend remedies to any adverse effects on the public interest which it has identified (see Chapter 17, paragraphs 17.31–17.33, for the substance of these remedies, and paragraphs 18.63–18.67 below for the procedure in implementing them).

The Competition Commission will wish to consider hypothetical remedies, and invite comments both from the main parties and from third parties (complainants, customers and so on). It will invite comments by way of writ-

---

[57] Monopolies and Mergers Commission information brief, 'MMC writes to providers of underwriting services for share issues', 11 May 1998. See also report in the *Daily Telegraph* the following day, 12 May 1998: 'MMC puts forward shake-up for rules on underwriting'.

ten submission and oral hearing—either as part of the 'issues' stage or separately at a subsequent stage. The fact that hypothetical remedies are discussed does not mean that the Commission has concluded that there are adverse effects to the public interest; it cannot reveal its conclusions until the report is published, but it still needs to consult the parties on any remedies it may wish to propose.[58]

(iv) **Preparing the report**   **18.56**

As the monopoly investigation draws to its close, the Competition Commission must prepare its report, which must be submitted to the Secretary of State within the time limit set for the investigation (at the time of the monopoly reference), and which is subsequently published by the Secretary of State.

The report typically includes a series of factual chapters describing, in turn: the nature of the relevant market; the main parties (in particular, the party or parties forming the alleged monopoly situation); and the evidence given by each of the main parties and by the most important other parties (complainants, customers, etc) as to the existence of the monopoly situation and the public interest issues. There is also a 'conclusions' chapter, setting out the Competition Commission's own assessment; this is normally the first full chapter of the report (and is preceded by a brief 'summary' of the report, of about two or three pages).

In the 'conclusions' chapter, the Competition Commission *must* set out its response to the questions set out in the monopoly reference (see paragraph 18.22 above) and, if it concludes that there is a monopoly situation which operates (or may operate) against the public interest, *may* include recommendations as to action to remedy those adverse effects.[59] The conclusions are decided by the members of the group. They will not always agree, and in a group which is evenly divided, the chairman of the group has a casting vote.[60] Sometimes one or more members of the group who disagree with the majority view on the conclusions insist on their 'dissenting view' being recorded in the conclusions chapter.

Before the report is submitted to the Secretary of State, the main parties and third parties are shown the passages from the factual chapters which are relevant to themselves, and are asked to submit last-minute corrections on any questions of factual accuracy. Neither the 'conclusions' chapter nor the summary is ever disclosed at this stage. This stage is also the first opportunity for the parties to request the excision from the report of commercially confidential material (see paragraph 18.60 below).

---

[58] Ibid.
[59] Fair Trading Act 1973, s 54(3)(b).
[60] Competition Act 1998, Sch 7, para 21.

Submitting the Report to the Secretary of State

18.57 At the end of the investigation, the report is submitted to the Secretary of State (at the Department of Trade and Industry), who then needs to consider its conclusion and recommendations, and prepare for publication of the report and an announcement of what action (if any) will be taken in the light of the report.

At this stage, a copy of the report is sent to the OFT, and the Secretary of State must—before any announcement—take account of any advice given by the OFT in respect of the report.[61]

E. Publication and Announcement by the Secretary of State

18.58 At least a month elapses before the Secretary of State publishes a report. If the Competition Commission has concluded that there is a monopoly situation which operates (or may operate) against the public interest, the Secretary of State also has to consider possible remedies, and this may prolong the period before publication and announcement.

18.59 In theory, this period is *not* an opportunity for further submissions or representations to be made by interested parties (the monopoly investigation was the opportunity for this). However, in practice, where the investigation relates to particularly 'political' or 'high-profile' matters, there can sometimes be advantages in lobbying, particularly through Members of Parliament and the news media.

Protecting Confidential Information

18.60 Parties will naturally be concerned that commercially confidential information which they submitted to the Competition Commission should not be included in the published report. There are essentially two opportunities for requesting this:

- First, before the report is passed to the Secretary of State, the parties—on being shown the draft chapters from the report—may request that confidential information be exercised from the report before it is submitted to the Secretary of State. Excisions are allowed in respect of:

  (i) any matter relating to an individual's private affairs, where publication of that matter would or might seriously and prejudicially affect that individual's interests; or

  (ii) any matter relating specifically to the affairs of a 'body of persons' whether corporate or unincorporate where publication would or might seriously

---

[61] Fair Trading Act 1973, s 86.

affect the interests of that body unless the inclusion of that matter relating to that body is necessary for the purposes of the report.[62]

- Secondly, in the period between the report going to the Secretary of State and its publication, the parties may submit requests to the Department of Trade and Industry that confidential material in the report should be excised before it is published. The Secretary of State will grant such requests if he considers that:

(i) publication would be against the public interest; or

(ii) the information relates to the private affairs of an individual, whose interests would be seriously and prejudicially affected by publication, and publication would not actually be in the public interest; or

(iii) the information relates specifically to the affairs of a particular person (which may include a company) whose interests would be seriously and prejudicially affected by publication, and publication would not actually be in the public interest.[63]

Mechanics of Publication

On the day of publication, the Competition Commission report—together with a press notice summarising the report's conclusions and the Secretary of State's announcement—is issued by the Department of Trade and Industry at 11.00 am precisely (or 3.00 pm if an announcement is made in Parliament, which will be the case for politically 'high-profile' investigations). At that point the parties alleged to form the monopoly situation may each collect one copy from the DTI's main offices at 1 Victoria Street, London, SW1.[64] Simultaneously, there is an electronic release of the press notice on the Stock Exchange Regulatory News Service. The parties named in the report as comprising the monopoly situation are given 24 hours' notice before publication (but, by virtue of section 69 of the Competition Act 1998, are not given prior sighting of the report itself). **18.61**

In order to benefit from the 24 hours' notice and the right to collect a copy from the DTI, the parties named as comprising the monopoly situation should make a request in advance for this to the DTI.[65] **18.62**

---

[62] Ibid, s 82(1).
[63] Ibid, s 83(3) and (3A).
[64] Further copies become available to anyone during the afternoon of that day, and may be obtained from The Stationery Office.
[65] The request form is published as Annex A to the DTI's booklet, 'Guidance on DTI Procedures for Handling Monopoly References and Reports' (London, DTI, 1998).

F. Remedies—Procedure

18.63 Action may only be taken by the Secretary of State if the Competition Commission concludes that there is a monopoly situation and that facts which it has uncovered in its investigation operate, or may be expected to operate, against the public interest.[66]

18.64 Such conclusions must be supported by at least two-thirds of the members of the group who conducted the investigation if any action is to be taken.[67]

18.65 A discussion of the nature of the remedies which might be adopted is in Chapter 17, paragraphs 17.31–17.33, of this book.

18.66 As regards the procedures, the Secretary of State must take into account any recommendations on remedies which have been included in the Competition Commission's report, but is not bound to follow these. Generally, the Secretary of State's announcement at the time of the report's publication will set out the Secretary of State's views on the remedies which are needed (although in particularly controversial cases the Secretary of State will initiate a further period of consultation). The OFT is required to negotiate with the party whose conduct needs to be remedied suitable legally-binding '**undertakings**' which those parties give to the Secretary of State, under FTA, section 88. If the parties fail to give acceptable undertakings, the Secretary of State is empowered to impose remedies by way of an **order** under FTA, section 56 (in fact, the Secretary of State is entitled to impose the remedies by order even without seeking undertakings from the parties, but in practice it is thought better to obtain the remedies with the co-operation of the parties).

18.67 These remedies, whether given by 'undertakings' under FTA, section 88, or by orders under FTA, section 56, are legally enforceable:

(i) Undertakings (whether given after a Competition Commission report, or as an alternative to a Competition Commission investigation[68]):

- If there is a breach, it is possible for the Crown (ie the government) to bring civil proceedings for injunctive or other relief.[69]

- As to whether third parties may bring such action, the legislation seems to suggest that this is the case, but it has been held that normally only the government may enforce undertakings, other than in exceptional circumstances such as where the undertakings conferred direct benefits (such as reduced prices) on a private party.[70]

---

[66] Ibid, s 56(1).
[67] Competition Act 1998, Sch 7, para 20.
[68] See above, paras 18.27–18.35 and 18.66 (using new numbering).
[69] Fair Trading Act 1973, s 93A(2), read with s 93(2).
[70] *Mid Kent Holdings v General Utilities* [1997] 2 WLR 14, [1996] 3 All ER 132.

- If, following such civil proceedings, the court makes an order granting an injunction or other relief, subsequent breach of that court order is punishable as contempt of court.

(ii) Orders:

- If an order is breached, the Crown (ie the government) may bring civil proceedings for an injunction or any other appropriate relief.[71]

- The legislation specifically also states that it does not limit the rights of any other person to bring civil proceedings in respect of breach, or apprehended breach, of an order,[72] but that is only if such a right already exists, and it is thought unlikely that third parties have such a right save in exceptional circumstances (as with undertakings).[73]

- If, following such civil proceedings, the court makes an order granting an injunction or other relief, subsequent breach of that court order is punishable as contempt of court.

---

[71] Fair Trading Act 1973, s 93(1).
[72] Fair Trading Act 1973, s 92(2).
[73] *Mid Kent Holdings v General Utilities*, n 70 above.

PART VIII

NEW REGIME FOR UTILITY REGULATION

19

CHANGES IN UTILITY REGULATION

A. Overview

The utility sectors which emerged from the UK privatisations of the 1980s and **19.01** early 1990s are subject to a special system of economic regulation, recognising their particular circumstances in the national economy. This special regime is reflected in the Competition Act 1998.

The sectors concerned—telecommunications, gas, electricity, water and rail- **19.02** ways—have been marked by almost continuous change since privatisation. The regulatory regime has had to develop rapidly in consequence. This process of change is continuing, and any survey of utility regulation in the UK is necessarily a 'snapshot', with further developments likely in the near future. At the time of the passing of the Competition Act in 1998, the principal features of the system of UK utility regulation can be summarised as follows:

- Initially, the privatised utilities were largely seen as 'natural monopolies' which were not subject to normal competitive forces, but needed to be specially regulated to control pricing and maintain quality and service standards. There was only a limited role for normal competition law. However, recent years have seen an increase in the possibilities of competition and the emergence of markets, culminating in the opening to competition of domestic gas and electricity supplies in 1998.

- The sector regulators have the primary statutory responsibility for enforcing the regulatory regime. There is a separate regulator for each of the main utility sectors (telecommunications, gas, electricity, water and railways). Each sector regulator is appointed by the government under the statute which privatised the sector, and each exercises its regulatory powers over the utility companies primarily through statutory powers to enforce conditions (as to pricing, quality, etc.) which are in the licences granted to the utility companies.

- The Competition Act 1998 gives the sector regulators powers to apply the Chapter I and Chapter II prohibition to companies in their sectors. These powers are exercisable concurrently with those of the OFT.

- Other regulatory functions reflect the broader social role of the utilities, and it is thought that these will need to be retained by the regulators alongside their Competition Act functions. In 1998, the Government announced proposals for reform in this area.

Each of these aspects is considered, in turn, in the following paragraphs.

B. Background: From Natural Monopolies to Emerging Markets

19.03 Until the mid-1980s, the major public utilities in the UK—telecommunications, gas, electricity, water and railways—were all monopoly nationalised industries. The Conservative government began the process of 'privatising' them one-by-one, as part of its broader political objective of reducing the role of the State in the economy.

19.04 By and large, however, these industries remained monopolistic in the initial stages after privatisation and, particularly in the early years, there was little attempt to introduce market competition. This partly reflected a financial concern on the part of the government at the time of privatisation: the fear that shareholders would be unwilling to subscribe for shares in any of the companies being privatised if the revenue stream of those companies were threatened by their having to face competition. However, there was also a more fundamental difficulty. This was that many of the utilities were 'natural monopolies', or were at least believed to be natural monopolies: that is, it was in the nature of those utilities that it was only economically feasible to have one company providing the service (for example, it would be wasteful and economically senseless to have two competing water suppliers, with duplicate reservoirs and pipe networks, serving the same markets).

19.05 Accordingly, the State telecommunications monopoly, British Telecom, was transferred to the private sector in 1984 as a single entity (although in subsequent years it was gradually deprived of its legal monopolies over the services it provided). The same was true of the State gas supplier, British Gas, which was privatised in 1986. By the time of the privatisation of the electricity industry, in 1990–1, widespread public concern at the lack of competition in the newly privatised industries induced the government to break up the State generating company into three competing companies in England and Wales, and a separate transmission company—but, at the level of local distribution and supply, the twelve regional electricity companies covering England and Wales were all transferred to the private sector, with each retaining its local monopoly. When the water industry was privatised, at around the same time, the existing companies were allowed to retain their local monopolies over water and sewerage provision. Finally, in the mid-1990s, the rail industry was privatised, with one company, Railtrack, holding a monopoly of the country's rail network, and individual private train-operating companies being granted monopoly rights over the routes franchised to them.

19.06 But the fact that it proved initially difficult to expose the privatised monopolies to market competition did not mean that the government was complacent about the possibility that the new privatised companies would exercise, and could abuse, market power. A structure of regulation was established as a substitute for market competition. Each Act of Parliament effecting a privatisation[1] accompanied the privatisation measures with a system of utility regulation, operating through the grant of licences to the individual privatised companies. Each licence contains conditions with which the company must comply, these conditions being designed to prevent the company from abusing its market power as a monopoly or near-monopoly. The licence conditions are enforced by sector regulators, each of which was established under the relevant Act of Parliament with responsibility for one specific sector (see paragraphs 19.12–19.13 below).

19.07 This system of regulation was explicitly designed to address the lack of market competition in the privatised utility sectors, ensuring at least some control over the exercise of market power by the previously-nationalised monopoly company. Thus, for example, in the 1988 White Paper paving the way for privatisation of the electricity industry, the government foresaw regulation of the industry in these terms:

> Even after privatisation, the supply activities of the distribution companies and the national grid company [responsible for transmission] will remain, in large part, natural monopolies. An effective regulatory regime will therefore be established by legislation, to promote competition and to safeguard the interests of customers . . . The regulatory system will be designed to provide each company in the industry with

---

[1] The Telecommunications Act 1984, the Gas Act 1986, the Electricity Act 1989, the Water Act 1989 (superseded by the Water Industry Act 1991), and the Railways Act 1993.

incentives to operate more efficiently and to ensure that the benefits are shared with customers.[2]

19.08 However, in the years following the initial privatisations, many of the monopolies have gradually transformed into competitive markets. This has been achieved mainly by a series of government measures to liberalise the sectors, removing legal monopolies and enabling new market entry, but also (in the case of British Gas) by splitting up the privatised monopoly. A major advancement in the process of developing market competition occurred in 1998:

- In telecommunications, liberalisation began in the early 1980s, even before the privatisation of British Telecom, with the removal of BT's monopoly over the provision of telephone sets, and the licensing of a competing company, Mercury, to provide basic switched services in the UK and international services. Following a White Paper in 1991, other new entrants were granted licences to operate fixed-link telecommunications services. In the meantime, technology created further challenges to market power, with the emergence of substitutable or near-substitutable services such as mobile telephones, cable television and e-mail.

- In the gas industry, where British Gas was privatised in 1986 as a single vertically-integrated company, enjoying monopoly rights over both the on-shore pipeline network and also supply to end-users (other than major industrial users). A decade later, however, the company was broken up, with BG demerging its trading business into a new company, Centrica, and with the requirement that all its monopoly rights over supplies to domestic customers should be removed by 1998.

- In the electricity industry, there had already been competition in generation from the outset, with the break-up of the old Central Electricity Generating Board into three competing generating companies in England and Wales. Subsequently, other parties were granted licences to compete in generation. At the local level, the regional electricity companies had, immediately prior to privatisation, enjoyed monopolies of both distribution and supply in their licensed areas. However, their monopoly rights over supply were gradually removed under an eight-year rolling programme: in the period 1990–4, competition was allowed in respect of supply to end-users consuming more than one megawatt (mainly large businesses); after 1994, the threshold was reduced to 100 kilowatts (affecting medium-sized businesses); and in 1998, the supply monopolies were required to be abolished altogether.

19.09 As a result of these developments—culminating in the opening of domestic gas and electricity supplies to full competition in 1998–99—it has become realistic to see

---

[2] White Paper, *Privatising Electricity*, Cm 322, Feb 1988, paras 50 and 51.

market competition as a way of controlling prices and maintaining quality and service standards in the utility sectors (rather than having to rely on direct regulatory intervention through enforcement of licence conditions). With the emergence of markets in the utility sectors, it becomes increasingly important to ensure, as in any other sector of the economy, that market competition is not restricted or distorted—and that requires the direct application of competition law to the utilities.

Of course, it would be an exaggeration to characterise all the utility sectors as com-   **19.10**
petitive markets. Some sectors, such as the supply of water, still appear to be natural monopolies, in which it seems very difficult to introduce genuine market competition (even though, in the case of water, the sector regulator, OFWAT, indicated in summer 1998 that it wished to extend competition). Moreover, even where legal monopolies have been removed, there may still be companies with market power or dominance. In telecommunications, although BT no longer enjoys its legal monopoly over the provisions of telephone services, it may still be said to enjoy a significant market position in certain key sectors; possibly because of customer inertia,[3] towards the end of the 1990s BT still retained around 90 per cent of domestic fixed exchange lines in the UK, and 84 per cent of retail revenues for UK fixed line telephony.[4]

However, any problems arising out of such market power can also now be effec-   **19.11**
tively addressed through *competition law*. As a result of the Competition Act 1998, and specifically the introduction of the 'Chapter II prohibition' on abuse of a dominant position, UK competition law now has for the first time an effective means of controlling and deterring abuses of market power, in place of the weak and slow provisions of the previous legislation.[5] It is significant that in spring 1998, when the Rail Regulator reported on the market position of the ROSCOs (the rolling stock companies, which lease trains to the train-operating companies), it concluded that:

> Whilst, at least in the medium term, the ROSCOs have market power, and therefore the potential to abuse it, regulation with powers of direction over pricing and investment does not offer the best way of dealing with such potential for abuse . . . [The] Rail Regulator should adopt a firm and proactive approach to the use of his powers under the Competition Bill, when available, in order to identify, monitor and police potential abuse of dominant positions.[6]

---

[3] Including customers' reluctance to switch to a competitor for fear of then having to change their telephone number; this problem is being addressed through proposals to introduce licence conditions on number portability.

[4] OFTEL, *UK Telecommunications Industry Market Information*, Jan 1997, Table 4; OFTEL, *Identification of Operators with Significant Market Power*, Apr 1998, paras 26 and 35.

[5] See Ch 1, paras 1.12–1.21.

[6] Office of the Rail Regulator, *Review of the Rolling Stock Market: Report to the Deputy Prime Minister*, May 1998, paras 1.23 and 1.28(ii). See also Office of the Rail Regulator press release ORR/98/16 of 15 May 1998. The ROSCOs had been the only major element of the railways industry not to have been brought under the direct regulatory control of a licensing regime on privatisation.

C. The Sector Regulators: Original Powers of Direct Regulatory Control

19.12 The sector regulators, and their original powers of direct regulatory control, were each established at the time of privatisation of the particular utility sector. The privatisation legislation, in each case, provided for the transfer of the nationalised utility company or companies to the private sector, and also for a system of regulation of those companies following privatisation. The privatised companies were each made subject to a licence granted by the government, containing conditions with which the company must comply, these conditions being designed to prevent the company from abusing its market power as a monopoly or near-monopoly. The licence conditions were to be enforced by sector regulators, each appointed under the relevant privatisation legislation, and each headed by an individual Director General, as follows:

- OFTEL, the Office of Telecommunications, headed by the Director General of Telecommunications;

- OFGAS, the Office of Gas Supply, headed by the Director General of Gas Supply;

- OFFER, the Office of Electricity Regulation, headed by the Director General of Electricity Supply;

- OFWAT, the Office of Water Services, headed by the Director General of Water Services;

- the ORR, the Office of the Rail Regulator, headed by the Rail Regulator.[7]

The sector regulators were given considerable powers to acquire information from the companies, and to enforce the licence conditions. The regulators were also entitled, in order to fulfil their statutory duties, to modify licence conditions (for example, by making them more stringent) and, if the licensed utility company concerned did not consent to such modification, to refer the question for adjudication to the Monopolies and Mergers Commission (forerunner of the Competition Commission).

19.13 The power to enforce licence conditions has enabled the sector regulators to constrain potential abuses of market power in a number of ways. Although there are variations between the different utility sectors, a number of basic features are common to all of them, including in particular:

(i) **Price controls** designed to exercise a downward pressure on pricing, by requiring prices to reduce annually in 'real' terms (ie after adjusting for inflation). This is expressed in licence conditions which allow prices to rise annu-

---

[7] There were also separate gas and electricity sector regulators for Northern Ireland.

498

ally by no more than 'RPI – *x*': that is, the annual movement in the retail prices index, measuring inflation, minus a percentage set by the regulator.[8]

(ii) **Quality and service standards** were set in the privatisation legislation and the licence as minimum requirements with which each company has to comply. In the electricity industry, for example, OFFER has powers to set performance standards for local public electricity suppliers, covering a range of criteria such as restoring electricity supplies after faults, keeping household appointments, responding quickly to letters querying bills, and so on.[9]

(iii) **'Interconnection' or 'use of system' obligations** are imposed in the licences of owners of infrastructure—BT owning the trunk telecommunications network, regional electricity companies owning the local distribution networks, British Gas owning the national gas pipelines—requiring them to grant 'third party access' to competitors in related markets, and to do so on generally reasonable and non-discriminatory terms. These provisions are designed to prevent companies which have market power through ownership of necessary infrastructure from abusing that market power by precluding competition in related markets where potential competitors require access to the infrastructure in order to be able to operate—that is, where the infrastructure acts as an 'essential facility' to competing in those related markets (access to a trunk telecommunications network, for example, is an essential facility to competing in the provision of domestic telephone services). This regulatory recognition that market power in the utility sectors can be abused by denying access to essential infrastructure mirrors the development in EC competition law of an 'essential facilities doctrine' where such refusals are considered to be an abuse of a dominant position in breach of Article 82 (formerly Article 86) of the EC Treaty (and, therefore, will be treated as an infringement of the Chapter II prohibition).[10]

D. Enforcing Competition: The Competition Act 1998

The Competition Act considerably widens the functions of the sector regulators **19.14** by giving them powers, to be exercised concurrently with those of the OFT, to enforce the new Chapter I and Chapter II prohibitions in the particular utility sectors for which they are responsible.

---

[8] The water industry is a partial exception, with provision for water companies' prices to rise, so as to enable capital investment in much needed quality improvements. Thus, instead of a formula of 'RPI – *x*', each water company is subjected to a cap of 'RPI + *K*', in which *K* can be, but has not always been, a positive number.

[9] Electricity Act 1989, ss 39 and 40; OFFER, *Annual Report 1991* (London, HMSO, 1992), 74–5.

[10] See eg *Sea Containers v Stena Sealink* [1994] OJ L15/8. See Ch 9, paras 9.61–9.78.

The Regulators' Existing Competition Powers

19.15   Even before the Competition Act, the sector regulators have had *some* responsibility for promoting competition in their sectors, in addition to their direct regulatory functions described in paragraphs 19.12–19.13 above.

19.16   Thus, for example, in each sector, the sector regulator has a general duty to promote competition.[11]

19.17   More specifically, the sector regulators were each given powers in their particular utility sectors to apply, concurrently with the OFT, existing competition legislation controlling abuses of market power: namely, the monopoly provisions of the Fair Trading Act 1973, and the anti-competitive practices provisions of the Competition Act 1980 (these latter provisions have now been repealed by the Competition Act 1998). Indeed, the concurrent powers to apply the monopoly provisions of the Fair Trading Act 1973 were applied by OFGAS when, in 1992, it made monopoly references to the Monopolies and Mergers Commission (now the Competition Commission); these monopoly investigations resulted in the requirement that British Gas's trading business should be separated from its pipeline business and also that there should be full competition in the supply of gas to domestic customers by 1998.[12]

19.18   However, these competition powers were limited. The regulators' powers to apply the existing legislation controlling abuses of market power suffered from the fundamental deficiencies of that legislation, in terms of ineffective deterrence and slow procedure.[13] Moreover, the sector regulators had no powers at all to apply the existing legislation on restrictive agreements, the RTPA; and, indeed, on privatisation the RTPA had been disapplied from gas supply agreements and from certain electricity and railway agreements.

Concurrent Powers under the Competition Act 1998: Policy Reasons

19.19   There were two main policy issues to be resolved, in connection with the utility sectors, when the new competition legislation was being considered. First, should the utility sectors be subject to the new Chapter I and Chapter II prohibitions? Secondly, if so, who should enforce the prohibitions in the utility sectors—the OFT, or sector regulators, or both?

19.20   On the first question, the increasing possibilities for competition in the utility sectors, as a result of the process (described in paragraphs 19.03–19.11) by which

---

[11] See: Telecommunications Act 1984, s 3(2)(b); Gas Act 1986 (as amended), s 4(1)(c) and (2)(c); Electricity Act 1989, s 3(1)(c); Water Industry Act 1991, s 2(3)(d); and Railways Act 1993, s 4(1)(d).

[12] Monopolies and Mergers Commission, *Gas*, Cm 2314, Aug 1993, and *British Gas plc*, Cm 2315, Aug 1993. Department of Trade and Industry press release, 'Heseltine announces decision on MMC report on gas industry', 21 Dec 1993.

markets had emerged in place of monopolies, led the government to the view that these sectors should now be subject to the full rigours of competition law. The new Chapter I and Chapter II should apply. Lord Simon of Highbury, the government minister responsible for the legislation in the House of Lords, rejected criticism that this was inconsistent with these sectors being subject to a framework of regulation:

> strong sector regulation has played a major part in securing consumer benefits in the regulated sectors. That has been possible only because the sectoral regulators have had the powers they need to do the job: to regulate in order to protect the consumer now; and, where feasible, to promote competition in order to protect the consumer in the future . . .
>
> Consequently, there is no clear distinction between sectoral regulation and the promotion of competition in those sectors . . . That is reflected in the regulators' responsibilities to enforce certain licence conditions which are aimed at market power issues. For example, there are licence conditions concerning price caps and prohibiting undue discrimination.[14]

As regards the second question, the government took the view that the sector reg- **19.21**
ulators should apply the new prohibitions in their sectors concurrently with the OFT.[15] Critics had argued that competition powers over the utility sectors should be vested solely in the competition authority (the OFT), as was the case in Italy and New Zealand, on the ground that the sector regulators lack experience in the application of UK or EC competition law—but, against this, it was felt that the sector regulators could bring their 'in-depth knowledge and experience to bear on the different sectors with their special characteristics'.[16] That was the reason for giving powers to the sector regulators, but why was it necessary that they should exercise these powers *concurrently* with the OFT (rather than, instead of the OFT)? Critics complained that, with a handful of different regulators applying the new prohibitions, inconsistencies were bound to develop. On behalf of the Government, however, Lord Simon insisted that there had to be concurrency because:

> we do not want gaps or litigation about whether [the OFT] or a regulator has jurisdiction[17]

—and questions of consistency could be dealt with by a procedure for consultation between the OFT and the sector regulators (see paragraph 19.32 below).

---

[13] See Ch 1, paras 1.13–1.16.

[14] Lord Simon of Highbury, *Hansard*, HL, vol 583, col 914 (25 Nov 1997).

[15] See, eg, Lord Borrie (former Director General of Fair Trading), House of Lords, *Hansard*, HL vol 582, col 1171 (30 Oct 1997); and Thomas Sharpe QC, 'Danger in Giving Regulators a Role as Competition Police', *The Times*, 23 Feb 1998.

[16] Don Cruickshank (then Director General of Telecommunications), 'Don Cruickshank: Competition on the line', *Financial Times*, 19 Feb 1998.

[17] Lord Simon of Highbury, House of Lords, *Hansard*, HL vol 586, col 1355 (5 Mar 1998).

The Regulators' Powers to Apply the Chapter I and Chapter II Prohibitions

19.22   The powers of the sector regulators to apply the new prohibitions, concurrently with the OFT, are set out in section 54 of the Competition Act 1998, read with Schedule 10. There are also useful draft guidelines published by the OFT.[18]

19.23   The powers are exercisable by the following regulators:

- OFTEL—for agreements or conduct which relate to 'commercial activities connected with telecommunications';

- OFGAS—for agreements or conduct which relate to the carrying on of activities involving the conveyance or supply of gas and ancillary activities (such as storage, meter reading, the provision of meters and the provision of pre-payment facilities);

- OFFER—for agreements or conduct which relate to 'commercial activities connected with the generation, transmission or supply of electricity';

- OFWAT—for agreements or conduct which relate to 'commercial activities connected with the supply of water or securing a supply of water or with the provision or securing of sewerage services';

- the Rail Regulator—for agreements or conduct which relate to 'the supply of railway services' as defined in the Railways Act 1993.[19]

19.24   The OFT's Director of Competition Policy has said that the powers which the sector regulators have in respect of the Chapter I and Chapter II prohibitions are 'generally stronger' than their powers of direct regulation under the privatisation statutes.[20] The main elements of those powers are as follows:

(i)   The sector regulator is given all the functions which the OFT has to apply the Chapter I and Chapter II prohibitions (subject to the exceptions in (iv) below).

(ii)   These functions may be exercised by each sector regulator with regard to agreements, decisions or concerted practices, or conduct, which relates to the matters for which the sector regulator is responsible (as indicated above).

---

[18] Office of Fair Trading, 'Competition Act 1998: Concurrent Application to Regulated Industries', (OFT 405).

[19] Competition Act 1998, s 54(1), read with Sch 10, paras 1, 2(6), 3(5), 4(5), 5(6) and 6(5). There are equivalent provisions for the sector regulators for gas and electricity in Northern Ireland. OFGAS's functions are defined by reference to the Gas Act 1986 (as amended by the Gas Act 1995), s 36A(3), read with s 36A(4) and s 5(1). The definition of 'railway services' in the Railways Act 1993 does not include the provision (eg by leasing) of rolling stock, but it is thought that this falls within the definition of matters which 'relate to' their supply: see Office of the Rail Regulator, n 6 above, para 5.69.

[20] Bloom, M., 'The impact of the Competition Bill', in McCrudden, C. (ed), *Regulation and Deregulation* (Oxford, Clarendon Press, 1999), 235.

(iii) The sector regulator is to exercise these functions 'concurrently with' the OFT.

(iv) The only exceptions are the OFT's functions of issuing procedural rules in connection with the two prohibitions (under section 51), and of issuing guidance as to penalties/fines (under section 38(1) to (6))—both of which remain the sole preserve of the OFT.[21]

(v) The implications of this are that, in its particular sphere of responsibility, the sector regulator has powers—parallel to those of the OFT—to:

- investigate suspected infringements of the Chapter I and Chapter II prohibitions—including the power to enter premises (the so-called 'dawn raid');

- examine notified agreements and conduct;

- issues decisions and guidance on notified agreements and conduct;

- grant individual exemptions in respect of agreements under the Chapter I prohibition;

- recommend to the Secretary of State the grant of UK block exemptions;

- make directions requiring termination or modification of an agreement or conduct, and obtain a Court order to enforce such directions;

- impose penalties (fines) for infringements, taking account of the OFT's guidance on penalties;

- impose interim measures;

- publish general advice and information about the application and enforcement of the prohibitions (except in respect of penalties).

19.25 In addition, each sector regulator continues to exercise the OFT's functions in relation to monopoly investigations, also concurrently with the OFT, and in respect of monopoly situations within that sector regulator's sphere of responsibility. The government intends that full use of monopoly investigations should be made in the regulated utility sectors, including scale monopoly investigations (even if there has been no prior finding of an infringement of the Chapter II prohibition).[22]

Whom to Approach—the OFT or the Sector Regulator?

19.26 The major practical issue raised by the grant of concurrent functions is the question of whom a party should approach if it wishes to make a notification or a complaint under the Chapter I or Chapter II prohibition in connection with a regulated utility—the OFT or the relevant sector regulator?

---

[21] Competition Act 1998, Sch 10.
[22] Department of Trade and Industry 'A Fair Deal for Consumers: Modernising the Framework for Utility Regulation—the Response to Consultation', July 1998, 20. See also: OFT, n 18 above, para 4.8.

19.27 Arrangements or conduct within the ambit of the prohibitions will often involve more than one sector. For example, there may be agreements between a gas and electricity company, or between a telecommunications and a non-regulated company. Similarly, alleged abusive conduct may be carried out by companies which operate in a number of regulated sectors (for example, gas and electricity, or electricity and water). In those cases, the danger is that the sector regulator's limited jurisdiction (ie in respect only of its sphere of responsibility) will mean that the notification or complaint could not be fully handled if addressed to the sector regulator.

19.28 The following rules apply:

- **Notifications (for guidance or decision)** *must* **be sent to the OFT, with an extra copy for any sector regulator who, in the applicant's opinion, may have concurrent jurisdiction (such copy to be submitted to the OFT).[23] In addition, a further copy of the notification** *should* **be sent directly to the sector regulator concerned.[24] If the OFT considers that a sector regulator has or may have jurisdiction, it sends a copy of the notification to the sector regulator, and informs the applicant in writing of this.[25]**

- **Complaints, including applications for interim measures, must be sent to either the OFT or the sector regulator, but not to both—they may be transferred by one to the other.[26]**

The applicant or complainant will be notified 'as soon as practicable' of which authority is dealing with the case.[27] All subsequent correspondence and evidence should be submitted to that authority.

19.29 This still leaves the question of who will generally deal with the matter and, for complainants, which body should be approached. The OFT's guidelines state:

> . . . it is the subject matter to which the agreement or conduct relates rather than the identity of the undertakings involved which will determine whether there is concurrent jurisdiction . . .

> In general, an agreement or conduct which falls within the industry sector of a regulator . . . will be dealt with by that regulator, although in some cases the Director General of Fair Trading [head of the OFT] will deal with such a case. The general principle will be that a case will be dealt with by whichever of the Director General of Fair Trading or the relevant regulator is better, or best, placed to do so. The factors considered in determining which of the Director General or regulators deals with the matter include the sectoral knowledge of a regulator; any previous contacts

---

[23] Office of Fair Trading, Formal Consultation draft, 'Competition Act 1998: The Draft Procedural Rules' proposed by the Director General of Fair Trading, (OFT 411), R 3(3).
[24] OFT, n 18 above, paras 3.3 and 4.5
[25] OFT, n 23 above, R 8.
[26] OFT, n 18 above, para 3.5.
[27] OFT, n 23 above, R 8(2); n 18 above, para 3,3,

between the parties or complainants and a regulator, or with the Director General of Fair Trading; and any recent experience in dealing with any of the undertakings or similar issues which may be involved in the proceedings.[28]

In any event, the OFT and sector regulators with which it shares concurrent jurisdiction will meet in a 'Concurrency Working Party' which will: decide who should handle the case; act as a forum for the exchange of information (within the constraints of the confidentiality obligations in section 55 of the Act—see paragraph 19.33 below), and develop guidelines.[29]

In terms of addressing complaints, it is suggested that, where the relevant markets affected by the agreement or conduct are confined to the sphere of responsibility of just one sector regulator, it is sensible to address any complaint to that sector regulator, since it will have the industry expertise to apply the relevant law in the most appropriate way. Otherwise, however, where the affected markets include more than one regulated sector, or a regulated sector and an unregulated sector, it would probably be more sensible to address complaints to the OFT—as no single sector regulator would have the competence to deal with it, and the risk of addressing it to a sector regulator is that it would be handled by a number of different authorities. **19.30**

Complaints about licence conditions will remain the sole preserve of the sector regulator, and will not be a matter for the OFT. However, where it is 'more appropriate' for the regulator to proceed under the Chapter I or Chapter II prohibition, the regulator's duty to take licence enforcement action ceases to apply;[30] the parties will then be informed that the prohibitions are being applied instead. Complaints alleging breach both of licence conditions and of the prohibitions 'in relation to the same subject matter' would normally be considered by the regulator.[30a] **19.31**

Achieving Consistency Among the OFT and the Sector Regulators

As a result of concurrency, the Chapter I and Chapter II prohibitions will be applied by eight different authorities—the OFT, plus the seven sector regulators identified in Schedule 10 (including two for Northern Ireland). This has created considerable concerns about inconsistent application of the prohibitions (as discussed in paragraphs 19.19–19.21). A number of legal and procedural mechanisms are intended to remove the dangers of inconsistency, including the following: **19.32**

(i) As a result of section 60 of the Act, both the OFT and the sector regulators are obliged to apply the prohibitions consistently with EC case law under

---

[28] OFT, n 18 above, paras 2.2 and 3.1.
[29] Ibid, paras 3.7 and 3.8.
[30] Ibid, para 4.3.
[30a] Ibid, para 3.5.

Articles 81 and 82 (formerly 85 and 86). This is a significant constraint on their ability to go off in different directions when interpreting the prohibitions, and should create an overall framework of consistency.

(ii) In addition, as a matter of practicality, as the OFT's Director of Competition Policy has pointed out, 'it is anticipated that the vast majority of decisions taken under the new legislation will be those made by the [OFT] rather than the sectoral regulators because of the much greater jurisdictional coverage of the former than the latter. It is the decisions which will drive the case law.'

(iii) Moreover, the fact that the OFT has sole right to produce procedural rules and guidance on penalties (see paragraph 19.24 (iv)) is itself a safeguard for consistency.

(iv) These safeguards are reinforced by obligations on the OFT and the sector regulators to consult one another:

- In each of the privatisation statutes outlining the functions of the relevant sector regulators, there is a specific obligation on the OFT and the relevant sector regulator to consult each other before exercising competition powers in relation to that sector regulator's sphere of responsibility and preventing either the OFT or the sector regulator from exercising its competition functions if the other has already done so in relation to the same matter.[31]

- Although the OFT has the sole right to issue procedural rules, if they relate to a matter in respect of which a sector regulator exercises concurrent jurisdiction, it must consult that sector regulator.[32]

- Similarly, although the OFT has sole rights to issue guidance on penalties, if such guidance relates to a matter in respect of which a sector regulator exercises concurrent jurisdiction, the OFT must consult that regulator when preparing the guidance.[33]

- Where the OFT publishes general advice or information relating to a matter in respect of which a sector regulator exercises concurrent jurisdiction, it must consult that regulator[34].

- Since general guidance and advice may also be published by sector regulators (it is not the sole preserve of the OFT), any sector regulator doing so must also consult the OFT and the other sector regulators.[35]

---

[31] These provisions, as a result of amendments to the privatisation statutes introduced by the Competition Act 1998, extend to application of the Chapter I and Chapter II prohibitions. See Telecommunications Act 1984, s 50(4); Gas Act 1986, s 36A(5); Electricity Act 1989, s 43(4); Water Industry Act 1991, s 31(5) and (6); and Railways Act 1993, s 67(4).

[32] Competition Act 1998, s 51(4).

[33] Ibid, s 38(7).

[34] Ibid, s 52(7).

[35] Ibid, s 52(8).

- The Concurrency Working Party (see para 19.29 above) will enable the OFT and the sector regulators to work together to ensure that the guidelines are developed as a single set—covering notifications, prohibitions, penalties, market definitions, the transitional arrangements and concurrency itself.[36]
- The Secretary of State has powers under section 54(4) to (6) of the Competition Act to make regulations to co-ordinate the performance of concurrent functions of the OFT and the sector regulators, so putting the Concurrency Working Party on a statutory basis if necessary. It is not yet clear whether such regulations will in fact be needed.[37]

Protecting Confidential Company Information

The general protection for confidential company information, under section 55 of the Competition Act, is subject to a number of exceptions which are of particular relevance where the OFT and the sector regulators have concurrent jurisdiction. In particular: **19.33**

- Information obtained by the sector regulators when exercising their investigatory functions under the Competition Act may be used by them for their general regulatory functions (although, when the sector regulators do this, any subsequent disclosure is subject to the restrictions on disclosure in the Competition Act).
- Information obtained by the sector regulators in the exercise of their general regulatory powers may be used by the sector regulators or by the OFT in the exercise of their Competition Act powers.
- Information obtained by the OFT or the sector regulators, in exercise either of Competition Act powers or general regulatory powers, may be passed to the European Commission to facilitate the performance of any of its functions under EC competition law.[38]

Special Transitional Provisions for Certain Utilities

The Competition Act contains transitional provisions which give businesses time to adjust their agreements and arrangements before becoming subject to the Chapter I prohibition. These transitional provisions are set out in Schedule 13 (and are described in Chapter 11 of this book). **19.34**

---

[36] Bloom, M., n 20 above.
[37] OFT, n 18 above, para 2.5.
[38] Competition Act 1998 s 55(3), read with Sch 11. See also Office of Fair Trading, n 18 above, paras 5.2 and 5.3.

19.35 In addition to the general transitional provisions, Schedule 13 lays down special transitional provisions which provide further protection for certain types of agreement in the gas, electricity and railways sectors.

19.36 In very broad terms, the special transitional provisions grant a 'transitional period' (ie a period during which the Chapter I prohibition does not apply) lasting for five years after the 'starting date' for (a) pre-existing agreements which benefited from disapplication of the RTPA[39] under the relevant sector legislation and also (b) other agreements, pre-existing or new, in respect of which the Secretary of State with the regulators have made a 'transitional order'.

19.37 In terms of definition, the 'starting date' is the date when the Chapter I prohibition generally comes into force, 1 March 2000. The date five years after the starting date is therefore 1 March 2005.

19.38 The special rules may be summarised as follows:

(i) In the electricity sector, an agreement benefits from a transitional period, ending five years after the starting date in any of the following circumstances:

- if it is an agreement, made before the starting date, to which the RTPA does not apply immediately before the starting date by virtue of an order under the Electricity Act 1989, section 100;[40]

- if it is an agreement made or varied at any time after the starting date, to which the RTPA (if it were still in force) would have been disapplied as at that date by virtue of an order under the Electricity Act 1989, section 100;[41] or

- if it is an agreement, whether made before or after the starting date, which relates to the generation, transmission or supply of electricity, and in respect of which the Secretary of State has made a 'transitional order' (having consulted the OFT and OFTEL).[42]

(ii) In the gas sector, an agreement benefits from a transitional period, ending five years after the starting date in any of the following circumstances:

- if it is an agreement, made before the starting date, to which the RTPA does not apply immediately before the starting date by virtue of the Gas Act 1986, section 62, or an order made under the Gas Act 1986, section 62, or an order made under the Gas (Northern Ireland) Order 1996, article 41;[43]

- if it is an agreement made or varied at any date after the starting date, to which the RTPA (if it were still in force) would have been disapplied as at

---

[39] Restrictive Trade Practices Act 1976.
[40] Competition Act 1998, Sch 13, para 28(1).
[41] Sch 13, para 28(2)–(4).
[42] Sch 13, para 29.
[43] Sch 13, paras 30(1) and 32(1).

that date by virtue of the Gas Act 1986, section 62, or an order made under that provision, or an order made under the Gas (Northern Ireland) Order 1986, article 41;[44] or

- if it is an agreement, whether made before or after the starting date), which is of a description falling within Gas Act 1986, section 62(2)(a) and (b) or section 62(2A)(a) and (b),[45] and in respect of which the Secretary of State has made a 'transitional order' (after consulting the OFT and OFGAS).[46]

(iii) In the railways sector, an agreement benefits from a transitional period ending five years after the starting date in any of the following circumstances:

- if it is an agreement, made before the starting date, to which the RTPA does not apply immediately before the starting date by virtue of the Railways Act 1993, section 131(1);[47]

- if it is an agreement, made before the starting date, in respect of which a direction under the Railways Act 1993, section 131(3) is in force immediately before the starting date;[48] or

- to the extent that it is an agreement, whether made before or after the starting date, which is required or approved by the Secretary of State or the Rail Regulator under the Railways Act 1993 (other than section 131), or under an agreement required or approved by the Secretary of State or the Rail Regulator under that Act, or under a licence granted under Part I of that Act.[49]

A variation to such an agreement, if it has the effect that it is no longer one to which the RTPA would not have applied or one to which a transitional order applies, deprives the agreement of the benefit of the transitional period.[50]

E. Other Regulatory Functions: Proposals for Reform

The emergence of market competition in the utilities sectors, and of stronger UK **19.39** competition law, has supplanted many of the direct regulatory functions which

---

[44] Sch 13, para 30(2)–(4), and 32(2)–(4).

[45] That is: either an agreement made on or after 28 Nov 1985 which contains provisions relating to (or to activities connected with) the supply otherwise than under a s 7A(1) licence of gas won under the authority of a petroleum production licence; or an agreement made on or after 2 Mar 1995 which contains provisions relating to (or to activities connected with) the introduction of gas into, taking out of gas from, or use by gas shippers of, a pipe-line system or storage facility operated by a public gas transporter.

[46] Sch 13, para 31.

[47] Sch 13, para 34(2).

[48] Sch 13, para 34(2). No s131(3) direction has ever been given.

[49] Sch 13, para 34(3).

[50] Office of Fair Trading, Formal Consultation Draft, 'Competition Act 1998: Transitional Arrangements', (OFT 406), para 4.10.

the sector regulators have traditionally exercised through enforcing licence conditions. To the extent that those original functions had been designed to control abuses of market power on the part of natural monopolists, that purpose is now largely served by the sector regulators' concurrent powers under the Competition Act. As noted above, where a matter can more appropriately be dealt with under the Chapter I or Chapter II prohibition, the regulator's duty to take licence enforcement action ceases to apply.[51]

19.40 However, there remains a continuing need for the sector regulators' traditional functions to be exercised. To a limited extent the application of the Chapter I and Chapter II prohibitions to utilities is constrained by the exclusion in Schedule 3 paragraph 4, for services of general economic interest, and in cases where that exclusion applies it is envisaged that 'the regulators' ability to ensure that services are available throughout the UK is particularly relevant'.[52]

19.41 Moreover, market competition, reinforced by competition law, cannot supplant all the original functions of the sector regulators.[53] Utility regulation has other functions than simply the promotion of competition and the prevention of abuses of market power. In particular, it has what may be termed a 'social function'—meeting certain social needs which even the most perfectly functioning competitive markets cannot be relied on to satisfy. This is because the utilities, unlike other sectors of the economy (such as the supply of motor cars or of advertising services), are regarded as providing services which are virtually essential to modern life. These are a social good which, it is widely held, everyone in society is entitled to enjoy, virtually regardless of how rich or poor they are, or of where in the country they happen to live. To that extent, the utility sectors are treated comparably with health and education, rather than with motor cars and advertising.

19.42 Consequently, the system of utility regulation instituted on privatisation included licence conditions designed to meet social objectives, as well as to prevent abuses of market power. These have included:

- universal service obligations—statutory requirements and/or licence conditions on British Telecom,[54] on gas suppliers,[55] on public electricity suppliers[56]

---

[51] OFT, n 18 above, para 4.3.

[52] OFT, n 18 above, paras 4.4–4.6. See Ch 5, paras 5.32–5.40 above on the exclusion for services of general economic interest.

[53] For a detailed discussion of this issue, see: Grenfell, M., 'Can Competition Law Supplant Utilities Regulation?', in McCrudden, C. (ed), *Regulation and Deregulation* (Oxford, Clarendon Press, 1999), 221.

[54] Licence granted to British Telecommunications plc under the Telecommunications Act 1984, Condition 1.

[55] Department of Trade and Industry/OFGAS, Standard Conditions of Gas Suppliers' Licences as modified to Mar 1997, Condition 2(1).

[56] Electricity Act 1989, s 16.

and on water suppliers[57] to supply *every* potential domestic customer in the area in which it is licensed to supply (regardless of whether such supply is commercially profitable or not);

- obligations to supply special facilities for elderly, disabled, blind and deaf customers;[58]

- licence conditions, and Codes of Practice, protecting vulnerable sectors of society who are unable to pay bills on time from having their supplies disconnected.[59]

Because of these broader 'social' functions of the sector regulators, in 1998 the **19.43** Government, as well as granting them concurrent powers under the Competition Act, issued proposals to reform and strengthen their direct regulatory powers under the licensing regime.[60] In some ways, the proposals were most notable for what they did not say: the government did not propose that the sector regulators should be required to change the basic 'RPI – *x*' price cap formula, in spite of criticisms which the Labour Party had made in Opposition that the formula was insufficiently stringent and enabled many utility companies to make 'excess profits'. However, some of the proposals were nevertheless fairly radical, and were designed to enhance the 'social' aspects of the sector regulators' functions. The most important proposals were as follows:

(i)   the imposition on the sector regulators of a 'primary duty' of **consumer protection**;

(ii) the sector regulators should have regard to statutory guidance, to be issued by Ministers, on **social and environmental issues** when exercising their statutory functions of regulation;

(iii) the establishment of **independent consumer councils** 'to protect the interests of all consumers, including the disadvantaged';

(iv) the amalgamation of OFGAS and OFFER into a **single energy sector regulator**;

(v)   in the regulatory bodies for energy and for telecommunications (now OFTEL), **executive boards should take over the functions of the individual Director General**;

---

[57] Water Industry Act 1991, s 37(1).
[58] eg, in the gas supply licence (Conditions 17 and 18), and in the public electricity supply licence (Condition 20).
[59] eg, the OFWAT guidelines to water companies to assist customers who are in default on their bill payments before proceeding to disconnection (OFWAT Annual Report 1991, 39–40), and Condition 20 of the gas supply licence prohibiting disconnection during the winter months (Oct to Mar) of old age pensioners who are in default.
[60] Department of Trade and Industry press release on the reform of utility regulation, 27 July 1998; Green Paper, *A Fair Deal for Consumers: Modernising the Framework for Utility Regulation*, Department of Trade and Industry, Cm 3898, Mar 1998.

(vi)　the imposition on these sector regulators of a statutory **duty to publish** reasons for their key decisions;

(vii)　**price caps** to be more clearly linked to customer service standards.

19.44　At the time of writing, these proposals have not yet been given legislative form, and it remains to be seen how they will develop. It remains to be seen, also, how well such reforms of the sector regulators' 'social' functions will sit with their new competition functions under the Chapter I and Chapter II prohibitions.

APPENDICES

APPENDIX 1

Competition Act 1998

CHAPTER 41

ARRANGEMENT OF SECTIONS

PART I
COMPETITION

CHAPTER I
AGREEMENTS

Introduction

Section
1. Enactments replaced.

The prohibition

2. Agreements etc. preventing, restricting or distorting competition.

Excluded agreements

3. Excluded agreements.

Exemptions

4. Individual exemptions.
5. Cancellation etc. of individual exemptions.
6. Block exemptions.
7. Block exemptions: opposition.
8. Block exemptions: procedure.
9. The criteria for individual and block exemptions.
10. Parallel exemptions.
11. Exemption for certain other agreements.

Notification

12. Requests for Director to examine agreements.
13. Notification for guidance.
14. Notification for a decision.
15. Effect of guidance.
16. Effect of a decision that the Chapter I prohibition has not been infringed.

CHAPTER II
ABUSE OF DOMINANT POSITION

Introduction

CHAPTER III
INVESTIGATION AND ENFORCEMENT

Investigations

Enforcement

Offences

CHAPTER IV
THE COMPETITION COMMISSION AND APPEALS

The Commission

Appeals

CHAPTER V
MISCELLANEOUS

Vertical agreements and land agreements

Director's rules, guidance and fees

Regulators

Confidentiality and immunity from defamation

Findings of fact by Director

Interpretation and governing principles

Part II
Investigations in relation to Articles 85 and 86

Part III
Monopolies

Part IV
Supplemental and Transitional

Competition Act 1998

1998 Chapter 41

An Act to make provision about competition and the abuse of a dominant position in the market; to confer powers in relation to investigations conducted in connection with Article 85 or 86 of the treaty establishing the European Community; to amend the Fair Trading Act 1973 in relation to information which may be required in connection with investigations under that Act; to make provision with respect to the meaning of 'supply of services' in the Fair Trading Act 1973; and for connected purposes.

[9th November 1998]

BE IT ENACTED by the Queen's most Excellent Majesty, by and with the advice and consent of the Lords Spiritual and Temporal, and Commons, in this present Parliament assembled, and by the authority of the same, as follows:—

PART I
COMPETITION

CHAPTER I
AGREEMENTS

Introduction

Enactments replaced

CA.01 1. The following shall cease to have effect—

(a) the Restrictive Practices Court Art 1976 (c. 33).

(b) the Restrictive Trade Practices Act 1976 (c. 34),

(c) the Resale Prices Act 1976 (c. 53), and

(d) the Restrictive Trade Practices Act 1977 (c. 19).

The prohibition

Agreements etc. preventing, restricting or distorting competition

CA.02 2.—(1) Subject to section 3, agreements between undertakings, decisions by associations of undertakings or concerted practices which—

(a) may affect trade within the United Kingdom, and

(b) have as their object or effect the prevention, restriction or distortion of competition within the United Kingdom,

are prohibited unless they are exempt in accordance with the provisions of this Part.

(2) Subsection (1) applies, in particular, to agreements, decisions or practices which—

(a) directly or indirectly fix purchase or selling prices or any other trading conditions;

(b) limit or control production, markets, technical development or investment;

(c) share markets or sources of supply;

(d) apply dissimilar conditions to equivalent transactions with other trading parties, thereby placing them at a competitive disadvantage;

(e) make the conclusion of contracts subject to acceptance by the other parties of supplementary obligations which, by their nature or according to commercial usage, have no connection with the subject of such contracts.

(3) Subsection (1) applies only if the agreement, decision or practice is, or is intended to be, implemented in the United Kingdom.

(4) Any agreement or decision which is prohibited by subsection (1) is void.

(5) A provision of this Part which is expressed to apply to, or in relation to, an agreement is to be read as applying equally to, or in relation to, a decision by an association of undertakings or a concerted practice (but with any necessary modifications).

(6) Subsection (5) does not apply where the context otherwise requires.

(7) In this section 'the United Kingdom' means, in relation to an agreement which operates or is intended to operate only in a part of the United Kingdom, that part.

(8) The prohibition imposed by subsection (1) is referred to in this Act as 'the Chapter I prohibition'.

Excluded agreements

3.—(1) The Chapter I prohibition does not apply in any of the cases in which it is **CA.03** excluded by or as a result of—

(a) Schedule 1 (mergers and concentrations);

(b) Schedule 2 (competition scrutiny under other enactments);

(c) Schedule 3 (planning obligations and other general exclusions); or

(d) Schedule 4 (professional rules).

(2) The Secretary of State may at any time by order amend Schedule 1, with respect to the Chapter I prohibition, by—

(a) providing for one or more additional exclusions; or

(b) amending or removing any provision (whether or not it has been added by an order under this subsection).

(3) The Secretary of State may at any time by order amend Schedule 3, with respect to the Chapter I prohibition, by—

(a) providing for one or more additional exclusions; or

(b) amending or removing any provision—

(i) added by an order under this subsection; or

(ii) included in paragraph 1, 2, 8 or 9 of Schedule 3.

(4) The power under subsection (3) to provide for an additional exclusion may be exercised only if it appears to the Secretary of State that agreements which fall within the additional exclusion—

(a) do not in general have an adverse effect on competition; or

(b) are, in general, best considered under Chapter II or the Fair Trading Act 1973.

(5) An order under subsection (2)(a) or (3)(a) may include provision (similar to that made with respect to any other exclusion provided by the relevant Schedule) for the exclusion concerned to cease to apply to a particular agreement.

(6) Schedule 3 also gives the Secretary of State power to exclude agreements from the Chapter I prohibition in certain circumstances.

Exemptions

Individual exemptions

CA.04 4.—(1) The Director may grant an exemption from the Chapter I prohibition with respect to a particular agreement if—

(a) a request for an exemption has been made to him under section 14 by a party to the agreement; and

(b) the agreement is one to which section 9 applies.

(2) An exemption granted under this section is referred to in this Part as an individual exemption.

(3) The exemption—

(a) may be granted subject to such conditions or obligations as the Director considers it appropriate to impose; and

(b) has effect for such period as the Director considers appropriate.

(4) That period must be specified in the grant of the exemption.

(5) An individual exemption may be granted so as to have effect from a date earlier than that on which it is granted.

(6) On an application made in such a way as may be specified by rules under section 51, the Director may extend the period for which an exemption has effect; but, if the rules so provide, he may do so only in specified circumstances.

Cancellation etc. of individual exemptions

CA.05 5.—(1) If the Director has reasonable grounds for believing that there has been a material change of circumstance since he granted an individual exemption, he may by notice in writing—

(a) cancel the exemption;

(b) vary or remove any condition or obligation; or

(c) impose one or more additional conditions or obligations.

(2) If the Director has a reasonable suspicion that the information on which he based his decision to grant an individual exemption was incomplete, false or misleading in a material particular, he may by notice in writing take any of the steps mentioned in subsection (1).

(3) Breach of a condition has the effect of cancelling the exemption.

(4) Failure to comply with an obligation allows the Director, by notice in writing, to take any of the steps mentioned in subsection (1).

(5) Any step taken by the Director under subsection (1), (2) or (4) has effect from such time as may be specified in the notice.

(6) If an exemption is cancelled under subsection (2) or (4), the date specified in the notice cancelling it may be earlier than the date on which the notice is given.

(7) The Director may act under subsection (1), (2) or (4) on his own initiative or on a complaint made by any person.

Block exemptions

6.—(1) If agreements which fall within a particular category of agreement are, in the opinion of the Director, likely to be agreements to which section 9 applies, the Director may recommend that the Secretary of State make an order specifying that category for the purposes of this section.   **CA.06**

(2) The Secretary of State may make an order ('a block exemption order') giving effect to such a recommendation—

    (a) in the form in which the recommendation is made; or

    (b) subject to such modifications as he considers appropriate.

(3) An agreement which falls within a category specified in a block exemption order is exempt from the Chapter I prohibition.

(4) An exemption under this section is referred to in this Part as a block exemption.

(5) A block exemption order may impose conditions or obligations subject to which a block exemption is to have effect.

(6) A block exemption order may provide—

    (a) that breach of a condition imposed by the order has the effect of cancelling the block exemption in respect of an agreement;

    (b) that if there is a failure to comply with an obligation imposed by the order, the Director may, by notice in writing, cancel the block exemption in respect of the agreement;

    (c) that if the Director considers that a particular agreement is not one to which section 9 applies, he may cancel the block exemption in respect of that agreement.

(7) A block exemption order may provide that the order is to cease to have effect at the end of a specified period.

(8) In this section and section 7 'specified' means specified in a block exemption order.

Block exemptions: opposition

7.—(1) A block exemption order may provide that a party to an agreement which   **CA.07**

523

(a) does not qualify for the block exemption created by the order, but

(b) satisfies specified criteria,

may notify the Director of the agreement for the purposes of subsection (2).

(2) An agreement which is notified under any provision included in a block exemption order by virtue of subsection (1) is to be treated, as from the end of the notice period, as falling within a category specified in a block exemption order unless the Director—

(a) is opposed to its being so treated; and

(b) gives notice in writing to the party concerned of his opposition before the end of that period.

(3) If the Director gives notice of his opposition under subsection (2), the notification under subsection (1) is to be treated as both notification under section 14 and as a request for an individual exemption made under subsection (3) of that section.

(4) In this section 'notice period' means such period as may be specified with a view to giving the Director sufficient time to consider whether to oppose under subsection (2).

Block exemptions: procedure

CA.08 8.—(1) Before making a recommendation under section 6(1), the Director must—

(a) publish details of his proposed recommendation in such a way as he thinks most suitable for bringing it to the attention of those likely to be affected; and

(b) consider any representations about it which are made to him.

(2) If the Secretary of State proposes to give effect to such a recommendation subject to modifications, he must inform the Director of the proposed modifications and take into account any comments made by the Director.

(3) If, in the opinion of the Director, it is appropriate to vary or revoke a block exemption order he may make a recommendation to that effect to the Secretary of State.

(4) Subsection (1) also applies to any proposed recommendation under subsection (3).

(5) Before exercising his power to vary or revoke a block exemption order (in a case where there has been no recommendation under subsection (3)), the Secretary of State must—

(a) inform the Director of the proposed variation or revocation; and

(b) take into account any comments made by the Director.

(6) A block exemption order may provide for a block exemption to have effect from a date earlier than that on which the order is made.

The criteria for individual and block exemptions

CA.09 9. This section applies to any agreement which—

(a) contributes to—

(i) improving production or distribution; or

(ii) promoting technical or economic progress,

while allowing consumers a fair share of the resulting benefit; but

(b) does not—

    (i) impose on the undertakings concerned restrictions which are not indispensable to the attainment of those objectives; or

    (ii) afford the undertakings concerned the possibility of eliminating competition in respect of a substantial part of the products in question.

Parallel exemptions

10.—(1) An agreement is exempt from the Chapter I prohibition if it is exempt from the Community prohibition—   **CA.10**

    (a) by virtue of a Regulation;

    (b) because it has been given exemption by the Commission; or

    (c) because it has been notified to the Commission under the appropriate opposition or objection procedure and—

        (i) the time for opposing, or objecting to, the agreement has expired and the Commission has not opposed it; or

        (ii) the Commission has opposed, or objected to, the agreement but has withdrawn its opposition or objection.

(2) An agreement is exempt from the Chapter I prohibition if it does not affect trade between Member States but otherwise falls within a category of agreement which is exempt from the Community prohibition by virtue of a Regulation.

(3) An exemption from the Chapter I prohibition under this section is referred to in this Part as a parallel exemption.

(4) A parallel exemption—

    (a) takes effect on the date on which the relevant exemption from the Community prohibition takes effect or, in the case of a parallel exemption under subsection (2), would take effect if the agreement in question affected trade between Member States; and

    (b) ceases to have effect—

        (i) if the relevant exemption from the Community prohibition ceases to have effect; or

        (ii) on being cancelled by virtue of subsection (5) or (7).

(5) In such circumstances and manner as may be specified in rules made under section 51, the Director may—

    (a) impose conditions or obligations subject to which a parallel exemption is to have effect;

    (b) vary or remove any such condition or obligation;

    (c) impose one or more additional conditions or obligations;

    (d) cancel the exemption.

(6) In such circumstances as may be specified in rules made under section 51, the date from which cancellation of an exemption is to take effect may be earlier than the date on which notice of cancellation is given.

(7) Breach of a condition imposed by the Director has the effect of cancelling the exemption.

(8) In exercising his powers under this section, the Director may require any person who is a party to the agreement in question to give him such information as he may require.

(9) For the purpose of this section references to an agreement being exempt from the Community prohibition are to be read as including references to the prohibition being inapplicable to the agreement by virtue of a Regulation or a decision by the Commission.

(10) In this section—

'the Community prohibition' means the prohibition contained in—

    (a) paragraph 1 of Article 85;

    (b) any corresponding provision replacing, or otherwise derived from, that provision;

    (c) such other Regulation as the Secretary of State may by order specify; and

'Regulation' means a Regulation adopted by the Commission or by the Council.

(11) This section has effect in relation to the prohibition contained in paragraph 1 of Article 53 of the EEA Agreement (and the EFTA Surveillance Authority) as it has effect in relation to the Community prohibition (and the Commission) subject to any modifications which the Secretary of State may by order prescribe.

Exemption for certain other agreements

CA.11 11.—(1) The fact that a ruling may be given by virtue of Article 88 of the Treaty on the question whether or not agreements of a particular kind are prohibited by Article 85 does not prevent such agreements from being subject to the Chapter I prohibition.

(2) But the Secretary of State may by regulations make such provision as he considers appropriate for the purpose of granting an exemption from the Chapter I prohibition, in prescribed circumstances, in respect of such agreements.

(3) An exemption from the Chapter I prohibition by virtue of regulations under this section is referred to in this Part as a section 11 exemption.

Notification

Requests for Director to examine agreements

CA.12 12.—(1) Sections 13 and 14 provide for an agreement to be examined by the Director on the application of a party to the agreement who thinks that it may infringe the Chapter I prohibition.

(2) Schedule 5 provides for the procedure to be followed—

    (a) by any person making such an application; and

(b) by the Director, in considering such an application.

(3) The Secretary of State may by regulations make provision as to the application of sections 13 to 16 and Schedule 5, with such modifications (if any) as may be prescribed, in cases where the Director—

(a) has given a direction withdrawing an exclusion; or

(b) is considering whether to give such a direction.

Notification for guidance

13.—(1) A party to an agreement who applies for the agreement to be examined under this section must—   **CA.13**

(a) notify the Director of the agreement; and

(b) apply to him for guidance.

(2) On an application under this section, the Director may give the applicant guidance as to whether or not, in his view, the agreement is likely to infringe the Chapter I prohibition.

(3) If the Director considers that the agreement is likely to infringe the prohibition if it is not exempt, his guidance may indicate—

(a) whether the agreement is likely to be exempt from the prohibition under—

(i) a block exemption;

(ii) a parallel exemption; or

(iii) a section 11 exemption; or

(b) whether he would be likely to grant the agreement an individual exemption if asked to do so.

(4) If an agreement to which the prohibition applies has been notified to the Director under this section, no penalty is to be imposed under this Part in respect of any infringement of the prohibition by the agreement which occurs during the period—

(a) beginning with the date on which notification was given; and

(b) ending with such date as may be specified in a notice in writing given to the applicant by the Director when the application has been determined.

(5) The date specified in a notice under subsection (4)(b) may not be earlier than the date on which the notice is given.

Notification for a decision

14.—(1) A party to an agreement who applies for the agreement to be examined under this section must—   **CA.14**

(a) notify the Director of the agreement; and

(b) apply to him for a decision.

(2) On an application under this section, the Director may make a decision as to—

(a) whether the Chapter I prohibition has been infringed; and

(b) if it has not been infringed, whether that is because of the effect of an exclusion or because the agreement is exempt from the prohibition.

(3) If an agreement is notified to the Director under this section, the application may include a request for the agreement to which it relates to be granted an individual exemption.

(4) If an agreement to which the prohibition applies has been notified to the Director under this section, no penalty is to be imposed under this Part in respect of any infringement or the prohibition by the agreement which occurs during the period—

(a) beginning with the date on which notification was given; and

(b) ending with such date as may be specified in a notice in writing given to the applicant by the Director when the application has been determined.

(5) The date specified in a notice under subsection (4)(b) may not be earlier than the date on which the notice is given.

Effect of guidance

CA.15 15.—(1) This section applies to an agreement if the Director has determined an application under section 13 by giving guidance that—

(a) the agreement is unlikely to infringe the Chapter I prohibition, regardless of whether or not it is exempt;

(b) the agreement is likely to be exempt under—

(i) a block exemption;

(ii) a parallel exemption; or

(iii) a section 11 exemption; or

(c) he would be likely to grant the agreement an individual exemption if asked to do so.

(2) The Director is to take no further action under this Part with respect to an agreement to which this section applies, unless—

(a) he has reasonable grounds for believing that there has been a material change of circumstance since he gave his guidance;

(b) he has a reasonable suspicion that the information on which he based his guidance was incomplete, false or misleading in a material particular;

(c) one of the parties to the agreement applies to him for a decision under section 14 with respect to the agreement; or

(d) a complaint about the agreement has been made to him by a person who is not a party to the agreement.

(3) No penalty may be imposed under this Part in respect of any infringement of the Chapter I prohibition by an agreement to which this section applies.

(4) But the Director may remove the immunity given by subsection (3) if—

(a) he takes action under this Part with respect to the agreement in one of the circumstances mentioned in subsection (2);

(b) he considers it likely that the agreement will infringe the prohibition; and

(c) he gives notice in writing to the party on whose application the guidance was given that he is removing the immunity as from the date specified in his notice.

(5) If the Director has a reasonable suspicion that information—

(a) on which he based his guidance, and

(b) which was provided to him by a party to the agreement,

was incomplete, false or misleading in a material particular, the date specified in a notice under subsection (4)(c) may be earlier than the date on which the notice is given.

Effect of a decision that the Chapter I prohibition has not been infringed

16.—(1) This section applies to an agreement if the Director has determined an application under section 14 by making a decision that the agreement has not infringed the Chapter I prohibition. **CA.16**

(2) The Director is to take no further action under this Part with respect to the agreement unless—

(a) he has reasonable grounds for believing that there has been a material change of circumstance since he gave his decision; or

(b) he has a reasonable suspicion that the information on which he based his decision was incomplete, false or misleading in a material particular.

(3) No penalty may be imposed under this Part in respect of any infringement of the Chapter I prohibition by an agreement to which this section applies.

(4) But the Director may remove the immunity given by subsection (3) if—

(a) he takes action under this part with respect to the agreement in one of the circumstances mentioned in subsection (2);

(b) he considers that it is likely that the agreement will infringe the prohibition; and

(c) he gives notice in writing to the party on whose application the decision was made that he is removing the immunity as from the date specified in his notice.

(5) If the Director has a reasonable suspicion that information—

(a) on which he based his decision, and

(b) which was provided to him by a party to the agreement,

was incomplete, false or misleading in a material particular, the date specified in a notice under subsection (4)(c) may be earlier than the date on which the notice is given.

CHAPTER II
ABUSE OF DOMINANT POSITION

Introduction

Enactments replaced

17. Sections 2 to 10 of the Competition Act 1980 (control of anti-competitive practices) shall cease to have effect. **CA.17**

The prohibition

Abuse of dominant position

CA.18   18.—(1) Subject to section 19, any conduct on the part of one or more undertakings which amounts to the abuse of a dominant position in a market is prohibited if it may affect trade within the United Kingdom.

(2) Conduct may, in particular, constitute such an abuse if it consists in—

(a) directly or indirectly imposing unfair purchase or selling prices or other unfair trading conditions;

(b) limiting production, markets or technical development to the prejudice of consumers;

(c) applying dissimilar conditions to equivalent transactions with other trading parties, thereby placing them at a competitive disadvantage;

(d) making the conclusion of contracts subject to acceptance by the other parties of supplementary obligations which, by their nature or according to commercial usage, have no connection with the subject of the contracts.

(3) In this section—

'dominant position' means a dominant position within the United Kingdom; and

'the United Kingdom' means the United Kingdom or any part of it.

(4) The prohibition imposed by subsection (1) is referred to in this Act as 'the Chapter II prohibition'.

Excluded cases

CA.19   19.—(1) The Chapter II prohibition does not apply in any of the cases in which it is excluded by or as a result of—

(a) Schedule 1 (mergers and concentrations); or

(b) Schedule 3 (general exclusions).

(2) The Secretary of State may at any time by order amend Schedule 1, with respect to the Chapter II prohibition, by—

(a) providing for one or more additional exclusions; or

(b) amending or removing any provision (whether or not it has been added by an order under this subsection).

(3) The Secretary of State may at any time by order amend paragraph 8 of Schedule 3 with respect to the Chapter II prohibition.

(4) Schedule 3 also gives the Secretary of State power to provide that the Chapter II prohibition is not to apply in certain circumstances.

Notification

Requests for Director to consider conduct

CA.20   20.—(1) Sections 21 and 22 provide for conduct of a person which that person thinks may infringe the Chapter II prohibition to be considered by the Director on the application of that person.

(2) Schedule 6 provides for the procedure to be followed—

    (a) by any person making an application, and

    (b) by the Director, in considering an application.

Notification for guidance

21.—(1) A person who applies for conduct to be considered under this section must—   **CA.21**

    (a) notify the Director of it; and

    (b) apply to him for guidance.

(2) On an application under this section, the Director may give the applicant guidance as to whether or not, in his view, the conduct is likely to infringe the Chapter II prohibition.

Notification for a decision

22.—(1) A person who applies for conduct to be considered under this section must—   **CA.22**

    (a) notify the Director of it; and

    (b) apply to him for a decision.

(2) On an application under this section, the Director may make a decision as to—

    (a) whether the Chapter II prohibition has been infringed; and

    (b) if it has not been infringed, whether that is because of the effect of an exclusion.

Effect of guidance

23.—(1) This section applies to conduct if the Director has determined an application   **CA.23** under section 21 by giving guidance that the conduct is unlikely to infringe the Chapter II prohibition.

(2) The Director is to take no further action under this Part with respect to the conduct to which this section applies, unless—

    (a) he has reasonable grounds for believing that there has been a material change of circumstance since he gave his guidance;

    (b) he has a reasonable suspicion that the information on which he based his guidance was incomplete, false or misleading in a material particular; or

    (c) a complaint about the conduct has been made to him.

(3) No penalty may be imposed under this Part in respect of any infringement of the Chapter II prohibition by conduct to which this section applies.

(4) But the Director may remove the immunity given by subsection (3) if—

    (a) he takes action under this Part with respect to the conduct in one of the circumstances mentioned in subsection (2);

    (b) he considers that it is likely that the conduct will infringe the prohibition; and

    (c) he gives notice in writing to the undertaking on whose application the guidance was given that he is removing the immunity as from the date specified in his notice.

(5) If the Director has a reasonable suspicion that information—

(a) on which he based his guidance, and

(b) which was provided to him by an undertaking engaging in the conduct,

was incomplete, false or misleading in a material particular, the date specified in a notice under subsection (4)(c) may be earlier than the date on which the notice is given.

Effect of a decision that the Chapter II prohibition has not been infringed

CA.24   24.—(1) This section applies to conduct if the Director has determined an application under section 22 by making a decision that the conduct has not infringed the Chapter II prohibition.

(2) The Director is to take no further action under this Part with respect to the conduct unless—

(a) he has reasonable grounds for believing that there has been a material change of circumstances since he gave his decision; or

(b) he has a reasonable suspicion that the information on which he based his decision was incomplete, false or misleading in a material particular.

(3) No penalty may be imposed under this Part in respect of any infringement of the Chapter II prohibition by conduct to which this section applies.

(4) But the Director may remove the immunity given by subsection (3) if—

(a) he takes action under this Part with respect to the conduct in one of the circumstances mentioned in subsection (2);

(b) he considers that it is likely that the conduct will infringe the prohibition; and

(c) he gives notice in writing to the undertaking on whose application the decision was made that he is removing the immunity as from the date specified in his notice.

(5) If the Director has a reasonable suspicion that information—

(a) on which he based his decision, and

(b) which was provided to him by an undertaking engaging in the conduct,

was incomplete, false or misleading in a material particular, the date specified in a notice under subsection (4)(c) may be earlier than the date on which the notice is given.

CHAPTER III

INVESTIGATION AND ENFORCEMENT

Investigations

Director's power to investigate

CA.25   25. The Director may conduct an investigation if there are reasonable grounds for suspecting—

(a) that the Chapter I prohibition has been infringed; or

(b) that the Chapter II prohibition has been infringed.

Powers when conducting investigations

26.—(1) For the purposes of an investigation under section 25, the Director may require **CA.26**
any person to produce to him a specified document, or to provide him with specified
information, which he considers relates to any matter relevant to the investigation.

(2) The power conferred by subsection (1) is to be exercised by a notice in writing.

(3) A notice under subsection (2) must indicate—

    (a) the subject matter and purpose of the investigation; and

    (b) the nature of the offences created by sections 42 to 44.

(4) In subsection (1) 'specified' means—

    (a) specified, or described, in the notice; or

    (b) falling within a category which is specified, or described, in the notice.

(5) The Director may also specify in the notice—

    (a) the time and place at which any document is to be produced or any information
    is to be provided;

    (b) the manner and form in which it is to be provided.

(6) The power under this section to require a person to produce a document includes
power—

    (a) if the document is produced—

        (i) to take copies of it or extracts from it;

        (ii) to require him, or any person who is a present or past officer of his, or is or was
        at any time employed by him, to provide an explanation of the document;

    (b) if the document is not produced, to require him to state, to the best of his knowl-
    edge and belief, where it is.

Power to enter premises without warrant

27.—(1) Any officer of the Director who is authorised in writing by the Director to do so **CA.27**
('an investigating officer') may enter any premises in connection with an investigation
under section 25.

(2) No investigating officer is to enter any premises in the exercise of his powers under
this section unless he has given to the occupier of the premises a written notice which—

    (a) gives at least two working days' notice of the intended entry;

    (b) indicates the subject matter and purpose of the investigation; and

    (c) indicates the nature of the offences created by sections 42 to 44.

(3) Subsection (2) does not apply—

    (a) if the Director has a reasonable suspicion that the premises are, or have been,
    occupied by—

        (i) a party to an agreement which he is investigating under section 25(a); or

      (ii) an undertaking the conduct of which he is investigating under section 25(b); or

   (b) if the investigating officer has taken all such steps as are reasonably practicable to give notice but has not been able to do so.

(4) In a case falling within subsection (3), the power of entry conferred by subsection (1) is to be exercised by the investigating officer on production of—

   (a) evidence of his authorisation; and

   (b) a document containing the information referred to in subsection (2)(b) and (c).

(5) An investigating officer entering any premises under this section may—

   (a) take with him such equipment as appears to him to be necessary;

   (b) require any person on the premises—

      (i) to produce any document which he considers relates to any matter relevant to the investigation; and

      (ii) if the document is produced, to provide an explanation of it;

   (c) require any person to state, to the best of his knowledge and belief, where any such document is to be found;

   (d) take copies of, or extracts from, any document which is produced;

   (e) require any information which is held in a computer and is accessible from the premises and which the investigating officer considers relates to any matter relevant to the investigation, to be produced in a form—

      (i) in which it can be taken away; and

      (ii) in which it is visible and legible.

Power to enter premises under a warrant

CA.28 28.—(1) On an application made by the Director to the court in accordance with rules of court, a judge may issue a warrant if he is satisfied that—

   (a) there are reasonable grounds for suspecting that there are on any premises documents—

      (i) the production of which has been required under section 26 or 27; and

      (ii) which have not been produced as required;

   (b) there are reasonable grounds for suspecting that—

      (i) there are on any premises documents which the Director has power under section 26 to require to be produced; and

      (ii) if the documents were required to be produced, they would not be produced but would be concealed, removed, tampered with or destroyed; or

   (c) an investigating officer has attempted to enter premises in the exercise of his powers under section 27 but has been unable to do so and that there are reasonable grounds for suspecting that there are on the premises documents the production of which could have been required under that section.

(2) A warrant under this section shall authorise a named officer of the Director, and any other of his officers whom he has authorised in writing to accompany the named officer—

(a) to enter the premises specified in the warrant, using such force as is reasonably necessary for the purpose;

(b) to search the premises and take copies or, or extracts from, any document appearing to be of a kind in respect of which the application under subsection (1) was granted ('the relevant kind');

(c) to take possession of any documents appearing to be of the relevant kind if—

(i) such action appears to be necessary for preserving the documents or preventing interference with them; or

(ii) it is not reasonably practicable to take copies of the documents on the premises;

(d) to take any other steps which appear to be necessary for the purpose mentioned in paragraph (c)(i);

(e) to require any person to provide an explanation of any document appearing to be of the relevant kind or to state, to the best of his knowledge and belief, where it may be found;

(f) to require any information which is held in a computer and is accessible from the premises and which the named officer considers relates to any matter relevant to the investigation, to be produced in a form—

(i) in which it can be taken away; and

(ii) in which it is visible and legible.

(3) If, in the case of a warrant under subsection (1)(b), the judge is satisfied that it is reasonable to suspect that there are also on the premises other documents relating to the investigation concerned, the warrant shall also authorise action mentioned in subsection (2) to be taken in relation to any such document.

(4) Any person entering premises by virtue of a warrant under this section may take with him such equipment as appears to him to be necessary.

(5) On leaving any premises which he has entered by virtue of a warrant under this section, the named officer must, if the premises are unoccupied or the occupier is temporarily absent, leave them as effectively secured as he found them.

(6) A warrant under this section continues in force until the end of the period of one month beginning with the day on which it is issued.

(7) Any document of which possession is taken under subsection (2)(c) may be retained for a period of three months.

Entry of premises under warrant: supplementary   **CA.29**

29.—(1) A warrant issued under section 28 must indicate—

(a) the subject matter and purpose of the investigation;

(b) the nature of the offences created by sections 42 to 44.

(2) The powers conferred by section 28 are to be exercised on production of a warrant issued under that section.

(3) If there is no one at the premises when the named officer proposes to execute such a warrant he must, before executing it—

(a) take such steps as are reasonable in all the circumstances to inform the occupier of the intended entry; and

(b) if the occupier is informed, afford him or his legal or other representative a reasonable opportunity to be present when the warrant is executed.

(4) If the named officer is unable to inform the occupier of the intended entry he must, when executing the warrant, leave a copy of it in a prominent place on the premises.

(5) In this section—

'named officer' means the officer named in the warrant; and

'occupier', in relation to any premises, means a person whom the named officer reasonably believes is the occupier of those premises.

Privileged communications

CA.30 30.—(1) A person shall not be required, under any provision of this Part, to produce or disclose a privileged communication.

(2) 'Privileged communication' means a communication—

(a) between a professional legal adviser and his client; or

(b) made in connection with, or in contemplation of, legal proceedings and for the purposes of those proceedings,

which in proceedings in the High Court would be protected from disclosure on grounds of legal professional privilege.

(3) In the application of this section to Scotland—

(a) references to the High Court are to be read as references to the Court of Session; and

(b) the reference to legal professional privilege is to be read as a reference to confidentiality of communications.

Decisions following an investigation

CA.31 31.—(1) Subsection (2) applies if, as the result of an investigation conducted under section 25, the Director proposes to make—

(a) a decision that the Chapter I prohibition has been infringed, or

(b) a decision that the Chapter II prohibition has been infringed.

(2) Before making the decision, the Director must—

(a) give written notice to the person (or persons) likely to be affected by the proposed decision; and

(b) give that person (or those persons) an opportunity to make representations.

Enforcement

Directions in relation to agreements

32.—(1) If the Director has made a decision that an agreement infringes the Chapter I **CA.32** prohibition, he may give to such person or persons as he considers appropriate such directions as he considers appropriate to bring the infringement to an end.

(2) Subsection (1) applies whether the Director's decision is made on his own initiative or on an application made to him under this Part.

(3) A direction under this section may, in particular, include provision—

(a) requiring the parties to the agreement to modify the agreement; or

(b) requiring them to terminate the agreement.

(4) A direction under this section must be given in writing.

Directions in relation to conduct

33.—(1) If the Director has made a decision that conduct infringes the Chapter II pro- **CA.33** hibition, he may give to such person or persons as he considers appropriate such directions as he considers appropriate to bring the infringement to an end.

(2) Subsection (1) applies whether the Director's decision is made on his own initiative or on an application made to him under this Part.

(3) A direction under this section may, in particular, include provision—

(a) requiring the person concerned to modify the conduct in question; or

(b) requiring him to cease that conduct.

(4) A direction under this section must be given in writing.

Enforcement of directions

34.—(1) If a person fails, without reasonable excuse, to comply with a direction under **CA.34** section 32 or 33, the Director may apply to the court for an order—

(a) requiring the defaulter to make good his default within a time specified in the order; or

(b) if the direction related to anything to be done in the management or administration of an undertaking, requiring the undertaking or any of its officers to do it.

(2) An order of the court under subsection (1) may provide for all of the costs of, or incidental to, the application for the order to be borne by—

(a) the person in default; or

(b) any officer of an undertaking who is responsible for the default.

(3) In the application of subsection (2) to Scotland, the reference to 'costs' is to be read as a reference to 'expenses'.

Interim measures

CA.35   35.—(1) This section applies if the Director—

   (a) has a reasonable suspicion that the Chapter I prohibition has been infringed; or

   (b) has a reasonable suspicion that the Chapter II prohibition has been infringed,

but has not completed his investigation into the matter.

   (2) If the Director considers that it is necessary for him to act under this section as a matter of urgency for the purpose—

   (a) of preventing serious, irreparable damage to a particular person or category of person, or

   (b) of protecting the public interest,

he may give such directions as he considers appropriate for that purpose.

   (3) Before giving a direction under this section, the Director must—

   (a) give written notice to the person (or persons) to whom he proposes to give the direction; and

   (b) give that person (or each of them) an opportunity to make representations.

   (4) A notice under subsection (3) must indicate the nature of the direction which the Director is proposing to give and his reasons for wishing to give it.

   (5) A direction given under this section has effect while subsection (1) applies, but may be replaced if the circumstances permit by a direction under section 32 or (as appropriate) section 33.

   (6) In the case of a suspected infringement of the Chapter I prohibition, sections 32(3) and 34 also apply to directions given under this section.

   (7) In the case of a suspected infringement of the Chapter II prohibition, sections 33(3) and 34 also apply to directions given under this section.

Penalty for infringing Chapter I or Chapter II prohibition

CA.36   36.—(1) On making a decision that an agreement has infringed the Chapter I prohibition, the Director may require an undertaking which is a party to the agreement to pay him a penalty in respect of the infringement.

   (2) On making a decision that conduct has infringed the Chapter II prohibition, the Director may require the undertaking concerned to pay him a penalty in respect of the infringement.

   (3) The Director may impose a penalty on an undertaking under subsection (1) or (2) only if he is satisfied that the infringement has been committed intentionally or negligently by the undertaking.

   (4) Subsection (1) is subject to section 39 and does not apply if the Director is satisfied that the undertaking acted on the reasonable assumption that that section gave it immunity in respect of the agreement.

(5) Subsection (2) is subject to section 40 and does not apply if the Director is satisfied that the undertaking acted on the reasonable assumption that that section gave it immunity in respect of the conduct.

(6) Notice of a penalty under this section must—

(a) be in writing; and

(b) specify the date before which the penalty is required to be paid.

(7) The date specified must not be earlier than the end of the period within which an appeal against the notice may be brought under section 46.

(8) No fixed penalty by the Director under this section may exceed 10% of the turnover of the undertaking (determined in accordance with such provisions as may be specified in an order made by the Secretary of State).

(9) Any sums received by the Director under this section are to be paid into the Consolidated fund.

Recovery of penalties

37.—(1) If the specified date in a penalty notice has passed and—   **CA.37**

(a) the period during which an appeal against the imposition, or amount, of the penalty may be made has expired without an appeal having been made, or

(b) such an appeal has been made and determined,

the Director may recover from the undertaking, as a civil debt due to him, any amount payable under the penalty notice which remains outstanding.

(2) In this section—

'penalty notice' means a notice given under section 36; and

'specified date' means the date specified in the penalty notice.

The appropriate level of a penalty

38.—(1) The Director must prepare and publish guidance as to the appropriate amount   **CA.38**
of any penalty under this Part.

(2) The Director may at any time alter the guidance.

(3) If the guidance is altered, the Director must publish it as altered.

(4) No guidance is to be published under this section without the approval of the Secretary of State.

(5) The Director may, after consulting the Secretary of State, choose how he publishes his guidance.

(6) If the Director is preparing or altering guidance under this section he must consult such persons as he considers appropriate.

(7) If the proposed guidance or alteration relates to a matter in respect of which a regulator exercises concurrent jurisdiction, those consulted must include that regulator.

(8) When setting the amount of a penalty under this Part, the Director must have regard to the guidance for the time being in force under this section.

(9) If a penalty or a fine has been imposed by the Commission, or by a court or other body in another Member State, in respect of an agreement or conduct, the Director, an appeal tribunal or the appropriate court must take that penalty or fine into account when setting the amount of a penalty under this Part in relation to that agreement or conduct.

(10) In subsection (9) 'the appropriate court' means—

   (a) in relation to England and Wales, the Court of Appeal;

   (b) in relation to Scotland, the Court of Session;

   (c) in relation to Northern Ireland, the Court of Appeal in Northern Ireland;

   (d) the House of Lords.

Limited immunity for small agreements

CA.39 39.—(1) In this section 'small agreement' means an agreement—

   (a) which falls within a category prescribed for the purposes of this section; but

   (b) is not a price fixing agreement.

(2) The criteria by reference to which a category of agreement is prescribed may, in particular, include—

   (a) the combined turnover of the parties to the agreement (determined in accordance with prescribed provisions);

   (b) the share of the market affected by the agreement (determined in that way).

(3) A party to a small agreement is immune from the effect of section 36(1); but the Director may withdraw that immunity under subsection (4).

(4) If the Director has investigated a small agreement, he may make a decision withdrawing the immunity given by subsection (3) if, as a result of his investigation, he considers that the agreement is likely to infringe the Chapter I prohibition.

(5) The Director must give each of the parties in respect of which immunity is withdrawn written notice of his decision to withdraw the immunity.

(6) A decision under subsection (4) takes effect on such date ('the withdrawal date') as may be specified in the decision.

(7) The withdrawal date must be a date after the date on which the decision is made.

(8) In determining the withdrawal date, the Director must have regard to the amount of time which the parties are likely to require in order to secure that there is no further infringement of the Chapter I prohibition with respect to the agreement.

(9) In subsection (1) 'price fixing agreement' means an agreement which has as its object or effect, or one of its objects or effects, restricting the freedom of a party to the agreement to determine the price to be charged (otherwise than as between that party and another party to the agreement) for the product, service or other matter to which the agreement relates.

Limited immunity in relation to the Chapter II prohibition

40.—(1) In this section 'conduct of minor significance' means conduct which falls   **CA.40** within a category prescribed for the purposes of this section.

(2) The criteria by reference to which a category is prescribed may, in particular, include—

    (a) the turnover of the person whose conduct it is (determined in accordance with prescribed provisions);

    (b) the share of the market affected by the conduct (determined in that way).

(3) A person is immune from the effect of section 36(2) if his conduct is conduct of minor significance; but the Director may withdraw that immunity under subsection (4).

(4) If the Director has investigated conduct of minor significance, he may make a decision withdrawing the immunity given by subsection (3) if, as a result of his investigation, he considers that the conduct is likely to infringe the Chapter II prohibition.

(5) The Director must give the person, or persons, whose immunity has been withdrawn written notice of his decision to withdraw the immunity.

(6) A decision under subsection (4) takes effect at such date ('the withdrawal date') as may be specified in the decision.

(7) The withdrawal date must be a date after the date on which the decision is made.

(8) In determining the withdrawal date, the Director must have regard to the amount of time which the person or persons affected are likely to require in order to secure that there is no further infringement of the Chapter II prohibition.

Agreements notified to the Commission

41.—(1) This section applies if a party to an agreement which may infringe the Chapter   **CA.41** I prohibition has notified the agreement to the Commission for a decision as to whether an exemption will be granted under Article 85 with respect to the agreement.

(2) A penalty may not be required to be paid under this Part in respect of any infringement of the Chapter I prohibition after notification but before the Commission determines the matter.

(3) If the Commission withdraws the benefit of provisional immunity from penalties with respect to the agreement, subsection (2) ceases to apply as from the date on which that benefit is withdrawn.

(4) The fact that an agreement has been notified to the Commission does not prevent the Director from investigating it under this Part.

(5) In this section 'provisional immunity from penalties' has such meaning as may be prescribed.

Offences

42.—(1) A person is guilty of an offence if he fails to comply with a requirement imposed   **CA.42** on him under section 26, 27 or 28.

(2) If a person is charged with an offence under subsection (1) in respect of a requirement to produce a document, it is a defence for him to prove—

(a) that the document was not in his possession or under his control; and

(b) that it was not reasonably practicable for him to comply with the requirement.

(3) If a person is charged with an offence under subsection (1) in respect of a requirement—

(a) to provide information;

(b) to provide an explanation of a document; or

(c) to state where a document is to be found,

it is a defence for him to prove that he had a reasonable excuse for failing to comply with the requirement.

(4) Failure to comply with a requirement imposed under section 26 or 27 is not an offence if the person imposing the requirement has failed to act in accordance with that section.

(5) A person is guilty of an offence if he intentionally obstructs an officer acting in the exercise of his powers under section 27.

(6) A person guilty of an offence under subsection (1) or (5) is liable—

(a) on summary conviction, to a fine not exceeding the statutory maximum;

(b) on conviction on indictment, to a fine.

(7) A person who intentionally obstructs an officer in the exercise of his powers under a warrant issued under section 28 is guilty of an offence and liable—

(a) on summary conviction, to a fine not exceeding the statutory maximum;

(b) on conviction on indictment, to imprisonment for a term not exceeding two years or to a fine or to both.

Destroying or falsifying documents

CA.43 43.—(1) A person is guilty of an offence if, having been required to produce a document under section 25, 27 or 28—

(a) he intentionally or recklessly destroys or otherwise disposes of it, falsifies it or conceals it; or

(b) he causes or permits its destruction, disposal, falsification or concealment.

(2) A person guilty of an offence under subsection (1) is liable—

(a) on summary conviction, to a fine not exceeding the statutory maximum;

(b) on conviction on indictment, to imprisonment for a term not exceeding two years or to a fine or to both.

False or misleading information

CA.44 44.—(1) If information is provided by a person to the Director in connection with any function of the Director under this Part, that person is guilty of an offence if—

(a) the information is false or misleading in a material particular; and

(b) he knows that it is or is reckless as to whether it is.

(2) A person who—

(a) provides any information to another person, knowing the information to be false or misleading in a material particular; or

(b) recklessly provides any information to another person which is false or misleading in a material particular,

knowing that the information is to be used for the purpose of providing information to the Director in connection with any of his functions under this Part, is guilty of an offence.

(3) A person guilty of an offence under this section is liable—

(a) on summary conviction, to a fine not exceeding the statutory maximum;

(b) on conviction on indictment, to imprisonment for a term not exceeding two years or to a fine or to both.

CHAPTER IV
THE COMPETITION COMMISSION AND APPEALS

The Commission

45.—(1) There is to be a body corporate known as the Competition Commission. **CA.45**

(2) The Commission is to have such functions as are conferred on it by or as a result of this Act.

(3) The Monopolies and Mergers Commission is dissolved and its functions are transferred to the Competition Commission.

(4) In any enactment, instrument or other document, any reference to the Monopolies and Mergers Commission which has continuing effect is to be read as a reference to the Competition Commission.

(5) The Secretary of State may by order make such consequential, supplemental and incidental provision as he considers appropriate in connection with—

(a) the dissolution of the Monopolies and Mergers Commission; and

(b) the transfer of functions effected by subsection (3).

(6) An order made under subsection (5) may, in particular, include provision—

(a) for the transfer of property, rights, obligations and liabilities and the continuation of proceedings, investigations and other matters; or

(b) amending any enactment which makes provision with respect to the Monopolies and Mergers Commission or any of its functions.

(7) Schedule 7 Makes further provision about the Competition Commission.

Appeals

Appealable decisions

CA.46 46.—(1) Any party to an agreement in respect of which the Director has made a decision may appeal to the Competition Commission against, or with respect to, the decision.

(2) Any person in respect of whose conduct the Director has made a decision may appeal to the Competition Commission against, or with respect to, the decision.

(3) In this section 'decision' means a decision of the Director—

(a) as to whether the Chapter I prohibition has been infringed;

(b) as to whether the Chapter II prohibition has been infringed;

(c) as to whether to grant an individual exemption;

(d) in respect of an individual exemption—

   (i) as to whether to impose any condition or obligation under section 4(3)(a) or 5(1)(c);

   (ii) where such a condition or obligation has been imposed, as to the condition or obligation;

   (iii) as to the period fixed under section 4(3)(b); or

   (iv) as to the date fixed under section 4(5);

(e) as to—

   (i) whether to extend the period for which an individual exemption has effect, or

   (ii) the period of any such extension;

(f) cancelling an exemption;

(g) as to the imposition of any penalty under section 36 or as to the amount of any such penalty;

(h) withdrawing or varying any of the decisions in paragraphs (a) to (f) following an application under section 4791),

and includes a direction given under section 32, 33 or 35 and such other decision as may be prescribed.

(4) Except in the case of an appeal against the imposition, or the amount, of a penalty, the making of an appeal under this section does not suspend the effect of the decision to which the appeal relates.

(5) Part I of Schedule 8 makes further provision about appeals.

Third party appeals

CA.47 47.—(1) A person who does not fall within section 46(1) or (2) may apply to the Director asking him to withdraw or vary a decision ('the relevant decision') falling within paragraphs (a) to (f) or section 46(3) or such other decision as may be prescribed.

(2) The application must—

(a) be made in writing, within such period as the Director may specify in rules under section 51; and

(b) give the applicant's reasons for considering that the relevant decision should be withdrawn or (as the case may be) varied.

(3) If the Director decides—

(a) that the applicant does not have a sufficient interest in the relevant decision;

(b) that, in the case of an applicant claiming to represent persons who have such an interest, the applicant does not represent such persons; or

(c) that the persons represented by the applicant do not have such an interest,

he must notify the applicant of his decision.

(4) If the Director, having considered the application, decides that it does not show sufficient reason why he should withdraw or vary the relevant decision, he must notify the applicant of his decision.

(5) Otherwise, the Director must deal with the application in accordance with such procedure as may be specified in rules under section 51.

(6) The applicant may appeal to the Competition Commission against a decision of the Director notified under subsection (3) or (4).

(7) The making of an application does not suspend the effect of the relevant decision.

Appeal tribunals

48.—(1) Any appeal made to the Competition Commission under section 46 or 47 is to be determined by an appeal tribunal. **CA.48**

(2) The Secretary of State may, after consulting the President of the Competition Commission Appeal Tribunals and such other persons as he considers appropriate, make rules with respect to appeals and appeal tribunals.

(3) The rules may confer functions on the President.

(4) Part II of Schedule 8 makes further provision about rules made under this section but is not to be taken as restricting the Secretary of State's powers under this section.

Appeals on point of law etc.

49.—(1) An appeal lies— **CA.49**

(a) on a point of law arising from a decision of an appeal tribunal; or

(b) from any decision of an appeal tribunal as to the amount of a penalty.

(2) An appeal under this section may be made only—

(a) to the appropriate court;

(b) with leave; and

(c) at the instance of a party or at the instance of a person who has a sufficient interest in the matter.

(3) Rules under section 48 may make provision for regulating or prescribing any matters incidental to or consequential upon an appeal under this section.

(4) In subsection (2)—

'the appropriate court' means—

(a) in relation to proceedings before a tribunal in England and Wales, the Court of Appeal;

(b) in relation to proceedings before a tribunal in Scotland, the Court of Session;

(c) in relation to proceedings before a tribunal in Northern Ireland, the Court of Appeal in Northern Ireland;

'leave' means leave of the tribunal in question or of the appropriate court; and

'party', in relation to a decision, means a person who was a party to the proceedings in which the decision was made.

Chapter V

Miscellaneous

Vertical agreements and land agreements

CA.50 50.—(1) The Secretary of State may by order provide for any provision of this Part to apply in relation to—

(a) vertical agreements; or

(b) land agreements,

with such modifications as may be prescribed.

(2) An order may, in particular, provide for exclusions or exemptions, or otherwise provide for prescribed provisions not to apply, in relation to—

(a) vertical agreements, or land agreements, in general; or

(b) vertical agreements, or land agreements, or any prescribed description.

(3) An order may empower the Director to give directions to the effect that in prescribed circumstances an exclusion, exemption or modification is not to apply (or is to apply in a particular way) in relation to an individual agreement.

(4) Subsections (2) and (3) are not to be read as limiting the powers conferred by section 71.

(5) In this section—

'land agreement' and 'vertical agreement' have such meaning as may be prescribed; and

'prescribed' means prescribed by an order.

Director's rules, guidance and fees

51.—(1) The Director may make such rules about procedural and other matters in con-   **CA.51**
nection with the carrying into effect of the provisions of this Part as he considers appropriate.

(2) Schedule 9 makes further provision about rules made under this section but is not
to be taken as restricting the Director's powers under this section.

(3) If the Director is preparing rules under this section he must consult such persons as
he considers appropriate.

(4) If the proposed rules relate to a matter in respect of which a regulator exercises concurrent jurisdiction, those consulted must include that regulator.

(5) No rule made by the Director is to come into operation until it has been approved
by an order made by the Secretary of State.

(6) The Secretary of State may approve any rule made by the Director—

   (a) in the form in which it is submitted; or

   (b) subject to such modifications as he considers appropriate.

(7) If the Secretary of State proposes to approve a rule subject to modifications he must
inform the Director of the proposed modifications and take into account any comments
made by the Director.

(8) Subsections (5) to (7) apply also to any alteration of the rules made by the Director.

(9) The Secretary of State may, after consulting the Director, by order vary or revoke
any rules made under this section.

(10) If the Secretary of State considers that rules should be made under this section
with respect to a particular matter he may direct the Director to exercise his powers under
this section and make rules about that matter.

Advice and information

52.—(1) As soon as is reasonably practicable after the passing of this Act, the Director   **CA.52**
must prepare and publish general advice and information about—

   (a) the application of the Chapter I prohibition and the Chapter II prohibition; and

   (b) the enforcement of those prohibitions.

(2) The Director may at any time publish revised, or new, advice or information.

(3) Advice and information published under this section must be prepared with a view
to—

   (a) explaining provisions of this Part to persons who are likely to be affected by
       them; and

   (b) indicating how the Director expects such provisions to operate.

(4) Advice (or information) published by virtue of subsection (3)(b) may include
advice (or information) about the factors which the Director may take into account in

considering whether, and if so how, to exercise a power conferred on him by Chapter I, II or III.

(5) Any advice or information published by the Director under this section is to be published in such form and in such manner as he considers appropriate.

(6) If the Director is preparing any advice or information under this section he must consult such persons as he considers appropriate.

(7) If the proposed advice or information relates to a matter in respect of which a regulator exercises concurrent jurisdiction, those consulted must include that regulator.

(8) In preparing any advice or information under this section about a matter in respect of which he may exercise functions under this Part, a regulator must consult—

> (a) the Director;
>
> (b) the other regulators; and
>
> (c) such other persons as he considers appropriate.

Fees

CA.53 53.—(1) The Director may charge fees, or specified amounts, in connection with the exercise by him of specified functions under this Part.

(2) Rules may, in particular, provide—

> (a) for the amount of any fee to be calculated by reference to matters which may include—
>
>> (i) the turnover of any party to an agreement (determined in such manner as may be specified);
>>
>> (ii) the turnover of a person whose conduct the Director is to consider (determined in that way);
>
> (b) for different amounts to be specified in connection with different functions;
>
> (c) for the repayment by the Director of the whole or part of a fee in specified circumstances;
>
> (d) that an application or notice is not to be regarded as duly made or given unless the appropriate fee is paid.

(3) In this section—

> (a) 'rules' means rules made by the Director under section 51; and
>
> (b) 'specified' means specified in rules.

Regulators

CA.54 54.—(1) In this Part 'regulator' means any person mentioned in paragraphs (a) to (g) or paragraph 1 of Schedule 10.

(2) Parts II and III of Schedule 10 provide for functions of the Director under this Part to be exercisable concurrently by regulators.

(3) Parts IV and V of Schedule 10 make minor and consequential amendments in connection with the regulators' competition functions.

(4) The Secretary of State may make regulations for the purpose of co-ordinating the performance of functions under this Part ('Part I functions') which are exercisable concurrently by two or more competent persons as a result of any provision made by Part II or III of Schedule 10.

(5) The regulations may, in particular, make provision—

(a) as to the procedure to be followed by competent persons when determining who is to exercise Part I functions in a particular case;

(b) as to the steps which must be taken before a competent person exercises, in a particular case, such Part I functions as may be prescribed;

(c) as to the procedure for determining, in a particular case, questions arising as to which competent person is to exercise Part I functions in respect of the case;

(d) for Part I functions in a particular case to be exercised jointly—

(i) by the Director and one or more regulators; or

(ii) by two or more regulators,

and as to the procedure to be followed in such cases;

(e) as to the circumstances in which the exercise by a competent person of such Part I functions as may be prescribed is to preclude the exercise of such functions by another such person;

(f) for cases in respect of which Part I functions are being, or have been, exercised by a competent person to be transferred to another such person;

(g) for the person ('A') exercising Part I functions in a particular case—

(i) to appoint another competent person ('B') to exercise Part I functions on A's behalf in relation to the case; or

(ii) to appoint officers of B (with B's consent) to act as officers of A in relation to the case;

(h) for notification as to who is exercising Part I functions in respect of a particular case.

(6) Provision made by virtue of subsection (5)(c) may provide for questions to be referred to and determined by the Secretary or State or by such other person as may be prescribed.

(7) 'Competent person' means the Director or any of the regulators.

Confidentiality and immunity from defamation

General restrictions on disclosure of information

55.—(1) No information which—   **CA.55**

(a) has been obtained under or as a result of any provision of this Part; and

(b) relates to the affairs of any individual or to any particular business of an undertaking, is to be disclosed during the lifetime of that individual or while that business continues to be carried on, unless the condition mentioned in subsection (2) is satisfied.

(2) The condition is that consent to the disclosure has been obtained from—

(a) a person from whom the information was initially obtained under or as a result of any provision of this Part (if the identity of that person is known); and

(b) if different—

(i) the individual to whose affairs the information relates; or

(ii) the person for the time being carrying on the business to which the information relates.

(3) Subsection (1) does not apply to a disclosure of information—

(a) made for the purpose of—

(i) facilitating the performance of any relevant functions of a designated person;

(ii) facilitating the performance of any functions of the Commission in respect of Community law about competition;

(iii) facilitating the performance by the Comptroller and Auditor General of any of his functions;

(iv) criminal proceedings in any part of the United Kingdom;

(b) made with a view to the institution of, or otherwise for the purposes of, civil proceedings brought under or in connection with this Part;

(c) made in connection with the investigation of any criminal offence triable in the United Kingdom or in any part of the United Kingdom; or

(d) which is required to meet a Community obligation.

(4) In subsection (3) 'relevant functions' and 'designated person' have the meaning given in Schedule 11.

(5) Subsection (1) also does not apply to a disclosure of information made for the purpose of facilitating the performance of specified functions of any specified person.

(6) In subsection (5) 'specified' means specified in an order made by the Secretary of State.

(7) If information is disclosed to the public in circumstances in which the disclosure does not contravene subsection (1), that subsection does not prevent its further disclosure by any person.

(8) A person who contravenes this section is guilty of an offence and liable—

(a) on summary conviction, to a fine not exceeding the statutory maximum; or

(b) on conviction on indictment, to imprisonment for a term not exceeding two years or to a fine or to both.

Director and Secretary of State to have regard to certain matters in relation to the disclosure of information

56.—(1) This section applies if the Secretary of State or the Director is considering whether to disclose any information acquired by him under, or as a result of, any provision of this Part.

CA.56

(2) He must have regard to the need for excluding, so far as is practicable, information the disclosure of which would in his opinion be contrary to the public interest.

(3) He must also have regard to—

(a) the need for excluding, so far as is practicable—

(i) commercial information the disclosure of which would, or might, in his opinion, significantly harm the legitimate business interests of the undertaking to which it relates; or

(ii) information relating to the private affairs of an individual the disclosure of which would, or might, in his opinion, significantly harm his interests; and

(b) the extent to which the disclosure is necessary for the purposes for which the Secretary of State or the Director is proposing to make the disclosure.

Defamation

57. For the purposes of the law relating to defamation, absolute privilege attaches to any advice, guidance, notice or direction given, or decision made, by the Director in the exercise of any of his functions under this Part.

CA.57

Findings of fact by Director

58.—(1) Unless the court directs otherwise or the Director has decided to take further action in accordance with section 16(2) or 24(2), a Director's finding which is relevant to an issue arising in Part I proceedings is binding on the parties if—

CA.58

(a) the time for bringing an appeal in respect of the finding has expired and the relevant party has not brought such an appeal; or

(b) the decision of an appeal tribunal on such an appeal has confirmed the finding.

(2) In this section—

'a Director's finding' means a finding of fact made by the Director in the course of—

(a) determining an application for a decision under section 14 or 22; or

(b) conducting an investigation under section 25;

'Part I proceedings' means proceedings—

(a) in respect of an alleged infringement of the Chapter I prohibition or of the Chapter II prohibition; but

(b) which are brought otherwise than by the Director;

'relevant party' means—

(a) in relation to the Chapter I prohibition, a party to the agreement which is alleged to have infringed the prohibition; and

(b) in relation to the Chapter II prohibition, the undertaking whose conduct is alleged to have infringed the prohibition.

(3) Rules of court may make provision in respect of assistance to be given by the Director to the court in Part I proceedings.

Interpretation and governing principles

CA.59 59.—(1) In this Part—

'appeal tribunal' means an appeal tribunal established in accordance with the provisions of Part III of Schedule 7 for the purpose of hearing an appeal under section 46 or 47;

'Article 85' means Article 85 of the Treaty;

'Article 86' means Article 86 of the Treaty;

'block exemption' has the meaning given in section 6(4);

'block exemption order' has the meaning given in section 6(2);

'the Chapter I prohibition' has the meaning given in section 2(8);

'the Chapter II prohibition' has the meaning given in section 18(4);

'the Commission' (except in relation to the Competition Commission) means the European Commission;

'the Council' means the Council of the European Union;

'the court', except in sections 58 and 60 and the expression 'European Court', means—

(a) in England and Wales, the High Court;

(b) in Scotland, the Court of Session; and

(c) in Northern Ireland, the High Court;

'the Director' means the Director General of Fair Trading;

'document' includes information recorded in any form;

'the EEA Agreement' means the Agreement on the European Economic Area signed at Oporto on 2nd May 1992 as it has effect for the time being;

'the European Court' means the Court of Justice of the European Communities and includes the Court of First Instance;

'individual exemption' has the meaning given in section 4(2);

'information' includes estimates and forecasts;

'investigating officer' has the meaning given in section 27(1);

'Minister of the Crown' has the same meaning as in the Ministers of the Crown Act 1975;

'officer', in relation to a body corporate, includes a director, manager or secretary and, in relation to a partnership in Scotland, includes a partner;

'parallel exemption' has the meaning given in section 10(3);

'person', in addition to the meaning given by the Interpretation Act 1978, includes any undertaking;

'premises' does not include domestic premises unless—

    (a) they are also used in connection with the affairs of an undertaking; or

    (b) documents relating to the affairs of an undertaking are kept there,

but does include any vehicle;

'prescribed' means prescribed by regulations made by the Secretary of State;

'regulator' has the meaning given by section 54;

'section 11 exemption' has the meaning given in section 11(3); and

'the Treaty' means the treaty establishing the European Community.

(2) The fact that to a limited extent the Chapter I prohibition does not apply to an agreement, because of an exclusion provided by or under this Part of any other enactment, does not require those provisions of the agreement to which the exclusion relates to be disregarded when considering whether the agreement infringes the prohibition for other reasons.

(3) For the purposes of this Part, the power to require information, in relation to information recorded otherwise than in a legible form, includes power to require a copy of it in a legible form.

(4) Any power conferred on the Director by this Part to require information includes power to require any document which he believes may contain that information.

Principles to be applied in determining questions

60.—(1) The purpose of this section is to ensure that so far as is possible (having regard **CA.60** to any relevant differences between the provisions concerned), questions arising under this Part in relation to competition within the United Kingdom are dealt with in a manner which is consistent with the treatment of corresponding questions arising in Community law in relation to competition within the Community.

(2) At any time when the court determines a question arising under this Part, it must act (so far as is compatible with the provisions of this Part and whether or not it would otherwise be required to do so) with a view to securing that there is no inconsistency between—

    (a) the principles applied, and decisions reached, by the court in determining that question; and

    (b) the principles laid down by the Treaty and the European Court, and any relevant decision of that Court, as applicable at that time in determining any corresponding question arising in Community law.

(3) The court must, in addition, have regard to any relevant decision or statement of the Commission.

(4) Subsections (2) and (3) also apply to—

    (a) the Director; and

    (b) any person acting on behalf of the Director, in connection with any matter arising under this Part.

(5) In subsections (2) and (3), 'court' means any court or tribunal.

(6) In subsections (2)(b) and (3), 'decision' includes a decision as to—

(a) the interpretation of any provision of Community law;

(b) the civil liability of an undertaking for harm caused by its infringement of Community Law.

PART II
INVESTIGATIONS IN RELATION TO ARTICLES 85 AND 86

Introduction

CA.61 61.—(1) In this Part—

'Article 85' and 'Article 86' have the same meaning as in Part I;

'authorised officer', in relation to the Director, means an officer to whom an authorisation has been given under subsection (2);

'the Commission' means the European Commission;

'the Director' means the Director General of Fair Trading;

'Commission investigation' means an investigation ordered by a decision of the Commission under a prescribed provision of Community law relating to Article 85 or 86;

'Director's investigation' means an investigation conducted by the Director at the request of the Commission under a prescribed provision of Community law relating to Article 85 or 86;

'Director's special investigation' means a Director's investigation conducted at the request of the Commission in connection with a Commission investigation;

'prescribed' means prescribed by order made by the Secretary of State;

'premises' means—

(a) in relation to a Commission investigation, any premises, land or means of transport which an official of the Commission has power to enter in the course of the investigation; and

(b) in relation to a Director's investigation, any premises, land or means of transport which an official of the Commission would have power to enter if the investigation were being conducted by the Commission.

(2) For the purposes of a Director's investigation, an officer of the Director to whom an authorisation has been given has the powers of an official authorised by the Commission in connection with a Commission investigation under the relevant provision.

(3) 'Authorisation' means an authorisation given in writing by the Director which—

(a) identifies the officer;

(b) specifies the subject matter and purpose of the investigation; and

(c) draws attention to any penalties which a person may incur in connection with the investigation under the relevant provision of Community law.

Power to enter premises: Commission investigations

62.—(1) A judge of the High Court may issue a warrant if satisfied, on an application **CA.62** made to the High Court in accordance with rules of court by the Director, that a Commission investigation is being, or is likely to be, obstructed.

(2) A Commission investigation is being obstructed if—

(a) an official of the Commission ('the Commission official'), exercising his power in accordance with the provision under which the investigation is being conducted, has attempted to enter premises but has been unable to do so; and

(b) there are reasonable grounds for suspecting that there are books or records on the premises which the Commission official has power to examine.

(3) A Commission investigation is also being obstructed if there are reasonable grounds for suspecting that there are books or records on the premises—

(a) the production of which has been required by an official of the Commission exercising his power in accordance with the provision under which the investigation is being conducted; and

(b) which have not been produced as required.

(4) A Commission investigation is likely to be obstructed if—

(a) an official of the Commission ('the Commission official') is authorised for the purpose of the investigation;

(b) there are reasonable grounds for suspecting that there are books or records on the premises which the Commission official has power to examine; and

(c) there are also reasonable grounds for suspecting that, if the Commission official attempted to exercise his power to examine any of the books or records, they would not be produced but would be concealed, removed, tampered with or destroyed.

(5) A warrant under this section shall authorise—

(a) a named officer of the Director;

(b) any other of his officers whom he has authorised in writing to accompany the named officer; and

(c) any official of the Commission authorised for the purpose of the Commission investigation,

to enter the premises specified in the warrant, and search for books and records which the official has the power to examine, using such force as is reasonably necessary for the purpose.

(6) Any person entering any premises by virtue of a warrant under this section may take with him such equipment as appears to him to be necessary.

(7) On leaving any premises entered by virtue of the warrant the named officer must, if the premises are unoccupied or the occupier is temporarily absent, leave them as effectively secured as he found them.

(8) A warrant under this section continues in force until the end of the period of one month beginning with the day on which it is issued.

(9) In the application of this section to Scotland, references to the High Court are to be read as references to the Court of Session.

Power to enter premises: Director's special investigations

CA.63 63.—(1) A judge of the High Court may issue a warrant if satisfied, on an application made to the High Court in accordance with rules of court by the Director, that a Director's special investigation is being, or is likely to be, obstructed.

(2) A Director's special investigation is being obstructed if—

(a) an authorised officer of the Director has attempted to enter premises but has been unable to do so;

(b) the officer has produced his authorisation to the undertaking, or association of undertakings, concerned; and

(c) there are reasonable grounds for suspecting that there are books or records on the premises which the officer has power to examine.

(3) A Director's special investigation is also being obstructed if—

(a) there are reasonable grounds for suspecting that there are books or records on the premises which an authorised officer of the Director has power to examine;

(b) the officer has produced his authorisation to the undertaking, or association of undertakings, and has required production of the books or records; and

(c) the books and records have not been produced as required.

(4) A Director's special investigation is likely to be obstructed if—

(a) there are reasonable grounds for suspecting that there are books or records on the premises which an authorised officer of the Director has power to examine; and

(b) there are also reasonable grounds for suspecting that, if the officer attempted to exercise his power to examine any of the books or records, they would not be produced but would be concealed, removed, tampered with or destroyed.

(5) A warrant under this section shall authorise—

(a) a named authorised officer of the Director;

(b) any other authorised officer accompanying the named officer; and

(c) any named official of the Commission,

to enter the premises specified in the warrant, and search for books and records which the authorised officer has power to examine, using such force as is reasonably necessary for the purpose.

(6) Any person entering any premises by virtue of a warrant under this section may take with him such equipment as appears to him to be necessary.

(7) On leaving any premises which he has entered by virtue of the warrant the named officer must, if the premises are unoccupied or the occupier is temporarily absent, leave them as effectively secured as he found them.

(8) A warrant under this section continues in force until the end of the period of one month beginning with the day on which it is issued.

(9) In the application of this section to Scotland, references to the high Court are to be read as references to the Court of Session.

Entry of premises under sections 62 and 63: supplementary

64.—(1) A warrant issued under section 62 or 63 must indicate—   **CA.64**

    (a) the subject matter and purpose of the investigation;

    (b) the nature of the offence created by section 65.

(2) The powers conferred by section 62 or 63 are to be exercised on production of a warrant issued under that section.

(3) If there is no one at the premises when the named officer proposes to execute such a warrant he must, before executing it—

    (a) take such steps as are reasonable in all the circumstances to inform the occupier of the intended entry; and

    (b) if the occupier is informed, afford him or his legal or other representative a reasonable opportunity to be present when the warrant is executed.

(4) If the named officer is unable to inform the occupier of the intended entry he must, when executing the warrant, leave a copy of it in a prominent place on the premises.

(5) In this section—

'named officer' means the officer named in the warrant; and

'occupier', in relation to any premises, means a person whom the named officer reasonably believes is the occupier of those premises.

Offences

65.—(1) A person is guilty of an offence if he intentionally obstructs any person in the   **CA.65**
exercise of his powers under a warrant issued under section 62 or 63.

(2) A person guilty of an offence under subsection (1) is liable—

    (a) on summary conviction, to a fine not exceeding the statutory maximum;

    (b) on conviction on indictment, to imprisonment for a term not exceeding two years or to a fine or to both.

PART III

MONOPOLIES

Monopoly investigations: general

CA.66 66.—(1) Section 44 of the Fair Trading Act 1973 (power of the Director to require information about monopoly situations) is amended as follows.

(2) In subsection (1), for the words after paragraph (b) substitute—

'the Director may exercise the powers conferred by subsection (2) below for the purpose of assisting him in determining whether to take either of the following decisions with regard to that situation.'

(3) After subsection (1) insert—

'1(A) Those decisions are—

(a) whether to make a monopoly reference with respect to the existence or possible existence or the situation;

(b) whether, instead to make a proposal under section 56A below for the Secretary of State to accept undertakings.'

(4) For subsection (2) substitute—

'(2) In the circumstances and for the purpose mentioned in subsection (1) above, the Director may,

(a) require any person within subsection (3) below to produce to the Director, at a specified time and place;

(i) any specified documents; or

(ii) any document which falls within a specified category,

which are in his custody or under his control and which are relevant;

(b) require any person within subsection (3) below who is carrying on a business to give the Director specified estimates, forecasts, returns, or other information, and specify the time at which and the form and manner in which the estimates, forecasts, returns or information are to be given;

(c) enter any premises used by a person within subsection (3) below for business purposes, and—

(i) require any person on the premises to produce any documents on the premises which are in his custody or under his control and which are relevant;

(ii) require any person on the premises to give the Director such explanation of the documents as he may require.

(3) A person is within this subsection if—

(a) he produces goods of the description in question in the United Kingdom;

(b) he supplies goods or (as the case may be) services of the description in question in the United Kingdom; or

(c) such goods (or services) are supplied to him in the United Kingdom.

(4) The power to impose a requirement under subsection (2)(a) or (b) above is to be exercised by notice in writing served on the person on whom the requirement is imposed; and 'specified' in those provisions means specified or otherwise described in the notice, and 'specify' is to be read accordingly.

(5) The power under subsection (2)(a) above to require a person ('the person notified') to produce a document includes power—

  (a) if the document is produced—

    (i)   to take copies of it or extracts from it;

    (ii) to require the person notified, or any person who is a present or past officer of his, or is or was at any time employed by him, to provide an explanation of the document;

  (b) if the document is not produced, to require the person notified to state, to the best of his knowledge and belief, where it is.

(6) Nothing in this section confers power to compel any person—

  (a) to produce any document which he could not be compelled to produce in civil proceedings before the High Court or, in Scotland, the Court of Session; or

  (b) in complying with any requirement for the giving of information, to give any information which he could not be compelled to give in evidence in such proceedings.

(7) No person has to comply with a requirement imposed under subsection (2) above by a person acting under an authorisation under paragraph 7 of Schedule 1 to this Act unless evidence of the authorisation has, if required, been produced.

(8) For the purposes of subsection (2) above—

  (a) a document is relevant if—

    (i)   it is relevant to a decision mentioned in subsection (1A) above; and

    (ii) the powers conferred by this section are exercised in relation to the document for the purpose of assisting the Director in determining whether to take that decision;

  (b) 'document' includes information recorded in any form; and

  (c) in relation to information recorded otherwise than in legible form, the power to require its production includes power to require production of it in legible form, so far as the means to do so are within the custody or under the control of the person on whom the requirement is imposed.'

(5) The amendments made by this section and section 67 have effect in relation to sectoral regulators in accordance with paragraph 1 of Schedule 10.

Offences

67.—(1) Section 46 of the Fair Trading Act 1973 is amended as follows.   **CA.67**

  (2) Omit subsections (1) and (2).

(3) At the end insert—

'(4) Any person who refuses of wilfully neglects to comply with a requirement imposed under section 4492) above is guilty of an offence and liable—

(a) on summary conviction, to a fine not exceeding the prescribed sum; or

(b) on conviction on indictment, to imprisonment for a term not exceeding two years or to a fine or to both.

(5) If a person is charged with an offence under subsection (4) in respect of a requirement to produce a document, it is a defence for him to prove—

(a) that the document was not in his possession or under his control; and

(b) that it was not reasonably practicable for him to comply with the requirement.

(6) If a person is charged with an offence under subsection (4) in respect of a requirement—

(a) to provide an explanation of a document; or

(b) to state where a document is to be found,

it is a defence for him to prove that he had a reasonable excuse for failing to comply with the requirement.

(7) A person who intentionally obstructs the Director in the exercise of his powers under section 44 is guilty of an offence and liable—

(a) on summary conviction, to a fine not exceeding the prescribed sum;

(b) on conviction on indictment, to a fine.

(8) A person who wilfully alters, suppresses or destroys any document which he has been required to produce under section 4492) is guilty of an offence and liable—

(a) on summary conviction, to a fine not exceeding the prescribed sum;

(b) on conviction on indictment, to imprisonment for a term not exceeding two years or to a fine or to both.'

Services relating to use of land

CA.68 68. In section 137 of the Fair Trading Act 1973, after subsection (2) insert—

'3(a) The Secretary of State may by order made by statutory instrument—

(a) provide that 'the supply of services' in the provisions of this Act is to include, or to cease to include, any activity specified in the order which consists in, or in making arrangements in connection with, permitting the use of land; and

(b) for that purpose, amend or repeal any of paragraphs (c), (d), (e) or (g) of subsection (3) above.

(3B) No order under subsection (3A) above is to be made unless a draft of the order has been laid before Parliament and approved by a resolution of each House of Parliament.

(3C) The provisions of Schedule 9 to this Act apply in the case of a draft of any such order as they apply in the case of a draft of an order to which section 91(1) above applies.'

Reports: monopoly references

69. In section 83 of the Fair Trading Act 1973—   **CA.69**

  (a) in subsection (1), omit 'Subject to subsection (1A) below'; and

  (b) omit subsection (1A) (reports on monopoly references to be transmitted to certain persons at least twenty-four hours before laying before Parliament).

PART IV
SUPPLEMENTAL AND TRANSITIONAL

Contracts as to patented products etc.

70. Sections 44 and 45 of the Patents Act 1977 shall cease to have effect.   **CA.70**

Regulations, orders and rules

71.—(1) Any power to make regulations or orders which is conferred by this act is exercisable by statutory instrument.   **CA.71**

  (2) The power to make rules which is conferred by section 48 is exercisable by statutory instrument.

  (3) Any statutory instrument made under this Act may—

  (a) contain such incidental, supplemental, consequential and transitional provision as the Secretary of State considers appropriate; and

  (b) make different provision for different cases.

  (4) No order is to be made under—

  (a) section 3;

  (b) section 19;

  (c) section 36(8);

  (d) section 50; or

  (e) paragraph 6(3) of Schedule 4,

unless a draft of the order has been laid before Parliament and approved by a resolution of each House.

  (5) Any statutory instrument made under this Act, apart from one made—

  (a) under any of the provisions mentioned in subsection (4); or

  (b) under section 76(3),

shall be subject to annulment by a resolution of either House of Parliament.

Offences by bodies corporate etc.

72.—(1) This section applies to an offence under any of sections 42 to 44, 55(8) or 65.   **CA.72**

  (2) If an offence committed by a body corporate is proved—

  (a) to have been committed with the consent or connivance of an officer; or

(b) to be attributable to any neglect on his part,

the officer as well as the body corporate is guilty of the offence and liable to be proceeded against and punished accordingly.

(3) In subsection (2) 'officer', in relation to a body corporate, means a director, manager, secretary or other similar officer of the body, or a person purporting to act in any such capacity.

(4) If the affairs of a body corporate are managed by its members, subsection (2) applies in relation to the acts and defaults of a member in connection with his functions of management as if he were a director of the body corporate.

(5) If an offence committee by a partnership in Scotland is proved—

(a) to have been committee with the consent or connivance of a partner; or

(b) to be attributable to any neglect on his part,

the partner as well as the partnership is guilty of the offence and liable to be proceeded against and punished accordingly.

(6) In subsection (5) 'partner' includes a person purporting to act as a partner.

Crown application

CA.73 73.—(1) Any provision made by or under this Act binds the Crown except that—

(a) the Crown is not criminally liable as a result of any such provision;

(b) the Crown is not liable for any penalty under any such provision; and

(c) nothing in this Act affects Her Majesty in her private capacity.

(2) Subsection (1)(a) does not affect the application of any provision of this Act in relation to persons in the public service of the Crown.

(3) Subsection (1)(c) is to be interpreted as if section 38(3) of the Crown Proceedings Act 1947 (interpretation of references in that Act to Her Majesty in her private capacity) were contained in this Act.

(4) If, in respect of a suspected infringement of the Chapter I prohibition or of the Chapter II prohibition otherwise than by the Crown or a person in the public service of the Crown, an investigation is conducted under section 25—

(a) the power conferred by section 27 may not be exercised in relation to land which is occupied by a government department, or otherwise for purposes of the Crown, without the written consent of the appropriate person; and

(b) section 28 does not apply in relation to land so occupied.

(5) In any case in which consent is required under subsection (4), the person who is the appropriate person in relation to that case is to be determined in accordance with regulations made by the Secretary of State.

(6) Sections 62 and 63 do not apply in relation to land which is occupied by a government department, or otherwise for purposes of the Crown, unless the matter being inves-

tigated is a suspected infringement by the Crown or by a person in the public service of the Crown.

(7) In subsection (6) 'infringement' means an infringement of Community law relating to Article 85 or 86 of the Treaty establishing the European Community.

(8) If the Secretary of State certifies that it appears to him to be in the interests of national security that the powers of entry—

(a) conferred by section 27; or

(b) that may be conferred by a warrant under section 28, 62 or 63,

should not be exercisable in relation to premises held or used by or on behalf of the Crown and which are specified in the certificate, those powers are not exercisable in relation to those premises.

(9) Any amendment, repeal or revocation made by this Act binds the Crown to the extent that the enactment amended, repealed or revoked binds the Crown.

Amendments, transitional provisions, savings and repeals

74.—(1) The minor and consequential amendments set out in Schedule 12 are to have effect.　　　　**CA.74**

(2) The transitional provisions and savings set out in Schedule 13 are to have effect.

(3) The enactments set out in Schedule 14 are repealed.

Consequential and supplementary provision

75.—(1) The Secretary of State may by order make such incidental, consequential, transitional or supplemental provision as he thinks necessary or expedient for the general purposes, or any particular purpose, of this Act or in consequence of any of its provisions or for giving full effect to it.　　　　**CA.75**

(2) An order under subsection (1) may, in particular, make provision

(a) for enabling any person by whom any powers will become exercisable, on a date specified by or under this Act, by virtue of any provision made by or under this Act to take before that date any steps which are necessary as a preliminary to the exercise of those powers;

(b) for making savings, or additional savings, from the effect of any repeal made by or under this Act.

(3) Amendments made under this section shall be in addition, and without prejudice, to those made by or under any other provision of this Act.

(4) No other provision of this Act restricts the powers conferred by this section.

Short title, commencement and extent

76.—(1) This Act may be cited as the Competition Act 1998.　　　　**CA.76**

(2) Sections 71 and 75 and this section and paragraphs 1 to 7 and 35 of Schedule 13 come into force on the passing of this Act.

(3) The other provisions of this Act come into force on such day as the Secretary of State may by order appoint; and different days may be appointed for different purposes.

(4) This Act extends to Northern Ireland.

SCHEDULES

SCHEDULE 1
EXCLUSIONS: MERGERS AND CONCENTRATIONS

PART I
MERGERS

Enterprises ceasing to be distinct: the Chapter I prohibition

1.—(1) To the extent to which agreement (either on its own or when taken together with **CA.77** another agreement) results, or if carried out would result, in any two enterprises ceasing to be distinct enterprises for the purposes of Part V of the Fair Trading Act 1973 ('the 1973 Act'), the Chapter I prohibition does not apply to the agreement.

(2) The exclusion provided by sub-paragraph (1) extends to any provision directly related and necessary to the implementation of the merger provisions.

(3) In sub-paragraph (2) 'merger provisions' means the provisions of the agreement which cause, or if carried out would cause, the agreement to have the result mentioned in sub-paragraph (1).

(4) Section 65 of the 1973 Act applies for the purposes of this paragraph as if—

(a) in subsection (3) (circumstances in which a person or group of persons may be treated as having control of an enterprise); and

(b) in subsection (4) (circumstances in which a person or group of persons may be treated as bringing an enterprise under their control),

for 'may' there were substituted 'must'.

Enterprises ceasing to be distinct: the Chapter II prohibition

2.—(1) To the extent to which conduct (either on its own or when taken together with **CA.78** other conduct)—

(a) results in any two enterprises ceasing to be distinct enterprises for the purposes of Part V of the 1973 Act), or

(b) is directly related and necessary to the attainment of the result mentioned in paragraph (a),

the Chapter II prohibition does not apply to that conduct.

(2) Section 65 of the 1973 Act applies for the purposes of this paragraph as it applies for the purposes of paragraph 1.

Transfer of a newspaper or of newspaper assets

3.—(1) The Chapter I prohibition does not apply to an agreement to the extent to which **CA.79** it constitutes, or would if carried out constitute, a transfer of a newspaper or of newspaper assets for the purposes of section 57 of the 1973 Act.

(2) The Chapter II prohibition does not apply to conduct (either on its own or when taken together with other conduct) to the extent to which—

(a) it constitutes such a transfer; or

(b) it is directly related and necessary to the implementation of the transfer.

(3) The exclusion provided by sub-paragraph (1) extends to any provision directly related and necessary to the implementation of the transfer.

Withdrawal of the paragraph 1 exclusion

CA.80 4.—(1) The exclusion provided by paragraph 1 does not apply to a particular agreement if the Director gives a direction under this paragraph to that effect.

(2) If the Director is considering whether to give a direction under this paragraph, he may by notice in writing require any party to the agreement in question to give him such information in connection with the agreement as he may require.

(3) The Director may give a direction under this paragraph only as provided in sub-paragraph (4) or (5).

(4) If at the end of such period as may be specified in rules under section 51 a person has failed, without reasonable excuse, to comply with a requirement imposed under sub-paragraph (2), the Director may give a direction under this paragraph.

(5) The Director may also give a direction under this paragraph if—

    (a) he considers—

        (i) that the agreement will, if not excluded, infringe the Chapter I prohibition; and

        (ii) that he is not likely to grant it an unconditional individual exemption; and

    (b) the agreement is not a protected agreement.

(6) For the purposes of sub-paragraph (5), an individual exemption is unconditional if no conditions or obligations are imposed in respect of it under section 4(3)(a).

(7) A direction under this paragraph—

    (a) must be in writing;

    (b) may be made so as to have effect from a date specified in the direction (which may not be earlier than the date on which it is given).

Protected agreements

CA.81 5. An agreement is a protected agreement for the purposes of paragraph 4 if—

    (a) the Secretary of State has announced his decision not to make a merger reference to the Competition Commission under section 64 of the 1973 Act in connection with the agreement;

    (b) the Secretary of State has made a merger reference to the Competition Commission under section 64 of the 1973 Act in connection with the agreement and the Commission has found that the agreement has given rise to, or would if carried out give rise to, a merger situation qualifying for investigation;

    (c) the agreement does not fall within sub-paragraph (a) or (b) but has given rise to, or would if carried out give rise to, enterprises to which it relates being regarded under section 65 of the 1973 Act as ceasing to be distinct enterprises (otherwise than as the result of subsection (3) or (4)(b) of that section); or

(d) the Secretary of State has made a merger reference to the Competition Commission under section 32 of the Water Industry Act 1991 in connection with the agreement and the Commission has found that the agreement has given rise to, or would if carried out give rise to, a merger of the kind to which that section applies.

PART II

CONCENTRATIONS SUBJECT TO EC CONTROLS

Enterprises ceasing to be distinct: the Chapter I prohibition

6.—(1) To the extent to which an agreement (either on its own or when taken together **CA.82** with another agreement) gives rise to, or would if carried out give rise to, a concentration, the Chapter I prohibition does not apply to the agreement if the Merger Regulation gives the Commission exclusive jurisdiction in the matter.

(2) To the extent to which conduct (either on its own or when taken together with other conduct) gives rise to, or would if pursued give rise to, a concentration, the Chapter II prohibition does not apply to the conduct if the Merger Regulation gives the Commission exclusive jurisdiction in the matter.

(3) In this paragraph—

'concentration' means a concentration with a Community dimension within the meaning of Articles 1 and 3 of the Merger Regulation; and

'Merger Regulation' means Council Regulation (EEC) No. 4064/89 of 21st December 1989 on the control of concentrations between undertakings as amended by Council Regulation (EC) No. 1310/97 of 30th June 1997.

SCHEDULE 2

EXCLUSIONS: OTHER COMPETITION SCRUTINY

PART I

FINANCIAL SERVICES

The Financial Services Act 1986 (c. 60)

1.—(1) The Financial Services Act 1986 is amended as follows. **CA.83**

(2) For section 125 (effect of the Restrictive Trade Practices Act 1976), substitute—

125.—(1) The Chapter I prohibition does not apply to an agreement for the constitution of—

(a) a recognised self-regulating organisation;

(b) a recognised investment exchange; or

(c) a recognised clearing house,

to the extent to which the agreement relates to the regulating provisions of the body concerned.

(2) Subject to subsection (3) below, the Chapter I prohibition does not apply to an agreement for the constitution of—

567

   (a) a self-regulating organisation;

   (b) an investment exchange; or

   (c) a clearing house,

to the extent to which the agreement relates to the regulating provisions of the body concerned.

(3) The exclusion provided by subsection (2) above applies only if—

   (a) the body has applied for a recognition order in accordance with the provisions of this Act; and

   (b) the application has not been determined.

(4) The Chapter I prohibition does not apply to a decision made by—

   (a) a recognised self-regulating organisation;

   (b) a recognised investment exchange; or

   (c) a recognised clearing house,

to the extent to which the decision relates to any of that body's regulating provisions or specified practices.

(5) The Chapter I prohibition does not apply to the specified practices of—

   (a) a recognised self-regulating organisation, a recognised investment exchange or a recognised clearing house; or

   (b) a person who is subject to—

     (i) the rules of one of those bodies; or

     (ii) the statements of principle, rules, regulations or codes of practice made by a designated agency in the exercise of functions transferred to it by a delegation order.

(6) The Chapter I prohibition does not apply to any agreement the parties to which consist of or include—

   (a) a recognised self-regulating organisation, a recognised investment exchange or a recognised clearing house; or

   (b) a person who is subject to—

     (i) the rules of one of those bodies; or

     (ii) the statements of principle, rules, regulations or codes of practice made by a designated agency in the exercise of functions transferred to it by a delegation order,

to the extent to which the agreement consists of provisions the inclusion of which is required or contemplated by any of the body's regulating provisions or specified practices or by the statements of principle, rules, regulations or codes of practice of the agency.

(7) The Chapter I prohibition does not apply to—

   (a) any clearing arrangements; or

(b) any agreement between a recognised investment exchange and a recognised clearing house, to the extent to which the agreement consists of provisions the inclusion of which in the agreement is required or contemplated by any clearing arrangements.

(8) If the recognition order in respect of a body of the kind mentioned in subsection (1)(a), (b) or (c) above is revoked, subsections (1) and (4) to (7) above are to have effect as if that body had continued to be recognised until the end of the period of six months beginning with the day on which the revocation took effect.

(9) In this section—

'the Chapter I prohibition' means the prohibition imposed by section 2(1) of the Competition Act 1998;

'regulating provisions' means—

(a) in relation to a self-regulating organisation, any rules made, or guidance issued, by the organisation;

(b) in relation to an investment exchange, any rules made, or guidance issued, by the exchange;

(c) in relation to a clearing house, any rules made, or guidance issued, by the clearing house;

'specified practices' means—

(a) in the case of a recognised self-regulating organisation, the practices mentioned in section 119(2)(a)(ii) and (iii) above (read with section 119(5) and (6)(a));

(b) in the case of a recognised investment exchange, the practices mentioned in section 119(2)(b)(ii) and (iii) above (read with section 119(5) and (6)(b));

(c) in the case of a recognised clearing house, the practices mentioned in section 119(2)(c)(ii) and (iii) above (read with section 119(5) and (6)(b));

(d) in the case of a person who is subject to the statements of principle, rules, regulations or codes of practice issued or made by a designated agency in the exercise of functions transferred to it by a delegation order, the practices mentioned in section 121(2)(c) above (read with section 121(4));

and expressions used in this section which are also used in Part I of the Competition Act 1998 are to be interpreted in the same way as for the purposes of that Part of that Act.'

(3) Omit section 126 (certain practices not to constitute anti-competitive practices for the purposes of the Competition Act 1980).

(4) For section 127 (modification of statutory provisions in relation to recognised professional bodies), substitute—

'127.—(1) This section applies to—

(a) any agreement for the constitution of a recognised professional body to the extent to which it relates to the rules or guidance of that body relating to the carrying on of investment business by persons certified by it ('investment business rules'); and

(b) any other agreement, the parties to which consist of or include—

(i) a recognised professional body;

(ii) a person certified by such a body; or

(iii) a member of such a body,

and which contains a provision required or contemplated by that body's investment business rules.

(2) If it appears to the Treasury, in relation to some or all of the provisions of an agreement to which this section applies—

(a) that the provisions in question do not have, and are not intended or likely to have, to any significant extent the effect of restricting, distorting or preventing competition; or

(b) that the effect of restricting, distorting or preventing competition which the provisions in question do have, or are intended or are likely to have, is not greater than is necessary for the protection of investors,

the Treasury may make a declaration to that effect.

(3) If the Treasury make a declaration under this section, the Chapter I prohibition does not apply to the agreement to the extent to which the agreement consists of provisions to which the declaration relates.

(4) If the Treasury are satisfied that there has been a material change of circumstances, they may—

(a) revoke a declaration made under this section, if they consider that the grounds on which it was made no longer exist;

(b) vary such a declaration, if they consider that there are grounds for making a different declaration; or

(c) make a declaration even though they have notified the Director of their intention not to do so.

(5) If the Treasury make, vary or revoke a declaration under this section they must notify the Director of their decision.

(6) If the Director proposes to exercise any Chapter III powers in respect of any provisions of an agreement to which this section applies, he must—

(a) notify the Treasury of his intention to do so; and

(b) give the Treasury particulars of the agreement and such other information—

(i) as he considers will assist the Treasury to decide whether to exercise their powers under this section; or

(ii) as the Treasury may request.

(7) The Director may not exercise his Chapter III powers in respect of any provisions of an agreement to which this section applies, unless the Treasury—

(a) have notified him that they have not made a declaration in respect of those provisions under this section and that they do not intend to make such a declaration; or

(b) have revoked a declaration under this section and a period of six months beginning with the date on which the revocation took effect has expires.

(8) A declaration under this section ceases to have effect if the agreement to which it relates ceases to be one to which this section applies.

(9) In this section—

'the Chapter I prohibition' means the prohibition imposed by section 2(1) of the Competition Act 1998,

'Chapter III powers' means the powers given to the Director by Chapter III of Part I of that Act so far as they relate to the Chapter I prohibition, and

expressions used in this section which are also used in Part I of the Competition Act 1998 are to be interpreted in the same way as for the purposes of that Part of that Act.

(10) In this section references to an agreement are to be read as applying equally to, or in relation to, a decision or concerted practice.

(11) In the application of this section to decisions and concerted practices, references to provisions of an agreement are to be read as references to elements of a decision or concerted practice.'

PART II

COMPANIES

The Companies Act 1989 (c. 40)

2.—(1) The Companies Act 1989 is amended as follows.

CA.84

(2) In Schedule 14, for paragraph 9 (exclusion of certain agreements from the Restrictive Trade Practices Act 1976), substitute—

'*The Competition Act 1998*

9.—(1) The Chapter I prohibition does not apply to an agreement for the constitution of a recognised supervisory of qualifying body to the extent to which it relates to—

(a) rules of, or guidance issued by, the body; and

(b) incidental matters connected with the rules or guidance.

(2) The Chapter I prohibition does not apply to an agreement the parties to which consist of or include—

(a) a recognised supervisory or qualifying body; or

(b) any person mentioned in paragraph 3(5) or (6) above,

to the extent to which the agreement consists of provisions the inclusion of which in the agreement is required or contemplated by the rules or guidance of that body.

(3) The Chapter I prohibition does not apply to the practices mentioned in paragraph 3(4)(a) and (b) above.

(4) Where a recognition order is revoked, sub-paragraphs (1) to (3) above are to continue to apply for a period of six months beginning with the day on which the revocation takes effect, as if the order were still in force.

(5) In this paragraph—

(a) 'the Chapter I prohibition' means the prohibition imposed by section 2(1) of the Competition Act 1998;

(b) references to an agreement are to be read as applying equally to, or in relation to, a decision or concerted practice,

and expressions used in this paragraph which are also used in Part I of the Competition Act 1998 are to be interpreted in the same way as for the purposes of that Part of that Act.

(6) In the application of this paragraph to decisions and concerted practices, references to provisions of an agreement are to be read as references to elements of a decision or concerted practice.'

The Companies (Northern Ireland) Order 1990 (SI 1990/593 (NI 5))

CA.85 3.—(1) The Companies (Northern Ireland) Order 1990 is amended as follows.

(2) In Schedule 14, for paragraph 9 (exclusion of certain agreements from the Restrictive Trade Practices Act 1976), substitute—

'*The Competition Act 1998*

9.—(1) The Chapter I prohibition does not apply to an agreement for the constitution of a recognised supervisory or qualifying body to the extent to which it relates to—

(a) rules of, or guidance issued by, the body; and

(b) incidental matters connected with the rules or guidance.

(2) The Chapter I prohibition does not apply to an agreement the parties to which consist of or include—

(a) a recognised supervisory or qualifying body; or

(b) any person mentioned in paragraph 3(5) or (6),

to the extent to which the agreement consists of provisions the inclusion of which in the agreement is required or contemplated by the rules or guidance of that body.

(3) The Chapter I prohibition does not apply to the practices mentioned in paragraph 3(4)(a) and (b).

(4) Where a recognition order is revoked, sub-paragraphs (1) to (3) are to continue to apply for a period of 6 months beginning with the day on which the revocation takes effect, as if the order were still in force.

(5) In this paragraph—

(a) 'the Chapter I prohibition' means the prohibition imposed by section 2(1) of the Competition Act 1998,

(b) references to an agreement are to be read as applying equally to, or in relation to, a decision or concerted practice,

and expressions used in this paragraph which are also used in Part I of the Competition Act 1998 are to be interpreted in the same way as for the purposes of that Part of that Act.

(6) In the application of this paragraph to decisions and concerted practices, references to provisions of an agreement are to be read as references to elements of a decision or concerted practice.'

PART III

BROADCASTING

The Broadcasting Act 1990 (c. 42)

4.—(1) The Broadcasting Act 1990 is amended as follows.

CA.86

(2) In section 194A (which modifies the Restrictive Trade Practices Act 1976 in its application to agreements relating to Channel 3 news provision), for subsections (2) to (6), substitute—

'(2) If, having sought the advice of the Director, it appears to the Secretary of State, in relation to some or all of the provisions of a relevant agreement, that the conditions mentioned in subsection (3) are satisfied, he may make a declaration to that effect.

(3) The conditions are that—

(a) the provisions in question do not have, and are not intended or likely to have, to any significant extent the effect of restricting, distorting or preventing competition; or

(b) the effect of restricting, distorting or preventing competition which the provisions in question do have or are intended or are likely to have, is not greater than is necessary—

(i) in the case of a relevant agreement falling within subsection (1)(a), for securing the appointment by holders of regional Channel 3 licences of a single body corporate to be the appointed news provider for the purposes of section 31(2), or

(ii) in the case of a relevant agreement falling within subsection (1)(b), for compliance by them with conditions included in their licences by virtue of section 31(1) and (2).

(4) If the Secretary of State makes a declaration under this section, the Chapter I prohibition does not apply to the agreement to the extent to which the agreement consists of provisions to which the declaration relates.

(5) If the Secretary of State is satisfied that there has been a material change of circumstances, he may—

(a) revoke a declaration made under this section, if he considers that the grounds on which it was made no longer exist;

(b) vary such a declaration, if he considers that there are grounds for making a different declaration; or

(c) make a declaration, even though he has notified the Director of his intention not to do so.

(6) If the Secretary of State makes, varies or revokes a declaration under this section, he must notify the Director of his decision.

(7) The Director may not exercise any Chapter III powers in respect of a relevant agreement, unless,—

(a) he has notified the Secretary of State of his intention to do so; and

(b) the Secretary of State—

   (i) has notified the Director that he has not made a declaration in respect of the agreement, or provisions of the agreement, under this section and that he does not intend to make such a declaration; or

   (ii) has revoked a declaration under this section and a period of six months beginning with the date on which the revocation took effect has expired.

(8) If the Director proposes to exercise any Chapter III powers in respect of a relevant agreement, he must give the Secretary of State particulars of the agreement and such other information—

(a) as he considers will assist the Secretary of State to decide whether to exercise his powers under this section, or

(b) as the Secretary of State may request.

(9) In this section—

'the Chapter I prohibition' means the prohibition imposed by section 2(1) of the Competition Act 1998;

'Chapter III powers' means the powers given to the Director by Chapter III of Part I of that Act so far as they relate to the Chapter I prohibition;

'Director' means the Director General of Fair Trading;

'regional Channel 3 licence' has the same meaning as in part I;

and expressions used in this section which are also used in Part I of the Competition Act are to be interpreted in the same way as for the purposes of that Part of that Act.

(10) In this section references to an agreement are to be read as applying equally to, or in relation to, a decision or concerted practice.

(11) In the application of this section to decisions and concerted practices, references to provisions of an agreement are to be read as references to elements of a decision or concerted practice.'

Networking arrangements under the Broadcasting Act 1990 (c. 42)

5.—(1) The Chapter I prohibition does not apply in respect of any networking arrange- **CA.87** ments to the extent to which they—

    (a) are subject to Schedule 4 to the Broadcasting Act 1990 (competition references with respect to networking arrangements); or

    (b) contain provisions which have been considered under that Schedule.

(2) The Independent Television Commission ('ITC') must publish a list of the networking arrangements which in their opinion are excluded from the Chapter I prohibition by virtue of sub-paragraph (1).

(3) The ITC must—

    (a) consult the Director before publishing the list; and

    (b) publish the list in such a way as they think most suitable for bringing it to the attention of persons who, in their opinion, would be affected by, or likely to have an interest in, it.

(4) In this paragraph 'networking arrangements' means—

    (a) any arrangement entered into as mentioned in section 39(4) or (7)(b) of the Broadcasting Act 1990; or

    (b) any agreements—

        (i) which do not constitute arrangements of the kind mentioned in paragraph (a), but

        (ii) which are made for the purpose mentioned in section 39(1) of that Act; or

    (c) any modification of the arrangements or agreements mentioned in paragraph (a) or (b).

PART IV

ENVIRONMENTAL PROTECTION

Producer responsibility obligations

6.—(1) The Environment Act 1995 is amended as follows. **CA.88**

(2) In section 94(1) (supplementary provisions about regulations imposing producer responsibility obligations on prescribed persons), after paragraph (o), insert—

'(oa) the exclusion or modification of any provision of Part I of the Competition Act 1998 in relation to exemption schemes or in relation to any agreement, decision or concerted practice at least one of the parties to which is an operator of an exemption scheme;'.

(3) After section 94(6), insert—

'(6A) Expressions used in paragraph (oa) of subsection (1) above which are also used in Part I of the Competition Act 1998 are to be interpreted in the same way as for the purposes of that Part of that Act.'

(4) After section 94, insert—

94A.—(1) For the purposes of this section, the relevant paragraphs are paragraphs (n), (o), (oa) and (ya) of section 94(1) above.

(2) Regulations made by virtue of any of the relevant paragraphs may include transitional provision in respect of agreements or exemption schemes—

    (a) in respect of which information has been required for the purposes of competition scrutiny under any regulation made by virtue of paragraph (ya);

    (b) which are being, or have been, considered for the purposes of competition scrutiny under any regulation made by virtue of paragraph (n) or (ya); or

    (c) in respect of which provisions of the Restrictive Trade Practices Acts 1976 and 1977 have been modified or excluded in accordance with any regulation made by virtue of paragraph (o).

(3) Subsections (2), (3), (5) to (7) and (10) of section 93 above do not apply to a statutory instrument which contains only regulations made by virtue of any of the relevant paragraphs or subsection (2) above.

(4) Such a statutory instrument shall be subject to annulment in pursuance of a resolution of either House of Parliament.'

SCHEDULE 3
GENERAL EXCLUSIONS

Planning obligations

CA.89 1.—(1) The Chapter I prohibition does not apply to an agreement—

    (a) to the extent to which it is a planning obligation;

    (b) which is made under section 75 (agreements regulating development or use of land) or 246 (agreements relating to Crown land) of the Town and Country Planning (Scotland) Act 1997; or

    (c) which is made under Article 40 of the Planning (Northern Ireland) Order 1991.

(2) In sub-paragraph (1)(a), 'planning obligation' means—

    (a) a planning obligation for the purposes of section 106 of the Town and Country Planning Act 1990; or

    (b) a planning obligation for the purposes of section 299A of that Act.

Section 21(2) agreements

CA.90 2.–(1) The Chapter I prohibition does not apply to an agreement in respect of which a direction under section 21(2) of the Restrictive Trade Practices Act 1976 is in force immediately before the coming into force of section 2 ('a section 21(2) agreement').

(2) If a material variation is made to a section 21(2) agreement, sub-paragraph (1) ceases to apply to the agreement on the coming into force of the variation.

(3) Sub-paragraph (1) does not apply to a particular section 21(2) agreement if the Director gives a direction under this paragraph to that effect.

(4) If the Director is considering whether to give a direction under this paragraph, he may by notice in writing require any party to the agreement in question to give him such information in connection with the agreement as he may require.

(5) The Director may give a direction under this paragraph only as provided in sub-paragraph (6) or (7).

(6) If at the end of such period as may be specified in rules under section 51 a person has failed, without reasonable excuse, to comply with a requirement imposed under sub-paragraph (4), the Director may give a direction under this paragraph.

(7) The Director may also give a direction under this paragraph if he considers—

    (a) that the agreement will, if not excluded, infringe the Chapter I prohibition; and

    (b) that he is not likely to grant it an unconditional individual exemption.

(8) For the purposes of sub-paragraph (7) an individual exemption is unconditional if no conditions or obligations are imposed in respect of it under section 4(3)(a).

(9) A direction under this paragraph—

    (a) must be in writing;

    (b) may be made so as to have effect from a date specified in the direction (which may not be earlier than the date on which it is given).

EEA Regulated Markets

3.—(1) The Chapter I prohibition does not apply to an agreement for the constitution **CA.91** of an EEA regulated market to the extent to which the agreement relates to any of the rules made, or guidance issued, by that market.

(2) The Chapter I prohibition does not apply to a decision made by an EEA regulated market, to the extent to which the decision relates to any of the market's regulating provisions.

(3) The Chapter I prohibition does not apply to—

    (a) any practices of an EEA regulated market; or

    (b) any practices which are trading practices in relation to an EEA regulated marked.

(4) The Chapter I prohibition does not apply to an agreement the parties to which are or include—

    (a) an EEA regulated market; or

    (b) a person who is subject to the rules of that market,

to the extent to which the agreement consists of provisions the inclusion of which is required or contemplated by the regulating provisions of that market.

(5) In this paragraph—

'EEA regulated market' is a market which—

(a) is listed by an EEA State other than the United Kingdom pursuant to article 16 of Council Directive No. 93/22/EEC of 10th May 1993 on investment services in the securities field; and

(b) operates without any requirement that a person dealing on the market should have a physical presence in the EEA State from which any trading facilities are provided or on any trading floor that the market may have;

'EEA State' means a State which is a contracting party to the EEA Agreement;

'regulating provisions', in relation to an EEA regulated market, means—

(a) rules made, or guidance issued, by that market;

(b) practices of that market; or

(c) practices which, in relation to that market, are trading practices;

'trading practices', in relation to an EEA regulated market, means practices of persons who are subject to the rules made by that market, and—

(a) which relate to business in respect of which those persons are subject to the rules of that market, and which are required or contemplated by those rules or by guidance issued by that market; or

(b) which are otherwise attributable to the conduct of that market as such.

Services of general economic interest etc

CA.92 4. Neither the Chapter I prohibition nor the Chapter II prohibition applies to an undertaking entrusted with the operation of services of general economic interest or having the character of a revenue-producing monopoly in so far as the prohibition would obstruct the performance, in law or in fact, of the particular tasks assigned to that undertaking.

Compliance with legal requirements

CA.93 5.—(1) The Chapter I prohibition does not apply to an agreement to the extent to which it is made in order to comply with a legal requirement.

(2) The Chapter II prohibition does not apply to conduct to the extent to which it is engaged in an order to comply with a legal requirement.

(3) In this paragraph 'legal requirement' means a requirement—

(a) imposed by or under any enactment in force in the United Kingdom;

(b) imposed by or under the Treaty or the EEA Agreement and having legal effect in the United Kingdom without further enactment; or

(c) imposed by or under the law in force in another Member State and having legal effect in the United Kingdom.

Avoidance of conflict with international obligations

CA.94 6.—(1) If the Secretary of State is satisfied that, in order to avoid a conflict between provisions of this Part and an international obligation of the United Kingdom, it would be appropriate for the Chapter I prohibition not to apply to—

(a) a particular agreement; or

(b) any agreement of a particular description,

he may by order exclude the agreement, or agreements of that description, from the Chapter I prohibition.

(2) An order under sub-paragraph (1) may make provision for the exclusion of the agreement or agreements to which the order applies, or of such of them as may be specified, only in specified circumstances.

(3) An order under sub-paragraph (1) may also provide that the Chapter I prohibition is deemed never to have applied in relation to the agreement or agreements, or in relation to such of them as may be specified.

(4) If the Secretary of State is satisfied that, in order to avoid a conflict between provisions of this Part and an international obligation of the United Kingdom, it would be appropriate for the Chapter II prohibition not to apply in particular circumstances, he may by order provide for it not to apply in such circumstances as may be specified.

(5) An order under sub-paragraph (4) may provide that the Chapter II prohibition is to be deemed never to have applied in relation to specified conduct.

(6) An international arrangement relating to civil aviation and designated by an order made by the Secretary of State is to be treated as an international obligation for the purposes of this paragraph.

(7) In this paragraph and paragraph 7 'specified' means specified in the order.

Public policy

7.—(1) If the Secretary of State is satisfied that there are exceptional and compelling reasons of public policy why the Chapter I prohibition ought not to apply to— **CA.95**

(a) a particular agreement; or

(b) any agreement of a particular description,

he may by order exclude the agreement, or agreements of that description, from the Chapter I prohibition.

(2) An order under sub-paragraph (1) may make provision for the exclusion of the agreement or agreements to which the order applies, or of such of them as may be specified, only in specified circumstances.

(3) An order under sub-paragraph (1) may also provide that the Chapter I prohibition is to be deemed never to have applied in relation to the agreement or agreements, or in relation to such of them as may be specified.

(4) If the Secretary of State is satisfied that there are exceptional and compelling reasons of public policy why the Chapter II prohibition ought not to apply in particular circumstances, he may by order provide for it not to apply in such circumstances as may be specified.

(5) An order under sub-paragraph (4) may provide that the Chapter II prohibition is to be deemed never to have applied in relation to specified conduct.

Coal and steel

CA.96 8.—(1) The Chapter I prohibition does not apply to an agreement which relates to a coal or steel product to the extent to which the ECSC Treaty gives the Commission exclusive jurisdiction in the matter.

(2) Sub-paragraph (1) ceases to have effect on the date on which the ECSC Treaty expires ('the expiry date').

(3) The Chapter II prohibition does not apply to conduct which relates to a coal or steel product to the extent to which the ECSC Treaty gives the Commission exclusive jurisdiction in the matter.

(4) Sub-paragraph (3) ceases to have effect on the expiry date.

(5) In this paragraph—

'coal or steel product' means any product of a kind listed in Annex I to the ECSC Treaty; and

'ECSC Treaty' means the Treaty establishing the European Coal and Steel Community.

Agricultural products

CA.97 9.—(1) The Chapter I prohibition does not apply to an agreement to the extent to which it relates to production of or trade in an agricultural product and—

(a) forms an integral part of a national market organisation;

(b) is necessary for the attainment of the objectives set out in Article 39 of the Treaty; or

(c) is an agreement of farmers or farmers' associations (or associations of such associations) belonging to a single member State which concerns—

(i) the production or sale of agricultural products; or

(ii) the use of joint facilities for the storage, treatment or processing of agricultural products,

and under which there is no obligation to charge identical prices.

(2) If the Commission determines that an agreement does not fulfil the conditions specified by the provision for agricultural products for exclusion from Article 85(1), the exclusion provided by this paragraph ('the agriculture exclusion') is to be treated as ceasing to apply to the agreement on the date of the decision.

(3) The agriculture exclusion does not apply to a particular agreement if the Director gives a direction under this paragraph to that effect.

(4) If the Director is considering whether to give a direction under this paragraph, he may by notice in writing require any party to the agreement in question to give him such information in connection with the agreement as he may require.

(5) The Director may give a direction under this paragraph only as provided in sub-paragraph (6) or (7).

(6) If at the end of such period as may be specified in rules under section 51 a person has failed, without reasonable excuse, to comply with a requirement imposed under sub-paragraph (4), the Director may give a direction under this paragraph.

(7) The Director may also give a direction under this paragraph if he considers that an agreement (whether or not he considers that it infringes the Chapter I prohibition) is likely, or is intended, substantially and unjustifiably to prevent, restrict or distort competition in relation to an agricultural product.

(8) A direction under this paragraph—

(a) must be in writing;

(b) may be made so as to have effect from a date specified in the direction (which may not be earlier than the date on which it is given).

(9) In this paragraph—

'agricultural product' means any product of a kind listed in Annex II to the Treaty; and

'provision for agricultural products' means Council Regulation (EEC) No. 26/62 of 4th April 1962 applying certain rules of competition to production of and trade in agricultural products.

SCHEDULE 4
PROFESSIONAL RULES

PART I
EXCLUSION

General

1.—(1) To the extent to which an agreement (either on its own or when taken together   **CA.98** with another agreement)—

(a) constitutes a designated professional rule;

(b) imposes obligations arising from designated professional rules; or

(c) constitutes an agreement to act in accordance with such rules,

the Chapter I prohibition does not apply to the agreement.

(2) In this Schedule—

'designated' means designated by the Secretary of State under paragraph 2;

'professional rules' means rules regulating a professional service or the persons providing, or wishing to provide, that service;

'professional service' means any of the services described in Part II of this Schedule; and

'rules' includes regulations, codes of practice and statements of principle.

Designated rules

2.—(1) The Secretary of State must establish and maintain a list designating, for the purposes of this Schedule, rules—

(a) which are notified to him under paragraph 3; and

(b) which, in his opinion, are professional rules.

(2) The list is to be established, and any alteration in the list is to be effected, by an order made by the Secretary of State.

(3) The designation of any rule is to have effect from such date (which may be earlier than the date on which the order listing it is made) as may be specified in that order.

Application for designation

CA.99 3.—(1) Anybody regulating a professional service or the persons who provide, or wish to provide, that service may apply to the Secretary of State for rules of that body to be designated.

(2) An application under this paragraph must—

(a) be accompanied by a copy of the rules to which it relates; and

(b) be made in the prescribed manner.

Alterations

4.—(1) A rule does not cease to be a designated professional rule merely because it is altered.

(2) If such a rule is altered (whether by being modified, revoked or replaced), the body concerned must notify the Secretary of State and the Director of the alteration as soon as is reasonably practicable.

Reviewing the list

5.—(1) The Secretary of State must send to the Director—

(a) a copy of any order made under paragraph 2; and

(b) a copy of the professional rules to which the order relates.

(2) The Director must—

(a) retain any copy of a professional rule which is sent to him under sub-paragraph (1)(b) so long as the rule remains in force;

(b) maintain a copy of the list, as altered from time to time; and

(c) keep the list under review.

(3) If the Director considers

(a) that, with a view to restricting the exclusion provided by this Schedule, some or all of the rules of a particular body should no longer be designated; or

(b) that rules which are not designated should be designated,

he must advise the Secretary of State accordingly.

Removal from the list

6.—(1) This paragraph applies if the Secretary of State receives advice under paragraph 5(3)(a).

(2) If it appears to the Secretary of State that another Minister of the Crown has functions in relation to the professional service concerned, he must consult that Minister.

(3) If it appears to the Secretary of State, having considered the Director's advice and the advice of any other Minister resulting from consultation under sub-paragraph (2), that the rules in question should no longer be designated, he may by order revoke their designation.

(4) Revocation of a designation is to have effect from such date as the order revoking it may specify.

Inspection

7.—(1) Any person may inspect, and take a copy of—

(a) any entry in the list of designated professional rules as kept by the Director under paragraph 5(2); or

(b) any copy of professional rules retained by him under paragraph 5(1).

(2) The right conferred by sub-paragraph (1) is to be exercised only—

(a) at a time which is reasonable;

(b) on payment of such fee as the Director may determine; and

(c) at such offices of his as the Director may direct.

PART II
PROFESSIONAL SERVICES

Legal

8. The services of barristers, advocates or solicitors. **CA.100**

Medical

9. The provision of medical or surgical advice or attendance and the performance of surgical operations.

Dental

10. Any services falling within the practice of dentistry within the meaning of the Dentists Act 1984.

Ophthalmic

11. The testing of sight.

Veterinary

12. Any services which constitute veterinary surgery within the meaning of the Veterinary Surgeons Act 1966.

Nursing

13. The services of nurses.

Midwifery

14. The services of midwives.

Physiotherapy

15. The services of physiotherapists.

Chiropody

16. The services of chiropodists.

Architectural

17. The services of architects.

Accounting and auditing

18. The making or preparation of accounts or accounting records and the examination, verification and auditing of financial statements.

Insolvency

19. Insolvency services within the meaning of section 428 of the Insolvency Act 1986.

Patent agency

20. The services of registered patent agents (within the meaning of Part V of the Copyright, Designs and Patents Act 1988).

21. The services of persons carrying on for gain in the United Kingdom the business of acting as agents or other representatives for or obtaining European patents or for the purpose of conducting proceedings in relation to applications for or otherwise in connection with such patents before the European Patent Office or the comptroller and whose names appear on the European list (within the meaning of Part V of the Copyright, Designs and Patents Act 1988).

Parliamentary agency

22. The services of parliamentary agents entered in the register in either House of Parliament as agents entitled to practise both in promoting and in opposing Bills.

Surveying

23. The services of surveyors of land, of quantity surveyors, of surveyors of buildings or other structures and of surveyors of ships.

Engineering and technology etc

24. The services of persons practising or employed as consultants in the field of—

    (a) civil engineering;

    (b) mechanical, aeronautical, marine, electrical or electronic engineering;

    (c) mining, quarrying, soil analysis or other forms of mineralogy or geology;

    (d) agronomy, forestry, livestock rearing or ecology;

    (e) metallurgy, chemistry, biochemistry or physics; or

    (f) any other form of engineering or technology analogous to those mentioned in sub-paragraphs (a) to (e).

Educational

25. The provision of education or training.

Religious

26. The services of ministers of religion.

SCHEDULE 5
NOTIFICATION UNDER CHAPTER I: PROCEDURE

Terms used

1. In this Schedule—

'applicant' means the person making an application to which this Schedule applies;

'application' means an application under section 13 or an application under section 14;

'application for guidance' means an application under section 13;

'application for a decision' means an application under section 14;

'rules' means rules made by the Director under section 51; and

'specified' means specified in the rules.

CA.101

General rules about applications

2.—(1) An application must be made in accordance with rules.

CA.102

(2) A party to an agreement who makes an application must take all reasonable steps to notify all other parties to the agreement of whom he is aware—

(a) that the application has been made; and

(b) as to whether it is for guidance or a decision.

(3) Notification under sub-paragraph (2) must be in the specified manner.

Preliminary investigation

3.—(1) If, after a preliminary investigation of an application, the Director considers that it is likely—

CA.103

(a) that the agreement concerned will infringe the Chapter I prohibition, and

(b) that it would not be appropriate to grant the agreement an individual exemption,

he may make a decision ('a provisional decision') under this paragraph.

(2) If the Director makes a provisional decision—

(a) the Director must notify the applicant in writing of his provisional decision; and

(b) section 13(4) or (as the case may be) section 14(4) is to be taken as never having applied.

(3) When making a provisional decision, the Director must follow such procedure as may be specified.

(4) A provisional decision does not affect the final determination of an application.

(5) If the Director has given notice to the applicant under sub-paragraph (2) in respect of an application for a decision, he may continue with the application under section 14.

Procedure on application for guidance

4. When determining an application for guidance, the Director must follow such procedure as may be specified.

CA.104

CA.105 5.—(1) When determining an application for a decision, the Director must follow such procedure as may be specified.

(2) The Director must arrange for the application to be published in such a way as he thinks most suitable for bringing it to the attention of those likely to be affected by it, unless he is satisfied that it will be sufficient for him to seek information from one or more particular persons other than the applicant.

(3) In determining the application, the Director must take into account any representations made to him by persons other than the applicant.

Publication of decisions

CA.106 6. If the Director determines an application for a decision he must publish his decision, together with his reasons for making it, in such manner as may be specified.

Delay by the Director

CA.107 7.—(1) This paragraph applies if the court is satisfied, on the application of a person aggrieved by the failure of the Director to determine an application for a decision in accordance with the specified procedure, that there has been undue delay on the part of the Director in determining the application.

(2) The court may give such directions to the Director as it considers appropriate for securing that the application is determined without unnecessary further delay.

SCHEDULE 6
NOTIFICATION UNDER CHAPTER II: PROCEDURE

CA.108   *Terms used*

1. In this Schedule—

'applicant' means the person making an application to which this Schedule applies;

'application' means an application under section 21 or an application under section 22;

'application for guidance' means an application under section 21;

'application for a decision' means an application under section 22;

'other party', in relation to conduct of two or more persons, means one of those persons other than the applicant;

'rules' means rules made by the Director under section 51; and

'specified' means specified in the rules.

CA.109   *General rules about applications*

2.—(1) An application must be made in accordance with rules.

(2) If the conduct to which an application relates is conduct of two or more persons, the applicant must take all reasonable steps to notify all of the other parties of whom he is aware—

(a) that the application has been made; and

(b) as to whether it is for guidance or a decision.

(3) Notification under sub-paragraph (2) must be in the specified manner.

Preliminary investigation

3.—(1) If, after a preliminary investigation of an application, the Director considers that **CA.110** it is likely that the conduct concerned will infringe the Chapter II prohibition, he may make a decision ('a provisional decision') under this paragraph.

(2) If the Director makes a provisional decision, he must notify the applicant in writing of that decision.

(3) When making a provisional decision, the Director must follow such procedure as may be specified.

(4) A provisional decision does not affect the final determination of an application.

(5) If the Director has given notice to the applicant under sub-paragraph (2) in respect of an application for a decision, he may continue with the application under section 22.

Procedure on application for guidance

4. When determining an application for guidance, the Director must follow such proce- **CA.111** dure as may be specified.

Procedure on application for a decision

5.—(1) When determining an application for a decision, the Director must follow such **CA.112** procedure as may be specified.

(2) The Director must arrange for the application to be published in such a way as he thinks most suitable for bringing it to the attention of those likely to be affected by it, unless he is satisfied that it will be sufficient for him to seek information from one or more particular persons other than the applicant.

(3) In determining the application, the Director must take into account any representations made to him by persons other than the applicant.

Publication of decisions

6. If the Director determines an application for a decision he must publish his decision, **CA.113** together with his reasons for making it, in such manner as may be specified.

Delay by the Director

7.—(1) This paragraph applies if the court is satisfied, on the application of a person **CA.114** aggrieved by the failure of the Director to determine an application for a decision in accordance with the specified procedure, that there has been undue delay on the part of the Director in determining the application.

(2) The court may give such directions to the Director as it considers appropriate for securing that the application is determined without unnecessary further delay.

SCHEDULE 7
THE COMPETITION COMMISSION

PART I
GENERAL

Interpretation

CA.115 1. In this Schedule—

'the 1973 Act' means the Fair Trading Act 1973;

'appeal panel member' means a member appointed under paragraph 2(1)(a);

'Chairman' means the chairman of the Commission;

'the Commission' means the Competition Commission;

'Council' has the meaning given in paragraph 5;

'general functions' means any functions of the Commission other than functions—

(a) in connection with appeals under this Act; or

(b) which are to be discharged by the Council;

'member' means a member of the Commission;

'newspaper merger reference' means a newspaper merger reference under section 59 of the 1973 Act;

'President' has the meaning given by paragraph 4(2);

'reporting panel member' means a member appointed under paragraph 2(1)(b);

'secretary' means the secretary of the Commission appointed under paragraph 9; and

'specialist panel member' means a member appointed under any of the provisions mentioned in paragraph 2(1)(d).

Membership of the Commission

CA.116 2.—(1) The Commission is to consist of—

(a) members appointed by the Secretary of State to form a panel for the purposes of the Commission's functions in relation to appeals;

(b) members appointed by the Secretary of State to form a panel for the purposes of the Commission's general functions;

(c) members appointed (in accordance with paragraph 15(5)) from the panel maintained under paragraph 22;

(d) members appointed by the Secretary of State under or by virtue of—

(i) section 12(4) or 14(8) or the Water Industry Act 1991;

(ii) section 12(9) of the Electricity Act 1989;

(iii) section 13(10) of the Telecommunications Act 1984;

(iv) Article 15(9) of the Electricity (Northern Ireland) Order 1992.

(2) A person who is appointed as a member of a kind mentioned in one of paragraphs (a) to (c) of sub-paragraph (3) may also be appointed as a member of either or both of the other kinds mentioned in those paragraphs.

(3) The kinds of member are—

    (a) an appeal panel member;

    (b) a reporting panel member;

    (c) a specialist panel member.

(4) Before appointing a person who is qualified for appointment to the panel of chairmen (see paragraph 26(2)), the Secretary of State must consult the Lord Chancellor or Lord Advocate, as he considers appropriate.

(5) The validity of the Commission's proceedings is not affected by a defect in the appointment of a member.

Chairman and deputy chairmen

3.—(1) The Commission is to have a chairman appointed by the Secretary of State from   **CA.117** among the reporting panel members.

(2) The Secretary of State may appoint one or more of the reporting panel members to act as deputy chairman.

(3) The Chairman, and any deputy chairman, may resign that office at any time by notice in writing addressed to the Secretary of State.

(4) If the Chairman (or a deputy chairman) ceases to be a member he also ceases to be Chairman (or a deputy chairman).

(5) If the Chairman is absent or otherwise unable to act, or there is no chairman, any of his functions may be performed—

    (a) if there is one deputy chairman, by him;

    (b) if there is more than one—

        (i) by the deputy chairman designated by the Secretary of State; or

        (ii) if no such designation has been made, by the deputy chairman designated by the deputy chairmen;

    (c) if there is no deputy chairman able to act—

        (i) by the member designated by the Secretary of State; or

        (ii) if no such designation has been made, by the member designated by the Commission.

President

4.—(1) The Secretary of State must appoint one of the appeal panel members to preside   **CA.118** over the discharge of the Commission's functions in relation to appeals.

(2) The member so appointed is to be known as the President of the Competition Commission Appeal Tribunals (but is referred to in this Schedule as 'the President').

(3) The Secretary of State may not appoint a person to be the President unless that person—

    (a) has a ten year general qualification within the meaning of section 71 of the Courts and Legal Services Act 1990;

(b) is an advocate or solicitor in Scotland of at least ten years' standing; or

(ii) a member of the Bar of Northern Ireland of at least ten years' standing; or

(ii) a solicitor of the Supreme Court of Northern Ireland of at least ten years' standing,

and appears to the Secretary of State to have appropriate experience and knowledge of competition law and practice.

(4) Before appointing the President, the Secretary of State must consult the Lord Chancellor of Lord Advocate, as he considers appropriate.

(5) If the President ceases to be a member he also ceases to be President.

The Council

CA.119 5.—(1) The Commission is to have a management board to be known as the Competition Commission Council (but referred to in this Schedule as 'the Council').

(2) The Council is to consist of—

(a) the Chairman;

(b) the President;

(c) such other members as the Secretary of State may appoint; and

(d) the secretary.

(3) In exercising its functions under paragraphs 3 and 7 to 12 and paragraph 5 of Schedule 8, the Commission is to act through the Council.

(4) The Council may determine its own procedure including, in particular, its quorum.

(5) The Chairman (and any person acting as Chairman) is to have a casting vote on any question being decided by the Council.

Term of office

CA.120 6.—(1) Subject to the provisions of this Schedule, each member is to hold and vacate office in accordance with the terms of his appointment.

(2) A person is not to be appointed as a member for more than five years at a time.

(3) Any member may at any time resign by notice in writing addressed to the Secretary of State.

(4) The Secretary of State may remove a member on the ground of incapacity or misbehaviour.

(5) No person is to be prevented from being appointed as a member merely because he has previously been a member.

Expenses, remuneration and pensions

CA.121 7.—(1) The Secretary of State shall pay to the Commission such sums as he considers appropriate to enable it to perform its functions.

(2) The Commission may pay, or make provision for paying, to or in respect of each member such salaries or other remuneration and such pensions, allowances, fees, expenses or gratuities as the Secretary of State may determine.

(3) If a person ceases to be a member otherwise than on the expiry of his term of office and it appears to the Secretary of State that there are special circumstances which make it right for him to receive compensation, the Commission may make a payment to him of such amount as the Secretary of State may determine.

(4) The approval of the Treasury is required for—

(a) any payment under sub-paragraph (1);

(b) any determination of the Secretary of State under sub-paragraph (2) or (3).

The Commission's powers

8. Subject to the provisions of this Schedule, the Commission has power to do anything **CA.122** (except borrow money)—

(a) calculated to facilitate the discharge of its functions; or

(b) incidental or conducive to the discharge of its functions.

Staff

9.—(1) The Commission is to have a secretary, appointed by the Secretary of State on **CA.123** such terms and conditions of service as he considers appropriate.

(2) The approval of the Treasury is required as to those terms and conditions.

(3) Before appointing a person to be secretary, the Secretary of State must consult the Chairman and the President.

(4) Subject to obtaining the approval of—

(a) the Secretary of State, as to numbers; and

(b) the Secretary of State and Treasury, as to terms and conditions of service,

the Commission may appoint such staff as it thinks appropriate.

Procedure

10. Subject to any provision made by or under this Act, the Commission may regulate its **CA.124** own procedure.

Application of seal and proof of instruments

11.—(1) The application of the seal of the Commission must be authenticated by the sig- **CA.125** nature of the secretary or of some other person authorised for the purpose.

(2) Sub-paragraph (1) does not apply in relation to any document which is or is to be signed in accordance with the law of Scotland.

(3) A document purporting to be duly executed under the seal of the Commission—

(a) is to be received in evidence; and

(b) is to be taken to have been so executed unless the contrary is proved.

Accounts

CA.126 12.—(1) The Commission must—

(a) keep proper accounts and proper records in relation to its accounts;

(b) prepare a statement of accounts in respect of each of its financial years; and

(c) send copies of the statement to the Secretary of State and to the Comptroller and Auditor General before the end of the month of August next following the financial year to which the statement relates.

(2) The statement of accounts must comply with any directions given by the Secretary of State with the approval of the Treasury as to—

(a) the information to be contained in it;

(b) the manner in which the information contained in it is to be presented; or

(c) the methods and principles according to which the statement is to be prepared,

and must contain such additional information as the Secretary of State may with the approval of the Treasury require to be provided for informing Parliament.

(3) The Comptroller and Auditor General must—

(a) examine, certify and report on each statement received by him as a result of this paragraph; and

(b) lay copies of each statement and of his report before each House of Parliament.

(4) In this paragraph 'financial year' means the period beginning with the date on which the Commission is established and ending with March 31st next, and each successive period of twelve months.

Status

CA.127 13.—(1) The Commission is not to be regarded as the servant or agent of the Crown or as enjoying any status, privilege or immunity of the Crown.

(2) The Commission's property is not to be regarded as property of, or held on behalf of, the Crown.

PART II

PERFORMANCE OF THE COMMISSION'S GENERAL FUNCTIONS

Interpretation

CA.128 14. In this Part of this Schedule 'group' means a group selected under paragraph 15.

Discharge of certain functions by groups

CA.129 15.—(1) Except where sub-paragraph (7) gives the Chairman power to act on his own, any general function of the Commission must be performed through a group selected for the purpose by the Chairman.

(2) The group must consist of at least three persons one of whom may be the Chairman.

(3) In selecting the members of the group, the Chairman must comply with any requirement as to its constitution imposed by any enactment applying to specialist panel members.

(4) If the functions to be performed through the group relate to a newspaper merger reference, the group must, subject to sub-paragraph (5), consist of such reporting panel members as the Chairman may select.

(5) The Secretary of State may appoint one, two or three persons from the panel maintained under paragraph 22 to be members and, if he does so, the group—

(a) must include that member or those members; and

(b) if there are three such members, may (if the Chairman so decides) consist entirely of those members.

(6) Subject to sub-paragraphs (2) to (5), a group must consist of reporting panel members or specialist panel members selected by the Chairman.

(7) While a group is being constituted to perform a particular general function of the Commission, the Chairman may—

(a) take such steps (falling within that general function) as he considers appropriate to facilitate the work of the group when it has been constituted; or

(b) exercise the power conferred by section 75(5) of the 1973 Act (setting aside references).

Chairmen of groups

16. The Chairman must appoint one of the members of a group to act as the chairman of the group.   **CA.130**

Replacement of member of group

17.—(1) If, during the proceedings of a group—   **CA.131**

(a) a member of the group ceases to be a member of the Commission;

(b) the Chairman is satisfied that a member of the group will be unable for a substantial period to perform his duties as a member of the group; or

(c) it appears to the Chairman that because of a particular interest of a member of the group it is inappropriate for him to remain in the group,

the Chairman may appoint a replacement.

(2) The Chairman may also at any time appoint any reporting panel member to be an additional member of a group.

Attendance of other members

18.—(1) At the invitation of the chairman of a group, any reporting panel member who is not a member of the group may attend meetings or otherwise take part in the proceedings of the group.   **CA.132**

(2) But any person attending in response to such an invitation may not—

(a) vote in any proceedings of the group; or

(b) have a statement of his dissent from a conclusion of the group included in a report made by them.

(3) Nothing in sub-paragraph (1) is to be taken to prevent a group, or a member of a group, from consulting any member of the Commission with respect to any matter or question with which the group is concerned.

Procedure

CA.133 19.—(1) Subject to any special or general directions given by the Secretary of State, each group may determine its own procedure.

(2) Each group may, in particular, determine its quorum and determine—

(a) the extent, if any, to which persons interested or claiming to be interested in the subject-matter of the reference are allowed—

(i) to be present or to be heard, either by themselves or by their representatives;

(ii) to cross-examine witnesses; or

(iii) otherwise to take part; and

(b) the extent, if any, to which sittings of the group are to be held in public.

(3) In determining its procedure a group must have regard to any guidance issued by the Chairman.

(4) Before issuing any guidance for the purposes of this paragraph the Chairman must consult the members of the Commission.

Effect of exercise of functions by group

CA.134 20.—(1) Subject to sub-paragraph (2), anything done by or in relation to a group in, or in connection with, the performance of functions to be performed by the group is to have the same effect as if done by or in relation to the Commission.

(2) For the purposes of—

(a) sections 56 and 73 of the 1973 Act;

(b) section 19A of the Agricultural Marketing Act 1958;

(c) Articles 23 and 42 of the Agricultural Marketing (Northern Ireland) Order 1982,

a conclusion contained in a report of a group is to be disregarded if the conclusion is not that of at least two-thirds of the members of the group.

Casting votes

CA.135 21. The chairman of a group is to have a casting vote on any question to be decided by the group.

Newspaper merger references

CA.136 22. The Secretary of State must maintain a panel of persons whom he regards as suitable for selection as members of a group constituted in connection with a newspaper merger reference.

Part III

Appeals

Interpretation

23. In this Part of this Schedule—   **CA.137**

'panel of chairmen' means the panel appointed under paragraph 26; and

'tribunal' means an appeal tribunal constituted in accordance with paragraph 27.

Training of appeal panel members

24. The President must arrange such training for appeal panel members as he considers **CA.138** appropriate.

Acting President

25. If the President is absent or otherwise unable to act, the Secretary of State may **CA.139** appoint as acting president an appeal panel member who is qualified to act as chairman of a tribunal.

Panel of tribunal chairmen

25.—(1) There is to be a panel of appeal panel members appointed by the Secretary of **CA.140** State for the purposes of providing chairman of appeal tribunals established under this Part of this Schedule.

(2) A person is qualified for appointment to the panel of chairmen only if—

    (a) he has a seven year general qualification within the meaning of section 71 of the Courts and Legal Services Act 1990;

    (b) he is an advocate or solicitor in Scotland of at least seven years' standing; or

    (c) he is—

        (i) a member of the Bar of Northern Ireland of at least seven years' standing; or

        (ii) a solicitor of the Supreme Court of Northern Ireland of at least seven years' standing,

and appears to the Secretary of State to have appropriate experience and knowledge of competition law and practice.

Constitution of tribunals

27.—(1) On receipt of a notice of appeal, the President must constitute an appeal tri- **CA.141** bunal to deal with the appeal.

(2) An appeal tribunal is to consist of—

    (a) a chairman, who must be either the President or a person appointed by him to be chairman from the panel of chairmen; and

    (b) two other appeal panel members appointed by the President.

PART IV

MISCELLANEOUS

Disqualification of members for House of Commons

CA.142 28. In Part II of Schedule 1 to the House of Commons Disqualification Act 1975 (bodies of which all members are disqualified) insert at the appropriate place—

'The Competition Commission'.

Disqualification of members for Northern Ireland Assembly

CA.143 29. In Part II of Schedule 1 to the Northern Ireland Assembly Disqualification Act 1975 (bodies of which all members are disqualified) insert at the appropriate place—

'The Competition Commission'.

PART V

TRANSITIONAL PROVISIONS

Interpretation

CA.144 30. In this Part of this Schedule—

'commencement date' means the date on which section 45 comes into force; and

'MMC' means the Monopolies and Mergers Commission.

Chairman

CA.145 31.—(1) The person who is Chairman of the MMC immediately before the commencement date is on that date to become both a member of the Commission and its chairman as if he had been duly appointed under paragraphs 2(1)(b) and 3.

(2) He is to hold office as Chairman of the Commission for the remainder of the period for which he was appointed as Chairman of the MMC and on the terms on which he was so appointed.

Deputy chairmen

CA.146 32. The persons who are deputy chairmen of the MMC immediately before the commencement date are on that date to become deputy chairmen of the Commission as if they had been duly appointed under paragraph 3(2).

Reporting panel members

CA.147 33.—(1) The persons who are members of the MMC immediately before the commencement date are on that date to become members of the Commission as if they had been duly appointed under paragraph 2(1)(b).

(2) Each of them is to hold office as a member for the remainder of the period for which he was appointed as a member of the MMC and on the terms on which he was so appointed.

Specialist panel members

CA.148 34.—(1) The persons who are members of the MMC immediately before the commencement date by virtue of appointments made under any of the enactments mentioned

596

in paragraph 2(1)(d) are on that date to become members of the Commission as if they had been duly appointed to the Commission under the enactment in question.

(2) Each of them is to hold office as a member for such period and on such terms as the Secretary of State may determine.

Secretary

35. The person who is the secretary of the MMC immediately before the commencement date is on that date to become the secretary of the Commission as if duly appointed under paragraph 9, on the same terms and conditions. **CA.149**

Council

36.—(1) The members who become deputy chairmen of the Commission under paragraph 32 are also to become members of the Council as if they had been duly appointed under paragraph 5(2)(c). **CA.150**

(2) Each of them is to hold office as a member of the Council for such period as the Secretary of State determines.

SCHEDULE 8
APPEALS

PART I
GENERAL

Interpretation

1. In this Schedule— **CA.151**

'the chairman' means a person appointed as chairman of a tribunal in accordance with paragraph 27(2)(a) of Schedule 7;

'the President' means the President of the Competition Commission Appeal Tribunals appointed under paragraph 4 of Schedule 7;

'rules' means rules made by the Secretary of State under section 48;

'specified' means specified in rules;

'tribunal' means an appeal tribunal constituted in accordance with paragraph 27 of Schedule 7.

General procedure

2.—(1) An appeal to the Competition Commission must be made by sending a notice of appeal to the Commission within the specified period. **CA.152**

(2) The notice of appeal must set out the grounds of appeal in sufficient detail to indicate—

(a) under which provision of this Act the appeal is brought;

(b) to what extent (if any) the appellant contends that the decision against, or with respect to which, the appeal is brought was based on an error of fact or was wrong in law; and

(c) to what extent (if any) the appellant is appealing against the Director's exercise of his discretion in making the disputed decision.

(3) The tribunal may give an appellant leave to amend the grounds of appeal identified in the notice of appeal.

Decisions of the tribunal

CA.153 3.—(1) The tribunal must determine the appeal on the merits by reference to the grounds of appeal set out in the notice of appeal.

(2) The tribunal may confirm or set aside the decision which is the subject of the appeal, or any part of it, and may—

(a) remit the matter to the Director;

(b) impose or revoke, or vary the amount of, a penalty;

(c) grant or cancel an individual exemption or vary any conditions or obligations imposed in relation to the exemption by the Director;

(d) give such directions, or take such other steps, as the Director could himself have given or taken; or

(e) make any other decision which the Director could himself have made.

(3) Any decision of the tribunal on an appeal has the same effect, and may be enforced in the same manner, as a decision of the Director.

(4) If the tribunal confirms the decision which is the subject of the appeal it may nevertheless set aside any finding of fact on which the decision was based.

CA.154 4.—(1) A decision of the tribunal may be taken by a majority.

(2) The decision must—

(a) state whether it was unanimous or taken by a majority; and

(b) be recorded in a document which—

(i) contains a statement of the reasons for the decision; and

(ii) is signed and dated by the chairman of the tribunal.

(3) When the tribunal is preparing the document mentioned in sub-paragraph (2)(b), section 56 is to apply to the tribunal as it applies to the Director.

(4) The President must make such arrangements for the publication of the tribunal's decision as he considers appropriate.

PART II
RULES

Registrar of Appeal Tribunals

CA.155 5.—(1) Rules may provide for the appointment by the Competition Commission, with the approval of the Secretary of State, of a Registrar of Appeal Tribunals.

(2) The rules may, in particular—

(a) specify the qualifications for appointment as Registrar; and

(b) provide for specified functions relating to appeals to be exercised by the Registrar in specified circumstances.

Notice of appeal

6. Rules may make provision— **CA.156**

(a) as to the period within which appeals must be brought;

(b) as to the form of the notice of appeal and as to the information which must be given in the notice;

(c) with respect to amendment of a notice of appeal;

(d) with respect to acknowledgement of a notice of appeal.

Response to the appeal

7. Rules may provide for the tribunal to reject an appeal if— **CA.157**

(a) it considers that the notice of appeal reveals no valid ground of appeal; or

(b) it is satisfied that the appellant has habitually and persistently and without any reasonable ground—

　(i) instituted vexatious proceedings, whether against the same person or against different persons; or

　(ii) made vexatious applications in any proceedings.

Pre-hearing reviews and preliminary matters

8.—(1) Rules may make provision— **CA.158**

(a) for the carrying-out by the tribunal of a preliminary consideration of proceedings (a 'pre-hearing review'); and

(b) for enabling such powers to be exercised in connection with a pre-hearing review as may be specified.

(2) If rules make provision of the kind mentioned in sub-paragraph (1), they may also include—

(a) provision for security; and

(b) supplemental provision.

(3) In sub-paragraph (2) 'provision for security' means provision authorising a tribunal carrying out a pre-hearing review under the rules, in specified circumstances, to make an order requiring a party to the proceedings, if he wishes to continue to participate in them, to pay a deposit of an amount not exceeding such sum—

(a) as may be specified; or

(b) as may be calculated in accordance with specified provisions.

(4) In sub-paragraph (2) 'supplemental provision' means any provision as to—

(a) the manner in which the amount of such a deposit is to be determined;

(b) the consequences of non-payment of such a deposit; and

(c) the circumstances in which any such deposit, or any part of it, may be—

    (i) refunded to the person who paid it; or

    (ii) paid to another party to the proceedings.

Conduct of the hearing

CA.159 9.—(1) Rules may make provision—

(a) as to the manner in which appeals are to be conducted, including provision for any hearing to be held in private if the tribunal considers it appropriate because it may be considering information of a kind to which section 56 applies;

(b) as to the persons entitled to appear on behalf of the parties;

(c) for requiring persons to attend to give evidence and produce documents and for authorising the administration of oaths to witnesses;

(d) as to the evidence which may be required or admitted in proceedings before the tribunal and the extent to which it should be oral or written;

(e) allowing the tribunal to fix time limits with respect to any aspect of the proceedings before it and to extend any time limit (whether or not it has expired);

(f) for enabling the tribunal to refer a matter back to the Director if it appears to the tribunal that the matter has not been adequately investigated;

(g) for enabling the tribunal, on the application of any party to the proceedings before it or on its own initiative—

    (i) in England or Wales or Northern Ireland, to order the disclosure between, or the production by, the parties of documents or classes of documents;

    (ii) in Scotland, to order such recovery or inspection of documents as might be ordered by a sheriff;

(h) for the appointment of experts for the purposes of any proceedings before the tribunal;

(i) for the award of costs or expenses, including any allowances payable to persons in connection with their attendance before the tribunal;

(j) for taxing or otherwise settling any costs or expenses directed to be paid by the tribunal and for the enforcement of any such direction.

(2) A person who without reasonable excuse fails to comply with—

(a) any requirement imposed by virtue of sub-paragraph 91)(c); or

(b) any requirement with respect to the disclosure, production, recovery or inspection of documents which is imposed by virtue of sub-paragraph (1)(g),

is guilty of an offence and liable on summary conviction to a fine not exceeding level 3 on the standard scale.

Interest

CA.160 10.—(1) Rules may make provision—

(a) as to the circumstances in which the tribunal may order that interest is payable;

(b) for the manner in which and the periods by reference to which interest is to be calculated and paid.

(2) The rules may, in particular, provide that compound interest is to be payable if the tribunal—

(a) upholds a decision of the Director to impose a penalty; or

(b) does not reduce a penalty so imposed by more than a specified percentage,

but in such a case the rules may not provide that interest is to be payable in respect of any period before the date on which the appeal was brought.

Fees

11.—(1) Rules may provide— **CA.161**

(a) for fees to be chargeable in respect of specified costs of proceedings before the tribunal;

(b) for the amount of such costs to be determined by the tribunal.

(2) Any sums received in consequence of rules under this paragraph are to be paid into the Consolidated Fund.

Withdrawing an appeal

12. Rules may make provision— **CA.162**

(a) that a party who has brought an appeal may not withdraw it without the leave of—

(i) the tribunal, or

(ii) in specified circumstances, the President or the Registrar;

(b) for the tribunal to grant leave to withdraw the appeal on such conditions as it considers appropriate;

(c) enabling the tribunal to publish any decision which it could have made had the appeal not been withdrawn;

(d) as to the effect of withdrawal of an appeal;

(e) as to any procedure to be followed if parties to proceedings on an appeal agree to settle.

Interim orders

13.—(1) Rules may provide for the tribunal to make an order ('an interim order') grant- **CA.163**
ing, on an interim basis, any remedy which the tribunal would have power to grant in its final decision.

(2) An interim order may, in particular, suspend the effect of a decision made by the Director or vary the conditions or obligations attached to an exemption.

(3) Rules may also make provision giving the tribunal powers similar to those given to the Director by section 35.

CA.164   14. Rules may make provision—

    (a) for a person who is not a party to proceedings on an appeal to be joined in those proceedings;

    (b) for appeals to be consolidated on such terms as the tribunal thinks appropriate in such circumstances as may be specified.

SCHEDULE 9
DIRECTOR'S RULES

General

CA.165   1. In this Schedule—

'application for guidance' means an application for guidance under section 13 or 21;

'application for a decision' means an application for a decision under section 14 or 22;

'guidance' means guidance given under section 13 or 21;

'rules' means rules made by the Director under section 51; and

'specified' means specified in rules.

Applications

CA.166   2. Rules may make provision—

    (a) as to the form and manner in which an application for guidance or an application for a decision must be made;

    (b) for the procedure to be followed in dealing with the application;

    (c) for the application to be dealt with in accordance with a timetable;

    (d) as to the documents and information which must be given to the Director in connection with the application;

    (e) requiring the applicant to give such notice of the application, to such other persons, as may be specified;

    (f) as to the consequences of a failure to comply with any rule made by virtue of sub-paragraph (e);

    (g) as to the procedure to be followed when the application is subject to the concurrent jurisdiction of the Director and a regulator.

Provisional decisions

CA.167   3. Rules may make provision as to the procedure to be followed by the Director when making a provisional decision under paragraph 3 of Schedule 5 or paragraph 3 of Schedule 6.

Guidance

CA.168   4. Rules may make provision as to—

    (a) the form and manner in which guidance is to be given;

(b) the procedure to be followed if—

    (i) the Director takes further action with respect to an agreement after giving guidance that it is not likely to infringe the Chapter I prohibition; or

    (ii) the Director takes further action with respect to conduct after giving guidance that it is not likely to infringe the Chapter II prohibition.

Decisions

5.—(1) Rules may make provision as to—   **CA.169**

    (a) the form and manner in which notice of any decision is to be given;

    (b) the person or persons to whom the notice is to be given;

    (c) the manner in which the Director is to publish a decision;

    (d) the procedure to be followed if—

      (i) the Director takes further action with respect to an agreement after having decided that it does not infringe the Chapter I prohibition; or

      (ii) the Director takes further action with respect to conduct after having decided that it does not infringe the Chapter II prohibition.

(2) In this paragraph 'decision' means a decision of the Director (whether or not made on an application)—

    (a) as to whether or not an agreement has infringed the Chapter I prohibition; or

    (b) as to whether or not conduct has infringed the Chapter II prohibition,

and, in the case of an application for a decision under section 14 which includes a request for an individual exemption, includes a decision as to whether or not to grant the exemption.

Individual exemptions

6. Rules may make provision as to—   **CA.170**

    (a) the procedure to be followed by the Director when deciding whether, in accordance with section 5—

      (i) to cancel an individual exemption that he has granted;

      (ii) to vary or remove any of its conditions or obligations; or

      (iii) to impose additional conditions or obligations;

    (b) the form and manner in which notice of such a decision is to be given.

7. Rules may make provision as to—

    (a) the form and manner in which an application under section 4(6) for the extension of an individual exemption is to be made;

    (b) the circumstances in which the Director will consider such an application;

    (c) the procedure to be followed by the Director when deciding whether to grant such an application;

    (d) the form and manner in which notice of such a decision is to be given.

CA.171 8. Rules may make provision as to—

(a) the form and manner in which notice of an agreement is to be given to the Director under subsection (1) of section 7;

(b) the procedure to be followed by the Director if he is acting under subsection (2) of that section;

(c) as to the procedure to be followed by the Director if he cancels a block exemption.

Parallel exemptions

CA.172 9. Rules may make provision as to—

(a) the circumstances in which the Director may—

(i) impose conditions or obligations in relation to a parallel exemption;

(ii) vary or remove any such conditions or obligations;

(iii) impose additional conditions or obligations; or

(iv) cancel the exemption;

(b) as to the procedure to be followed by the Director if he is acting under section 10(5);

(c) the form and manner in which notice of a decision to take any of the steps in subparagraph (a) is to be given;

(d) the circumstances in which an exemption may be cancelled with retrospective effect.

Section 11 exemptions

CA.173 10. Rules may, with respect to any exemption provided by regulations made under section 11, make provision similar to that made with respect to parallel exemptions by section 10 or by rules under paragraph 9.

Directions withdrawing exclusions

CA.174 11. Rules may make provision as to the factors which the Director may take into account when he is determining the date on which a direction given under paragraph 4(1) of Schedule 1 or paragraph 2(3) or 9(3) of Schedule 3 is to have effect.

Disclosure of information

CA.175 12.—(1) Rules may make provision as to the circumstances in which the Director is to be required, before disclosing information given to him by a third party in connection with the exercise of any of the Director's functions under Part I, to give notice, and an opportunity to make representations, to the third party.

(2) In relation to the agreement (or conduct) concerned, 'third party' means a person who is not a party to the agreement (or who has not engaged in the conduct).

Applications made under section 47

CA.176 13. Rules may make provision as to—

(a) the period within which an application under section 47(1) must be made;

(b) the procedure to be followed by the Director in dealing with the application;

(c) the person or persons to whom notice of the Director's response to the application is to be given.

Enforcement

14. Rules may make provision as to the procedure to be followed when the Director takes action under any of sections 32 to 41 with respect to the enforcement of the provisions of this Part. **CA.177**

SCHEDULE 10
REGULATORS

PART I
MONOPOLIES

1. The amendments of the Fair Trading Act 1973 made by sections 66 and 67 of this Act are to have effect, not only in relation to the jurisdiction of the Director under the provisions amended, but also in relation to the jurisdiction under those provisions of each of the following— **CA.178**

(a) the Director General of Telecommunications;

(b) the Director General of Electricity Supply;

(c) the Director General of Electricity Supply for Northern Ireland;

(d) the Director General of Water Services;

(e) the Rail Regulator;

(f) the Director General of Gas Supply; and

(g) the Director General of Gas for Northern Ireland.

PART II
THE PROHIBITIONS

Telecommunications

2.—(1) In consequence of the repeal by this Act of provisions of the Competition Act 1980, the functions transferred by subsection (3) of section 50 of the Telecommunications Act 1984 (functions under 1973 and 1980 Acts) are no longer exercisable by the Director General of Telecommunications. **CA.179**

(2) Accordingly, that Act is amended as follows.

(3) In section 3 (general duties of Secretary of State and Director), in subsection (3)(b), for 'section 50' substitute 'section 50(1) or (2)'.

(4) In section 3, after subsection (3A), insert—

'(3B) Subsections (1) and (2) above do not apply in relation to anything done by the Director in exercise of functions assigned to him by section 50(3) below ("Competition Act functions").'

(3C) The Director may nevertheless, when exercising any Competition Act function, have regard to any matter in respect of which a duty is imposed by subsection (1) or 92) above ("a general matter"), if it is a matter to which the Director General of Fair Trading could have regard when exercising that function; but that is not to be taken as implying that, in relation to any of the matters mentioned in subsection (3) or (3A) above, regard may not be had to any general matter.'

(5) Section 50 is amended as follows.

(6) For subsection (3) substitute—

'(3) The Director shall be entitled to exercise, concurrently with the director General of Fair Trading, the functions of that Director under the provisions of Part I of the Competition Act 1998 (other than sections 38(1) to (6) and 51), so far as relating to—

    (a) agreements, decisions or concerted practices of the kind mentioned in section 2(1) of that Act; or

    (b) conduct of the kind mentioned in section 18(1) of that Act,

which relate to commercial activities connected with telecommunications.

(3A) So far as necessary for the purposes of, or in connection with, the provisions of subsection (3) above, references in Part I of the Competition Act 1998 to the Director General of Fair Trading are to be read as including a reference to the Director (except in sections 38(1) to (6), 51, 52(6) and (8) and 54 of that Act and in any other provision of that Act where the context otherwise requires).'

(7) In subsection (4), omit paragraph (c) and the 'and' immediately after it.

(8) In subsection (5), omit 'or (3)'.

(9) In subsection (6), for paragraph (b) substitute—

'(b) Part I of the Competition Act 1998 (other than sections 38(1) to (6) and 51),'.

(10) In subsection (7), omit 'or the 1980 Act'.

Gas

CA.180 3.—(1) In consequence of the repeal by this Act of provisions of the Competition Act 1980, the functions transferred by subsection (3) of section 36A of the Gas Act 1986 (functions with respect to competition) are no longer exercisable by the Director General of Gas Supply.

(2) Accordingly, that Act is amended as follows.

(3) In section 4 (general duties of Secretary of State and Director), after subsection (3), insert—

'(3A) Subsections (1) to (3) above and section 4A below do not apply in relation to anything done by the Director in the exercise of functions assigned to him by section 36A below ("Competition Act functions").

(3B) The Director may nevertheless, when exercising any Competition Act function, have regard to any matter in respect of which a duty is imposed by any of subsections (1) to (3) above or section 4A below, if it is a matter to which the Director General of Fair Trading could have regard when exercising that function.'

(4) Section 36A is amended as follows.

(5) For subsection (3) substitute—

'(3) The Director shall be entitled to exercise, concurrently with the Director General of Fair Trading, the functions of that Director under the provisions of Part I of the Competition Act 1998 (other than sections 38(1) to (6) and 51), so far as relating to—

(a) agreements, decisions or concerted practices of the kind mentioned in section 2(1) of that Act; or

(b) conduct of the kind mentioned in section 18(1) of that Act,

which relate to the carrying on of activities to which this subsection applies.

(3A) So far as necessary for the purposes of, or in connection with, the provisions of subsection (3) above, references in Part I of the Competition Act 1998 to the Director General of Fair Trading are to be read as including a reference to the Director (except in sections 38(1) to (6), 51, 52(6) and (8) and 54 of that Act and in any other provision of that Act where the context otherwise requires).'

(6) In subsection (5)—

(a) for 'transferred by', in each place, substitute 'mentioned in';

(b) after paragraph (b), insert 'and';

(c) omit paragraph (d) and the 'and' immediately before it.

(7) In subsection (6), omit 'or (3)'.

(8) In subsection (7), for paragraph (b) substitute—

'(b) Part I of the Competition Act 1998 (other than sections 38(1) to (6) and 51),'.

(9) In subsection (8)—

(a) omit 'or under the 1980 Act';

(b) for 'or (3) above' substitute 'above and paragraph 1 of Schedule 10 to the Competition Act 1998'.

(10) In subsection (9), omit 'or the 1980 Act'.

(11) In subsection (10), for the words from 'transferred' to the end substitute 'mentioned in subsection (2) or (3) above.'

Electricity

4.—(1) In consequence of the repeal by this Act of provisions of the Competition Act 1980, the functions transferred by subsection (3) of section 43 of the Electricity Act 1989 (functions with respect to competition) are no longer exercisable by the Director General of Electricity Supply.   **CA.181**

(2) Accordingly, that Act is amended as follows.

(3) In section 3 (general duties of Secretary of State and Director), after subsection (6), insert—

> '(6A) Subsections (1) to (5) above do not apply in relation to anything done by the Director in the exercise of functions assigned to him by section 43(3) below ("Competition Act functions").
>
> (6B) The Director may nevertheless, when exercising any Competition Act function, have regard to any matter in respect of which a duty is imposed by any of subsections (1) to (5) above ("a general matter"), if it is a matter to which the Director General of Fair Trading could have regard when exercising that function; but that is not to be taken as implying that, in the exercise of any function mentioned in subsection (6) above, regard may not be had to any general matter.'

(4) Section 43 is amended as follows.

(5) For subsection (3) substitute—

> '(3) The Director shall be entitled to exercise, concurrently with the Director General of Fair Trading, the functions of that Director under the provisions of Part I of the Competition Act 1998 (other than sections 38(1) to (6) and 51), so far as relating to—
>
> > (a) agreements, decisions or concerted practices of the kind mentioned in section 2(1) of that Act; or
> >
> > (b) conduct of the kind mentioned in section 18(1) of that Act,
>
> which relate to Commercial activities connected with the generation, transmission or supply of electricity.
>
> (3A) So far as necessary for the purposes of, or in connection with, the provisions of subsection (3) above, references in Part I of the Competition Act 1998 to the Director General of Fair Trading are to be read as including a reference to the Director (except in sections 38(1) to (6), 51, 52(6) and (8) and 54 of that Act and in any other provision of that Act where the context otherwise requires).'

(6) In subsection (4), omit paragraph (c) and the 'and' immediately after it.

(7) In subsection (6), for paragraph (b) substitute—

> '(b) Part I of the Competition Act 1998 (other than sections 38(1) to (6) and 51),'.

(9) In subsection (7), omit 'or the 1980 Act'.

Water

CA.182 5.—(1) In consequence of the repeal by this Act of provisions of the Competition Act 1980, the functions exercisable by virtue of subsection (3) of section 31 of the Water Industry Act 1991 (functions of Director with respect to competition) are no longer exercisable by the Director General of Water Services.

(2) Accordingly, that Act is amended as follows.

(3) In section 2 (general duties with respect to water industry), in subsection (6)(a), at the beginning, insert 'subject to subsection (6A) below'.

(4) In section 2, after subsection (6), insert—

'(6A) Subsections (2) to (4) above do not apply in relation to anything done by the Director in exercise of functions assigned to him by section 31(3) below ("Competition Act functions").

(6B) The Director may nevertheless, when exercising any competition Act function, have regard to any matter in respect of which a duty is imposed by any of subsections (2) to (4) above, if it is a matter to which the Director General of Fair Trading could have regard when exercising that function.'

(5) Section 31 is amended as follows.

(6) For subsection (3) substitute—

'(3) The Director shall be entitled to exercise, concurrently with the Director General of Fair Trading, the functions of that Director under the provisions of Part I of the Competition Act 1998 (other than sections 38(1) to (6) and 51), so far as relating to—

(a) agreements, decisions or concerted practices of the kind mentioned in section 2(1) of that Act; or

(b) conduct of the kind mentioned in section 18(1) of that Act,

which relate to commercial activities connected with the supply of water or securing a supply of water or with the provision or securing of sewerage services.'

(7) In subsection (4)—

(a) for 'to (3)' substitute 'and (2)';

(b) omit paragraph (c) and the 'and' immediately before it.

(8) After subsection (4), insert—

'(4A) So far as necessary for the purposes of, or in connection with, the provisions of subsection (3) above, references in Part I of the Competition Act 1998 to the Director General of Fair Trading are to be read as including a reference to the Director (except in sections 38(1) to (6), 51, 52(6) and (8) and 54 of that Act and in any other provision of that Act where the context otherwise requires).'

(9) In subsection (5), omit 'or in subsection (3) above'.

(10) In subsection (6) omit 'or in subsection (3) above'.

(11) In subsection (7), omit 'or (3)'.

(12) In subsection (8), for paragraph (b) substitute—

'(b) Part I of the Competition Act 1998 (other than sections 38(1) to (6) and 51),'.

(13) In subsection (9), omit 'or the 1980 Act'.

Railways

CA.183 6.—(1) In consequence of the repeal by this Act of provisions of the Competition Act 1980, the functions transferred by subsection (3) of section 67 of the Railways Act 1993 (respective functions of the Regulator and the Director etc) are no longer exercisable by the Rail Regulator.

(2) Accordingly, that Act is amended as follows.

(3) In section 4 (general duties of the Secretary of State and the Regulator), after subsection (7), insert—

'(7A) Subsections (1) to (6) above do not apply in relation to anything done by the Regulator in the exercise of functions assigned to him by section 67(3) below ("Competition Act functions").

(7B) The Regulator may nevertheless, when exercising any Competition Act function, have regard to any matter in respect of which a duty is imposed by any of subsections (1) to (6) above, if it is a matter to which the Director General of Fair Trading could have regard when exercising that function.'

(4) Section 67 is amended as follows.

(5) For subsection (3) substitute—

'(3) The Regulator shall be entitled to exercise, concurrently with the Director, the functions of the Director under the provisions of Part I of the Competition Act 1998 (other than sections 38(1) to (6) and 51), so far as relating to—

(a) agreements, decisions or concerted practices of the kind mentioned in section 2(1) of that Act; or

(b) conduct of the kind mentioned in section 18(1) of that Act,

which relate to the supply of railway services.

(3A) So far as necessary for the purposes of, or in connection with, the provisions of subsection for the purposes of, or in connection with, the provisions of subsection (3) above, references in Part I of the Competition Act 1998 to the Director are to be read as including a reference to the Regulator (except in sections 38(1) to (6), 51, 52(6) and (8) and 54 of that Act and in any other provision of that Act where the context otherwise requires).'

(6) In subsection (4), omit paragraph (c) and the 'and' immediately after it.

(7) In subsection (6)(a), omit 'or (3)'.

(8) In subsection (8), for paragraph (b) substitute—

'(b) Part I of the Competition Act 1998 (other than sections 38(1) to (6) and 51),'.

(9) In subsection (9)—

(a) omit 'or under the 1980 Act';

(b) for 'or (3) above' substitute 'above and paragraph 1 of Schedule 10 to the Competition Act 1998'.

PART III

THE PROHIBITIONS: NORTHERN IRELAND

Electricity

7.—(1) In consequence of the repeal by this Act of the provisions of the Competition Act 1980, the functions transferred by paragraph (3) of Article 46 of the Electricity (Northern Ireland) Order 1992 (functions with respect to competition) are no longer exercisable by the Director General of Electricity Supply for Northern Ireland.

CA.184

(2) Accordingly, that Order is amended as follows.

(3) In Article 6 (general duties of the Director), after paragraph (2), add—

'(3) Paragraph (1) does not apply in relation to anything done by the Director in the exercise of functions assigned to him by Article 46(3) ("Competition Act functions").

(4) The Director may nevertheless, when exercising any Competition Act function, have regard to any matter in respect of which a duty is imposed by paragraph (1) ("a general matter"), if it is a matter to which the Director General of Fair Trading could have regard when exercising that function; but that is not to be taken as implying that, in the exercise of any function mentioned in Article 4(7) or paragraph (2), regard may not be had to any general matter.'

(4) Article 46 is amended as follows.

(5) For paragraph (3) substitute—

'(3) The Director shall be entitled to exercise, concurrently with the Director General of Fair Trading, the functions of that Director under the provisions of Part I of the Competition Act 1998 (other than sections 38(1) to (6) and 51), so far as relating to—

(a) agreements, decisions or concerted practices of the kind mentioned in section 2(1) of that Act; or

(b) conduct of the kind mentioned in section 18(1) of that Act,

which relate to commercial activities connected with the generation, transmission or supply of electricity.

(3A) So far as necessary for the purposes of, or in connection with, the provisions of paragraph (3), references in Part I of the Competition Act 1998 to the Director General of Fair Trading are to be read as including a reference to the Director (except in sections 38(1) to (6), 51, 52(6) and (8) and 54 of that Act and in any other provision of that Act where the context otherwise requires).'

(6) In paragraph (4), omit sub-paragraph (c) and the 'and' immediately after it.

(7) In paragraph (5), omit 'or (3)'.

(8) In paragraph (6), for sub-paragraph (b) substitute—

'(b) Part I of the Competition Act 1998 (other than sections 38(1) to (6) and 51),'.

(9) In paragraph (7), omit 'or the 1980 Act'.

Gas

CA.185 8.—(1) In consequence of the repeal by this Act of provisions of the Competition Act 1980, the functions transferred by paragraph (3) of Article 23 of the Gas (Northern Ireland) Order 1996 (functions with respect to competition) are no longer exercisable by the Director General of Gas for Northern Ireland.

(2) Accordingly, that Order is amended as follows.

(3) In Article 5 (general duties of the Department and Director), after paragraph (4), insert—

'(4A) Paragraphs (2) to (4) do not apply in relation to anything done by the Director in the exercise of functions assigned to him by Article 23(3) ("Competition Act functions").

(4B) The Director may nevertheless, when exercising any Competition Act function, have regard to any matter in respect of which a duty is imposed by any of paragraphs (2) to (4), if it is a matter to which the Director General of Fair Trading could have regard when exercising that function.'

(4) Article 23 is amended as follows.

(5) For paragraph (3) substitute—

'(3) The Director shall be entitled to exercise, concurrently with the Director General of Fair Trading, the functions of that Director under the provisions of Part I of the Competition Act 1998 (other than sections 38(1) to (6) and 51), so far as relating to—

(a) agreements, decisions or concerted practices of the kind mentioned in section 2(1) of that Act, or

(b) conduct of the kind mentioned in section 18(1) of that Act,

connected with the conveyance, storage or supply of gas.

(3A) So far as necessary for the purposes of, or in connection with, the provisions of paragraph (3), references in Part I of the Competition Act 1998 to the Director General of Fair Trading are to be read as including a reference to the Director (except in sections 38(1) to (6), 51, 52(6) and (8) and 54 of that Act and in any other provision of that Act where the context otherwise requires).'

(6) In paragraph (40—

(a) for 'transferred by', in each place, substitute 'mentioned in';

(b) after sub-paragraph (b), insert 'and';

(c) omit sub-paragraph (d) and the 'and' immediately before it.

(7) In paragraph (5), omit 'or (3)'.

(8) In paragraph (6), for sub-paragraph (b) substitute—

'(b) Part I of the Competition Act 1998 (other than sections 38(1) to (6) and 51),'.

(9) In paragraph (7)—

    (a) omit 'or under the 1980 Act';

    (b) for 'or (3)' substitute 'and paragraph 1 of Schedule 10 to the Competition Act 1998'.

(10) In paragraph (8), omit 'or the 1980 Act'.

(11) In paragraph (9), for the words from 'transferred' to the end substitute 'mentioned in paragraph (2) or (3)'.

PART IV

UTILITIES: MINOR AND CONSEQUENTIAL AMENDMENTS

The Telecommunications Act 1984 (c. 12)

9.—(1) The Telecommunications Act 1984 is amended as follows.   **CA.186**

(2) In section 13 (licence modification references to Competition Commission) for subsections (9) and (10) substitute—

    '(9) The provisions mentioned in subsection (9A) are to apply in relation to references under this section as if—

        (a) the functions of the Competition Commission in relation to those references were functions under the Fair Trading Act 1973 (in this Act referred to as "the 1973 Act");

        (b) the expression "merger reference" included a reference under this section;

        (c) in section 70 of the 1973 Act—

            (i) references to the Secretary of State were references to the Director, and

            (ii) the reference to three months were a reference to six months.

    (9A) The provisions are—

        (a) sections 70 (time limit for report on merger) and 85 (attendance of witnesses and production of documents) of the 1973 Act;

        (b) Part II of Schedule 7 to the Competition Act 1998 (performance of the Competition Commission's general functions); and

        (c) section 24 of the Competition Act 1980 (modification of provisions about performance of such functions).

    (10) For the purposes of references under this section, the Secretary of State is to appoint not less than three members of the Competition Commission.

    (10A) In selecting a group to perform the Commission's functions in relation to any such reference, the chairman of the Commission must select up to three of the members appointed under subsection (10) to be members of the group.'

(3) In section 14, omit subsection (2) (which falls with the repeal of the Restrictive Trade Practices Act 1976).

(4) In section 16 (securing compliance with licence conditions), in subsection (5), after paragraph (a), omit 'or' and after paragraph (b), insert 'or

613

(c) that the most appropriate way of proceeding is under the Competition Act 1998.'

(5) In section 50 (functions under 1973 and 1980 Acts), after subsection (6), insert—

'(6A) Section 93B of the 1973 Act (offences of supplying false or misleading information) is to have effect so far as relating to functions exercisable by the Director by virtue of—

(a) subsection (2) above and paragraph 1 of Schedule 10 to the Competition Act 1998; or

(b) paragraph 1 of Schedule 2 to the Deregulation and Contracting Out Act 1994,

as if the reference in section 93B(1)(a) to the Director General of Fair Trading included a reference to the Director.'

(6) In section 95 (modification by orders under other enactments)—

(a) in subsection (1), omit 'or section 10(2)(a) of the 1980 Act';

(b) in subsection (2)—

(i) after paragraph (a), insert 'or';

(ii) omit paragraph (c) and the 'or' immediately before it;

(c) in subsection (3), omit 'or the 1980 Act'.

(7) In section 101(3) (general restrictions on disclosure of information)—

(a) omit paragraphs (d) and (e) (which refer to the Restrictive Trade Practices Act 1976 and the Resale Prices act 1976);

(b) after paragraph (m), insert—

'(n) and the Competition Act 1998'.

(8) At the end of section 101, insert—

'(6) Information obtained by the Director in the exercise of functions which are exercisable concurrently with the Director General of Fair Trading under Part I of the Competition Act 1998 is subject to sections 55 and 56 of that Act (disclosure) and not to subsections (1) to (5) of this section.'

The Gas Act 1986 (c. 44)

CA.187 10.—(1) The Gas Act 1986 is amended as follows.

(2) In section 24 (modification references to the Competition Commission), for subsection (7) substitute—

'(7) The provisions mentioned in subsection (7A) are to apply in relation to references under this section as if—

(a) the functions of the Competition Commission in relation to those references were functions under the Fair Trading Act 1973;

(b) the expression 'merger reference' included a reference under this section;

614

(c) in section 70 of the Fair Trading Act 1973—

(i) references to the Secretary of State were a references to the Director, and

(ii) the reference to three months were a reference to six months.

(7A) The provisions are—

(a) sections 70 (time limit for report on merger) and 85 (attendance of witnesses and production of documents) of the Fair Trading Act 1973;

(b) Part II of Schedule 7 to the Competition Act 1998 (performance of the Competition Commission's general functions); and

(c) section 24 of the Competition Act 1980 (modification of provisions about performance of such functions).'

(3) In section 25, omit subsection (2) (which falls with the repeal of the Restrictive Trade Practices Act 1976).

(4) In section 27 (modification by order under other enactments)—

(a) in subsection (1), omit 'or section 10(2)(a) of the Competition Act 1980';

(b) in subsection (3)(a), omit from 'or' to 'competition reference';

(c) in subsection (6), omit 'or the said Act of 1980'.

(5) In section 28 (orders for securing compliance with certain provisions), in subsection (5), after paragraph (aa), omit 'or' and after paragraph (b), insert 'or

(c) that the most appropriate way of proceeding is under the Competition Act 1998.'

(6) In section 42(3) (general restrictions on disclosure of information)—

(a) omit paragraphs (e) and (f) (which refer to the Restrictive Trade Practices Act 1976 and the Resale Prices Act 1976);

(b) after paragraph (b), insert—

'(o) the Competition Act 1998'.

(7) At the end of section 42, insert—

'(7) Information obtained by the Director in the exercise of functions which are exercisable concurrently with the Director General of Fair Trading under Part I of the Competition Act 1998 is subject to sections 55 and 56 of that Act (disclosure) and not to subsections (1) to (6) of this section.'

The Water Act 1989 (c. 15)

11. In section 174(3) of the Water Act 1989 (general restrictions on disclosure of information)— **CA.188**

(a) omit paragraphs (d) and (e) (which refer to the Restrictive Trade Practices Act 1976 and the Resale Prices Act 1976);

(b) after paragraph (l), insert—

'(ll) the Competition Act 1998'.

The Electricity Act 1989 (c. 29)

CA.189 12.—(1) The Electricity Act 1989 is amended as follows.

(2) In section 12 (modification references to Competition Commission), for subsections (8) and 99) substitute—

'(8) The provisions mentioned in subsection (8A) are to apply in relation to references under this section as if—

(a) the functions of the Competition Commission in relation to those references were functions under the 1973 Act;

(b) the expression "merger reference" included a reference under this section;

(c) in section 70 of the 1973 Act—

(i) references to the Secretary of State were references to the Director, and

(ii) the reference to three months were a reference to six months.

(8A) The provisions are—

(a) sections 70 (time limit for report on merger) and 85 (attendance of witnesses and production of documents) of the 1973 Act;

(b) Part II of Schedule 7 to the Competition Act 1998 (performance of the Competition Commission's general functions); and

(c) section 24 of the 1980 Act (modification of provisions about performance of such functions).

(9) For the purposes of references under this section, the Secretary of State is to appoint not less than eight members of the Competition Commission.

(9A) In selecting a group to perform the Commission's functions in relation to any such reference, the chairman of the Commission must select up to three of the members appointed under subsection (9) to be members of the group.'

(3) In section 13, omit subsection (2) (which falls with the repeal of the Restrictive Trade Practices Act 1976).

(4) In section 15 (modification by order under other enactments)—

(a) in subsection (1), omit paragraph (b) and the 'or' immediately before it;

(b) in subsection (2)—

(i) after paragraph (a), insert 'or';

(ii) omit paragraph (c) and the 'or' immediately before it;

(c) in subsection (3), omit 'or the 1980 Act'.

(5) In section 25 (orders for securing compliance), in subsection (5), after paragraph (b), omit 'or' and after paragraph (c), insert 'or

(d) that the most appropriate way of proceeding is under the Competition Act 1998.'

(6) In section 43 (functions with respect to competition), after subsection (6), insert—

'(6A) Section 93B of the 1973 Act (offences of supplying false or misleading information) is to have effect so far as relating to functions exercisable by the Director by virtue of—

(a) subsection (2) above and paragraph 1 of Schedule 10 to the Competition Act 1998; or

(b) paragraph 4 of Schedule 2 to the Deregulation and Contracting Out Act 1994,

as if the reference in section 93B(1)(a) to the Director General of Fair Trading included a reference to the Director.'

(7) In section 57(3) (general restrictions on disclosure of information)—

(a) omit paragraphs (d) and (e) (which refer to the Restrictive Trade Practices Act 1976 and the Resale Prices Act 1976);

(b) after paragraph (no), insert—

'(nop) the Competition Act 1998'.

(8) At the end of section 57, insert—

'(7) Information obtained by the Director in the exercise of functions which are exercisable concurrently with the Director General of Fair Trading under Part I of the Competition Act 1998 is subject to sections 55 and 56 of that Act (disclosure) and not to subsections (1) to (6) of this section.'

The Water Industry Act 1991 (c. 56)

13.—(1) The Water Industry Act 1991 is amended as follows.   **CA.190**

(2) In section 12(5) (determination under conditions of appointment)—

(a) after 'this Act', insert 'or';

(b) omit 'or the 1980 Act'.

(3) In section 14 (modification references to Competition Commission), for subsections (7) and (8) substitute—

'(7) The provisions mentioned in subsection (7A) are to apply in relation to references under this section as if—

(a) the functions of the Competition Commission in relation to those references were functions under the 1973 Act;

(b) the expression "merger reference" included a reference under this section;

(c) in section 70 of the 1973 Act—

(i) references to the Secretary of State were references to the Director, and

(ii) the reference to three months were a reference to six months.

(7A) The provisions are—

(a) sections 70 (time limit for report on merger) and 85 (attendance of witnesses and production of documents) of the 1973 Act;

(b) Part II of Schedule 7 to the Competition Act 1998 (performance of the Competition Commission's general functions); and

(c) section 24 of the 1980 Act (modification of provisions about performance of such functions).

(8) For the purposes of references under this section, the Secretary of State is to appoint not less than eight members of the Competition Commission.

(8A) In selecting a group to perform the Commission's functions in relation to any such reference, the chairman of the Commission must select one or more of the members appointed under subsection (8) to be members of the group.'

(4) In section 15, omit subsection (2) (which falls with the repeal of the Restrictive Trade Practices Act 1976).

(5) In section 17 (modification by order under other enactments)—

(a) in subsection (1), omit paragraph (b) and the 'or' immediately before it;

(b) in subsection (2)—

(i) after paragraph (a), insert 'or';

(ii) omit paragraph (c) and the 'or' immediately before it;

(c) in subsection (4), omit 'or the 1980 Act'.

(6) In section 19 (exceptions to duty to enforce), after subsection (1), insert—

'(1A) The Director shall not be required to make an enforcement order, or to confirm a provisional enforcement order, if he is satisfied that the most appropriate way of proceeding is under the Competition Act 1998.'

(7) In section 19(3), after 'subsection (1) above', insert 'or, in the case of the Director, is satisfied as mentioned in subsection (1A) above.'

(8) In section 31 (functions of Director with respect to competition), after subsection (8), insert—

'(8A) Section 93B of the 1973 Act (offences of supplying false or misleading information) is to have effect so far as relating to functions exercisable by the Director by virtue of—

(a) subsection (2) above and paragraph 1 of Schedule 10 to the Competition Act 1998; or

(b) paragraph 8 of Schedule 2 to the Deregulation and Contracting Out Act 1994,

as if the reference in section 93B(1)(a) to the Director General of Fair Trading included a reference to the Director.'

(9) After section 206(9) (restriction on disclosure of information), insert—

'(9A) Information obtained by the Director in the exercise of functions which are exercisable concurrently with the Director General of Fair Trading under Part I of the Competition Act 1998 is subject to sections 55 and 56 of that Act (disclosure) and not to subsections (1) to (9) of this section.'

(10) In Schedule 15 (disclosure of information), in Part II (enactments in respect of which disclosure may be made)—

(a) omit the entries relating to the Restrictive Trade Practices Act 1976 and the Resale Prices Act 1976;

(b) after the entry relating to the Railways Act 1993, insert the entry—

'The Competition Act 1998'.

The Water Resources Act 1991 (c. 57)

14. In Schedule 24 to the Water Resources Act 1991 (disclosure of information), in part II (enactments in respect of which disclosure may be made)— **CA.191**

(a) omit the entries relating to the Restrictive Trade Practices Act 1976 and the Resale Prices Act 1976;

(b) after the entry relating to the Coal Industry Act 1994, insert the entry—

'The Competition Act 1998'.

The Railways Act 1993 (c. 43)

15.—(1) The Railways Act 1993 is amended as follows. **CA.192**

(2) In section 13 (modification references to the Competition Commission), for subsection (8) substitute—

'(8) The provisions mentioned in subsection (8A) are to apply in relation to references under this section as if—

(a) the functions of the Competition Commission in relation to those references were functions under the 1973 Act;

(b) the expression "merger reference" included a reference under this section;

(c) in section 70 of the 1973 Act—

(i) references to the Secretary of State were references to the Director, and

(ii) the reference to three months were a reference to six months.

(8A) The provisions are—

(a) sections 70 (time limit for report on merger) and 85 (attendance of witnesses and production of documents) of the 1973 Act;

(b) Part II of Schedule 7 to the Competition Act (performance of the Competition Commission's general functions); and

(c) section 24 of the Competition Act 1980 (in this Part referred to as "the 1980 Act") (modification of provisions about performance of such functions).'

(3) In section 14, omit subsection (2) (which falls with the repeal of the Restrictive Trade Practices Act 1976).

(4) In section 16 (modification by order under other enactments)—

    (a) in subsection (1), omit paragraph (b) and the 'or' immediately before it;

    (b) in subsection (2)—

        (i) after paragraph (a), insert 'or';

        (ii) omit paragraph (c) and the 'or' immediately before it;

    (c) in subsection (5), omit 'or the 1980 Act'.

(5) In section 22, after subsection (6), insert—

    '(6A) Neither the Director General of Fair Trading nor the Regulator may exercise, in respect of an access agreement, the powers given by section 32 (enforcement directions) or section 35(2) (interim directions) of the Competition Act 1998.

    (6B) Subsection (6A) does not apply to the exercise of the powers given by section 35(2) in respect of conduct—

        (a) which is connected with an access agreement; and

        (b) in respect of which section 35(1)(b) of that Act applies.'

(6) In section 55 (orders for securing compliance), after subsection (5), insert—

    '(5A) The Regulator shall not make a final order, or make or confirm a provisional order, in relation to a licence holder or person under closure restrictions if he is satisfied that the most appropriate way of proceeding is under the Competition Act 1998.'

(7) In section 55—

    (a) in subsection (6), after 'subsection (5)', insert 'or (5A)';

    (b) in subsection (11), for 'subsection (10)' substitute 'subsections (5A) and (10)'.

(8) Omit section 131 (modification of Restrictive Trade Practices Act 1976).

(9) In section 145(3) (general restrictions on disclosure of information)—

    (a) omit paragraphs (d) and (e) (which refer to the Restrictive Trade Practices Act 1976 and the Resale Prices Act 1976);

    (b) after paragraph (q), insert—

    '(qq) the Competition Act 1998.'

(10) After section 145(6), insert—

    '(6A) Information obtained by the Regulator in the exercise of functions which are exercisable concurrently with the Director General of Fair Trading under Part I of the Competition Act 1998 is subject to sections 55 and 56 of that Act (disclosure) and not to subsections (1) to (6) of this section.'

The Channel Tunnel Rail Link Act 1996 (c. 61)

CA.193 16.—(1) The Channel Tunnel Rail Link Act 1996 is amended as follows.

(2) In section 21 (duties as to exercise of regulatory functions), in subsection (6), at the end of the paragraph about regulatory functions, insert 'other than any functions assigned to him by virtue of section 67(3) of that Act ("Competition Act functions").

(7) The Regulator may, when exercising any competition Act function, have regard to any matter to which he would have regard if—

(a) he were under the duty imposed by subsection (1) or (2) above in relation to that function; and

(b) the matter is one to which the Director General of Fair Trading could have regard if he were exercising that function.'

(3) In section 22 (restriction of functions in relation to competition etc), for subsection (3) substitute—

'(3) The Rail Regulator shall not be entitled to exercise any functions assigned to him by section 67(3) of the Railways Act 1993 (by virtue of which he exercises concurrently with the Director General of Fair Trading certain functions under Part I of the Competition Act so far as relating to matters connected with the supply of railway services) in relation to—

(a) any agreements, decisions or concerted practices of the kind mentioned in section 2(1) of that Act that have been entered into or taken by, or

(b) any conduct of the kind mentioned in section 18(1) of that Act that has been engaged in by,

a rail link undertaker in connection with the supply of railway services, so far as relating to the rail link.'

PART V
MINOR AND CONSEQUENTIAL AMENDMENTS: NORTHERN IRELAND

The Electricity (Northern Ireland) Order 1992

17.—(1) The Electricity (Northern Ireland) Order 1992 is amended as follows.   **CA.194**

(2) In Article 15 (modification references to Competition Commission), for paragraphs (8) and (9) substitute—

'(8) The provisions mentioned in paragraph (8A) are to apply in relation to references under this Article as if—

(a) the functions of the Competition Commission in relation to those references were functions under the 1973 Act;

(b) "merger reference" included a reference under this Article;

(c) in section 70 of the 1973 Act—

  (i) references to the Secretary of State were references to the Director, and

  (ii) the reference to three months were a reference to six months.

(8A) The provisions are—

(a) sections 70 (time limit for report on merger) and 85 (attendance of witnesses and production of documents) of the 1973 Act;

(b) Part II of Schedule 7 to the Competition Act 1998 (performance of the Competition Commission's general functions); and

(c) section 24 of the 1980 Act (modification of provisions about performance of such functions).

(9) The Secretary of State may appoint members of the Competition Commission for the purposes of references under this Article.

(9A) In selecting a group to perform the Commission's functions in relation to any such reference, the chairman of the Commission must select up to three of the members appointed under paragraph (9) to be members of the group.'

(3) In Article 16, omit paragraph (2) (which falls with the repeal of the Restrictive Trade Practices act 1976).

(4) In Article 18 (modification by order under other statutory provisions)—

(a) in paragraph (1), omit sub-paragraph (b) and the 'or' immediately before it;

(b) in paragraph (20—

(i) after sub-paragraph (a), insert 'or';

(ii) omit sub-paragraph (c) and the 'or' immediately before it;

(c) in paragraph (3), omit 'or the 1980 Act'.

(5) In Article 28 (orders for securing compliance), in paragraph (5), after sub-paragraph (b), omit 'or' and after sub-paragraph (c), insert 'or

(d) that the most appropriate way of proceeding is under the Competition Act 1998.'

(6) In Article 46 (functions with respect to competition), after paragraph (6), insert—

'(6A) Section 93B of the 1973 Act (offences of supplying false or misleading information) is to have effect so far as relating to functions exercisable by the Director by virtue of—

(a) paragraph (2) and paragraph 1 of Schedule 10 to the Competition Act 1998, or

(b) paragraph 5 of Schedule 2 to the Deregulation and Contracting Out Act 1994,

as if the reference in section 93B(1)(a) to the Director General of Fair Trading included a reference to the Director.'

(7) In Article 61(3) (general restrictions on disclosure of information)—

(a) omit sub-paragraphs (f) and (g) (which refer to the Restrictive Trade Practices Act 1976 and the Resale Prices Act 1976);

(b) after sub-paragraph (t), add—

'(u) the Competition Act 1998'.

(8) At the end of Article 61, insert—

'(7) Information obtained by the Director in the exercise of functions which are exercisable concurrently with the Director General of Fair Trading under Part I of the Competition Act 1998 is subject to sections 55 and 56 of that Act (disclosure) and not to paragraphs (1) to (6).'

(9) In Schedule 12, omit paragraph 16 (which amends the Restrictive Trade Practices Act 1976).

The Gas (Northern Ireland) Order 1996

18.—(1) The Gas (Northern Ireland) Order 1996 is amended as follows.   **CA.195**

(2) In Article 15 (modification references to the Competition Commission), for paragraph (9) substitute

'(9) The provisions mentioned in paragraph (9A) are to apply in relation to references under this Article as if—

    (a) the functions of the Competition Commission in relation to those references were functions under the 1973 Act;

    (b) "merger reference" included a reference under this Article;

    (c) in section 70 of the 1973 Act—

        (i) references to the Secretary of State were references to the Director; and

        (ii) the reference to three months were a reference to six months.

(9A) The provisions are—

    (a) sections 70 (time limit for report on merger) and 85 (attendance of witnesses and production of documents) of the 1973 Act;

    (b) Part II of Schedule 7 to the Competition Act 1998 (performance of the Competition Commission's general functions); and

    (c) section 24 of the 1980 Act (modification of provisions about performance of such functions).'

(3) In Article 16, omit paragraph (2) (which falls with the repeal of the Restrictive Trade Practices Act 1976).

(4) In Article 18 (modification by order under other statutory provisions)—

    (a) in paragraph (1), omit sub-paragraph (b) and the 'or' immediately before it;

    (b) in paragraph (3)—

        (i) after sub-paragraph (a), insert 'or';

        (ii) omit sub-paragraph (c) and the 'or' immediately before it;

    (c) in paragraph (5), omit 'or the 1980 Act'.

(5) In Article 19 (orders for securing compliance), in paragraph 95), after sub-paragraph (b), omit 'or' and after sub-paragraph (c), insert 'or

    (d) that the most appropriate way of proceeding is under the Competition Act 1998.'

(6) In Article 44(4) (general restrictions on disclosure of information)—

    (a) omit sub-paragraphs (f) and (g) (which refer to the Restrictive Trade Practices Act 1976 and the Resale Prices Act 1976);

(b) after sub-paragraph (u), add—

'(v) the competition Act 1998'.

(7) At the end of Article 44, insert—

'(8) Information obtained by the Director in the exercise of functions which are exercisable concurrently with the Director General of Fair Trading under Part I of the Competition Act 1998 is subject to sections 55 and 56 of that Act (disclosure) and not to paragraphs (1) to (7).'

SCHEDULE 11

INTERPRETATION OF SECTION 55

Relevant functions

CA.196 1. In section 55(3) 'relevant functions' means any function under—

(a) Part I of any enactment repealed in consequence of Part I;

(b) the Fair Trading Act 1973 (c. 41) or the Competition Act 1980 (c. 21);

(c) the Estate Agents Act 1979 (c. 38);

(d) the Telecommunications Act 1984 (c. 12);

(e) the Gas Act 1986 (c. 44) or the Gas Act 1995 (c. 45);

(f) the Gas (Northern Ireland) Order 1996;

(g) the Airports Act 1986 (c. 31) or Part IV of the Airports (Northern Ireland) Order 1994;

(h) the Financial Services Act 1986 (c. 60);

(i) the Electricity Act 1989 (c. 29) or the Electricity (Northern Ireland) Order 1992;

(j) the Broadcasting Act 1990 (c. 42) or the Broadcasting Act 1996 (c. 55);

(k) the Courts and Legal Services Act 1990 (c. 41);

(l) the Water Industry Act 1991 (c. 56), the Water Resources Act 1991 (c. 57), the Statutory Water Companies Act 1991 (c. 58), the Land Drainage Act 1991 (c. 59) and the Water Consolidation (Consequential Provisions) Act 1991 (c. 60);

(m) the Railways Act 1993 (c. 43);

(n) the Coal Industry Act 1994 (c. 21);

(o) the EC Competition Law (Articles 88 and 89) Enforcement Regulations 1996;

(p) any subordinate legislation made (whether before or after the passing of this Act) for the purpose of implementing Council Directive No. 91/440/EEC of 29th July 1991 on the development of the Community's railways, Council Directive No. 95/18/EC of 19th June 1995 on the licensing of railway undertakings or Council directive No. 95/19/EC of 19th June 1995 on the allocation of railway infrastructure capacity and the charging of infrastructure fees.

Designated persons

CA.197 2. In section 55(3) 'designated person' means any of the following—

(a) the Director;

(b) the Director General of Telecommunications;

(c) the Independent Television Commission;

(d) the Director General of Gas Supply;

(e) the Director General of Gas for Northern Ireland;

(f) the Civil Aviation Authority;

(g) the Director General of Water Services;

(h) the Director General of Electricity Supply;

(i) the Director General of Electricity Supply for Northern Ireland;

(j) the Rail Regulator;

(k) the Director of Passenger Rail Franchising;

(l) the International Rail Regulator;

(m) the Authorised Conveyancing Practitioners Board;

(n) the Scottish Conveyancing and Executry Services Board;

(o) the Coal Authority;

(p) the Monopolies and Mergers Commission;

(q) the Competition Commission;

(r) the Securities and Investments Board;

(s) any Minister of the Crown or any Northern Ireland department.

SCHEDULE 12

MINOR AND CONSEQUENTIAL AMENDMENTS

The Fair Trading Act 1973 (c. 41)

1.—(1) The Fair Trading Act 1973 is amended as follows.   **CA.198**

(2) Omit section 4 and Schedule 3 (which make provision in respect of the Monopolies and Mergers Commission).

(3) Omit—

(a) section 10(2);

(b) section 54(5);

(c) section 78(3);

(d) paragraph 3(1) and (2) of Schedule 8,

(which fall with the repeal of the Restrictive Trade Practices Act 1976).

(4) In section 10 (supplementary provisions about monopoly situations), in subsection (8), for 'to (7)' substitute 'and (3) to (7)'.

(5) In sections 35 and 37 to 41, for 'the Restrictive Practices Court', in each place, substitute 'a relevant Court'.

(6) After section 41, insert—

'Meaning of "relevant Court".

41A. In this Part of this Act, "relevant Court", in relation to proceedings in respect of a course of conduct contained in the course of a business, means any of the following courts in whose jurisdiction that business is carried on—

(a) in England and Wales or Northern Ireland, the High Court;

(b) in Scotland, the Court of Session.'

(7) In section 42 (appeals from decisions or orders of courts under Part III)—

(a) in subsection (1), at the end, add '; but this subsection is subject to subsection (3) of this section';

(b) in subsection (2)(b), after 'Scotland', insert 'from the sheriff court'; and

(c) after subsection (2), add—

'(3) A decision or order of the Court of Session as the relevant Court may be reviewed, whether on a question of fact or on a question of law, by reclaiming to the Inner House.'

(8) Omit section 45 (power of the Director to require information about complex monopoly situations).

(9) In section 81 (procedure in carrying out investigations)—

(a) in subsection (1)—

(i) in the words before paragraph (a), omit from 'and the Commission' to 'of this Act)';

(ii) in paragraph (b), omit 'or the Commission, as the case may be,' and 'or of the Commission';

(b) in subsection (2), omit 'or the Commission' and 'or of the Commission'; and

(c) in subsection (3), omit from 'and, in the case,' to '85 of this Act' and 'or the Commission, as the case may be,'.

(10) In section 85 (attendance of witnesses and production of documents on investigations by Competition Commission of references under the Fair Trading Act 1973), in subsection (1)(b)—

(a) after 'purpose', insert '(i)';

(b) after the second 'notice', insert 'or

(ii) any document which falls within a category of document which is specified, or described, in the notice,'.

(11) In section 85, in subsection (1)(c), after 'estimates' (in both places), insert 'forecasts'.

(12) In section 85, after subsection (1), insert—

'(1A) For the purposes of subsection (1) above—

(a) 'document' includes information recorded in any form;

(b) the power to require the production of documents includes power to take copies of, or extracts from, any document produced; and

(c) in relation to information recorded otherwise than in legible form, the power to require it to be produced includes power to require it to be produced in legible form, so far as the means to do so are within the custody or under the control of the person on whom the requirement is imposed.'

(13) In section 85(2), for 'any such investigation' substitute 'an investigation of the kind mentioned in subsection (1)'.

(14) In section 133 (general restrictions on disclosure of information), in subsection (2)(a), after 'the Coal Industry 1994' insert 'or the Competition Act 1998'.

(15) In section 135(1) (financial provisions)—

(a) in the words before paragraph (a) and in paragraph (b), omit 'or the Commission'; and

(b) omit paragraph (a).

The Energy Act 1976 (c. 76)

2. In the Energy Act 1976, omit section 5 (temporary relief from restrictive practices law in relation to certain agreements connected with petroleum). **CA.199**

The Estate Agents Act 1979 (c. 38)

3. In section 10(3) of the Estate Agents Act 1979 (restriction on disclosure of information), in paragraph (a)— **CA.200**

(a) omit 'or the Restrictive Trade Practices Act 1976'; and

(b) after 'the Coal Industry Act 1994', insert 'or the Competition Act 1998'.

The Competition Act 1980 (c. 21)

4.—(1) The Competition Act 1980 is amended as follows. **CA.201**

(2) In section 11(8) (public bodies and other persons referred to the Commission), omit paragraph (b) and the 'and' immediately before it.

(3) For section 11(9) (which makes provision for certain functions of the Competition Commission under the Fair Trading Act 1973 to apply in relation to references under the Competition Act 1980) substitute—

'(9) The provisions mentioned in subsection (9A) are to apply in relation to a reference under this section as if—

(a) the functions of the Competition Commission under this section were functions under the Fair Trading Act 1973;

(b) the expression "merger reference" included a reference to the Commission under this section; and

(c) in paragraph 20(2)(a) of Schedule 7 to the Competition Act 1998, the reference to section 56 of the Fair Trading Act 1973 were a reference to section 12 below.

(9A) The provisions are—

    (a) sections 70 (time limit for report on merger), 84 (public interest) and 85 (attendance of witnesses and production of documents) of the Fair Trading Act 1973; and

    (b) Part II of Schedule 7 to the Competition act 1998 (performance of the Competition Commission's general functions).'

(4) In section 13 (investigation of prices directed by Secretary of State)—

    (a) in subsection (1), omit from 'but the giving' to the end;

    (b) for subsection (6) substitute—

'(6) For the purposes of an investigation under this section the Director may, by notice in writing signed by him—

    (a) require any person to produce—

        (i) at a time and a place specified in the notice,

        (ii) to the Director or to any person appointed by him for the purpose,

any documents which are specified or described in the notice and which are documents in his custody or under his control and relating to any matter relevant to the investigation; or

    (b) require any person carrying on any business to—

        (i) furnish to the Director such estimates, forecasts, returns or other information as may be specified or described in the notice; and

        (ii) specify the time, manner and form in which any such estimates, forecasts, returns or information are to be furnished.

(7) No person shall be compelled, for the purpose of any investigation under this section—

    (a) to produce any document which he could not be compelled to produce in civil proceedings before the High Court or, in Scotland, the Court of Session; or

    (b) in complying with any requirement for the furnishing of information, to give any information which he could not be compelled to give in evidence in such proceedings.

(8) Subsections (6) to (8) of section 85 of the Fair Trading Act 1973 (enforcement provisions relating to notices requiring production of documents etc) shall apply in relation to a notice under subsection (6) above as they apply in relation to a notice under section 85(1) but as if, in section 85(7), for the words from "any one" to "the Commission" there were substituted "the Director." '

(5) In section 15 (special provisions for agricultural schemes) omit subsections (2)(b), (3) and (4).

(6) In section 16 (reports), omit subsection (3).

(7) In section 17 (publication etc of reports)—

(a) in subsections (1) and (3) to (5), omit '8(1)';

(b) in subsection (2), omit '8(1) or'; and

(c) in subsection (6), for 'sections 9, 10 or' substitute 'section'.

(8) In section 19(3) (restriction on disclosure of information), omit paragraphs (d) and (e).

(9) In section 19(3), after paragraph (q), insert—

'(r) the Competition Act 1998'.

(10) In section 19(5)(a), omit 'or in anything published under section 4(2)(a) above'.

(11) Omit section 22 (which amends the Fair Trading Act 1973).

(12) In section 24(1) (modifications of provisions about performance of Commission's functions), for from 'Part II' to the 'Commission' substitute 'Part II of Schedule 7 to the Competition Act 1998 (performance of the Competition Commission's general functions)'.

(13) Omit sections 25 to 30 (amendments of the Restrictive Trade Practices Act 1976).

(14) In section 31 (orders and regulations)—

(a) omit subsection (2); and

(b) in subsection (3), omit '10'.

(15) In section 33 (short title etc)—

(a) in subsection (2), for 'sections 2 to 24' substitute 'sections 11 to 13 and sections 15 to 24';

(b) omit subsections (3) and (4).

Magistrates' Courts (Northern Ireland) Order 1981 (SI 1981/1675 (NI 26))

5. In Schedule 6 to the Magistrates' Courts (Northern Ireland) Order 1981, omit paragraphs 42 and 43 (which amend the Restrictive Trade Practices Act 1976). **CA.202**

Agricultural Marketing (Northern Ireland) Order 1981 (SI 1982/1080 (NI 12))

6. In Schedule 8 to the Agricultural Marketing (Northern Ireland) Order 1982— **CA.203**

(a) omit the entry relating to paragraph 16(2) of Schedule 3 to the Fair Trading Act 1973; and

(b) in the entry relating to the Competition Act 1980—

(i) for 'sections' substitute 'section';

(ii) omit 'and 15(3)'.

The Airports Act 1986 (c. 31)

7.—(1) The Airports Act 1986 is amended as follows. **CA.204**

(2) In section 44 (which makes provision about references by the CAA to the Competition Commission), for subsection (3) substitute—

'(3) The provisions mentioned in subsection (3A) are to apply in relation to references under this section as if—

(a) the functions of the Competition Commission in relation to those references were functions under the 1973 ACT;

(b) the expression "merger reference" included a reference under this section;

(c) in section 70 of the 1973 Act—

(i) references to the Secretary of State were references to the CAA; and

(ii) the reference to three months were a reference to six months.

(3A) The provisions are—

(a) sections 70 (time limit for report on merger) and 85 (attendance of witnesses and production of documents) of the 1973 Act;

(b) Part II of Schedule 7 to the Competition Act 1998 (performance of the Competition Commission's general functions); and

(c) section 24 of the 1980 Act (modification of provisions about performance of such functions).'

(3) In section 45, omit subsection (3) (which falls with the repeal of the Restrictive Trade Practices Act 1976).

(4) In section 54 (orders under the 1973 Act or 1980 Act modifying or revoking conditions)—

(a) in subsection (1), omit 'or section 10(2)(a) of the 1980 Act';

(b) in subsection (3), omit paragraph (c) and the 'or' immediately before it;

(c) in subsection (4), omit 'or the 1980 Act'.

(5) In section 56 (co-ordination of exercise of functions by CAA and Director General of Fair Trading), in paragraph (a)(ii), omit 'or the 1980 Act'.

The Financial Services Act 1986 (c. 60)

CA.205 8. In Schedule 11 to the Financial Services Act 1986, in paragraph 12—

(a) in sub-paragraph (1), omit '126';

(b) omit sub-paragraph (2).

The Companies Consolidation (Consequential Provisions) (Northern Ireland) Order 1986 (SI 1986/1035 (NI 9))

CA.206 9. In Part II of Schedule 1 to the Companies Consolidation (Consequential Provisions) (Northern Ireland) Order 1986, omit the entries relating to the Restrictive Trade Practices Act 1976 and the Resale Prices Act 1976.

The Consumer Protection Act 1987 (c. 43)

CA.207 10. In section 38(3) of the Consumer Protection act 1987 (restrictions on disclosure of information)—

(a) omit paragraphs (e) and (f); and

(b) after paragraph (o), insert—

'(p) the Competition Act 1998.'

The Channel Tunnel Act 1987 (c. 53)

11. In section 33 of the Channel Tunnel Act 1987—   **CA.208**

(a) in subsection (2) omit paragraph (c) and the 'and' immediately before it;

(b) in subsection (5), omit paragraphs (b) and (c).

The Road Traffic (Consequential Provisions) Act 1988 (c. 54)

12. In Schedule 3 to the Road Traffic (Consequential Provisions) Act 1988 (consequen- **CA.209**
tial amendments), omit paragraph 19.

The Companies Act 1989 (c. 40)

13. In Schedule 20 to the Companies Act 1989 (amendments about mergers and related **CA.210**
matters), omit paragraphs 21 to 24.

The Broadcasting Act 1990 (c. 42)

14.—(1) The Broadcasting Act 1990 is amended as follows.   **CA.211**

(2) In section 193 (modification of networking arrangements in consequence of reports under competition legislation)—

(a) in subsection (2), omit paragraph (c) and the 'and' immediately before it;

(b) in subsection (4), omit 'or the Competition Act 1980'.

(3) In Schedule 4 (which makes provision for references to the Director or the Competition Commission in respect of networking arrangements), in paragraph 4, for sub-paragraph (7) substitute—

'(7) The provisions mentioned in sub-paragraph (7A) are to apply in relation to references under this paragraph as if—

(a) the functions of the Competition Commission in relation to those references were functions under the Fair Trading Act 1973;

(b) the expression "merger reference" included a reference under this paragraph.

(7A) The provisions are—

(a) section 85 of the Fair Trading Act 1973 (attendance of witnesses and production of documents);

(b) Part II of Schedule 7 to the Competition Act 1998 (performance of the Competition Commission's general functions); and

(c) section 24 of the Competition Act 1980 (modification of provisions about performance of such functions).'

The Tribunals and Inquiries Act 1992 (c. 53)

15. In Schedule 1 to the Tribunals and Inquiries Act 1992 (tribunals under the supervi- **CA.212**
sion of the Council on Tribunals), after paragraph 9, insert—

'Competition   9A. An appeal tribunal established
                                                under section 48 of the Competition
                                                Act 1998.'

The Osteopaths Act 1993 (c. 21)

CA.213 16. Section 33 of the Osteopaths Act 1993 (competition and anti-competitive practices) is amended as follows—

(a) in subsection (4), omit paragraph (b) and the 'or' immediately before it;

(b) in subsection (5), omit 'or section 20 of the Act of 1980'.

The Chiropractors Act 1995 (c. 17)

CA.214 17. Section 33 of the Chiropractors Act 1994 (competition and anti-competitive practices) is amended as follows—

(a) in subsection (4), omit paragraph (b) and the 'or' immediately before it;

(b) in subsection (5), omit 'or section 10 of the Act of 1980'.

The Coal Industry Act 1994 (c. 21)

CA.215 18. In section 59(4) of the Coal Industry Act 1994 (information to be kept confidential by the Coal Authority)—

(a) omit paragraphs (e) and (f); and

(b) after paragraph (m), insert—

'(n) the Competition Act 1998.'

The Deregulation and Contracting Out Act 1994 (c. 40)

CA.216 19.—(1) The Deregulation and Contracting Out Act 1994 is amended as follows.

(2) Omit—

(a) section 10 (restrictive trade practices: non-notifiable agreements); and

(b) section 11 (registration of commercially sensitive information).

(3) In section 12 (anti-competitive practices: competition references), omit subsections (1) to (6).

(4) In Schedule 4, omit paragraph 1.

(5) In Schedule 11 (miscellaneous deregulatory provisions: consequential amendments), in paragraph 4, omit sub-paragraphs (3) to (7).

The Airports (Northern Ireland) Order 1994 (SI 1994/426 (NI 1))

CA.217 20.—(1) The Airports (Northern Ireland) Order 1994 is amended as follows.

(2) In Article 35 (which makes provision about references by the CAA to the Competition Commission), for paragraph (3) substitute—

'(3) The provisions mentioned in paragraph (3A) are to apply in relation to references under Article 34 as if—

(a) the functions of the Competition Commission in relation to those references were functions under the 1973 Act;

(b) the expression "merger reference" included a reference under that Article;

(c) in section 70 of the 1973 Act—

　　(i) references to the Secretary of State were references to the Director, and

　　(ii) the reference to three months were a reference to six months.

(3A) The provisions are—

(a) sections 70 (time limit for report on merger) and 85 (attendance of witnesses and production of documents) of the 1973 Act;

(b) Part II of Schedule 7 to the Competition Act 1998 (performance of the Competition Commission's general functions); and

(c) section 24 of the 1980 Act (modification of provisions about performance of such functions).'

(3) In Article 86, omit paragraph (3) (which falls with the repeal of the Restrictive Trade Practices Act 1976).

(4) In Article 45 (orders under the 1973 Act or 1980 Act modifying or revoking conditions)—

(a) in paragraph (1), omit 'or section 10(2)(a) or the 1980 Act';

(b) in paragraph (3), omit sub-paragraph (c) and the 'or' immediately before it;

(c) in paragraph (4), omit 'or the 1980 Act'.

(5) In Article 47 (co-ordination of exercise of functions by CAA and Director of Fair Trading), in paragraph (a)(ii), omit 'or the 1980 Act'.

(6) In Schedule 9, omit paragraph 5 (which amends the Restrictive Trade Practices Act 1976).

The Broadcasting Act 1996 (c. 55)

21. In section 77 of the Broadcasting Act 1996 (which modifies the Restrictive Trade Practices Act 1976 in its application to agreements relating to Channel 3 news provision), omit subsection (2). **CA.218**

SCHEDULE 13
TRANSITIONAL PROVISIONS AND SAVINGS

PART I
GENERAL

Interpretation

1.—(1) In this Schedule— **CA.219**

'RPA' means the Resale Prices Act 1976;

'RTPA' means the Restrictive Trade Practices Act 1976;

'continuing proceedings' has the meaning given by paragraph 15;

'the Court' means the Restrictive Practices Court;

'Director' means the Director General of Fair Trading;

'document' includes information recorded in any form;

'enactment date' means the date on which this act is passed;

'information' includes estimates and forecasts;

'interim period' means the period beginning on the enactment date and ending immediately before the starting date;

'prescribed' means prescribed by an order made by the Secretary of State;

'regulator' means any person mentioned in paragraphs (a) to (g) of paragraph 1 of Schedule 10;

'starting date' means the date on which section 2 comes into force;

'transitional period' means the transitional period provided for in Chapter III and IV of Part IV of this Schedule.

(2) Sections 30, 44, 51, 53, 55, 56, 57 and 59(3) and (4) and paragraph 12 of Schedule 9 ('the applied provisions') apply for the purposes of this Schedule as they apply for the purposes of Part I of this Act.

(3) Section 2(5) applies for the purposes of any provisions of this Schedule which are concerned with the operation of the Chapter I prohibition as it applies for the purposes of Part I of this Act.

(4) In relation to any of the matters in respect of which a regulator may exercise powers as a result of paragraph 35(1), the applied provisions are to have effect as if references to the Director included references to the regulator.

(5) The fact that to a limited extent the Chapter I prohibition does not apply to an agreement, because a transitional period is provided by virtue of this Schedule, does not require those provisions of the agreement in respect of which there is a transitional period to be disregarded when considering whether the agreement infringes the prohibition for other reasons.

General power to make transitional provision and savings

CA.220 2.—(1) Nothing in this Schedule affects the power of the Secretary of State under section 75 to make transitional provisions or savings.

(2) An order under that section may modify any provision made by this Schedule.

Advice and information

CA.221 3.—(1) The Director may publish advice and information explaining provisions of this Schedule to persons who are likely to be affected by them.

(2) Any advice or information published by the Director under this paragraph is to be published in such form and manner as he considers appropriate.

PART II

DURING THE INTERIM PERIOD

Block exemptions

4.—(1) The Secretary of State may, at any time during the interim period, make one or **CA.222** more orders for the purpose of providing block exemptions which are effective on the starting date.

(2) An order under this paragraph has the effect as if properly made under section 6.

Certain agreements to be non-notifiable agreements

5. An agreement which— **CA.223**

(a) is made during the interim period, and

(b) satisfies the conditions set out in paragraphs (a), (c) and (d) of section 27A(1) or the RTPA,

is to be treated as a non-notifiable agreement for the purposes of the RTPA.

Application of RTPA during the interim period

6. In relation to agreements made during the interim period— **CA.224**

(a) the Director is no longer under the duty to take proceedings imposed by section 1(2)(c) of the RTPA but may continue to do so;

(b) section 21 of that Act has effect as if subsections (1) and (2) were omitted; and

(c) section 35(1) of that Act has effect as if the words 'or within such further time as the Director may, upon application made within that time, allow' were omitted.

Guidance

7.—(1) Sub-paragraphs (2) to (4) apply in relation to agreements made during the **CA.225** interim period.

(2) An application may be made to the Director in anticipation of the coming into force of section 13 in accordance with directions given by the Director and such an application is to have effect on and after the starting date as if properly made under section 13.

(3) The Director may, in response to such an application—

(a) give guidance in anticipation of the coming into force of section 2; or

(b) on and after the starting date, give guidance under section 15 as if the application had been properly made under section 13.

(4) Any guidance so given is to have effect on and after the starting date as if properly given under section 15.

PART III

ON THE STARTING DATE

Applications which fall

CA.226   8.—(1) Proceedings in respect of an application which is made to the Court under any of the provisions mentioned in sub-paragraph (2), but which is not determined before the starting date, cease on that date.

(2) The provisions are—

(a) sections 2(2), 35(3), 37(1) and 40(1) of the RTPA and paragraph 5 of Schedule 4 to that Act;

(b) section 491) of the RTPA so far as the application relates to an order under section 2(2) of that Act; and

(c) section 25(2) of the RPA.

(3) The power of the Court to make an order for costs in relation to any proceedings is not affected by anything in this paragraph or by the repeals made by section 1.

Orders and approvals which fall

9.—(1) An order in force immediately before the starting date under—

(a) section 2(2), 29(1), 30(1), 33(4), 35(3) or 37(1) of the RTPA; or

(b) section 25(2) of the RPA,

ceases to have effect on that date.

(2) An approval in force immediately before the starting date under section 32 of the RTPA ceases to have effect on that date.

PART IV

ON AND AFTER THE STARTING DATE

CHAPTER I

GENERAL

Duty of Director to maintain register etc

CA.227   10.—(1) This paragraph applies even though the relevant provisions of the RTPA are repealed by this Act.

(2) The Director is to continue on and after the starting date to be under the duty imposed by section 1(2)(a) of the RTPA to maintain a register in respect of agreements—

(a) particulars of which are, on the starting date, entered or filed on the register;

(b) which fall within sub-paragraph (4);

(c) which immediately before the starting date are the subject of proceedings under the RTPA which do not cease on that date by virtue of this Schedule; or

(d) in relation to which a court gives directions to the Director after the starting date on the course of proceedings in which a question arises as to whether an agreement was, before that date—

    (i)   one to which the RTPA applied;

    (ii) subject to registration under that Act;

    (iii) a non-notifiable agreement for the purposes of that Act.

(3) The Director is to continue on and after the starting date to be under the duties imposed by section 1(2)(a) and (b) of the RTPA of compiling a register of agreements and entering or filing certain particulars of the register, but only in respect of agreements of a kind referred to in paragraph (b), (c) or (d) of sub-paragraph (2).

(4) An agreement falls within this sub-paragraph if—

  (a) it is subject to registration under the RTPA but—

    (i)   it is not a non-notifiable agreement within the meaning of section 27A of the RTPA, or

    (ii) it is not one to which paragraph 5 applies;

  (b) particulars of the agreement have been provided to the Director before the starting date; and

  (c) as at the starting date no entry or filing has been made in the register in respect of the agreement.

(5) Sections 23 and 27 of the RTPA are to apply after the starting date in respect of the register subject to such modifications, if any, as may be prescribed.

(6) In sub-paragraph (2)(d) 'court' means—

  (a) the High Court;

  (b) the Court of Appeal

  (c) the Court of Session;

  (d) the High Court or Court of Appeal in Northern Ireland; or

  (e) the House of Lords.

RTPA section 3 applications

11.—(1) Even though section 3 of the RTPA is repealed by this Act, its provisions (and **CA.228** so far as necessary that Act) are to continue to apply, with such modifications (if any) as may be prescribed—

  (a) in relation to a continuing application under that section; or

  (b) so as to allow an application to be made under that section on or after the starting date in respect of a continuing application under section 1(3) of the RTPA.

(2) 'Continuing application' means an application made, but not determined, before the starting date.

RTPA section 26 applications

12.—(1) Even though section 26 of the RTPA is repealed by this Act, its provisions (and **CA.229** so far as necessary that Act) are to continue to apply, with such modifications (if any) as may be prescribed, in relation to an application which is made under that section, but not determined, before the starting date.

(2) If an application under section 26 is determined on or after the starting date, this Schedule has effect in relation to the agreement concerned as if the application had been determined immediately before that date.

Right to bring civil proceedings

CA.230 13.—(1) Even though section 35 of the RTPA is repealed by this Act, its provisions (and so far as necessary that Act) are to continue to apply in respect of a person who, immediately before the starting date, has a right by virtue of section 27ZA or 35(2) of that Act to bring civil proceedings in respect of an agreement (but only so far as that right relates to any period before the starting date or, where there are continuing proceedings, the determination of the proceedings).

(2) Even though section 25 of the RPA is repealed by this Act, the provisions of that section (and so far as necessary that Act) are to continue to apply in respect of a person who, immediately before the starting date, has a right by virtue of subsection (3) of that section to bring civil proceedings (but only so far as that right relates to any period before the starting date or, where there are continuing proceedings, the determination of the proceedings).

CHAPTER II
CONTINUING PROCEEDINGS

The general rule

CA.231 14.—(1) The Chapter I prohibition does not apply to an agreement at any time when the agreement is the subject of continuing proceedings under the RTPA.

(2) The Chapter I prohibition does not apply to an agreement relating to goods which are the subject of continuing proceedings under section 16 or 17 of the RPA to the extent to which the agreement consists of exempt provisions.

(3) In sub-paragraph (2) 'exempt provisions' means those provisions of the agreement which would, disregarding section 14 of the RPA, be—

(a) void as a result of section 9(1) of the RPA; or

(b) unlawful as a result of section 9(2) or 11 of the RPA

(4) If the Chapter I prohibition does not apply to an agreement because of this paragraph, the provisions of, or made under, the RTPA or the RPA are to continue to have effect in relation to the agreement.

(5) The repeals made by section 1 do not affect—

(a) continuing proceedings; or

(b) proceedings of the kind referred to in paragraph 11 or 12 of this Schedule which are continuing after the starting date.

Meaning of 'continuing proceedings'

CA.232 15.—(1) For the purposes of this Schedule 'continuing proceedings' means proceedings in respect of an application made to the Court under the RTPA or the RPA, but not determined, before the starting date.

(2) But proceedings under section 3 or 26 of the RTPA to which paragraph 11 or 12 applies are not continuing proceedings.

(3) The question whether (for the purposes of Part III, or this Part, of this Schedule) an application application has been determined is to be decided in accordance with sub-paragraphs (4) and (5).

(4) If an appeal against the decision on the application is brought, the application is not determined until—

(a) the appeal is disposed of or withdrawn; or

(b) if as a result of the appeal the case is referred back to the Court—

(i) the expiry of the period within which an appeal ('the further appeal') in respect of the Court's decision on that reference could have been brought had this Act not been passed; or

(ii) if later, the date on which the further appeal is disposed of or withdrawn.

(5) Otherwise, the application is not determined until the expiry of the period within which any party to the application would have been able to bring an appeal against the decision on the application had this Act not been passed.

RTPA section 4 proceedings

16. Proceedings on an application for an order under section 4 of the RTPA are also con- **CA.233**
tinuing proceedings if—

(a) leave to make the application is applied for before the starting date but the proceedings in respect of that application for leave are not determined before that date; or

(b) leave to make an application for an order under that section is granted before the starting date but the application itself is not made before that date.

RPA section 16 or 17 proceedings

17. Proceedings on an application for an order under section 16 or 17 of the RPA are also **CA.234**
continuing proceedings if—

(a) leave to make the application is applied for before the starting date but the proceedings in respect of that application for leave are not determined before that date; or

(b) leave to make an application for an order under section 16 or 17 of the RPA is granted before the starting date, but the application itself is not made before that date.

Continuing proceedings which are discontinued

18.—(1) On an application made jointly to the Court by all the parties to any continu- **CA.235**
ing proceedings, the Court must, if it is satisfied that the parties wish it to do so, discontinue the proceedings.

(2) If, on an application under sub-paragraph (1) or for any other reason, the Court orders the proceedings to be discontinued, this Schedule has effect (subject to paragraphs

21 and 22) from the date on which the proceedings are discontinued as if they had never been instituted.

<h2 style="text-align:center">Chapter III
The Transitional Period</h2>

The general rule

CA.236 **19.**—(1) Except where this Chapter or Chapter IV provides otherwise, there is a transitional period, beginning on the starting date and lasting for one year, for any agreement made before the starting date.

(2) The Chapter I prohibition does not apply to an agreement to the extent to which there is a transitional period for the agreement.

(3) The Secretary of State may by regulations provide for sections 13 to 16 and Schedule 5 to apply with such modifications (if any) as may be specified in the regulations, in respect of applications to the Director about agreements for which there is a transitional period.

Cases for which there is no transitional period

CA.237 **20.**—(1) There is no transitional period for an agreement to the extent to which, immediately before the starting date, it is—

(a) void under section 2(1) or 35(1)(a) of the RTPA;

(b) the subject of an order under section 292) or 35(3) of the RTPA; or

(c) unlawful under section 1, 2 or 11 of the RPA or void under section 9 of that Act.

(2) There is no transitional period for an agreement to the extent to which, before the starting date, a person has acted unlawfully for the purposes of section 27ZA(2) or (3) of the RTPA in respect of the agreement.

(3) There is no transitional period for an agreement to which paragraph 25(4) applies.

(4) There is no transitional period for—

(a) an agreement in respect of which there are continuing proceedings; or

(b) an agreement relating to goods in respect of which there are continuing proceedings,

to the extent to which the agreement is, when the proceedings are determined, void or unlawful.

Continuing proceedings under the RTPA

CA.238 **21.** In the case of an agreement which is the subject of continuing proceedings under the RTPA, the transitional period begins—

(a) if the proceedings are discontinued, on the date of discontinuance;

(b) otherwise, when the proceedings are determined.

Continuing proceedings under the RPA

CA.239 **22.**—(1) In the case of an agreement relating to goods which are the subject of continuing proceedings under the RPA, the transitional period for the exempt provisions of the agreement begins—

(a) if the proceedings are discontinued, on the date of discontinuance;

(b) otherwise, when the proceedings are determined.

(2) In sub-paragraph (1) 'exempt provisions' has the meaning given by paragraph 14(3).

Provisions not contrary to public interest

23.—(1) To the extent to which an agreement contains provisions which, immediately before the starting date, are provisions which the Court has found not to be contrary to the public interest, the transitional period lasts for five years. **CA.240**

(2) Sub-paragraph (1) is subject to paragraph 20(4).

(3) To the extent to which an agreement which on the starting date is the subject of continuing proceedings is, when the proceedings are determined, found by the Court not to be contrary to the public interest, the transitional period lasts for five years.

Goods

24.—(1) In the case of an agreement relating to goods which, immediately before the starting date, are exempt under section 14 of the RPA, there is a transitional period for the agreement to the extent to which it consists of exempt provisions. **CA.241**

(2) Sub-paragraph (1) is subject to paragraph 20(4).

(3) In the case of an agreement relating to goods—

(a) which on the starting date are the subject of continuing proceedings, and

(b) which, when the proceedings are determined, are found to be exempt under section 14 of the RPA,

there is a transitional period for the agreement, to the extent to which it consists of exempt provisions.

(4) In each case, the transitional period lasts for five years.

(5) In sub-paragraphs 91) and (3) 'exempt provisions' means those provisions of the agreement which would, disregarding section 14 of the RPA, be—

(a) void as a result of section 9(1) or the RPA; or

(b) unlawful as a result of section 9(2) or 11 of the RPA.

Transitional period for certain agreements

25.—(1) This paragraph applies to agreements— **CA.242**

(a) which are subject to registration under the RTPA but which—

(i) are not non-notifiable agreements within the meaning of section 27A of the RTPA; or

(ii) are not agreements to which paragraph 5 applies; and

(b) in respect of which the time for furnishing relevant particulars as required by or under the RTPA expires on or after the starting date.

(2) 'Relevant particulars' means—

(a) particulars which are required to be furnished by virtue of section 24 of the RTPA; or

(b) particulars of any variation of an agreement which are required to be furnished by virtue of sections 24 and 27 of the RTPA.

(3) There is a transitional period of one year for an agreement to which this paragraph applies if—

(a) relevant particulars are furnished before the starting date; and

(b) no person has acted unlawfully (for the purposes of section 27ZA(2) or (3) of the RTPA) in respect of the agreement).

(4) If relevant particulars are not furnished by the starting date, section 35(1)(a) of the RTPA does not apply in relation to the agreement (unless sub-paragraph (5) applies).

(5) This sub-paragraph applies if a person falling within section 27ZA(2) or (3) of the RTPA has acted unlawfully for the purposes of those subsections in respect of the agreement.

Special cases

CA.243 26.—(1) In the case of an agreement in respect of which—

(a) a direction under section 127(2) of the Financial Services Act 1986 ('the 1986 Act') is in force immediately before the starting date; or

(b) a direction under section 194A(3) of the Broadcasting Act 1990 ('the 1990 Act') is in force immediately before the starting date,

the transitional period lasts for five years.

(2) To the extent to which an agreement is the subject of a declaration—

(a) made by the Treasury under section 127(3) of the 1986 Act; and

(b) in force immediately before the starting date,

the transitional period lasts for five years.

(3) Sub-paragraphs (1) and (2) do not affect the power of—

(a) the Treasury to make a declaration under section 127(2) of the 1986 Act (as amended by Schedule 2 to this Act);

(b) the Secretary of State to make a declaration under section 194A of the 1990 Act (as amended by Schedule 2 to this Act),

in respect of an agreement for which there is a transitional period.

CHAPTER IV

THE UTILITIES

General

CA.244 27. In this Chapter 'the relevant period' means the period beginning with the starting date and ending immediately before the fifth anniversary of that date.

Electricity

28.—(1) For an agreement to which, immediately before the starting date, the RTPA   **CA.245**
does not apply by virtue of a section 100 order, there is a transitional period—

  (a) beginning on the starting date; and

  (b) ending at the end of the relevant period.

(2) For an agreement which is made at any time after the starting date and to which, had the RTPA not been repealed, that Act would not at the time at which the agreement is made have applied by virtue of a section 100 order, there is a transitional period—

  (a) beginning on the date on which the agreement is made; and

  (b) ending at the end of the relevant period.

(3) For an agreement (whether made before or after the starting date) which, during the relevant period, is varied at any time in such a way that it becomes an agreement which, had the RTPA not been repealed, would at that time have been one to which that Act did not apply by virtue of a section 100 order, there is a transitional period—

  (a) beginning on the date on which the variation is made; and

  (b) ending at the end of the relevant period.

(4) If an agreement for which there is a transitional period as a result of sub-paragraph (1), (2) or (3) is varied during the relevant period, the transitional period for the agreement continues if, had the RTPA not been repealed, the agreement would have continued to be one to which that Act did not apply by virtue of a section 100 order.

(5) But if an agreement for which there is a transitional period as a result of sub-paragraph (1), (2) or (3) ceases to be one to which, had it not been repealed, the RTPA would not have applied by virtue of a section 100 order, the transitional period ends on the date on which the agreement so ceases.

(6) Sub-paragraph (3) is subject to paragraph 20.

(7) In this paragraph and paragraph 29—

  'section 100 order' means an order made under section 100 of the Electricity Act 1989; and

  expressions which are also used in Part I of the Electricity Act 1989 have the same meaning as in that Part.

Electricity: power to make transitional orders

29.—(1) There is a transitional period for an agreement (whether made before or after   **CA.246**
the starting date) relating to the generation, transmission or supply of electricity which—

  (a) is specified, or is of a description specified, in an order ('a transitional order') made by the Secretary of State (whether before or after the making of the agreement but before the end of the relevant period); and

  (b) satisfies such conditions as may be specified in the order.

(2) A transitional order may make provision as to when the transitional period in respect of such an agreement is to start or to be deemed to have started.

(3) The transitional period for such an agreement ends at the end of the relevant period.

(4) But if the agreement—

(a) ceases to be one to which a transitional order applies, or

(b) ceases to satisfy one or more of the conditions specified in the transitional order,

the transitional period ends on the date on which the agreement ceases.

(5) Before making a transitional order, the Secretary of State must consult the Director General of Electricity Supply and the Director.

(6) The conditions specified in a transitional order may include conditions which refer any matter to the Secretary of State for determination after such consultation as may be so specified.

(7) In the application of this paragraph to Northern Ireland, the reference in sub-paragraph (5) to the Director General of Electricity Supply is to be read as a reference to the Director General of Electricity Supply for Northern Ireland.

Gas

CA.247 30.—(1) For an agreement to which, immediately before the starting date, the RTPA does not apply by virtue of section 62 or a section 62 order, there is a transitional period—

(a) beginning on the starting date; and

(b) ending at the end of the relevant period.

(2) For an agreement which is made at any time after the starting date and to which, had the RTPA not been repealed, that Act would not at the time at which the agreement is made have applied by virtue of section 62 or a section 62 order, there is a transitional period—

(a) beginning on the date on which the agreement is made; and

(b) ending at the end of the relevant period.

(3) For an agreement (whether made before or after the starting date) which, during the relevant period, is varied at any time in such a way that it becomes an agreement which, had the RTPA not been repealed, would at that time have been one to which that Act did not apply by virtue of section 62 or a section 62 order, there is a transitional period—

(a) beginning on the date on which the variation is made; and

(b) ending at the end of the relevant period.

(4) If an agreement for which there is a transitional period as a result of sub-paragraph (1), (2) or (3) is varied during the relevant period, the transitional period for the agreement continues if, had the RTPA not been repealed, the agreement would have continued to be one to which that Act did not apply by virtue of section 62 or a section 62 order.

(5) But if an agreement for which there is a transitional period as a result of sub-paragraph (1), (2) or (3) ceases to be one to which, had it not been repealed, the RTPA

would not have applied by virtue of section 62 or a section 62 order, the transitional period ends on the date on which the agreement so ceases.

(6) Sub-paragraph (3) also applies in relation to a modification which is treated as an agreement made on or after 28th November 1985 by virtue of section 62(4).

(7) Sub-paragraph (3) is subject to paragraph 20.

(8) In this paragraph and paragraph 31—

'section 62' means section 62 of the Gas Act 1986;

'section 62 order' means an order made under section 62.

Gas: power to make transitional orders

31.—(1) There is a transitional period for an agreement of a description falling within **CA.248** section 62(2)(a) and (b) or section 62(2A)(a) and (b) which—

(a) is specified, or is of a description specified, in an order ('a transitional order') made by the Secretary of State (whether before or after the making of the agreement but before the end of the relevant period); and

(b) satisfies such conditions as may be specified in the order.

(2) A transitional order may make provision as to when the transitional period in respect of such agreement is to start or to be deemed to have started.

(3) The transitional period for such an agreement ends at the end of the relevant period.

(4) But if the agreement—

(a) ceases to be one to which a transitional order applies, or

(b) ceases to satisfy one or more of the conditions specified in the transitional order, the transitional period ends on the date when the agreement so ceases.

(5) Before making a transitional order, the Secretary of State must consult the Director General of Gas Supply and the Director.

(6) The conditions specified in a transitional order may include—

(a) conditions which are to be satisfied in relation to a time before the coming into force of this paragraph;

(b) conditions which refer any matter (which may be the general question whether the Chapter I prohibition should apply to a particular agreement) to the Secretary of State, the Director or the Director General of Gas Supply for determination after such consultation as may be so specified.

Gas: Northern Ireland

32.—(1) For an agreement to which, immediately before the starting date, the RTPA **CA.249** does not apply by virtue of an Article 41 order, there is a transitional period—

(a) beginning on the starting date; and

(b) ending at the end of the relevant period.

(2) For an agreement which is made at any time after the starting date and to which, had the RTPA not been repealed, that Act would not at the time at which the agreement is made have applied by virtue of an Article 41 order, there is a transitional period—

(a) beginning on the date of which the agreement is made; and

(b) ending at the end of the relevant period.

(3) For an agreement (whether made before or after the starting date) which, during the relevant period, is varied at any time in such a way that it becomes an agreement which, had the RTPA not been repealed, would at that time have been one to which that Act did not apply by virtue of an Article 41 order, there is a transitional period—

(a) beginning on the date on which the variation is made; and

(b) ending at the end of the relevant period.

(4) If an agreement for which there is a transitional period as a result of sub-paragraph (1), (2) or (3) is varied during the relevant period, the transitional period for the agreement continues if, had the RTPA not been repealed, the agreement would have continued to be one to which that Act did not apply by virtue of an Article 41 order.

(5) But if an agreement for which there is a transitional period as a result of sub-paragraph (1), (2) or (3) ceases to be one to which, had it not been repealed, the RTPA would not have applied by virtue of an Article 41 order, the transitional period ends on the date on which the agreement so ceases.

(6) Sub-paragraph (3) is subject to paragraph 20.

(7) In this paragraph and paragraph 33—

'Article 41 order' means an order under Article 41 of the Gas (Northern Ireland) Order 1996;

'Department' means the Department of Economic Development.

Gas: Northern Ireland—power to make transitional orders

CA.250 33.—(1) There is a transitional period for an agreement of a description falling within Article 31(1) which—

(a) is specified, or is of a description specified, in an order ('a transitional order') made by the Department (whether before or after the making of the agreement but before the end of the relevant period); and

(b) satisfies such conditions as may be specified in the order.

(2) A transitional order may make provision as to when the transitional period in respect of such an agreement is to start or to be deemed to have started.

(3) The transitional period for such an agreement ends at the end of the relevant period.

(4) But if the agreement—

(a) ceases to be one to which a transitional order applies, or

(b) ceases to satisfy one or more of the conditions specified in the transitional order,

the transitional period ends on the date when the agreement so ceases.

(5) Before making a transitional order, the Department must consult the Director General of Gas for Northern Ireland and the Director.

(6) The conditions specified in a transitional order may include conditions which refer to any matter (which may be the general question whether the Chapter I prohibition should apply to a particular agreement) to the Department for determination after such consultation as may be so specified.

Railways

34.—(1) In this paragraph—   **CA.251**

'section 131' means section 131 of the Railways Act 1993 ('the 1993 Act');

'section 131 agreement' means an agreement—

(a) to which the RTPA does not apply immediately before the starting date by virtue of section 131(1); or

(b) in respect of which a direction under section 131(3) is in force immediately before that date;

'non-exempt agreement' means an agreement relating to the provision of railway services (whether made before or after the starting date) which is not a section 131 agreement; and

'railway services' has the meaning given by section 82 of the 1993 Act.

(2) For a section 131 agreement there is a transitional period of five years.

(3) There is a transitional period for a non-exempt agreement to the extent to which the agreement is at any time before the end of the relevant period required or approved—

(a) by the Secretary of State or the Rail regulator in pursuance of any function assigned or transferred to him under or by virtue of any provision of the 1993 Act;

(b) by or under any agreement the making of which is required or approved by the Secretary of State or the Rail Regulator in the exercise of any such function; or

(c) by or under a licence granted under Part I of the 1993 Act.

(4) The transitional period conferred by sub-paragraph (3)—

(a) is to be taken to have begun on the starting date; and

(b) ends at the end of the relevant period.

(5) Sub-paragraph (3) is subject to paragraph 20.

(6) Any variation of a section 131 agreement on or after the starting date is to be treated, for the purposes of this paragraph, as a separate non-exempt agreement.

The regulators

35.—(1) Subject to sub-paragraph (3), each of the regulators may exercise, in respect of **CA.252**
sectoral matters and concurrently with the Director, the functions of the Director under paragraph 3, 7, 19(3), 36, 37, 38 or 39.

(2) In sub-paragraph (1) 'sectoral matters' means—

(a) in the case of the Director General of Telecommunications, the matters referred to in section 50(3) of the Telecommunications Act 1984;

(b) in the case of the Director General of Gas Supply, the matters referred to in section 36A(3) and (4) of the Gas Act 1986;

(c) in the case of the Director General of Electricity Supply, the matters referred to in section 43(3) of the Electricity Act 1989;

(d) in the case of the Director General of Electricity Supply for Northern Ireland, the matters referred to in Article 46(3) of the Electricity (Northern Ireland) Order 1992;

(e) in the case of the Director General of Water Services, the matters referred to in section 31(3) of the Water Industry Act 1991;

(f) in the case of the Rail Regulator, the matters referred to in section 67(3) of the Railways Act 1993;

(g) in the case of the Director General of Gas for Northern Ireland, the matters referred to in Article 23(3) of the Gas (Northern Ireland) Order 1996.

(3) The power to give directions in paragraph 7(2) is exercisable by the Director only but if the Director is preparing directions which relate to a matter in respect of which a regulator exercises concurrent jurisdiction, he must consult that regulator.

(4) Consultations conducted by the Director before the enactment date, with a view to preparing directions which have effect on or after that date, are to be taken to satisfy sub-paragraph (3).

(5) References to enactments in sub-paragraph (2) are to the enactments as amended by or under this Act.

CHAPTER V

EXTENDING THE TRANSITIONAL PERIOD

CA.253 36.—(1) A party to an agreement for which there is a transitional period may apply to the Director, not less than three months before the end of the period, for the period to be extended.

(2) The Director may (on his own initiative or on an application under sub-paragraph (1))—

(a) extend a one-year transitional period by not more than twelve months;

(b) extend a transitional period of any period other than one year by not more than six months.

(3) An application under sub-paragraph (1) must—

(a) be in such form as may be specified; and

(b) include such documents and information as may be specified.

(4) If the Director extends the transitional period under this paragraph, he must give notice in such form, and to such persons, as may be specified.

(5) The Director may not extend a transitional period more than once.

(6) In this paragraph—

'person' has the same meaning as in Part I; and

'specified' means specified in rules made by the Director under section 51.

Chapter VI

Terminating the Transitional Period

General

38.—(1) Subject to sub-paragraph (2), the Director may by a direction in writing termi- **CA.253** nate the transitional period for an agreement, but only in accordance with paragraph 38.

(2) The Director may not terminate the transitional period, nor exercise any of the powers in paragraph 38, in respect of an agreement which is excluded from the Chapter I prohibition by virtue of any of the provisions of Part I of this Act other than paragraph I of Schedule 1 or paragraph 2 or 9 of Schedule 3.

Circumstances in which the Director may terminate the transitional period

38.—(1) If the Director is considering whether to give a direction under paragraph 37 ('a **CA.254** direction'), he may in writing require any party to the agreement concerned to give him such information in connection with that agreement as he may require.

(2) If at the end of such period as may be specified in rules made under section 51, a person has failed, without reasonable excuse, to comply with a requirement imposed under sub-paragraph (1), the Director may give a direction.

(3) The Director may also give a direction if he considers—

    (a) that the agreement would, but for the transitional period or a relevant exclusion, infringe the Chapter I prohibition; and

    (b) that he would not be likely to grant the agreement an unconditional individual exemption.

(4) For the purposes of sub-paragraph (3) an individual exemption is unconditional if no conditions or obligations are imposed in respect of it under section 4 (3)(a).

(5) In this paragraph—

'person' has the same meaning as in Part I;

'relevant exclusion' means an exclusion under paragraph 1 of Schedule 1 or paragraph 2 or 9 of Schedule 3.

Procedural requirements on giving a paragraph 37 direction

39.—(1) The Director must specify in a direction under paragraph 37 ('a direction') the **CA.255** date on which it is to have effect (which must not be less than 28 days after the direction is given).

(2) Copies of the direction must be given to—

    (a) each of the parties concerned; and

(b) the Secretary of State,

not less than 28 days before the date on which the direction is to have effect.

(3) In relation to an agreement to which a direction applies, the transitional period (if it has not already ended) ends on the date specified in the direction unless, before that date, the direction is revoked by the Director or the Secretary of State.

(4) If a direction is revoked, the Director may give a further direction in respect of the same agreement only if he is satisfied that there has been a material change of circumstances since the revocation.

(5) If, as a result of paragraph 24(1) or (3), there is a transitional period in respect of provisions of an agreement relating to goods—

(a) which immediately before the starting date are exempt under section 14 of the RPA; or

(b) which, when continuing proceedings are determined, are found to be exempt under section 14 of the RPA,

the period is not affected by paragraph 37 or 38.

Part V

The Fair Trading Act 1973

References to the Monopolies and Mergers Commission

CA.256 40.—(1) If, on the date on which the repeal by this Act of a provision mentioned in sub-paragraph (2) comes into force, the Monopolies and Mergers Commission has not completed a reference which was made to it before that date, continued consideration of the reference may include consideration of a question which could not have been considered if the provision had not been repealed.

(2) The provisions are—

(a) sections 10(2), 54(5) and 78(3) and paragraph 3(1) and (2) of Schedule 8 to the Fair Trading Act 1973 (c. 41);

(b) section 11(8)(b) of the Competition Act 1980 (c. 21);

(c) section 14(2) of the Telecommunications Act 1984 (c. 12);

(d) section 45(3) of the Airports Act 1986 (c. 31);

(e) section 25(2) of the Gas Act 1986 (c. 44);

(f) section 13(2) of the Electricity Act 1989 (c. 29);

(g) section 15(2) of the Water Industry Act 1991 (c. 56);

(h) article 16(2) of the Electricity (Northern Ireland) Order 1992;

(i) section 14(2) of the Railways Act 1993 (c. 43);

(j) article 36(3) of the Airports (Northern Ireland) Order 1994;

(k) article 16(2) of the Gas (Northern Ireland) Order 1996.

Orders under Schedule 8

CA.257 41.—(1) In this paragraph—

'the 1973 Act' means the Fair Trading Act 1973;

'agreement means an agreement entered into before the date on which the repeal of the limiting provisions comes into force;

'the order' means an order under section 56 or 73 of the 1973 Act;

'the limiting provisions' means sub-paragraph (1) or (2) of paragraph 3 of Schedule 8 to the 1973 Act (limit on power to make orders under paragraph 1 or 2 of that Schedule) and includes any provision of the order included because of either of those sub-paragraphs; and

'transitional period' means the period which—

(a) begins on the day on which the repeal of the limiting provisions comes into force; and

(b) ends on the first anniversary of the starting date.

(2) Sub-paragraph (3) applies to any agreement to the extent to which it would have been unlawful (in accordance with the provisions of the order) but for the limiting provisions.

(3) As from the end of the transitional period, the order is to have effect in relation to the agreement as if the limiting provisions had never had effect.

Part III of the Act

42.—(1) The repeals made by section 1 do not affect any proceedings in respect of an **CA.258** application which is made to the Court under Part III of the Fair Trading Act 1973, but is not determined, before the starting date.

(2) The question whether (for the purposes of sub-paragraph (1)) an application has been determined is to be decided in accordance with sub-paragraphs (3) and (4).

(3) If an appeal against the decision on the application is brought, the application is not determined until—

(a) the appeal is disposed of or withdrawn; or

(b) if as a result of the appeal the case is referred back to the Court—

(i) the expiry of the period within which an appeal ('the further appeal') in respect of the Court's decision on that reference could have been brought had this Act not been passed; or

(ii) if later, the date on which the further appeal is disposed of or withdrawn.

(4) Otherwise, the application is not determined until the expiry of the period within which any party to the application would have been able to bring an appeal against the decision on the application had this Act not been passed.

(5) Any amendment made by Schedule 12 to this Act which substitutes references to a relevant Court for references to the Court is not to affect proceedings of the kind referred to in sub-paragraph (1).

PART VI

THE COMPETITION ACT 1980

Undertakings

CA.259 43.—(1) Subject to sub-paragraph (2), an undertaking accepted by the Director under section 4 or 9 of the Competition Act 1980 ceases to have effect on the coming into force of the repeal by this Act of that section.

(2) If the undertaking related to an agreement which on the starting date is the subject of continuing proceedings, the undertaking continues to have effect for the purposes of section 29 of the Competition Act 1980 until the proceedings are determined.

Application of sections 25 and 26

CA.260 44. The repeals made by section 1 do not affect—

(a) the operation of section 25 of the Competition Act 1980 in relation to an application under section 1(3) of the RTPA which is made before the starting date;

(b) an application under section 26 of the Competition Act 1980 which is made before the starting date.

PART VII

MISCELLANEOUS

Disclosure of information

CA.261 45.—(1) Section 55 of this Act applies in relation to information which, immediately before the starting date, is subject to section 41 of the RTPA as it applies in relation to information obtained under or as a result of Part I.

(2) But section 55 does not apply to any disclosure of information of the kind referred to in sub-paragraph (1) if the disclosure is made—

(a) for the purpose of facilitating the performance of functions of a designated person under the Control of Misleading Advertisements Regulations 1988; or

(b) for the purposes of any proceedings before the Court or of any other legal proceedings under the RTPA or the Fair Trading Act 1973 or the Control of Misleading Advertisements Regulations 1988.

(3) Section 56 applies in relation to information of the kind referred to in sub-paragraph (1) if particulars containing the information have been entered or filed on the special section of the register maintained by the Director under, or as a result of, section 27 of the RTPA or paragraph 10 of this Schedule.

(4) Section 55 has effect, in relation to the matters as to which section 41(2) of the RTPA had effect, as if it contained a provision similar to section 41(2).

The Court

CA.262 46. If it appears to the Lord Chancellor that a person who ceases to be a non-judicial member of the Court as a result of this Act should receive compensation for loss of office, he may pay to him out of moneys provided by Parliament such sum as he may with the approval of the Treasury determine.

SCHEDULE 14

REPEALS AND REVOCATIONS

PART I

REPEALS

Chapter	Short title	Extent of repeal	
1973 c. 41.	The Fair Trading Act 1973.	Section 4.	**CA.263**
		Section 10(2).	
		Section 45.	
		Section 54(5).	
		Section 78(3).	
		In section 81(1), in the words before paragraph (a), from 'and the Commission' to 'of this Act'); in paragraph (b), 'or the Commission, as the case may be' and 'or of the Commission'; in subsection (2), 'or the Commission' and 'or of the Commission' and in subsection (3), from 'and, in the case,' to '85 of this Act', and 'or the Commission, as the case may be,'.	
		In section 83, in subsection (1) 'Subject to subsection (1A) below' and subsection (1A).	
		In section 135(1), in the words before paragraph (a) and in paragraph (b), 'or the Commission', and paragraph (a).	
		Schedule 3.	
		In Schedule 8, paragraph 3(1) and (2).	
1976 c. 33.	The Restrictive Practices Court Act 1976.	The whole Act.	
1976 c. 34.	The Restrictive Trade Practices Act 1976.	The whole Act.	
1976 c. 53.	The Resale Prices Act 1976.	The whole Act.	
1976 c. 76.	The Energy Act 1976.	Section 5.	
1977 c. 19.	The Restrictive Trade Practices Act 1977.	The whole Act.	
1977 c. 37.	The Patents Act 1977.	Sections 44 and 45.	
1979 c.38.	The Estate Agents Act 1979.	In section 10(3), 'or the Restrictive Trade Practices Act 1976.'	
1980 c. 21.	The Competition Act 1980.	Sections 2 to 10.	
		In section 11(8), paragraph (b) and the 'and' immediately before it.	
		In section 13(1), from 'but the giving' to the end.	

653

Chapter	Short title	Extent of repeal
		In section 15, subsections (2)(b), (3) and (4).
		Section 16(3).
		In section 17, '8(1)' in subsections (1) and (3) to (5) and in subsection (2) '8(1) or'.
		In section 19(3), paragraph (d).
		In section 19(5)(a), 'or in anything published under section 4(2)(a) above'.
		Section 22.
		Sections 25 to 30.
		In section 31, subsection (2) and '10' in subsection (3).
		Section 33(3) and (4).
1984 c. 12.	The Telecommunications Act 1984.	Section 14(2).
		In section 16(5), the 'or' immediately after paragraph (a).
		In section 50(4), paragraph (c) and the 'and' immediately after it.
		In section 50(5), 'or (3)'.
		In section 50(7), 'or the 1980 Act'.
		In section 95(1), 'or section 10(2)(a) of the 1980 Act'.
		In section 95(2), paragraph (c) and the 'or' immediately before it.
		In section 95(3), 'or the 1980 Act'.
		In section 101(3), paragraphs (d) and (e).
1986 c. 31.	The Airports Act 1986.	Section 45(3).
		In section 54(1), 'or section 10(2)(a) of the 1980 Act'.
		In section 54(3), paragraph (c) and the 'or' immediately before it.
		In section 54(4), 'or the 1980 Act'.
		In section 56(a)(ii), 'or the 1980 Act'.
1986 c. 44.	The Gas Act 1986.	Section 25(2).
		In section 27(1), 'or section 10(2)(a) of the Competition Act 1980'.
		In section 27(3)(a), from 'or' to 'competition reference'.
		In section 27(6), 'or the said Act of 1980'.
		In section 28(5), the 'or' immediately after paragraph (aa).

Chapter	Short title	Extent of repeal
		In section 36A(5), paragraph (d) and the 'and' immediately before it.
		In section 36A(6), 'or (3)'.
		In section 36A(8), 'or under the 1980 Act'.
		In section 36A(9), 'or the 1980 Act'.
		In section 42(3), paragraphs (e) and (f).
1986 c. 60.	The Financial Services Act 1986.	Section 126.
1987 c. 43.	The Consumer Protection Act 1987.	In section 38(3), paragraphs (e) and (f).
1987 C. 53.	The Channel Tunnel Act 1987.	In section 33(2), paragraph (c) and the 'and' immediately before it.
		In section 33(5), paragraphs (b) and (c).
1988 c. 54.	The Road Traffic (Consequential Provisions) Act 1988.	In Schedule 3, paragraph 19.
1989 c. 16.	The Water Act 1989.	In section 174(3), paragraphs (d) and (e).
1989 c. 29.	The Electricity Act 1989.	Section 13(2).
		In section 15(1), paragraph (b) and the 'or' immediately before it.
		In section 15(2), paragraph (c) and the 'or' immediately before it.
		In section 15(3), 'or the 1980 Act'.
		In section 25(5), the 'or' immediately after paragraph (b).
		In section 43(4), paragraph (c) and the 'and' immediately after it.
		In section 43(5), 'or (3)'.
		In section 43(7), 'or the 1980 Act'.
		In section 57(3), paragraphs (d) and (e).
1989 c. 40.	The Companies Act 1989.	In Schedule 20, paragraphs 21 to 24.
1990 c. 42.	The Broadcasting Act 1990.	In section 193(2), paragraph (c) and the 'and' immediately before it.
		In section 193(4), 'or the Competition Act 1980'.
1991 c. 56.	The Water Industry Act 1991.	In section 12(5), 'or the 1980 Act'.
		Section 15(2).
		In section 17(1), paragraph (b) and the 'or' immediately before it.

Chapter	Short title	Extent of repeal
		In section 17(2), paragraph (c) and the 'or' immediately before it.
		In section 17(4), 'or the 1980 Act'.
		In section 31(4), paragraph (c) and the 'and' immediately before it.
		In section 31(5), 'or in subsection (3) above'.
		In section 31(6), 'or in subsection (3) above'.
		In section 31(7), 'or (3)'.
		In section 31(9), 'or the 1980 Act'.
		In Part II of Schedule 15, the entries relating to the Restrictive Trade Practices Act 1976 and the Resale Prices Act 1976.
1991 c. 57.	The Water Resources Act 1991.	In Part II of Schedule 24, the entries relating to the Restrictive Trade Practices Act 1976 and the Resale Prices Act 1976.
1993 c. 21.	The Osteopaths Act 1993.	In section 33(4), paragraph (b) and the 'or' immediately before it.
		In section 33(5), 'or section 10 of the Act of 1980'.
1993 c. 43.	The Railways Act 1993.	Section 14(2).
		In section 16(1), paragraph (b) and the 'or' immediately before it.
		In section 16(2), paragraph (c) and the 'or' immediately before it.
		In section 16(5), 'or the 1980 Act'.
		In section 67(4), paragraph (c) and the 'and' immediately after it.
		In section 67(6)(a), 'or (3)'.
		In section 67(9), 'or under the 1980 Act'.
		Section 131.
		In section 143(3), paragraphs (d) and (e).
1994 c. 17.	The Chiropractors Act 1994.	In section 33(4), paragraph (b) and the 'or' immediately before it.
		In section 33(5), 'or section 10 of the Act of 1980'.
1994 c. 21.	The Coal Industry Act 1994.	In section 59(4), paragraphs (e) and (f).
1994 c. 40.	The Deregulation and Contracting Out Act 1994.	Sections 10 and 11.
		In section 12, subsections (1) to (6).
		In Schedule 4, paragraph 1.

Chapter	Short title	Extent of repeal
1996 c. 55.	The Broadcasting Act 1996.	In Schedule 11, in paragraph 4, sub-paragraphs (3) to (6). Section 77(2).

PART II
REVOCATIONS

Reference	Title	Extent of revocation
SI 1981/1675 (NI 26).	The Magistrates Courts (Northern Ireland) Order 1981.	In Schedule 6, paragraphs 42 and 43.
SI 1982/1080 (NI 12).	The Agricultural Marketing (Northern Ireland) Order 1982.	In Schedule 8, the entry relating to paragraph 16(2) of Schedule 3 to the Fair Trading Act 1973 and in the entry relating to the Competition Act 1980, 'and 15(3)'.
SI 1986/1035 (NI 9).	The Companies Consolidation (Consequential Provisions) (Northern Ireland) Order 1986.	In Part II of Schedule 1, the entries relating to the Restrictive Trade Practices Act 1976 and the Resale Prices Act 1976.
SI 1992/231 (NI 1).	The Electricity (Northern Ireland) Order 1992.	Article 16(2). In Article 18— (a) in paragraph (1), sub-paragraph (b) and the 'or' immediately before it; (b) in paragraph (2), sub-paragraph (c) and the 'or' immediately before it; (c) in paragraph (3) 'or the 1980 Act'. In Article 28(5), the 'or' immediately after sub-paragraph (b). In Article 46— (a) in paragraph (4), sub-paragraph (c) and the 'and' immediately after it; (b) in paragraph (5), 'or (3)'; (c) in paragraph (7), 'or the 1980 Act'. Article 61(3)(f) and (g). In Schedule 12, paragraph 16.
SI 1994/426 (NI 1)	The Airports (Northern Ireland) Order 1994.	Article 36(3). In Article 45— (a) in paragraph (1), 'or section 10(2)(a) of the 1980 Act';

CA.264

Reference	Title	Extent of revocation
		(b) in paragraph (3), sub-paragraph (c) and the 'or' immediately before it;
		(c) in paragraph (4), 'or the 1980 Act'.
		In Article 47(a)(ii), 'or the 1980 Act'.
		In Schedule 9, paragraph 6.
SI 1996/275 (NI 2).	The Gas (Northern Ireland) Order 1996.	Article 16(2).
		In Article 18—
		(a) in paragraph (1), sub-paragraph (b) and the 'or' immediately before it;
		(b) in paragraph (3), sub-paragraph (c) and the 'or' immediately before it;
		(c) in paragraph (5), 'or the 1980 Act'.
		In Article 19(5), the 'or' immediately after sub-paragraph (b).
		In Article 23—
		(a) in paragraph (4), sub-paragraph (d) and the 'and' immediately before it;
		(b) in paragraph (5), 'or (3)';
		(c) in paragraph (7), 'or under the 1980 Act';
		(d) in paragraph (8), 'or the 1980 Act'.
		Article 44(4)(f) and (g).

APPENDIX 2

EARLY GUIDANCE: DIRECTIONS GIVEN BY THE DIRECTOR GENERAL OF FAIR TRADING UNDER PARAGRAPH 7(2) OF SCHEDULE 13 TO THE ACT

Form of Application

1. A person who wishes to apply under paragraph 7(2) of Schedule 13 for guidance in relation to an agreement shall in all cases submit Form EG to the Director General of Fair Trading.

Joint application

2. Where a joint application is made, Form EG shall be submitted to the Director General of Fair Trading by or on behalf of all the applicants, and a joint representative may be nominated in the application as authorised to submit and receive documents on behalf of some or all of the applicants.

Copies

3.—(1) Documents submitted as part of Form EG shall be either originals or true copies, and the applicant shall certify that each copy is a true copy of the original.

(2) Subject to paragraph (3) below, two copies of the information submitted as Form EG, in addition to the original, shall be submitted to the Director General of Fair Trading.

(3) If, in the applicant's opinion, one or more regulators has or may have concurrent jurisdiction with the Director General of Fair Trading under paragraph 7 of Schedule 13, one extra copy of the information submitted as Form EG shall be submitted to the Director General of Fair Trading for each such regulator.

Content of applications

4.—(1) Where the declaration which is submitted as part of Form EG is signed by a solicitor or other representative of an applicant, the information submitted as Form EG shall include written proof of that representative's authority to act on that applicant's behalf.

(2) The information submitted as Form EG shall, subject to paragraph (4) below, be correct and complete, and for these purposes information which is false or misleading shall be treated as incorrect or incomplete.

(3) If the applicant considers that any information contained in the application is confidential, in the sense given to that word by direction 11 below, he shall set out that information in a separate annex to the application marked 'confidential information' and explain why it should be treated as such.

(4) The Director may dispense with the obligation to submit any particular information, including any document, forming part of Form EG if he considers that such information or document is unnecessary for the examination of the case.

Effective date of application

5.—(1) Except where paragraph (3) below applies, an application shall have effect on the date on which it is received by the Director General of Fair Trading; an application received after 6 pm on a working day shall be treated as received on the next working day.

(2) The Director general of Fair Trading shall acknowledge receipt of an application to the applicant without delay.

(3) Where the Director finds that the information submitted as Form EG is incomplete in a material respect he shall, without delay, inform the applicant in writing of that fact; in such cases, the application, if otherwise made in accordance with these directions, shall have effect on the date on which the complete information is received by that Director, and information received after 6.00 pm on a working day shall be treated as received on the next working day.

(4) Material changes to the facts contained in an application of which the applicant knows, or ought reasonably to know, shall be communicated voluntarily and without delay:

(a) to the Director who is exercising jurisdiction under paragraph 7 of Schedule 13 in relation to the application; or

(b) where the applicant has not yet been informed of which Director that is, to the Director General of Fair Trading.

(5) If, on the expiry of the period of one month following the date on which an application has been received by the Director General of Fair Trading, the Director has not informed the applicant, under paragraph (3) above, that the application is incomplete in a material respect, the application, if made in accordance with these directions, shall be deemed to have become effective on the date of its receipt by the Director General of Fair Trading.

Notification of application to other parties

6.—(1) A party to an agreement who makes an application under paragraph 7(2) of Schedule 13 shall take all reasonable steps to:

(a) give written notification to all the other parties to the agreement of whom he is aware that the application has been made;

(b) give such notification within seven working days of the date on which the applicant receives acknowledgement of receipt of his application by the Director General of Fair Trading.

(2) The applicant shall provide a copy of such notification as is given under paragraph (1) above to the Director General of Fair Trading.

Concurrent jurisdiction

7.—(1) If the Director General of Fair Trading considers that a regulator has or may have concurrent jurisdiction under paragraph 7 or Schedule 13 to give guidance in response to an application made under paragraph 7(2) of Schedule 13, he shall:

    (a) as soon as practicable, send a copy of the information submitted as Form EG to the regulator; and

    (b) inform the applicant in writing that he has done so.

(2) As soon as practicable, the Director General of Fair Trading shall inform the applicant in writing of which Director is to exercise jurisdiction under paragraph 7 of Schedule 13 in relation to the application; if, subsequently, the application is transferred to a different Director who is to exercise such jurisdiction instead, the applicant shall be informed in writing of that fact.

Giving of guidance

8. Where the Director gives guidance to the applicant under sub-paragraph 7(3)(a) of Schedule 13, he shall do so in writing without delay after determining the application, stating the facts on which he bases the guidance and his reasons for it.

Withdrawal of guidance

9.—(1) If, having given guidance under sub-paragraph 7(3)(a) of Schedule 13 to the effect that:

    (a) the agreement is unlikely to infringe the Chapter I prohibition, regardless of whether or not it is exempt; or

    (b) the agreement is likely to be exempt under:

        (i) a block exemption;

        (ii) a parallel exemption; or

        (iii) a section 11 exemption; or

    (c) he would be likely to grant the agreement an individual exemption if asked to do so,

the Director proposes to withdraw that guidance before the date on which section 2 comes into force, he shall consult the person to whom he gave the guidance.

(2) Where the Director withdraws such guidance as is referred to in paragraph (1) above, he shall do so by giving written notice of the withdrawal to the person to whom he gave the guidance, stating his reasons for the withdrawal.

Confidential third party information

10.—(1) If a person who is not a party to the agreement to which an application made under paragraph 7(2) of Schedule 13 relates gives information to the Director in connection with the exercise of the Director's functions under paragraph 7 of Schedule 13 in relation to that agreement, and that person considers that any of the information is confidential, in the sense given to that word by direction 11 below, he shall set out the part of the information which he considers to be confidential in that sense in a separate annex marked 'confidential information' and explain why it should be treated as such.

(2) The Director shall, if he proposes to disclose any of the information contained in an annex provided in accordance with paragraph (1) above, consult the person who provided the information if it is practicable to do so.

Interpretation

11.—(1) In these directions—

(a) a reference to 'the applicant' is to be construed as being a reference to the applicant or to his duly authorised representative if written proof of the representative's authority to act on the applicant's behalf is included in the formation submitted as Form EG;

(b) 'a block exemption' is to be construed by reference to section 6;

(c) information is confidential if it is—

(i) commercial information the disclosure of which would, or might, significantly harm the legitimate business interests of the undertaking to which it relates; or

(ii) information relating to the private affairs of an individual the disclosure of which would, or might, significantly harm his interests;

(d) where the Director, if he proposes to take action, is required to consult a person, he shall—

(i) give written notice to the person in question, stating the action he proposes and his reasons for it; and

(ii) inform that person that any written representations made to the Director within the period specified in the notice will be considered;

(e) a reference to 'the Director' is to be construed as being a reference to the Director General of Fair Trading or to any regulator;

(f) 'Form EG' means the information, including any document, required to be provided by such form as is from time to time issued by the Director General of Fair Trading;

(g) 'an individual exemption' is to be construed by reference to section 4;

(h) 'a parallel exemption' is to be construed by reference to section 10;

(i) 'regulator' has the meaning given by section 59;

(j) 'a section 11 exemption' is to be construed by reference to section 11; and

(k) 'working day' means any day which is not Saturday, Sunday, an official holiday on which the Office of Fair Trading is closed, or any other day on which that office is closed.

(2) References in these directions to the 'Act' are to the Competition Act 1998 and references to numbered sections or schedules are to the sections or schedules so numbered in the Act.

APPENDIX 3

FORM FOR APPLICATIONS FOR EARLY GUIDANCE UNDER PARAGRAPH 7 OF SCHEDULE 13 TO THE COMPETITION ACT 1998

Part 1:   Notes

1.1   *Guidance in anticipation of the coming into force of Chapter I of the Act ('early guidance') is available for agreements made during the period beginning on 9 November 1998 (enactment date) and ending immediately before 1 March 2000 (the date on which the Chapter I prohibition comes into force). It may be applied for under paragraph 7 of Schedule 13 to the Act. Early guidance is not available in respect of the Chapter II prohibition. This form cannot be used for notifications made on or after 1 March 2000; Form N must be used for such notifications.*

1.2   *Although this document is described as 'a Form', it is essentially a check-list of information which must be supplied to the Director General of Fair Trading to enable him to determine an application for early guidance. Before completing the Form, reference should be made to the Early Guidance Directions of the Director General of Fair Trading issued on 26 November 1998.*

1.3   *The information must be correct and complete for the application to be effective.*

1.4   *The Form must be supplied in original version plus two copies, together with either an original or a certified copy, plus two further copies, of the agreement(s) and any relevant Annexes.*

1.5   *All applications for early guidance should be sent to the Director General of Fair Trading and marked for the attention of the 'Early Guidance Co-ordination Unit'.*

1.6   *The Act is enforced by the Director General of Fair Trading and, in relation to the regulated utility sectors shown in question 3.5 below, concurrently with the sector regulators; these have concurrent jurisdiction with the Director General to give early guidance. If any positive answer is given question 3.5, provide one further copy of the Form and attachments for each relevant regulator who may have concurrent jurisdiction. A copy of the Form (together with its Annexes and copies of agreements) should also be sent to the relevant regulator(s), if the agreement being notified may fall within their sector(s). In general, the relevant regulator will deal with the application. If the Director General considers that a regulator has, or may have, concurrent jurisdiction in relation to an agreement in respect of which an application for early guidance has been submitted, he will send a copy of the Form EG to the regulator(s) and inform the notifying party that he has done so.*

1.7   *Indicate clearly to which section of the Form any additional pages relate. The applica-tion* **must** *include the form of receipt at Part 3.* **Information which is regarded by the undertaking or undertakings as confidential should be clearly identified as such and placed in a separate identified annex. An explanation of why such information is regarded as confidential should also be provided.** *Applications may also be made on disk or using other electronic format: please telephone the enquiry point at the Office of Fair Trading on 0171 211 8989 before using this facility.*

1.8   **The Director General, or, of the applicant has been informed that a regulator is dealing with the application, that regulator, must be informed of any material changes which occur after application has been made and which may affect any information given in this Form.**

Part 2:   Information to be Provided by the Undertaking Notifying the Agreement

Number sections as below. In some cases, it may be possible to dispense with the requirement to provide information in all categories. This should be discussed with officials before making the application. **Information which is regarded by the undertaking(s) as confidential should be clearly identified as such and placed in a separate identified annex.**

1.   *The Undertaking(s) Submitting the Application*

1.1   the identity of the undertaking submitting the application (full name and address, name of representative, telephone and fax numbers, and brief description of the undertaking or association of undertakings). For a partnership, sole trader or other unincorporated body trading under a business name, give the name(s) and address(es) of the proprietor(s) or partners. Please quote any reference which should be used;

1.2   if acting on behalf of another undertaking, state in what capacity, eg solicitor;

Where the Form is signed by a solicitor or other representative, proof of authority to act on behalf of the undertaking submitting the application must be provided.

1.3   if the application is submitted by or on behalf of more than one undertaking, indi-cate whether a joint representative has been appointed. If so, give the details as requested in 1.1 above in respect of the joint representative. If not, give the details in respect of any representatives who have been authorised to act on behalf of each, or either, of the parties to the agreement, indicating who they represent;

1.4   the Standard Industrial Classification code for the relevant good(s) or service(s), if known. If the code is not known, describe the goods or services involved as fully and accurately as possible;

The directions issued by the Director General require a party to an agreement who makes an application for early guidance in respect of that agreement to take all reasonable steps to notify all other parties to the agreement of whom he is aware that the application has been made. In exceptional cases, it may not be practicable to inform all non-notifying parties to the notified agreement that it has been notified, if, for example, an agreement is concluded with a large number of undertakings. The notification to such other undertakings must be made (a) in writing; and (b) within seven working days of the applicant receiving the Director General's acknowledgment of receipt of his application. The applicant must send a copy of such notification to the Director General.

1.5   the full names, addresses (by registered office, where appropriate, and principal place of business, if different), telephone and fax numbers, nature of business, and brief description of any other parties to the agreement, decision or concerted practice ('the arrangement') being notified;

1.6   details of the steps to be taken to inform any other such parties that the application has been made and indicate whether the remaining parties have received a copy of the application with confidential information and business secrets deleted. State the reasons, if it is not practicable to inform other parties of the application in accordance with the requirements outlined above.

2.   *Purpose of the Application*

The Chapter I prohibition will not apply unless the arrangement has an 'appreciable effect' on competition, and an application for early guidance will not normally be appropriate when that is not the case. Further information is given in the guideline **The Competition Act 1998: the Chapter I prohibition.**

2.1   whether the arrangement that is the subject of the application is considered to be of a type which would benefit from any exclusion from the Chapter I prohibition. Specify the exclusion: give reasons why you are unsure whether the arrangement will be covered by the exclusion and why an application for early guidance is considered appropriate;

2.2   specify why it is considered that the Chapter I prohibition is likely to be infringed and whether the arrangement is likely to qualify (or in the case of an individual exemption, is likely to qualify if notified) for an exemption (individual, UK block exemption, parallel, or under section 11 of the Act);

3.   *Jurisdiction*

In general, when an arrangement is also caused by Article 85 of the EC Treaty, the Director General considers that the EC Commission is the more appropriate authority to whom notification should be made (see the guideline **The Competition Act 1998: the Chapter I prohibition***).*

3.1   why the arrangement is considered to be not caught by Article 85(1);

3.2   whether the arrangement is the subject of an application to the European Commission. If so, it would assist consideration of the application if three copies of the completed Form A/B and supporting documents, and one further copy if information has been given in response to question 3.5 below, were attached. It is unnecessary to repeat information given on Form A/B, but information specific to the UK market will be necessary (following the format in question 7.1) to the extent that it has not been given on Form A/B, and should be provided separately. Supply three copies of any 'comfort' letter received from the European Commission;

3.3 whether the arrangement is the subject of an application to any other national competition authority;

3.4 if the arrangement relates to transport by rail, road, inland waterway or to services ancillary to transport and is the subject of an application to the European Commission under Regulation 1017/68, it would similarly assist consideration of the application if three copies of the completed Form II and any supporting documents and one further copy if information has been given in response to question 3.5 below were attached;

3.5 whether the arrangement being notified relates to any one or more of:

    a commercial activities connected with telecommunications;

    b the shipping, conveyance or supply of gas and activities ancillary thereto;

    c commercial activities connected with the generation, transmission or supply of electricity;

    d commercial activities connected with the supply of water or securing a supply of water or with the provision or securing of sewerage services;

    e commercial activities connected with the generation, transmission or supply of electricity in Northern Ireland;

    f the conveyance, storage or supply of gas in Northern Ireland;

    g the supply of railway services.

Identify the sector regulator or regulators who may have concurrent jurisdiction with the Director General of Fair Trading to deal with the application for early guidance;

3.6 names and addresses, telephone and fax numbers, date and details, including case references, of any previous contacts with the Office of Fair Trading, a regulator, any other national competition authority, or the EC Commission, and of any proceedings in any national court in the European Community, relating to the arrangement being notified and of any relevant previous arrangements.

4. *Details of the Arrangement*

4.1 a brief description of the arrangement being notified (nature, content, purpose, date(s) and duration);

4.2 if written, attach either an original or a certified copy, together with two further copies, of the most recent version of the text of the arrangement being notified (technical details contained in know-how agreements, for example, may be omitted but omissions should be indicated); if not written, provide a full description;

4.3 identify any provisions in the arrangement which may restrict the parties in their freedom to take independent commercial decisions or to act on those decisions;

4.4 if the application related to a standard contract, the number expected to be concluded.

5. *Information on the Parties to the Arrangement and the Groups to which they belong*

5.1 for each undertaking identified in 1.5 above, the name of a contact, together with his or her address, telephone and fax numbers, and position held in the undertaking;

5.2 the corporate groups to which each undertaking belongs and the product and/or services market(s) in which the groups are active (hereafter called 'the relevant product market'); include one copy of the most recent consolidated annual report and accounts (or equivalent for unincorporated bodies) for each undertaking;

5.3 for each of the parties to the arrangement, provide a list of all undertakings belonging to the same group which are active in the same relevant product market(s), and those active in markets neighbouring the relevant product markets—that is, those which are not regarded by the consumer as fully interchangeable or substitutable for products in the defined relevant product market, as defined in question 6.1 below.

6. *The Relevant Prod...*

A rel... ...ervices regarded by the con-
sun... ...by reason of their character-
istic... ...normally considered when
deter... ...ccount, together with any
others...
— *the a... ...estion;*
— *any d...*
— *differe...*
— *the cost... ...ces; and*
— *establish... ...ice.*

The relevant... ...erned are involved
in the supply... ...e appreciably dif-
ferent from ne... ...mally considered
when determin... ...ccount, together
with any others...
— *the nature an... ...*
— *the existence o...*
— *appreciable dif... ...*
between neighb... ...substantial price differences
— *transport costs.*

6.1 In the light of the relevant factors given above (which are not exhaustive), explain the definitions of the relevant product and geographic markets which should be considered, with full reasons, in particular stating the specific products or services directly or indirectly affected by the application and other goods or services that may be viewed as substitutable, with reasons. If the relevant geographic market is considered to be an area smaller, or larger, than the whole of the United Kingdom, the boundaries considered applicable, with reasons. Give reasons for all assumptions or findings, and explain how the factors outlined above have been taken into account. Further details are in the guideline *The Competition Act 1998: Market Definition*;

6.2 provide a copy of the most recent in-house long-term market studies assessing or analysing the relevant markets (including any commissioned by the undertakings from outside consultants), and give references of any external studies of the relevant product market, and, where possible, include a copy of any such studies.

7.   *The Position of the Undertakings in the Relevant Product Markets*

The information required under this section relates to both the relevant geographic market and the relevant product market, for the groups of the parties as a whole. Market shares may be calculated either on the basis of value or volume. Justification for the figures provided must be given by reference to the sales or turnover of each of the undertakings in question. The source or sources of information should be given, and, where possible, a copy of the document from which information has been taken.

7.1 for each of the previous three calendar or financial years, as available, give:

a details of the market shares of each undertaking in the goods or services in the relevant product and geographic markets, as identified in 6.1 above, and, if different, in the UK, and in the European Community;

b estimates of market shares in the relevant product and geographic markets for each of the five main competitors of each of the undertakings, giving the undertaking's name, address, telephone and fax number, and, where possible, a contact name;

c identify the five main customers of each of the undertakings in the relevant product and geographic markets, giving the undertaking's name, address, telephone and fax number, and, where possible, a contact name;

d details of the undertakings' interests in, and arrangements with, any other companies competing in the relevant product and geographic market, together with details of their market shares, if known.

8.   *Market Entry and Potential Competition in the Relevant Product and Geographic Markets*

8.1 For all relevant product and geographic markets:

a describe the factors influencing entry into the relevant product market(s): that is, the barriers which exist to prevent undertakings not presently manufacturing goods within the relevant product market(s) from entering the market(s), taking account of, in particular but not exclusively, the extent to which:

— entry is regulated by the requirements of government authorisation or standard-setting, in any form, and any legal or regulatory controls on entry to the market(s);

— entry is influenced by the availability of raw materials;

— entry is influenced by the length of existing contracts between suppliers and customers;

— research and development and licensing patents, know-how and other rights are important

b describe the factors influencing entry in geographic terms: that is, the barriers that exist to prevent undertakings already producing and/or marketing goods within the relevant product market(s) outside the relevant geographic market(s) from extending sales into the relevant geographic market(s), taking account of, in particular but not exclusively, the importance of:

— trade barriers imposed by law, such as tariffs, quotas etc;

— local geographical specifications or technical requirements;

— procurement policies;

— the existence of adequate and available local distribution and retailing facilities;

— transport costs;

— strong consumer preference for local brands or products;

c In respect of new entrants in both product and geographic terms, state whether any new undertakings have entered the product market(s) in geographic areas where the undertakings sell, during the last three years. Identify the undertakings concerned by name, address, telephone and fax numbers and, where possible, a contact name, with best estimates of market shares of each in the relevant product and geographic markets.

9. *Negative Clearance*

9.1 state reasons for seeking 'negative clearance' (that is, the Director General should conclude that the arrangement will not be covered by the Chapter I prohibition). Indicate, for example, which provision or effects of the arrangement may breach the prohibition, and state the reasons why it is considered that the arrangements do not have the object or effect of preventing, restricting or distorting competition within the UK to an appreciable extent.

10. *Exemption*

The criteria which will be taken into account in considering applications for exemption are set out in section 9 of the Act.

10.1 if guidance on exemption from the Chapter I prohibition is sought, explain how the arrangements contribute to improving production or distribution and/or promoting technical or economic progress, and how consumers will be allowed a fair share of those benefits. Explain how each restrictive provision in the arrangements is indispensable to these objectives, and how the arrangements do not eliminate competition in respect of a substantial part of the relevant product or geographic market concerned.

11. Transitional Periods

11.1   if the arrangement is considered to benefit from any transitional periods during which the Chapter I prohibition does not apply, indicate the duration of the relevant transitional periods by reference to Schedule 13 to the Act.

12. Other Information

12.1   state:

      a whether this application should be considered as urgent. If so, give reasons;

      b any other information you consider may be helpful.

The application must conclude with the following declaration which is to be signed by or on behalf of all the applicants or notifying undertakings. Unsigned applications are invalid.

DECLARATION

The undersigned declare that all the information given above and in the . . . pages annexed hereto is correct to the best of their knowledge and belief, and that all estimates are identified as such and are their best estimates of the underlying facts.

Place and date ....

Signatures ....

....

Status ....

.... name(s) in block capitals

Part 3:   Acknowledgement of Receipt

This form will be returned to the address inserted below if the top half is completed by the undertaking lodging it.

to be completed by the undertaking making the application

To .... (name and address of applicant)

....

....

....

Your application dated ....

concerning ....

under reference ....

involving the following undertakings:

1. ....

2. .... [and others]

to be completed by the Office of Fair Trading

was received on ....

and registered under reference number

.... **Please quote this number in all correspondence**

In the event that this application is not complete in a material respect, you will be informed within one month of its receipt. If you are not informed within that time that it is considered to be incomplete, it is deemed to be effective on the date of its receipt.

INDEX